Covenant and Liberation

European University Studies
Europäische Hochschulschriften
Publications Universitaires Européennes

Series XXIII
Theology
Reihe XXIII   Série XXIII
Theologie
Théologie

Vol./Bd. 411

PETER LANG
Frankfurt am Main · Bern · New York · Paris

Christopher J. Baker

Covenant and Liberation

Giving new heart to God's endangered family

PETER LANG
Frankfurt am Main · Bern · New York · Paris

CIP-Titelaufnahme der Deutschen Bibliothek

Baker, Christopher J.:

Covenant and liberation : giving new heart to God's endangered family / Christopher J. Baker. -- Frankfurt am Main ; Bern ; New York ; Paris : Lang, 1991
   (European university studies: Ser. 23, Theology ; Vol. 411)
   ISBN 3-631-43479-0

NE: Europäische Hochschulschriften / 23

ISSN 0721-3409
ISBN 3-631-43479-0
© Verlag Peter Lang GmbH, Frankfurt am Main 1991
All rights reserved.

All parts of this publication are protected by copyright. Any utilisation outside the strict limits of the copyright law, without the permission of the publisher, is forbidden and liable to prosecution. This applies in particular to reproductions, translations, microfilming, and storage and processing in electronic retrieval systems.

Printed in Germany 1   3 4 5 6 7

DEDICATION

To my family
who first showed me
Christian family values

and

To the people of Peru
struggling to revive the
family spirit of the new covenant
at home and abroad.

CONTENTS

PREFACE AND ACKNOWLEDGEMENTS — XIV

INTRODUCTION — 1
  A: COVENANT CONCEPT AS CENTRAL TO BIBLE — 1
    1. Covenant as central to O.T. — 1
    2. Covenant as central to N.T. — 2
    3. Unity, continuity, fulfilment and surpassing of covenants — 2
    4. Fresh incentive to search the Scriptures — 3
  B: LIBERATION IS FOR COVENANT — 3
    1. Exodus as a paradigm for liberation — 3
    2. "Exodus" of Jesus as the definitive paradigm of liberation — 4
    3. O.T. liberation demands ongoing justice and compassion — 4
    4. Jesus' insistence on compassion and justice — 5
  C. AIMS AND METHODS — 5
    1. Aims — 5
    2. Methods — 6
    3. Hermeneutics — 7
    4. Commitment to the Church as a covenanted community — 8
  D. COVENANT IN RELATION TO SIGNS OF THE TIMES — 9
    1. Council Documents — 9
    2. Episcopal Conferences — 10
    3. International concern for our one planet — 13
  E. COVENANT IN INTERDISCIPLINARY DIALOGUE — 15
    1. Moral Theology and Christian ethics — 15
    2. Social sciences — 18
  F. COVENANTING FOR "JUSTICE, PEACE AND INTEGRITY OF CREATION" — 20
  NOTES — 21

CHAPTER 1: WHAT IS A BIBLICAL COVENANT? — 29
  A. INTERNATIONAL TREATIES (NON-BIBLICAL) — 29
    1. Wide range of Ancient Near Eastern treaties — 29
    2. Common elements in those international treaties — 30
    3. Different kinds of international treaties — 31
    4. Treaties or pacts within a kingdom — 31
    5. Application of treaty sanctions — 31
  B. BIBLICAL COVENANTS — 31
    1. Extensive use of covenant terms throughout the Bible — 31
    2. Divine and human covenants in the Bible — 32
    3. Principal features of the divine covenants — 32
    4. Towards a synthesis of divine covenants — 34
      a) Gradual unfolding of God's plan to reunite human family — 34

           b) Covenant embraces several different kinds of commitment 36
           c) Development of covenant is coherent if not homogeneous 38
NOTES 39

CHAPTER 2: INITIAL RUDIMENTARY COVENANTS 43
A: FROM CREATION TILL THE FLOOD (GEN 1 - 5) 44
    1. First creation account in Gen 2,4b - 3,24 (J) 44
    2. Later creation account in Gen 1,1 - 2,4a (P) 48
    3. Bonds of brotherhood violently broken by Cain: Gen 4 52
B. FROM FLOOD TO FAMILY OF ABRAHAM (GEN 6-11) 54
    1. The Universal covenant granted to Noah and family 55
    2. Expansion from Noah's family to that of Abraham:
       Gen 9,18 - c.11 57
NOTES 58

CHAPTER 3: COVENANT WITH ABRAHAM AND SARAH
       (GEN 12 - 50) 62
A. THE PROMISE TO ABRAHAM (GEN 12) 62
B. CONFIRMING THE PROMISE WITH A COVENANT
   (GEN 15 & 17) 63
    1. Yahweh "cuts a covenant" with Abram (Gen 15) 63
    2. God's covenant made more explicit in its demands (Gen 17) 65
C. THE PROMISE CONFIRMED BY OATH (GEN 22) 67
D. PROMISSORY COVENANT RENEWED WITH ISAAC AND
   JACOB (GEN 26 - 28) 68
E. THE FAILURE AND RESTORATION OF COVENANT KINSHIP
   (GEN 37 - 50) 70
NOTES 72

CHAPTER 4: COVENANT WITH A LIBERATED NATION
       (EXODUS) 75
A. EARLY LIFE AND FLIGHT OF MOSES (EX 1 - 2) 75
B. MOSES CALLED AND SENT BY GOD TO FREE
   HIS PEOPLE (EX 3 - 6) 76
C. MOSES CONFRONTS THE PHARAOH (EX 7 - 13) 78
D. DEFINITIVE CROSSING FROM SLAVERY TO FREEDOM
   (EX 14 - 18) 80
    1. Crossing the Sea of Reeds (Ex 14) 80
    2. The joyful song of victory (Ex 15) 81
    3. Providence of Yahweh in the wilderness (Ex 16 -18) 82
E. THE COVENANT SEALED AT SINAI (EX 19 - 24) 82
F. VIOLATION AND RENEWAL OF COVENANT AT SINAI
   (EX 32 - 34) 85
G. RELATION OF THE DECALOGUE TO THE COVENANT (EX 20) 87
H. THE SINAI COVENANT IN THE PRIESTLY TRADITION
   (EX 25 - 31. 35 - 40) 89

CONTENTS

I. COVENANT IDEALS UPHELD BY SABBATICAL AND
   JUBILEE YEARS (LEV 25)   90
NOTES   92

CHAPTER 5: COVENANT PROCLAIMED BY DEUTERONOMY AND DEUTERONOMIC HISTORY   98

A. THE BOOK OF DEUTERONOMY   98
   1. The origin, purpose and structure of Deuteronomy   98
   2. Expansion and actualization of the Ten Commandments (Dt 6 - 28)   100
   3. Elements of the treaty form in Deuteronomy   102

B. THE DEUTERONOMIC HISTORY (JOSHUA - 2 KINGS)   104
   1. The Book of Joshua   104
   2. The Book of Judges   105
   3. 1 & 2 Samuel   106
   4. 1 & 2 Kings   111

NOTES   113

CHAPTER 6: COVENANT IN PRE-EXILIC PROPHETS   118

Introduction   118

A. DURING THE ASSYRIAN EMPIRE   119
   1. Amos (in the Northern Kingdom)   119
   2. Hosea (in the Northern Kingdom)   121
   3. Micah (in the Southern Kingdom)   125
   4. Isaiah (in the Southern Kingdom)   127

B. PROPHETS DURING THE BABYLONIAN EMPIRE   133
   1. Jeremiah (in Jerusalem)   134

NOTES   141

CHAPTER 7: COVENANT IN EXILIC AND POST-EXILIC PROPHETS   146

B. (Cont.d) UNDER BABYLONIAN EMPIRE   146
   2. Ezekiel (in Babylon)   146
   3. Deutero-Isaiah (in Babylon)   150

C. DURING THE PERSIAN EMPIRE   155
   1. Trito-Isaiah (in Jerusalem)   155
   2. Zechariah (in Jerusalem)   157
   3. Malachi (in Jerusalem)   157
   4. Joel (in Jerusalem)   158

D. DURING THE GREEK PERIOD   159
   1. Baruch (among exiles of the Diaspora)   159
   2. Daniel (Babylonian background actualized for Jerusalem)   160

NOTES   163

CHAPTER 8: COVENANT IN CHRONICLER'S AND MACCABEAN HISTORY, IN WISDOM AND PSALMS, AND IN QUMRAN COMMUNITY	168
Introduction	168
A. COVENANT IN THE CHRONICLER'S HISTORY	168
B. COVENANT IN THE MACCABEAN HISTORY	171
C. COVENANT IN WISDOM LITERATURE	172
D. COVENANT IN THE PSALMS	177
E. COVENANT COMMUNITY OF QUMRAN	183
NOTES	188
CHAPTER 9: NEW COVENANT IN MARK AND MATTHEW	194
A. THE NEW COVENANT IN MARK'S GOSPEL	195
1. The Gospel of Jesus Christ	195
2. Jesus as a suffering Messiah	195
3. Jesus Christ as Son of God	196
4. Jesus as one teaching with authority	196
5. The Twelve as disciples accompanying Jesus	196
6. The way prepared by John the Baptist	196
7. The meaning of baptism in Jesus' mission	197
8. Jesus proclaiming the kingdom of God	197
9. Kingship and kinship for the covenant community	198
10. God as **Abba**, Father	199
11. Jesus as bridegroom	199
12. The new covenant's all-embracing commandment	200
13. Love of riches as opposed to love of poor people	200
14. Sharing bread and the eucharist	201
15. Jesus as messianic king	201
16. Jesus' concern for the Temple	202
17. Giving the "blood of the covenant"	203
18. The new covenant can extend God's reign to every land	204
19. The new covenant is the way to full resurrection	204
B. THE NEW COVENANT IN MATTHEW'S GOSPEL	205
1. The Infancy Narrative: Jesus as Son of David	205
2. The Infancy Narrative: Jesus as a new Moses	206
3. Sermon on the Mount: the spirit of the new covenant	206
a) The Beatitudes	207
b) Bringing to perfection the Law and the Prophets	210
c) The prayer of the covenant community	211
4. Jesus himself as messianic king	212
5. The Church as the new covenant community accepting God's reign	213
a) The narrative section (13,53 - c.17)	213
b) Discourse on a new community spirit (c.18)	214
6. The parousia and last judgment	215
a) The narrative section (cc.19 - 23)	215

b) The concluding discourse (cc.24 - 25)	215
7. "The blood of the covenant" for the forgiveness of sins	216
8. The commission to offer the new covenant to all nations	217
NOTES	218

CHAPTER 10: NEW COVENANT IN LUKE AND ACTS OF THE APOSTLES — 226

A. NEW COVENANT IN LUKE'S GOSPEL — 226
1. The Infancy Narrative in Lk — 227
   a) The consent of Mary to the mighty word of God — 227
   b) The promissory covenant with Abraham recalled — 227
   c) the importance of Jerusalem in Lk-Acts — 229
2. The inaugural address in Nazareth — 230
3. Beatitudes and parables — 233
   a) The Sermon on the Plain — 233
   b) Three Lucan parables — 234
4. The transfiguration - "speaking about his exodus" — 235
5. "This cup is the new covenant in my blood" — 236
   a) Eating the Jewish Passover and drinking the festal wine — 236
   b) "My body given for you...; ..the new covenant in my blood" — 237
   c) "Do this as my reminder" — 237
   d) "And now I confer a kingdom on you" — 238
   e) The words spoken from the cross — 239

B. THE NEW COVENANT IN ACTS — 240
1. Entry into the new covenant community — 240
2. Community fellowship and sharing — 241
3. Admission of Gentiles to the new covenant community — 242
4. Mission to the Gentiles "to the ends of the earth" — 243

NOTES — 245

CHAPTER 11: NEW COVENANT IN JOHN'S GOSPEL AND EPISTLES — 250

A. NEW COVENANT IN JOHN'S GOSPEL — 250
1. The Prologue (1,1-18) — 251
2. The Spirit of the new covenant (cc. 1 - 20) — 253
3. Messianic nuptials between Jesus and his disciples (c.2) — 254
4. The solemn declaration of "I AM" (cc. 4 - 18) — 254
5. "If the Son sets you free, you will indeed be free" (c.8) — 257
6. The new commandment of love (cc. 13 - 17) — 258
7. The risen Lord confirms the new covenant (cc. 20 - 21) — 261
   a) The appearance to Mary Magdalene (20,1-18) — 261
   b) The renewal of the covenant for Simon Peter (c.21) — 262

B. NEW COVENANT IN THE EPISTLES OF JOHN — 263
1. Love of God demands and inspires love of one another — 263

        2. The Spirit brings Christians an indwelling and knowledge of God 264
NOTES 266

CHAPTER 12: NEW COVENANT IN THE EPISTLES AND APOCALYPSE 272
A. IN 1 THESSALONIANS 272
B. IN 1-2 CORINTHIANS 274
    1. In 1 Corinthians 274
    2. In 2 Corinthians 277
C. IN ROMANS AND GALATIANS 280
D. IN EPHESIANS AND PHILEMON 284
    1. New covenant in Ephesians 284
    2. New covenant in Philemon 286
E. NEW COVENANT IN HEBREWS 289
    1. Jesus as Son of God and brother of us all (Heb 1 - 2) 289
    2. Jesus, as Son over God's household, is its high priest (3,1 - 5,10) 290
    3. Jesus as high priest is perfect, unique and eternal, superseding the priesthood of the Mosaic covenant (5,11 - 8,13) 290
    4. Jesus, "mediator of a new covenant", has offered himself as the perfect sacrifice (9,1 - 10,39) 291
    5. A pilgrim people called to follow faithfully the example of Jesus, mindful of "the blood of the covenant" (cc. 11 - 13) 293
F. NEW COVENANT IN 1 PETER 295
G. NEW COVENANT IN THE APOCALYPSE 297
    1. The blood of the Lamb inaugurating a new covenant 298
    2. The Church as the bride of the Lamb 300
NOTES 302

CHAPTER 13: COVENANT DIMENSION IN LIBERATION THEOLOGY 308
Introduction 308
A. WHAT IS LIBERATION THEOLOGY? 310
    1. A critical reflection 310
    2. On liberating praxis 311
    3. Accompanying a personal commitment to and with the poor 311
    4. A praxis to challenge and change political decisions 311
    5. A praxis which wants all history to reflect God's reign 312
    6. Continually evaluated in the light of the Word 313
B. COVENANT AND ALL CREATION 314
C. COVENANT CONFIRMING THE PROMISE 315
D. COVENANT CROWNING THE EXODUS 315
E. COVENANT AND LAND 317
F. KINGS UNDER COVENANT 319
G. COVENANT AND THE PROPHETS 320

H. COVENANT AND CULTURE	322
I. THE NEW COVENANT AND THE KINGDOM OF GOD	323
J. THE NEW COVENANT COMMUNITY AND POLITICS	326
K. THE NEW COVENANT AND ITS EUCHARISTIC RENEWAL	328
L. NEW COVENANT SPIRITUALITY AND LIBERATION	328
NOTES	332
BIBLIOGRAPHY	339

PREFACE AND ACKNOWLEDGEMENTS

Liberation has been keenly desired by many people in Latin America since the successful voyage there by Christopher Columbus in 1492, which led on to the arrival of the Spanish **conquistadores** (conquerors) accompanied by colonists and missionaries. There can be no denying that the sword and the cross arrived together and, at least from the point of view of the afflicted Indians, stayed together far too long. However, from the beginning of the "conquest" there were some missionaries, like the Dominican Bartolomé de las Casas, who strongly denounced the constant oppression and killing of the local Indians. By calling loudly and persistently during many decades of the 16th century for the liberation of those poor and unjustly treated people, las Casas sowed the seeds of liberation theology as we know it today in Latin America.

It is quite understandable that the people of Latin America are currently experiencing great difficulty in deciding on some suitable way to celebrate the 5th Centenary of Columbus's arrival. The Catholic Church is rightly calling for the celebration of 500 years of evangelization; those who still feel dispossessed and oppressed want it to be commemorated also as the 5th centenary of an invasion which robbed them of much of their rightful land and goods, of their traditional culture and personal dignity.

The main purpose in drawing attention to the harmful aspects of the arrival of the Spaniards (and later of the Portugese) is to rectify some of the most serious consequences of the original injustices. There are still many dehumanizing consequences of those early sinful attitudes, deeds and structures. A radical change of heart is necessary to allow Latin Americans of today to live in full freedom as God's people. That, to my mind, is the daunting challenge to be addressed by the next General Assembly of the Episcopal Conference of Latin America when it meets in 1992 in Santo Domingo.

The pastoral options which were made at Medellin and Puebla for the poor and for the youth will need to be given even greater force at Santo Domingo. Likewise their compassionate response to the cry for liberation from increasingly oppressive burdens on the poor should be clearly proclaimed once again in the name of Christ. May the new evangelization of Latin America, which John Paul II wants to spring from the celebration of the 5th Centenary, bear the stamp of a "communion and participation" of all God's people, as Medellin proposed. My suggestion would be to have the Pope declare 1992 a biblical-style Jubilee Year, with emphasis on liberation from modern bondage, especially external debt, and calling for a return of homes and lands to the poor, particularly in rural areas.

The present work on *Covenant and Liberation* has been written as a contribution towards those goals. While working for 11 years with the poor in Condevilla, a large parish in Lima, I have learnt a great deal from them and from our reflection together on the local situation in the light of the Scriptures.

Rereading the Scriptures with the poor and oppressed helped me to realize as never before that each person called into covenant with God is called at the same time to full liberation. Those years in Lima also kept me in constant touch with genuine liberation theology, so much so that it has become self-evident to me that a theology which is anti-liberation must be a false theology.

The many attacks on liberation theology have led in some cases to the murder of liberation theologians and more frequently to the murder of pastoral workers committed to the liberation of their people. This has moved me to offer here a sustained treatment of all the biblical covenants in which God was the initiator and one of the parties. The long story of those covenants runs from start to finish of the Bible. It provides overwhelming evidence that the liberation of a family or a nation was crowned with a covenant to ensure that their God-given freedom would be cherished within the bonds of kinship.

Nowadays the image of Noah's ark gives way to that of planet earth as the one and only spaceship in which the human family and the rest of our fellow creatures may survive. The global family and all its life-sustaining environment is now endangered. But the Son has been set over all his Father's household, to guide it according to the values of the new covenant sealed in his own blood. He brings the Spirit of the new covenant that can transform stony hearts so that they will share earth's limited resources with the rest of God's family. This aspect underlies the subtitle: *Giving new heart to God's endangered family.*

It has also influenced the whole approach of the ecumenical World Convocation on Justice, Peace and the Integrity of Creation, held in Seoul in March 1990. The participants concluded with a fourfold Act of Covenanting and recommended to the Seventh Assembly of the World Council of Churches that it endorse this process in Canberra in 1991.

The writing of this book began after a sabbatical year spent in research in Rome during 1986-87, and it was practically concluded before I left Lima in mid-'89. The biblical fields over which it has ranged are so vast that no scholar could hope to cover all the literature available on them. However, I think that committed Christian leaders and their apostolic teams should have on hand some kind of a non-specialist presentation, a reliable synthesis of the covenants, with an eye to their inspiring message for the family of God today. Because the story is so long, it may be wiser for some readers to take it a chapter at a time, especially if it is being used (as intended) to help groups reflect on their Christian praxis and in so doing become familiar with all the Scriptures.

Since my arrival in Ireland, events in Europe have made it obvious that liberation from a modern tyranny still leaves whole nations in need of a new foundation on which to build their free society. The breaking down of the Berlin Wall at the end of 1989 and the ensuing collapse of Marxist governments around and within USSR highlight the urgent need for such people to have a positive alternative to institutional oppression. Liberal capitalism cannot provide sufficient basis for safeguarding that new freedom. Like Latin America, Europe also needs to heed the invitation to accept the Spirit of the new covenant, accepting God as a partner in the construction of a united Europe where the common good will takes precedence over private profits.

ACKNOWLEDGEMENTS

My thanks now go to the many people who have helped in the preparation of this book:
— to my Columban confrères in Peru for granting me the time necessary for research and writing;
— to the people of Condevilla and adjacent sectors who taught me so much about covenant values in a harsh world and were also patient about the priority given to writing a book on that theme;
— to our staff at Sol de Oro for help with word processing and copying, as well as with accommodation whenever required;
— to John McGreevy and John Kelly for proof-reading each new chapter and suggesting improvements; likewise to my brother Leo and to Maurice Hogan for reading the finished manuscript and making a critique of it;
— to Columbans also in the US, Australia, the Philippines, Rome and Ireland who have helped me by their hospitality and encouragement over the past four years;
— to June Casey for helping with the finishing touches and photocopying of the manuscript in Navan, Ireland;
— to Hugh Smith for helping to finalize arrangements with the publisher, Peter Lang;
— to Ms Iris Kramer-Alcorn who acted on behalf of the publisher to guide me in submitting the manuscript for publication.

Biblical texts are taken from the New Jerusalem Bible, published and © 1985 by Darton, Longman & Todd Ltd and Doubleday & Co Inc, and are used with permission of the publishers. All other quotations or references are gratefully acknowledged in the Notes and Bibliography.

Navan, Transfiguration of our Lord, August 6, 1990.

ABBREVIATIONS

CBQ	Catholic Biblical Quarterly
ET	English Translation
FT	French Translation
IT	Italian Translation
JBC	Jerome Biblical Commentary (1968)
NAB	New American Bible
NCCHS	New Catholic Commentary on Holy Scripture
NJB	New Jerusalem Bible
NJBC	New Jerome Biblical Commentary (1989)
P-b	Paperback
ST/ Sp.T	Spanish Translation

Books of the Bible are abbreviated in the usual way of giving from one to five of the opening letters, e.g.:

1 & 2 K = 1 & 2 Kings; 1 & 2 M = 1 & 2 Maccabees; 1 & 2 P = 1 & 2 Peter;

1 & 2 Ch = 1 & 2 Chronicles; Ex = Exodus; Dt = Deuteronomy; Mk = Mark;

1 & 2 Cor = 1 & 2 Corinthians; Gen = Genesis; 1 & 2 Sam = 1 & 2 Samuel;

Phil = Philippians;

1 & 2 Thess = 1 & 2 Thessalonians.

Qumran documents:

CD	Covenant [of] Damascus
QH	Hymns of Thanksgiving
QM	Rule for the War
QS	Manual of Discipline
QSa	Rule of the Congregation

INTRODUCTION

This book has arisen from two converging convictions acquired by a lifetime related to God as encountered in the family circle, in others, especially the poor, in the Church and especially in its sacred Scripture. The first conviction is that the covenant concept is central to the entire Bible, enabling us to appreciate God's plan for the whole human family, a plan still unfolding in our own troubled world of today. The second conviction is that the new covenant under which we are now invited to live is the best way to consolidate whatever freedom we already possess, while demanding of us a wholehearted commitment to work for the integral liberation of every person.

As an exegete I have always been deeply interested in the way the covenant concept appears within the first chapters of Genesis and continues appearing at crucial points right through to the close of Revelation. The division of the Bible into Old Testament and New Testament arose from St Paul's contrasting the old covenant with the new in 1 Cor 3,6-14. Although we may regret that the Latin used **"testamentum"** instead of a word meaning explicitly "covenant", it does alert us to the difficulty of finding any one modern word that does full justice to either the original Hebrew **b^{e}rit** of the O.T. or the Greek **diatheke** of the N.T. That difficulty is dealt with in the opening chapter of this book. Suffice it to note here that I will be quoting extensively from the New Jerusalem Bible[1], which consistently uses "covenant" to translate those two original words wherever they occur. This is to treat them both as expressing the same basic biblical concept, which is nevertheless open to a wide variety of nuances. The particular shade of meaning has to be deduced from the text and general context in which it occurs.

As a missionary working with the poor in a suburban parish of Lima, Peru, since 1978, I have also been keenly interested in liberation theology, as a new way of doing theology, and as a movement to encourage a liberating praxis in solidarity with the poor and oppressed. Lima is the home city and archdiocese of an acknowledged father of liberation theology, Gustavo Gutiérrez, whose writings, lectures and summer schools have helped considerably to relate biblical covenant to modern yearning for integral liberation[2]. His Archbishop, Juan Cardinal Landázuri Ricketts, has always respected his search for pastorally conditioned and pastorally oriented theology.

The final chapter of this book attempts to indicate something of the rich possibilities for developing further the implications of the covenant with regard to liberation theology. Meanwhile the whole work keeps in mind how today's oppressed and afflicted are crying out for liberation.

A. COVENANT CONCEPT AS CENTRAL TO BIBLE

1. Covenant as central to O.T.

Biblical scholars in the latter half of this century have stressed the importance of the covenant in the religious and social life of Israel, as reflected throughout the O.T. Walter Eichrodt presented a fine "Theology of the Old Testament" centred around the covenant[3]. Bernhard Anderson has successfully introduced us to "The Living World of the Old Testament" by relating the story of Israel as the covenant community[4]. In a recent study Sharon Ringe can rightly claim: "To speak of a sovereign God in biblical terms in general, however, is not to describe an omnipotent God and insignificant human beings. The primary vehicle by which God's sovereignty finds expression is God's initiation of covenants with humankind — covenants that are offered anew when human beings violate them"[5]. The more detailed treatment of this topic in Chapter 1 is necessary in order to bring out the richness and variety of insights about the O.T. covenant, as well as differences of opinion that merit attention.

2. Covenant as central to N.T.

Readers of the N.T. readily agree with the many commentators who highlight the kingdom of God as central to the preaching of Jesus[6]. What is not nearly so commonly noted is the close connection between that kingdom and the new covenant. One could get the impression that the inauguration of the new covenant by Jesus at the Last Supper is somewhat marginal to the main theme of the kingdom. It could even be seen as a surprising ritual with little basis in all the previous ministry of Jesus, who is not recorded as mentioning the covenant explicitly anywhere else. The present work, however, will interpret the Gospel as firmly set within the framework of the O.T. covenant and its promises of a new covenant. In this setting Jesus can be seen as preparing his disciples constantly for the supreme hour in which he would declare the inauguration of the new covenant and go forth voluntarily to seal it for ever in his own lifeblood. The reign of God implies that the Father's will is known and freely accepted by his children. Jesus indicated that this is really at the heart of his new covenant by his own complete submission to the Father's will in the searching interlude between announcing that covenant and sealing it. "Father", he prayed in Gethsemani, "if you are willing, take this cup away from me. Nevertheless, let your will be done, not mine" (Lk 22,42).

3. Unity, continuity, fulfilment and surpassing of covenants

Another aim of this work is to indicate the development in the story of God's many initiatives in offering to enter into a covenant relationship with all creation(as in the days of Noah), or with one family (as in the case of Abraham and Sarah), or with one nation (like Israel at Mt Sinai), or with a royal family (as in the reign of David). All that leads up to the promise of a new covenant to replace the Mosaic covenant so badly broken by Israel before the destruction of Samaria and then of Jerusalem. The N.T. reveals both continuity and striking differences between the Mosaic covenant and the new covenant which brings it to perfection, surpasses it in crucial ways, and therefore replaces it[7]. One of the outstanding features of this new covenant is that of it being also a covenant of the Spirit, who sets off the nuclear fission needed to turn hearts of stone into truly human hearts again. Thanks to the indwelling of the Spirit the new covenant community is empowered to love God and all his human family with a little spark of God's own tenderness, compassion and fidelity. This is really the goal of calling humans into the covenant of love with God and with one another.

4. Fresh incentive to search the Scriptures

No book about the Scriptures can ever replace them. It achieves a good deal if it arouses a new enthusiasm and openness concerning the way in which God seeks to communicate himself to us through his word. For this reason I earnestly invite and urge all readers of this present work to keep the Bible itself open at the pages under consideration. One of my hopes in mentioning the New Jerusalem Bible is that its excellent introductions, footnotes and cross references will absolve me from duplicating that wealth of helpful information. My own experience has been that an understanding of the covenant relationship contributes enormously towards an understanding of the entire Bible. Because it has proved to be a many faceted relationship, I willingly share whatever light has been shed on it for me by thousands of others during many decades of reading and ongoing community reflection related to pastoral involvement.

B. LIBERATION IS FOR COVENANT

1. Exodus as a paradigm for liberation

One of the principal biblical images recalled by liberation theologians is that of the exodus of Israel from their Egyptian slavery. A recent issue of Concilium confirms this point[8]. What has struck me during the past twelve years working in Latin America is the need to relate the political liberation of Exodus more explicitly and fully to the covenant. Yahweh set his people free from slavery in Egypt precisely in order to invite them to enter as free people into a covenant with himself, their **Go'el**, their Liberator, who had just acted so spectacularly as their saving Kinsman. In other words, Exodus itself indicates quite clearly that liberation of the Israelites was <u>from slavery</u> and <u>for covenant with Yahweh</u>. The rest of Israel's history shows how indispensable was fidelity to that covenant for their growth in freedom and social justice[9]. Without that they quickly found new forms of bondage even within their own nation and in the promised land.

Equally important for understanding why Yahweh redeemed the Israelites is his earlier promissory covenant with Abraham, Sarah and their descendants. We will see that covenant emerging as even more basic than the Mosaic one in N.T. writers like Luke and Paul[10]. Then further reflection leads us right back to the earliest chapters of Genesis as the most fundamental of all. In the light of Christ as the perfect image of the Father, we now realise that all people have been made in the image and likeness of God so that they might enter freely into a relationship of love with God and each other. Genesis anticipates Exodus in its teaching, through many simple stories, that human life depends on the development of a truly family spirit. The evasive question of the first murderer, "Am I my brother's guardian?" (Gen 4,9), really cries out for the answer "Yes!" The implications of this theme have given rise to a striking book by L. Alonso Schökel, who stresses that Genesis is the richest book of the O.T.

on the conduct expected between brothers and sisters[11]. It is very significant that Moses' first attempt to intervene as a defender of the Hebrews is inspired by kinship. Having effectively stopped an Egyptian from hurting a Hebrew, Moses is then disturbed to see two Hebrews fighting. He demanded of the main offender, "What do you mean by hitting your own kinsman?"(Ex 2,13). In short, Exodus as a paradigm for liberation must include Yahweh's loving fidelity prior to his intervention in Egypt, then his persistent call for a corresponding fidelity on Israel's part during and after their liberation from slavery.

2. "Exodus" of Jesus as the definitive paradigm of liberation

At the time of the transfiguration of Jesus, Moses and Elijah were speaking with him about the "exodus" he was to accomplish in Jerusalem(Lk 9,31). Here we have Luke linking Jesus' mission as Liberator and Mediator of the new covenant with that of Moses. It is by his death, resurrection, and ascension, according to Lk and Acts, that the definitive "exodus" is achieved, that fully integral liberation is made possible for all Christ's brothers and sisters. Moreover, the risen Christ has become the way into the more perfect promised land. Humanity's goal is to reach an ever deepening communion with the Father, in whatever land they may be. All lands can become a dwelling place for God the Father among his human family. With Father, Son and Holy Spirit as our covenant partners, we are called and commissioned to work together to transform all lands into one great kingdom of God. Now that the risen Christ has walked the dusty roads of this planet, there is reason to expect that "the new heaven and the new earth" will find our race enjoying eternal life on mother earth duly transformed. Meanwhile our task is to work in union with our Liberator to make this world a fitting home for the entire human family. This entails working to transform any unjust or oppressive structure, be it economic, political, social or domestic. Redemption through Christ is so abundant as to break the power of sin in private and public affairs, but always respecting the freedom and innate dignity of the sinners. Normally the gifts of God demand a constant and loving service of others, as exemplified to the utmost limit in the life of Jesus. This is really the inescapable demand if we are in earnest about accepting his "exodus" to the Father as our own paradigm today.

3. O.T. liberation demands ongoing justice and compassion

As we shall see in considering the early covenants, especially that of Mt Sinai, a feature that distinguishes them from ancient non-biblical treaties between other nations is an emphasis on upright moral conduct between members of the covenanted nation. The ancient treaties were content to stipulate how kings, for example, were to behave towards each other, but neither bound the other to enforce a high standard of morality on his own subjects. Yahweh, on the other hand, gave his covenant partner, Israel, more commandments about their community conduct than about honouring himself as their only God. The more we ponder the O.T. the more we realise that God will not accept honour from those who are dishonouring his living image in their neighbour. Yahweh emerges as one whose covenant demands a conduct that reflects, however faintly, something of his own compassion and justice towards everybody. One of the most striking consequences of this is the demand not only to act justly, but to make every effort to restore justice when it has been violated, as Pietro Bovati shows convincingly in his large book on the topic. He gives as the reason for this that O.T. justice(**sedaqa**) "expresses not so much the reference of an individual to an ethical norm but rather the relationship between two beings"[12]. That relationship is what covenant must protect.

4. Jesus' insistence on compassion and justice

In preparing the way for the new covenant, Jesus draws out the interior qualities necessary to carry out properly what was already laid down in the Law. Some aspects of that are touched on in our reflection on what each gospel accentuates. Here it will suffice to mention how Mt, for instance, records two occasions on which Jesus defends himself or his disciples against critics by quoting the prophet Hosea: "Mercy is what pleases me, not sacrifice" (9,13 and 12,7). In Hosea the word here translated as mercy is, in Hebrew, that famous **hesed**, so frequently used to designate the loving loyalty expected between covenant partners[13]. Later in Mt, Jesus has to denounce the scribes and Pharisees: "You have neglected the weightier matters of the Law — justice, mercy, good faith!"(23,23). Constantly by such teaching, as by his personal example, Jesus manifests what kind of liberation he has in mind. It is obviously for a society or kingdom in which the members will give top priority to justice, God-like mercy and compassion. He could demand this of his disciples because it was his own way of life: "the Son of man came not to be served but to serve, and to give his life as a ransom for many"(Mt 20,28)[14]. His solidarity with all those depending on him to act as their liberating **Go'el** led him onwards to Jerusalem, willing to sacrifice his own life for them.

C. AIMS AND METHODS

1. Aims

The principal aim of this work, therefore, is to present a continuous and unified story of covenant as it emerges from beginning to end of the Bible. A complementary aim is to offer some help to theologians and all those committed to the integral liberation of our one human family. This will be a popular presentation by an exegete mindful of the current plea that people be told by the specialists not only what God has said in the past, but also what what he is saying to us today through his biblical word[15].

As an Australian missionary doing pastoral work with some of the desperately poor of Latin America, I must bear in mind the viewpoints and major concerns of the First World as well as of the Third World, while not forgetting the afflicted people of the Fourth World, nor those of the socialist Second World, for they too "live, move and exist" in the one God(Acts 17,28). It is in a spirit of solidarity with the poor, the oppressed, the marginated, and the suffering that I have been moved to offer this modest contribution towards an already rich literature about liberation. This has now become such a vast field that my work is necessarily limited to touching on those key points where the covenant seems to offer valuable insights.

My hope is to facilitate the understanding of the entire range of biblical covenants, culminating in the new covenant under which we are now invited to live. This should provide a good background and abundant motivation for reflecting further on daily life and commitment to those not yet fully free. Liberation through the crucified and risen Christ is <u>from</u> sin and all its consequences, including all forms of social injustice and the unjust structures that help injustice to flourish and enslave. That liberation is also <u>for</u> the necessary freedom of body and spirit to accept the new covenant, then to live fully according to its gifts and demands. These make quite explicit many of the kingdom values frequently proposed by liberation theologians without reference to the new covenant as such.

My contention is that the concept and reality of covenant can help us to accept generously our part as covenant partners of the Father, Son and Holy Spirit. Called, sent out to others and accompanied by such Partners, we share personally and community-wise in Christ's mission to proclaim the new covenant. The covenant relationship favours our own growth in freedom, while at the same time it urges us ever more insistently to risk our all so that others, too, may enjoy the full freedom of the children of God within the covenant community.

2. Methods

In keeping with its character as a popular presentation, this work follows mainly the model of each biblical book being a unified whole having one responsible final author. This method of literary criticism is now frequently termed synchronic. It accepts that the literary work to be interpreted is a coherent message from its final author, even if it is obvious that he has had to pull together quite different earlier units. The faithful usually approach the biblical books with the presumption that each book makes sense as it now stands. They expect to find some common themes running through it and emphasising a central insight or experience of God's people.

At the same time, another valid model for analysing each biblical book must be taken into account. Its model is a book gradually formed by different literary units from different decades and even different centuries. It is well described by Luis Alonso Schökel as a sedimentation model, for it is somewhat like an initial rock upon which layer after layer of sediment settle and practically merge with the rock. However, the expert can indicate where each layer begins and ends. This method gives great importance to determining the date of each layer, with its particular line of interest and argument. The method is called analysis of redactions, as each literary layer is joined to another by a redactor, one who edits an existing document to make it ready for publication. Exegetes avail of this model in order to try and reconstruct the particular concern and orientation discernible in each layer. Their method is termed diachronic, since the material is viewed as spread across much time. Many contributions have been made by such analysis to our understanding of how the covenant ideas arose and developed in Israel[16]. These are kept constantly in mind, even if not frequently acknowledged here.

This work takes up the references to covenant in the Bible a book at a time, more or less in the chronological order of the main events and persons involved in this or that covenant. For example, the covenant involving Noah is treated before the one at Mount Sinai, even if various literary strands about Mount Sinai might be even earlier than those about the Noachic covenant.

Blocks of biblical books are also generally taken up as a block, for instance the Pentateuch, then the six books that are commonly treated as the Deuteronomistic History, namely Joshua, Judges, 1 & 2 Samuel, 1 & 2 Kings. The books of the prophets and the wisdom literature are another two blocks that emerged over spans of many centuries, including centuries of which the Deuteronomistic History also tells us a good deal. Book by book and block by block is intended to simplify following the Bible.

3. Hermeneutics

A helpful distinction is made these days between exegesis and hermeneutics. Exegesis is now thought of mainly as the diligent effort to interpret and explain what the word of God meant at the time it was written down by the inspired writers. Hermeneutics, on other hand, is thought of as the effort to explain what God is saying through those words to his people of today, in their own setting. Their current situation, interests, and burning questions seem so far removed from those of the biblical writers that they may experience great difficulty in bridging that gap. Hermeneutics therefore attempts to bring out more clearly how God is still speaking to us here and now through his inspired word. The various human authors who wrote down God's word are long since dead, but he himself, the principal Author, is still alive and dynamically present in the midst of his reading or listening people of today.

What hermeneutics wants to bring about, therefore, is described by H.G. Gadamer as a "fusion of horizons", although Alonso Schökel would prefer "a readjustment of horizons"[17]. The horizon or perspective of the biblical writer has to become closely related to the horizon of the modern reader. This of course implies that the reader knows and understands his own reality, as well as grasping something of the biblical writer's reality.

Paul Ricoeur has also helped in this field by his insight into the "reservoir of meaning" which a literary work contains, beyond the original meaning that the writer himself may have had in mind as he wrote down his message for readers[18]. Once a human author has committed his message to writing and published it, he does not control the future readers, especially those of later centuries. A literary work therefore is capable of calling forth ideas and inspiration that may surpass what the author had in mind, and yet they have legitimately been drawn out of his work. Biblical images, symbols, metaphors, allegories, parables, paradigms, as well as key concepts, all have great power to capture the interest of modern readers[19]. They can all help us to broaden our own horizon and enrich our whole pattern of thinking, for images and symbols especially free us to cross gorges or break down walls in our approach to contemporary issues.

From this it follows that constant dialogue has to be established between modern daily life and the Bible[20]. One way of ensuring this is to bring the most pressing questions of family and social life to interrogate the Bible. A precedent for this is seen in the case of the Jews of Beroea, who felt challenged by Paul's preaching of the Gospel: "every day they studied the scriptures to check whether it was true"(Acts 17,11)[21].

4. Commitment to the Church as a covenanted community

Exegesis, in explaining what God has said, and hermeneutics, in interpreting what God is saying today through his biblical word, both depend heavily on the living tradition within God's people, both Jewish and Christian. The Christian Church traces back its living roots through Jesus Christ to David, Moses, Abraham and Sarah, Noah and family, Adam and Eve, and so to the Creator and Father of the entire human family. It treasures the Bible as its precious heritage that has emerged from within that first covenanted people and has been significantly enriched within the new covenant community of apostolic times. To that Church the Scriptures have been entrusted, to be preserved without adulteration, to be proclaimed with loving fidelity, to be confirmed by courageous partnership with God through Christ.

It is within the Church, therefore, that all the faithful have access to the living tradition which must guide the whole community as such in its current reflection on how to interpret God's word in today's language. This has to continue in the same Spirit that inspired the preacher in Deuteronomy: "Yahweh our God made a covenant with us at Horeb. Yahweh made this covenant not with our ancestors, but with us, with all of us alive here today"(5,2-3). Many implications of this have been set forth clearly by Robert Daly and collaborators in their book "Christian Biblical Ethics", with its significant subtitle "From Biblical Revelation to Contemporary Christian Praxis: Method and Content", with an added line: "In Consultation with C.B.A. Task Force"[22]. In his own contribution, Daly declares: "Biblical revelation is not something that happened then, got completed or 'bottled' at the end of the apostolic age, and comes to us now only in its bottled form. ..... For 'Christian Biblical Revelation' has not only taken place, it is in reality still taking place in and through both individual and communal experience..."[23].

Praxis is now a key word for indicating the ongoing reflection on the relationship between God's word and the Church's efforts to live it out fully in its current practice. Hence praxis is more than just the practice, or a firm decision to improve this or that practice, or even a solemn Council Constitution that has come from reflection on modern Church practice. Praxis implies an abiding attitude and effective method of reflecting constantly on what is going on today between the Church and all our world. For instance, where we are aware of people being ground into the dirt on which they are compelled by poverty to eat and sleep, we bring this awareness with us as we read anew the Scriptures, above all as we share with the very poor in their biblical reflection.

INTRODUCTION

Together we search the Scriptures, asking them to throw more light on what Yahweh and Jesus of Nazareth are calling us to do about this kind of unjust and dehumanizing situation. Almost every page of the Bible assures us that God is always just and compassionate himself, leading him to demand the same of his people. Guided and given fresh hope by this kind of reflection, we return to reflect again on local conditions and analyse more closely whatever factors are preventing our people from living the kind life that our Father has in mind for them.

We also keep reflecting on the Church's pastoral commitment to work in solidarity with the poor, as the Church of the poor[24]. Is the Church — taken to include all its members — continuing effectively the liberating and saving mission of her Founder and Model? In what ways could her involvement be improved today, in keeping with our insights from God's word and our community's evaluation of the present reality? No definitive answer is given, but each provisional answer must be tested in further reflection on the Bible, as must the new light from God's word for today be brought to bear once more on the Church's efforts towards integral liberation of each and every person[25]. Much remains to be said in the final chapter about the implications of integral liberation for this world's history, economics, politics, social structures etc.[26].

D. COVENANT IN RELATION TO SIGNS OF THE TIMES

1. Council Documents

Two of the most influential documents from Vatican II, "On the Church" and "On the Church in the Modern World," underlined the unity of the whole human race. The latter document declares, for example: "God, who has fatherly concern for everyone, has willed that all men should constitute one family and treat one another in a spirit of brotherhood"(#24)[27]. This is another way of describing the call of all to accept the new covenant of love and kinship with the Father and with one another.

The Extraordinary Synod of 1985, reflecting on Vatican II twenty years after it concluded, issued a message to all the people of God. It is an invitation to intensify the effort to know and understand the Council documents. "It is also a question of putting them more deeply into practice: in communion with Christ present in the Church(**Lumen Gentium**), in listening to the Word of God(**Dei Verbum**), in the holy liturgy (**Sacrosanctum Concilium**), in the service of mankind (**Gaudium et Spes**)". "Through this Church", it declares, "God offers an anticipation and a promise of the communion to which he calls all mankind"[28].

The message later touches on a vision of humanity dear to Paul VI, shared by Vatican II, and frequently recalled by John Paul II: "God has not made us for death but for life. We are not condemned to divisions and wars but called to fraternity and peace. .... For mankind there is a path ... which leads to a civilization of sharing, solidarity and love. We propose to work with all of you towards the realization of this civilization of love, which is God's design for humanity..."29.

My contention is that this "civilization of love" requires that we Christians take seriously and live out fully the new covenant of love. There is no other way in which the Church can fulfil the new commandment given by Jesus on the night he inaugurated the new covenant: "You must love one another as I have loved you. It is by your love for one another that everyone will recognise you as my disciples"(Jn 13,34-35). Only to the extent that the Church practises and proclaims this kind of love can she be a really convincing "sacrament of the unity of the whole human race", as John Paul II put it in his closing homily30.

Genuine Christ-like covenant love is both ingathering and outgoing. It gathers together into one people of God those who freely accept it, moving them constantly to share generously and to serve joyfully within their own community. It also impels them to reach out to every neighbour in need or bondage. Some of the greatest challenges and burdens to be confronted in today's world are mentioned by the Synod, including "those related to lack of respect for human life, the suppression of civil and religious liberties, contempt for the rights of families, social discrimination, economic imbalance, insurmountable debts and the problems of international security, the race for more powerful and terrible arms"31. These are all aspects of world affairs that lead to misery and death for hundreds of millions of God's family, and cry out with as many tongues for genuine solidarity with them in their grim struggle for liberation and active participation in the new civilization of love. Covenant commitment demands that we not only thank our firstborn Brother for delivering himself up as **Go'el** for us; it also demands that we be willing to spend our own life and talents in working in humble partnership with him as kinspeople for any brother or sister held today in cruel bondage.

2. Episcopal Conferences

Vatican II certainly opened up new horizons for the Bishops gathered from all countries and cultures. Fresh impetus was also given to national and regional Episcopal Conferences. They continue to reflect on contemporary concerns along the lines of the Council, making it really relevant for their own regions. Here we can only touch on four outstanding documents that have come forth from such Conferences in North and South America. They amplify what has already been said about the signs of the times and how the Church can best respond to them. They are also representative of the Church active in the First and Third Worlds, with a keen awareness now of the great economic gap between North and South. Many of the issues they highlight are germane to any reflection on the meaning and demands of the new covenant today. What follows now is only a small indication of the many key issues and lines of pastoral action emerging therefrom.

Medellin, Columbia, was the city chosen for the Second General Assembly of the Episcopal Conference of Latin America (CELAM) in 1968. It was inaugurated by Paul VI, who expressed confidence that the Conference would "offer its service of truth and love for the construction of a new, modern and

Christian civilization"[32]. The Bishops themselves said at the conclusion that their reflection had been directed towards "the search for a new and more intense presence of the Church in the actual transformation of Latin America, in the light of Vatican II"[33]. In confronting the rampant injustices that cause huge numbers to live in misery, they recall that the law of love is fundamental for the transformation of the world and is "the dynamism which should move Christians to bring about justice in the world"[34].

They declare likewise that "peace is the fruit of love, the expression of fraternity among people, a fraternity established by Christ, the Prince of Peace, as he reconciled all with the Father"[35]. They confront the "tremendous injustices which keep the majority of our people in a painful poverty, which in many cases is close to an inhuman misery. A mute cry goes forth from millions who seek from their pastors a liberation which does not come to them from any side"[36]. After recalling the prophets' denunciation of similar injustices, the Bishops declare that pastoral preference must be given to the poor, and the Church itself "will present before the world a clear and unmistakable sign of the poverty of her Lord"[37].

Puebla in Mexico was the venue for the Third General Assembly of CELAM, inaugurated by the recently elected John Paul II. The Pope set the pattern for Puebla's clear endorsement of Medellin's "preferential option for the poor" when he stated that today "the growing wealth of a few continues parallel to the growing misery of the masses"[38]. Puebla re-echoed that aspect of poverty, decrying that "our countries produce, on an international level, rich people who all the time grow richer at the cost of poor people who all the time become poorer"[39]. It proceeds to describe in moving terms how such inhuman poverty on all sides is stamped on human faces, e.g.
- faces of children, constantly battered by poverty before and after birth;
- faces of youth, disoriented, frustrated, without training or occupation;
- faces of indigenous and afro-american peoples, the poorest among the poor;
- faces of campesinos, often left landless, dependent, exploited, excluded;
- faces of workers, often badly paid, unable to form effective unions;
- faces of the underemployed, the unemployed and the sacked;
- faces of the marginated and impoverished migrants to the cities;
- faces of the elderly, marginated as "non-producers in society";
- faces of women in particular among the above, for they are "doubly oppressed and marginated"[40].

The evangelization of Latin America, which is the theme of the whole document, is therefore viewed consistently in relation to those millions on whose brow the crown of thorns presses in[41]. Their liberation from all forms of bondage due to sin, both personal and social, has to be realized in history.

As it is being realised in history, integral liberation must embrace all dimensions of human life, including the social, political, economic, and cultural. The Bishops urge a "liberating evangelization", capable of dethroning the idol of money, which they see as a basic deviation of both liberal capitalism and

Marxist collectivism. Allied to them can be the ideology of "State Security" as an absolute, whereby a ruling elite oppresses all opposition[42]. The risen Christ, as "Lord of our history and inspirer of a true social change", calls us to share fully in his resurrection and the ongoing transformation of the whole created world[43]. Moreover, he continues to identify himself with the poorest. Puebla repeatedly announces its "preferential option for the poor", renewing the clear, prophetic and solidary option taken earlier at Medellin[44]. This leads it to opt for pastoral priorities that defend and promote the rights of all the poor.

A second preferential option is made in favour of the youth of Latin America, on whom the Church depends so much for present and future evangelization. Youth must be helped to become active participants in the Church in the whole of its transforming mission[45]. For me, one pregnant sentence expresses well what Puebla desires: "The continent needs people aware that God is calling us to act in covenant with him"[46].

Pastoral Letters of U.S. National Conference of Catholic Bishops

In 1983 the Bishops issued "The Challenge of Peace: God's Promise and Our Response" — A Pastoral Letter on War and Peace. Peace is described in biblical terms as a gift coming from God, yet demanding right order among peoples and within all creation. "The right relationship between the people and God (in Israel) was grounded in and expressed by a covenantal union. ... Peace is a special characteristic of this covenant", hence through Ezekiel God could promise a new and everlasting covenant of peace. Through Jesus Christ he has now established that covenant[47].

In evaluating the morality of the nuclear arms buildup and any form of nuclear war, they reject nuclear war completely. "We see with increasing clarity the political folly of a system which threatens mutual suicide, the psychological damage this does to ordinary people, especially the young, the economic distortion of priorities — billions readily spent for destructive instruments while pitched battles are waged daily in our legislatures over much smaller amounts for the homeless, the hungry, and the helpless here and abroad"[48].

War and peace have become inescapable global issues for the entire human family. "Either we shall learn to resolve these problems together, or we shall destroy one another. Mutual security and survival require a new vision of the world as one interdependent planet. We have rights and duties not only within our diverse national communities but within the larger world community"[49]. The Conclusion explains that these complex issues have been addressed by the Bishops in fidelity to their call by Jesus to be peacemakers. "Peacemaking is not an optional commitment". They want all people to unite in setting up a truly effective international authority to find an enduring substitute for war. At present the threat of war holds the world in bondage from which peacemakers, with God's help, could set it free. "A better world is here for human hands and hearts and minds to make"[50].

In 1986 the same NCCB issued a Pastoral Letter on "Economic Justice for All: Catholic Social Teaching and the U.S. Economy". It manifests many of the same concerns voiced at Medellin and Puebla, including a "fundamental option for the poor", which is later said to be called today the "preferential option for the poor"[51]. The biblical covenant is frequently referred to as the basis and model of how to treat others, e.g. "The justice that was the sign of God's covenant with Israel was measured by how the poor and unprotected — the widow, the orphan and the stranger — were treated. The kingdom that Jesus proclaimed in his word and ministry excludes no one"[52]. Or again: "The focal points of Israel's faith — creation, covenant and community — provide a foundation for reflection on issues of economic and social justice"[53]. A gripping example of how Mosaic laws tried to protect the small family farmer is seen in the Jubilee Year, when accumulated lands and their enslaved owners had to be set free again[54]. As Christians we are called to acknowledge God as "our covenant partner", who enables us to live also in community and partnership with others[55].

Not only must economic measures be judged by their impact on the poor at home, but also on the poor around the world. This global vision and solidarity with the entire human family is a feature of the Letter. This shines through in discussing the budget of $300 billion for military purposes[56], the moral obligation on farmers to grow food for the world's hungry[57], the constant widening of the gap between the rich nations and the poor nations[58], and the urgent need to create an effective international political entity to defend and promote the global common good[59].

In short, "because Jesus' command to love our neighbor is universal, we hold that the life of each person on this globe is sacred". The Letter concludes by touching on the essence of "a new covenant of love": "Love implies concern for all — especially the poor — and a continued search for those social and economic structures that permit everyone to share in a community.."[60].

3. International concern for our one planet

Parallel to the growing awareness that we are all members of the one human family is a gradual realisation that we all have to share just one home — planet earth. To foul any part of our planet is fouling the one and only home we have. If we wreck this home, there is no other one to which we can go for shelter. This growing concern can be seen in a report prepared for the U.N. Conference on the Human Environment. The report was submitted by Barbara Ward and René Dubos, who edited the written contributions of a 152-member committee of environmental experts drawn from 58 countries. It has been published under the title: "Only One Earth — The Care and Maintenance of a small Planet"[61]. Its introduction declares: "As we enter the global phase of human evolution it becomes obvious that each man has two countries, his own and Planet Earth"[62]. A strong warning is sounded that humans need to show much greater wisdom than previously if their behaviour is not to destroy the fine balance of their whole planetary environment. Without that environment life for humans would cease[63]. An appeal is also made for the recognition of all nations' interdependence and basic common humanity. "If this vision of unity — which is not a vision only but a hard and inescapable scientific fact — can become part of the common insight of all the inhabitants of Planet Earth, then we may find that, beyond all our inevitable pluralisms, we can achieve just enough unity of purpose to build a human world"[64]. In its final pages the report notes the prevailing attitude which it has tried valiantly to change: (at present) "world institutions are not backed by any sense of planetary commitment. ... The planet is not yet a centre of rational loyalty for all mankind"[65].

The impact of modern industrialization on the ecology is well evaluated in E.F. Schumacher's "Small is Beautiful" — Economics as if People Mattered. He warns: "Of all the changes introduced by man into the household of nature, large-scale nuclear fission is undoubtedly the most dangerous and profound. As a result, ionising radiation has become the most serious agent of pollution on the environment and the greatest threat to man's survival on earth. ... Yet..the hazard remains, and such is the thraldom of the religion of economics that the only question that appears to interest either governments or the public is whether 'it pays'"[66]. Leaving aside the increasing capacity of many nations to produce nuclear bombs, we must realise that radio-active nuclear waste still remains highly toxic, it can't be destroyed, it can only be stored somewhere. To continue building nuclear power stations before this generation knows how to dispose safely of nuclear waste seems extremely dangerous to our human family and its one planetary home[67].

This kind of profoundly disturbing situation and its bearing on what the Creator has entrusted to us has led the German theologian Jurgen Moltmann to write: "Today exploitation, oppression, alienation, the destruction of nature and inner despair make up the vicious circle in which we are killing ourselves and our world"[68]. These are modern oppressions from which our whole family needs to be fully liberated. For the Christian, this must be an ongoing process oriented towards the full freedom promised as the new creation through Christ. He guides us and all creation towards the End intended by the Father[69]. Creation, the economy of salvation/liberation, ecology, man-made economic systems and eschatology are all inseparably linked.

A recent book by Sean McDonagh, "To Care for the Earth" — A call to a new theology[70], appeals to the story of how we humans have emerged with this beautiful "garden planet of the universe" over a "magnificent span of twenty billion years". It reminds us that "human beings are part of the family of the living" and that in us "the whole universe reflects upon itself and celebrates its own wonderful journey"[71]. The title of the book is expanded in the assertion: "Our human vocation is not to despoil, plunder and pillage, but to foster, nurture, bless and give thanks"[72].

Both themes of covenant and liberation are taken up, e.g. in speaking of Gen. ch 9 on the Noachic covenant between God and every living creature: "This inclusive covenant is at the heart of stewardship . The harmony that should exist between human beings and the natural world emerges from this understanding of interdependence"[72]. With regard to liberation: "Today it is vital for humans and the earth that liberation theology begins to include liberation for every species and the Earth itself. ... Unless the environment is preserved, social justice for all human beings, not to mention other creatures, will simply be a dream"[73].

E. COVENANT IN INTERDISCIPLINARY DIALOGUE

1. Moral theology and Christian ethics

These two disciplines are already so closely related that it will suffice for our purposes to treat them together. The person of Jesus Christ, his own example, his whole teaching, above all his new and all pervading law of love are seen as underlying both disciplines. In both fields more attention is being given to the biblical covenant as an indispensable foundation for maintaining the right relationship to God, to oneself and to all neighbours. This approach is to be acknowledged and encouraged by all that follows in the present work. Today we are the ones who should have what Fritz Chenderlin calls "an awareness of the uniqueness of the 'now' vantage point on the forward edge of the wave of finite being, and of the capacity that gives for living an accumulated wealth of experience never before available"[74]. Here we can only mention a few authors, but ones who provide sufficiently wide bibliographies for years of further study, reflection and practical application to modern life around the globe.

Bernard Häring's writings over the past twenty five years have emphasised the centrality of Christ, his law of love, and increasingly the new covenant dimension in moral theology. For instance, in "The Law of Christ" he says: "The law of the Christian is Christ Himself in Person." A few pages on: "Christ as sole teacher of the New Covenant founded in His sacrifice on Calvary establishes a new law sealed with the Blood of the New Covenant. ... What is new in the moral preaching of Jesus is not antithesis to the Old Testament, but its fulfillment"[75]. Vol 2 is devoted to "Life in Fellowship with God" and "Love in Human Fellowship" — both themes relating Christian love to a "partnership in this incomprehensible love of God for us"[76].

In his more recent "Free and Faithful in Christ", Häring states: "God's saving and liberating action becomes the main motif for life. He makes a new covenant with Moses and the people, and all of Israel's morality is covenant morality"[77]. This "key concept and leitmotif of the O.T." is found to be also at the heart of the N.T.: "That Christ is the fulfilment of the covenant and is, himself, the new covenant, is expressed in many forms"[78]. Vol 2 amplifies this basic reality: "In the God-Man, Jesus Christ, there is a unique and indissoluble covenant between the divine and human natures. ... The covenant relation (of Christians) is not an addition to faith but an essential component of it." Further on: "Christ is the Covenant of the people, solidarity incarnate, who is equally near to all cultures and traditions, bringing all home into the one covenant"[79].

Charles Curran & Richard McCormick have edited a book dealing specifically with : "The Use of Scripture in Moral Theology"[80], in which they note: "In the last two decades Catholic moral theology has given much more importance to the Scriptures, but there is no general agreement about exactly how the Bible should be used in a systematic moral theology." They accept that, on the level of determining the meaning of any text within the Bible itself, "the ethicist will be heavily dependent on the professional exegete" and moreover "the particular text must be seen in relation to the whole Bible"[81]. They also insist on the need to relate the Bible to "the other sources of ethical wisdom and knowledge for the discipline of moral theology"(including tradition, magisterium, human experience and reason)[82].

In the same volume Hans Schürmann & Philippe Delhaye treat of "Actual Impact of the Moral Norms of the N.T.". They indicate that the exemplary conduct of Jesus and his own words making explicit the fundamental attitude of love suffice to establish the commandment of love as the 'law of Christ'[83]. Likewise Edouard Hamel sees the person of Christ as pervading all our morality: "There is continuity between the two covenants, but this continuity is guaranteed and measured by the person of Jesus which remains, in Paul, the central theme of his theology and of his moral law. The key to a proper understanding of N.T. morality is, therefore, not Paul's criticism of the law but the person of Jesus, heart of the Pauline and Christian kerygma"[84].

Robert Daly considers Christian ethics as "a part or division of Christian theology" and as such can be called "moral theology"[85]. Given that exegetes and systematic theologians tend to work in clearly demarcated zones, he recommends more commitment to a "community of scholarship"[86]. He also presents Christian biblical ethics as both a science and an art. As science it implies accurate knowledge of what we are and should do; as an art it implies the virtue necessary to translate such knowledge into consistently good conduct and right living. "Great art, of course, usually results from the marriage of great talent with great technique"[87].

For William Spohn, "Ethics is the more organized and abstract expression of morality, our ordinary experience of discovering what is worth living for and trying to live for it." With regard to the use of Scripture in ethics for today's believers, he declares: "The Christian belief that the same Spirit that inspired the authors of Scripture still inspires the use of Scripture in the Church today gives us hope of a faithful continuity with those early believers. The meaning of a specific scriptural passage _then_ has a controlling influence on its meaning _now_"[88](italics are his). An important aspect of covenant morality according to the Decalogue is touched on: "The call of covenant morality rests on profound gratitude for an undeserved deliverance"[89].

Exegetes like Rudolf Schnackenburg and Ceslaus Spicq have provided extensive coverage of N.T. morality[90]. The latter has recently concentrated on what the Bible suggests about religious knowledge which inspires and directs action[91]. He finds that biblical morality is to do the will of God made known to and interiorized by the mind and heart of the believer. The life of the incarnate Son of God was to accomplish his Father's will. The 'New Man in Christ' is given the perception to judge in each case what is the will of God. A characteristic of the new covenant is that the Christian's conscience, enlightened and strengthened by God, becomes the expression of God's will[92].

A penetrating exegesis along this line, but concentrating on a limited number of Pauline texts, is given by T.J. Deidun in "New Covenant Morality in Paul"[93]. His preface states: "This study deals with important aspects of christian morality in the perspective that is characteristic of Paul, that of the New Covenant. .... It discusses the novelty of the Church's self-understanding — Christians form the People of the New Covenant — and the centrality of the New Covenant in Paul's theology[94] (author's italics). Commenting on Phil 2,12f. he says: "it is this wonder of the New Covenant wrought in the heart of human freedom that constitutes the ground of the christian imperative and of christian morality"[95]. On Gal 5,22f. he comments: "Christian life is a yielding to what God has done in Christ, and what he now does in us through the Spirit of Christ"[96]. We shall return, when discussing the Pauline epistles, to other valuable insights given by this exegete. Here it is worth giving one of his conclusions: "The most general conclusion regarding Pauline ethics is that the theology of the New Covenant provides a most useful and comprehensive framework within which to view the larger issues and more special problems raised by Paul's understanding of christian morality"[97].

A recent work of Francisco Moreno Rejón, "Salvar la Vida de Los Pobres", presents clearly the most pressing ethical dimensions of a Latin American theology of liberation, with special reference to the contemporary Peruvian reality[98]. Solidarity with the poor, for whom abject poverty brings so much death, urges him to "elaborate an ethics of life starting from the threatened and precarious life of the poor. ... ... What demands are made on us by the Peruvian context in which we are called to proclaim the God of life who heals, saves and frees us in Christ?"[99]. A basic demand is that the moral theologian himself should not simply know about the dehumanizing reality but live it, perceive it in community with the poor, and be personally committed to struggle with them to change the situation. From such involvement in praxis arises the ongoing reflection for a systematic ethics, which must in turn be reflected on and evaluated in relation to the community's current experience. Thus a new (or modified) praxis can emerge, and so on[100]. Allied to this is the constant effort to read, preferably in a community of the poor, the Scriptures "with the eyes and the heart of the poor". The Bible read that way is "the inevitable pole of reference for ethics"[101].

Roger Haight in "An Alternative Vision" — An Interpretation of Liberation Theology — observes perceptively concerning its ethics: "..the effects of the operation of the Spirit are precisely to release freedom from bondage, to open it up and free it for commitment on all its levels, but with special focus on ethical action in the social arena"[102]. He agrees that the human person is so socially constituted that he can't ignore life's social dimensions and demands. "In a pluralist society social ministry dealing with public structures must be objectively reasoned and pubicly argued by means of middle axioms, that is, socio-economic, political, and ethical principles, through which Christian values are brought to bear on society in a reasonable way"[103].

The universal dimension of God's reign and hence of the Church's mission to the world is well portrayed by Donald Senior and Carroll Stuhlmueller in "The Biblical Foundations for Mission"[104]: "The church's call to be universal touches the very issues that seem to perplex the church today: the impact of liberation theology, the urgent challenge of global justice and peace, debates over pluralism in dogma and praxis, dialogue with Judaism and non-Christian religions, church government, the emergence of new forms of ministry, the role of women. Having to struggle with such issues is a necessary consequence of belief in a universal gospel. ... (By sharing their religious experience) Christians attempt to fulfill the divine mandate given to the church that humanity reflect God's own life as one people drawn together in love and respect" [105].

2. Social sciences

These are concerned with many matters already mentioned under signs of the times and Christian ethics. Our manner of following the biblical covenants right through the history of Israel and the Church of the N.T. requires constant attention to their economic, political, and sociological dimensions. There is more awareness today among both exegetes and liberation theologians that interdisciplinary collaboration is called for in these areas. Norbert Lohfink brings out well the proper outlook with regard to the "this-worldly" transformation made possible and demanded by the arrival of God's kingdom in our midst: "The Bible conceives the comprehensive character of the Kingdom of God now in this world. That would mean that the human management of economic affairs would itself have to belong to the lordship of God... In the biblical sense, the Kingdom of God means the transformation of this world, including its economic dimension. ... God wills with divine passion to implement his lordship already in this world and this society"[106]. It would be quite wrong to think that the N.T. has done away with the economic dimension of God's reign, as though only the afterlife in heaven mattered now[107].

Sharon Ringe likewise sees a continuity in the imagery of the Jubilee Year, which Jesus used in opening his own mission to Israel. "Through these images", she says, "of the one who as the Christ heralds the Jubilee of God's reign, we might find the courage to struggle for justice and peace, and to dare to yearn for the time of liberty acceptable to God"[108].

A strong advocate of the social sciences as a necessary ingredient for speaking about God in the midst of dehumanizing poverty is Gustavo Gutiérrez. He insists repeatedly: "Our conversion to the Lord implies this conversion to the neighbor. ... To be converted is to commit oneself to the process of the liberation of the poor and oppressed, to commit oneself lucidly, generously but also with an analysis of the situation and a strategy of action"[109]. Later in the same work he points out: "Peace, justice, love and freedom are not private realities.... They are social realities, implying a historical liberation. A poorly understood spiritualization has often made us forget the human consequences of the eschatological promises and the power to transform unjust social structures which they imply"[110].

How social analysis helps us to know, interpret and engage effectively in changing the oppressive reality of the poor is well explained by him in "La verdad los hará libres" — confrontaciones[111]. This kind of social analysis, he insists, is a meeting between theology and the social sciences, not with "marxist analysis" as such, even though the latter offers some valuable insights. He refers back to the same theme in: "The Power of the Poor in History". There he has praised "an ongoing dialogue with the sciences". He sees the challenge for theology in Latin America to be not from the nonbeliever but "from the nonperson". — "They question first of all our economic, social, political and cultural world"[112]. To proclaim convincingly to them that God is Father, we must be actively committed with them as brothers and sisters in battling against all oppressive social structures[113].

A good example of the way social scientists are contributing to the solution of contemporary world problems is furnished by the Swedish sociologist and economist, Gunnar Myrdal, in "The Challenge of World Poverty. A World Anti-Poverty Programme in Outline"[114]. In three big areas especially he indicates some indispensable steps for meeting the present world-wide challenge:

The first area is that of prevailing attitudes and moral values. The egalitarian ideal needs to become much more firmly rooted in public institutions as well as in the hearts of the majority of the people. "The underprivileged have to become conscious of their demands for greater equality and fight for their realization"[115]. Education is an important factor in changing people's attitudes with regard to economic issues and encouraging commitment to changing economic systems to benefit rather than impoverish large masses of people. First World governments, banks, armed forces, and academics so far have favoured the richer sectors in the Third World and rarely the poor. Too often this has really increased the control of minority groups over the bulk of their own increasingly impoverished people[116].

A second area is the ownership and use of land in developing countries. The grave shortage of food in such countries should be met by greatly increasing agricultural production. Better methods are available, but even more radical a need is to let the millions of poor agricultural workers own a piece of land. This is an "immensely important, practical and concrete aspect of the equality issue"[117]. Landlords of large estates frequently use their profits to invest in urban projects instead of in their farms or on their farm labourers and their country towns. Farms in countries where millions are looking for work should be as labour intensive as possible, avoiding the purchase of costly imported machinery which replaces the human worker[118].

The third area is that of the responsibility of the economists themselves to be completely professional, making their own careful analysis of all the relevant factors, including the human ones. If people themselves need to be changed in order to permit a truly healthy economy that will ensure the well-being of all the population, then that factor is relevant even for an economist. "The social scientists", he claims, "represent the main link between rational and actual policy choices. Among them we economists, as planners and actual advisers to peoples and their governments, dominate their inter-relation"[119]. One big hazard for the economist is that he can so easily accept as true and universally valid the policy of his own government, whereas he should assess it critically to see if it represents a bias. Biases are the usual fruit of any country's culture, hence are unintentional and often not even noticed. However, a bias carried in to evaluate some other country's situation can be extremely misleading. "Generally speaking, a purge of bias from economic research will lead to policy conclusions demanding radical reforms in underdeveloped countries and radical changes in the aid and trade policies of developed countries.."[120]. He also urges economists to write to convince the non-specialists as well as fellow-economists. After all, "science is never anything more than highly rationalized common sense"[121].

F. COVENANTING FOR "JUSTICE, PEACE, AND THE INTEGRITY OF CREATION"

In March 1990 the World Council of Churches (WCC) held a Convocation in Seoul, Korea, on "Justice, Peace and the Integrity of Creation" (JPIC). Not only has it shown how those three themes are now inseparably linked together throughout the world , but it has also called on Christians to commit themselves to work together in the spirit of the biblical covenants. The Convocation was able to make a fourfold "Act of Covenanting" as its participants' response "to the threats of injustice, violence and the degradation of the human environment". The kind of commitment proposed included "concrete action out of renewed faithfulness to the covenant". The participants were also committing themselves to raise the same issues within their own churches and "to report on progress to the Seventh Assembly of the World Council of Churches in February 1991".

The four areas for which the Act of Covenanting was made were as follows:

1. "For a just economic order", at local and international levels, with special attention to the current bondage to foreign debt suffered by hundreds of millions of people;
2. "For the true security of all nations and peoples", with demilitarization, an end to militarism, and with the adoption of non-violence as a force to bring about liberation;
3. "For preserving the gift of the earth's atmosphere and to nurture and sustain the world's life", with an effort to live "in harmony with creation's integrity";
4. "For the eradication of racism and discrimination on national and international levels for all people", with a sustained effort to break down all walls erected through sins of racism.

That fourfold commitment is recalled in the Final Approved Message from the Convocation, which begins with a reference to covenant: "Now is the time to commit ourselves anew to God's covenant. ... All life on earth is threatened by injustice, war and the destruction of creation because we have turned away from God's covenant."

The Act of Covenanting was seen as a crucial step leading up to the Seventh General Assembly of WCC to take place in Canberra, Australia. The Seoul Convocation carries an appeal to the WCC "officially to make its own this ecumenical process of covenanting for JPIC and at its forthcoming Seventh Assembly to assure its continuation"[122] (emphasis added).

Because the manuscript for this book had already been completed and put into the hands of publishers well before that Convocation took place in Seoul, this is all that can be said of it for the present. Hopefully it will suffice to draw attention to the extraordinary prominence given to covenant by the Convocation. Many practical implications of covenant commitment in the midst of today's struggles for life are presented. They suggest various ways in which modern Christians can commit themselves to work together ecumenically in the Spirit of the new covenant. As the WCC is to take up these themes at the forthcoming General Assembly, it is to be hoped that they are thoroughly endorsed and publicized. And may this book also help in some way to confirm the importance of covenant for effective ecumenical dialogue and personal commitment to the many poor people still in bondage today.

NOTES

1. H.Wansbrough (Gen.Ed.), The New Jerusalem Bible (London: Darton, Longman and Todd, 1985).
2. G. Gutiérrez, A Theology of Liberation (E.T. by Sister Caridad Ida & John Eagleson, London: S.C.M., 1974). Cf. 36; 157: "The Covenant gives full meaning to the liberation from Egypt; one makes no sense without the other... The Covenant and the liberation from Egypt were different aspects of the same movement, a movement which led to encounter with God".
3. W. Eichrodt, Theology of the Old Testament, 2 vols. (Philadelphia: E.T. by J. Baker, Westminster Press, 1961 and 1967).
4. B. Anderson, The Living World of the Old Testament (Harlow, Essex, 1978³).
5. S. Ringe, Jesus, Liberation And the Biblical Jubilee (Philadelphia: Fortress Press, 1985), 96.
6. R. Schnackenburg, God's Rule and Kingdom (London: E.T. J. Murray, Burns & Oates, 1968²); J. Jeremias, Abba, y El Mensaje Central del Nuevo Testamento (Salamanca: S.T. by A. Ortiz & others, Sigueme, 1983²); J. Fuellenbach, Kingdom of God — Central Message of Jesus (Class Notes, Nemi; and Rome: Pontifical Gregorian University, 1986).

7. S. Lyonnet, Il Nuovo Testamento alla luce dell'Antico (Brescia: Paideia, 1971) esp.9-26 on the unity of the two Testaments; A. Vanhoye, Our Priest is Christ (Rome: E.T. by M. Richards,Pontifical Biblical Institute, 1977), e.g. 11: "Resemblances, differences, superiority; such are the three relationships that must be noted in regard to Christ's high-priesthood when compared with the ancient worship"; L. Sabourin, The Bible and Christ — the unity of the two Testaments (New York: Alba House, 1980).
8. B.van Iersel & A. Weiler(Eds.), Concilium N.189 (Feb. 1987) devoted to a single theme: "Exodus — A Lasting Paradigm", on which some 14 contributors offer reflections. Cf. also Michael Walzer, Exodus and Revolution (New York: Basic Books, 1985), in which many of the political lessons and their diverse application in other countries are considered.
9. J. Bright, A History of Israel (Philadelphia: Westminster, 1972^2).
10. The "**Magnificat**" and "**Benedictus**" both recall the promise to Abraham, but do not mention the covenant through Moses(Lk 1,46-55.68-79). Cf. Gal 3 & 4; Rm 4 & 9-11 on the basic role of Abraham and the promise to him.
11. L. Alonso Schökel, ¿Dónde está tu hermano? —Textos de fraternidad en el libro de Génesis (Valencia, Institución San Jerónimo, 1985). e.g. 13: "...creo que el Génesis es el libro más rico del Antiguo Testamento para tratar este tema(de la fraternidad)".
12. P. Bovati, Ristabilire la Giustizia (Rome: Biblical Institute, 1986), 10 and 17, where he stresses the biblical call to live in justice and to re-establish justice wherever it has been violated.
13. Cf. J.L. McKenzie, "Aspects of Old Testament Thought", in The Jerome Biblical Commentary (London: G. Chapman, 1968) 736-767, esp. 752-3 on covenant love and kinship, etc. Cf. P. Kalluveetil, Declaration and Covenant — A Comprehensive Review of Covenant Formulae from the Old Testament and the Ancient Near East (Rome: Pontifical Biblical Institute, 1982), p.48: "Still in some cases **hesed**'s covenant implication is so strong as to substitute for b^{e}rit. In such instances...**hesed** can be understood as a synonym for covenant".
14. Cf. documents On the Church, #27; The Church and the Modern World, #57; Bishops' Pastoral Office in the Church, #16; Ministry and Life of Priests, #12; Priestly Formation, #4.
15. Cf. W.Spohn, What Are They Saying About Scripture and Ethics? (New York: Paulist Press, 1984), esp. 3-4.
16. L. Alonso Schökel, Hermenéutica de la Palabra (Madrid:Hermenéutica Bíblica (Madrid: Cristiandad, 1986) 184-185.
17. Cf. ibid. 239-240. Also N.Gottwald(Ed.), The Bible and Liberation (Maryknoll: Orbis,1983^2) 2, where various chasms that the study attempts to bridge are mentioned, including those between "religion and the rest of life", "the past as 'dead history' and the present as 'real life'", and "biblical academics and popular lay Bible study". Cf. E. Schüssler Fiorenza, Bread Not Stone — The Challenge of Feminist Biblical Interpretation (Boston: Beacon Press, 1984), 31-8.

18. P. Ricoeur, Art. "Hacia una teología de la Palabra", in Exégesis y Hermenéutica (Madrid: Sp.T. G.Ballester, Cristiandad, 1976) 33-50, 237-253; and "Bosquejo de Conclusión", ibid. 225-234, esp. 230-1 where Ricoeur expounds the historical continuity between the text itself, its transmission and interpretation within the living community, which continues to be both interpreting and interpreted by the Word of God. Cf. C. Segre, Avviamento all'analisi del testo letterario (Torino: Einaudi, 1985), esp. 5-21 on how the reader enters into relation with the literature rather than directly with its author.
19. Cf. S. Ringe, op.cit, 4-6: "(Symbols) not only name meanings that already exist, but also evoke new meanings. Symbols give rise to thought." She prefers to speak of images, as being broader and more inclusive than symbols. "Images are rooted in particular social, cultural and political contexts. ... Images have the power to change one's world. ... Images bridge traditionally separate fields of inquiry and arenas of life." In the Editor's Foreword, x, W. Brueggemann highlights these aspects of Ringe's approach: "She sees that the social proposal of Jubilee has come to function as a powerful metaphor, so that what was sociology takes on a literary rhetorical power well beyond a specific social proposal. .. The metaphor now invites to a social possibility that lies well beyond the initial proposal." Furthermore, xi: "The metaphor as elusive and provocative social possibility continues to push forward into the life of the community wherever the text is taken seriously."
20. Cf. C. Mesters, Lecturas Bíblicas — guías de trabajo para un curso bíblico (S.T. N.Darrícal, Estella, Navarra: Verbo Divino, 1986), e.g. 18: "El fruto de la biblia es el sentido que la biblia tiene para nosotros" (italics his); also following pages 19-21 on "engaging gear" from life to Bible and Bible to life. Cf. his Flor Sin Defensa — Una Explicación de la Biblia a Partir del Pueblo (S.T. CLAR, Bogotá: CLAR, 1984). Also R. Haight, An Alternative Vision (New York: Paulist Press, 1985) 31: "Increasingly people will believe or not believe to the extent that systems of belief are experienced by people as meaningful or not for their human lives."
21. Cf. H. Bouillard's art.:"Exégesis, Hermenéutica y Teología. Problemas de Método", in Exégesis y Hermenéutica (Eds. R. Barthes & several others, S.T. by T.Ballester, Madrid: Cristianidad, 1976), 213-224. Cf. also E. Arens: La Biblia Es Para Todos, in El Quehacer Teológico desde el Perú (Eds. E. Arens & P Thai Hop, Lima: ISET, 1986) 73-95, e.g. 75: (Speaking of usual formation for exegetes): "No se nos introdujo adecuadamente en la hermenéutica bíblica, es decir, en el arte de interpretar el texto para el hombre de hoy."
22. New York: Paulist Press, 1984.
23. "The Science and the Art of Christian Ethics", op.cit. 119.
24. M. Farina, Chiesa di Poveri e Chiesa dei Poveri — La fondazione biblica di un tema conciliare (Roma, Libreria Ateneo Salesiano, 1986), esp. 167-207 on evangelical poverty in Luke, who singles out what was already determined by the risen Lord "che ha costituito la Nuova Alleanza e ha

inaugurato la nuova fraternità. La sequela di Gesù se realizza ora nella Chiesa e si traduce nella **agape—koinonia** che si concretizza anche nella condivisione dei beni(167)".

25. Cf. D.Lochhead, "The Liberation of the Bible", in N. Gottwald (Ed.) op.cit., 74-93, e.g. 78: "By praxis I mean the way theory and practice fit together. I say certain things; I hold to certain opinions; I do certain things. How are these things interrelated? How does what I think fit together with what I do?" Also F. Moreno R., Salvar La Vida De Los Pobres — aportes a la teología moral (Lima: CEP, 1986), 47-73, which includes a bibliography on "praxis" on p.49, note (5).
26. Cf. N. Lohfink, art.: "The Kingdom of God and the economy in the Bible", in Communio 13(1986), e.g. 220: "Between these images of two opposed worlds of economic activity there lies the Exodus: the exit from the State economic system of an oriental despot and the entry into a new social order of free brotherhood on Mt. Sinai. .... What Israel called 'redemption' was concretely a change of economic systems effected by God."
27. W. Abbott, The Documents of Vatican II (London: G. Chapman, 1966), 223. Cf. within same Pastoral Constitution #33, #40, #43, #55, #92; and in "The Church" #28.
28. The Extraordinary Synod — 1985 (Boston: St Paul Editions, n.d.) 32.
29. Ibid. 35. Cf. also John Paul II's Message in preparation for the World Day of Youth to be celebrated during his visit to Buenos Aires on Palm Sunday, 1987: "No puede haber auténtico crecimiento en la paz y en la justicia, en la verdad y en la libertad, si Cristo no se hace presente con su fuerza salvadora. La construcción de una civilización del amor requiere temples recios y perseverantes.." (Osservatore Romano, Nov. 30, 1986).
30. The Extraordinary Synod — 1985, 103.
31. Ibid. 34.
32. The Medellin Conclusions — The Church in the Present-day Transformation of Latin America in the Light of the Council (E.T. Division for Latin America — USSC, Washington,D.C.). The translations of Medellin, however, are my own; references given below are to facilitate further reading.
33. Ibid. Introduction, #8, 37.
34. Ibid. 1: Justice, #4, 42.
35. Ibid. 2: Peace, #14 c), 60.
36. Ibid. 14: Poverty of the Church, #2, 188.
37. Ibid. #18, 195. Cf. the Message from Medellin to the Peoples of Latin America concering "Commitments", ibid 28.
38. Inaugural Discourse, III,4, reprinted in Puebla — III Conferencia General del Episcopado Latinoamericano (Edition authorized by CELAM; Lima: Editorial Labrusa, 1982^4), 19.
39. Puebla, #30, 56.
40. Ibid. ##31-39, 56-57; and #1135, footnote 2.
41. Cf. Second Part, Ch. 2: What is Evangelizing?, 1-3, ##340-469.
42. Ibid. 4-5, ##470-562, 135-152.

NOTES

43. Ibid. #174; #175-181; #195-197(in which it is stated that the risen Christ is leading the world towards the fulness of "communion and participation", a goal ardently desired by Puebla); #276-8.
44. Ibid. #1134; cf. ##382; 707; 733; 769; and 1217.
45. Ibid. ##1186-7; 1218.
46. Ibid. #279.
47. (Washington, D.C.: United States Catholic Conference, 1983), #32, p.11; cf. #53, 17 which declares: "The way to union has been opened, the covenant of peace established. The risen Lord's gift of peace is inextricably bound to the call to follow Jesus and to continue the proclamation of God's reign."
48. ##132-134, p.42. Cf. F.X. Winter, Art.: After Tension, Detente: A Continuing Chronicle of European Episcopal Views on Nuclear Deterrence, in Theol. Studies 45(1984), 343-351. He is able to report that Bishops around the NATO countries have manifested a "consensus" in condemning all use of nuclear weapons, and in permitting the (temporary) retaining of a nuclear arsenal as a deterrent until complete dismantling of all nuclear arsenals has been agreed upon.
49. Ibid. #244, p.76.
50. Ibid. #333 and #337, pp.102-3.
51. This Pastoral Letter with its accompanying Pastoral Message is reprinted in Origins (Washington,D.C.: National Catholic News Service, Nov.27, 1986). The Message, #16, p.411: "As followers of Christ, we are challenged to make a fundamental'option for the poor' — to speak for the voiceless, to defend the defenseless, to assess lifestyles, policies and social institutions in terms of their impact on the poor. This 'option for the poor' does not mean pitting one group against another, but rather, strengthening the whole community by assisting those who are most vulnerable." The Letter, #52,p.418: "Such perspectives provide a basis for what today is called the 'preferential option for the poor'." Cf.#77, p.420; #88,p.421; #258,p.436.
52. Message, #16, p.411.
53. Pastoral #30, p.415; cf. #40, p.416-7, where it speaks of God coming to aid an oppressed people and to form them into a covenant community; and #330, p.444.
54. Ibid. #36, p.416.
55. Ibid. #41, p.417; cf. #79, p.420; #296, p.440, where it is said that "the unfinished business of the American experiment will call for new forms of cooperation and partnership..."; #297, p.441, calls for an expansion of economic participation, with a broader sharing of economic power.
56. Ibid. #20.p.414; cf. #294, p.440; and #320, p.443.
57. Ibid. #228, p.434; and ##282-4, p.439.
58. Ibid. #290, p.440.
59. Ibid. #261, p.437; and #323, p.443.
60. Ibid. #326, p.443; and #365, p.448.
61. Harmondsworth, Middlesex: Penguin Books, 1972.

62. op.cit. 32.
63. Ibid. 87.
64. Ibid. 297.
65. Ibid. 298.
66. New York: Harper and Row, 1973, pp.135-6.
67. Ibid. 136-145.
68. J. Moltmann, The Future of Creation. Collected Essays (E.T. S.C.M. Press, Philadelphia: Fortress Press, 1979) p.110.
69. Ibid. 103-108.
70. London: G. Chapman, 1986.
71. Ibid. 80; cf. 78 and 86.
72. Ibid. 123.
73. Ibid. 203. Cf. id., The Greening of the Church(London: G. Chapman, 1989).
74. F. Chenderlin, 'Do This as My Memorial' — The Semantic and Conceptual Background and Value of **anamnesis** in 1 Cor 11:24-25 (Rome: Pontifical Biblical Institute, 1982), 35.
75. B. Häring, The Law of Christ, 3 Vols.(E.T. E.Kaiser, Cork: Mercier Press, 1963, and Vol 3 1967), Foreword vii; and p.4.
76. Vol. 2, 353; cf. id. The Liberty of the Children of God (E.T. P. O'Shaughnessy, London: G. Chapman, 1967) 18.
77. B. Häring, Free and Faithful in Christ, — Moral Theology for Clergy and Laity, 3 Vols.(New York: Seabury Press, I, 1978; 2, 1979; 3, 1981); Vol 1, p.9.
78. Ibid. 15.
79. Op.cit., Vol 2, 217 and 301.
80. C.E. Curran & R. A. McCormick(Eds.), Moral Theology N°4: The Use of Scripture in Moral Theology (New York: Paulist Press. 1984).
81. Ibid. Foreword vii.
82. Ibid. viii.
83. Ibid. 95-99; cf. R. N. Longenecker, N.T. Social Ethics for Today (Grand Rapids: W. Eerdmans, 1984) esp. 26-28 on "A Proposed Understanding of N.T. Ethics."
84. E. Hamel, Art. "Scripture, the Soul of Moral Theology?", in Curran & McCormick(Eds.) op.cit., 121-122.
85. R. Daly, op.cit. 66-67.
86. Ibid. 37.
87. Ibid. 115.
88. W. Spohn, What Are They Saying About Scripture and Ethics?, 3-4.
89. Ibid. 5.
90. R. Schnackenburg, The Moral Teaching of the N.T. (E.T. J. Holland-Smith & W.J. O'Hara, London: Burns & Oates, 1965). Cf. C. Spicq, Théologie Morale du N.T. , Tome I & II (Paris: Gabaldi, 1970^4).
91. C. Spicq, Connaissance et Morale dans la Bible (Paris: Ed. du Cerf, 1985), 9.
92. Ibid. 8; 47-48; and 87.

93. T.J. Deidun, New Covenant Morality in Paul (Rome: Biblical Institute, 1981).
94. Ibid. Preface xi.
95. Ibid. 69.
96. Ibid. 83; cf. 136: "Only by interpreting the christian faith experience in the theological context of the New Covenant is it possible to appreciate the unique wonder of christian love for what it is —'through and through a Divine work' and, at the same time, truly the act of the acting human subject."
97. Ibid. 227; cf. 228 for a further conclusion: "Thus in the New Covenant, religion and morality are inseparable, for religion is eminently moral and morality is eminently religious."
98. F. Moreno Rejón, Salvar la Vida de los Pobres — aportes a la teología moral, 24 and 29. P.13, ftn. (5) refers to his thesis published under the title of "Teología Moral desde los pobres. La moral en la reflexión teológica desde América Latina" (Madrid: PS Editorial, 1986).
99. Id., Salvar la Vida, 24-25.
100. Ibid. 73; cf. 65; 91; and 105.
101. Ibid. 100. Cf. E. Dussel, Ethics and the Theology of Liberation(E.T. B.F. McWilliams, Maryknoll: Orbis, 1978), esp. 28-51, e.g. 49: "If I am able to make institutions work for the good of the poor, I am complying with the demands of the gospel. Excessive private property leads to an economic system of subjugation. ..... Only by identifying itself with the poor can the church liberate the world from an unjust system."
102. (New York: Paulist Press, 1985), 12.
103. Ibid. 223-8.
104. (London: SCM Press, 1983).
105. Ibid. 3.
106. N. Lohfink, Art. cit. in Communio 13(1986), 218.
107. Ibid. 230.
108. S. Ringe, op.cit. 15.
109. G. Gutiérrez, A Theology of Liberation , 205;   cf. 213-250 on "Eschatology and Politics".
110. Ibid. 167.
111. (Lima: CEP, 1986), esp. 75-112 on Theology and the Social Sciences. It is significant that the Instruction "Sobre Libertad Cristiana y Liberación", issued by the Congregation for Doctrine and Faith in 1986 (reprinted Madrid: BAC, 1986) also refers many times to the implications of the Gospel with regard to social, economic and political structures, e.g. #42; #57; ##60-68; ##74-75; #80; and #81: "The direct aim of this reflection in depth is the elaboration and launching of daring programmes of action directed towards the socio-economic liberation of millions of men and women whose situation of economic, social and political oppression proves intolerable."
112. G. Gutiérrez, The Power of the Poor — Selected writings (London: SCM Press, 1983), p.57.

113. Ibid. 72; cf. 47: "Furthermore, it was thought, politics belonged to a particular sector of society specially called to this responsibility. But today, those who have made the option for commitment to liberation look upon the political as a dimension that embraces, and demandingly conditions, the entirety of human endeavors. Politics is the global condition, the collective field, of human accomplishment." Cf. Donal Dorr, Option for the Poor — A Hundred Years of Vatican Social Teaching (Dublin: Gill & Macmillan, 1983), who indicates in the Introduction that his concern is with the question "that must be the first item on the social justice agenda and at the same time underpins all the rest: what does the Church have to say to, or about, those who are the victims of a society that is structurally unjust?"(p.3).
114. G. Myrdal (Hammonsville: Penguin, 1970).
115. Ibid. 88.
116. Ibid. 21; 186; 210; 211-251 on the "Soft State", where bribery and corruption derail attempts at social reform; 258-9; 306; 356-7; 404; 451.
117. Ibid. 111.
118. Ibid. 108-114; 385; 425.
119. Ibid. 417.
120. Ibid. 417-428.
121. Ibid. 428.
122. Final Document: Justice Peace Integrity of Creation (Geneva: World Council of Churches, Central Committee, March 1990). Cf. John Paul II's Message for Jan. 1, 1990 (World Peace Day) on "Peace with God the Creator, Peace with all Creation", which devotes much attention to ecological issues as integral to the search for justice and peace.

CHAPTER 1: WHAT IS A BIBLICAL COVENANT?

A. INTERNATIONAL TREATIES (NON-BIBLICAL)

1. Wide range of ancient Near Eastern treaties:
Thanks to the diligent work of archaeologists and experts in ancient languages, especially during the last century and a half, we now have access to a rich variety of ancient treaty documents. They have been found in the excavations of ancient cities all round the Ancient Near East, some from well before the days of Abraham, others about a thousand years after that. They are precious witnesses to the way treaties were drawn up and sealed in nations frequently in touch with the Hebrews of the Bible. It throws considerable light on a practice that appears as a normal way to enter into a mutual agreement, generally involving explicit obligations accepted under oath and carrying detailed sanctions. Here we can only mention a few samples from Mesopotamia, from the Land of Hatti, from Syria and Egypt.

a) Sumerian "Vulture Stele" from Lagash, about 2,500 B.C., recording how Eannatum bound the defeated men of Umma to keep various stipulations, according to an oath sworn in the name of the god Nin-ki. Those Sumerians were a leading civilization in the southernmost part of Mesopotamia, where one of their leading cities was Ur, said to be the birthplace of Abraham many centuries later[1].

b) Akkad and Elam entered into a treaty towards the end of the 3rd millenium B.C. The document, found in Susa, records how the conquered ruler of Elam swears fidelity to king Naram-Sin of Akkad. The oath is sworn before the gods of Akkad and Elam; curses and blessings are listed[2]. Akkad was the centre of a powerful Semitic kingdom under Sargon (c.2,500 B.C.). It included Ur within its borders. From c. 2,000 B.C. other Semites, namely the Amorites, took control over much of Mesopotamia.

Concerning the above-mentioned "Vulture Stele" and the "Naram-Sin Tablet", D.McCarthy remarks: "In both cases it is the defeated people or subordinate prince who is subject to the stipulation and who takes the oath.."[3].

c) Mari Letter, sent c. 1730 B.C. by Isme-Dagan to his brother says: "Let us swear a mighty oath between us... Let us establish a lasting brotherhood between us"[4]. Mari was also an important city on the middle Euphrates from the time of the first Sumerian kingdom and endured till the reign of the great Hammurabi of Babylon(c.1700 B.C.). Akkadian language was used and developed there over millenniums.

d) Syrian Treaty between Abb-An and Yarimlim, c.1680 B.C., which may indicate the significance of the frequent O.T. phrase "to cut a covenant", for the treaty declares: "Abba-An is bound to Yarimlim by oath and he has cut the throat of a sheep. If he lets go of the hem of the cloak of Abba-An, he shall forfeit the cities and territory"[5]. Syria also frequently influenced the Hebrews, lying as it did between Mesopotamia and Canaan, being controlled by Aramaeans from about 1200 B.C. Jacob, the father of the twelve tribes, is said to have been been "a wandering Aramaean"(Dt 26,5). From c.500 B.C. Aramaic even became the common language of Palestine.

e) Hittite and Egyptian rulers, Hattusilis III and Ramses II, made a treaty as equals about 1280 B.C., at Kadesh on the Orontes river. Copies are extant in Akkadian cuneiform (i.e. "wedge-shaped") writing and in Egyptian hieroglyphs; translations of both can be seen in Pritchard's great selection of "Ancient Near Eastern Texts"[6]. This provides us, in the view of G. Mendenhall, with "the classical example" of a parity treaty[7]. For us it is doubly significant, because this Ramses II was quite likely the Pharaoh of the oppression in the days of Moses, while the Hittites have left their stamp on the form for making international treaties. This particular treaty is one of non-aggression, "peace and brotherhood between us forever". The rulers call on a thousand gods and goddesses of each country as witnesses, to back up the blessings or curses mentioned on "this tablet of silver".

f) Ugaritic king Niqmadu pledged himself to the Hittite king Shuppilu-liumash by a vassal treaty, declaring: " I am the servant... of the Sun, the Great king, my lord. Towards the enemy of my lord I am an enemy, and towards the friend of my lord, a friend"[8]. P. Kalluveetil finds in this case that "the declaration of vassalage is the only act mentioned in order to express the establishing of the treaty relationship."[9].

g) Assyrian king Ashurnirari imposed a vassal treaty on the Syrian prince Mati'ilu, about 754 B.C., acting out a menacing curse by the substitution of a ritual ram, explaining: "This head is not the head of a ram; (it is) the head of Mati'ilu ... the head of his sons, his nobles, his people, .. if Mati'ilu sins against this treaty"[10]. This has added significance for us in that Assyria at that time was already a big threat to the Northern Kingdom of Israel, which it completely overran within the following thirty years. Prophets and other biblical writers saw that also as a terrible sanction suffered by Israel for violating its covenant with Yahweh.

2. Common elements in those international treaties

We have now sampled treaties made over a period of some 1800 years, involving rulers of practically all the major empires from southern Mesopotamia, up to the Hittite land of Hatti, and down to Egypt. This was during a time span starting long before Abraham and stretching well beyond Moses or David. Nevertheless, D. McCarthy has good grounds for maintaining that "at one point or another the early Mesopotamian, the Hittite, and relatively late Syrian and Assyrian texts link together across a long span of history. ... . To summarize: we find in the treaties a common basic structure with the overlord proclaiming a set of stipulations and the underling obliged to accept them under divine sanction"[11].

Such examples are typical of many ancient treaties that led G. Mendenhall to pick out six elements that recur in Hittite vassal treaties[12]:
1) Preamble or Titulature, identifying the giver of the treaty by his titles, etc.
2) Historical prologue, recalling previous relations between the two parties, especially the benevolent deeds of the overlord.

3) The stipulations, mainly the obligations imposed upon and accepted by the vassal party.
4) Provision for deposit in the temple and periodic public reading, obviously to emphasise the sacredness and seriousness of the treaty.
5) List of gods as witnesses, naming many gods of both parties.
6) The curses and blessings formula, which provides the religious sanctions for violation or observance of the whole treaty.
As we might expect, not every element had to be rigidly spelt out in every such treaty.
3. Different kinds of international treaties
a) Parity treaty: a treaty between two partners who commit themselves as equals, as in the case of Hattusilis III and Ramses II mentioned above in 1e).
b) Vassal treaty: one in which a conquered or weaker king is bound to the stronger king as to his overlord, as in the case of Mati'ilu given above in 1g).
4. Treaties or pacts within a kingdom
Various legal declarations are shown by P. Kalluveetil to use formulae that sufficed to set up a legal relationship or public bond between two parties, e.g. in the areas of adoption, marriage, service and slavery. "Adoption and marriage", he notes in this context, "are connected with the concept of pact"[13].
5. Application of the treaty sanctions
Unlike our modern international treaties, every such treaty was a sacred commitment. The imposition of the sanctions was primarily the task of the various national gods invoked explicitly at the solemn sealing of the treaty. Fidelity to the treaty terms facilitated peace and mutual collaboration between the parties, both of whom could expect to receive the blessings invoked upon loyal partners. On the other hand, serious violation of the treaty by one party left him and his kingdom open to swift and often terrible sanctions carried out in the name of the offended national gods. Obviously the vassal king would have to rely much more on the gods to punish the overlord who violated his part of the treaty. At least he could with an easy conscience look for a treaty with some other king to safeguard his kingdom and to impose the sanctions deserved by the faithless partner.

B. BIBLICAL COVENANTS
1. Extensive use of covenant terms throughout the Bible
a)In the Old Testament
The Hebrew word b^{e}rit is found by P. Buis to occur some 287 times in the Hebrew (Textus Masoreticus) Bible[14]. This does not include, therefore, other occurrences of the equivalent term in the deuterocanonical books such as 1 & 2 Maccabees. B^{e}rit is first used in Gen 6,18 and 9,9 to describe the new relationship established by God with Noah and family, as well as with all creation. From there on it is used frequently in "the Law of Moses, the Prophets and the Psalms", to use our Lord's summary of the Scriptures being fulfilled by him(Lk 24, 44).

b) In the New Testament

The word **diatheke** occurs some 33 times in the Greek N.T., rarely in the Synoptic gospels, not at all in John's gospel or epistles, a little more often in Paul's writings, and reflected upon in depth in Hebrews. It is Paul's references in 2 Cor 3,6.14 to **kaine diatheke** and **palaia diatheke** that have led to our division of the whole Bible into New Testament and Old Testament. It could more accurately have been called Old Covenant and New Covenant, since Paul was referring without doubt to the Mosaic Covenant and the Christian Covenant. This itself is some indication of how central covenant is to the entire Bible.

c) Several other terms to express a covenant relationship

Not every instance of a biblical covenant is termed explicitlyeither **b^{e}rit** or **diatheke**. The reality can be detected from the context, thanks to other loaded words such as **ḥesed**(= loving kindness; loyal love), **'emeth**(=truth; fidelity; enduring loyalty as promised), and **shalom**(=peace; general well-being). Another N.T. example would be the (Greek) word **koinonia**(=communion; community sharing; comradeship). After giving more than 70 packed pages of examples from non-biblical treaties and biblical covenants described only through synonyms or some other indications, P. Kalluveetil can conclude: "The word **b^{e}rit** does not adequately express the full richness of the OT covenant concept. Our synonym and non-synonym texts demonstate the existence of non-**b^{e}rit** covenants"[15]. Even a cryptic phrase like "oil is brought to Egypt"(Hosea 12,2) can be used as the synonymous parallel to "they make a covenant with Assyria". D. McCarthy argues well that, in the context, bringing oil to the Egyptian king would be "a direct allusion to a form of covenant making"[16].

2. Divine and human covenants in the Bible

A *divine* covenant has God as one of the actual parties to the covenant, e.g.between God and Abraham(Gen 15). A *human* covenant is one between humans, even though God is the chief witness and upholder of it, e.g. between Jacob and his uncle Laban(Gen 31). In the N.T. the most likely example is where James, Cephas and John, as Paul says, "offered their right hands to Barnabas and to me as a sign of partnership (**koinonia**): we were to go to the gentiles and they to the circumcised"(Gal 2,9).

From here on we will only use the term covenant when dealing with biblical covenants, whereas non-biblical alliances or pacts will be referred to always as treaties. When we speak of a human covenant, therefore, it will be one found within the Bible. This will apply likewise to any mention of a divine covenant — it must be one mentioned in the Bible, even if not explicitly called there either **b^{e}rit** or **diatheke**.

3. Principal features of the divine covenants

Much of what follows will be true also of human covenants, which actually help us perceive many of the implications of the divine covenants.

However, our scope is more the unfolding of God's plan through the divine covenants.

a) Content

Content is most obvious in the terms of the agreement, in the covenant stipulations or commitments, which spell out the way in which the special relationship is to be lived out. Above all, each covenant expesses or implies a mutual obligation to preserve **hesed**(loving kindness), **'emeth**(loyalty), and **shalom**(peace, integral well-being).

All these three are essential and amount to an undertaking to live in a harmonious family relationship. They are also mutual obligations, since a covenant is by its very nature a relationship entered into and accepted voluntarily by two parties. For a treaty a ruthless king might impose his own stipulations on a terrified vassal, but God does not make his covenants that way. So a covenant remains truly bilateral, even though what is actually mentioned in the text seems to be all one-sided, e.g. in a promissory covenant[17].

On God's part, his loving kindness is already manifested in initiating the particular covenant — without that there would be no covenant. His loyalty is shown by remaining completely faithful to his commitment, often in the form of promised blessing and enduring well-being for the human party. The peace he offers implies great mercy and compassion with regard to human sinners, making possible forgiveness, reconciliation, and renewed partnership in shaping the family or national history.

On the humans' part, covenant love and loyalty demand that they live out fully the demands either stipulated or implied. The Ten Commandments were to spell out the basic conduct not only with regard to God, but also within the human community that had been called together as God's people. The human response within such a covenant is basically one of loving service and trusting compliance with the will of Yahweh as communicated through the encounter.

b) Form of covenant

The human covenants made among the Hebrews indicate that the basic form was a mutual accepting of obligations under oath. This form also underlies the divine covenants, being made explicit in the case of Abraham to whom God bound himself by oath(Gen 22)[18]. Often the oath is left implicit, since God's every word is as firm as an oath, while Israel's acceptance of it with God as witness binds them like an oath. Some other form may replace it, because, as D. McCarthy rightly asserts, "it is simply a fact that there are many different forms of covenant and these different forms imply different meanings"[19]. He also draws attention to the way Genesis distinguishes between "cutting a covenant" and simply "swearing", used absolutely — "'To swear' taken by itself is enough to imply a covenant"[20].

Mendenhall and others following him thought that the Sinai covenant was drawn up from the start in close parallel to the form of contemporary Hittite treaties. Ongoing studies, however, are concluding that it was mainly the Deuteronomistic writers who presented it clearly in that form[21]. We shall discuss this, together with details about the content of each covenant, as we move through the biblical presentation in more or less chronological order. We will be alert to the way such covenants can presuppose so much about both content and form that they may be recorded with surprisingly little detail to establish an irrevocable commitment of both parties[22].

c) Ritual for sealing a covenant

In this area the biblical people manifest more variety than found in the sealing of international treaties. Their semi-nomadic background and their own cultic traditions have led them to confirm or seal a covenant by a sacrifice, by sprinkling of blood, by a sacred meal(i.e. eating reverently something already handed over to God, who then permits it to be shared with his people or family), as well as by a solemn promise or an oath, especially in a cultic setting. These ancient rites conveyed more to the Hebrews than did a lengthy written document, for they signified that a close family or even a "blood" relationship had been established[23].

4. Towards a synthesis of divine covenants

a) Gradual unfolding of God's plan to reunite the human family

In this section we have a short preview of the main lines to be followed in the rest of our reflection. The following juxtaposition of so many seemingly different and even disconnected covenants should forestall any over-enthusiastic effort to force everything into one strict (or preconceived) model or form of covenant. Each covenant was initiated and formulated to some extent at least by God, then eventually recorded for us under his inspiration. It is of paramount importance to let God communicate with us as freely as possible through each such text within its context. While we keep in mind traditional explanations of it, we are also looking at it from today's vantage point, seeking more light on our own world's most urgent questions.

1) Initial relationship through creating man and woman as image of God

Gen 1-3 seems indispensable as the foundation for all future growth in mutual relationships between the Creator and his people. By creating man and woman "in his own image and likeness" God made them capable of free, intelligent, personal and social life, a life open to ever deepening relationships through language and other signs. They are capable of marriage, the fundamental human covenant that receives increasing importance right through to the "marriage of the Lamb" (Rev.19-22). It emerges as the best image of all to represent the divine covenant as well.

2) Covenant with Noah's family and all creation

Gen 6 and 9 are the first texts to speak explicitly of covenant, a divine one in which God promises that there will never again be "a flood to devastate the earth"(9,11). It appears as completely one-sided as far as stated commitments go, and yet we are told that before the flood began Noah was a good man who "walked with God"(6,9), and after the flood he offered sacrifice. In other words, much is left implicit about the response expected of Noah and family with regard to that covenant. The new beginning granted to the human race carries with it a brighter hope than in the case of Adam and Eve.

3) Covenant with Abraham and Sarah

Gen 12-22 abounds in details of how God called this couple to become the parents of a chosen family and eventually a chosen people, to be the vehicles of blessings for all other peoples as well. The principal promises are confirmed by covenant(15 and 17) and also by oath(22). Here again the promises made by God are unconditional, i.e. they don't depend on the obedience of the human partners to the covenant. Nevertheless the whole context indicates that faith and obedience are a vital part of the human response.

4) Covenant through Moses with all Israel

Exodus 19-20; 24; and 32-34 are the key chapters in describing how Yahweh, the liberator of the Israelites from Egyptian slavery, entered into a covenant with them all at Mt. Sinai. This time it is more obviously a two-sided commitment, for the Israelites declare: "Whatever Yahweh has said, we will do"(19,7-8). Through Moses Yahweh gives them the Ten Commandments(20), and they seal the covenant through the sprinkling of sacrificial blood and by a sacred meal(24). All too soon fidelity to their solemn word is forgotten in the incident of the Golden Calf. Yahweh heeds the plea of Moses not to wipe out the sinful people, and the covenant is renewed, but not without some severe sanctions against those who remained deaf to Moses' call to side with him.

Deuteronomy depicts Moses recalling this covenant to the Israelites poised to enter the Promised Land, so that this new generation born free in the desert will live up to its responsibilities.

Then Joshua 23-24 tells of a decisive renewal and extension of that Mosaic covenant, after the land has been occupied and distributed among all the tribes except that of Levi.

5) Covenant with Phinehas assuring "priesthood for ever"

Numbers 25 tells of a "covenant of peace" granted by Yahweh to the zealous priest Phinehas, a grandson of Aaron. Again it is in the form of a promise: "To him and his descendants after him, this covenant will assure the priesthood for ever. ... he will have the right to perform the ritual of expiation for the Israelites"(25,13).

6) Covenant with David and his house

2 Samuel 7 records a prophecy of Nathan in which Yahweh promises David a dynasty and a throne "secure for ever". In this particular chapter the word covenant is not used, but in a later chapter we find among the last words of David: "Yes, my House stands firm with God; he has made an eternal covenant with me"(23,5). Once again first impressions would suggest that Nathan simply passed on a promise, but for David the circumstances call for a covenantal response from him.

Davidic kings such as Asa(2 Chron 14-15) and Josiah(2 Kings 22-23) took seriously their responsibility for maintaining not only the Davidic covenant but the Mosaic one as well.

7) From a broken Mosaic covenant to the promise of a new covenant

Despite valiant efforts of prophets, priests, sages, upright citizens and some Davidic kings, the Israelites as a people did not live up to the minimum demands of the covenant. This was seen by sacred writers as a major factor in bringing disaster upon both the northern kingdom("Israel") and the southern kingdom("Judah"), culminating in the destruction of Jerusalem itself and the Babylonian exile.

Such shattering disasters raised the question as to whether the Mosaic covenant had been so disregarded by the people as to put an end to it. It was a bilateral covenant; by so frequently refusing to keep their side of it, the Israelites had forfeited any right to hold Yahweh to his side of it. In this context came forth prophecies from Jeremiah(31), Ezekiel(34 and 36-37), and Deutero-Isaiah(42 and 54) promising a new covenant, one more effective in bringing pardon for sin and the abiding spirit of Yahweh to ensure fidelity this time.

A group of Essenes at Qumran on the edge of the Dead Sea, from about 135 B.C. to 68 A.D., called themselves the community of the new covenant, but for them this meant that they were trying hard to live out fully a complete observance of the renewed Mosaic covenant.

8) The new covenant proclaimed and sealed by Jesus Christ

In the Gospel account it is only at the Last Supper that Jesus mentions explicitly the new covenant, which he says is to be (sealed) in his own blood as it is shed for all for the forgiveness of sin(Lk 22,20; Mt 26,28). In Hebrews (especially 8-10 and 12-13) it is made clearer that the risen Christ is "the mediator of a new covenant"(9,15). Having entered the presence of the Father, bringing with him his own blood "that sealed an eternal covenant"(13,20; cf. 9,12), he has opened up a living way by which his brothers and sisters may also enter into the presence and perfection of their heavenly Father. This, after all, is the true goal of the divine covenants - full and everlasting communion with the Divine Persons and between all members of their restored human family.

b) Covenant embraces several different kinds of commitment

This is really the root cause of so many seemingly conflicting opinions about what merits the title of covenant. The problem is even more acute in languages like Italian, Spanish and French, where the words "alleanza", "alianza", and "alliance" carry implications of a mutually accepted alliance, bringing new obligations to both parties. P. Buis, for example, is quite justified in concluding from a meticulous analysis of all uses of b^erit in the Hebrew Bible that three quarters of such texts do not speak of a reciprocal agreement between God and his people, a dialogue in act in which man constructs his history with God. "Alliance peut recouvrir plusieurs realités différents"[24]. He remarks that this poses a pressing problem for translators, who would like to use the one French word to translate the same recurring Hebrew word, but it seems necessary to use different words that capture better the particular shade of meaning in each context. On the other hand, he agrees that to do full justice to the original overtones, it may be more satisfactory to use the same French word throughout (e.g. "alliance"), while indicating in a footnote the specific nuance each time[25].

This is a better approach than that of those who take the divine covenants to be unilateral, always administered by God, who thus is really unfolding and extending one single covenant from Noah to Abraham, to Moses, to David and on to Christ[26]. It would also help to avoid the mistaken conclusion reached by D. Hillers: "The Essenes had a covenant, but it was not new; the Christians had something new, but it was not a covenant"[27]. C. Westermann is another scholar who cannot accept that Gen 15,18, for instance, is talking about a covenant between Yahweh and Abraham, partly because here b^erit "must have a broader meaning"[28]. His translation renders it as "Yahweh gave Abraham the solemn assurance"[29].

The divine covenants certainly vary with regard to the commitment which they make explicit, for it can be:
i) unilateral, with God alone binding himself by a promise;
ii) unilateral, with Israel alone stating explicitly its new commitment due to the covenant, e.g. as in Joshua 24(where Jahweh's previous fidelity to all his promises is recalled);
iii) bilateral, with God and Israel both accepting new obligations, as at Mt Sinai(Exod 19-20);
iv) implicitly bilateral, with God imposing obligations on Israel, but in virtue of his benefits already given, together with the assurance that "today he makes you a nation for himself",e.g. as in Deut 29[30].

It must also be noted that a parity covenant strictly so called cannot be made between God and his people,for there is no equality. This has led many to speak instead of a vassal covenant, corresponding to the vassal treaty between a powerful king and a weaker king. If this term is used, though, it does not include the non-biblical nuances of an agreement imposed by means of armed force or overwhelming fear such as conquering kings wielded against weaker kings. The invitation of Yahweh to enter into a covenant with him is always a gracious gesture carrying promises of greater wellbeing.

The word **diatheke** was well chosen by the Greek Septuagint version of the Old Testament to translate the Hebrew b^erit(in most texts). The basic meaning of **diatheke** is not a bilateral treaty, but a disposition, arrangement, especially of property, and in common Greek usage often refers to a disposition made by a last will and testament of one person. The word **syntheke** does frequently mean a bilateral treaty, so it was available for the Septuagint translators, who nevertheless preferred **diatheke**. We may conclude that they have chosen the latter word because it is flexible enough to express best the various shades of meaning conveyed to them by b^erit. A "disposition" can be by means of one will only, or by a last will and testament, or it can be by mutual consent and include mutual obligations.

This is the word that has passed into the New Testament as well, first in texts that are taken from the O.T., then in the texts which speak explicitly of the "disposition" established by Jesus Christ between his Father and the human race. A major concern of the present work is to draw out the real meaning and practical consequences of this new **diatheke**. At the Last Supper it seems to be all one-sided, something bequeathed by Jesus as a farewell gift, with the most obvious obligation being to keep on celebrating it as his memorial. We shall see, however, that the increasingly frequent references these days to "the new covenant" is fully justified and motivates us to reflect more deeply on our own covenant commitments.

c) Development of covenant is coherent if not homogeneous

In attempting to arrive at a synthesis of the divine covenants we will obviously need a broad understanding of the English word covenant. Fortunately it does convey the basic idea of agreement, engagement, dispensation or disposition, especially with reference to the divine economy of salvation[31]. The root meaning is a coming together(Latin: con-venire). On the other hand, it leaves fairly open the kind of agreement involved.

The key to entering and following the seemingly inconsistent path of the crucial covenants mentioned earlier under 4 a) is to recognise that each one does involve a mutual relationship. D. McCarthy could reflect aloud: "It seems legitimate to consider a sure promise as a covenant. ... The essential thing seems to have been that an obligatory relationship was formed"[32]. P. Kalluveetil notes the same latitude for the human covenants: "And **berith** itself is not a univocal concept, it could comprise relationships of different kinds"[33]. The relationship expected as the fruit of biblical covenants is one of family or kinship.

The divine covenants emerge as God's initiative in manifesting and deepening some bonds that already exist between him and his people. This aspect can also be detected in the human covenants described, e.g. between David and Jonathan(1 Sam 20,11-23). They were far from enemies prior to entering into a solemn covenant[34]. We might well take as our working description of covenant that it is a solemn and externally manifested commitment which strengthens kinship and family concern between both parties.

In the light of this we can go along with exegetes and biblical theologians who see covenant as a central concept, which also helps to show forth the unity of the Bible. Among such authors, as well as those already mentioned, can be found the following kind of comments:

— J. Jocz: "It is therefore no exaggeration to say that covenantal theology is at the root of biblical thinking. ... from beginning to end biblical theology is founded upon the premise of the covenant"[35].

— J. Croatto: "The theme of the covenant is central to the Bible. The present work aims to show that the covenant is a basic expression of biblical theology, something like the backbone which supports it and gives it unity"[36].

— F.C. Prussner (recalling G. Von Rad's position):"The inner history of Israel's faith appears here as the history of two covenants"[37] (namely of Sinai and with David). While we accept both these covenants as important, they should not be thought of as rendering the others unimportant.

— L. Krinetzki: "God reveals himself throughout the history of the old and of the new covenant as the Faithful One, who keeps his word in spite of all the human failures..."[38].

— T.E. McComiskey: "The purpose of this volume is to examine the theological importance of the covenantal structure of redemptive history. The central thesis is that the major redemptive covenants are structured bicovenantly"[39].

— R.E. Clements: "Wherein lay the distinctiveness of the canonical prophets? We have sought to show throughout this study that it lay in their particular relationship to, and concern with, the covenant between Yahweh and Israel"[40].

— R. Sklba sketches a synthesis of redemption and covenant theology based especially on Yahweh as **Go'el** (Redeemer), for "at Sinai the Israelites ...came to understand that Yahweh had accepted them as His own relatives and kinsfolk"[41].

— J. Galot emphasises that Jesus, as the Suffering Servant, is himself the final covenant, being the perfect representative of both God and his people. And "Pentecost is therefore the consummation of the covenant; thanks to the outpouring of the Spirit, the Church is the people that belongs to God"[42].

In short, with Jesus Christ and the Spirit to light up and draw to perfection the earlier steps towards an enduring family relationship with God the Father, the main synthesis is already a living reality. The challenge for us is to live according to that reality and, through ongoing reflection within God's family, become more convincing in proclaiming it to all the world. Our proclamation must carry with it a cordial invitation to all members of our race.

NOTES

1. Cf. D.J. McCarthy, Treaty and Covenant: A Study in Form in the Ancient Oriental Documents and in the O.T. (Rome: Pontifical Biblical Institute, 1963), 16. Cf. S.N. Kramer, The Sumerians: Their History, Culture and Character (Chicago: University of Chicago, 1963).
2. D.J. McCarthy, op.cit. 18-20.
3. ibid. 20. Cf. P. Kalluveetil, Declaration and Covenant, 98.
4. D.J. McCarthy, op.cit. 20. Cf. P. Kalluveetil, op.cit. 97-98
5. D.J. McCarthy, ibid. 52.
6. J.B. Pritchard, Ancient Near Eastern Texts Relating to the Old Testament (Princeton University Press, 1950) 199-203. Cf. D.J. McCarthy, Institution and Narrative (Rome: Biblical Institute,1985) 72, note 18 on this treaty.
7. G.E. Mendenhall, Law and Covenant in Israel and the Ancient Near East (Pittsburgh,Pa.: The Biblical Colloquium, 1955)29-30. Cf. O.R. Gurney, The Hittites (Hammonsville: Penguin, 1952). Also on ancient Hittite documents, cf. R.E. Brown, Recent Discoveries and the Biblical World (Wilmington, Delaware, Glazier, 1983), 21 (on Ebla); 30-33 (on Boghazkoy).
8. P. Kalluveetil, op.cit. 97.
9. Ibid.
10. D.J. McCarthy, Treaty and Covenant, p.71. Cf. id. , Institution and Narrative, 121.
11. D.J. McCarthy, Treaty and Covenant, 80 and 93.

12. G.E. Mendenhall, op.cit. 31-35. Cf. K. Baltzer, The Covenant Formulary in O.T., Jewish and Early Christian Writings (Oxford: E.T. by D.E. Green, Blackwell, 1971), 9.
13. P. Kalluveetil, op.cit. 107.
14. P. Buis, La Notion de l'Alliance dans l'A.T.(Paris: Cerf, Lectio Divina, 1976), 15.
15. P. Kalluveetil, op.cit. 91; see all ch.3 from 17-91.
16. D.J. McCarthy, Institution and Narrative, p.15; see 14-20; also id., Old Testament Covenant (Oxford: B.Blackwell, 1973) 51-52: "Thus the anointing of the king signifies his vassalship, his special union with the divine sovereign of Egypt giving him a kind of untouchable holiness himself. Here is a sign, a rite constituting a vassal kingship with all the features characteristic of the position of Yahweh's anointed king."
17. Id., Institution and Narrative, 66: "Covenant-making, then, is a complex action, and so is its result. .... It is not simply the act, nor the obligation on one party which results from the act, nor anything else so simple. One will expect it to involve all parties both as a relationship and as an act. It cannot usually come about unless all join in making it, and it means nothing unless all are somehow involved in it, even tied by it."
18. Cf. S. Porubcan, Il Patto Nuovo in Is. 40-46 (Rome: Pontifical Biblical Institute, 1958), 57 and 77. Cf. D.J. McCarthy, op.cit. 13 on the importance of the oath in affirming a covenant.
19. D.J. McCarthy, ibid. 4.
20. Ibid. 5.
21. Id., in both Treaty and Covenant, 172, and O.T. Covenant, 29. Cf. G. Fohrer, Introduction to the O.T. (E.T. by D. Green, London: S.P.C.K., 1970), 73: "The Sinai covenant does not follow the treaty pattern. ... Even the alleged parallels themselves are dubious... The relationship of Israel to Yahweh does not correspond to the bond between a vassal and his Lord."
22 P.Buis, op.cit. 30, where he explains that the Hebrew 'olam means irrevocable, not eternal or everlasting.
23. P. Kalluveetil, op.cit. 91: "The OT does not have a fixed form for realizing a pact. The oath is the most important factor, but is not the sine-qua-non element. Rites such as eating together, pouring out libations, giving and accepting presents, shaking hands, holding the hem of the garment ... can by themselves effect a covenant. ... These covenant-enacting rites are destined to establish relationship or union between the partners. In some covenant contexts oral declarations of relationship occur." On the Bedouin background to meals and kinship, cf. J. Pedersen, Israel, Its Life and Culture (Oxford University Press, I-II, 1926) esp. 263-310. On rite to establish "blood relationship" by mingling of the partners' blood, cf. M. Noone, The Islands Saw It, (Dublin: Helicon Press, n.d.) 64-66, where he tells of Majellan's surprise to be invited to enter into this kind of pact by a Filipino chief, Kolambu, on Good Friday, 1521. On Easter Sunday the chief permitted Majellan to erect a Cross on a nearby hill, whereby, unbeknown to the chief, the island was also being claimed for the King of

Spain. That this is still very close to the ancient biblical practice can be judged against what G. Quell says about the latter: "One might say that the idea of the covenant, or the natural covenant, is the state of fellowship posited among blood brothers and to be observed by them. ... an analogous legal relationship can be established only by means of a fictional blood relationship." - Art. re **Diatheke** in G. Kittel's Theological Dictionary of the N.T.(E.T. by G.W. Bromiley, Grand Rapids: Eerdmans, 1964) II, 114.
24. P. Buis, op.cit. 7.
25. Ibid. 45.
26. O.P. Robertson, The Christ of the Covenants (Grand Rapids: Baker Book House, 1980), esp. 27-52 on the unity of the divine covenants: e. g. "The covenants of Abraham, Moses, and David actually are successive stages of a single covenant. ... the new covenant promised to Israel represents the consummate fulfillment of the earlier covenants"(41). Cf. W.J. Dumbrell, Covenant and Creation — An O.T. Covenantal Theology (Exeter, Devon: Paternoster Press, 1984), e.g. 41: "It would follow from our analysis of Gen.1-9 that there can be only one divine covenant, and also that any theology of covenant must begin with Gen.1:1. All else in covenant theology which progressively occurs in the O.T. will be deducible from this basic relationship."
27. D.R. Hillers, Covenant: The History of a Biblical Idea (Baltimore: John Hopkins Press, 1969), p.188.
28. C. Westermann, Genesis 12-36 - A Commentary (E.T. by J.J. Scullion, London: SPCK, 1985) 228-229.
29. Ibid. 213.
30. A. Vanhoye, La Nuova Alleanza Nel Nuovo Testamento (Rome, Pontifical Biblical Institute, Class Notes, 1984), A4-A35 where he treats of "b^{e}rit e alleanza nell'A.T."(A.T. referring to Old Testament).
31. Cf. E.M. Kirkpatrick (Editor), Chambers Twentieth Century Dictionary (Edinburgh: W.& R. Chambers, 1983).
32. D.J. McCarthy, Old Testament Covenant, 81.
33. P. Kalluveetil, op.cit. 6; cf. p.3 note 12. Cf. J. Bishop, The Covenant: A Reading (Springfield, Illinois: Templegate Publishers, 1982), 28: "The Bible differs from other ancient (non-Abrahamic) religions, as from modern ideologies, in that it declares that religious relation is ultimate across the board. Relation is what revelation reveals. And the covenant is the means of relation, as soon as that has been explicitly consented to. Once relation is admitted, I may still obey or rebel...; but I cannot help becoming Somebody 'before the face of' Somebody Else to the infinite degree." On the importance of relation in religion, cf. also J. Thornhill, "Is Religion the Enemy of Faith?", in Theol. Studies 45(1984), 254-274. e.g. 274: "Mircea Eliade's insight into man's religious experience as essentially relational ... seems of great moment for Christian theology as it takes up this problem."
34. D.J. McCarthy, Institution and Narrative, 65: "Covenant-making occurs when a relationship already exists. The point is to define and affirm the

connection. This is the case in all the examples in Genesis; it is usually so in the deuteronomistic examples as well." ... ... 66: "As a totality involving an action, a thing done or made, it(covenant) regularly implicates all the parties involved in it. This is clear in the negotiations which aim at defining some aspect of a relationship or relationships which include all the parties and which already exist. That is, it does not create a connection but presupposes one."

35. Jakob Jocz, The Covenant. — A Theology of Human Destiny (Grand Rapids: Eerdmans, 1968) 9 and 13; cf. 124: "Salvation in biblical terms implies an I-Thou relationship. God does not offer something, but Himself."
36. J. Severino Croatto, Alizanza y Experiencia Salvífica en la Biblia (Buenos Aires: Ediciones Paulinas, 1964) 13; cf. later expansion of this work in Historia de la Salvación — La experiencia religiosa del Pueblo de Dios (ibid. 1966) e.g. 28: "Y toda la historia bíblica — con las dos Alianzas centrales (la del Sinai y la de Cristo) — delinea los rasgos típicos de la economía de la salvación."
37. F.C. Prussner, "The Covenant of David and the Problem of Unity in O.T. Theology", in Transitions in Biblical Scholarship, Ed. by J.C. Rylaarsdam (Chicago: University of Chicago Press, 1968) 31; cf. 41, where he claims that "the total picture of Israel's faith" can be viewed "as the history of two covenants", namely the Sinaitic and the Davidic. (In dealing with the Noachic and Abrahamic covenants, we shall insist that they always remain as a backdrop, even if the other pair highlighted by Prussner do receive more frequent attention in the O.T.).
38. L. Krinetzki, L'Alliance de Dieu Avec les Hommes (Paris: Editions du Cerf, 1970) 110.
39. T.E. McComiskey, The Covenants of Promise — A Theology of O.T. Covenants (Nottingham: Inter-Varsity Press, 1985) 10.
40. R.E. Clements, Prophecy and Covenant (London: S.C.M., 1965) 127.
41. R. Sklba, "The Redeemer of Israel", in Catholic Biblical Quarterly 34(1972) 1-18; quotation is from 11. Cf. W. Most, "A Biblical Theology of Redemption in a Covenant Framework", also in C.B.Q. 29(1967) 1-19.
42. J. Galot, Gesù Liberatore (Rome : I.T. by C. Ciani & A. Cappelli, Florentina, 1978) 117-120, and quotation is from 439. Cf. his earlier work, of which this one is an updating: La Rédemption Mystère d'Alliance (Rome: M/L , 1965), e.g. 19: "C'est sous la forme d'une alliance que Yahvé avait présenté ses relations avec le peuple juif, et c'est à la conclusion d'une alliance que le Christ a rapporté son sacrifice. Dans la perspective d'alliance, qui est capitale, viennent s'encadrer les divers aspects de l'oeuvre salvifique."

CHAPTER 2: INITIAL RUDIMENTARY COVENANTS

We come now to reflect on the first eleven chapters of the Bible, which tell of primeval events, such as the origins of the universe and the human race. This serves as the backdrop to the origin and divine call of the Hebrews in the remainder of Genesis and all the Pentateuch. These early chapters use simple, popular language that reflects much of the common heritage of the Ancient Near East with regard to myths and legends. As J.L. McKenzie points out: "the literature of the Hebrews manifests a wide acquaintance with the mythology and folklore of both Mesopotamia and Canaan. It is no longer possible to assert that the Hebrews ingnored them or refused to allude to them"[1]. Myth is being increasingly recognised as a rich medium through which primitive peoples expessed their deepest insights and aspirations concerning their origins, their gods, their place in the universe, their destiny, and even the origins of the most ancient human institutions. "In all these", observes McKenzie, "the myth ultimately goes to the unknown underlying reality, whether this reality be explicitly identified as a divine personal being or not"[2].

Having laid to rest the fear of a few decades ago, that myths were just primitive fiction about false gods acting in human ways, we can better appreciate the confident reworking of widespread ancient myths by our biblical writers. This approach is excellently vindicated by C. Westermann in his monumental commentary "Genesis 1-11", e.g. "...stories of the creation of the world and of mankind are spread over the whole earth and throughout the whole of humanity; they reach from the oldest, primitive cultures to the high cultures and beyond." Again: "The Yahwistic author of Gen 2 was not saying anything new to his listeners when he spoke of the creation of humanity from the earth; it was an ancient theme, well-known to the world in which Israel lived."[3]. Westermann brings out clearly the significance of this biblical use of "primeval story" for relating what was special to Israel to what was common to all humankind[4]. Just as biblical writers have adapted their neighbours' laws, wisdom and poetry in accordance with their faith in Yahweh, so also they have availed of their earlier myths as part of a common heritage.

To understand what is being said these days about the human authors of the Pentateuch, we need to know the commonly accepted theory that there are four distinct "streams of tradition" discernible. Each stream is thought to have reached a written form which we can still detect within the final redaction of the Pentateuch. The first of these, the Yahwistic (J), took shape in Jerusalem during the reign of Solomon, hence is dated about 950 B.C. The Elohistic (E) is dated a little later, in the 9th century, and is situated in the Northern Kingdom. The Deuteronomic (D) seems to have moved from the Northern Kingdom to the Southern and crystallized about the time of Josiah, late 7th century. Finally the Priestly (P) tradition took shape during the Exile and was finalized by the time of Ezra in 5th century B.C.[5]. Of these, only J and P have contributed to Gen 1-11. Because J represents a tradition at a stage some 500 years earlier than that of P, we will take J's account of creation in Gen 2,4b-3,24 before that of P in 1,1—2,4a. Our main concern will be to draw out any elements of covenant hinted at in either account. Obviously the primeval stories they retell were circulating long before there were official treaties with set form and content, so we should not expect more than hints of a covenant relationship. Such hints, however, are extremely important as a basis for the more explicit universal and national covenants that follow, as well as for the covenant of love between man and wife, parents and children, brothers and sisters.

A. FROM CREATION TILL THE FLOOD (GEN 1-5)
1. First creation account in Gen 2,4b-3,24 (J)

This section is assigned to the Yahwist, the writer who is presumed to have drawn together and presented a unified story of God's people reaching back beyond Abraham right to creation. He is deservedly honoured by Peter Ellis as "The Yahwist — The Bible's First Theologian", for being "an ancient genius who could be called — and with equal justice — the Hebrew Homer, 'the father of theology', the earliest monumental theologian in history"[6]. An attempt to present "The Yahwist Saga" in continuous form, from Gen 2 to Num 35, is given in an appendix to Ellis's pioneering work. The Yahwist tells his story in vivid and popular language, redolent of myth, folklore and legend, but also thoroughly imbued with the deep faith of Israel learnt from many extraordinary encounters with Yahweh. The language and appeal may be universal, but the central message is unique.

The Yahwist's creation account is a unified story moving on easily from one scene to the next. It begins by mentioning a few things still needed when Yahweh had made heaven and earth: there had been no rain and there was no one to till the earth. So Yahweh forms man from dust of the earth and breathes into him the breath of life, and kindly places him "in the garden of Eden, to cultivate and take care of it"(2,15). It was a well watered garden, adequate to support life for mankind, as also for birds and beasts.

As the man acts like Yahweh's viceroy, naming the other creatures, he experiences the pangs of solitude at not finding any suitable helpmate or partner. This brings out what Yahweh had already observed: "It is not good for man to be alone. I will make a suitable partner for him"(3,18 as in The New American Bible)[7]. This translation brings out well the nuance of reciprocity and companionship as well as help. Moreover, the Hebrew word **'ezer** (= help, helper) is nearly always reserved for the kind of help that only God can proffer, in situations of grave risk to life, thus an indispensable help for survival. For the man, the great danger mentioned is solitude, aloneness. As J-L. Ska comments on our text: "Life is only truly what it is from the moment when one can share it and transmit it"[8].

The special creation of woman from man's rib emphasises the one common nature of man and woman, as the joyful cry of the man, in poetic form, indicates when he beholds his partner: "This one at last is bone of my bones and flesh of my flesh! "(2,23). In the partnership of marriage "they become one flesh"(2,24). The significance of the rib has been clarified by Sumerian literature,in which the word for rib is also the word for life. "The Sumerian Lady of the Rib (NIN-TI) is also the Lady of Life, (again NIN-TI), the life-giver. But this is exactly what Eve is"[9]. C. Westermann's finding is also pertinent here: "Gen 2 is unique among the creation myths of the whole of the Ancient Near East in its appreciation of the meaning of woman, i.e., that human existence is a partnership of man and woman"[10].

The first couple had access to the tree of life, but also one limitation had been set by Yahweh. They were forbidden under pain of death to eat of the tree of knowledge of good and evil. In this command we see again the power of speech, whereby Yahweh can speak to humans and enter into personal relationship with them. As events soon prove, they too can enter into dialogue with God, for they are capable of responding. Yahweh makes it clear that they are responsible to him for their choices.

The snake enters the story as the subtle tempter, a creature that symbolises understanding of earth, life and the seasons. Cleverly he persuades the woman that the forbidden fruit, far from harming humans, will make them like gods, able to decide for themselves what is right or wrong. No sooner had they broken God's command than "their eyes were opened and they realised they were naked"(3,7). They felt shame and loss of confidence in each other; they also felt fear of Yahweh, trying to hide from him in the bushes.

On finding them, Yahweh promptly opens an enquiry into what they had done, speaking to man, woman and snake. The verdict and specific consequences are communicated to snake, woman and man. The snake and the soil are cursed, but not the couple. The death penalty is not carried out immediately,but after a toilsome and troublesome life humans will return to the earth from which they were formed. By following their own desires instead of accepting the will of Yahweh, they now face suffering in what should have been happy roles — the woman as wife and mother, the man as tiller of the land. The kindness of the Judge breaks through the narrative as he provides tunics of skin for the guilty couple, to whom he wishes to restore their sense of dignity and value despite one serious failure. Their expulsion from the garden of Eden shuts off their access to the tree of life, while cherubim with flashing sword forestall any hope of returning there.

Does the Yahwist's story here depict a rudimentary covenant? The Yahwist is certainly interested in divine and human covenants as he continues his story from Abraham on to Moses. At least a significant proportion of the following covenants have been attributed to J:
— Gen 15: Abraham is granted a covenant with Yahweh;
— Gen 21,22-34: Covenant between Abraham and Abimelech;
— Gen 26,23-33: Covenant between Isaac and Abimelech;
— Gen 31,36-54: Covenant between Jacob and Laban;

— Exod 24,1-11: Covenant between Yahweh and Israel;
— Exod 34,1-28: Renewal of the Sinai covenant[11].

Allowing for ongoing scholarly debates about the extent of the Yahwist's hand in those six covenants, there is adequate evidence that he was well aware of covenant-making at crucial moments.

Many commentators accept that the Yahwist has also been influenced by covenant thinking and covenant patterns in his creation account. In the view of L. Alonso Schökel: "The narratives of Gn 2-3 is simply the classical outline of salvation history. There is a minor pattern, that of the covenant"[12]. P. Ellis also mentions that "the shattering of this covenant by Adam ends the initial economy of salvation"[13]. For A.D. Galloway, "Covenant is the freely given faithfulness of God upon which our faith rests. ..... Creation takes place in the free, unforced, unshakable will of God. It therefore has the character of God's initial covenant. He creates what is other than himself in order to have that kind of relationship with it"[14]. W. Vogels claims: "We have therefore discovered nearly all the elements belonging to the covenant-formulary. ... The Yahwist used the elements very freely, independently from a rigid structure and projected them into the past to present the relation between God and mankind as a covenant-relationship"[15]. The fundamental connection between creation and covenant is also accepted by T.E. McComiskey: "In the relationship that God established with mankind and the created world, certain strictures were placed on creation that obtain to this day. Thus the emphasis on 'creation' rather than 'works' in the more recent designation <u>covenant of creation</u>(author's italics) is more consonant with the intent of the context. Adam thus functioned as a representative of all mankind as he received the announcement of the divine disposition"[16]. Here the words relationship, covenant and disposition are well chosen with regard to God's plan in creation.

As well as the relationship of benevolence and dialogue inaugurated between Yahweh and the first couple, the relationship between the human partners themselves is of supreme importance in any biblical covenant. Being created as equal partners, they are capable of entering into such a full covenant of love as to become "one flesh" (2,24), one living 'body' whose parts collaborate in harmony for the good of the whole. Reflecting on the phrase "a helper fit for him", C. Westermann concludes: "What is meant is the personal community of man and woman in the broadest sense — bodily and spiritual community, mutual help and understanding, joy and contentment in each other"[17]. Likewise he explains the phrase "one flesh" as "describing human existence as a whole under the aspect of corporality" and "as spiritual unity, the most complete personal community"[18]. This love is so strong as to draw man to leave his own parents and "<u>stay fast</u> by his wife" — "It is amazing that this one word presents the basic involvement of man and woman as something given and rooted in the very act of creation. .... The love of man and woman receives here a unique evaluation"[19].

With keen appreciation of what might have been, Phyllis Trible concludes her treatment of Gen 2-3 by saying: "The divine, human, animal and plant

INITIAL RUDIMENTARY COVENANTS

world are all adversely affected. Indeed, the image of God male and female has participated in a tragedy of disobedience. Estranged from each other, the man and woman are banished from the garden and barred forever from the tree of life. Truly, a love story has gone awry. Yet Gen 2-3 is not the only word in scripture on human sexuality. What it forfeits in tragedy, the Song of Songs redeems in joy"[20].

We are now in a position to draw out and coordinate the elements of covenant that have been discerned in the Yahwist's story of creation, stewardship, partnership, temptation, disobedience and expulsion from the garden holding the tree of life.

With regard to the international treaty form, we need not expect it in a primeval story, even though some have detected traces of: i) a brief history of Yahweh's benefits;
ii) one fundamental stipulation in typically Israelite apodictic form: "...you are not to eat; for, the day you eat of that, you are doomed to die"(Gen 2,17), plus the commission to cultivate and care for God's special garden;
iii) a sanction involving life or death.

With regard to the content, the Yahwist uses simple, non-legal language to describe rather than define the relationship between Yahweh and the couple. Nevertheless his masterly description suggests an implicit covenant initiated entirely by Yahweh, who benevolently invites the couple to collaborate in caring for their garden home so as to have access to the tree of life. In all this they must accept certain limitations to their independence, remaining attentive to the known laws of their Creator.

At first the whole atmosphere is one of profound peace and harmony, of friendship and partnership between all concerned. Then in creeps a disruptive element in the form of a snake, who cleverly tempts them to disregard Yahweh's command. Although no oath has been taken, both man and woman show clearly that they knew of their obligation not to eat the forbidden fruit. Their sudden feeling of shame in each other's presence and fugitives' fear at Yahweh's approach manifest a radical change in their relationship because of the transgression. In place of friendship there is now fear, in place of peace there is now turmoil and shame.

Yahweh, the offended party, arrives in the evening to call the culprits to account for their free but mistaken choice. He imposes the penalties merited by the violation of their part of the covenant, in a manner that is really spelling out to them the consequences of their sinful disregard of his just command. Contrary to earthly sovereigns, Yahweh does not impose nor carry out any curse on the violators themselves "for", as he declares later with regard to Israel, "I am God, not man"(Hosea 11,9). He curses only the snake and the soil — which the snake must eat and mankind must work very hard in order to eat. Despite human efforts to sustain life, with access to the tree of life now barred, death and return to the earth is to be the lot of mankind. The frightening cherubim and flaming sword denote the finality of the banishment from the garden of Eden, from Paradise, as well as an atmosphere of warfare instead of peace. Hence we may justifiably say that a rudimentary covenant of friendship and peace has been definitively shattered. All subsequent events in salvation history are to be directed towards the restoration of the human family to peace and abiding kinship with Yahweh, the Creator and also the Lord of history. Only by the new covenant is access to the fulness of life with God and each other opened up to all our race[21].

2. Later creation account in Gen 1,1-2,4a (P)

As mentioned above, the Priestly tradition emerged in written form in the fifth century B.C., after the Exile. By that time, in the midst of captivity and subsequent liberation, a battered but resurrected Israel had long reflected on the power of God's word. For instance, the well-named Book of Consolation of Deutero-Isaiah, reassured the exiles of Babylon: "...so it is with the word that goes forth from my mouth: it will not return to me unfulfilled or before having carried out my good pleasure and having achieved what it was sent to do"(55,11). This conviction runs right through P's account of creation. Ten times over it gives a word of God that immediately has its fulfilment, beginning with "Let there be light" (Gen 1,3-29)[22].

At the same time, this account also avails of the ancient heritage of creation stories to narrate how, "In the beginning, God created heaven and earth" (1,1). From a situation of darkness, emptiness and boundless waters, God sets about methodically to create light, to push back waters so that heaven and earth can emerge, then to fill all parts with a rich variety of living creatures — flowering, flying, swimming, creeping, or running wild. As the crowning work which best reflects the Creator's own image, he makes humans. They are able to understand the personal blessing addressed to them and to accept responsibly his special commission concerning all the other living creatures. This Priestly author draws disparate materials and traditions into an organic unity by distributing the divine Artist's work over six working days, followed by a delightful climax: "God blessed the seventh day and made it holy, because on that day he rested after all his work of creating" (2,3).

P's account contains much more poetry than J's. Whereas J's account rises to a short poetic cry as the man beholds his partner, P's account has a poetic strain running through it and intermingled with the prose. As C. Westermann notes, "Gen 1 contains a fusion of poetry and prose that is unique in the Old Testament"[23]. It has been carefully constructed and placed as a solemn introduction to all that follows in the Bible and beyond it. Everything begins here!

To what extent, then, is this Priestly writer interested in covenant? As in the case of J, we can point to constant interest in covenants on the part of P.:
—Gen 6,18 and 9,8-17: Covenant with Noah and family;
—Gen 17: Covenant with Abraham and Sarah and family;
—Exod 19,1-2; 24,15b-18a; Covenant with Israel at Mt. Sinai[24]; and 25-26 and 40 (where the "Ark of the Testimony" is so called because it contains inscribed stones as witnesses to the covenant clauses):
—Numb 25,10-13: Covenant with the priest Phinehas.

Despite such interest in later covenants, P cannot be said to portray any covenant in the creation narrative. What it does describe quite clearly, however, is the unmistakable basis of all covenant relation-ships between the Creator and humans. That basis is given by God's creation of man and woman to his own image and likeness(Gen 1,26-27).

First of all,we are alerted to this as a high point of creation by the special deliberation of God saying: "Let us make man(=humans) in our own image, in the likeness of ourselves"(1,26). Then we have a prime example of the pattern of word and fulfilment, for immediately "God created man in the image of himself, ... male and female he created
them. God blessed them, saying to them, 'Be fruitful, multiply, fill the earth and subdue it'. ...God saw all he had made, and indeed it was very good"(1,27-31). The divine Artist was justifiably satisfied with that vast and beautiful masterpiece. The first seven words had made a world with light, fertile land,and innumerable species blessed with life. Then came the self-portrait of the Artist, not carved on stone nor painted on canvas, but imprinted permanently on man and woman. P. indicates that the image of God is so deeply stamped on humans that they pass it on as they pass on their own likeness to their children(Gen 5,1-3 and 9,6).

When we try to determine more fully why P regarded humans as constituting an image of God, we realise that it must be associated with their capacity to recognize and converse with their Creator. O. Robertson is justified in asserting: "By the very act of creating man to his own image and likeness, God established a unique relationship between himself and creation"[25]. It is likewise in the area of relationship that C. Westermann, after a careful review of other opinions, finds the most plausible explanation of the text, e.g.: "What God decides to create must be something that has a relationship to him just as in the Sumerian and Babylonian texts people are related to the creator god as servants of the gods"[26]. Moreover: "The relationship to God is not something which is added to human existence; humans are created in such a way that their very existence is intended to be their relationship to God"[27]. To give full force to these remarks, it must also be noted that Westermann insists strongly that the creation text is talking about an action of God and "not the nature of human beings"[28].

Needless to say, any reflection on such a fundamental text is quite entitled to search for aspects of the relationship that would help to explain why it projects the Creator's image and likeness. One obvious aspect in Gen 1 is that God can entrust humans with the responsibility of ruling the rest of the living things so carefully created. Humans must have greater dignity and capacity for such trust than the creatures they are appointed to watch over. It is not far-fetched to see humans here as viceroys of the majestic Creator, to whom they themselves are subject. This limits their power and should always guide them in its exercise. One little hint of the moderation expected is contained in the directive that humans are to be vegetarians(1,29)! For P the kind of service expected of humans is not to wait on capricious gods but to make visible an outgoing God's concern for all this magnificent creation.[29].

The very fact that God can speak to humans and be understood by them shows that dialogue and a spirit of collaboration are possible between them. What is also noteworthy in Gen 1 is that humans were not created "according to their species", but all belong to the one human species, each and every one is to be a living image of the Creator. This means they can have dialogue as partners of equal dignity and enter into personal relationships with each other. In fact God does explicitly unite them in marriage by blessing them and endowing them with the inner dynamism necessary to share their life and bring forth children sufficient to "fill the earth"(1,28). The children themselves, as we shall soon see in the case of Cain and Abel, are also called to relate to one another with mutual respect and concern.

J.Bishop is one who accepts "the intuition that reality is essentially relational. To that extent this argument may be taken as descending from the style of thought originally associated with Buber and Brunner in theology and MacMurray in philosophy., For covenant is simply the Biblical name for relation as soon as this becomes absolute"(i.e.,as he indicates, "between me and Somebody Else to the infinite degree")[30] (emphasis added). W.Dumbrell also regards relationship as the key, claiming: "It would follow from our analysis of Gen 1-9 that there can be only one divine covenant, and also that any theology of covenant must begin with Gen 1:1. All else in covenant theology which progressively occurs in the O.T. will be deducible from this basic relationship"[31]. While agreeing with him that Gen 1 marks the beginning of an openness to some kind of covenant relationship, we differ considerably with regard to the variety of ways in which covenants were established on that common basis. They have much in common and are interconnected, yet differ sufficiently to be treated as distinct covenants.

Another important aspect of "image and likeness" is that at the time of the Exile those same two nouns are used by Ezekiel and Deutero-Isaiah. Both authors use them in cultic settings, and both use them in strong condemnations of idolatry. E.g. Ezek 7,19-20: "They used to pride themselves on the beauty of their jewellery, out of which they made their loathsome images.... I shall hand it over as plunder to foreigners". In 16,8-17 Yahweh reproaches his faithless bride for doing the same thing. In 23,14-15, God again denounces Jerusalem for being moved by "wall-carvings of men, pictures of Chaldaeans" to go chasing after them and so deserting him to whom she was betrothed. Deutero-Isaiah 40-46 has several equally stinging attacks on idolatry, e.g. in 40,18: "To whom can you compare God? What image can you contrive of him?" After describing how craftsman and goldsmith fashion an idol and have to be careful in setting it up so that it does not totter, he contrasts that to the "Holy One", exclaiming: "Lift your eyes and look: he who created these things leads out their army in order, summoning each of them by name"(40,26).

Furthermore, all this must be seen against the prohibition recorded in both traditions of the Ten Commandments: "You shall not make yourself a carved image or any likeness of anything in heaven above or on earth beneath or in the waters under the earth. You shall not bow down to them or serve them"(Exod 20,4; cf. Deut 5,8-9). Although different Hebrew words are used here for image and likeness, it certainly emphasises their connection with idolatry. The inferiority of lifeless idols is pinpointed by a post-exilic Psalm: "These have mouths but say nothing, have eyes but see nothing, have ears but hear nothing .... have feet but cannot walk"(115,5-7). P's daring assertion that God has already made an acceptable image and likeness of himself can therefore be related to the realm of community worship and holiness. It is saying that nothing less than living humans able to speak, see, hear and walk freely can safely be thought of as an image of the living God[32].

Obviously they are not to be worshipped, but to worship and to freely reflect in their daily life something of the holiness of God, a theme dear to the Priestly tradition: "Be holy, for I, Yahweh your God am holy"(Lev 19,2). Following closely on this comes the still more famous command: "You will love your neighbour as yourself. I am Yahweh" (19,18). Self-love here is seen to be not only good, but the norm for loving the neighbour. To be an acceptable norm before Yahweh, what is loved in self and neighbour must also be related to him as image to the Artisan, as reflection to the Creator seen in the mirror.

That we are not doing violence to P's train of thought in the creation story may be gauged from its conclusion. While it is true to regard the creation of man and woman as the climax of the six days of creation, only on the seventh day is the high point of the whole story reached. All attention is on God while he rests that day, making it for ever a unique day in every week, as "God blessed the seventh day and made it holy, because on that day he rested from all the work he had been doing"(Gen 2,3). The sabbath as blessed and made holy by the Creator must somehow share in his own holiness, his own transcendence and freedom with regard to work.

Once again we find that this has entered both traditional listings of the Ten Commandments, and very significantly both stress the strict obligation to rest from work that day. It requires the entire household, including servants, slaves, aliens, even domestic animals, to rest likewise from their labours. God's sabbath rest is also linked up with the rest he made possible for Israel by freeing them from slavery: "Remember that you were once a slave in Egypt, and that Yahweh your God brought you out of there with mighty hand and outstretched arm; this is why Yahweh your God has commanded you to keep the Sabbath day"(cf.Deut 5,12-15; Exod 20,8-11). The sabbath rest thus sets a mandatory rhythm to weekly work and leisure, putting it in harmony with God's creative power and eternal rest. Man and woman cannot reflect a true likeness of their Creator unless they also have some leisure to pause and see how very good creation really is. Joyful appreciation should lead on to praise of the Creator.

The Lord of creation who created time and seasons and recurring "holy-days" is shown here to be quite consistent with the Lord of all history as well. No theology of liberation can afford to pass over in silence this aspect of cyclic leisure and holi-days, lest political liberation result in bondage to work for the system, or even for greedy individuals. L. Epsztein rightly hails the sabbath rest as "one of the most revolutionary ideas of the Bible", as well as "the most characteristic institution of Judaism", signifying "a victory of the spiritual over the temporal"[33].

With regard to P's facility in blending Israel's history with creation stories, an observation of Westermann is apposite: "It is not possible to regard Gen 1 directly and without reservation as the beginning of salvation history or even as its preparation. The reason why this chapter is at the beginning of the Bible is so that all of God's subsequent actions — <u>his dealings with humankind</u>, the history of his people, <u>the election and the covenant</u> — may be seen against the broader canvas of his work in creation"[34] (emphasis added).

To conclude this reflection and recall its aim of relating the creation account to divine covenants, an exhortation of John Paul II will serve well: "...the status of image and likeness of God obliges you to act in conformity with what you are. Be faithful, then, to the Covenant that God the Creator has made with you, a creature, from the beginning"[35].

3. Bonds of brotherhood violently broken by Cain: Gen 4

In this chapter the Yahwist takes up the story of the first family, which suffers a major blow when Cain murders his brother Abel. Seven times over in quick succession the word brother is repeated(4,2-11), and as many times some word indicating attacking or killing is used. The scene unfolds before God, to whom both brothers offer sacrifice. "The first of his flock and some of their fat as well" offered by Abel is accepted by Yahweh, presumably because it represents a generous effort to offer something precious. Cain's sacrifice of "some of the produce of the soil" did not win God's approval, perhaps because he made no effort to select the firstfruits or the best.

Yahweh by no means ignores the attempt of Cain, but takes the opportunity to warn him that "sin is lurking at the door, hungry to get you. You can still master him "(4,7). Sadly, it is sin — mentioned by name for the first time in the Bible — that masters Cain, who invites Abel into open country and murders him. As in the case of the first couple, Yahweh soon confronts the culprit and conducts an enquiry into the murder. In line with ancient trial procedures, the accused is called on to say what happened, in the hope of him admitting his guilt and helping to restore justice[36].

Cain, however, refuses to admit any knowledge of his brother's whereabouts. He also rejects any responsibility for his brother's welfare, asking: "Am I my brother's guardian?"(4,9). While Cain would expect the answer No!, for the Yahwist the answer must be a strong Yes![37]. God as Judge cannot be deaf to the accusing cry of Abel's blood. Blood for the Israelites was regarded as the seat of life, hence the Lord of life was deeply concerned to hear a destroyed life crying out from the earth, the place of the dead. To take away a brother's life is to take away the precious gift which best reflects God's life and generosity.

The verdict is severe as God curses Cain himself and banishes him from the ground desecrated by blood shed unjustly. Cain appeals against the sentence which seems to make survival impossible for him, so Yahweh grants him a protective mark to forestall any blood vengeance. This is an important guide to restraint in dealing with violent people, especially as the following verses indicate that Cain became the forefather of settled town dwellers and artisans[38]. His victim Abel was also replaced for the injured parents by another brother, Seth, whose son Enosh "was the first to invoke the name of Yahweh"(4,26). Sin will remain "lurking at the door of the tent", but not unchallenged by Yahweh.

Two features of the story have a special bearing on our theme. First is the offering of sacrifice to Yahweh by primitive mankind, as something expressive of the desire to relate more fully with the God who blesses both fields and flocks. Moreover, Yahweh does not simply accept it willy-nilly; he responds quite differently to Cain and Abel. Perhaps more striking still is that the stern confrontation with Cain is not to question him about a poor offering but about the murder of his brother. At that stage there was no talk about restoring the balance of justice by offering the Judge another sacrifice. The crime had been committed within the human family and the consequences affected Cain's participation within that family ever afterwards. He was banished as an unwanted outcast and so became "a restless wanderer",one who had also "left Yahweh's presence"(4,12-16). In short, Yahweh emerges as one who is the defender of human life and demands an account of those who shed their brother's lifeblood. "Thou shalt not kill" is written deep in human hearts, right from the start of our race.

Which brings us to the second significant feature, the relation of this to all the Yahwist has to say about covenants and explicit covenant obligations. J. Miranda has rightly drawn attention to that "cry" of Abel's blood which moved Yahweh to intervene as the champion of justice, as he was later to intervene at the "cry" of the Hebrews oppressed in Egypt. In reacting to the cry of Abel's blood, Yahweh does so "before there were covenants, patriarchs, promises and commandments. ... In this verse it is immediately apparent that Genesis was written completely under the inspiration of Exodus and as a prologue to the irruption of Yahweh's justice, which, in saving a people from oppression, would determine history"[39]. Miranda, however, insists that the basis of Yahweh's intervention in both cases was the "cry" and not any formal promise or covenant.

This would seem correct only if we see Yahweh's intervention as stemming from his saving justice in binding himself to bless all nations through the family of Abraham. Seen in this light, his promise and special treatment of the Hebrews was fulfilling a solemn promise, but at the same time it was the manifestation of the Creator of all peoples, all of whose "cries" were certainly reaching him. Thus the universal dimension of Gen 4 is undeniable — murder of any brother anywhere sets off a piercing "cry" that the just Yahweh will not let pass unattended.

Israel itself had that made very explicit through many laws which they took as an integral part of their commitment to Yahweh by the Mosaic covenant, e.g. in the so-called "Code of the Covenant": "Anyone who by violence causes a death must be put to death. ... But should any person dare to kill another with deliberate planning,you will take that person even from my altar to be put to death." (Note the way cult is ruled out as a shelter for such murderers.) ... "Do not cause the death of the innocent or upright, and do not acquit the guilty. You will accept no bribes, for a bribe blinds the clear-sighted"(Exod 21,12.14; 23,7-8). (Note here the stress on defending justice and the life of the innocent by a fair trial, parallel to Yahweh's judgement of Cain.) This Code has "points of contact with the Code of Hammurabi, with the Hittite Code and with the Decree of Horemheb"(of Egypt), and is considered older than the Jahwist's writing[40].

In other words, brotherhood and a divinely given right to life are even more fundamental and universal than any covenant stipulations. What Yahweh intends, therefore, in granting a covenant to one family must be to inspire in that other party a deeper commitment to these admirable family values. Acceptance of this is seen in the lead-up to the great liberation from Egyptian slavery through a true son of Abraham. Moses was moved to begin trying to better the lot of the Hebrew slaves precisely because "while he was watching their forced labour he also saw an Egyptian striking a Hebrew, one of his kinsmen. ...(Moses) killed the Egyptian and hid him in the sand"(Exod 2,11-12). Next day Moses tried again to defend a kinsman, this time against a brother Hebrew. The rejection and denouncing of Moses by his own kinsman forced him to flee from Egypt, frustrated in that first attempt to defend his own kith and kin[41].

The Yahwist thus illustrates clearly the way in which the ever just God normally intervenes to restore justice and freedom by sending somebody like Moses. Those in need of justice and liberation have to accept the solidarity of kinspeople or abort their liberation[42]. Similarly, after the liberation from Egypt, the Israelites were called on by God through Moses to reconfirm their family spirit and values. More on this when we come to Mount Sinai!

Among the descendants of Cain is mentioned Lamech, a further indication that murder and other forms of violence beget ever greater violence. Lamech appears boasting of killing those that hurt him, as if he were entitled to demand vengeance "seventy-sevenfold"(4,24).

Gen 5, from P, is important as linking the first couple with Noah and family, bringing out at the same time the effectiveness of God's blessing to impart ever expanding life[43].

B. FROM FLOOD TO FAMILY OF ABRAHAM (GEN 6-11)

Gen 3-4 has narrated the profound rupture of harmony between humans as married partners, as brothers, as members of one united family, as responsible stewards over living nature, and as tillers of the earth. The next two primeval stories to be considered now are the Flood and the Tower of Babel. The first, in cc.6-9, tells how human violence became so intolerable before the Creator that he decided to drown out the corruption and let the human family start off afresh from Noah's family. The other, in c.11, tells how

INITIAL RUDIMENTARY COVENANTS

pride was thwarted as confusion of languages prevented the city tower reaching heaven as a merely human achievement. The whole section concludes by stretching forward through genealogies to the immediate forebears of Abraham and Sarah, through whom both the Yahwist and Priestly writer can enter into salvation history.

1. The universal covenant granted to Noah and family: Gen 6-9

The account of the Flood in these chapters is a careful juxtaposition of material from both J and P. Such respect is shown for each tradition that we know fairly well which tradition is responsible for each section. An intriguing aspect is that we can put together a reasonable Flood story using the pieces preserved from each tradition. Still more gripping is the cosmic dimension and universal import of such an apparently simple story. It presents an extemely critical step in creation, when human wickedness has reached the point of making the Creator "regret" that he had made human beings(Gen 6,6). Strong words are used here to describe the wickedness, words connoting "violence, injury, oppression", and "corruption, rottenness", and "lawlessness"(6,5-13).

Inexorably the Creator unleashes the waters of chaos to join together again and sweep over the dry land intended for human life. But one family is saved by God, that of the upright Noah, one who "walked with God"(6,9). In fact God warns Noah of the impending flood and instructs him how to build the Ark in which to save himself and his family, so that human life may start afresh on a purified earth after the Flood. A central point is the covenant, which God first mentions to Noah before the Flood starts: "But with you I shall establish my covenant"(6,18). In the middle of the Flood, which had drowned all other breathing things, God remembered Noah(8,l), mindful of his promise already given and being fulfilled by saving the family in the Ark. As soon as Noah and family were able to step out of the Ark onto Mount Ararat, they responded to God by building an altar on which to offer up sacrifice. In J's account, "Yahweh smelt the pleasing smell and said to himself, 'Never again will I curse the earth because of human beings, ... never again will I strike down every living thing as I have done' "(8,21). Yahweh goes on to promise the constancy of days and seasons "as long as earth endures". This is of utmost importance, as C. Westermann points out, for subsequent saving events in the "linear" time of history do not abrogate "the course of cyclic time established in 8:20-22. Rather it retains its significance for everything that happens. A substantial part of the working out of God's blessing takes place within the cycle established here; the working out of God's saving action takes place in contingent events.."[44].

P's account recalls various steps of the original creation in c.1, e.g. the blessing on Noah and family: "Breed, multiply, and fill the earth"(9,1). This time murder is explicitly forbidden, because of God's image in humans(9,6). Of significance for our linking of image with covenant in Gen 1 is that here in c.9 P passes immediately from the sacredness of life in God's image to speak seven times over of covenant (vv.8-17). Many striking details of the covenant are simply announced by God: "I am now establishing my covenant with you and with your descendants to come, and with every living creature that was with you. ... never again shall all living things be destroyed by the waters of a flood" (9,9-11). The rainbow is to be the sign and a constant reminder to God of this covenant.

Since the term **b^{e}rit** occurs here for the first time in Gen, being used by P eight times in 6,18 and 9,8-17, we must consider what kind of covenant is meant. There can be no doubt that the initiative is entirely God's, that he mentions no obligations as binding on Noah's family because of the covenant as such, that it is unconditional and an "eternal covenant between God and every living creature on earth"(9,16). There is no ceremony to seal it, for God's declaration is what establishes this unique covenant. It is so unique that C. Westermann seriously questions "whether there is any parallel between the covenant with Noah and that with Abraham". In view of it being extended to animals as well, "there can be no question of what is usually understood by covenant or what is later called the promise"[45]. What it describes is "a relationship between God and humanity in which the initiative is all on one side"[46] (emphasis added).

Those penetrating observations help clarify in what sense P employs the word "covenant" as central to his teaching about God's intervention to save humankind from self-destruction, as well as to save the rest of creation from the total chaos which humans might otherwise cause again by their violence. With good reason J-L Ska gives as a consequence of this particular account: "Noah's experience becomes paradigmatic. With him we can survive the flood and live the new beginning of the universe. ... It is only with Noah, for instance, that we can discover the cosmos' new order that hinges upon God's covenant and his memory of it"[47]. W. Vogels likewise judges: "To the priestly writer there is no doubt that God concluded a 'covenant' with mankind, long before his covenant with Israel"[48].

We must recall here the conclusion of D. McCarthy: "With regard to its religious use: **b^{e}rit**, when applied to the relation of man to God, must carry some of its rich associations with complex relationships with it"[49] (emphasis added). What, then, are the dominant elements in the new relationship established unilaterally with Noah's family and yet called a covenant? It is evident that the relationship has to be two-sided, and looking now at cc.6-9 as a whole, we can discern what new elements have affected the relationship.

On God's part, he announces the covenant before the flood, enables one family and pairs of other living creatures to be saved from the universal destruction, kindly shuts them in the ark, remembers them during the flood and sends a wind to help return conditions to normal, then accepts their sacrifice back on dry land, promises never to curse earth again and to ensure stability of cyclic time and seasons, renews for the surviving family and its descendants the blessing of life, fertility, and stewardship over the earth. Even the rainbow is mentioned as a sign of the covenant by which God intends to remind himself of his solemn commitment.

On the part of Noah's family, the narrative emphasises from the start that Noah(as responsible leader of the family) has "won God's favour","a good and

INITIAL RUDIMENTARY COVENANTS

upright man,and one who walked with God" (6,8-9), very obedient in all that concerned the building and stocking the ark, doing "exactly as God commanded him" (6,22; cf. 7,16). As soon as they could set foot on dry land again, they built an altar and offered sacrifice to Yahweh, who was pleased with it. In renewing the blessing upon them, God mentioned explicitly the grave obligation to respect human life, for failure in that area had been largely responsible for the previous violence, and was the biggest threat to the life and development of the new family. In this way, the Creator does call for a better relationship between himself and all future humans, as well between humans themselves, above all in helping to cherish life instead of destroying it. Both J and P have shown a keen awareness that sin will continue among humans, "because their heart contrives evil from their infancy"(8,21). God will gradually bring about a change in such stony hearts.

2. Expansion from Noah's family to that of Abraham: Gen 9,18-c.11

Just as a genealogy including Noah leads up to the flood, so also after the flood comes another genealogy which includes the descendants of Noah's sons. Shem merits special attention as from him the line runs on to Abraham. The cursing of Ham,"the father of Canaan"(9,18) for disrespect towards his father Noah is noteworthy. Noah declares that Canaan "shall be his brother's meanest slave"(9,25). The story stems from prehistoric times and reflects in its final form something of the enslavement of Canaanites conquered by the Israelites. Unfortunately it has mistakenly been used to justify slavery of all kinds of people, including millions enslaved by Christians. North, Central and South America are still experiencing the aftermath of an unjust and unchristian practice. Even in this first mention of primitive slavery, it is as a severe punishment brought upon a son for gravely disrupting the proper relationship between father and son. In ancient times the father had to rely on decent sons to restore the balance and prevent the family disintegrating. We shall meet other biblical views of slavery in later covenant texts, not to mention liberationist writings.

The ample genealogies of cc. 10 are evidence of how fruitful was God's blessing and how diverse were the nations spreading out across the known world. Nevertheless such growth in population and progress in civilization was not without its temptations. The Yahwist, with usual vividness, tells of a proud attempt to build a brick tower reaching heaven and winning fame for themselves(11,1-4). Yahweh intervened to confuse their language and "scatter them all over the world" (11,7-9). God thus forestalled "the possibility of overstepping the limits"[50]. The human city already bespeaks a lengthy concerted effort of its citizens, but experience had taught the ancient Israelites that a powerful city can dehumanize those within and around it. Capital-ism means more than accumulating money! A variety of scattered nations would also permit a wider variety of cultures and initiatives in the advance of civilization.

The closing genealogy of c.11 presents the family tree of Abram and Sarai, telling that Abram's father Terah brought them with him from "Ur of the Chaldaeans". They settled much further north in Mesopotamia, in a city called

Haran. With this the stage has been well set for the emergence of Abraham's family to become the living channel through which the blessing of God would flow outwards to all nations.

NOTES

1. J.L. McKenzie, Myths and Realities: Studies in Biblical Theology (London: G. Chapman, 1963) 171; cf. all Part III, 83-200.
2. Ibid. 191; cf. 200: "The Hebrew intuition of the ineffable reality which revealed itself to man as the personal reality behind the succession of phenomena, the agent of the great cosmic event which we call creation, the reality from which all things came, in which they exist, and to which they must return, was not the creation of mythical form or of logical discourse, but a direct and personal experience of God as the 'Thou' to whom the human 'I' must respond. But they had no media through which they could enunciate the ineffable reality except the patterns of thought and speech which they inherited from their civilization".
3. C. Westermann, Genesis 1-11, (London: E.T. by J. Scullion, SPCK 1984) 19 and 36.
4. Ibid. 64-69.
5. Cf. The New Jerusalem Bible, 7-11. Also La Nueva Biblia Española, 21.
6. P. Ellis, The Yahwist — The Bible's First Theologian (Notre Dame, Indiana: Fides Publishers, 1968) viii. He explains further the stature of the Yahwist: "Coming at the beginning, and with all the disadvantages of a pioneer, he nevertheless launched the writing of theology, gave to the Israel founded by Moses the thrust and momentum given later by St. Paul to the New Israel founded by Christ".
7. The New American Bible, (New York: Thomas Nelson,1983).
8. J-L. Ska, "Je vais lui faire un allié qui soit son homologue" (Gn 2,18) — A propos du terme 'ezer — "aide", in Biblica 65(1984), 233-238; cf. esp.238.
9. D. McCarthy, Institution and Narrative, 292. Cf. C. Westermann, op.cit. 230.
10. C. Westermann, op.cit. 232; cf. on same page further comment on "a helper fit for him": "What is meant is the personal community of man and woman in the broadest sense — bodily and spiritual community, mutual help and understanding, joy and contentment in each other."
11. Cf. D. McCarthy, op.cit. 3-13 for treatment of the human covenants thought to be described by the Yahwist in Genesis. C. Westermann, op.cit. 347 and 423 does not accept some of the examples used as being from the Yahwist. Cf. The footnotes of the New Jerusalem Bible for indications of pentateuchal texts attributed to the Yahwist or other traditions.
12. L. Alonso Schökel, Motivos Sapienciales y De Alianza En Gen 2-3, in Biblica 43(1962), 295-316; English form, Sapiential and Covenant themes in Genesis 2-3, in Theology Digest 13(1965) 3-10. Part quoted is p.6.

NOTES

13. P. Ellis, Men and Message of the Old Testament (Collegeville, Minnesota: Liturgical Press, 1963) 23.
14. A.D. Galloway,"Creation and Covenant" in R.McKinney (Ed.) Creation Christ And Culture — Studies in Honour of F.F. Torrance (Edinburgh: T. & T. Clark, 1976) 108-118; part quoted is 111-112.
15. W. Vogels, God's Universal Covenant — A Biblical Study (Ottawa: University of Ottawa Press, 1979) 25.
16. T. E. McComiskey, The Covenants of Promise — A Theology of O.T. Covenants, 220.
17. C. Westermann, op.cit. 232.
18. Ibid. 233.
19. Ibid. 234.
20. P. Trible, God and the Rhetoric of Sexuality (Philadelphia: Fortress Press, 1978) 143 — see whole section 72-143.
21. Cf. S. Porubcan, Il Patto Nuovo in Is.40-66, 275: "La nostra definizione ... del Patto Nuovo della salvezza: Ripristino dei rapporti di favore (hesed) tra Dio e l'umanità di prima del peccato".
22. Cf. J-L Ska, Class Notes on Gen 1-11 (Rome: Biblical Institute, 1986-7) 1-14.
23. C. Westermann, op.cit. 90.
24. Cf. D.R. Hillers, Covenant: The History of a Biblical Idea, 158: "An important part of 'P' articulation of history is a sequence of covenants with God." Again: "It seems ... that **'eduth** is actually another name for covenant." Further light on this is given by P. Kalluveetil, Declaration and Covenant, 30-31 and 56; he finds: "Another term belonging to the same root is **'edut**. Like the Akkadian ade and the Aramaic **'dn/'dy'** it refers to stipulations of covenant and sometimes stands by metonymy for covenant itself. In 2 Kg 11,12 it appears in connexion with the pact betwen the king and the people"(31).
25. O.P. Robertson, The Christ of the Covenants, 67. Cf. W. Dumbrell, Covenant and Creation, 32: "A pledge of divine obligation does not follow the development of mutual relationships... but by the very nature of such a pledge it must be coterminous with the onset of the relationship itself." We would not rule out that God could intitiate a better relationship with people who already recognise some ties with God, e.g. Noah's family.
26. C. Westermann, op.cit. 157. Cf. P.C. Hodgson, New Birth of Freedom, 122-126 on 'Homo Liber as Imago Dei', e.g. 123-124: "In the Genesis passage, human freedom is defined in terms of certain constitutive relationships: the relationship to God, in whose image (as the Free One) we are created; ... and the relationship between man and woman as the primordial community in which human beings can be free 'for the other'. Freedom is not an individualistic but a communal, relational concept ..."
27. C. Westermann, op.cit. 158.
28. Ibid. 155.
29. Cf. J-L. Ska, Class Notes on Gen 1-11, pp.9-11. Cf. C. Westermann, op.cit. 468: "The explanation given of Gen 1:26-28 shows that it is not a

question of a quality in people but of the fact that God has created people as his counterpart and that humans can have a history with God. The image and likeness of God is only there in the relationship between God and the individual. Murder then is a direct attack on God's right of dominion. Every murderer confronts God; murder is direct and unbridled revolt against God."

30. J. Bishop, The Covenant: A Reading, 8.
31. W. Dumbrell, op.cit. 41.
32. J. Miranda, Marx and the Bible— A Critique of the Philosophy of Oppression (New York: E.T. by J. Eagleson, Orbis, 1974) 35-76, with helpful reflections on the prohibition against making dead images of God. Such images may be seen but they cannot speak, whereas the biblical God does speak without being seen(cf Dt 4,12).
33. Leon Epsztein, La Justice Social dans le Proche-Orient et le Peuple de la Bible (Paris: Cerf, 1983) 211; 207; 210; cf. also 212: "En cessant d'être serviteur des 'pharaons extérieurs et intérieux', le fidèle se mettra au service de Dieu et, par conséquent, de l'humanité" (E.T. by J. Bowden: Social Justice in the Ancient Near East and the People of the Bible ; London: SCM Press, 1986.)
34. C. Westermann, op.cit. 175.
35. John Paul II, Talk on November 12, 1986, as reported in "Osservatore Romano", English Ed., Nov. 17, 1986.
36. P. Bovati, Ristabilire la Giustizia , 64; whole ch. 2 on "The Accusation" , 51-77, indicates how deeply this aspect influenced the biblical pursuit of justice. God can play the role of Accuser as well as Judge, before whom the accused may speak up but not lie. We will see that the end of history, if it is to conclude with full justice, must entail a great Last Judgment.
37. J. Navone, "The Dynamic of the Question in the Search for God", in Review for Religious 45, N°6 (1986) 876-891, e.g. 881: "Jewish and Christian Scriptures are the expression of responding love inspired by the gift of the Spirit of love for the God who speaks in his question and answer." Also 886: "The answers to the basic questions that Jesus Christ raises are given to those who are willing to share his life of costly self-transcendence, or way of the cross. The answers to his questions are learned in the authentic coresponsibility of those who live in the Spirit of Jesus Christ within his New Covenant community"(emphasis added). Here Navone touches on the sense of responsibility that God expects of every family member at all times, including Cain.
38. C. Westermann, op.cit. 331-344 on musicians, artisans and metallurgists among Cain's descendants, whereas for Seth the emphasis is on his son Enosh as being "the first to invoke the name Yahweh" (Gen 4,26), leading W. to conclude: "When J in the same context also associates the beginning of the worship of God with primeval time, he is pointing out that worship is as determinative for the whole history of humankind as is the work of civilization and that its universal aspect should not be lost sight of by way of the partial" (344).

NOTES

39. J. Miranda, op.cit. 89; cf. 95: "Moreover, the gratuitous beneficence of Yahweh's love for mankind consists, according to the Yahwist, precisely in Yahweh's breaking into our history to achieve a justice which all previous history had shown that men were not able to achieve. All the tribes of the earth will be blessed in Abraham 'because' Yahweh 'has singled out' the people of Israel to teach the whole world how to achieve 'justice and right'".
40. The New Jerusalem Bible, 107, note j.
41. Cf. P. Ellis, The Yahwist, 269-270 on this text as from J. The N.J.B. regards it as such, but adverts to other views.
42. Cf. L. Alonso Schökel, ¿Dónde está tu Hermano?, 323-4: "La solidaridad exige interesarse activamente por el hermano en dificultad." Cf. E. Malatesta, Interiority and Covenant — A Study of **'einai 'en** and **menein 'en** in the First Letter of St John (Rome: Pontifical Biblical Institute, 1978) 257: "The author builds his reflections [in 1 Jn 3,11-24] around the contrasting examples of Cain who out of envious hatred killed his brother, and Jesus who out of selfless love gave His life so that all might live."
43. C. Westermann, op.cit. 345-362 on genealogies of Gen 5, e.g. 348: "P is saying here that the plan of God in creating human beings is spelling itself out. The blessing and its power have been bestowed on the creature. The imperative, 'be fruitful and multiply and fill the earth', is being carried out in Gen 5. The power of the blessing shows itself effective in the relentless rhythm and steady successsion of generations that stretch out across time."
44. Ibid. 458.
45. Ibid. 470-471.
46. Ibid. 473.
47. J-L Ska, Class Notes on Gen 1-11, 39; cf. 42: "The hinge of this renewal is the 'covenant' (6,18; 9,8-17; and 8,1). ... And the new universe rests upon God's remembrance of his covenant (9,15.16). .... The basic function of the covenant is stylistically underlined by the central position of 8,1 in the structure, as by the key function of 8,1 in the narrative structure." (Emphasis added.)
48. W. Vogels, op.cit. 30. Cf. O.P. Robertson, op.cit. 121: "The covenant with Noah possesses a distinctively universalistic aspect. The particular stress on the cosmic dimensions of the covenant with Noah should be noted in this regard. The whole of the created universe, including the totality of humanity, benefits from this covenant."
49. D. McCarthy, op.cit. 4l.
50. C. Westermann, op.cit. 555: "In both places [Gen 3 and ll] J is saying that this aspiration merely hides within itself the possiblity of overstepping the limits and that it is precisely here that human existence is in such great danger. Behind Gen 11:1-9 stands the idea of human ambition which only revealed itself in the course of human history in conjunction with the great achievements of civilization."

CHAPTER 3: COVENANT WITH ABRAHAM AND SARAH (GEN 12-50)

A. THE PROMISE TO ABRAM (GEN 12)

Yahweh breaks into the life and destiny of Abram and Sarai by calling them to leave the security of their own kindred and country, to set off for a country which he will show them[1]. With this unexpected call comes also the astonishing promise: "and I shall make you a great nation, I shall bless you and make your name famous; you are to be a blessing!
I shall bless those who bless you,
and shall curse those who curse you,
and all clans on earth
will bless themselves by you" (Gen 12,2-3).

The initiative was completely with Yahweh, who had prepared for this moment through the earlier creation and blessings recounted in the primeval stories right from the first couple. The response, however, must be given freely by the chosen couple, who unreservedly accept the call with all the cutting of old ties: "So Abram went as Yahweh had told him ... Abram took his wife Sarai, his nephew Lot, all the possessions they had amassed and the people they had acquired in Haran. They set off for the land of Canaan, and arrived there" (Gen 12,4-5). The divine call and the human response play a central role in all that follows with regard to the family of Abraham and also with regard to all the nations on earth. It is therefore basic as well for our understanding of the Abrahamic covenant, which can only confirm and clarify a few of the implications of the promise.

In no way can this gratuitous and unconditional promise be terminated by its recipients. Individuals and even a whole community may freely forfeit their participation in the promised blessing, but that will not lead God to cancel his promise for everybody else. With reason the covenant granted to confirm this promise is often referred to as a promissory covenant. The emphasis throughout is on the promise and not on covenant stipulations accepted by the human party. Moreover, the promise already mentions blessings and curses, ruling out that these will become like the usual sanctions put at the end of international treaties.

Although recorded cryptically, the core promise already announces blessings that are to be personal, national and universal:
personal: "I shall bless you (Abram) and make your name famous; you are to be a blessing" (v.2);
national: "I shall make you a great nation" (v.2);
universal: "all the clans on earth will bless themselves by you" (v.3).

The remaining stories from Gen 12 -25 also add the promise of the land of Canaan for the descendants of Abraham and Sarah, e.g. in 12,7; 13,14-17; 15,7.18; 17,8. This "promised land" is considered by C.Westermann to be a later addition to the ancient patriarchal traditions[2]. Be that as it may, the

Yahwist's account of the covenant in Gen 15, then the Priestly account of it in Gen 17, both emphasise the promise of that land as an element confirmed by the covenant.

Having accepted the gracious but demanding call of Yahweh, Abram and Sarai — as they are called until God changes their names to Abraham and Sarah (Gen 17) — set off with their sizable household for the land of Canaan. Their story from then on is that of an expanding family, frequently journeying from place to place as semi-nomads, shifting their herds to the fringes of more settled towns and fields. Ancient places that appear in their stories are Shechem, Bethel, Ai, Salem (later Jerusalem), the Negeb, Hebron, Kadesh, Lahai Roi, Beersheba, and as far afield as Egypt when famine makes it a necessity. These stories have obviously been preserved as precious family traditions, handed on orally from one generation to the next. No doubt they were adapted to later audiences, but they still retain many ancient elements that reflect faithfully the period of the patriarchs. Excavations and other efforts during the last two centuries to unlock the past have thrown a great deal of light on the Mesopotamia, Canaan and Egypt of Abraham's time, perhaps between 19th to 17th centuries B.C.[3].

Pertinent to our reflection is the noble way in which Abram, recalling "we are kinsmen" (13,8), gave his nephew Lot first choice of the lands available for grazing, in order to put an end to their shepherds fighting. Lot's choice of fertile lands near Sodom was soon to involve his whole family in the consequences of city corruption and violence. For his part, Abram went on further south to Hebron, erecting there an altar to Yahweh as he had done earlier on reaching Bethel(13,18; 12,8). Like Noah, Abram leads his household in public worship of Yahweh. Another glimpse of family loyalty is provided by the story of the way Abram acted quickly and courageously as **go'el** (redeeming kinsman) to rescue all Lot's household from foreign invaders (14,11-16). Even with regard to the booty captured in that operation, Abram insisted: "For myself, nothing..." (14,24). Such glimpses are pertinent to the covenant we are about to discuss, since they show Abram responding well to God and kinspeople. This is in keeping with the call and promise already freely accepted. It is against this background that the present text of Genesis can describe God's confirming of the promise as a covenant, availing of traditions from J (15) and P (17). Covenant can bring out more forcefully than promise the aspect of new and deeper relationships between the two parties. As stated in the case of the Noachic covenant, one-sided initiative in establishing a covenant does not rule out a better two-sided relationship springing from that covenant.

B. CONFIRMING THE PROMISE WITH A COVENANT (GEN 15 AND 17)

1. Yahweh "cuts a covenant" with Abram (Gen 15)

As it now stands, ch.15 tells of two distinct difficulties of Abram, one concerning a son and heir, the other a promised land (vv. 1-6 and 7-21). Both

preoccupations are allayed by Yahweh. He promises a son to Abram and innumerable descendants. So "Abram put his faith in Yahweh and this was reckoned to him as uprightness"(v.6).
With regard to the land, Yahweh renews the promise to give him the land of Canaan as his possession. When Abram asks, "How can I know that I shall possess it?", Yahweh directs him to proceed with a covenant-cutting ceremony. Abram cuts in two a heifer, she-goat and ram, placing each half opposite the other. After driving off birds of prey, Abram fell into a trance after sunset and experienced a deep dread. Finally "there appeared a smoking firepot and a flaming torch passing between the animals' pieces. That day Yahweh made a covenant with Abram in these terms: 'To your descendants I give this country....'"(vv.17-18).

The "smoking firepot and flaming torch" , perhaps two ways of describing the one fiery object, represent Yahweh passing between the sacrificed animals. The symbolism would be the acceptance of a curse in the event of violating the solemn promise given to Abram, a daring image for Hebrews to allow where Yahweh is involved. However, it is a roundabout way of stressing that there is no way Yahweh will bring a curse upon himself. In other words, it is unthinkable that he will fail in his promise. Worthy of note in 15,18 is that the Hebrew text says that Yahweh **karat b^{e}rit** (= cut a covenant) with Abram, which helps us grasp some of the significance of the seemingly strange ritual performed by Abram at Yahweh's instigation. Precisely because only Yahweh is thought to have passed between the cut pieces, the one-sidedness of obligation accepted is further highlighted. Had Abram also walked between the pieces, he too would have been accepting a covenant obligation under threat of a curse for any violation on his part.

The lack of mutuality of obligations underlies the rejection of this particular **b^{e}rit** as a covenant by C. Westermann. To avoid misunderstanding, it is indispensable to look closely at what exactly he says. He insists that "Gen. 15:17-21 does not present the concluding of a covenant between God and Abraham which established from that moment on a mutual covenantal relationship, but rather God's assurance or promise to Abraham solemnized by a rite. ... ... If **berit** here does not mean 'covenant' but a solemn promise or oath(N. Lohfink), then the text is not dealing with a covenant which God concludes with Abraham, but with the solemn confirmation by oath of the promise of the land. ... The text of Gen. 15 ceases to have any relevance for the whole question of a patriarchal covenant.."[4].

We agree with Westermann that the rite does solemnly confirm the existing promise, and does not make it dependent subsequently on covenant fidelity on the part of Abraham or his descendants. We differ from Westermann, however, when he sees the rite as only equivalent to an oath, not a covenant of any kind. Ch. 22 does speak explicitly of God "swearing" an oath to confirm the promise; here in 15 it speaks explicitly of **b^{e}rit**, which we consider to carry with it overtones of a new covenantal relationship. The obligations for Abraham are left unstated but are there implicitly, for a covenant connotes mutual agreement to live in peace with an abiding attitude of family-style loyalty.

In this we accept D. McCarthy's conclusion drawn from the nature of the irrevocable promise by the "God of the fathers" to "nomads on the way to sedentarization": "Further, since such a promise was **ipso facto** a covenant of one sort, it is entirely reasonable to hold some form of actual covenant with the patriarchs.."5..(emphasis added). Here he is speaking of a real covenant, not merely a later construct projected back. Consequently we cannot agree that Gen 15 has no relevance for the kind of covenant we are talking about. On the contrary, it seems an important text for delineating some nuances of the covenant, which Gen 17 can make much more obvious. The sealing of the new covenant, as we shall see, also leaves a great deal implicit with regard to the human response expected. Its emphasis also is on a new kind of family relationship rather than on covenant stipulations. It continues to fulfil that promissory covenant without abrogating it, whereas it does supersede and replace the Mosaic covenant. The faith, justice, and compliance of Abram with Yahweh's word all help towards the final **shalom** (peace) promised in 15,15.

Ch.16 tells the story of Ishmael's birth from the Egyptian slave-girl Hagar, who had run away because Sarai treated her so badly. She preferred freedom in the scorching desert rather than maltreatment as a slave. Although the Hebrew mistress had felt entitled to maltreat an Egyptian slave, Yahweh heard the latter's "cries of distress" (v.11) and promised innumerable descendants through her son. Hagar went back to bear her son to Abram, who named him Ishmael.

2. God's covenant made more explicit in its demands (Gen 17)

This time the Priestly writer uses the word covenant even more persistently than he did to depict the Noachic covenant. Right from the start comes the divine command, "Walk in my presence and be blameless" (v.1 - New English Bible). To walk before God and to be blameless are exactly what P mentioned earlier as distinguishing Noah from his contemporaries (Gen 6,9). Similarly, God does not wait for any explicit reply, but takes the initiative in declaring: "For my part, this is my covenant with you: you will become the father of many nations. And you are no longer to be called Abram; your name is to be Abraham" (17,4-5). God establishes the covenant between himself and Abraham's family "in perpetuity" (or, as P. Buis would translate, irrevocably). Here again "the entire land of Canaan" is promised to Abraham and his descendants (v.8). The sign of this covenant is to be circumcision, and even male slaves within the household are to be circumcised. Any uncircumcised male "must be cut off from his people" (v.14).

Then comes the amazing clarification that the son and heir to this promissory covenant will be born from Abraham and Sarah — as Sarai is renamed by God (vv.15-16). Abraham understandably laughs at the idea of a son in their old age, and he proceeds to ask God to settle for Ishmael instead. God simply explains that Sarah will bear a son to Abraham, who will call him Isaac. "And I shall maintain my covenant with him, a covenant in perpetuity, to be his God and the God of his descendants after him" (vv.17-19). Ishmael will be blessed indeed, ensuring that he, too, will grow into a great nation. The chosen people are to come from a free couple, both of them free to cooperate with God and with each other in the transmission of a life so crucial in the whole history of mankind. As Eve has been called "the mother of all those who live"(Gen 3,20), Sarah could well be called "the mother of all the free". The importance of Sarah is remembered by Deutero-Isaiah as a motive for continuing trust in God's guidance of Israel: "Consider the rock from which you were hewn, the quarry from which you were dug. Consider Abraham your father and Sarah who gave you birth. When I called him he was the only one but I blessed him and made him numerous" (51,2)[6].

To keep his part of the covenant, Abraham immediately had himself and all the males of his household circumcised, including Ishmael. The story is taken up from the Yahwist tradition, telling of Yahweh's visit to tell Abraham and Sarah that they are to have a son within the year. This time it is Sarah who laughs at hearing such an incredible announcement (Gen 18,1-12). Yahweh seizes the opportunity to reassure Sarah, "Nothing is impossible for Yahweh" (v.14).

Abraham accompanies Yahweh in keeping with oriental concern for the parting guest. This provides the setting for their famous dialogue about sparing Sodom for the sake of even ten just people. Yahweh treats Abraham with the confidence shown to one of the family, through whom he plans to channel the blessing and saving knowledge to all nations. "For I have singled him out to command his sons and his family after him to keep the way of Yahweh by doing what is upright and just, so that Yahweh can carry out for Abraham what he has promised him"(v.19). The text brings out clearly the importance of Abraham's free response and moral leadership with regard to the actualization of Yahweh's promise. Again we must conclude that, while the promise is unconditional, it carries with it the constant demand of faith and just conduct[7]. Rejection of God in a personal encounter or serious injustice to others will lead to the offenders being cut off from their share in the promise. This in turn makes it seem reasonable for both the Yahwist and the Priestly writers to associate the promise with covenant. Admittedly there is a certain blurring of the line of demarcation between the two, but there is no contradiction.

The preeminence of justice is stressed by Abraham's appeal to Yahweh to spare Sodom if even ten just people can be found there: "Is the judge of the whole world not to act justly?" (v.25). Subsequent events indicate that the "outcry" reaching Yahweh from Sodom was in fact due to a very sinful city, which was thereupon destroyed. Lot and his daughters alone escaped with their lives. When Abraham hurried back at sunrise, "he saw the smoke rising from the ground like smoke from a furnace"(19,28).

Ch. 20 tells of how God protected the future mother, Sarah, from Abimelech, who had to restore her to Abraham. This would seem to be a doublet of the story of God's intervention to rescue Sarah from an Egyptian pharaoh (Gen 12,10-20). Both stories again underline the special role of Sarah, whom God constantly watches over as a precious person in the plan of salvation[8].

Finally, in their old age, Abraham and Sarah can laugh for joy at the birth of their son Isaac (21,1-7). On the other hand, the arrival of the new son and heir had serious repercussions for Hagar and Ishmael. Sarah could no longer tolerate their presence once Isaac was weaned, whereas Abraham was "greatly distressed" at the prospect of sending away the son whom he also cherished, not to mention the spirited and long-suffering mother, Hagar. Only on being assured by God that Ishmael would become the father of a great nation did Abraham do what Sarah wanted. Hagar and Ishmael were sent off into the wilderness, and soon suffered the harsh consequences of being alone. Death was staring them in the face when God "heard the boy crying" and enabled Hagar to find water. From then on "God was with the boy" and blessed him as promised (21,15-21). The special blessing promised to Abraham and Sarah will be transmitted through the line of Isaac, but this should never be regarded as limiting God's right to bless others beyond that line. The end in view is the blessing of all the families on earth. Ishmael's receives it as an anticipation.

C. THE PROMISE CONFIRMED BY OATH (GEN 22)

In this incident the demand made upon Abraham precedes the confirming of the promise, when he is requested to sacrifice his only free-born son, the son through whom God had promised to make a great nation as a channel of blessing for all the other nations. The obedient way Abraham sets off with Isaac for the sacrifice forms one of the most poignant stories of the Bible[9]. Abraham displays an obedience without limit, not even in the matter of sacrificing his only son and hope for the future. At the last moment God makes it clear that he does not want human sacrifice, even though he does want unreserved obedience . He declares: "I swear by my own self that because you have done this, because you have not refused me your own beloved son, I will shower blessings on you and make your descendants as numerous as the stars of heaven ... All nations on earth will bless themselves by your descendants, because you have obeyed my command" (vv.16-18).

Oath-taking was one of the most common ways to confirm the content of a covenant or treaty, in fact D. McCarthy notes of the international treaties: "It would seem that the same   legal-literary form, essentially stipulations sanctioned by oath, was used to express these treaty relationships all through two millennia of ancient Near Eastern history"[10]. Again: "..the treaty form is essentially a development of the ancient oath formula, i.e., a conditioned self-curse which would be activated if the oath were broken"[11]. It is worth recalling a parallel conclusion reached by P. Kalluveetil concerning biblical covenants: "The OT does not have a fixed form for realizing a pact. <u>The oath is the most important factor,</u> but it is not the sine-qua-non element"[12](emphasis added). Hence we may legitimately interpret Gen 22 as a solemn confirmation of the existing promissory covenant.

Only God is said to swear, but he links his oath explicitly with the way Abraham's fidelity has been unwavering despite the agonizing test: "because you have done this, because you have not refused me your own beloved son, ..

because you have obeyed my command" (vv.16-18). In such a context, the fact that only God takes the oath does not imply that Abraham steps out of his existing relationship of confident loyalty towards God. Everything points rather to a new level of relationship between God and Abraham. The more Abraham grasps the goodness and fidelity of God, the more does he respond with trusting faith and obedient justice. He and Sarah become models to be followed by all future families who wish to share in the promised blessing.

The closing years of their own full lives are peaceful, Sarah being the first to die. A first plot of land is purchased in the promised land, in the field of Machpelah. There Sarah is laid to rest. After the marriage of Isaac and Rebekah, and after Abraham had other children by Keturah and concubines, he too was gathered to his fathers. Ishmael rejoined his former playmate Isaac to bury with fitting solemnity their father Abraham, beside Sarah in the plot of Machpelah(Gen 25,1-11).

The reflection of F.E.Peters on "The children of Abraham" is relevant here before we leave Abraham and Sarah. "Judaism, Christianity and Islam are all children born of the same Father and reared in the bosom of Abraham. They grew to adulthood in the rich spiritual climate of the Near East, and though they have lived together all their lives, now in their maturity they stand apart and regard their family resemblances and conditioned differences with astonishment, disbelief, or disdain. ... Rich parallels of attitude and institution exist among these three religions that acknowledge, in varying degrees, their evolution one out of the other"[13].

Abraham and Sarah are also models of a pilgrim spirituality which encourages the people of God throughout the Bible to "walk before his face" and move on confidently to wherever he calls them. It still inspires missionaries of today to leave their own birthplace and culture to set off into the unknown. "The style of missionary life demands the spirit of the wanderer and of the provisional."... Even after establishing some community in another culture, the missionary must have "a readiness to journey and be uprooted when the moment comes"[14]. A similar spirit is rightly advocated for those who would enter seriously into the struggle of the poor and downtrodden for their liberation. As R. McAfee Brown puts it, "something of the Abrahamic quality will have to invest the lives of those who take on the task of liberation today. The degree of our ability to respond will not finally rest on the soundness of our analysis.. but on the extent of our willingness to risk our security on behalf of the insecurities of others"[15].

D. PROMISSORY COVENANT RENEWED WITH ISAAC AND JACOB (GEN 26-28)

We are told quite simply that "after Abraham's death, God blessed his son Isaac"(25,11), who at that time was settled in the southern part of Canaan where he had grown up. He married Rebekah, who bore him the famous twins Esau and Jacob. During a time of famine God reassured Isaac: "I shall be with you and bless you, for I shall give all these countries to you and your descendants in fulfilment of the oath I swore to your father Abraham. I shall make your descendants as numerous as the stars of heaven,.. and all nations on earth will bless themselves by your descendants, in return for Abraham's obedience, for he kept my charge, my commandments" (Gen 26,3-5). Not a great deal is recorded about the life or character of Isaac, but enough is given to set him firmly for ever as the link between Abraham and Jacob. God is called "the God of Abraham, Isaac and Jacob".

As the second twin to be born, Jacob considers it necessary to resort to unfair means to make sure he gets the birthright of the firstborn. The biblical account of their struggle even within the womb mentions Yahweh's declaration to Rebekah, "the elder will serve the younger". We may presume that what Jacob tries to do later on is to make doubly sure that anything special comes his way rather than Esau's.

Because of the antagonism his treatment of Esau had aroused, Jacob set off to Haran. On his journey he stopped the night at Bethel, where he dreamed of the ladder reaching up to heaven, with angels going up and down. That makes a worthy setting for the special message imparted that night to Jacob: "I, Yahweh, am the God of Abraham your father, and the God of Isaac. The ground on which you are lying I shall give to you and your descendants. Your descendants will be as plentiful as the dust on the ground; ... and all clans on earth will bless themselves by you and your descendants. Be sure I am with you; ... for I shall never desert you until I have done what I have promised you" (Gen 28,13-15).

As in the previous promises made to Abraham and Isaac, here again the promise centres upon a numerous progeny to be a blessing for all other families, and on the land of Canaan which will be given to Jacob's descendants. The working out of the promise is described in several chapters covering Jacob's marriage to Leah and Rachel, his twenty years of tough work for his wily uncle Laban, his eventual escape with a large household and plentiful herds, his traumatic encounter and reconciliation with Esau near the river Jabbok (Gen 29-33). So abundantly had Jacob and his whole household been blessed that he was able to restore to Esau the honour and blessing of which he had deprived him[16]. On returning safely to Canaan, Jacob settles on the outskirts of Shechem. The rape of his daughter Dinah stirs his sons to massacre the men of Shechem, with the result that the family move on to Bethel (Gen 34). There Jacob encounters once again the God who has by now fulfilled the promise to keep Jacob safe in all his journeying and to grant him numerous offspring. In gratitude he sets up an altar and memorial stone in Bethel, in keeping with the vow he had made there before setting out for Haran (Gen 28,20-22). God changes Jacob's name to Israel.

His twelfth son, Benjamin, is born near Bethlehem, but Rachel dies in giving birth to him. From these twelve sons are to come the twelve tribes of Israel. Finally Jacob returns to his father Isaac in Hebron, where Isaac dies. Jacob and Esau meet once again to bury him there(Gen 35). A considerable list of Esau's descendants, who became chieftains and later kings in Edom, are a further indication that the blessing of Jacob did not prevent God from blessing Esau and his household as well (Gen 36).

E. FAILURE AND RESTORATION OF COVENANT KINSHIP (GEN 37-50)

This so-called Joseph cycle serves to explain how the family of Jacob had to move out of Canaan and go down to Egypt. For our purposes, it presents impressive examples of lack of family loyalty followed by noble gestures of family reconciliation. It also shows God continuing to accompany Joseph more than ever once his own brothers had sold him into slavery out of jealousy. As it now stands, the whole cycle is a fairly well unified story in which can be detected J, E (Elohistic) and P traditions. Like the earlier patriarchal stories, it cannot be linked with any particular pharaoh or date now known from Egyptian studies. However, a careful consideration of these chapters 37-50 in the light of current knowledge about ancient Egypt has led J. Vergote to conclude that they do display a familiarity with life there from the time of the "New Kingdom" (about 1550 B.C. on)[17].

We also know now that Egypt was invaded and conquered by the Hyksos in the 18th c.B.C. They set up their fortress-capital at Avaris (Tanis) in the Nile delta, to guard their northeastern frontier. They seem to have been largely a Semitic people with a variety of other racial groups, coming down from Canaan and beyond. They founded the 15th Dynasty of Egypt, then ruled for nearly a century from Avaris, being finally expelled around 1550 B.C. "It is tempting", as B. Anderson says, "to connect the Hyksos movement into Egypt with the biblical story of the descent of Jacob and his family into Egypt. ... According to the biblical narratives the Hebrew settlement in the Goshen area ..was near Pharaoh's court... When Ahmose expelled the Hyksos, Avaris was destroyed and the capital was moved back to Thebes. ... The patriarchal migration may well have occurred on the fringe of the Hyksos population movement"[18].

Once the Hyksos had been expelled, the "New Kingdom" began in Egypt and endured for about five hundred years. It seems plausible, therefore, to hold that the Joseph cycle preserves memories of some kind of entry into Egypt during Hyksos supremacy there. Subsequent centuries would have been under the "Middle Kingdom" of local Egyptian kings, less sympathetic to Semites still waxing strong within the kingdom.

Joseph, then, appears as an outstanding member of the chosen family, a young man caught up in his own dreams and able to interpret them as presaging a special role for himself. That coming on top of the special affection shown him by Jacob proved too much for his brothers. The spectre of Cain rears itself again, as they plan his murder. Fortunately Reuben in one tradition, Judah in another, cannot accept the blood of their own brother on their hands. "Shed no blood", pleads Reuben (37,22); "What do we gain by killing our brother and covering up his blood?", asks Judah (37,26). They manage to save his life, but at the cost of Joseph being sold into slavery. While he was being carried off by traders to Egypt, his bright tunic was sent back soaked in goat's blood to deceive Jacob into thinking he was dead. Their crime against a brother had also vitiated their relationship with the grieving father. Once again it is an eloquent warning that promised blessings do not ward off painful blows even from those within the chosen family. If such a family chooses to make slaves of its own household, they must face the day of "reckoning" for it (Gen 42,21-22).

On the other hand, the hated, exiled and enslaved brother found favour with his new master, Potiphar, for "God was with Joseph" and "Yahweh blessed the Egyptian's household out of consideration for Joseph"(39,2.5). Even within that household, the wife tempted Joseph to adultery, but he refused to betray the trust of his master or to sin against God. For that reason he was falsely denounced and thrown into prison, where Yahweh still "showed him <u>faithful love</u> (**hesed**)" (39,21). This word **hesed** has overtones of covenant fidelity and kindness, even more obvious in the context where Joseph is unjustly suffering because of his loyalty to Yahweh. So Joseph is enabled to interpret well the dreams of his fellow-prisoners, explaining to pharaoh's butler that he was soon to be released, whereas the baker had to be told of his impending hanging.

The butler eventually persuaded the pharaoh to fetch Joseph out of prison to interpret his ominous dreams as well. Joseph declared, "Not I, God will give Pharaoh a favourable answer" (41,16). He interpreted the dreams so convincingly as pointing to seven years of plenty to be followed by seven years of famine that Pharaoh appointed him as vizier or governor of all Egypt. His wisdom and competence as an honest administrator served in God's providence to enable all Egypt and their neighbours to survive the terrible famine when it hit. Among those best served were to be found Joseph's own brothers. The story reaches great heights as it reveals the searching of hearts when they come face to face with the brother they had hated and wronged so badly.

In the first encounters Joseph left his brothers in ignorance as to his real identity, and from overhearing their conversations he could sense a more noble attitude on their part with regard to Jacob and Benjamin. Astutely he got them to bring Benjamin with them to Egypt the next time they needed grain. Once his only full brother, Benjamin, arrived, he feasted with all his brothers. Weeping with emotion he revealed to them: "I am Joseph your brother, whom you sold into Egypt. But now, do not grieve, do not reproach yourselves for having sold me here, since God sent me before you to preserve your lives" (45,4-5). He went on to insist that they immediately bring Jacob and all their own families to settle in the rich Nile delta. The Pharaoh endorsed the invitation and provided wagons to help them move.

Once Jacob and his numerous household had settled in Goshen, Jacob blessed the two sons of Joseph and Asenath, his Egyptian wife. The blessing of Ephraim and Manasseh recalls that of their forefathers, as Jacob prays over them: "May the God in whose presence my fathers Abraham and Isaac walked ... bless these boys, so that my name may live on in them... and they grow into teeming multitudes on earth! ... By you shall Israel bless itself, saying, 'God make you like Ephraim and Manasseh'" (48,15-20). There is also a very long farewell blessing of the twelve sons, in which occurs the allusion, "the sceptre shall not pass from Judah" (49,10). Already the promissory covenant with the patriarchs can be perceived as extending onwards towards the Davidic covenant.

When Jacob died, Joseph saw to it that he was embalmed and then given a fitting burial back in the cave of Machpelah, to rest beside Abraham and Sarah. The guilty brothers feared that, without the restraining influence of their father, Joseph might at last punish them. To forestall this they begged forgiveness and asked him to accept them as slaves. Joseph was still magnanimous, refusing to enslave them. He repeated that God had used their maltreatment of him to bring about "the survival of a numerous people" (50,20). The reconciliation of the brothers was complete, so that as free people they might go forward with the unique mission entrusted to them by the Lord of all nations.

NOTES

1. R. McAfee Brown, "Liberation Theology: Paralyzing Threat or Creative Challenge?", in G. H. Anderson and T. F. Stransky (Ed.s), Mission Trends No.4: Liberation Theologies (New York: Paulist Press; and Grand Rapids: Eerdmans, 1979), 3-24.
2. C. Westermann, Genesis 12-36 — A Commentary (E.T. by J. Scullion, London: SPCK, 1985), 155.
3. Cf. B. Vawter, On Genesis : A New Reading (London: G. Chapman, 1977). For a wealth of background material, cf. R. De Vaux, Histoire ancienne d'Israël (Paris: J. Gabalda, 2 Vol. 1971-1973).
4. C. Westermann, op.cit. 113; cf. 577: "The programmatic promise of 12:1-3 extends beyond to the nations of the world. The promises, therefore, make the patriarchal story an indispensable component of the rest of the Old Testament; their fulfillment proceeds step by step through the history of the people of God...The promises to the patriarchs become a link between the O.T. and the N.T. ... The same is true for the covenant; the original meaning of b^{e}rit is a solemn, binding obligation and it is used in this sense to designate God's promise to Abraham in Gen. 15. In Gen. 17 its meaning is extended to <u>a reciprocal obligation</u>, the 'covenant'" (emphasis added).
5. D. McCarthy, Old Testament Covenant, 48-49; cf. 81: "It seems legitimate to consider a sure promise as a covenant. After all, the O.T. had no single necessary form for expressing or making covenants. The essential thing seems to have been that an obligatory relationship was formed. ... An obligation is <u>to</u> someone or <u>between</u> parties, that is, it necessarily involves a relationship. Surely a promise from God was a firm basis for obligation, a fixed relationship we may still call covenant."
6. C. Mesters, Abrahan y Sara (Spanish T. by W. Alvarez; Madrid: Ediciones Paulinas, 1981).
7. J. Miranda, Marx and the Bible, 116; and 216, where he reflects: "The works of men were not able to achieve justice. This is the thesis of the Yahwist in Gen. 2-11; Abraham, however, believed that Yahweh would achieve justice by intervening in our history(Gen. 15 and 18)".
8. C. Westermann, op.cit. 158, where he asserts: "Salvation history <u>as rescue history</u> did not begin with Abraham, but with the exodus. Rescue, insofar

NOTES

as it is rescue vis-a-vis man, has always an effect of separation; with rescue a particular history begins. By contrast, the promise of blessing to Abraham is aimed at a blessing which embraces mankind"(emphasis added). We can accept this point of view, and clarify that the kind of salvation we have in mind is greater than political or social liberation. We regard this kind of salvation as rescuing even individuals like Cain or like Joseph's brothers from some of the consequences of their sins. The God of justice who promises blessing is implicitly promising to overcome the consequences of hearts that "contrive evil from their infancy"(Gen 8,21). Because from Abraham and Sarah a family begins to have its particular history of such salvation or friendship with God, with vitality enough to have some impact on descendants like Moses, we may speak of it as salvation history.

9. Cf. ibid. 355: "It has often been said that Gen 22 is one of the most beautiful narratives in the Old Testament, and that it also has a special place among the narratives of world literature. Its extraordinary, frightening dimension one can only experience with empathy; a commentary can do no more than hint at it."

10. D. McCarthy, op. cit. 26; cf. 31, where he notes that in international treaties "the emphasis is on the oath, the human act of taking on a solemn obligation, so much so that the very word for 'treaty' is taken from the oath in Akkadian, Hittite, and Aramaic, but not in ordinary Hebrew."

11. Ibid. 34; cf. 41 and 57.

12. P. Kalluveetil, Declaration and Covenant, 91; cf.39 and 87-8.

13. F.E. Peters, Children of Abraham — Judaism/ Christianity/ Islam (New Jersey: Princeton University Press, 1982; pb. 1984), Preface ix. Cf. C. Westermann, op. cit. 403: "Only by surveying the whole content of the Abraham traditions can one grasp that the figure of Abraham has a history, unique in breadth and depth, which leads through the Old Testament, the New Testament, and the Koran right into the present life of the three religions. ... Because he is neither the father of a people nor the founder of a religion, he can be father for Jews, Christians and Muslims alike." Another aspect of Abraham singled out in this "Retrospect" bears directly on our understanding of covenant: "The third matter common to the texts [Gen 12-25] is Abraham's obvious relationship to God. Everything that happens, happens between Abraham and God, God and Abraham. The relationship is simply an element of human existence..."(404) (emphasis added).

14. Departamento de Vocaciones de CELAM, Dar desde nuestra Pobreza — Vocación Misionera de Amerérica Latina (Bogotá: CELAM. 1986) 232: "El estilo de vida misionera exige el espíritu de lo itinerante y de lo provisorio. ... ...El misionero está en tensión entre su arraigo y compromiso con una comunidad local, y su disponibilidad para itinerar y desarraigarse llegado el momento."

15. R. McAfee Brown, art.cit., 23.

16. Cf. C. Westermann, op.cit. 510 g74, where he points out that the word used by Jacob when begging Esau to accept his "gift" was precisely b^erakah(Gen 33,11), a word commonly used for "blessing". "The b^erakah, coming from Jacob, gives back the blessing that he had once stolen. Jacob had fled because of the consequences of his trickery; he now restores to his brother what he had taken by trickery."
17. J. Vergote, Joseph en Egypte (Louvain: University of Louvain Press, 1959).
18. B. Anderson, The Living World of the Old Testament, 40; cf. all section 38-41 on "The Descent into Egypt".

CHAPTER 4: COVENANT WITH A LIBERATED NATION (EXODUS)

A. EARLY LIFE AND FLIGHT OF MOSES (EX 1-2)

The book of Exodus in its opening lines bridges the gap of perhaps three centuries between the death of Joseph and the birth of Moses. During that time the descendants of Jacob's twelve sons had flourished in Egypt, growing into a such a large and powerful people that the king began to treat them as a threat to national security. They were used harshly for forced labour, building store cities like Pithom and Rameses in the Nile Delta. The name of the latter city, in the light of many other little indications, points to the mighty Rameses II(1290-1224 B.C.), of the 19th Dynasty, as the pharaoh of the oppression of the Israelites. There were attempts at genocide, first through the midwives being ordered to kill any newborn Hebrew boy. That failed, because the midwives were God-fearing women who answered back courageously to the oppressing pharaoh. Next he ordered everyone to throw any such baby boys into the river.

Moses was born to a family of the tribe of Levi in the midst of that oppression and serious threat to the survival of his people. His own survival was certainly in jeopardy, but a kindly princess saved him from the river and adopted him herself. She availed of Moses' own mother to act as his wet-nurse. Having been handed back to pharaoh's daughter, Moses grew up in the Egyptian court and became well versed in their highly developed culture. Egypt already had behind it more than two thousand years of writing, and only a few centuries less of unified government under a king, which had encouraged the development of great architecture and huge buildings, of excellent arts and crafts, of wisdom and religious literature. Egypt had reached a peak in several of those areas during the 18th Dynasty, so its influence was still being felt in the days of Moses[1]. As in the case of Joseph, God was bringing good out of the injustice done to Moses and his family, for Moses was sufficiently well educated to become a great leader of his own people and to confront the pharaoh on their behalf.

A turning point came in Moses' life when he defended one of his oppressed kinsmen against an Egyptian who was striking him. Moses killed and buried the Egyptian. When he tried to defend another kinsman against a fellow Hebrew, he was rejected as having no right to intervene. "'And who has appointed you', the man retorted, 'to be prince over us and judge?'"(Ex 2,14). To make sure of undermining Moses' position, that kinsman taunted him about killing the Egyptian. Word soon got back to the pharaoh, as Moses had feared, forcing him to flee for his life out of Egypt. That incident illustrates well both the lack of true brotherhood between the Hebrews themselves and the fear of Moses, which ruled out any further assistance to his enslaved people. Left to himself he had no hope of liberating them.

He went to Midian and settled with the hospitable Midianite priest, Reuel (also called Jethro), who gave his daughter Zipporah in marriage to Moses. In return, Moses worked many years as a shepherd looking after Jethro's flock in the area of Mount Horeb. According to Stephen's speech before he was stoned, Moses was forty when he fled from Egypt, and spent forty years in the land of Midian (Acts 7,23-30). Given that "Moses was a hundred and twenty years old when he died" (Dt 34,7), Stephen has divided his life neatly into three equal periods, leaving the final forty years for what now follows, namely his mission as liberator.

B. MOSES CALLED AND SENT BY GOD TO FREE HIS PEOPLE (EX 3 - 6)

Meanwhile back in Egypt, "the Israelites, groaning in their slavery, cried out for help and from the depths of their slavery their cry came up to God. God heard their groaning; God remembered his covenant with Abraham, Isaac and Jacob" (Ex 2,23-24). This introduction is attributed to the P tradition, especially as it mentions the Abrahamic covenant explicitly, as it does twice more when its account is resumed in ch.6,2ff. There Yahweh also promises to lead them out of slavery and into that land promised to their forefathers (vv.4-9).

The earlier J and E traditions found in cc. 3-4 contain a vivid account of the way Yahweh suddenly broke in to change Moses' quiet life in the wilderness. The burning bush caught Moses' attention, then God was revealed to him as "the God of Abraham, the God of Isaac and the God of Jacob" (Ex 3,6). Here again God declares., "I have indeed seen the misery of my people in Egypt. I have heard them crying on account of their taskmasters. Yes, I am well aware of their sufferings. And I have come down to rescue them from the clutches of the Egyptians and to bring them up out of that country, to a country broad and rich, to country flowing with milk and honey, to the home of the Canaanites.." (Ex 3,7-8). Then comes the mission of Moses: "So now I am sending you to Pharaoh, for you to bring my people the Israelites out of Egypt" (v.10).

Not surprisingly, a reluctant Moses counters: "Who am I to go to Pharaoh and bring the Israelites out of Egypt?" To which God replies, as in many such situations of a reluctant envoy[2], "I shall be with you" (v.12). The first sign mentioned is that the liberated people will come back to worship God "on this mountain". That the freedom to worship Yahweh as their God is of prime importance in the whole story of the exodus can be gauged by the way in which it is repeated more than twenty times from here until Pharaoh finally agrees to let the Israelites go free to do just that[3].

In the E account there follows the revelation of the liberating God's special name, Yahweh (Ex 3,13-15), meaning "I am he who is" (v.14). Some think it should be taken as part of the causative form of the verb, in which case it would mean "I am the one who causes to be". Still others take it as implying rather "I am the one who is present"(and always able to control events). It remains, therefore, a living word of God rich in implications that no amount of reflection can exhaust. For the Israelites, Yahweh is the sacred name of the

God who set them free from slavery, entered into covenant with them as a free people, and led them through many hardships into the promised land.

In response to further hesitations expressed by Moses, Yahweh granted him power to perform signs to help convince the Israelites themselves concerning his otherwise incredible mission (Ex 4,1-9). Next Yahweh had to overcome Moses' objection that he was "slow and hesitant of speech", with the result that his brother Aaron was granted to him as an eloquent spokesman (vv. 10-17). Sufficiently reassured, Moses set off resolutely with Zipporah and their son Gershom to confront the Israelites and the new pharaoh. Moses was instructed to tell him: "This is what Yahweh says: Israel is my first-born son" (4,22). The death of Pharaoh's own first-born son is threatened as a punishment for his obstinacy in letting Israel go free. As M. Vellanickal notes, Israel's sonship is a kind of covenantal sonship, since covenant has a family aspect[4].

The mention of Israel being the first-born son also leaves room for other peoples to be welcomed into the family as additional children[5]. Which serves to remind us once more that the call of Israel is a call to service of the other nations as well. Its own liberation is intended as a model and also as a means for the liberation of all enslaved or oppressed people[6]. Yet another aspect is that when God does intervene to save an oppressed people, that very intervention puts the oppressor under judgment at the same time[7]. The enormity of Moses' task may be glimpsed through the strange incident of his encounter with Yahweh on the long trek back to Egypt (4,24-26). It is reminiscent of that feeling of dread or struggle before God experienced by Abraham (Gen 15) and Jacob (Gen 32) at crucial moments of their life and mission.

Aaron met Moses in the desert, and together they were able to convince and gladden the Israelites by means of their good news and signs from Yahweh. The reaction of Pharaoh was just the opposite when they conveyed to him Yahweh's demand, "Let my people go.."(5,1). He rejected any knowledge of Yahweh and would concede him no rights over any people within Egypt. After all, Pharaoh regarded himself as an important god in human form, being thought of as the son of Ra, the Sun-god. On principle he could not tolerate any foreign god talking about some of Egypt's slaves as "my people". They were all Pharaoh's people, and he immediately set about to make that quite plain to all concerned.

As is usual among oppressors and slave-masters, he thought the quickest way to snuff out any further thought of liberation would be to treat the petitioners more harshly than before. Those whose forced labour was making bricks, for example, were given quotas too high to be met, and their foremen were flogged for not seeing to it that quotas were met on time. Understandably the afflicted people told Moses that he had only given the king an excuse to kill them off. Moses for his part turned to ask Yahweh pointedly, "Why did you send me? Ever since I came to Pharaoh and spoke to him in your name, he has ill-treated this people, and you have done nothing at all about rescuing your people" (5,22-23).

C. MOSES CONFRONTS THE PHARAOH (EX 7-13)

This section opens with an assurance that Yahweh will overcome the hardness of Pharaoh's heart by working many signs and wonders: "Since Pharaoh will not listen to you, I shall lay my hand on Egypt and with great acts of judgement lead my armies, my people, the Israelites, out of Egypt. And the Egyptians will know that I am Yahweh.." (7,4-5). Not only will Yahweh set his chosen people free, but also use the occasion to show the Egyptians their helplessness when confronted with his power and justice. One of the most fundamental lessons which Pharaoh had to learn was that Yahweh did not accept him as a god, hence he did not respect his claim to keep the Israelites as his slaves. This is still a lesson of great importance for today, when this or that State acts as though it were a god, entitled to crush the rights of any person within the country, or even of those seeking refuge beyond it[8].

The way in which Yahweh began to show his power to the Egyptians was through striking signs and wonders, which are traditionally called the "ten plagues". They are mainly natural phenomena that are impressive because they come at the bidding of Moses and Aaron, and each is presented as a sign of God's right to have his people set free to go out and worship him in the wilderness. As J. Plastaras has observed, this refrain is common to all six plagues attributed to J tradition[9]. He also draws attention to the different emphasis in four plagues taken from P tradition, which stresses the word of God spoken and then taking effect(as we noted right from P's creation account in Gen 1)[10]. The plague of boils (Ex 9,8-12) provides a good example of this.

Another way of numbering and dividing up the plagues is given by D. McCarthy, who takes the changing of Moses' staff into a snake as the first of the ten "plagues" recounted from Ex 7,8 to 10,27. They make up five pairs carefully constructed in a "concentric scheme", in which the first corresponds exactly to the last, the second to the second last, and so on[11]. The most serious plague, that of the death of the first-born, remains outside this literary unit. It is announced in ch.11 and carried out in ch.12, where it is related to the Passover, then in ch. 13 it is related to the consecration of Israel's first-born to Yahweh. It is in ch.14 that he finds strong links with the "ten plagues" given before cc.11-13. Which leads him to suggest that there was originally a joyful liturgical celebration of the "Crossing of the Reed See", during which the stories of the earlier 10 plagues were also recounted[12]. That would leave cc.11-13 apart, having their cultic setting in the Passover celebration. His treatment of these texts brings out well the part played by religious celebrations in preserving, interpreting and rearranging the founding events of Israel.

All those earlier plagues proved insufficient to wring from Pharaoh the necessary permission to leave his country. Yahweh then assured Moses that the last plague in store for Egypt would really change Pharaoh's heart sufficiently to make him let the Israelites go at last. All the first-born in Egypt were to die. Before the final plague struck, the Israelites were told to celebrate the Passover. Part of that rite was to sprinkle some blood of the paschal lamb or goat on the door-posts and lintels of the houses, so that the Destroyer would "pass over" those houses, leaving their first-born alive. The paschal meal was to be observed always as a "memorial"(Ex 12,14) of the way Yahweh passed through "to execute justice on all the gods of Egypt"(Ex 12,12), and passed over the homes of his people Israel, then led them forth that very night from slavery to freedom beyond the reach of Pharaoh.

A memorial for the Israelites was a re-living, a re-presentation of the past saving event, whereby those celebrating it were also set free for wholehearted service of the same living Yahweh. A memorial also "reminded" God of his commitment to the people. When God "remembered Noah"(Gen 8,1), or when he heard "the groaning of the Israelites enslaved by the Egyptians" and said, "I have remembered my covenant"(Ex 6,5), he was moved to act effectively as their special covenant partner, to rescue them from a threat to their survival as his adopted family. The memorial, then, made the wonder of the exodus a source of new strength and confidence for each participant[13]. It obviously helped likewise to orient them anew in forging their future with Yahweh, now duly "reminded" of the present situation in relation to past struggles and rescues. The willingness of Jahweh to be reminded of Israel's troubles is implied by the striking comparison made: "The night when Yahweh kept vigil to bring them out of Egypt must be kept as a vigil in honour of Yahweh by all Israelites, for all generations" (Ex 12,42).

In cc. 12-13 we now find that two other religious practices have also been tied in with the exodus and the paschal meal, namely the feast of Unleavened Bread (12,15-20) and the consecration of all Israelite first-born to Yahweh(13,11-16). Such a combination is yet another indication of how constant celebrations tend to broaden the scope of an ancient feast and permit it to give greater significance to other early practices as well.

The death of the Egyptian first-born moved Pharaoh immediately to summon Moses and tell him, "Up, leave my subjects, you and the Israelites! Go and worship Yahweh as you have asked!" (12,31). As well as the Israelites, "a mixed crowd went with them, and flocks and herds.." (12,38). Presumably quite a few others who had been caught up in forced labour gangs decided to throw in their lot with the Israelites, to escape with them. The presence of herds would mean that the old semi-nomadic skills of the Hebrews had not disappeared altogether, for grazing spots were difficult to find in the wilderness. Even in this, Moses had been providentially prepared by many years as shepherd in the wilderness towards which he was now setting out with them all.

A ring of finality about their departure can be heard in the cryptic reference to Moses taking with him the bones of Joseph, in keeping with the oath he had exacted from his people. Joseph had been confident that one day God would "visit his people" to lead them out of Egypt, and he wanted his mummified body to be taken out, too (13,19). Moses may have talked to

Pharaoh about going out to worship Yahweh for a few days, but he had no intention of coming back again afterwards.

D. DEFINITIVE CROSSING FROM SLAVERY TO FREEDOM (EX 14 - 18)

1. Crossing of the Sea of Reeds (Ex 14)

This chapter is so rich in content and so carefully forged into a literary unit that it truly proclaims an irreversible crossing from slavery under Pharaoh to freedom under Yahweh. Its gripping narrative and symbolism serve to sum up for us the central issue in the prolonged confrontation between Yahweh and Pharaoh, as J-L. Ska amply demonstrates in "Le Passage de la Mer"[14]. While Moses is outstanding as the faithful servant, it is Yahweh himself whose "glory" is seen so clearly that even the humiliated Egyptians recognise it. Yahweh, symbolised by a pillar of cloud or fire, is right with the Israelites as they pass through the divided waters and emerge on the other shore as a new born nation, free at last. Looking back to the other shore they see it strewn with the lifeless bodies of their former slave-masters[15].

The escape from Egypt has been immortalized as a dramatic experience, one that Israel could never forget. They had reached the Reed Sea, guided by Yahweh, but meanwhile Pharaoh once again had changed his mind and regretted loosing the Israelites from his "service" (Ex 14,5). He still could not accept that his slaves should go free to serve some foreign god instead of himself and his kingdom, so he decided to go and recapture them. The unrelenting hardness of heart of the oppressor still remained as a big obstacle to Yahweh's plan for his people[16].

As soon as the Israelites saw the Egyptian chariots closing in on them from behind, while the sea barred their way forward, they were terrified. "They cried out to Yahweh for help"(v.10), but also turned on Moses for having brought them out to face this kind of death in the desert. They reminded him in no uncertain terms that they were against leaving Egypt in the first place, that they had wanted to remain "serving" the Egyptians rather than risk death in the desert. It must be noted that the Hebrew word '**abad** means to serve another, whether as slave or freeman. In the context it expresses the readiness of the Israelites to go along with Pharaoh and return to the assured, if tough, life as his slave-labourers. Such a crisis point must be faced in any process of escape from bondage. Years of bondage tend to break down human initiative and confidence in withstanding the final assaults or more subtle persuasion of erstwhile oppressors[17].

To counter their crumbling morale, Moses told them to remain calm and see how Yahweh was going to rescue them (literally: 'today you will see the salvation of Yahweh' - v.13). Facing alone the might of Pharaoh, Israel could easily have been dragged back into slavery. But they were not alone at the crucial showdown. Yahweh adverted to their cry, and ordered Moses, "Tell the Israelites to march on" (v.15). That simple command was the reply to their talk of going back to Egypt. Moses has only to raise his staff and stretch out his hand over the sea to divide its waters, revealing dry ground on which the Israelites were able to pass over to safety. The power of separating the waters to allow dry land to appear recalls the creation scene of Gen 1. The way the pillar of cloud moved to the rearguard of the Israelites was another symbol of the Creator separating his people definitively from their slave-masters. "Let my people go!" had been disobeyed for the last time![18].

Unwilling to let the Israelites slip out of the military trap, the charioteers gave chase and "went into the sea after them"(v.23). Then they were the ones trapped as their chariots bogged and they sensed the danger. At last they came to grasp the real situation, admitting defeat and exclaiming, "Let us flee from Israel, for Yahweh is fighting on their side against the Egyptians!" (v.25). They were still trying to flee back to firm sand when, at Moses' bidding, the sea closed over them and their horses. All were drowned, and "Israel saw the Egyptians lying dead on the sea-shore"(v.30). In its fear, Israel had talked of death in the desert, but now it could see that its pursuers were the ones whom death had struck down as if in the primeval waters of chaos.

The effect of that "mighty deed", which had won them definitive liberation from Pharaoh's clutches, was sufficient to change their wavering hearts. Now "the people revered Yahweh and put their faith in Yahweh and in Moses, his servant" (v.31). Very significantly, their newly enkindled faith lets them recognise in Moses what each of them is now free to be—a servant (**'ebed**) of Yahweh, instead of a slave of Pharaoh.

2. The joyful song of victory (Ex 15)

Ch. 15 retains something of the triumphant mood and exuberant faith of the Israelites as they sing of Yahweh's victory on their behalf. It bears the stamp of very early poetry, and most likely was embellished during centuries of cultic recital in reliving that epic crossing to freedom. The opening verse gives the refrain: "I shall sing to Yahweh, for he has covered himself in glory, horse and rider he has thrown into the sea"(v.1). In many ways it proclaims, "To him I owe my deliverance"(v.2). It rehearses the most dramatic moments of the epic. Of particular relevance for our theme is the covenant language used in v.13: "In your faithful love (**hesed**) you led out the people you had redeemed"(by acting as their **go'el**, their responsible relative). There are some who regard Ex 1-15 as adequate to serve as the O.T. model or paradigm for liberation[19]. They have here a good indication of the way Israel linked its liberation to Yahweh's covenant commitment, even before the liberated nation formalized its commitment to Yahweh at Mt. Sinai. With good reason Yahweh will remind them there, "You have seen for yourselves what I did to the Egyptians and how I carried you away on eagle's wings and brought you to me" (Ex 19,4). Like the sealing of the new covenant, that of the Sinai covenant marked the climax and not a sudden beginning of the covenant relationship.

Another pregnant phrase of the song occurs in v.18: "Yahweh will be king for ever." Yahweh's decisive victory over the king regarded as a god by the Egyptians, coupled with his saving presence in the midst of the Israelites now freed from Pharaoh, meant that Yahweh was undisputed Sovereign over them. For their part, they gladly accepted Yahweh as their King, indeed it was to remain always a basic conviction of Israel. This obviously will colour the basic attitude of Israel towards any expression of God's will for them, whether as specific covenant demands or not.

3. Providence of Yahweh in the wilderness (Ex 16-18)

As a literary device to recall something of the remainder of the journey to Mt Sinai, these chapters give examples of various hardships and threats to survival which they had to overcome. It illustrates how Yahweh accompanied them on that journey and saw to it that they did not perish nor return voluntarily to the "flesh pots" (16,3) of Egypt. When they cried out about the danger of starving to death in the desert, they were given the manna(16,1-36). Because they longed for some meat as well, they were supplied with quail(v.13). Similarly, when thirst threatened to kill off their surviving livestock and themselves, they were close to stoning Moses, who then managed to draw water by striking a rock. That overcame a serious crisis, when the people were losing faith and demanding, "Is Yahweh with us, or not?"(17,1-7).

In a battle against the Amalekites, the intercession of Moses was crowned by a victory of Joshua's men (17,8-16). Finally, when Moses met Jethro and was reunited with his wife and two sons, he accepted the advice of Jethro to appoint judges. The idea was to lighten Moses' heavy burden as the only judge, and to ensure a more rapid "justice for the people"(18,1-26). In Egypt the goddess Ma'at was regarded as maintaining truth and justice through the pharaoh[20]. Now Israel looked to their judges as upholders of Yahweh's sovereign justice.

E. THE COVENANT SEALED AT SINAI (EX 19 - 24)

We are told that the Israelites reached Sinai three months after leaving Egypt. Presumably Moses' intention in returning to the holy spot whence he had been sent was to "worship Yahweh", in keeping with his repeated requests to Pharaoh. Like Jacob in returning to Bethel to worship there again after his successful encounters with Laban and Esau, Moses returned to Mt Sinai. He wanted to worship Yahweh, to give praise for the wonderful way in which his mission had been accomplished against all odds. But unlike Jacob, Moses was now the leader of a nation in the making. The time had come to make explicit and celebrate publicly what had gradually been accomplished for Israel through his mission. Yahweh had liberated the Israelites from forced slavery to Egypt so that as a free people they might serve the one God who really is. In so doing, they would also ensure that they could remain free and not begin to enslave one another or any stranger coming to live among them.

The main descriptions of how the covenant was arranged and sealed are found in cc. 19 and 24, with a list of the Ten Commandments in ch. 20 not fully tied in to the narrative. Then in ch. 32 comes a serious breaking of the covenant through the making of a golden calf, so cc. 33-34 tell of how Moses was able to persuade Yahweh to renew the covenant with a repentant people.

The material in those chapters seems to have been drawn mainly from the J and E traditions, which have been so combined as to make it difficult now to pinpoint where each starts or finishes. It has been found that E tradition is more to the fore in cc. 19, 20 and 24, whereas J stands out in the renewal of cc. 33-34. Perhaps the redactor who combined the precious traditions chose the present form as a way of preserving two different accounts of the same Sinai covenant[21]. As it now stands, however, it presents a striking resumé of Israel's core experience over the centuries, namely covenant commitment, violation of covenant, and covenant renewal. The glory of the free Israelites was to make a covenant with their Liberator; their abuse of freedom was to break that covenant. We shall consider separately the sealing at Sinai, then the renewal.

The initiative to enter into a covenant came from God, with "Moses his servant" as the faithful mediator. After reminding the Israelites how he had carried them away from Egypt "on eagle's wings" and brought them to himself(Ex 19,4), God invites them into covenant: "So now, if you are really prepared to obey me and keep my covenant, you, out of all peoples, shall be my personal possession, for the whole world is mine. For me you shall be a kingdom of priests, a holy nation"(vv.5-6). Here God calls for global obedience, and for unreserved keeping of his covenant. What is offered on God's side is to accept Israel as his very own possession, parallel to the way a king may have a country estate which is special in comparison to the rest of his realm. The mention of Israel as "a kingdom of priests, a holy nation" is a corollary of their song that "Yahweh will be king for ever"(Ex 15,18). A king implies a kingdom, a nation over which he reigns and which he can represent in his own person. The puzzling combination, "a kingdom of priests", must explain the distinctive character of this kingdom in relation to its worship of God. Where the king of the nation is also its God, a religious response is of prime importance from all the kingdom. The text may well mean that all the people will be so united to God through the covenant that each one will be called on to share in the worship of God through praise, sacrifice, and all daily life directed towards him.

The other phrase, "a holy nation", confirms that the priority expected of the covenanted people will be related to a sharing in God's own holiness. Humans become holy only by personal and community association with the all-holy God. In short, Israel was being invited to accept and confirm outwardly a unique relationship with God whereby it would, as a community and a kingdom, always worship God in holiness and justice. Israel could not obey God nor keep his covenant without being both holy and just itself.

Although God could have imposed some kind of an oath of fidelity to himself as king over the redeemed Israelites, the Sinai covenant differs in many ways from the ancient suzerainty treaties. We find that Moses was sent expressly to discuss with the people the offer of a covenant. Then "the people all replied with one accord, 'Whatever Yahweh has said, we will do'" (Ex 19,7-8)[22]. Reverting to the eagle imagery, the fledgelings have gained sufficient size and confidence to attempt free flight. From here on they have the capacity to soar to new heights in Yahweh's company, or to fly far away from their true "nest" if they so choose.

Only after the people had freely agreed did God proceed to the next stage, that of an awesome theophany. It was to indicate his special presence and personal communication to those chosen people. At the same time, it served to impress on its witnesses an awareness of God's transcendence, of his mysterious separation from his own world. The manifestation of God through mighty storm and frightening volcano is told in a way that suggests frequent repetition in a cultic celebration with plenty of trumpet blasts, smoke and incense, blazing torches, etc. M. Newman has followed this lead far enough to deduce that different celebrations and theological emphases among the southern and northern tribes of Israel shaped the J and E traditions respectively[23].

The account of the actual rite for sealing the covenant at Sinai is given quite briefly in ch. 24. As already mentioned, the predominant tradition incorporated here is from E, in vv.3-8. In those few verses are to be found both the essential content and the solemn rite of the covenant destined to guide Israel for many centuries. The content or clauses of the covenant are stated simply as "all Yahweh's words and all the laws" (24,3). As when the covenant was first offered, so now the people all agreed to the general terms, declaring, "All the words Yahweh has spoken we will carry out. Moses put all Yahweh's words into writing"(vv.3-4). He also built an altar and set around it twelve stones to represent the twelve tribes. Bullocks were sacrificed and offered as communion sacrifices, which would indicate that part of them would be eaten afterwards by the participants. It was a fitting sacrifice for the occasion, as the aim of the covenant was to consolidate the communion between both parties, as well as between the Israelites themselves.

Half the blood of the sacrificed bullocks was taken to sprinkle the altar, representing God; the other half was to be sprinkled over the people. Moses took "the Book of the Covenant" and read it out to all the people, who for the third time expressed their voluntary commitment to this covenant: "We shall do everything that Yahweh has said; we shall obey"(v.7). Only then did Moses sprinkle the remaining sacrificial blood over the people, declaring, "This is the blood of the covenant which Yahweh has made with you, entailing all these stipulations" (v.8). The sprinkling of the blood on both altar and people was a symbolic rite manifesting that the life given back to God in sacrifice had then been imparted to the people open to accept it. Blood as the seat of life was strictly reserved to God, so to experience such a sprinkling of sacred blood conveyed to them in tangible form that they really had been consecrated as a "holy nation". Even more than the altar, they now were set apart for the worship of God and the mediation of his blessing to others. That altar surrounded by twelve big stones would remain as a silent witness to the covenant at the foot of Mt Sinai; Israel was called to be henceforth a living and articulate witness to this covenant, not only in the wilderness but also in Canaan, a busy crossroads where many ancient civilizations and empires clashed.

The E tradition makes it abundantly clear that Israel had committed itself irrevocably to obey all the words of the covenant, as made known through Moses and even written down in the Book of the Covenant. The writing of "the law and the commandment" on "stone tablets" is even attributed to God (v.12; cf. 31,18). It does not, however, give details as to what those words or covenant stipulations were at that time. The Ten Commandments now neatly listed in ch.20 are certainly in the general vein of E tradition, but they also seem somewhat apart from the actual narrative about Sinai (or Horeb, as some traditions call the holy mountain). Similarly the detailed laws now found together in cc. 21-23, often referred to for convenience as "the book or code of the covenant", seem to have reached that form after the occupation of the promised land.

We will look more closely at the valuable material in cc. 20-23 later on, after dealing with the renewal of the covenant at Sinai. They have been touched on here to clarify the general character of Yahweh's original demands. Because those demands are left so general, some commentators have gone to the extent of rejecting or minimizing the Sinai experience as a covenant in any form[24]. Such views seem to us understandable but not the best explanation of the earliest traditions concerning those events. We find more convincing the interpretation of those who hold for a historical covenant rite at Sinai, while accepting that it was not drawn up in the form of an ancient international treaty. In a nutshell, it was a genuine covenant but not in that sort of treaty form[25]. We insist on this point, partly because it confirms that liberation from Egypt was for a covenant with the Liberator, and partly for the light it throws on later developments in covenant thinking among Israel's kings, prophets and inspired writers.

Before leaving ch.24, it is worth noting that another rite for sealing the covenant is that of the sacred meal eaten by Moses, Aaron and another "seventy elders", who "actually gazed on God" on the holy mountain and yet lived through that mystic encounter. That tradition is more likely from J than E, so we bear it in mind as we take up the predominantly J tradition in what follows.

F. VIOLATION AND RENEWAL OF THE COVENANT AT SINAI (EX 32-34)

Ch. 32 presupposes a sizable group among the Israelites who could not tolerate the austere limits placed by Moses on fashioning images to represent

God. While Moses was absent for a long time on the mountain, they were able to persuade the people and even Aaron to make a golden bull-calf from the jewellery they had brought out of Egypt. This was not meant to replace Yahweh, but rather to serve as a kind of footstool to denote his presence and power to grant fertility to the people and their flocks. Moses was sent back quickly by Yahweh, who talked of wiping out all those obstinate people and replacing them by a great nation from Moses. Through the intercession of Moses, who reminded God of his solemn promise under oath to Abraham, Isaac and Jacob, the extreme punishment was averted. On reaching the people who were still celebrating" a feast to Yahweh" around the golden calf, Moses threw down and broke the stone tablets containing the words of the covenant, making it plain that the covenant itself was broken. The confrontation between Moses and the rebels was so sharp that Moses called on the loyal Levites to put them to the sword. We are told that "about three thousand men perished that day"(v.28). That gives some indication of the seriousness of the move to oust the ageing Moses as leader once liberation had been achieved[26].

Moses continued to plead with Yahweh to spare and pardon his people, to accompany them still on their journey to the promised land(ch.33). Yahweh was moved to invite Moses to bring two more stone tablets with him to the mountain top, and there"Yahweh descended in a cloud and stood with him.."(34,1-5). Yahweh made known to Moses the divine qualities: "Yahweh, God of tenderness and compassion, slow to anger, rich in faithful love and constancy , maintaining his faithful love to thousands, forgiving fault, crime and sin..(vv.6-7). Twice the word **hesed** occurs here, and in the first case it is part of the very common pair, 'love and fidelity', which really sum up what covenant is about. A covenant is established because of Yahweh's gratuitous love, then maintained thanks to his 'truth', fidelity, constancy.

In that atmosphere Yahweh declared to Moses, "Look, I am now making a covenant: I shall work such wonders at the head of your whole people as have never been worked in any other country or nation, and all the people round you will see what Yahweh can do..(v.10). A covenant is shown here to be much more than setting free a people from political and economic slavery. That was certainly the first enormous step with regard to Israel, but because of Yahweh's concern to put an end to slavery and oppression among all peoples, he pledges to remain at the head of this recently liberated people, Israel. Yahweh does not promise that Israel will be enabled to go back and enslave the Egyptians. On the contrary, he promises that "all the people around you will see what Yahweh can do"(v.10), namely he can lead even the most enslaved of peoples to their rightful freedom and dignity. As Creator and Redeemer of Israel he drew them into a positive relationship with himself and with one another, to perpetuate and radiate their hard-won freedom. The compassion with which they had been rescued from slavery to Pharaoh was still operative to rescue them from the consequences of their sin and rejection of "Moses, his servant".

This time the commands given are interwoven with the rest of the narrative, being mainly concerned with cultic requirements. They insist strongly on worshipping no other god besides Yahweh, on casting no metal gods, on avoiding pacts with the idolatrous occupants of Canaan, who would lead them into religious prostitution. The sabbath rest is again strongly emphasised, and the annual observance of big feasts such as the Passover and Pentecost is required. After giving these commands, "Yahweh then said to Moses, 'Put these words in writing, for they are the terms of the covenant which I have made with you and with Israel'" (v.27). This section about Moses on the mountain for forty days closes by saying that, obeying Yahweh's orders, Moses "wrote the words of the covenant — the Ten Words" (v.28).

It is likely that the phrase, "the Ten Words", is a later addition, and several of the cultic laws include material from later settled life in Canaan, e.g. that the sabbath rest must be observed "even during ploughing and harvesting"(v.21). On the other hand, there is good reason to accept as ancient the more fundamental commandments concerning the exclusive worship of Yahweh, "a jealous God", together with the prohibition of making images. These are very close to the beginning of the Decalogue given in Ex 20, and could well be the substance of what was demanded right from the Sinai experience[27].

The conclusion of ch.34 tells how Moses simply passed on to the people "all the orders that Yahweh had given to him on Mount Sinai" (v.32). His closeness to God was symbolized by a face so radiant that he had to cover it with a veil as soon as he finished speaking to them(vv.33-35). Nothing is said here of a rite to seal the covenant, but we must look for that back in ch.24, where a few lines from the J tradition tell of Moses and the elders eating a sacred meal on the mountain top (vv.1-2 and 9-11). That would have been the original climax to J's account of the Sinai covenant, for a meal could seal a covenant[28].

G. RELATION OF THE DECALOGUE TO THE COVENANT (EX 20)

Before leaving J and E traditions, we must reflect a few moments on the Decalogue, about which many worthwhile books have been written [31]. Here we can only indicate very briefly how central it is to the whole book of Exodus. The Decalogue is placed in the centre of the book (20,1-21), and serves there as an inspired synthesis of what Yahweh has done for the Israelites and what is expected of them as the "special possession" of Yahweh. Its location between the call to covenant (ch.19) and the sealing of the covenant(ch.24) gives it the status of a covenant document, one that enshrines the quintessence of the unique relationship established between Yahweh and Israel. We are not saying that these Ten Commandments are word for word with what was written on the two stone tablets on Mt Sinai, but rather that they capture accurately, under divine inspiration, Israel's own understanding of the encounter as it was lived out and celebrated over the centuries[32]. The way the Decalogue is found in fairly much the same form in Deut 5 as here in an otherwise very different book would suggest that both books are really drawing on an independent source.

The personal "I - Thou" relationship that has been established by the liberation of Israel from slavery shines through from the opening words: "I am Yahweh your God who has brought you out of Egypt, where you lived as slaves. You shall have no other gods to rival me" (vv.2-3). (The Hebrew uses the singular, "thou - thee" right through the Decalogue). The basis of all the Commandments that follow is fixed forever in that historical intervention of Yahweh to lift a people out of slavery. It also reveals the prevalent spirit in which such a kind and faithful God wishes to communicate something of those qualities to the liberated nation. The Decalogue is rightly hailed as the foundation of justice in Israel — justice towards their Redeemer and justice towards one another[33]. God's role as Creator of heaven, earth and sea is also recalled by vv. 4 and 11, underscoring his right to be listened to attentively by Israel. Like creation and redemption from slavery, so also making known his will to Israel is a great gift. A caring God makes clear the limits which it would be rebellious to cross.

A glimpse of the love expected in serving this "jealous God" is found after the prohibition of bowing down to idols: "I act with faithful love (**hesed**) towards thousands of those who love me and keep my commandments" (v.6). This should colour all discussion of law as compared to gospel, since Yahweh expects love to be the real motive for loyalty, a loyalty not so much to "law" as to the self-revealing God and his ennobling "instruction". Seen in this light, the Commandments are not cold "covenant clauses" to be kept in order to win favour instead of punishment before Yahweh. They are guidelines for preserving and strengthening the family spirit, the friendship, so generously made possible through the exodus and the solemn covenant[34].

The first commandments call for exclusive worship of Yahweh, a complete avoidance of idols, and a profound respect for the name of God. The next two commandments serve as a transition from duties towards Yahweh to duties towards one another. The seventh day each week is to be kept holy "as a Sabbath for Yahweh your God"(v.10). In that way it is directly related to Yahweh, as calling upon parents to imitate the way God rested after six days of creation. But this also means that the parents must grant, with a touch of divine generosity, a day of rest to their children, their servants, and the aliens of their household. In Dt 5,12-15 the sabbath rest is linked explicitly with the liberation of Israel itself from slavery in Egypt. Now Israel must show the world that every sabbath is a celebration of freedom from slavery, as well as an invitation to enter with joy into the Creator's mysterious "rest".

The other transitional commandment concerns the children of the household. They are told to honour their parents, "so that you might live long in the land that Yahweh your God is giving you" (v.12). P. Bovati perceives here a close link between the parents and Yahweh, in whose mission they participate, and also between the parents and the promised land, for they are the bearers of the promise from one generation to the next[35].

The remaining five (or, in Catholic listing, six) commandments give short,pithy prohibitions against killing, adultery, stealing, false witness, and coveting the neigbour's wife or goods (vv.12-17). This selection reflects a keen sense of morality flowing from an historic encounter with Yahweh. From a wealth of ancient laws, Israel has singled out these ten as most important according to the criterion of its new relationship with Yahweh. To them Yahweh had initially been made known as the God of the patriarchs, then experienced in depth as the God of the exodus and of the Sinai theophany. Those historical events founded Israel as a new, independent and "holy nation", having as its refined "constitution" the Ten Commandments.

H. THE SINAI COVENANT IN THE PRIESTLY TRADITION (EX 25-31. 35-40)

Perhaps the most striking aspect of P tradition is its lavish use of the word "covenant" with regard to both Noah and Abraham (Gen 6-9 and 17). In the same spirit it refers back to the "covenant" with Abraham of which God is mindful when he hears the groaning of the Israelites in their slavery (Ex 2,23-25). Twice more the Abrahamic "covenant" is recalled when telling of Moses' call (Ex 6,4-5). Moses is sent by Yahweh to tell the people, "I shall take you as my people and I shall be your God" (v.7). That phrase occurs frequently in the Bible as a summary of the covenant relationship[29], but P seems to avoid deliberately the actual term "covenant" for describing what happened at Sinai.

It does, however, tell with much detail of the making of the ark of the Testimony, so called because in the ark was placed the Testimony (Ex 40,20). The Testimony (**'edut**) means here the words (on stone tablets) of the covenant, so that the placing of this ark of the Testimony in the Dwelling, within the Meeting Tent, would be a constant reminder of the covenant. The ark is referred to in other biblical texts as the ark of the covenant (e.g. Joshua 3-6). In recalling how God ordered the sabbath rest, it presents the sabbath rest itself as though that were "an eternal covenant" (31,17), to be a sign between Yahweh and Israel for ever. We would expect the sabbath to be called a sign of the Mosaic covenant, which included the commandment of sabbath rest. One explanation of such reticence about a Mosaic "covenant" is that the P tradition took final shape after the destruction of Jerusalem and the Exile, by which time the hope of Israel was springing from promissory covenants rather than the conditional Mosaic covenant, with its sanctions of blessings or curses[30]. The ark of the Testimony had also been lost, after the words of Yahweh to which it witnessed had been badly neglected. The "glory of Yahweh" which filled the Dwelling when the ark was first placed in it (Ex 40,34-35), was to be seen leaving Jerusalem by Ezekiel before the city was captured and burnt (Ezek 10,18-22).

I. COVENANT IDEALS UPHELD BY SABBATICAL AND JUBILEE YEARS (LEV 25)

A law about setting Hebrew slaves free after six years, and another law about making every seventh year a whole year of rest, for the land and its workers, are also found in the so-called "Book of the Covenant" (Ex 23,10-11). It is only in Lev 25, however, that the law concerning a sabbath of sabbath years, i.e. a jubilee after seven times seven years, is recorded and explained. This law comes after a restatement of the one about keeping the sabbath year of the land, which is thereby given an amazing new dimension[36]. Such a jubilee year is to be a year of remission during which debts must be forgiven, ancestral lands must be returned to their dispossessed owners, and any Hebrew slaves must be set free without ransom (vv.8-55).

Lev 25 must be seen within the framework of the "Holiness Code", which extends from cc.17 to 26. Its overriding concern is expressed in 19,2: "Speak to the whole community of Israelites and say: 'Be holy, for I, Yahweh your God, am holy'". As well as recalling the commandments to love parents and to observe the sabbath(v.3), it gives two other fundamental principles governing social relations in Israel: "You will not exploit or rob your fellow"(v.13); and "You will love your neighbour as yourself" (v.18)[37]. Jesus found in the latter commandment the complement to that of loving God wholeheartedly (cf.Mt 22,34-43). We shall also see the importance he gave to the jubilee year of Lev 25, an aspect very ably expounded by S. Ringe in "Jesus, Liberation and the Biblical Jubilee"[38].

There is every reason for taking the jubilee legislation within the Code of Holiness as a direct practical application of Yahweh's demands that Israelites be holy and love their neighbour. This is borne out by such phrases about the jubilee as: "The jubilee will be <u>a holy thing</u> for you (25,12); and "So you <u>will not exploit one another</u>" (25,17). It was obviously meant to repair the grave social evils caused by loss of farmlands, homes and personal freedom, whether through natural disasters or greedy exploitation by the rich and powerful. Yahweh insists that the land is his gift to the Israelites, but a gift that must be used always in keeping with the Donor's intention: "Land will not be sold absolutely, for the land belongs to me, and you are only strangers and guests of mine. You will allow a right of redemption over all ancestral property" (vv.23-24). In the case of a person unable to redeem his ancestral property, it must be returned to him gratis in the jubilee year (v.28)[39].

There follows quite detailed legislation about the setting free of Israelites held as virtual slaves (vv.35-55). They would be mainly the families whose small farms had failed to keep them solvent. As a result they were forced to give over their farm as a "live-gage", to use R. North's terminology, rather than a mort-gage[40]. In the first place, an Israelite is not to be treated as a slave, but like a hired worker or guest, until the jubilee year, unless some relative ransoms him beforehand. Yahweh again insists on his special claim on these impoverished people: "For they are my servants whom I have brought out of

Egypt, and they may not be bought and sold as slaves. You will not oppress your brother-Israelites harshly but will fear your God"(vv.42-43). The liberation of any virtually enslaved Israelite is shown to be fully consistent with the status of all Israel as a nation set free from slavery gratuitously by Yahweh. They all then freely pledged themselves to be his servants. So Yahweh forbids the Israelites to "go back to Egypt" in the basic matter of slavery.

It is difficult to put a date on the Code of Holiness as it now stands. It has some ancient material which would fit in well with conditions at the time of the first Occupation of the promised land, when wise leaders saw the danger of rapid loss of tribal land and personal freedom. There are also indications, though, that the Code has been redacted to make it more relevant to conditions at the time of the re-occupation of the land after the Babylonian exile[41]. As practically all of Leviticus is attributed to the Priestly tradition, it is feasible to posit that this Code, including its jubilee laws, was given its present shape during or shortly after the exile[42].

In answer to the question still being raised in our day as to whether the jubilee was ever observed in Israel, R. North thinks it fair to say both Yes! and No![43]. He points out that the jubilee is not said to be recurrent. In its original form it could have been aimed at an immediate social reform to counter an alarming deterioration with regard to family lands and families being forced to sell themselves into slavery to other Israelites. The principles at stake, however, were permanent, being vital for Israel's continuance as a genuine covenanted community. The reduction of the people of the land to such dehumanizing poverty and slavery by their fellow-Israelites was a denial of community kinship and justice.

We do find echoes of the jubilee spirit in the story of Ruth, whom Boaz married as the kinsman **go'el** willing to preserve the family and property of Ruth's deceased husband(Ruth 2-4). Then in the outspoken prophets of social justice like Amos and Micah, as we shall see in more detail, the accumulation of properties and the enslavement of Israelites is denounced as an evil leading to the destruction of the nation[44]. Even after the chastening experience of the exile, Nehemiah had to intervene very strongly to order the richer Jews around Jerusalem to stop the process of enslaving anew their fellow-Jews, who had complained explicitly to Nehemiah, "we shall have to sell our sons and daughters into slavery" (Neh 5,5). The way Nehemiah was able to get the offenders to return the fields, orchards and houses, as well as to cancel the debts (Neh 5,11-13) presupposed the spirit of the jubilee. Through the imagery of the jubilee used in Trito-Isaiah(58 and 61), its profound implications were able to emerge in the programmatic discourse of Jesus in Nazareth (Lk 4,16-22).

The Holiness Code concludes with a long list of blessings and curses as sanctions for the covenant demands. The final blessing promised for fidelity once more harks back to Yahweh's historical intervention to end his people's slavery: "I shall live among you; I shall be your God and you will be my people, I, Yahweh your God, who brought you out of Egypt so that you should be their slaves no longer, and who broke the bonds of your yoke and made you walk with head held high" (Lev 26,12-13). Among the threatened curses it mentions forcefully the way the land will be given a prolonged sabbath rest due to enemy occupation: "As it lies deserted it will rest, as it never did on your Sabbaths when you were living there"(26,35; cf.v.43).

Despite all infidelities on Israel's part, God promises to remember his covenant with Abraham, Isaac and Jacob (v.42). Also, "For their sake I shall remember the covenant I made with those first generations that I brought out of Egypt while other nations watched, so that I could be their God, I, Yahweh"(v.45). Here, the word b^{e}rit is used, as in the earlier verse where Yahweh calls it plainly "my covenant" (v.15). This at least is a further indication that P tradition did regard it as a full covenant. It also realized the shattering consequences that befell Israel for neglecting its part of that covenant. If we are proposing the exodus as our paradigm for liberation, this is a further reminder that any liberated nation can throw away its freedom by not heeding the goal of an exodus achieved in God's name: "so that I could be their God.." (v.45). Total and integral liberation, sustained by Yahweh as covenant partner for ever, is the true goal of the first exodus[44].

NOTES

1. Cf. A. Erman and H. Ranke, La Civilisation Égyptienne (F.T. by C. Mathien; Paris: Payot, 1985 — Photocopy of 1963 ed.), e.g. ll: "A un autre égard encore, l'Égypte est pour nous pleine d'enseignements. Dans aucun autre pays, la tradition historique ne présente aussi peu de lacunes. ... Pouvoir suivre un peuple, le même peuple, durant plus de cinq millénaires, ... c'est une chose que l'histoire ne nous permet d'observer que dans ce seul cas." Cf. J.A. Wilson, The Culture of Ancient Egypt (Chicago: Chicago University Press, p-b. 1963).
2. J. Plastaras, The God of Exodus — The Theology of the Exodus Narratives (Milwaukee: Bruce, 1966), esp. 74-82 on the pattern of a reluctant envoy of God.
3. Given the bearing which this aspect of being set free to serve Yahweh has on our entire understanding of the exodus, the following listing may help dispel any doubts: Ex 3,12.18; 4,23.31; 5,1.3.8.17; 7,26; 8,16.21.22.23.25; 9,1.13; 10,3.7.9.11.24.25; 12,31 being the capitulation of Pharaoh: "Go and worship Yahweh as you have asked!"
4. Cf. M. Vellanickal, The Divine Sonship of Christians in the Johannine Writings (Rome: Pontifical Biblical Institute, 1970), 13: "So Yahweh liberated Israel in order to establish this Covenantal relationship and thus Israel's sonship becomes a Covenantal sonship."
5. J. Plastaras, op.cit. 111.
6. W. Vogels, God's Universal Covenant, 49: "Israel was taken from among the nations to be at the service of the nations. Election and covenant are thus not an end in themselves, but a means towards something else."
7. J. Plastaras, op.cit. 180: "Yahweh was not simply a bloodthirsty war god. Whenever he had to do battle, it had been as the just Judge coming to the

aid of the helpless and oppressed." Cf. P. Hodgson, New Birth of Freedom, 24-25, where he quotes Abraham Lincoln's words connecting "the scourge of war" and the previous injustice done to the slaves: "Yet, if God wills that it continue, until all the wealth piled up by the bond-man's 250 years of unrequited toil should be sunk, and until every drop of blood drawn with the lash, shall be paid with another drawn with the sword, as was said 3000 years ago, so still it must be said, 'The judgments of the Lord are true and righteous altogether'"
8. Cf. J.L. Sicre, Los Dioses Olvidados — Poder y Riqueza en los Profetas Preexílicos (Madrid: Ediciones de Cristiandad, 1979) 23-25, where he points out that to divinize the ruler is not so far-reaching and dangerous for today as to divinize the State itself.
9. J. Plastaras, op.cit. 126.
10. Ibid. 127-128.
11. D.J. McCarthy, Institution and Narrative, 115-126.
12. Ibid. 135-158; e.g. 158: :"From this point of view the connection between the story of the plagues and that of the Sea of Reeds miracle is significant since the Sea of Reeds probably gives us a cultic locus. The tradition about events at the Sea of Reeds was certainly originally distinct from that of the Passover, and these events were celebrated in the cult, as is shown, among other things, by the existence of a liturgical poem about it in Exod 15,1-18. Why could the **legenda** for this liturgy not have been the nucleus around which the elaborate story of Moses' dealings with the Pharaoh, the story of the plagues, grew?".
13. Cf. J. Jocz, The Covenant, 194: "This paradox of Passover [salvation entails suffering] symbolizes not only Israel's condition but the condition of humanity at large: man is born to freedom but never quite reaches the promised land." Again, 195: "The cup of joy is tempered by the bread of affliction .. and the bitter herbs."
14. J. L. Ska, Le Passage de la Mer (Rome: Biblical Institute Press, 1986, esp. 53-60 and 97-106 on the confrontation with Pharaoh and his judgment at the Sea of Reeds. Ska prefers to speak of judgment rather than invoke the "holy war" theme.
15. Ibid. 174: "En guise de résumé, on pourrait proposer la définition suivante du miracle de la mer comme 'naissance' d'Israël: immergé dans les eaux des origines, plongé dans la nuit cosmique, Israël est séparé par le feu de son passé d'esclave en Egypte et conduit par ce même feu vers la lumière de sa vie nouvelle et libre; cette vie lui est offerte parce qu'il a vaincu la peur pour se risquer dans l'inconnu de l'au-delà; elle est inaccessible à l'Egypte qui ne cherche qu'à perpétuer son passé."
16. Cf. R. Burns, "The Book of Exodus", in Concilium 189 (Feb. 1987), pp.11-21, esp. 16
17. Cf. P. Lapide, "Exodus in Jewish Tradition", in same issue of Concilium, pp.47-55, esp. 53-55 on the lessons offered for contemporary liberators and teachers. The third lesson he mentions is that "the bread of freedom was hard and dry", making the flesh-pots of Egypt enticing again. It

needed a generation of children born free in the desert to go ahead effectively with the "entry into freedom".
18. Cf. J.L. Ska, op.cit. 82-96.
19. Cf. J. Severino Croatto, "The Socio-historical and Hermeneutical Relevance of the Exodus", in the same issue of Concilium, pp.125-133, e.g. 126 where he mentions Ex 1-15 as the normative text, the "kerygma of liberation", to be taken with the "exodus theme" as it appears throughout the Bible. Cf. also E. Dussel, "Exodus as a Paradigm in Liberation Theology", same Concilium, pp.83-92, where he rightly says that in Latin America "liberation theology from its very beginning understood the paradigm of the Exodus as its fundamental scheme"(83). He also gives a diagrammatic schema to show the kind of paradigm provided by Exodus. It is noteworthy that "covenant" does not appear in it, but he does mention "the kingdom" and "community of life", relating them expressly to the Land.
20. Cf. L. Epsztein, Social Justice in the Ancient Near East and the People of the Bible (E.T. by John Bowden; London: SCM 1983), esp. 17-42 on the role of Ma'at in ancient Egypt, e.g. 18: "Maat, the personification of values like order, justice and truth .. played a central role. She was intimately connected with two chief gods (Re, the sungod, and Osiris, the god of the dead) and thus had close relationship with the king, who was the representative of divine order on earth." Cf. also P. Bovati, Ristabilire la Giustizia, 17, where he asserts that the Bible, in speaking of the relations between God and people, assigns a privileged place to juridical language. His whole work indicates how this reflects God's constant concern that justice prevail and be acknowledged as such, even by those who have been brought to judgment.
21. Cf. J. Plastaras, op.cit 218-220. Cf. New Jerusalem Bible footnotes for likely division between traditions in these texts.
22. Cf. P. Hodgson, op.cit. 228, where he reflects on some aspects of the symbol, 'kingdom of God': "It is also a realm of freedom — a liberated communion of free subjects, founded on the power of God's grace. God's kingdom is a kingdom of freedom, a 'place' where freedom prevails as the defining relationship among human beings instead of the bondage and alienation that ordinarily characterize human affairs."
23. Cf. M. Newman, The People of the Covenant (New York: Abingdon Press, 1962) esp. 51-54, e.g. 54: "The covenant event was re-enacted in the cult, and the cult legend both described and perpetuated the cult ceremony." (On the previous page he had made it clear that the cult legends "reflect an actual event".) Cf. J. Plastaras, op.cit. 248-252.
24. Cf. J. Miranda, Marx and the Bible, 140: "The entire conception of the O.T. which the theology professors, the spiritual writers and the New Testament exegetes have fashioned for themselves and now profess has to be radically modified if it can be demonstrated that the idea of covenant is from the seventh century." He gives too much weight to the fact that the international treaty form cannot be found in the earlier biblical traditions

about covenant. Cf. R.E. Clements, "Covenant and Canon in the Old Testament", in R.McKinney (Ed.), Creation Christ and Culture — Studies in honour of F.F. Torrance (Edinburgh: T & T Clark, 1976), 1-12, e.g. 3: "it (b^{e}rit) was not used in the earliest sources to describe the Sinai event, except in a relatively minor way(Exod. 34:10)." ... "It is the Deuteronomic literature of the seventh and sixth centuries B.C. which has given the term a new meaning and currency as the key concept by which the relationship between God and Israel is to be understood."

25. Cf. J. Bright, Covenant and Promise — The Future in the Preaching of Pre-exilic Prophets (London: SCM, 1977) 24: "It (Israel's eschatological hope) must be sought in Israel's understanding of her God and his activity in history, and specifically in her belief that God had chosen her to be his people, delivered her from bondage, entered into a covenant with her, and extended to her his promises." Cf. D. McCarthy, Old Testament Covenant, 29; 54; 71; and 57: "The Sinai texts do not show the covenant form, and the origins of apodictic law and so of the Decalogue are to be sought elsewhere than in the treaties." Cf. id., Institution and Narrative, 42-53.

26. Cf. M. Walzer, Exodus and Revolution (New York: Basic Books, 1985) 55-61.

27. Cf. R. de Vaux, Histoire Ancienne d'Israël: Dès Origines à l'Installation en Canaan (= Vol. 1), esp. 369-440.

28. Cf. D. McCarthy, O.T. Covenant, 30: "In any event, the covenant between Yahweh and Israel described in the Sinai narrative was a covenant based upon some sort of blood and sacrificial rite or, in another version (Exod 24:11), a covenant meal uniting Yahweh and the people, through which a quasi-familial relation was set up between the two."

29. Cf. D. McCarthy, G. Mendenhall, R. Smend, Per una Teologia del Patto nell'Antico Testamento (It. tr. by M. Bracchi & others; Torino: Marietti, 1972), esp. the contribution of R.Smend, "La Formula di Alleanza", 123-153, in which he argues that the "pair" ("my people/your God") did not exist until the State of Israel came into existence, although the relation so described had its beginnings with the exodus(see e.g. 143).

30. Cf. J. Plastaras, op.cit. 265-275. Cf. M. Newman, op.cit. 91, where he refers to the Ark as a kind of "portable Sinai".

31. Cf. E. Nielsen, The Ten Commandments in New Perspective (London: SCM, 1968), esp. 132ff. on the historical problem of the Decalogue. He posits that, while the first four commandments could go back to Moses, the remainder would be from the time of the monarchy, when a "basic law" was hammered out for judges.

32. Cf. P. Bovati, Giustizia e Ingiustizia nell'Antico Testamento, Mimeographed Class Notes (Roma: Biblical Institute, 1986/87) 2-33, where he discusses in detail the wording and significance of the Decalogue, including the message it conveys as a literary unit.

33. Cf. L. Epsztein, op.cit., esp. 83-134, where he indicates the development in social laws as Israel became more settled. He picks out many laws to safeguard social justice, and also finds, "The aims pursued by the social

legislation of the Torah are closely correlated with the ideal of the prophets" (104). Cf. P. Bovati, Ristabilire la Giustizia, 358-362, his conclusion to the work, reaffirming that God appears as "partner" who confronts the other but always with the prospect of a reconciliation. In other cases, where God appears as just Judge to rectify an injustice between humans, he acts in favour of the weak who are being crushed by the arrogant powerful.

34. M. Wyschogrod, "La Torah en tant que Loi dans le Judaisme", in SIDIC XIX,n.3 (1986), Ed. Française (Roma), 10-16, in which he rightly insists that for the Jew Torah means Teaching and not (isolated) law. "La réponse se trouve fondamentalement dans l'amour par lequel ce peuple se sent aimé de Dieu" (p.14).
35. Cf. P. Bovati, Giustizia e Ingiustizia..., 31-33 on honouring parents; also 40-43 on the way love, respect, obedience, and service give unity to all the Law.
36. R. North, Sociology of the Biblical Jubilee (Roma: Pontifical Biblical Institute, 1954), e.g. 3: "Moreover, literary criticism proves the strict jubilee-notion to be a quite ancient kernel of an otherwise ramified and incoherent legal chapter. ... ... The permanent theological contribution of the law is that God's ownership, with the expanding family as its vehicle, subordinates particular property acquisitions to the general welfare".
37. Cf. N. Lohfink, art.cit. , 222-226.
38. S. Ringe, Jesus, Liberation and the Biblical Jubilee, e.g.33-49 on "Jesus as Herald of Liberation".
39. Cf. W. Brueggemann, The Land — Place as Gift, Promise, and Challenge in Biblical Faith (Philadelphia: Fortress Press, 1977) e.g. in the Preface : "Israel simply told its children what had been seen and heard. In the telling Israel discerned itself characteristically in the crunch between Yahweh and his land. ... For the believing community of the church, it is not absolute history, but it is 'our' history, and probably our destiny is hidden in this history of land and landlessness."
40. R. North, op.cit. p.2.
41. Ibid. 212: "The jubilee law presumes an agrarian economy of primitive simplicity. This would fit either the Occupation or the Esdran era. But the dispirited return from Babylon was unsuited to idealistic demands. The slave-release of Nehemias, being absolute, stems from a wholly later atmosphere than Lv 25, which acknowledges slavery and fixes its term."
42. S. Ringe, op.cit. 26, where she considers that the jubilee legislation seems to contain pieces of ancient material which were "probably woven together as part of the Holiness Code by a priestly editor of the late exilic or postexilic period."
43. R. North, op.cit., 1; also 212 re Jubilee not being said to be recurrent; and 231: "The perennial contribution of Lv 25 to the treasury of religious certitudes is that the self-subsistent expanding family is the basis of a healthy divine worship. ... Economic reform is intended not on the civil or secular plane, but as a form of worship."

44. J.L. Sicre, Con Los Pobres de la Tierra — La Justicia Social en los Profetas de Israel (Madrid: Ediciones Cristiandad, 1984), esp. 165 for influence of covenant on Amos, and 313 for similar influence on Micah.
45. D. Tracey, "Exodus: Theological Reflection", in Concilium 189, pp.118-124, e.g. 119: "For Exodus demands a resolutely this-worldly spirituality as it demands an historical and political, not a private or individualist understanding of Christian salvation-as-total-liberation."

CHAPTER 5 :

COVENANT PROCLAIMED BY DEUTERONOMY AND DEUTERONOMIC HISTORY

A. THE BOOK OF DEUTERONOMY

The final book of the Pentateuch, and hence of the Torah, is called Deuteronomy, due to a remark in Dt 17,18 in the Septuagint (Greek) version that an Israelite king must write out for himself this **deuteronomion** (=second law). In the same vein is another observation in 28,69: "These are the words of the covenant which Yahweh ordered Moses to make with the Israelites in Moab, in addition to the covenant which he had made with them at Horeb." Deuteronomy depicts the aged Moses giving his farewell discourse in sight of the promised land, which he had glimpsed from afar but would never enter. In fervent exhortatory tones he recalls the Sinai (or Horeb) covenant, as well as the crucial experiences before and after that awesome encounter with Yahweh[1]. He presents it as a call to respond with love and obedience to the manifest love and fidelity of Yahweh. To respond wholeheartedly is to choose life and ensure permanent possession of the fine land they are about to be given by Yahweh. To serve other gods and forget Yahweh would be to choose death and forfeit their land.

This spirit of Deuteronomy has left its mark very clearly on the historical books, which the Hebrew Bible calls "the Former Prophets", namely Joshua, Judges, 1 & 2 Samuel, 1 & 2 Kings. For that reason it is now usual to refer to all six books together as "Deuteronomic History". This title is intended to bring out that the formation of Deuteronomy itself and the prolonged redactions of the early history books involved an ongoing "school" imbued with the ideals and enthusiasm now enshrined in Deuteronomy and reflected in all those books. We shall consider first the book of Deuteronomy, then each of the six history books, because they are all concerned with fidelity to the Mosaic covenant as the only way to maintain peaceful possession of the promised land.

It is highly significant that Moses warns his people sternly that the alternative would be a return to slavery in Egypt — if they could manage to sell themselves there in their desperation to survive!: "Yahweh will send you back to Egypt... And there you will want to offer yourselves for sale to your enemies as serving men and women, but no one will buy you" (Dt 28,68). A further reason for considering all this material in some detail is that Deuteronomy does present the Mosaic covenant in treaty form[2].

1. THE ORIGIN, PURPOSE AND STRUCTURE OF DEUTERONOMY

The origin of Deuteronomy is generally placed in the Northern Kingdom, "Israel", which had broken away from Jerusalem and the house of David in order to establish its own capital in Shechem and then Samaria. The book has an affinity with the Northern prophets such as Elijah and Elisha, Amos and Hosea. Jeremiah of Anathoth was preaching in Jerusalem when king

Josiah instituted a big reform there after the finding of the "book of the Law" in the Temple (2 K 22-23), about 622 B.C. What was found was probably the major part of Deuteronomy, perhaps chapters 12-26, or even much of cc 5-28. In any case, Jeremiah has many points in common with Deuteronomy, not the least being his frequent denunciations of infidelity to Yahweh, and his promise of a new covenant with a new spirit to make its observance a reality. It is presumed that priests from the Northern kingdom had brought the basic texts of Deuteronomy to Jerusalem after the Assyrians had destroyed Samaria in 721 B.C. and put an end to that whole kingdom. The Jerusalem redaction of Deuteronomy stresses the law of one central sanctuary only, obviously the Temple. Once Jerusalem itself had been destroyed by the Babylonians in 587 B.C., the finishing touches would have been given to Deuteronomy during the Exile in Babylon[3].

One obvious purpose of Deuteronomy is to urge all its readers and their listeners to take completely to heart the spirit and the laws of the covenant. In many ways Moses' appeal reaches right to to the latest generation of Israel, e.g. "Yahweh our God made a covenant with us at Horeb. Yahweh made this covenant not with our ancestors, but with us, with all of us alive here today" (Dt 5,2-3). All through it runs an appeal to the heart of Israel, exhorting the nation to respond with love in gratitude and loyalty to Yahweh's own prior love for Israel[4]. This aspect is all the more important in view of the prominence given to the treaty form and the obvious stress on the conditional nature of the Sinai covenant.

It would be most unjust to Deuteronomy to accuse it of being mainly an attempt to move Israel by a system of legalistic rewards and punishments. Blessings and curses, life and death are certainly offered in direct relation to the observance of covenant requirements. The greatest and central requirement, however, is forcefully proclaimed early on: "Listen, Israel: Yahweh our God is the one, the only Yahweh. You must love Yahweh your God with all your heart... Let the words I enjoin on you today stay in your heart" (6,4-5)[5]. It is also made abundantly clear that Yahweh is so merciful and mindful of his oath to the patriarchs that he will be ready to pardon violators of the covenant if they turn back to him in the midst of disaster (cf. 4,25-31; 30,1-10).

The literary structure of Deuteronomy as it now stands sets the so-called Deuteronomic Code firmly in the middle, cc. 12 - 26. Immediately before it is found a kind of introductory discourse of Moses (cc.5-11). He begins by recalling the ten commandments as the nucleus of the covenant (c.5) and later mentioning how the "Ten Words" were to be inscribed on stone tablets and put into the ark (10,1-9). Interior conviction is so vital that the heart itself must be circumcised (10,16), for "you must love Yahweh" (11,1) and "beware of letting your heart be seduced" (11,16).

Immediately after the Code come mainly lists of curses, blessings and more curses (cc.27 -28), followed by another covenant discourse of Moses,which could stand as a unit by itself (cc. 29 - 30). As D. McCarthy has observed, this corresponds well to a similar independent covenant speech of

Moses in c.4, with the result that the central block of cc.5 - 28 is now framed by these covenant speeches, each having the treaty form and yet each promising survival and renewal after covenant violations[6].

Cc.1-3 give an important element of the treaty form, namely the historical prologue, in which is recalled what Yahweh has done for Israel between Egypt and Moab. At the other end of the book we also have some more history, such as the handing on of authority to Joshua as Moses' successor (31), followed by the farewell Song of Moses and his blessings upon the tribes (32 - 33), then Deuteronomy, and with it the Pentateuch, closes reverently with the death of Moses (34).

2. EXPANSION AND ACTUALIZATION OF THE TEN COMMANDMENTS (DT 6 - 28)

A close reading of these central chapters reveals that these are an extension and updated interpretation of the heart of the Mosaic covenant, which here, as in Exod. 20, is presented as summed up well in the ten commandments. As noted in treating of Exodus, they may have been the précis arrived at by centuries of living out and reflecting upon the Exodus-Sinai experience. For Israel, as for Christ and the Church, the ten commandments do retain the quintessence of what Yahweh asks of his people. In view of all that, it is worth noting here at least some of the most striking cases of a commandment being actualized for later generations.

The first commandment as given in Dt 5,6-7 says, "I am Yahweh your God who brought you out of Egypt... You will have no gods other than me". We have already had cause to quote the way Dt 6,4 adds a new dimension to that basic commandment by insisting, "You must love Yahweh your God with all your heart.."

The commandment forbidding worship of other gods or the making of idols or images in Dt 5,7-9 is amplified frequently, e.g. 8,19: "if you follow other gods.. you will perish"; 12,29-31 is a warning against being drawn after Canaanite gods; 13,3-17 warns against being seduced by dreamers or false prophets to go after other gods; such seducers must be put to death; cf. 28,63-64 on being exiled to where stone and wooden gods are worshipped. An interesting reason for the prohibition against making images is given in 4,15-16: "Since you saw no shape that day at Horeb when Yahweh spoke to you from the heart of the fire, see that you do not corrupt yourselves by making an image in the shape of anything whatever."

The commandment in 5,11 against using the name of Yahweh in vain or for what is false finds one stern application in 18,20: "the prophet who presumes to say something in my name which I have not commanded him to say, .. that prophet must die."

The commandment to observe and keep holy the Sabbath day is already amplified in 5,12-15, where it is linked with the idea of putting an end to unremitting and dehumanizing slave labour, such as Israel itself had suffered until liberated from Egypt by Yahweh.

The commandment in 5,16 to honour father and mother is strengthened by 21,18-21, ruling that a persistently rebellious son can be stoned to death after a hearing of his case at the town gate. Such a son would also merit the curse mentioned in 27,16.

The commandment against killing in 5,17 is to have its sanction against a cold-blooded murderer, even a city of refuge (19,11-13). Even the finding of an abandoned murder victim in open country calls for a sacrifice in the nearest town, to beg forgiveness for the shedding of innocent blood (21,1-9). A curse is invoked on anyone "who secretly strikes down his neighbour" (27,24).

The command against adultery in 5,18 is expanded in 22,22ff., where the death penalty is mentioned for adultery, and likewise for rape of a betrothed girl. The rights of wives taken from among prisoners (21,10-14), and the rights of unloved wives (21,15-17), and of divorced wives (24,1-4) are spelt out.

The commandment against stealing in 5,19 finds an echo at least in the injunction against displacing the neighbour's boundary (19,14; cf 27,17 for the corresponding curse), and again in the law against keeping false weights and measures (25,13-16). An amplification can be seen in the rules against charging a brother interest on a loan (23,20-21) or holding overnight a cloak given as a pledge by some poor person (24,12-13), or withholding a poor man's wages once the day's work has finished (24,14-15). Going beyond the stated commandments, there are several exhortations to be kind to the stranger, the widow and the orphan, e.g. 24,17-22, with a corresponding curse in 27,19: "Accursed be anyone who violates the rights of the foreigner, the orphan and the widow."

The commandment in 5,20 against giving false witness is strengthened in 19,16 by calling for the same punishment upon the false witness as he would have caused to the innocent party.

The final commandment(s) in 5,21 against coveting the neighbour's wife or servants or belongings is strengthened by the spirit of the sabbatical year in 15,1-18: "At the end of every seven years, you must grant remission." This means remission of debts, the returning of things taken as a pledge, and also the setting free of any enslaved Hebrews who have not opted to remain on as slaves within the household. The motivation is clearly stated, "Remember that you were once a slave in Egypt and that Yahweh your God redeemed you; that is why I am giving you this order today" (15,15). Another concession to strangers living within Israel is that the Edomites and Egyptians are not to be regarded as detestable, since the first are relatives and the others once welcomed Israel to reside in their country (23,7-8). To us, Deuteronomy often seems too nationalistic and fiercely anti-foreign, but Yahweh and those more aware of his gratuitous love for all people tried to moderate excesses in this regard. Third generation Edomites and Egyptians born in Israel, for instance, could be admitted into the assembly of God's people (23,8), and so enter fully into the covenanted community.

Another important contribution to the maintenance of the covenant standards is demanded of those who should be guardians of the covenant[7]. These were firstly the judges in every town, whose duty it was "to mete out justice to the people", impartially and beyond bribing, for "strict justice must be your ideal" (16,18-20). In more difficult cases, recourse is to be had to an official levitical judge (17,8-13). Next comes the king, who is nonetheless under the covenant himself and bound to treat other Israelites truly as his brothers and sisters (17,14-20). Then the rights and duties of levitical priests are outlined, especially "the duties of the sacred ministry" (18,1-8; cf.10,6-9 on the choice of the tribe of Levi "to carry the ark of Yahweh's covenant", etc.). Finally the role of the prophet "like Moses" is stressed, for through prophets Yahweh continues to speak authoritatively to the people (18,9-22). We will hear more of all these charismatic and hereditary servants of the covenant in the Deuteronomic history and beyond it.

3. ELEMENTS OF THE TREATY FORM IN DEUTERONOMY

Many elements of the treaty form can be found in the central core (5 - 28), and also in each of the discourses that introduce it (4) and follow it (29-30)[8]. Here, however, we shall treat the book as a whole, to avoid repetitions and to present in order clear examples of all six main elements of the treaty form. In this listing (of treaty elements) we are still following that of G. Mendenhall[9].

i) Preamble or Titulature: 5,6: "I am Yahweh your God who brought you out of Egypt, out of the place of slave-labour."

ii) Historical Prologue: Cc. 1-3 recall many of the favours shown to Israel from Horeb (or Sinai) to Moab. Cc.6-11 mention an even wider variety of Yahweh's mighty deeds right from Egypt and even recalling the promises to the patriarchs. 29,1-8 also recalls the liberation from Egypt and the protection granted in the usually destructive desert.

iii) The stipulations of the treaty: Ch. 5 with the commandments and cc.12-26 with the Code of "laws and customs which you must keep in the country which Yahweh.. is giving you as yours" (12,1), form a substantial set of obligations assumed by Israel. Yahweh's part is to continue treating Israel as a chosen people and to bless them in keeping with the solemn promises given to them, e.g. to grant them peaceful and prosperous life in their (new) land (cc.4-ll; 28,1-14; 30,15-20).

iv) Provisions for the deposit of a copy of the treaty in a sanctuary and for a regular reading of it, etc.: In 10,1-5 Moses recalls Yahweh's instructions to him about putting the "Ten Words", inscribed afresh on two more stone tablets, into the ark. The ark (of the covenant) was a little portable shrine, so that wherever its protecting tent was pitched, there was the principal sanctuary of early Israel. One of the main tenets of king Josiah's reform was that the Temple in Jerusalem had to become the only official sanctuary for all Israel, north as well as south. 11,26-32 refers to setting "the blessing on Mount Gerizim and the curse on Mount Ebal" (v.29), which is clarified in 27,1-10. The people are told: "You must set up tall stones, coat them with lime and on them write all the words of this Law... When you have crossed the Jordan, you must erect these stones on Mount Ebal" (vv.2-4). Moses also commanded that there should be a public proclamation of the Law to the assembly every seven years, during the feast of Tabernacles (or Shelters) (31,9-13).

v) List of gods as witnesses to the treaty: In 4,26 Moses declares: "Today I call heaven and earth to witness against you — [when you have grown corrupt] you will quickly vanish from the country which you are crossing the Jordan to possess." Later on Moses gives the alternatives: "Today, I call heaven and earth to witness against you: I am offering you life or death, blessing or curse. Choose life, then" (30,19; cf. 31,28). Similarly "the book of the Law" is to be laid beside the ark of the covenant of Yahweh "as evidence against you" (31,25-26).

vi) List of blessings and curses as sanctions: Curses are listed in 27,11-26; 28,15-68; and 29,17-28. Blessings are given in 28,1-14; many promises are scattered throughout the book, more in the line of what Yahweh wants to give Israel if only it will remain faithful and open to life as God's partner.

What emerges from such a detailed comparison with political treaties is that Deuteronomy likes to present the Mosaic covenant in treaty form. On the other hand, it by no means limits Israel's relation-ship with Yahweh to that of a bilateral and conditional treaty. We need only recall the persistently fervent and moving appeals for love and faithful obedience, such as children show to their parents. In fact, this image is found in Dt 8,5-6: "Learn from this that Yahweh your God was training you as a man trains his child, and keep the commandments of Yahweh.." Similarly in 14,1: "You are children of Yahweh your God." Towards the end of this whole book, the one most influenced by treaty terminology, is placed the Song of Moses, in which Yahweh is referred to as the father who made Israel(32,5-6) and guarded it "as the pupil of his eye" (32,10). In short, Deuteronomy's use of treaty language and form is aimed primarily at moving Israel to treasure and honour in daily life its covenant, which far surpasses any secular vassal treaty. We conclude with D. McCarthy: "There is the fact that the father-son image appears in connections which are relevant to covenant and treaty. .. It is not without significance that Deuteronomy sees nothing incongruous about basing a law safeguarding the essential relationship to Yahweh on an appeal to the father-son relationship"[10].

B. THE DEUTERONOMIC HISTORY (JOSHUA - 2 KINGS)

1. THE BOOK OF JOSHUA

In common with all six books comprising the Deuteronomic History, the Book of Joshua contains much ancient material from traditions both oral and written, which have been edited and re-edited about the time of Josiah and during the Exile. By means of these redactions the Deuteronomic group were able to evaluate the history of Israel from the Occupation to the Exile by their criterion of promise and covenant. This deep reflection is really a theology, a study of what God is revealing through the ongoing history of Israel, with all its successes and disasters. Israel's relation to the promised land during this period has been perceptively denoted by W. Brueggemann as "entry and exit"[11]. Our main interest lies in the way the covenant has been used as the yardstick by which to measure the success or failure of Israel, especially as represented by their leaders.

Fortunately Joshua was filled with the spirit of Moses and remained very faithful to the covenant. Thanks to his sterling leadership and military skills, Israel did take possession of much of Canaan and each tribe, apart from Levi, was allotted its territory. The final chapters of Joshua tell of his farewell discourses in which, like the dying Moses, he strongly urges continuing fidelity to Yahweh and the covenant. Ch. 23 expresses well the central concern of Joshua: "Acknowledge with all your heart and soul that of all the promises made to you by Yahweh your God, not one has failed" (v.14). This is followed by a stern warning: "by the same token, Yahweh will fulfil all his threats against you, even to exterminating you from this fine country given you by Yahweh your God" (v.15).

It is in ch. 24 as it now stands that we are told of Joshua's great national renewal of the covenant at Shechem, where "all the tribes of Israel" are invited to renew — or accept for the first time — their commitment to the Mosaic covenant. We can take it as an extension of that covenant to many inhabitants of Canaan who felt kinship with Joshua's people but had not experienced the exodus nor Sinai theophany nor the wandering in the wilderness[12]. Thanks to Deuteronomic reworking of a genuinely ancient basic tradition, all the usual treaty elements can now be discerned in Jos 24[13]:
i) The preamble (v.1-2).

ii) Historical prologue (vv.2-13).
iii) Stipulation (v.14 — undivided loyalty to Yahweh).
iv) Curses and blessings (vv.19-20 with "threats" and an oblique reference to Yahweh being good to them).
v) Witnesses to the treaty (v.22 - the people themselves are said to be "witnesses" to themselves; v.26-27 — "a large stone" taken and set up there, "under the oak tree in Yahweh's sanctuary", to be "a witness to us").
vi) A copy of the covenant (vv.25-26 — drawn up by Joshua in "the Book of the Law of God").
vii) An added feature is the fourfold declaration of the people that they freely and fully want to serve Yahweh (vv. 16-18; 21. 22. 24). These are regarded by Baltzer as equivalent to confirming the covenant by oath. In any case, such a public declaration by the assembly in a cultic setting was a sufficiently solemn sealing of the covenant on their part. The occupation of the land was off to a promising start!

2. THE BOOK OF JUDGES

This takes up the story of Israel following on the death of Joshua, but it also indicates that the conquest and occupation was by no means a fait accompli. Various tribes still had to struggle hard in order to get possession of their territories. Moreover, plenty of other inhabitants of Canaan and adjacent territories were ready to attack this or that tribe to win control of their area. A key concept of the Deuteronomic redactors is given in Jg 2,11-23, namely that after Joshua there was a recurring cycle of sin, oppression by enemies, crying out to God in distress, liberation by some judge seized by the spirit of God, and stability during the lifetime of the judge, then a further lapse into infidelity.

This kind of cycle continues on to the end of the Deuteronomic history, which stops with Israel in exile and presumably crying out once more for liberation, which Yahweh can be expected to bring about once Israel has sufficiently repented. Another refrain has a bearing on the place of the monarchy, since it attributes lawless conditions to the lack of a king in Israel (e.g. 17,6; 18,1; 19,1; 21,25).

The Judges themselves were called and inspired by God to be first of all military leaders to free their tribe from armed enemies. Once liberation had been achieved, then they continued on as civil rulers and judges to settle disputes among their people. They were charismatic leaders, appearing sporadically, each Judge helping one or a few tribes, and they were not replaced when they died[14]. They were not meant to replace the normal loose inter-tribal loyalty based on kinship and strengthened by covenant commitment. The Judge Gideon refused the title of kingship, insisting that "Yahweh shall rule you" (8,23). Later on his son had himself declared king of Shechem, but he was killed in an early campaign (ch.9).

3. 1 & 2 SAMUEL

These two books were originally given as one work in the Hebrew Bible, and yet the have obviously been compiled and re-edited from a wide variety of traditions. They preserve for us some of the most gripping stories of ancient literature, such as the rise and tragedy of Saul, the escapades and unifying reign of David, narrowly surviving the revolt of his spirited son Absalom. They seem to have been incorporated into the development of the Deuteronomic history with great respect for the earlier sources. At times two traditions are preserved, enabling us to see widely differing attitudes, e.g. towards the place of a monarchy within Israel(1 Sam 8 - 15). This is really the crucial issue for our work, too, because the monarchy was entrusted with the government of people who had to retain Yahweh as their undisputed King. This had as a corollary that the monarch's rule had to be in keeping with and subordinate to Yahweh's will as made known through the Mosaic covenant. In brief, the monarch had to be an exemplary defender of the covenant, not an obstacle to it. Much of what is frequently referred to as anti-monarchical consists of texts which evaluated kingship as posing a big risk to basic covenant values. The transition from Judges to a stable monarchy is seen in 1 & 2 Samuel, as serious objections are overcome and God eventually promises to make the house of David secure for ever.

Of obvious interest to our reflection is the prominence given in the early chapters of 1 Samuel to the ark of the covenant at Shiloh, then in the hands of the Philistines, and later brought back to a spot near Jerusalem(cc.3 - 7). It was David who eventually had the ark brought right into his capital city, Jerusalem (2 Sam 6). He wanted to build a fitting temple for it, but that task was carried out by his son, Solomon. All of which points up the importance which those kings attached to the covenant itself, for that was the obvious symbolism of the ark of the covenant.

There is rich symbolism in Samuel as the man of God involved, however reluctantly at first, in the transition from occasional charismatic Judges to an enduring dynastic monarchy ruling all Israel. Samuel himself was an outstanding Judge with the distinction of being called to judge all Israel. Likewise he was the last of the Judges, because he was also the seer through whom Yahweh guided the nation when it demanded a king "like the other nations". In reply to Samuel's warning about the disadvantages and limitations accompanying kingship, the people insisted, "We are determined to have a king, so that we can be like the other nations" (Sam 8,5.19-20).To him fell the jarring task of designating and anointing, in God's name, the farmer Saul as first king of Israel — and therefore the replacement of Samuel himself as political leader. Then when Saul failed, Samuel as God's spokesman had the disagreeable task of designating and anointing the young shepherd, David, to replace the dynasty of Saul. The symbolism in all this is that Yahweh moved the charismatic Judge and seer to grant, with the reservations we shall see, Israel's request for an institutional, dynastic form of government.

The profound significance of the prophets' role in establishing and guiding kingship in Israel has been well brought out by A. Campbell in his recent monograph "Of Prophets and Kings — A Late Ninth Century Document". He posits the hypothesis that there was a "prophetic record" telling of the anointing of Saul, David, and Jehu, and that "all three [episodes] have been put together to express the conviction that God's guidance of his people was manifested through the action of a prophet empowered to designate Israel's kings through the rite of anointing"[15]. He also finds that there is good reason to include a substantial part of Nathan's promise to David (2 Sam 7,1-17) in the "prophetic record".

The fundamental import of that (hypothetical) record is that it "proclaimed a view of history in which God's will was paramount. Kings originated from Yahweh's will, manifested through the prophets"[16].

The great influence of prophets on the emergence and conduct of the first four kings of Israel can be gauged by the forthright way in which Samuel denounced Saul(1 Sam 13,8-14; 15,22-23), Nathan denounced David(2 Sam 12,1-15), Ahijah denounced Solomon (1 K 11,29-39), and Shemaiah denounced Rehoboam, son of Solomon: "Yahweh says this: Do not go to make war on your brothers" (1 K 12, 22-24).

Seen against this wider prophetic background and spirit, the seemingly conflicting reactions of Samuel are really an honest airing of national soul-searching when faced with such a powerful institution as the monarchy. The material presented in 1 Sam 8 - 12 suffices to alert all generations to the earlier values which must be preserved, as well as the dangers of oppression and dehumanization which have to be avoided at all costs. Samuel objected to the impulsive way in which Israel acted as though Yahweh were no longer an adequate King (cf. 12,12), as though the Judges he raised up were unsatisfactory, and as though it were time for Israel to base its security on human kings just like the other nations were doing. They were not sufficiently concerned about the high price that kings in other nations demanded in terms of human lives, possessions and personal dignity. Once Samuel had led the people to realise their "sin" and ask forgiveness of God, then he could reassure them that Yahweh would not desert them, unless they acted persistently with wickedness. In that case, he warned them plainly, "you and your king will perish" (12,24)[17].

Much light has been thrown on this matter by G. E. Gerbrandt in "Kingship According to the Deuteronomistic History", where he rightly claims: "In other words, the correct question with which to confront the Deuteronomist is not whether he was anti-kingship or pro-kingship. Rather, we need to ask what kind of kingship he saw as ideal for Israel, or what role kingship was expected to play for Israel"[18]. One of the modern authors whom he mentions as having already moved in that direction is D.McCarthy[19]. With regard to the king's responsibility to honour and uphold the covenant in his kingdom, the Deuteronomist presupposes that "the king's role was to make sure that the covenant was observed in Israel. Practically, he could be called the <u>covenant administrator</u>"[20] (author's emphasis).

A somewhat similar dimension of kingship is given by S. Talmon in "King, Cult and Calendar in Ancient Israel", who asserts: "The idea of state and the concept of monarchy are one. ... Similarly, both Israel and her neighbors conceived of divine rule as monarchical"[21]. Since God remains always the supreme King over Israel, "Socio-political leadership, in any form, is viewed in the Bible as a function of God's divine Covenant with Israel"[22].

That this was the overriding concern manifested through Samuel can be seen by the juxtaposition of the pros and cons of having a human king to rule Israel. One the one hand, Yahweh is moved to grant such a king precisely because of the misery of the people whose cry of anguish has reached him (1 Sam 9,16). That is reminiscent of the harsh situation in Egypt from which Moses was enabled to deliver them(1 Sam 8,17; 12,6). Saul is made known to Samuel by Yahweh declaring: "This is the man of whom I said to you, 'He is to govern my people'" (9,17). Shortly after Saul had been anointed by Samuel as leader of the people, "the spirit of God seized on him" (10,1-11)[23]. These are indications that Saul was meant to be much more than simply a king "like other nations have". He was designated, anointed, and empowered by the spirit of God to rule as a kind of viceroy[24].

On the other hand, not even Yahweh's viceroy was to rule as though completely autonomous, nor even as one no longer bound by covenant ties to the rest of his brothers and sisters(cf. the stipulation in Dt 17,15: "The appointment of a king must be made from your own brothers"). The immediate reason for granting a king was to win more stable relief from Philistine oppression, hence the need to forewarn against the excesses of monarchy. The end result could well be, as Samuel warns, that "you yourselves will become his slaves" (8,17).

The reign of Saul achieved some respite from the Philistines, but the burdens of kingship proved too much for him, as if the change were too great for him to cope with[25]. For not obeying the voice of God coming to him through Samuel, Saul found himself rejected. He remained on as king until he died in the battle of Mt Gilboa, but David had long since been designated and anointed by Samuel as his successor. David was accepted in Hebron as king over Judah for seven years, and then as king over all Israel for another 33 years. As soon as he captured the city of Jerusalem, he made that undisputed "city of David" his new capital. He quickly showed his desire to integrate kingly power with deep respect for Yahweh's worship by having the ark of the covenant brought to Jerusalem.

It was on the occasion of his discussions with Nathan about the need to house the ark in a worthy temple that David received an extraordinary promise. Yahweh took the initiative away from David, promising instead to make David's own house secure. This culminated in the famous words, "Your dynasty and your sovereignty will ever stand firm before me and your throne be for ever secure" (2 Sam 7,16). Here the Davidic monarchy obviously receives a new dimension within Israel, now that God has freely committed himself to grant security and "rest" to his people through David's dynasty. As previously for all Israel, so now for David's heir Yahweh promises, "I shall be a father to him and he a son to me; if he does wrong, I shall punish him with a rod such as men use, ... But my faithful love will never be withdrawn from him as I withdrew it from Saul" (vv.14-15).

D. McCarthy argues convincingly that Nathan's promise in 2 Sam 7 is a key text for the Deuteronomic historian, on a par with the speech of Moses in Dt 31 and that of Joshua in Jos 23[26]. Like Moses, David is referred to by Yahweh as "my servant David". In fact, "for the D writer, the Davidic covenant continues and specifies the older [Mosaic] one. David's covenant does not compete with the people's covenant as an independent, parallel means to Yahweh's grace; rather, through David the whole people receives the divine favor"[27]. Because in David's case God's promise is unconditional and irrevocable, it has much in common with the promissory covenant granted to Abraham(Gen 15). It, too, offers an unshakeable basis for hope when the Sinai covenant has been so violated as to bring down some of its frightening sanctions. The Deuteronomic history goes on to show that loyalty to the Mosaic covenant remained the criterion by which to judge events - and even Davidic kings - right through until the monarchy was overthrown.

This brings us to the big question as to what kind of a covenant was granted to David and his dynasty. While it appears in 2 Sam 7 as a unilateral and unconditional promise, David's last words recall it fondly as a covenant: " Yes, my House stands firm with God: he has made an eternal covenant with me" (2 Sam 23,5). Ps 89 sings of Yahweh's faithful love and constancy towards David and his royal house, e.g. "I have made a covenant with my Chosen One, sworn an oath to my servant David: I have made your dynasty firm for ever" (vv. 3-4). Again, "I shall maintain my faithful love for him always, my covenant with him will stay firm" (v.28). Perhaps the most surprising reference is found in Deutero-Isaiah, where God consoles the Jewish exiles in Babylon: "I shall make an everlasting covenant with you in fulfilment of the favours promised to David" (55,3). Long after the return from exile, and when four centuries had gone by without any king in Jerusalem, Sirach still recalls of David that the Lord "gave him a royal covenant, and a glorious throne in Israel" (47,11).

As we explained when treating of the Abrahamic covenant, a solemn promise by God to a chosen servant can establish a new kind of relationship between the two parties. At the moment of giving the promise to David, Yahweh indicates its scope: "I took you from the pasture, from following the sheep, to be leader of my people Israel. ... I am going to provide a place for my people Israel .. and there they will live and never be disturbed again. ... I shall grant you rest from all your enemies" (2 Sam 7,8-11). From this, as from the historical unfolding of the promised dynasty, it can be seen that Israel was still a theocracy, a nation whose civil as well as religious government was determined by God-given laws. When necessary, it was further guided by prophetic interventions. So David was keenly aware of being entrusted by God with power and promises far beyond his merits: "Who am I, Lord Yahweh, and what is my lineage, for you to have led me as far as this?" (2 Sam 7,18).

Explicit mention is made of corrective punishment for any wrongdoing, even though it could not cancel the promise. Moreover, the stinging rebuke given to David after his sins of adultery and homicide confirm that the king was still bound to live under the Mosaic covenant. Similar prophetic rebukes or denunciations are to be found in the history of subsequent kings. Because a kingdom's conduct and values depended so much on its king, a divinely appointed king like David had an added responsibility to lead by example evermore than by laws or structures. Samuel had said of David that "Yahweh has discovered a man after his own heart and designated him as leader of his people" (1 Sam 13,14). At David's anointing by Samuel, "the spirit of Yahweh seized on David from that day onwards" (1 Sam 16,13). Much of David's greatness lay in his openness to God and to many fellow-servants of God, such as the prophets, priests, Levite guardians of the ark, cultic singers, sages, his trusted warriors, as well as to his various wives and troublesome children. David saw to it that "his" city of Jerusalem could become also the special dwelling place of Yahweh[28]. He was, then, sincerely committed to maintaining covenant loyalty towards both Yahweh and his fellow Israelites, avoiding the usual pitfalls of kingship (cf. Dt 17; 1 Sam 8,10-22; 10,25). Solomon, for his part, tended to overshadow the Temple by building his own much more grandiose palace adjoining it. At least that impressive complex was a public symbol of the close links between Yahweh's house and the house of David.

A recent commentary on 1 & 2 Samuel by R.P. Gordon also emphasises the centrality of the Davidic dynasty : "2 Sam 7 is rightly regarded as an 'ideological summit', not only in the 'Deuteronomistic history' but also in the Old Testament as a whole. ... .. We shall not be exaggerating the importance of the Nathan oracle, therefore, if we see it as the matrix of biblical messianism"[29]. As we shall be returning to messianism in the prophets, suffice it to note here that Nathan's great promise opened the way for linking God's rule with the political rule and religious orientation of an anointed "servant" ruler in Jerusalem.

To sum up the place of the Davidic covenant in the development of the whole biblical understanding of covenant, we may truly say that it provided a precious new dimension for the interplay between Yahweh's loving kindness and a powerful socio-political institution. It opened the way for Yahweh's reign to enter into public life and gradually transform it — provided the kings and their kingdom were willing to be transformed. From wanting a king like other nations had, Israel was being led to accept a king quite different to what other nations had, a king completely "after God's own heart". The irrevocable nature of the covenant with David's house kept alive the hope that Yahweh would raise up a descendant to bring in a lasting reign of justice and peace[30].

B 4. 1 & 2 KINGS

After a long struggle for succession to the throne, Solomon was proclaimed king before David's death. As David came to be remembered as "the singer of the songs of Israel" (2 Sam 23,1) and patron of the Psalms, so his son Solomon came to be regarded as the patron of Wisdom in Israel. The background for it is seen in the prayer of Solomon at Gibeon, where he prayed, "So give your servant a heart to understand how to govern your people, how to discern between good and evil". Yahweh promised to grant him "a heart wise and shrewd" (1 K 3,9-14; cf.5,9-14). This was intended to help Solomon rule over God's people and to follow personally God's "ways", "laws" and "commandments" as David had done (1 K 3,9-14; cf.5,9-14).

As mentioned above, it was Solomon who built the first Temple in Jerusalem, and then a much more elaborate palace for himself and his all-too-numerous wives and concubines. Such large buildings and so many dependants living around the palace led him into the pitfalls adverted to by Samuel. He "raised a levy throughout Israel for forced labour" (1 K 5,27; cf. 11,28). There was also a great corps of officials and a large army, including plenty of charioteers. The royal table required hundreds of animals and birds per day. Taxes and other revenues rolled in to the royal coffers (1 K 10,14-25)[31]. The hundreds of wives of royal rank also had an adverse effect on Solomon, so keen was he to show interest in their foreign gods — "his heart was not wholly with Yahweh as his father David's had been" (1 K 11,4).

The rumblings of a revolt against Solomon came when an energetic Ephraimite, Jeroboam, was told by the prophet Ahijah that Yahweh was going to give him the ten northern tribes of Israel to have as a kingdom independent of Jerusalem. Presumably news of it got back to Solomon, for he tried to kill Jeroboam. He managed to flee to Egypt, where the pharaoh received him kindly (1 K 11,17-40). Once Rehoboam succeeded Solomon on the throne, Jeroboam returned from Egypt and came with the northern tribes to demand better treatment from the new king. Rehoboam told them that he would treat them with much greater harshness than Solomon had. Having heard for themselves that kinship and covenant evidently counted for nothing any more, the northern tribes responded, "What share have we in David? ... Away to your tents, Israel!" That was the start of the schism between the southern kingdom, Judah, and the northern kingdom, confusingly termed "Israel", although it comprised only ten of the twelves tribes of greater Israel.

In order to put a stop to the usual pilgrimages up to the Jerusalem, Jeroboam had golden calves set up in Bethel and Dan, repeating Aaron's presentation of the golden calf at Sinai: "Here is your God, Israel, who brought you out of Egypt" (1 K 12,28). This time the prophet Ahijah had to denounce Jeroboam in the strongest terms for having made "idols of cast metal" and led his people away from Yahweh and not only from the harsh king of Jerusalem. According to the Deuteronomic history, Jeroboam and all the kings of the nine dynasties that quickly displaced one another in "Israel" were bad kings. They all allowed the shrines of the golden calves to continue, and many other commandments were broken. God continued to invite them back through great prophets like Elijah and Elisha, Amos and Hosea. The most moving example of defence of covenant values against a ruthless monarch is the case of Naboth and king Ahab (not to mention queen Jezebel). Ahab had Naboth murdered so he could get vacant possession of his vineyard, but Elijah denounced him to his face and foretold the massacre of all his house(1 K 21). The whole northern kingdom ended with the destruction of its capital, Samaria, by the Assyrians in 721 B.C. Many were led off into exile around Niniveh, and Samaria was repopulated with foreigners also deported willy-nilly.

In Judah, some kings like Asa and Hezeklah were evaluated as good kings. As we might expect, Josiah, the king who implemented a big reform in keeping with "the Book of the Covenant discovered in the Temple of Yahweh" (2 K 23,2), is considered excellent. In Deuteronomic terminology he is praised: "No king before him turned to Yahweh as he did, with all his heart, all his soul, all his strength, in perfect loyalty to the Law of Moses; nor did any king like him arise again" (2 K 23,25). Josiah was so impressed by the contents of the Book of the Covenant that he assembled all the people at the Temple. There he read out the entire contents of the Book, then he "bound himself by the covenant before Yahweh ...to carry out the terms of the covenant. .. All the people pledged their allegiance to the covenant" (2 K 23, 2-3).

Part of the reform was to abolish the high places in any territory under his control, which by then (about 621 B.C.) included a good deal of the breakaway northern kingdom. He also ordered the people to celebrate the Passover according to the Book of the Covenant. For our central theme, Josiah provides the clearest example of a Davidic king who saw his own role as a champion of the Mosaic covenant as preached in Deuteronomy. There is no hint of him thinking that the promise to David's house made fidelity to the Sinai covenant unnecessary. What is also striking in these final pages of 2 Kings is that the promise to David was not regarded as sufficient to ward off the destruction of his city, Jerusalem. For "Yahweh did not renounce the heat of his great anger which had been aroused against Judah by all the provocations which Manasseh had caused him. Yahweh said, 'I shall thrust Judah way from me too, as I have already thrust Israel' " (2 K 23,26-27)[32].

After narrating the last harrowing years of Jerusalem, which was relentlessly broken down and destroyed by the Babylonians in 587 B.C., the Deuteronomic history ends on a note of hope. It tells of the release of king Jehoiachin from prison in Babylon and his new status as a permanent guest at the Babylonian king's table (2 K 25,27-30). The throne in Jerusalem was destroyed, but the house of David survived, still a bearer of the promise to be fulfilled through the birth of an outstanding son of David (cf. Mt 1,10-17, in which Jehoiachin figures under the name of Jechoniah, and stress is laid on the exile by counting fourteen generations from David to the exile, then another fourteen generations from the exile to Jesus the Christ)[33]

NOTES

1. H. Cunliffe-Jones, Deuteronomy —The Preaching of the Covenant (London: Torch Bible p-b., S.C.M., 1964).
2. D. McCarthy, Old Testament Covenant, 28: "To take the clearest example, there can be no doubt that Deuteronomy does show some kind of relationship to the literary form of these treaties." 72: "Moreover, it has long been my contention that the parallel with the treaties is clearest in Deuteronomy and the Deuteronomistic passages."
3. Cf. O. Eissfeldt, The Old Testament — An Introduction (New York: E.T. by P. Ackroyd, Harper and Row, 1965) 233: "But D [= Deuteronomy] also remained authoritative law for the period of the exile and beyond, and so

the editions which we now have may have originated first in the exile."
Cf. M. Weinfeld, "Traces of Assyrian Treaty Formulae in Deuteronomy", in Biblica 46 (1965), 417-427. Cf. J. Blenkinsopp, "Deuteronomy", in The New Jerome Biblical Commentary (NJBC), 95 re a "decisive" redaction of Deuteronomy during the exile.

4. Cf. W. Eichrodt, Theology of the O.T., I, 55-56. Cf. D. McCarthy, Treaty and Covenant, 118, where he speaks of a "theology of the heart" in Dt.

5. Cf. W.L. Moran, "Ancient Near Eastern Background of Love of God in Dt.", in Catholic Biblical Quarterly 25(1963), 77-87; also his "Deuteronomy", in New Catholic Commentary on Holy Scripture (London: Nelson, 1969) 256-276. Cf. J.A. Thompson, Deuteronomy, (London: Tyndale Commentary, Inter-Varsity Press, 1974).

6. D. McCarthy, Treaty and Covenant, 131-140.

7. W. Eichrodt, op.cit., I, 289-456 on "Instruments of the Covenant", whom he divides conveniently into "charismatic", such as Judges and prophets, and "official", such as priests and kings.

8. Cf. D. McCarthy, op. cit., 121-140, wherein the various elements common to the treaties and to Dt. are discussed.

9. G. Mendenhall, Law and Covenant in Israel and the Ancient Near East, 32-34.

10. D. McCarthy, Institution and Narrative, 303; cf. all 301-304.

11. W. Brueggemann, The Land, 73: "The major temptation is to use up the land in wasteful, careless, self-indulgent ways and so lose it." 75-76: "Other kings ... incline to control the land as possession. This king is to manage the land as a gift entrusted to him but never possessed by him. ... It is not to control the land, but to enhance the land for the sake of the covenant partners, to whom the king is bound by common loyalties and memories" (emphasis added).

12. Cf. M. Noth, The History of Israel (London: E.T. by P. Ackroyd, A. & C. Black, 1960^2) esp. 53-138 on "Israel as the Confederation of the Twelve Tribes", even though today many question his term "amphictyony" to describe the confederation. Cf. W. Beyerlin, Origins and History of the Oldest Sinaitic Traditions (Oxford: E.T. by S. Rudman, Blackwell, 1965), where he proposes a much greater continuity than does M. Noth between the Sinai and Shechem covenants, e.g .151: "The same Sinaitic covenant by which the desert-community was conscious of being bound to Yahweh is renewed at Shechem with reference to the tribal union."

13. Cf. K. Baltzer, The Covenant Formulary (Oxford: E.T. by D. Green, Blackwell, 1971) 19-27. Cf. McCarthy, Treaty and Covenant, 145-149.

NOTES

14. Cf. J.A. Soggin, Le Livre de Juges (F.T. by C. Lanoir, Genève. 1987), e.g. 9-10 on the various offices of Judges, and 11 for a reflection on the cycle of sin, oppression, etc., which occurs often enough to give the impression that history simply repeats itself.
15. A. Campbell, Of Prophets and Kings — A Late 9th-Century Document (1 Sam 1 - 2 K 10) (Washington D.C.: C.B.A.A. Monograph Series 17, 1986) 23.
16. Ibid., 81: "To sum up: there is good reason to include 2 Sam 7:1a, 2-5, 7-10, 11b-12, 14-17 in the Prophetic Record". The final text quoted in the body of our work is from 204.
17. D. McCarthy, Institution and Narrative, 213-224. In concluding his interpretation of 1 Sam 8 - 12, he says, "The kingship has been integrated into the fundamental relationship between Yahweh and the people and that relationship reaffirmed. A crisis has been described and resolved in narrative terms and in theological, and a new era can begin" (224).
18. G.E. Gerbrandt, Kingship According to the Deuteronistic (sic) History (Atlanta, Georgia: Scholars Press, 1986) 41;
19. Ibid. 43.
20. Ibid. 99; cf. 191; 194: "Rather, according to the Deuteronomist, the political success or failure of a king was entirely dependent upon the degree to which Israel obeyed the covenant. Political success could thus only be achieved by a king thorough fulfilling his responsibility as covenant administrator."
21. S. Talmon, King, Cult and Calendar in Ancient Israel (Jerusalem: Magnes Press, 1986) 11; cf. 12-13.
22. Ibid. 14.
23. C. Stuhlmueller, in Part I of The Biblical Foundations For Mission, 22: "The key phrase, linking Moses with David, turns out to be 'the spirit of the Lord', the divine force by which extraordinary acts were accomplished. This <u>charismatic spirit</u>, by which God broke into human life, formed a key element of Mosaic religion" (author's emphasis).
24. W. Brueggemann, The Land, 79: "Neither the king nor anyone else is permitted to take the land of covenant and turn it into absolute, royal space." By failing badly in that respect, "Solomon creates a situation not unlike that of Pharaoh" (86). Cf. L. Epsztein, Social Justice in the A.N.E., 104-108 on the Israelite king as an upholder of the social laws and hence of social justice.
25. Cf. R. North, "The Trauma of King Saul", in The Bible Today, 1967, 2048-2059.
26. Cf. D. McCarthy, Institution and Narrative, 127-134.
27. Ibid. 132.

28. J. Bright, Covenant and Promise, 53: "In bringing it [ark of the covenant] to Jerusalem, David made that city the religious, as well as the political, capital of his realm and, what is more, forged a link between the newly created state and Israel's ancient order which enabled him to advertise the state as the legitimate successor of the tribal league and the patron and protector of the sacred institutions of the past." Also 71: "But whatever their historical relationships may have been, it appears that in time the Davidic covenant came to be viewed, in some circles at least, as no less than a renewal and extension of the promises to Abraham." Cf. M. Newman, The People of the Covenant — From Moses to the Monarchy, in which he develops the hypothesis that around Jerusalem their covenant theology stressed the covenant with a priestly dynasty and then the Davidic dynasty, whereas in the north of Israel, the stress was on the (conditional) covenant between Yahweh and all the people.
29. R.P. Gordon, 1 & 2 Samuel — A Commentary (Exeter: Paternoster Press, 1986), 235-236. Cf. G. Gerbrandt, op.cit., p.158-160, where he points out that David gets 40 chapters and then all the kings after him only get 46 chapters between them. He also insists that the Nathan prophecy is at the centre of the David stories. Also, 173: "In David already the Mosaic law and the Davidic promise are combined. The Deuteronomist considers both to be effective within Israel."
30. Cf. F.C. Fensham, "The Covenant as Giving Expression to the Relationship Between Old and New Testament", in Tyndale Bulletin 22 (1971) 82-94, e.g.on concluding page: "These three covenants [of Abraham, Moses, David] have one important aspect in common, the promise by God to his people or to His elected favourites."
31. W. Brueggemann, op.cit., 72: "The second history of Israel is the history on the other side of the Jordan. It is the history of <u>landed Israel in the process of losing the land</u>" (author's emphasis). 79-88 considers the ways in which Solomon was trying to "domesticate God" and hence "the God of the Temple is subordinated to the royal regime" (87). Cf. D. McCarthy, Kings and Prophets (Milwaukee: Bruce, 1968) 31, on Solomon's heavy taxes and corvée. Cf. S. Talmon, op.cit., 27.
32. Cf. J. Coert Rylaardsam, "Jewish-Christian Relationships: The Two Covenants and the Dilemmas of Christology", in J. I. Cook (Ed.) Grace Upon Grace (Essays in Honor of L.J. Kuyper) (Grand Rapids: W. Eerdmans, 1975), where he finds the Davidic covenant obscuring some of the freedom and responsibility evoked by the Sinai covenant and the Torah (78). However, 81: "In the story of the meeting of the two covenants, the so-called reformation of king Josiah must count as a major reassertion of the perspective of the Davidic dynasty and of Zion and its temple by giving

them a setting in the historically and communally oriented traditions of Shechem."
33. R.E. Brown, The Birth of the Messiah — A Commentary on the Infancy Narratives in Matthew and Luke (New York: Image Books, Doubleday, 1979) 83, where he also mentions that the Jechoniah of Mt's genealogy would have been the grandson of good king Josiah.

CHAPTER 6: COVENANT IN PRE-EXILIC PROPHETS

INTRODUCTION

The Jews refer to the books containing the Deuteronomic history as the "Former Prophets", whereas they speak of the "Latter Prophets" to designate the books of the prophets we are about to consider. We have already seen something of the way prophets helped to charter and evaluate the history of Israel until the time of the Babylonian exile. Now we are better prepared to grasp the enormous task entrusted to the "Latter Prophets", those prophets whose powerful preaching has come down to us in the books which bear their names.

Our word prophet comes from the Greek word **prophetes**, meaning one who speaks for/ on behalf of (somebody). This was used to translate the Hebrew word **nabi'**, one called or calling out [enthused]. These prophets, therefore, were spokesmen called by Yahweh to guide Israel in many of its most critical situations, and to assess publicly, in God's name, what was happening to the nation. Their primary charism was to preach the word of God as faithful heralds, nevertheless from the time of Amos onward the prophetic oracles were also written down. These were gradually collected and edited to form impressive literary works, generally in poetic form[1]. God's all-pervading word made such an impact on the prophets' own understanding of creation and salvation history that they were inspired to express it to the nation in poetry. To relish their message — which is also God's — we need to read it, listen to it, meditate on it as poetry. They certainly offer us a great deal of theology, discourse about God, but in poetic discourse, not dull classroom notes.

The content of their preaching was usually related directly to the situation of their people, with the result that it ranges over an enormous field. It often recalls the past interventions of Yahweh that shaped Israel, it evaluates a current situation in the light of God's gifts and demands, frequently denouncing infidelities, but also making known more good news. It also arouses the nation to keep moving forward towards the more perfect fulfilment of God's great promises with regard to its destiny and universal mission. A helpful summary of the teaching of the prophets can be found in The New Jerusalem Bible under the headings of (i) monotheism, (ii) morality, and (iii) future salvation [including messianism][2].

A fine outline of "the cardinal points of the content" is given by L. Alonso Schökel & J. Sicre under these headings:
a) The oracle as instruction, norm or concrete disposition;
b) the oracle as an interpretation of historical events;
c) the oracle as accusation and condemnation;
d) the oracle as promise[3]. What is particularly striking for our own theme is that explicit mention is made of the covenant in explaining three out of four of those cardinal points. In short, the oracles actualize the precepts, the blessings and the curses of the covenant. Although b) is not linked here explicitly to the

covenant, it could well be, since the prophets did interpret history partly in the light of the exodus and Sinai events. Added light came from the earlier patriarchal promises and the later messianic promises, as well as from God's unfathomable goodness and wisdom that kept springing surprises. For "for my thoughts are not your thoughts, and my ways are not your ways, declares Yahweh" (Is 55,8).

The period during which such prophets and their groups of writing disciples were active extended from about 750 to 400 B.C., with a few works like Deutero-Zechariah (cc.9-14) and Daniel being still later. The destruction of Jerusalem in 587 B.C. and the Exile in Babylon had so many repercussions that it is normal to speak of pre-exilic and post-exilic prophets. This chapter will take up the pre-exilic prophets, leaving the next chapter for exilic and post-exilic prophets. To make it easier to view each prophet against his particular international background, we shall treat of them in four groups according to which of the four empires was dominant in their day:
— the Assyrian Empire (c. 880 - 612 B.C.); an exile to Nineveh;
— the Babylonian Empire (612 - 539 B.C.); the exile to Babylon;
— the Persian Empire (539 - 331 B.C.); return from exile;
— the Greek Empire (-s) (331 - 63 B.C.).

Given that the covenant has exercised a considerable influence on the prophets in their assessment of fidelity towards Yahweh and conduct towards the neighbour, we cannot attempt to dwell on every text which shows some evidence of this. We will take up only the most outstanding examples in some prophets of each of the periods mentioned above. The aim is not to prove that prophets were interested in the covenants granted through Abraham, Moses and David. It is rather to seek new insights into the whole nature of those covenants and their meaning as perceived by new generations in Israel — or in exile. We also wish to catch something of the special features of the new covenant which several prophets announced with fervent hope in the wake of a badly broken Mosaic covenant.

A. DURING THE ASSYRIAN EMPIRE

1. AMOS (IN THE NORTHERN KINGDOM)

"Yahweh roars from Zion and makes himself heard from Jerusalem" (Amos 1,2). These words serve as a fitting introduction to the first of all those prophets whose own words have continued ever since to make Yahweh's roar reverberate around Israel and later right around the world. Amos was a shepherd from Tekoa near Bethlehem when Yahweh took him from his flock, saying, "Go and prophesy to my people Israel" (7,15). The reaction of Amos and his acceptance of the commission finds an echo in his comment: "The lion roars: who is not afraid? Lord Yahweh has spoken: who will not prophesy?" (3,8).

Two features of the lion's roar strike us in the opening chapters (1-2), first that Yahweh roars out against several non-Israelites nations for their brutal injustices against other peoples. Then within "Israel"(= northern kingdom) the roar is against social injustice and heartlessness towards the poor, "because they have sold the upright for silver and the poor for a pair of sandals" (2,6). Amos makes quite clear how repugnant is the enslavement of the conquered and the impoverished, above all among the Israelites whom Yahweh had set free from slavery in Egypt[4].

Cc. 3-6 then concentrate on "Israel", recalling at the start its standing as Yahweh's special family "which I brought up from Egypt: You alone have I intimately known of all the families of earth, that is why I shall punish you for all your wrong-doings" (3,1-2). What stand out as their worst sins are: the luxury of the rich which makes them increasingly heartless towards the poor; the prevalence of social injustice and a breakdown of public justice, because the judges are corrupted by bribes; empty, merely external cultic religious observances, giving rise to a false security that these guarantee divine protection. Amos announces in strong rural imagery the terminal disaster that will come upon the kingdom because of its corruption and obstinacy in the face of repeated warnings. Like a refrain rings out the reproach, "and still you would not come back to me" (4,6.8.9.10.11). The climax is powerful after recalling so much resistance: "Israel, prepare to meet your God!" (4,12).

Commenting on this poem, B. Anderson writes: "In this case, Amos was not speaking to the larger problem of natural evils that engulf all peoples but, specifically, to Israel's failure in her covenant responsibility"[5]. For their part, Alonso Schökel and Sicre suggest that we also move on to the alternative offered in 5,4.6: "Seek out Yahweh and you will survive". This would correspond to the option offered by Moses: "I am offering you life or death, blessing or curse" (Dt 30,19)[6]. In other words, the dire threats of punishment are given as yet one more appeal for a change of heart, without which "Israel" cannot escape the punishment. Invasion, destruction, and deportation are threatened. In that case, only a remnant will survive, and that after unspeakable sufferings, e.g. "Seek good and not evil so that you may survive .. Hate evil, love good, let justice reign at the city gate: it may be that Yahweh, God Sabaoth, will take pity on the remnant of Joseph" (5,14-15). It is expressed more vividly in 3,12: "As the shepherd rescues two legs or the tip of an ear from the lion's mouth, so will the children of Israel be salvaged."

Cc.5 - 6 amplify what it will mean for the heartless rich to meet their God. Amos is the first prophet to speak of "the Day of the Lord", a day of reckoning. Far from vindicating those living in luxury, worshipping Mammon rather than Yahweh in their palaces "crammed with violence and extortion" (3,10)[7], that Day "will mean darkness, not light" (5,18). "On that day .. I shall turn your festivals into mourning .. and it shall end like the bitterest of days" (8,9-10). However, it will not be a Day without hope of a new beginning for the poor and the enslaved, because the corrupt Israelites responsible for much of their misery will be uprooted, killed or deported — "they will now go into captivity, heading the column of captives. The sprawlers' revelry is over" (6,7).

Cc.7 - 9 record five visions of Amos which also announce the proximate judgment and punishment of "all the sinners of my people" (9,10). The visions are interconnected, progressing from threats of locusts and drought, which Amos averts by his intercession, to visions in which Yahweh declares: "The time is ripe for my people Israel; I will not continue to overlook their offences" (8,2). After the third vision, which depicts the destruction of the northern sanctuaries and even the House of Jeroboam II, there comes a short account of the confrontation of Amos with Amaziah, the priest of the royal sanctuary of Bethel. Amaziah tells Amos to go back home to Judah, as he was now forbidden to preach any more around Bethel. In defiance of such a ban, Amos went on to forewarn of disaster and exile for Amaziah himself (7,10-17). The visions are followed by a few verses, probably from a later century, which promise restoration for "the tottering hut of David" and for "the fortunes of my people Israel" (9,ll.14).

To what extent did Amos draw on the covenant in his preaching? He never used the word covenant in addressing Israel, so we need to look more closely to discern the implicit allusions to the Mosaic covenant. Yahweh does refer to Israel as the special "family" which he brought up from Egypt (3,2; 9,7), and which spent forty years in the desert (5,25). Several times Yahweh calls them "my people" (7,8.15; 8,2; 9,7), and once alerts them, "Israel, prepare to meet your God" (4,12). The kind of solidarity, compassion and concern for all their fellow-Israelites which Amos expects of the well-to-do, as well as justice and uprightness, would be quite in line with the demands of covenant **hesed**. At the same time, several other influences would have accompanied that of the basic covenant, especially the wisdom and ancient legal traditions of Israel, plus the personal experience and rural values of Amos himself[8]. An important aspect stressed by Amos is that injustice, causing the re-enslavement of Israelites, had become institutionalized. That free choice taken by the oppressors was nothing less than opting for their own destruction, as well as the ongoing misery of their victims, the "upright" and the "poor"[9]. In our own day we should do our utmost to ensure that the lion's roar continues to reverberate around the world, for never have so many teeming millions of God's family been held in misery because a heartless minority live "secure" in modern "castles" crammed with luxuries enjoyed at the cost of their undernourished brothers and sisters.

2. HOSEA (IN THE NORTHERN KINGDOM)

Unlike Amos, Hosea, son of Beeri, was a native of the northern kingdom, whose king he referred to as "our king" (7,5). The only information we have about his personal life concerns his troubled marriage with Gomer, who bore him two sons and a daughter but abandoned him to live as a prostitute. With incredible love Hosea sought her out, redeemed her from her clients, and renewed their married life (cc.1-3). That much is made known, because it colours his entire message concerning the kind of union forged between Yahweh and Israel. If Amos is outstanding for his ringing denunciations of infidelity towards the neighbour, Hosea is remarkable for his condemnation of infidelity to Yahweh as the violation of a covenant of love. Hosea opened the way to describe that union as a marriage, so that infidelities are strongly denounced as adultery and prostitution.

Hosea could have begun his prophetic ministry in "Israel" while Amos was still active there, but Hosea continued on until only a few years prior to the destruction of Samaria by the Assyrians in 721 B.C. It is noteworthy that the book sets his ministry within the reigns of four kings of Judah, while mentioning only Jeroboam of "Israel" (1,1). This could well indicate that the book reached its final form around Jerusalem, after Samaria had been wiped out despite all the warnings of Amos and Hosea. It would seem that after the death of Jeroboam II, conditions deteriorated rapidly as the rattling of Assyrian chariots and swords grew ever more threatening for Samaria. Amos was the last voice to re-echo Yahweh's invitation to renew their covenant of love or be swept away as "not my people" (1,9). "Israel begins to pass out of existence .. into the nothingness from which God first drew her"[10]. In some ways the story of the adulterous wife is even more moving, because more revealing of Yahweh's tenacious, pursuing love, than the parable of the prodigal son (Lk 15,11-32). In any case, Hosea also anticipates that analogy in ch.11.

We do find explicit mention of covenant in later chapters of Hosea, both to do with Israel's breaking of the covenant: "But they have broken the covenant at Adam, there they have betrayed me" (6,7). Again: "Because they have violated my covenant and been unfaithful to my Law, in vain will they cry, 'My God'" (8,1-2). That the relationship between Yahweh and Israel is like a marriage can also be seen in the warning: "No merrymaking, Israel, for you, .. for you have deserted your God to play the whore. .. No more will they live in Yahweh's country; Ephraim will have to go back to Egypt and eat polluted food in Assyria" (9,1-3). We can therefore accept as beyond doubt that Hosea intended to depict his own marriage as a symbol of the covenant between Yahweh and Israel (cc.1-3). In that way the story of Hosea and Gomer was able to become the classic allegory of covenant love, estrangement and reconciliation.

On looking closely at cc.1-3, commentators have found that the text as we have it has been carefully arranged in a chiastic pattern, that is A-B-C - C-B-A, as follows:

A = 1,2-9 and 3,1-5 : the marriage of Hosea and Gomer;
B = 2,1-3 and 2,18-25 : the 3 children and their names;
C = 2,4-17 : the faithless wife as symbol of the people[11].

A: The opening words come as a shock, and yet they prove to be an apt prologue to the entire work of Hosea: "The beginning of what Yahweh said through Hosea: Yahweh said to Hosea, 'Go, marry a whore, and get children with a whore; for the country itself has become nothing but a whore by abandoning Yahweh' (1,2). We do not know for sure whether Gomer was already a prostitute when Hosea married her. The ominous names given to their three children certainly emphasise a grave crisis in relations between Yahweh and "Israel". The first son is named Jezreel, as a sign that God will "punish the House of Jehu for the bloodshed at Jezreel" (1,4). The daughter is named Lo-Ruhamah, for Yahweh says "I shall show no more pity for the House of Israel" (1,6). The youngest son has to be given the very disturbing name of Lo-Ammi, "for you are not my people and I do not exist for you" (1,9). So instead of continuing for them as "I am he who is" (Ex 3,14), Yahweh "is not". It is as though they now know nothing of Moses, nor the exodus, nor the covenant that welded them into Yahweh's people[12].

B: Immediately there comes a short oracle promising numerical growth similar to the patriarchal promises, a reunion of "Israel" and Judah under a single head (presumably of the line of David), and a reversal of the children's names: "Then call your brothers, 'My people', and your sisters, 'You have been pitied' (2,3). This has the ring of a redactor about it, because some of the points seem to go beyond the normal concerns expressed by Hosea. However, it has been well woven in to the chiastic pattern of the whole section. It matches the counterpart that is more obviously from Hosea, which we will look at shortly.

C: This central section really is the heart of what Hosea is proclaiming. "Here we come to the finest page of Hosea, to one of the great poems of the O.T. A poem of unrequited love living on in spite of all.."[13]. This poem opens like a lawsuit at court[14], and it is soon obvious that the one laying the charge against the adulterous mother is Yahweh, who states the case for divorce: "For she is no longer my wife nor am I her husband" (2,4). He recalls how she has disgraced herself by chasing after her lovers, for the sake of wool, flax, oil, drinks, etc.(2,7). Because of all her infidelity, Yahweh says, "I will block her way with thorns, and wall her in to stop her in her tracks" (2,8). This is not for spite or revenge. On the contrary, it is precisely to bring her to decide for herself, "I shall go back to my first husband, I was better off then than I am now" (2,9).

To make the most of her half-hearted return, Yahweh exclaims: "But look, I am going to seduce her and lead her into the desert and speak to her heart. .. There she will respond as when she was young, as on the day when she came up from Egypt" (2,16-17). We need only recall how Israel went from Egypt through the desert to Sinai to catch the overtones of what that "first love" entailed by way of covenant commitment. Then they were also tested by about forty years wandering in the desert, very dependent on Yahweh for their survival until they were led safely into the Land. Her response, therefore, will be positive, making possible a new beginning of mutual love.

B: The poem continues on by foretelling the outcome of that desert renewal: "When that day comes — declares Yahweh — you will call me 'My husband'" (2,18). After promising a pact of peace with all nature, and security from her enemies, Yahweh also promises his returned wife, "I shall betroth you to myself for ever, I shall betroth you in uprightness and justice, and faithful love and tenderness. Yes, I shall betroth you to myself in loyalty and in the knowledge of Yahweh" (2,21-22). These qualities of the restored conjugal love — justice, love, fidelity, a convincing knowledge/acknowledgement of God[15]

— are to be shared by both partners. Obviously they will have to be bestowed by Yahweh on the bride whose previous conduct was so lacking in them all. Moreover, the wife's children will need and hence receive them, too, so that the demands of the covenant will be met in daily dealings with one another, as well as with Yahweh. This much is implied by the closing lines of the poem: "I shall take pity on Lo-Ruhamah, I shall tell Lo-Ammi, 'You are my people', and he will say, 'You are my God'" (2,25). With those closing words Hosea gives a simple formula that is frequently used to sum up the covenant relationship between God and the people.

A: This ch.3 appears at first glance to be either a doublet of the first account of Hosea's marriage to a prostitute, or an account of another breakdown in the marriage after its renewal. In fact it is a matter of completing the literary construction, hence this last section is meant to correspond to the first one. What the author does, therefore, is make quite plain the symbolism of the human couple in relation to Yahweh and Israel[16]. Hosea is told to go and love an adulteress "as Yahweh loves the Israelites although they turn to other gods and love raisin cakes" (3,1). Obediently Hosea redeems Gomer and sets her a "long time" of probation, during which there must be no more prostitution — "for the Israelites will have to spend a long time without king or leader" (3,4).

The kingship in "Israel" had become indistinguishable from that of "other nations". J. Sicre has drawn attention to the way those kings had ceased entirely to rely on Yahweh and so looked to other kings to save them. At times it would be Egypt, at other times Assyria, so that those powers were really idols replacing Yahweh[17]. Such a monarchy, Hosea insisted, had to go, together with the worship of the golden calves in Bethel and Dan, as well as the widespread orgiastic rites miming Baal and goddesses of fertility. Those rites were supposed to ensure fertility of the fields, the flocks, the gardens, and of the Israelites themselves. Well might Yahweh protest concerning his faithless bride, "she had never realised before that I was the one who was giving her the grain, new wine and oil" (2,10). We can see in this example an added reason why Yahweh longs to share with Israel something of the marriage dowry mentioned above — loving concern and loyalty towards the partner and towards other Israelites. So often people turn to false gods in the hope of getting from them their daily bread and other necessities of life. When the people of God are without loving kindness, many act as though God has lost credibility.

The remainder of the book, cc.4-14, contain a large collection of oracles, with the emphasis still on the infidelities of "Israel" and the punishment that they are about to bring down on their whole kingdom. It opens fittingly with another lawsuit in which "Yahweh indicts the citizens of the country: there is no loyalty, no faithful love, no knowledge of God in the country" (4,1). That short section (vv.1-3) accuses the nation of having broken most of the ten commandments, with "bloodshed after bloodshed". For Hosea, those crimes are so many manifestations of the fundamental lack of covenant love, of **hesed**.

He reiterates the primacy of that loyal love when the Israelites say that they would like to come back and be healed. Yahweh declares that their love is as fickle as the morning mist. He demands something much more stable: "for faithful love is what pleases me, not sacrifice; knowledge of God, not burnt offerings" (6,6). That is such a striking resumé of Yahweh's mind that Jesus quotes it twice to defend his disciples against the Pharisees (Mt 9,13; 12,7).

We cannot leave Hosea without reflecting briefly on the second high point of his poetic description of Yahweh's own unquenchable love for the people no matter how poor their response. This time Israel is represented not as a bride but as a child. The poem commences: "When Israel was a child I loved him, and I called my son out of Egypt." Yahweh fondly taught Israel how to walk, how to eat, and how to experience parental affection. Because that child has become so deaf and impervious to God, he will be devoured by Assyria. That is the punishment such an obstinately rebellious son deserves, and yet it hurts Yahweh to contemplate it: "Ephraim, how could I part with you? Israel, how could I give you up? My heart within me is overwhelmed.. I will not give rein to my fierce anger, I will not destroy Ephraim again, for I am God, not man" (11,8-9). Those words give some indication of the enormous difference between the divine covenant and the contemporary international treaties. God retains full liberty to exercise love and seek a response in ways that go far beyond any human treaties. The use of covenant language is likewise a faltering effort to express a boundless love which seeks a wholehearted human response.

3. MICAH (IN THE SOUTHERN KINGDOM)

Micah was a prophet from Moresheth, south of Jerusalem and not very far from the home town of Amos. Judging from the kings mentioned in the introduction to the book, as well as from various events touched on later, Micah was active around Jerusalem from about 730-700 B.C. He was therefore a contemporary of Hosea for a short time, and of the great Isaiah in Jerusalem during all those years. He preached to the civil and religious leaders there a stinging condemnation of their cruel oppression of the poor, in fact he is ranked as one of the greatest champions of social justice among the prophets[18]. No other prophet goes so far in identifying the political and religious leaders guilty of oppressing and killing their own people, the "community of Yahweh" (2,5). The book alternates between threats of dire punishment for such injustices and promises of salvation, at least for a remnant. Some commentators think it likely that cc. 6-7 are due to a different author or editor than cc.1-5[19]. In both sections, however, the covenant can be discerned as a common denominator[20].

Although Micah does not mention covenant explicitly, his public denunciations of all the leaders and the powerful of Jerusalem presuppose that they were violating well known laws of Yahweh. In this vein are the words of God which conclude the whole first section: "In furious anger I shall wreak vengeance on the nations that have disobeyed me" (5,14). The second section is famous for its summary of Yahweh's demands: "Only this, to do what is right, to love loyalty (**hesed**) and to walk humbly with your God" (6,8). "Loyalty" certainly includes covenant loyalty, as we have seen more explicitly brought out in Hosea[21]. A further hint of this is given in the denunciation: "<u>The faithful have vanished from the land</u>: there is no one honest left. All of them are on the alert for blood, <u>every man hunting his brother</u> with a net" (7,2).

We shall limit our reflection now to cc. 2-3, which contain the strongest condemnation of social injustices in Jerusalem, that city of David on Mount Sion, where Yahweh's unique Temple stood. Ch. 2 announces disaster for the greedy landlords who lie awake plotting evil, then at dawn hurry off to carry out their plans, "since they have the power to do so" (2,1). That is another way of saying that they are shrewd in avoiding any clash with the local authorities. The laws and structures permit them to seize fields, houses, and the owner as well (2,2). But Yahweh is one authority that cannot be bribed, so "this breed" will lose everything when "my people's land has been divided up" (2,4). This is in line with the spirit of the Jubilee (Lev 25) and of Yahweh's enduring ownership of the land as in the Deuteronomic writings. In the new distribution it will be the dispossessed who will once again receive the land as their rightful heritage.

Next comes a denunciation of the cheap prophets who think that only favourable things can be prophesied for God's people. Micah replies that de facto such prophets and the oppressors they encourage are "the enemy to my people" (2,8). So not everybody in Jerusalem continues to belong automatically to God's people; grave injustices against other citizens suffice to exclude the offenders. They are snatching away the innocent man's cloak, evicting women from their homes, and depriving children of their God-given "glory" of being free children of Israel. To reduce the parents to homeless slaves involves their children also in ongoing slavery.

The chapter closes with a contrasting promise of restoration of "the remnant of Israel" (2,12), once again with a (good) king leading the way "and with Yahweh at their head". Then ch. 3 returns with greater vehemence to denounce those political and religious leaders responsible for oppressing their own people, instead of defending them against such blatant and even legalized injustice. To the "leaders" and "princes of the House of Israel" he says, "Surely you are the ones who ought to know what is right, and yet you hate what is good and love what is evil, skinning people alive, pulling the flesh off their bones, eating my people's flesh, stripping off their skin, breaking up their bones" (3,2-3). That gives a vivid picture of the oppressing princes and of their terribly maltreated victims, with whom Micah expresses his solidarity by calling them "my people"

Again, Micah confronts the prophets "who lead my people astray" (3,5), because they proclaim "peace" to anybody who will feed them. For being so mercenary they will be reduced to shame, confusion, and silence. "The sun will set for the prophets, and daylight will go black above them" (3,6). On the other hand, declares Micah, "Not so with me, I am full of strength (full of Yahweh's spirit), of the sense of right, of energy to accuse Jacob of his crime"

(3,8). Something of his energy to accuse is then unleashed against the leaders and princes "who detest justice, wresting it from its honest course, who build Zion with blood, and Jerusalem with iniquity" (3,9-10). The country prophet is far from overawed by the imposing buildings of Jerusalem nor its prosperous commercial zones. The cost has been the sacrifice of many lives and the dehumanizing of far too many survivors. That city which killed the prophets sent to it (and taunted Micah himself for talking "drivel" - 2,6) is here indicted for killing a great many humble citizens as well.

The very ones who should have protected the lives and dignity of Yahweh's people had opted for Mammon instead[22]. "Her leaders give verdicts for presents, her priests take a fee for their rulings, her prophets divine for money and yet they rely on Yahweh! 'Isn't Yahweh among us?' they say, 'No disaster is going to overtake us'" (3,11). Such a twisting of the promises associated with Yahweh's special presence to Israel and to worshippers on Zion had become, in Sicre's phrase, "a theology of oppression"[23]. Micah, however, cut right through that false confidence and despicable justification of injustice as though protected by Yahweh, the God of incorruptible justice, the Liberator of Israel from its slavery due to Egyptian injustice. In chilling words he conveys Yahweh's sentence upon them, and, sadly, upon the whole city sheltering such thoroughly institutionalized injustice: "That is why, thanks to you, Zion will become a ploughland, Jerusalem a heap of rubble and the Temple Mount a wooded height" (3,12).

There are good grounds for seeing in the term "a wooded height" another allusion to those "high places" where the worship was all too often idolatrous in some way. The same sentiment was expressed in the Hebrew text of 1,5: "What is the high place (**bamoth**) of Judah? Is it not Jerusalem?" That sort of talk would have sounded blasphemous to many of the city dwellers. Nonetheless, his scathing denunciations did help to bring a change of heart, so that the city was spared from the Assyrians. Micah's example was used in an effort to save the life of Jeremiah a century later when he prophesied that the Temple and Jerusalem would be wiped out (Jer 26).

A kind of corollary to the corruption of the princes of Jerusalem can be seen in cc. 4-5, which foretell that salvation will come for a remnant and the sovereignty will return to Jerusalem(ch.4). However, "a future ruler of Israel" will come, not from Jerusalem, but from lowly Bethlehem of Ephrathah (ch.5). The mention of a ruler from David's home town is a further indication of the way the Davidic covenant continued to provide a ray of hope.

4. ISAIAH (IN THE SOUTHERN KINGDOM)

Isaiah is regarded as the prince of the prophets because of both the content and the poetic expression of his oracles. As mentioned earlier, he was active in Jerusalem during all the ministry there of Micah. Whereas Micah was from the country and a relentless critic of the capital city's corrupt leaders, Isaiah gives the impression of being thoroughly at home in that city. We know that he received his prophetic mission in the Temple (ch.6), and that he could speak easily to kings (ch.7). His prophetic activity extended over the reigns of four kings of Judah and lasted nearly forty years (about 740 - 700 B.C.). During that time Samaria was destroyed by the Assyrians, and Isaiah by his wise counsels helped to save Jerusalem from a similar fate at the hands of Sennacherib in 701 B.C.

Isaiah speaks of having "disciples" in whose hearts his testimony and instruction were to be sealed up (8,16). No doubt some of them played a considerable part in collecting and editing his oracles, some of which he himself would have written down (30,8). Gradually other oracles from exilic and postexilic prophets were joined on to those of Isaiah. In our treatment we follow the generally accepted divisions of Isaiah (cc.1-39), Deutero-Isaiah (40-55), and Trito-Isaiah (56-66). Here we limit ourselves to the first part of Isaiah. Admittedly he does not use the word covenant except when speaking of a sinful treaty with death or with Egypt (28,18; 30,1-5). He certainly does recall relationships that are due to the Sinai covenant, as well as plenty more that are based on the Davidic covenant. F. Moriarty points to them as important factors for Isaiah: "To these [greed, hypocrisy and injustice] should be added the national loss of nerve that led its rulers to seek an accommodation with Assyria and her gods, thus undermining the very foundation of Judah's existence as a covenanted people." Some were "interpreting the covenant with David as a guarantee of absolute invincibility no matter what crimes were committed against Yahweh.."[24].

The first twelve chapters consist mainly of oracles given before the destruction of Samaria, hence during the early years of Isaiah's prophetic ministry. He displays a great concern for social justice, parallel with and influenced by the same concern of Amos proclaimed in the northern kingdom[25]. The remaining cc.13-39 manifest greater concern for political situations, at a time when the "super powers", Assyria and Egypt, pressured Judah to act as though Yahweh had ceased to be a power any more[26]. It is noteworthy that the famous "Immanuel" prophecies are found in the first section, in cc.6-12. For Isaiah (and the redactors), if the crippling social injustices were to be remedied, Jerusalem would have to have an exemplary Davidic king dedicated to justice. Hence he promises a worthy successor to David rather than to Moses. In any case, the predominant concern of Isaiah at all times is thrice-holy Yahweh Sabaoth, so majestic, so powerful, so renowned for the saving justice to overcome human injustice, so completely in control of Israel and all other nations.

The opening chapter immediately recalls two of the images used by Hosea when appealing for a return to covenant loyalty, namely those of the child and the bride. His first prophecy has Yahweh protesting, "I have reared children and brought them up, but they have rebelled against me. .. They have abandoned Yahweh, despised the Holy One of Israel" (1,2-4). Then in a lament for Jerusalem: "The faithful city, what a harlot she has become! Zion, once full of fair judgement, where saving justice used to dwell, but now assassins!"(1,21). The assassins are none other than the "princes" who are so greedy for bribes that "they show no justice to the orphan, and the widow's cause never reaches them" (1,23). That Isaiah accepted Deuteronomy's option of "life or death" can be seen in the closing line of that lament: "Rebels and sinners alike will be destroyed, and those who abandon Yahweh will perish" (1,28).

Ch. 3 has Yahweh accusing "the elders and princes of his people: "You are the ones who have ravaged the vineyard, the spoils of the poor are in your houses. By what right do you crush my people and grind the faces of the poor?" (vv.14-15). The two phrases underlined form a synonymous parallel, that is, "my people" is parallel to its equivalent, "the faces of the poor". This marks an important step towards the linking of the crushed poor with God, so that "the poor of Yahweh" are practically identified with "the people of Yahweh". Membership depends, in the view of Isaiah, on justice and compassion towards the poor, not merely on race or royal blood[27]. Further evidence of this comes in his threatened punishment of the proud and pompous women of Jerusalem with their "gorgeous clothes" and "jingling bangles". They will finish up with rope and sacking around the waist, and "brand marks instead of beauty" (3,16-24). Because of war ravages upon Zion's men, the once proud women will be desperate to find even one man to take away their disgrace of being childless (3,25-4,1). Disaster will be followed by the emergence of a purified remnant, after the Lord has "cleansed Jerusalem of the blood shed in her" (4,5).

In the beautiful "song of my friend for his vineyard", Isaiah describes how his "beloved had a vineyard", planted it with good vines, and yet found only sour grapes (5,1-2). The Beloved then enters to demand (through the mouth of his friend, the prophet) that the people judge "between me and my vineyard". He challenges them: "What more could I have done for my vineyard that I have not done? (5,3-4). Having done so much "for the plant he cherished", "he expected fair judgment, but found injustice, uprightness, but found cries of distress" (3,7). Once again we see the inescapable demand for personal justice and genuine public justice, properly upheld by all the institutions of the kingdom. It is important to recall here the purpose of these frequent "lawsuits" or "juridical controversies" to which Yahweh summons Israel.

P. Bovati shows clearly that their aim was above all to move the accused party to admit their failures before God, to repent and be reconciled, committing themselves thereby to live up to their obligations from then on. If God had to use threats of punishment in order to convince Israel that injustice was totally unacceptable, the purpose was still to achieve a change of heart, forgiveness and reconciliation. That puts this kind of "lawsuit" firmly within the wider context of covenant relationship. "If pardon is granted, it supposes that it is possible now to respect the word which binds both parties" (author's emphasis)[28].

As if to emphasise the kind of punishment that Yahweh has in mind to end the injustices and so bring relief to the victims, six woes are given. The first woe threatens those accumulating houses and fields so greedily that they will be the only citizens left in the country. All those deprived of fields, houses, and finally of their freedom, will have lost their rights as citizens to participate in public affairs. "In modern terms, Isaiah denounces the accumulation of capital in a few hands, while for the majority nothing is left but their work [with no right to participate in political life]"[29]. So Yahweh has sworn that "many houses will be brought to ruin". Connected with the accumulation of lands could be the hint of a later redistribution, "once the Holy One has displayed his holiness by his justice" (5,16): "Now the lambs will graze in their old pastures, and the fields laid waste by fat cattle will feed the kids" (5,17)[30]. The sixth woe threatens those wine bibbers "who acquit the guilty for a bribe and deny justice to the upright". They and their progeny will disappear "for having rejected the law of Yahweh Sabaoth" (5,24). This kind of woe comes close to saying that Yahweh cannot but impose some sanctions similar to those expressed in the covenant curses of Deuteronomy. To "reject the law of Yahweh" is to declare unilaterally that the covenant is finished.

The call of Isaiah is dated "in the year of King Uzziah's death". After experiencing the opening vision, which filled him with a profound sense of Yahweh's holiness and his own sinfulness, he exclaimed, "Woe is me! I am lost, for ... my eyes have seen the King, Yahweh Sabaoth" (6,5). It is obvious that his call left an indelible impression on his mind, because the holiness of Yahweh and the importance of the Lord as King "seated on a high and lofty throne" (6,1) colour all his prophecies. It must be kept in mind also by us in order to appreciate the role he attributes to the kings of David's faltering dynasty. King Yahweh will honour his promissory covenant with his human viceroy David, for through a good king will be established a kingdom of justice and peace. The whole call and commission of Isaiah therefore forms a fitting threshold to the Immanuel prophecies in cc.7-12.

Our consideration of them here has to be limited to a few of the most striking aspects relevant to the development of major covenant concerns. The prominence given to a Davidic child as the great source of hope and ultimate transformation of Israel has served ever since as a fertile seed-bed of messianic thought. The reign of Yahweh will be accepted voluntarily within human hearts and within the people of God through the inspired leadership of a mysterious Immanuel, "God-with-us". Immanuel therefore takes Israel forward to a new king "after the heart of God", rather than back to a simple renewal of the Mosaic covenant. There is a great stretching forward to God's time and ways of fulfilling such marvellously rich promises that no historic successor to David seems to have satisfied, at least not until the birth of Jesus in the humble town of David.

The first mention of Immanuel was made to Achaz, a king not very interested in receiving any sign from God. Isaiah told him plainly: "Listen now, House of David: .... The Lord will give you a sign in any case: It is this: the young woman is with child and will give birth to a son whom she will call Immanuel" (7,13-14). The occasion of the sign was to reassure Achaz that the threats of Samaria and Damascus against Jerusalem would come to nought. The House of David would not be toppled and wiped out by them. The short term fulfilment of that promise could have been the birth of a son, Ezechias, to

Achaz and his wife. Promises concerning prosperous times "such as have not been seen since Ephraim broke away from Judah" (7,17) remain open to a more perfect fulfilment later on.

Ch. 8 mentions that Isaiah and his wife, a prophetess, had another child with a symbolic name chosen by Yahweh — the equivalent of "Speedy-spoil, quick-booty"[31]. The first son also had a symbolic name — "a-remnant-shall-return" (7,3), a name summing up the alternation of threats and promises throughout Isaiah's ministry. He could stand with confidence despite the deafness of his contemporaries, pointing to the living symbols of God's concern: "Look, I and the children whom Yahweh has given me shall become signs and portents in Israel on behalf of Yahweh Sabaoth who dwells on Mount Zion" (8,18). Isaiah could rightly include himself, since his own name was also symbolic, meaning "Salvation-of-the-Lord". The chapter also alludes to a sweeping Assyrian invasion of Judah, over "the whole extent of your land, Immanuel". However, that flood will be dissipated, "for God is with us" (8,8.10).

Ch. 9 opens with another vista of desolation wrought by the ruthless Assyrians on areas around the Lake of Galilee. Then comes new light for those who have walked in the shadow of death, with the promise of liberation. "For the yoke that weighed on it, the bar across its shoulders, the rod of its oppressor, these you have broken as on the day of Midian" (9,3). Once again, that dramatic change is linked to Immanuel: "For a son has been born for us, a son has been given to us .. and this is the name he has been given, 'Wonder-Counsellor, Mighty-God, Eternal-Father, Prince-of-Peace" (9,5). The rejoicing indirectly praises God, when it is understood that the son has been given, not just to a royal couple, but "to us", to the whole kingdom.

Each of the four names (also given by God) refers to an important responsibility of the king — to be truly a counsellor, a (mighty) warrior, a father and a prince. Moreover, each of these roles is linked with God by the word qualifying it: a marvellous (or miraculous) counsellor, a God-like (or divine) warrior; an eternal (or everlasting) father; and a prince (empowered to ensure an enduring reign) of peace[32]. Immanuel will at last "secure and sustain" full peace "in fair judgement and integrity" (9,6). That pair, judgement and justice, frequently appears in the O.T. as indispensable before Yahweh can grant lasting peace.

A seventh woe, perhaps originally following the other six woes given in ch.5, for it is similar, warns: "Woe to those who enact unjust decrees, who compose oppressive legislation to deny justice to the weak and to cheat the humblest of my people of fair judgement, to make widows their prey and to rob the orphan." Here Isaiah makes perfectly clear who are the principal victims of "unjust decrees" and "oppressive legislation". This pair, being in synonymous parallel, indicates that official injustice begets legalized oppression. The oppressed are named as "the weak", "the humblest of my people","the widows" and "the orphan". The woe speaks of "the day of punishment" coming, a disaster bringing destitution, captivity and death to such oppressors of the very ones for whom Yahweh demands most compassion and public justice.

A positive result of suffering disaster is mentioned towards the end of the chapter, for a remnant will be spared and will return, in keeping with the name of Isaiah's elder son. With this in view, "a destruction has been decreed which will make justice overflow" (10,22). This illustrates very well Yahweh's plan in pursuing the unjust until they renounce injustice or bring about national disaster. Then, once disaster has struck in the form of foreign invaders such as the Assyrians, Yahweh will be with his people to liberate a humble remnant. "When that day comes, his [Assyria's] burden will fall from your shoulder, and his yoke from your neck" (10,27). In other words, Yahweh remains always compassionate and ready to liberate Israel again from foreign oppressors as well as from the national ones.

Ch. 11 opens with a further poetic description of the new shoot from the root of David. "On him will rest the spirit of Yahweh", endowing him with the gifts most essential for a truly charismatic leader of Yahweh's people: wisdom and insight, counsel and power, knowledge and fear of Yahweh (11,2). Those are gifts which will help enormously to make the Davidic king's reign conform to Yahweh's own designs for it. In direct contrast to the oppressive legislators mentioned in the final woe (ch.10), this ideal king "will judge the weak with integrity and give fair sentence for the humblest in the land" (11,4). Not only will he defend the weak and the lowly, but he will "bring death to the wicked" (11,5). A king who breaks the power of the unjust and the oppressor forestalls the more drastic intervention of Yahweh through invaders to put an end to rank injustice. The messianic peace will even extend to all the re-establishment of harmony with nature (11,6-9).

The remainder of the chapter has added another later promise concerning the role of "the root of David" in the return of the scattered exiles. As in the exodus of old, Yahweh will watch over the journey of this "remnant" back to their homeland (11,16). Once again the two rival kingdoms, "Israel" and Judah, will be reconciled and collaborate against outside enemies. That is at least a small pointer to the practical demands of the covenant if Israel wants to retain the Land entrusted to it for the good of all the people. It was definitely not intended to be a place of injustice and oppression like Egypt all over again, nor a land where brothers try to destroy one another in civil wars.

The Immanuel cycle closes with a psalm praising Yahweh, with triple repetition of the salvation granted (this time in keeping with the name of Isaiah himself). The closing lines hint again at the significance of Immanuel for Jerusalem: "Cry and shout for joy, you who live in Zion, For the Holy One of Israel is among you in his greatness" (12,6).

Before leaving Isaiah we must draw attention to his profound observations concerning Judah's efforts to enter into an alliance with Egypt. The circumstances and the spirit with which that was being attempted was denounced by Isaiah as equivalent to idolatry[33] The woe threatened by Yahweh also presupposes the existence of a prior covenant relationship with him: "Woe to the rebellious children — declares Yahweh — who make plans which do not come from me and make alliances not inspired by me, and so add sin to sin! They are leaving for Egypt without consulting me, to take refuge in Pharaoh's protection, to shelter in Egypt's shadow" (30,1-2). The sinful rebellion evidently consists in deserting Yahweh as their saving ally, and hurrying off to seek "shelter" and "protection" from Pharaoh instead. Given the usual biblical understanding that God is Israel's refuge, "it becomes clear that this power has occupied the place of God, turning itself into an idol"[34].

This interpretation is confirmed by a further denunciation of the same thing in the following chapter: "Woe to those going down to Egypt for help, who put their trust in horses, who rely on the quantity of chariots .. but do not look to the Holy One of Israel... The Egyptian is human, not divine" (31,1-3). Yahweh will simply "stretch out his hand", then both the Egyptians and their vassals will perish. The explicit denial of divinity to the Egyptian brings out well the prime objection against looking to Egypt for an alliance that might save Judah from the Assyrians. Isaiah looked on the whole scheme as putting Egypt in Yahweh's place, even though the delegates may not have put it in those terms. What has been abandoned in practice is not loyalty to the Davidic king, but loyalty to and wholehearted trust in Yahweh.

B. PROPHETS DURING THE BABYLONIAN EMPIRE

The supremacy of the Assyrian empire ended in flames with the destruction of their capital, Nineveh, by the Babylonians in 612 B.C.[35]. From then on it was the Babylonians who went from strength to strength, consolidating their power as far afield as Egypt. Judah was astride an important military route between Babylon and Egypt. King Josiah (ca.640-609 B.C.) had managed to cut free of Assyria's suzerainty over Judah, and he tried hard to carry through a sweeping religious reform to undo some of the damage done to Judah by the impious Manasseh. After Josiah died in a battle against Egypt, the rising Babylonian empire was soon knocking at Jerusalem's gates for recognition and tribute. Four more Davidic kings were caught up in schemes to thwart the Babylonians, but unfortunately they were deaf or openly hostile to the prophets Yahweh sent them with an urgent ultimatum for conversion and reconciliation. The threatened disaster struck hardest in ca.587 B.C. with the destruction of Jerusalem and the deportation of thousands to Babylon for a long exile.

The prophets in those days who spoke out most eloquently about the old covenant being so abandoned as to call forth the promise of a new one were Jeremiah, Ezekiel and Deutero-Isaiah. We include Jeremiah here among the pre-exilic prophets, because practically all his known ministry was in Jerusalem until the hour of its destruction. Ezekiel, on the other hand, is regarded as exilic or post-exilic, since his prophetic ministry commenced after he himself was already in exile with many others deported to Babylon. That occurred about a decade before the final rebellion of Jerusalem provoked its complete destruction by the Babylonians.

COVENANT AND LIBERATION

1. JEREMIAH (IN JERUSALEM)

Like Isaiah a century earlier, Jeremiah spent about forty years carrying out his prophetic ministry in Jerusalem, from ca. 627 - 587 B.C. His call came during the reign of Josiah, only five or six years before that king's religious reform based on the "Book of the Covenant" found in the Temple. We have very little information about Jeremiah's preaching during the lifetime of Josiah, but he is referred to as a good king (Jer 22,15-17). Interestingly enough, the only oracle dated explicitly in his reign is an invitation to "disloyal Israel" (as distinct from "her faithless sister Judah") to come back to Yahweh (3,6-13).

This alerts us to Jeremiah being a native of Anathoth, a town only a few kilometres north of Jerusalem but within the territory of Benjamin. Benjamin was Saul's tribe, and that tribe had always retained a lot of sympathy for the northern kingdom, although officially they had to belong to Jerusalem. It is possible that Jeremiah may even have gone up north to preach when the reform of Josiah extended in that direction as well (cf. 2 K 23,15-20). In any case, his poems and discourses display a kinship with Hosea and with the Deuteronomic preaching of faithful love toward Yahweh, the only reliable Lover of Israel.

Much more of the book can be associated with the reign of Jehoiachim, a crucial ten years beginning with his enthronement as a vassal of Egypt. Jeremiah was moved to denounce him personally as an oppressor of his "neighbour", whereas the king brazenly cut up and burnt a scroll of Jeremiah's prophecies. Jeremiah's daring denunciation of the corruption that could lead to the Temple itself being wiped out nearly cost him his own life. Presumably the "Confessions" of Jeremiah now found scattered from cc.11-20 speak largely of his anguish and rejection during those years.

Other prophecies and public reactions to them can be dated during the reign of Zedekiah, a king put on the throne by the Babylonians. They had deposed his young nephew, Jehoiakin, whom they led off to prison in Babylon. So at first Zedekias obeyed Babylon, but within ten years he was persuaded to rebel. Jeremiah was advising him and the city to surrender to the Babylonians. Thanks especially to the details given by Baruch about the hostile treatment of Jeremiah, we also know that he was arrested, beaten, tried, thrown into a dirty old well, then kept under arrest even after being pulled out of the well. He was still a prisoner when the Babylonians captured and destroyed Jerusalem. Eventually he was allowed to remain with the Jews who were not deported to Babylon, but despite all his prophetic warning to the contrary, a frightened group of rebels against Babylon dragged him with them to Egypt. We can only presume that his highly conflictive life ended there. His words, however, were obviously collected, treasured, edited, and enlarged by new prophetic touches.

The book is by no means a year-by-year account of Jeremiah's preaching, but commentaries help us follow developments in a general way. In what follows we will concentrate on the most explicit or obvious references to the Mosaic covenant, mainly telling of its violations. From there we will turn to the great promise of the new covenant that would bring with it a more radical and enduring change of heart to ensure its observance.

Jer 2,1 - 4,4 can be taken as yet another "lawsuit" conducted by Yahweh against faithless Israel (which includes Judah without forgetting any tribe). In ch.2 Yahweh begins his case against the accused: "I remember your faithful love (**hesed**), the affection of your bridal days, when you followed me through the desert" (v.2). Right from the start the image of the bride appears, and the language of covenant commitment, plus the desert experience recalled also by Hosea in his appeal for a renewal of married love[36]. The leading question challenges the accused: "What did your ancestors find wrong in me for them to have deserted me to follow Futility?" (v.5). The gift of the Land is recalled: "I brought you to a country of plenty.. but when you entered you defiled my country" (v.7). Jeremiah is rightly acclaimed as "the poet of the land", so frequent are his fond references to it as a precious heritage being so defiled as to be lost completely[37]. Then the current case is stated: "For my people have committed two crimes: they have abandoned me, the fountain of living water, and dug water-tanks for themselves, cracked water-tanks that hold no water" (v.13). To desert Yahweh is also to opt for a return to slavery, hence the jarring question: "Is Israel a slave? Was he born into serfdom, for him to be preyed on like this?"(v.14). Ominously this is linked explicitly with both the superpowers to whom Israel turns for "water" to survive: "What is the good of going to Egypt now to drink the water of the Nile? What is the good of going to Assyria to drink the water of the River?" (v.18). To abandon Yahweh has meant for Israel to "play the whore" uncontrollably, impervious to danger signals, exclaiming, "It is no use! No! For I love the Strangers and they are the ones I shall follow" (2,20.25). The whole people will be caught red-handed — "their kings, their chief men, their priests and their prophets" (v.26). Part of their infidelity to Yahweh has been their murderous treatment of the poor and the innocent: "The very skirts of your robe are stained with the blood of the poor, of innocent men you never caught breaking and entering" (v.34).

Ch.3 also opens with Yahweh's question as to whether it would be right to take back a divorced wife like Israel, now "totally polluted" by her many other lovers (v.1). It is high time she stopped calling out hypocritically to Yahweh, "My father! My beloved ever since I was young!" (v.4). She has long since ceased to act either as daughter or bride of Yahweh. Being proclaimed "in the days of King Josiah" (v.6), the accusation levelled at Judah in particular, that "she has come back to me not in sincerity, but only in pretence" (v.10), sounds like an evaluation of the nation after Josiah's big reform there. We know that the king and his people all renewed the Mosaic covenant publicly (2 K 23,1-3). Perhaps they soon went back on their pledge, as the slave-owners went back on their covenant in the days of Zedekiah (Jer 34). An urgent appeal is made to all Israel to return, both north and south. An interlude about messianic days in Jerusalem promises the reunion of both groups under "shepherds after my own heart" (v.15), like David was.

The "lawsuit" concludes in the opening verses of ch.4 with a promise reminiscent of the one made to Abraham, but this time the moral demands are made quite explicit: "If you come back to me, .. if you go roving no more, if you swear, 'As Yahweh lives!' truthfully, justly, uprightly, then the nations will bless themselves by him" (vv.1-2). This rules out hypocrisy and demands public justice as well as personal integrity. It amounts to a genuine change of heart, which is described as a circumcision of the heart (v.4; cf. 9,25). Circumcision was prescribed for Abraham as a sign of that promissory covenant with him and his descendants (Gen 17), then reconfirmed by the Mosaic law. From the Deuteronomic ideal of an interior "circumcision" (cf. Dt 10,16; 30,6), Jeremiah went on to promise the engraving of God's law on the heart (ch.31).

The lack of justice is exemplified by the men who trap their neighbours as though they were birds, so that "their houses are full of loot; they have grown rich and powerful because of it". Heartlessly they disregard the rights of the orphans and the needy (5,26-28). Or again: "For, from the least to greatest, they are all greedy for gain; prophet no less than priest, all of them practise fraud" (6,13). The extent of their fraud can be seen from the way such prophets are lulling the people into false security by saying, "Peace! Peace! (6,14). They pretend that peace can exist while they are all breaking the covenant. Biblical peace is very much the fruit of mutual fidelity to the covenant, whereas infidelity quickly erodes the family ties that would ensure peace.

Ch. 11,1-14 reads like prophetic support for Josiah's public renewal of the covenant: "Then Yahweh said to me, 'Proclaim the terms in the towns of Judah and in the streets of Jerusalem, saying, "Listen to the terms of this covenant and obey them." ... [Despite all this] Yahweh said to me, ...'The House of Israel and the House of Judah have broken my covenant which I made with their ancestors'" (vv.6.9.10).

The most memorable denunciation of Judah's crimes against the neighbour was delivered "at the gate of the Temple of Yahweh", at the start of Jehoiakim's reign (7,1; 26,1). It unmasked the intolerable reliance on the Temple to guarantee Jerusalem's safety no matter how much they exploited "the stranger, the orphan and the widow", or "shed innocent blood", or stole, committed adultery, perjured themselves, or ran after false gods (7,6-9). The ten commandments, also a summary of covenant obligations, are as shattered as the two original stone tablets that Moses threw down in blazing anger (cf.Ex 32,15-24). The Temple really serves them as "a den of bandits" (7,8-11). The option is given: "Amend your behaviour and your actions and I will let you stay in this place". Or the alternative: "I shall treat this Temple that bears my name... just as I treated Shiloh, and I shall drive you out of my sight" (7,3.14-15). Since Shiloh, an earlier sanctuary of the ark of the covenant, had been destroyed by the Philistines, then the current sanctuary could suffer a similar destruction. Yahweh has no obligation to protect a robbers' lair. On the contrary!

A further discourse on true worship recalls the one thing Yahweh requested "when I brought your ancestors out of Egypt", namely: "Listen to my voice, then I will be your God and you shall be my people" (7,23). That is clearly covenant language, giving the basic attitude demanded but seriously lacking in Judah. The people there, like so many of their ancestors, would not heed the word of God sent through "all my servants, the prophets" (7,25). They have instead "forsaken my Law which I gave them and have not listened to my voice or followed it, but have followed their own stubborn hearts, have followed the Baals" (9,12-13).

The reaction to Jeremiah's discourse in the Temple was immediate, but very hostile, according to the more biographical account given in ch.26, probably by his faithful secretary Baruch. In fact, much of cc.26-45 can be assigned to his records, especially texts speaking about Jeremiah in the third person. No sooner had Jeremiah finished warning the people about the destruction of their Temple and city than everybody grabbed him, saying menacingly, "You will die for this!" (26,8). "The chief men of Judah" were hurriedly assembled to judge him there at the Temple gate, to hear the case put bluntly by "the priests and prophets" : "This man deserves to die, since he has prophesied against this city" (v.11). Jeremiah corrected that distortion of his prophecy, which had been a plea to save the city through a change of conduct. Fortunately the chief men accepted that he was speaking in the name of Yahweh, as Micah had been when delivering a similar warning. By accepting Micah's warning Jerusalem had been spared the threatened destruction. The result of the trial this time was that Jeremiah "was not handed over to the people to be put to death" (v.24). Nor did that brush with death scare him from continuing to pass on Yahweh's word for another twenty turbulent years.

The courage of Jeremiah stands out in his explicit denunciation of Jehoiakim for defrauding, oppressing and murdering his neighbour, especially the poor workers constructing the fancy palace for him (22,13-17). It is unique among the written prophecies, but faithful to earlier prophets like Nathan and Elijah. Jeremiah protests indignantly at the way the king "makes his fellow-man work for nothing, without paying him his wages" (v.13). After recalling the "just and upright" conduct of Josiah, in particular his genuine concern for "the poor and the needy", Yahweh asks, "Is not that what it means to know me?" (vv.16-17). "Knowledge of God" in the prophets includes much more than theoretical knowledge or mere intellectual assent to some proposition about God.

To know God properly is also to acknowledge one's own experience of, and immersion in, a personal God, a God of wisdom, love and justice whose presence must colour all human life as well (cf. 9,23) Later, when speaking of the first lot of Judaeans taken to Babylon, Yahweh promises: 24,7: "I shall give them a heart to acknowledge that I am Yahweh". The close ties between this kind of knowledge of Yahweh and the covenant can be gauged by what follows: "They will be my people and I shall be their God, for they will return to me with all their heart" (24,7). In short, genuine knowledge of God is manifested and continually deepened by just conduct[38].

The role of the Davidic kings in safeguarding an effective knowledge of Yahweh has also been stated clearly in Jer 21, 11-14; 22,1-9 (where destruction of the palace is threatened if the kings permit the weakest of their people to be oppressed or murdered); and 23,1-6 (where Yahweh promises to raise up a new "Branch for David" whose name will be "Yahweh-is-our-Saving-Justice"). A striking example of vacillating royal leadership in promoting the covenant values is provided by the case of Zedekiah and the freeing of all Hebrew slaves. When the Babylonians were besieging Jerusalem, "Zedekiah had made a covenant with all the people in Jerusalem to issue a proclamation freeing their slaves: each man was to free his Hebrew slaves, men and women, no one was any longer to keep a brother Judaean in slavery" (34,8-9). The slaves were all set free as agreed. But as soon as the siege was lifted, the recently freed slaves were all rounded up again and reduced to slavery once again (34,11).

That covenant might not have meant much to Zedekiah and his people, but Yahweh immediately sent Jeremiah to convey his strong condemnation of their contempt for a solemn covenant . It had been made between humans, but sworn before Yahweh in the Temple. Moreover, it was a long overdue recognition of the implications of the Mosaic covenant, as Yahweh reminds them: "I made a covenant with your ancestors when I brought them out of Egypt, out of the house of slavery; it said: At the end of seven years each one you is to free his brother Hebrew who has sold himself to you.. Now, today you repented and did what pleases me by proclaiming freedom for your neighbour; you made a covenant before me in the Temple that bears my name. And then you changed your minds and, profaning my name, each of you has recovered his slaves .. and has forced them to become your slaves again" (vv.13-16). The evaluation is quoted at length, because it speaks volumes of Yahweh's attitude to slaves and their right to be free. As for their covenant-breaking slavemasters, Yahweh's sentence is that the Babylonians will be brought back to destroy the unjust city, leaving many corpses as "food for the birds of the sky and the animals of the earth" (vv.17-22).

Just as Jeremiah was called on to announce disaster because of violations of the covenant, he was also moved to foretell the granting of a new covenant. His long years of daring denunciations and fervent appeals for a change of heart obviously convinced him that words were no longer sufficient. Gradually he must have sensed deep in his own being that God's love would not be defeated by the stony hearts of an ungrateful people. The solution had to lie in God stepping in somehow to change those stony hearts, so that the people would honour their commitment to both God and neighbour. That led on to the clear prophecy of a new covenant as recorded in ch.31, making this the most important chapter of the book for understanding both the old and the new covenants.

We accept ch.31 as part of a collection of oracles in cc.30 - 33 about the restoration of Israel, both north and south. Ch.30 promises a messianic restoration after the return of the exiles, whose yoke and chains will be broken, so that once again "Israel and Judah will serve Yahweh their God and David their king whom I shall raise up for them" (vv.8-9). Covenant ties will also be renewed — "You will be my people and I shall be your God" (v.22).

Ch.31 opens with that refrain also, making explicit that "I shall be the God of all the families of Israel, and they will be my people" (v.1). Following the lead of Alonso Schökel and Sicre, we can treat the whole chapter as it has been finally redacted, while realising that several once separate blocks were used in its final redaction[39]. This helps us understand, for instance, why Israel seems to have referred originally to the northern kingdom rather than to all twelve tribes. Judah is now included in ways that suggest it needed to be brought in due to later developments, e.g. after Jerusalem had suffered deportations similar to those of Samaria. It is not necessary to know with certainty how much reshaping of his earlier prophecies was done by Jeremiah himself, nor when exactly his disciples may have added to them (with fresh inspiration)[40]. There is every reason to attribute the astonishing promise of the new covenant (vv.31-34) to Jeremiah in person, with the possible exception of the phrase "and the House of Judah" (v.31).

After opening with Yahweh's promise to renew the covenant relationship summed up by "your people/my God", ch.31 describes the return of a pardoned Israel through the desert to his "rest" (the Land). Yahweh explains why: "I have loved you with an everlasting love and so I still maintain my faithful love (**hesed**) for you. I shall build you once more, yes, you will be rebuilt" (vv.3-4). That will be fulfilling the frequent promise to save a remnant of Israel (v.7). Recalling the enduring affection of Yahweh expressed in Hosea ch.11, Yahweh here explains the incredible new beginning: "For I am a father to Israel, and Ephraim is my first-born son" (v.9). Rachel, the matriarch for Ephraim and Manasseh, as also for Benjamin, need weep no longer for all her lost children. "There is hope for your future after all, Yahweh declares, your children will return to their homeland" (v.17). Ephraim is such a dear son to Yahweh that he is remembered lovingly still (v.20). Then the image switches to that of the bride, being invited to come home again. "How long will you hesitate, rebellious daughter? For Yahweh is creating something new on earth: the Woman sets out to find her Husband again" (v.22).

That prepares the way for the promise of renewed fertility in the people as well as the cattle, for it will be a time "to build and to plant" (when Jeremiah could at last say from his grave: "mission accomplished" — cf. 1,10). Because it will offer a new beginning, the people will not feel that they are being punished for their fathers' sins. No! "But each will die for his own guilt" (v.30). The new generation will be responsible for its own conduct, and treated accordingly by God. Each one is to serve the common good wholeheartedly. Princes and judges, priests and prophets, parents and teachers are not the only ones in the community with responsibility for its welfare.

The promise reaches its peak with the solemn announcement: "Look, the days are coming, Yahweh declares, when I shall make a new covenant with the House of Israel (and the House of Judah), but not like the covenant I made with their ancestors the day I took them by the hand to bring them out of Egypt, a covenant which they broke, even though I was their Master" (vv.31-32). This is clearly more than a renewal, however enthusiastic, of the Mosaic covenant, the one sealed at Sinai when Yahweh had liberated them. It really will be a new covenant, different from the Mosaic covenant which so many Israelites had abandoned in practice. So the big difference is to be sought in the way the new covenant can be made effective as far as Israel is concerned. Yahweh's faithful love has never been in doubt; an adequate response to it, yes[41].

How then can human infidelity be remedied sufficiently to ensure the observance of a new covenant? The reply comes: "This is the covenant I shall make with the House of Israel when those days come, Yahweh declares. Within them I shall plant my Law, writing it on their hearts. Then I shall be their God and they will be my people" (v.33). So God will not give a new Moses another set of the Law chiselled on stone tablets. Instead, the Law will be chiselled by God deep into human hearts, the centre of knowledge and wisdom, of thoughts, attitudes and most importantly, of love[42]. Thanks to that interior transformation of the heart, "they will all know me, from the least to the greatest, Yahweh declares, since I shall forgive their guilt and never more call their sin to mind" (v.34). Since "to know God" is such a rich activity and abiding attitude, as we saw earlier, the new covenant will bring with it all that is necessary to acknowledge God with a personal conviction and persevering commitment.

The connection between "know me" and "since I shall forgive their guilt" is of utmost importance for Jeremiah, so frequently driven to denounce the sins of his people and the ever-widening rupture of the existing covenant. Many have spoken about God always preserving a "faithful remnant" with which to found a new Israel. However, Jeremiah is not simply promising a new covenant for the faithful few who never abandoned the old covenant. Here, as throughout cc.30 - 31, God, moved by an eternal and inexhaustible love, is calling back a rebellious and faithless Israel. Therefore the very basis of the new covenant attitude within each and every Israelite must include an acknowledgement of Yahweh's gratuitous love and the forgiveness prompted by such love. It is as though the pardon granted will open their hearts to the new kind of interior acknowledgement and full reconciliation envisaged under the new covenant[43].

What had been formerly written "with an iron pen, engraved with a diamond point" on their hearts was sin (17,1), which led them to idolatry and caused the loss of their "heritage" (17,4). This goes to the root of sin as denounced by Yahweh when they asked, "What sin have we committed?" They were told they were worse than their ancestors, "who abandoned me and did not keep my Law". "Look, each of you follows his own stubborn and wicked inclinations [Hebrew has "heart"], without listening to me" (16,10-12).

For Yahweh, therefore, to plant the Law within them by "writing it on their hearts" must entail forgiving and rubbing out the sin that had poisoned their hearts. On the positive side, God promises to implant the Law personally within the purified heart, obviating the need for any human teacher. To know that basic Law "by heart" and to let the heart be guided by it in all dealings with God or neighbour will be to "know God" in the biblical sense.

In contrast to the Sinai covenant, the new covenant will be "made" by God, not just offered and left in abeyance until the people accept its terms saying, "All that the Lord has said, we will do". Nor is any human mediator like Moses mentioned, nor any external rite to seal it and so make public its mutual acceptance. In these ways the promissory character of the new covenant is accentuated, linking it with the Abrahamic covenant, which Yahweh made gratuitously, unconditionally, and irrevocably[44].

Also reminiscent of the Abrahamic promise, which was sealed by a covenant and then confirmed by Yahweh's solemn oath, is the twofold oath given in the verses following Jeremiah's momentous oracle. As if calling on all creation to witness the new irrevocable promise,"Yahweh Sabaoth says this, 'Were this established order ever to pass away before me, Yahweh declares, then the race of Israel would also cease being a nation for ever before me'" (vv.35-6). The following verse has a similar cosmic oath declaring, in the same negative style, that Yahweh will never reject the whole race of Israel. We can also discern in that twofold oath a parallel with the treaty element whereby various witnesses, generally gods, were called upon to add solemnity and help enforce the sanctions.

The Creator of the universe, who also sees to its orderly running, is likewise committed to the unfolding of Israel's history as a people called to know Yahweh properly, so that through them all nations might be blessed (cf. 4,2). Although the short oracle in 31,31-34 is addressed to Israel, some hint of its more universal import can be found in the preliminary oracle: "Listen, nations, to the word of Yahweh. On the farthest coasts and islands proclaim it, say, 'He who scattered Israel is gathering him, will guard him as a shepherd guarding his flock'" (v.10). The miracle of the revived flock should teach other nations something about its Shepherd.

Ch. 33 rounds off the group of oracles foretelling the restoration of Jerusalem, the Temple, and all Israel. The emphasis this time is on a "Branch " for David "who will do what is just and upright in the country", so that at last Jerusalem may be called "Yahweh-is-our-Saving-Justice" (vv.15-16). Yahweh makes it perfectly clear here, as in ch.31, that the restoration will be something radical: "Look, I shall bring them remedy and cure; I shall cure them and reveal a new order of peace and loyalty to them " (v.6).

It is the mention of shepherds to look after the flocks again throughout the land that leads on to a solemn assurance that Yahweh will fulfil the promise — "my covenant with David my servant" (v.21). The mission of the promised "Branch" is obviously to serve Yahweh and the whole restored kingdom justly. So generous will be the restoration that heirs of David will be as numerous as the stars and the sands of the sea-shore. Which is to suggest that the blessing of abundant offspring promised to Abraham (as recalled in v.26) will somehow descend upon the house of David. A similar innumerable offspring is also promised to the levitical priests (vv.17-22). We can discern in this teeming multitude of future kings and priests a renewal of all Israel's mission as a chosen nation: "For me you shall be a kingdom of priests (Ex 19,6).

NOTES

1. Cf.: Alonso Schökel & J. Sicre (con S. Breton & E. Zurro): Profetas — Introducciones y Commentario, 2 Vol. (Madrid: Ediciones Cristiandad,

1987²) esp. 2-89 as general introduction. B. Vawter, The Conscience of Israel — Pre-exilic Prophets and Prophecy (New York: Sheed & Ward, 1961). H. Renckens, The Religion of Israel (New York: Sheed & Ward, 1966) esp. 227-275 on Prophets. G. Von Rad, The Message of the Prophets (E.T. by D. Stalker, London: S.C.M., 1968).
2. Cf. New Jerusalem Bible, 1157-1189 for introduction to the Prophets; 1162-1166 is on the teaching of the prophets.
3. Cf. Alonso Schökel & J. Sicre, op.cit. I, 24-25.
4. Cf. J. Sicre, Con Los Pobres, 141-153; also 130-132 on what Amos gives as desired by God, Heb. **mishpat** and **sedaqa** (= right and justice). The pair occurs in other prophets also.
5. B. Anderson, The Eighth Century Prophets — Amos: Hosea: Isaiah: Micah; Proclamation Commentaries (Ed.: F.R. McCurley) (Philadelphia: Fortress Press, 1978) 29.
6. Alonso Schökel & J. Sicre, op.cit. II, 974.
7. Cf. J. Sicre, Los Dioses Olvidados, 112;
8. Cf. J. Sicre, Con Los Pobres, 164.
9. Cf. Ibid. 129 and 145 re Amos and unjust institutions; 114 re the parallel between the upright and the 'anawim (afflicted, lowly, poor).
10. N. Flanagan, Amos, Hosea, Micah (Collegeville: O.T. Reading Guide, Liturgical Press, 1966) 29.
11. Alonso Schökel & J. Sicre, op.cit. II, 864
12. Ibid. 870. Cf. B. Anderson, op.cit. 29: "Hosea took the Sinaitic conditional covenant so seriously that he could even contemplate the possibility that Yahweh would terminate the covenant relationship."
13. Ibid. 874.
14. Cf. B. Gesmer, "The RIB or Controversy-Pattern in Hebrew Mentality", in M.Noth and W.W. Thomas (Gen. Editors), Wisdom in Israel and in the Ancient Near East, issued as Supplement III to Vetus Testamentum (Leiden: E.J. Brill, 1960) 120-137. Cf. W. Vogels, God's Universal Covenant, 5-6 on the pattern running from promise to Mosaic covenant to RIB to TODAH to promise of new covenant. He asserts: "This concept of covenant gives a perfect unity to the whole of salvation-history, which moves from promise to promise" (6). Cf. C. Giraudo, La Struttura Letteraria Della Preghiera Eucaristica (Rome: Biblical Institute, 1981) 13-16 for the relationship between covenant, RIB and TODA; also examples in parallel columns, inserted after 106.
15. Cf. D.J. McCarthy & R.E. Murphy, "Hosea", in NJBC, 221.
16. Cf. E. Rust, Covenant and Hope: A Study in the Theology of the Prophets (Waco, Texas: Word Books, 1972) 63: "There was certainly nothing contractual about the covenant love of Yahweh, for his steadfast covenant love and faithfulness were grounded in a free and unconditioned elective love. The emotional warmth that had driven Hosea to redeem his wife, keeping him faithful to her in her unfaithfulness, making him show her covenant love when such a response was lacking on her part, was a window through which the prophet saw the love of God."

17. Cf. J. Sicre, Los Dioses Olvidados, 34-50, e.g. 34: "Los políticos han dejado de confiar en Yahvé y necesitan un nuevo dios que los salve. Ese ídolo será unas veces Asiria, otras Egipto."
18. Cf. J. Sicre, Con Los Pobres, 250: "En Miqueas, último profeta del siglo VIII, la denuncia social alcanza sus cotas más altas."
19. Alonso Schökel & J. Sicre, op. cit. II, 1033 and 1039.
20. Cf. J. Sicre, Con Los Pobres, 313-314, where he posits that the catastrophe announced by Micah was based on the breaking of the covenant on the part of the authorities.
21. Cf. B. Anderson, op.cit. 49-50: "In Hosea 6:6 (and Micah 6:8), however, the word [hesed] applies to the people's reciprocal covenant obligation to God, obligation that also should be manifest in the faithful performance of responsibilities that strengthen and maintain the community."
22. Cf. J. Sicre, Los Dioses Olvidados, 128-129, where he points out that the city built with blood must be treated by Yahweh as a monument to Mammon. That cannot be tolerated.
23. J. Sicre, Con Los Pobres, 308.
24. F.L. Moriarty, "Isaiah 1-39", in Jerome Biblical Commentary, I, 265-267. Cf. B. Viviano "Isaiah" in NJBC, 230, stressing importance of the Davidic promises in Jerusalem.
25. J.Sicre, op.cit. 191.
26. Alonso Schökel & J. Sicre, op.cit. I, 109, where they contend that the message of Isaiah embraced two great issues: the social question during the first years of his activity and the political as from 734 B.C.
27. J. Sicre, op.cit. 213.
28. Cf. P. Bovati, Ristabilire la Giustizia, 67-77 on the purpose of the "lawsuit"; cf. all 19-148 concerning details of such divinely instigated "lawsuits" calling Israel to respond and to be moved to observe God's just demands in the future. Text quoted is 142 : "Non c'è alleanza senza legge. Se si perdona, si suppone che è possible ora rispettare la parola che impegna entrambi" (author's emphasis). Cf. F.L. Moriarty, art.cit. 267.
29. J. Sicre, op.cit. 219 on accumulation of houses and lands leading to accumulation of capital in the hands of a few to the detriment of many.
30. Alonso Schökel & J. Sicre, op.cit. I, 134-136, where they suggest that Is 1,17 be inserted between vv.9 and 10.
31. Cf. New Jerusalem Bible, ftn. to 8,1.
32. Cf. Alonso Schökel & J. Sicre, op.cit. I, 157.
33. J. Sicre, Los Dioses Olvidados, 51-64.
34. Ibid. 57: "Quien se refugia en Dios reconoce que puede ayudarle, confiesa la potencia salvífica del Señor. .. En vez de ello prefiere buscar refugio en Egipto. Resulta claro que esta potencia ha ocupado el puesto de Dios, convirtiéndose en un ídolo."
35. Cf: M.E.L. Mallowan, Nimrud, 2 Vol. (London: Collins, 1966), being a report on the prolonged excavations of biblical Calah, near ancient Nineveh. Also J. Curtis (Ed.) Fifty Years of Mesopotamian Discovery (London: British School of Archaeology in Iraq, 1982). The 50 years ran

from 1932-1982. Julian Reade's contribution on "Nimrud" (99-112) mentions the finding in Nimrud, in a temple of Nabu, a copy of the "Epic of Gilgamesh" and also copies of Vassal Treaties — "these last documents are in the form of agreements between Esarhadaddon and various Median chieftains from the eastern fringes of the empire: the chieftains swear to support Ashurbanipal as next King of Assyria, and <u>fearful curses are invoked for disloyalty</u>" (111) (emphasis added).

36. Cf. Alonso Schökel & J. Sicre, op.cit. I, 411: After saying that Jeremiah's message could be summed up by the word conversion, they assert: "Jeremías, siguiendo a Oseas, concibe las relaciones entre Dios y el pueblo en clave matrimonial. El pueblo, como una mujer infiel, ha abandonado a Dios; por eso debe convertirse, volver. .. Es cierto que Jeremías no usó esta imagen en años posteriores, pero el contenido de la misma siguió vivo en su mensaje."
37. Cf. W. Brueggemann, The Land, 107-129 on "The Push toward Landlessness — and Beyond". E.g. on Jeremiah: "In the O.T. he is the poet of the land par excellence" (107). On relation between covenant and the land: "It [land] is lost when it is taken from its covenant context" (121).
38. Cf. B. Anderson, op.cit. 54-7, e.g. 56-57: "The covenant lawsuit just considered helps us to understand the statement in Hosea 6:6 in which 'loyalty' (**hesed**) and 'knowledge of God' stand in synonymous poetic parallelism. Both terms refer to the kind of personal relationship with God that is manifest in social responsibility — in actions that help to restore the poor and weak to meaningful and fulfilling relationships in the community and thus foster and maintain peace." Cf. J. Sicre, Con Los Pobres, 360.
39. Alonso Schökel & J. Sicre, op.cit. I, 551-566.
40. Cf. G.P. Couturier, "Jeremiah", in NJBC, 288: (On cc.30-31 on the restoration and new covenant): "All agree that this section of Jeremiah's book constitutes a climax, and some would even say the apogee of all prophecy." On the actual promise of the new covenant (31,31-34): "This is the only time 'new covenant' is used in the OT." Cf. J. Bright, Jeremiah (New York: Anchor Bible, Doubleday, 1965) 287 on the same short oracle: "Although the passage may not preserve the prophet's **ipsissima verba**, it represents what might well be considered the high point of his theology. It is certainly one of the profoundest and most moving passages in the entire Bible." Id., Covenant and Promise, 11-28; and 140-170.
41. Cf. W. Vogels, La Promesse Royale de Yahweh Préparatoire a l'Alliance — Étude d'une forme littéraire de l'A.T. (Ottawa: L'Université d'Ottawa, 1970) 161, where he gives a general view of the progress of God's royal promise from the Sinai covenant to the royal promise of the new covenant.
42. E. Malatesta, Interiority and Covenant, 22-24 on the influence of Jer 31 and Ez 36 on 1 Jn, e.g. 24:"Indeed we believe that these expressions when in personal, reciprocal form, serve as the Johannine equivalent of the Covenant formula: 'I will be your God, and you shall be my people'

(which) has become 'God is Love, and he who remains in love remains in God, and God remains in him'."
43. P. Beauchamp, L'Un et l'Autre Testament — essai de lecture (Paris: Ed. du Seuil, 1976) 229-274 concerning "la nouvelle alliance", e.g. "La justice est donnée par Dieu directement. C'est lui qui fait d'autres coeurs, selon Jérémie et Ezéchiel. Il donne l'Esprit, son Esprit, qui est la justice." With respect to pardon being granted before the people have changed: "Le pardon précède la conversion selon plusieurs textes décisifs: le peuple est changé de se savoir pardonné, plutôt que pardonné parce qu'il change" (260). Also Tableau N° 6, 307 on new covenant features.
44. A. Vanhoye, La Nuova Alleanza Nel N.T., 23.

CHAPTER 7: COVENANT IN EXILIC AND POST-EXILIC PROPHETS

B.(cont.) UNDER BABYLONIAN EMPIRE

2. EZEKIEL (IN BABYLON)

Like Jeremiah, Ezekiel was from a priestly family, from around Jerusalem. To judge from his constant concern for the Temple, for details of worship there, for separating sacred from profane, legally clean from unclean, it would seem likely that Ezekiel was prepared to minister as a priest. In any case, his whole book reflects the interests of the Priestly circles, just as that of Jeremiah reflects those of the Deuteronomic circles[1]. At least a few years of his early prophetic ministry coincided with the closing years of Jeremiah's. However, while Jeremiah was struggling in Jerusalem to avert the final disaster, Ezekiel was already among the exiles that had been dragged off with young King Jehoiakin by the Babylonians in 597 B.C. According to the information supplied in his book, Ezekiel received his call to be a prophet in 592 B.C., and was active in Babylon at least until 571, that is, for some fifteen years after Jerusalem had been destroyed and a large number of fresh exiles had arrived in Babylon[2].

Ezekiel comes through to his readers as a most unusual character, a visionary and poet, whose visions seem too involved, whose style of communicating is heavy, whose frequent symbolic gestures and miming are surprising, and whose priorities in the midst of uprooted exiles are hard to fathom. There is a harsh ring about his denunciations of the sins of Israel right from the time of Moses until they had made Jerusalem such a city of blood that it would have to be wiped out(ch.22). On the other hand he does display a keen sensitivity to the demands of God for justice and holiness. Biting denunciations of social injustice go hand in hand with his concern for a restored Temple and liturgy. God evidently chose that unusual young priest from among the exiles in Babylon to be a profoundly disturbing prophet for fellow-exiles in a state of shock after being uprooted and held captive in the city of their gentile conquerors. His mission was to tell them God's message, "whether they listen or not"(3,11).

It is no wonder that his early preaching was not welcome to their ears, because it kept harping on the sinfulness and coming destruction of their still cherished Jerusalem(cf. cc.2-24). On the other hand, after the destruction of Jerusalem his message becomes one of fresh hope, promising a national resurrection, reoccupation of the Land, and rebuilding of the Temple(cc.33-48). What is most relevant to our particular theme is the way he seems to re-echo and develop Jeremiah's promise of a new covenant with emphasis on God granting a major change of heart. According to C. Begg, Jeremiah speaks explicitly of covenant (**berit**) 23 times, whereas Ezekiel does so 18 times, of which 7 are in reference to a future covenant[3]. We shall therefore touch on the chapters which contain such texts, as well as the main texts illustrating the covenant demands of a complete return to Yahweh and hence the effective eradication of social injustice in Israel or upon her.

Ch. 11 is often remembered for the vision of Yahweh's glory leaving Jerusalem, as it had also just left the Temple. What must also catch our attention is the denunciation levelled at its citizens: "You have filled this city with more and more of your victims; you have strewn its streets with victims" (v.6). In sharp contrast is the message to the exiles already in Babylon: "The Lord Yahweh says this: I shall gather you back from the peoples, I shall collect you in from the countries where you have been scattered and give you the land of Israel" (v.17). Through the gift of God's spirit they will be given a new heart, a "heart of flesh" to replace their "heart of stone", "so that they can keep my laws and respect my judgements and put them into practice. Then they will be my people and I shall be their God" (vv.19-20). Here we already have the keynote of Ezekiel's teaching on what will characterize the covenant after the return from exile. It will be observed properly thanks to the gift of a new spirit, resulting in a new heart.

In ch.16 Ezekiel takes up the theme of Jerusalem as Yahweh's bride, fondly cared for since birth. Yahweh reminds her that, when she had reached marriageable age, "I gave you my oath, I made a covenant with you .. and you became mine" (v.8). All too quickly she abandoned him to go chasing other lovers. She turned out to be worse than Samaria, an "elder sister". As in Hosea, a reconciliation is promised, after some chastisement: "For the Lord Yahweh says this: I shall treat you as you have deserved for making light of an oath and breaking a covenant, but I shall remember my covenant with you when you were a girl and shall conclude a covenant with you that will last for ever. And you for your part will remember your behaviour and feel ashamed of it" (vv. 59-61). The repentance will come after the granting of the everlasting covenant[4]. Having been brought back and experienced a change of heart, then Jerusalem "will know that I am Yahweh" (v.62). A similar long allegory is given in ch.23, in which the treaties made by Samaria and Jerusalem are shown to be idolatry (or "prostitution")[5]. It was all a desertion of Yahweh, who could rightly claim, "They belonged to me and bore sons and daughters" (23,4). In this chapter there is no talk of a reconciliation, but of handing over both wayward sisters to judgment.

In ch.18 the same proverb is quoted about parents eating sour grapes and their children's teeth being put on edge (v.2). Ezekiel, like Jeremiah, declares the proverb to be no longer applicable in the sense of innocent children suffering because of what their parents did. "The one who has sinned is the one who must die; a son is not to bear his father's guilt" (v.20). Each person will be judged according to his or her conduct. The invitation to reconciliation is noteworthy: "Repent, renounce all your crimes, avoid all occasions for guilt. Shake off all the crimes you have committed, and make yourselves a new heart and a new spirit! Why die, House of Israel?" (v.31). Here the change of heart and spirit is put up as an invitation to the people themselves, but elsewhere Ezekiel promises that God will effect the change. In line with the personal responsibility just mentioned, and the urging to avoid death, it is still necessary for each person to accept the proffered new heart and new spirit.

Ch.22 contains a chilling indictment of Jerusalem, "the blood-stained city". Every commandment has been broken with contempt for Yahweh, for the Temple, for the Sabbath, for parents, for wives, for the strangers, widows, and orphans. Money is lent to make a gain by extortion from fellow-citizens (v.12). Those who should be defending the afflicted people are found among the worst offenders - princes, priests, prophets, leaders, country people. Yahweh reluctantly concludes, "I have been looking for someone among them to build a barricade and oppose me in the breach, to defend the country and prevent me from destroying it; but I have found no one" (v.30)[6].

The destruction of that unfaithful city serves to convince the exiles that "there has been a prophet among them" (33,33). From that point on Ezekiel proceeds to console them, helping them to rebuild their shattered lives and national hopes. He promises, in ch.34, the replacement of bad shepherds who feed themselves rather than the sheep, ruling them "cruelly and harshly"(vv.4-8). Yahweh will become their shepherd, placing his "servant David" to be "ruler among them" (vv.11.24). Again there is promise of a future covenant: "I, Yahweh, have spoken. I shall make a covenant of peace with them. .. And they will know that I am Yahweh when I break the bars of their yoke and rescue them from the clutches of their slave-masters. No more will they be a prey to the nations, no more will the wild animals of the country devour them. .. So they will know that I, their God, am with them, and that they, the House of Israel, are my people" (vv.25-30). The close link between the covenant of peace and proper knowledge of Yahweh is striking, for it will be experiential knowledge that Yahweh has broken their iron yoke and rescued them "from the clutches of their slave-masters". In addition, it will be an inner conviction that Israel has become the people of Yahweh, whose name itself will be appreciated:"I, their God, am with them" (cf. Ex 3,13-15).

Ch.36 expands the promise concerning the restoration of Israel by a return of its scattered children to the Land, which Yahweh will accomplish to put an end to the scandal caused by Israel among the nations. The scandal is not that the Israelites are slaves as in Egypt, but that they themselves had deteriorated into such a sinful people in Canaan despite the first liberation and covenant[7]. Again the universal impact of the new covenant is mentioned: "And the nations will know that I am Yahweh .. when I display my holiness before them"(v.23). The order in which the return to the homeland and the reconciliation will be brought about is consistent with the earlier promises: "I shall pour clean water over you and you will be cleansed. .. I shall give you a new heart, and put a new spirit in you; I shall remove the heart of stone and give you a heart of flesh instead. I shall put my spirit in you, and make you keep my laws, and respect and practise my judgements. You will live in the land which I gave your ancestors. You will be my people and I shall be your God. .. Then you will remember your evil conduct and actions. You will loathe yourselves for your guilt" (vv.25-31).

As noted earlier (for Ez.11), Ezekiel tells of a return and cleansing, with the giving of a new heart and covenant, which will enable the people to realise and repent of the enormity of their past infidelities. This section also emphasises the role of God's spirit in "making" the people keep the divine laws and practise social justice fully. In line with the certainty that Yahweh's holiness and justice communicated to the people will prevail, the oracle concludes with promises of blessings (vv.29-38), but with no threat of curses. It reads like a commentary on the earlier promise of the new covenant in Jeremiah, hence it could well be intended as such. Jeremiah's words were also pondered among the exiles.

The astonishing vision in ch.37 of the dry bones being brought back to full human life at Yahweh's bidding is explained immediately: "Son of man, these bones are the whole House of Israel"(v.11). Yahweh goes on to explain further: "I am now going to open your graves and raise you from your graves, my people, and put my spirit in you, and lead you back to the soil of Israel. And you will know that I am Yahweh" (v.12). God's initiative reaches right into the grave, for what is promised is nothing less than a national resurrection of a dead nation, a shattered and hopeless people. They have lost their capital cities, both monarchies(of Samaria and Jerusalem), the Temple, and the Land promised to the Patriarchs and granted in the days of Joshua. Here again we must remark that God's concern is not the hard heart of some Pharaoh, but the hearts of the Israelites themselves. He has to reassure them that the change will be within them: " And you will know that I am Yahweh, when I open your graves .. and put my spirit in you, and you revive, and I resettle you on your own soil" (vv.13-14). The amazing new thing promised here is a return from the death chosen by Israel after they had been invited so often to choose life (cf.Deut 30,15-20).

Another consequence of the return will be a reunion of all the tribes under one king, healing the centuries-old schism. "My servant David will reign over them, one shepherd for all. .. I shall make a covenant of peace with them, an eternal covenant with them. .. I shall set my sanctuary among them for ever" (vv.15-28). The new covenant is to be effective, hence its designation again as "a covenant of peace". Because it is not merely provisional nor conditional this time, it will endure for ever, "an eternal covenant".

The final cc.40-48 present a vision of how the Temple is to be rebuilt in Jerusalem, how the city itself is to look, and how the Land is to be divided up in rectangular strips for the various tribes. Ezekiel as a priest was obviously extremely concerned for the proper restoration of the Temple and worship within it, this time not to be in any way overshadowed by the royal palace. The Priestly tradition in Exodus devotes about a dozen chapters to the ark of the covenant and the Dwelling. The glory of the Lord filled the Dwelling after its completion (cf. Ex 40,34). Parallel to that, Ezekiel is granted a vision of the glory of Yahweh returning to Jerusalem and filling the Temple, and he heard the words, "Son of man, this is the dais of my throne, the step on which I rest my feet. I shall live here among the Israelites for ever" (43,7). At least we can grasp something of what the rebuilding of the Temple would mean to the exiles. It was not intended to trap or manipulate Yahweh, but to serve as a constant reminder to the "priestly kingdom" of their commitment to the God living in their midst, offering them life sustained by loyal love.

3. DEUTERO-ISAIAH (IN BABYLON)

This is the name that has increasingly been used during the last two centuries to denote the anonymous author of Is 40-55. The indications found within those chapters point to a most penetrating prophet and superb poet active among the Babylonian exiles. References to the approach of Cyrus towards Babylon as liberator help date the period as around 550 B.C., hence about twenty years after Ezekiel's ministry there[8]. Whereas Ezekiel promised the exiles a restoration because of Yahweh's holiness, Deutero-Isaiah more often recalls God's compassion and everlasting love, as well as fidelity to every word spoken in promise before. Practically every major theme from creation to the rebuilding of Jerusalem is touched upon with keen perception and artistry. In view of the resurrection theme in Ez 37, it is understandable that the predominant message heralded by Deutero-Isaiah could be summed up as "creative redemption"[9].

He too takes up the promise of a new covenant, linking it with a mysterious suffering servant of Yahweh, then with the Noachic and the Davidic covenants. We will look mainly at those promises within their more immediate context. Moreover, the new exodus would not be towards a long-awaited promised land, but back to the God-given land they had already forfeited by their rebellion. Hence the profound realisation of the prophet that this exodus and reoccupation of the lost Land would require really a new creation[10]. Gratefully he acclaimed Yahweh as the Kinsman/Redeemer (**go'el**) who was also the Creator of Israel and the universe, as well as everything within it. So what no human kinsman could possibly achieve, Yahweh could and would accomplish through an all-powerful word creating something quite new[11].

Such a liberation from death and the marvels of the new exodus would likewise have a greater impact than the first exodus had on Egypt. This time the impact will extend to all nations, as they witness what Yahweh does and proclaims through the revived Israel. The previous prophets had manifested Yahweh's concern for the surrounding nations by many oracles denouncing their injustices (e.g. Is 13-23; Jer 46-51; Ez 25-32). Now the servant of Yahweh sent to tell of Israel's redemption has good news likewise for the other nations: "It is not enough for you to be my servant, to restore the tribes of Jacob and bring back the survivors of Israel; I shall make you a light to the nations so that my salvation may reach the remotest parts of the earth" (49,6).

The forty or fifty years living in a bustling Gentile city, remarkable for its huge temples and impressive religious celebrations, had many repercussions on the marginated deportees. They must have been thinking hard about the splendour of Babylonian religion compared to their own little gatherings on a Sabbath to read and reflect, to sing and pray about some kind of a future as Yahweh's people[12]. From that crucible of suffering and humiliation in the sight of gentiles confident that their gods reigned supreme, there emerged the true gold held up to the world by Deutero-Isaiah. God inspired him to broaden and enrich the hope kept alive by Ezekiel and other faithful exiles. His whole work is rightly described as a book of consolation, suggested by its opening lines, "Console my people" (40,1)[13].

Within the book are found four "Songs of the Servant of Yahweh", which seem to be from the same author and yet are somewhat detached from the texts surrounding them. Even so, commentators have great difficulty in determining the last verse of the first three Songs. This has led S. Porubcan to see in the first two Songs a "primary vision" followed by a "commentary", as follows:
first Song: A) 42,1-4;   B) 42,5-9
second Song: A) 49,1-6;   B) 49,7-13 [14].

The third Song he takes as being 50,4-11, which others limit to 50,4-9 [15].
The fourth Song is generally thought to be 52,13 - 53,12.
The four Songs together tell of a prophet faithful unto death, and whose sufferings are offered like a sacrifice pleading for the forgiveness of others.

The promise of a new covenant occurs precisely in those "commentaries" of the first two Songs, linking it directly with that mysterious servant of Yahweh. In two other passages a new covenant is associated also with the Noachic or Davidic covenants. We will now look mainly at those explicit promises within their more immediate context, while noting a few of the other texts replete with covenant imagery.

God reassures the exiles: "But you, Israel, my servant, .. I have chosen you, I have not rejected you, .. do not be alarmed, for I am your God" (41,8-10). Here the usual "my people/your God" is slightly altered to remind Israel that it is chosen to serve, so that through it "the glory of Yahweh will be revealed and all humanity will see it together, for the mouth of Yahweh has spoken. ..[And] the word of God remains for ever" (40,5-8).

In the first Servant Song it is Yahweh who speaks, to introduce the servant: "Here is my servant whom I uphold, my chosen one in whom my soul delights. I have sent my spirit upon him, he will bring fair judgement to the nations" (42,1). The servant will persevere faithfully until he has established justice and (divine) law (Heb. **torah**) on earth (v.4). Then comes the role of the servant with regard to a covenant: "I, Yahweh, have called you in saving justice, I have grasped you by the hand and shaped you; I have made you a covenant of the people and light to the nations, to open the eyes of the blind, to free captives from prison, and those who live in darkness from the dungeon. .. See how former predictions have come true. Fresh things I now reveal" (vv.6-9).

The extraordinary declaration that the servant in person has been made "a covenant for the people" must set him firmly on a level with Moses or David, if not even in a new category entirely. Moses was a mediator of the former conditional covenant, and David was the recipient of a covenant promising him a permanent dynasty. Of neither Moses nor David was it ever said that he himself was made a covenant for Israel. It sounds as though this chosen servant, so fondly called and shaped by Yahweh, is able to be the focalpoint in which Israel relates properly to Yahweh. We can gather from the four Songs that he was unreservedly open to God and dedicated to the full return of his people to God. He also surpasses previous prophets in being given explicitly as a light to other nations as well. Yet another remarkable aspect of the covenant made in his own person is that this is a covenant for liberation — "to open the eyes of the blind, to free captives..". The liberation from Egypt was to free the Israelites and enable them as free people to accept voluntarily the covenant at Sinai. Hence on that occasion, liberation was for covenant. In the servant's case, however, he is made a covenant in order that others may be set free; this time covenant is for liberation. The steps may be in a different order, but the redeeming God is the same for both liberations: "I am Yahweh, that is my name! I shall not yield my glory to another, nor my honour to idols" (v.8). Those words recall not only the call of Moses to go back to free his people from Egypt, but also the opening words of the Ten Commandments that sum up Sinai's charter. The verse, comments C. Stuhlmueller, "proclaims the sacred covenantal name of God. ... All nations may one day invoke this name, and in so doing express their prayer for God's continual presence"[16]. Surely this covenant must be included among the "fresh" things which Yahweh is only now revealing (v.9). The Hebrew adjective used here (**hadash**) is the same one that Jer 31,31 uses to announce the new covenant. Having drawn attention to that point, S. Porubcan concludes: "From here it is only a step to consider and call, even formally, this covenant a 'new covenant' "[17].

The second Servant Song, in its "primary vision" (49,1-6), has the servant himself telling of his call right from his mother's womb. He was carefully prepared to speak out God's word with force and sharpness. Despite everything, his toil seemed futile. God reassured him that the prophet's mission went beyond restoring Israel: "I shall make you a light to the nations so that my salvation may reach the remotest parts of earth" (v.6). The "commentary" (49,7-13) again has Yahweh speaking of the servant: "I have formed you and have appointed you to be the covenant for a people, to restore the land, to return ravaged properties, to say to prisoners, 'Come out', to those who are in darkness, 'Show yourselves' " (vv.8-9). As in the first Song, so here too the servant in person is appointed as the covenant. Now the scope of the covenant is extended to include the restoration of the Land and the return of lost properties to the homecoming exiles. All this is motive for rejoicing, "for Yahweh has consoled his people, is taking pity on his afflicted ones" (Hebrew: **'anawim**) (v.13).

It is difficult to be sure that vv.7-13 are still speaking of the one servant in person, rather than about the humble, "afflicted" group of Israelites committed to the new exodus and renewal of true community life back in Judah[18]. We realise that this is one of those passages in which the servant is described as an individual who embodies in his own person the revived exiles, hence he can represent the whole group. Due to that Hebrew concept of "corporate personality", in one verse the accent could be on the individual servant, in another verse on the whole people identified with him as servant[19].

The material restoration should not be taken as evidence that those verses at least have nothing to do with the new covenant, as if they only indicated a return to the covenant of Moses and Joshua. That would be to miss a vital point, namely that under the new covenant respect for the rights of the "afflicted humble ones" will be respected and social justice will prevail, so that such people won't soon be robbed again of their modest dwellings and ancestral lands. That spirit of a new Joshua could also be extended to the afflicted poor of other nations duly impressed by the example of a revitalised Israel.

The fourth Song is unique among all the prophecies, for the reader feels drawn into the crowd looking with astonishment and reflecting aloud on the innocent servant being put to death - and accepting it all to make amends for our rebellion (52,13 - 53,9). But his death is not the end of the Song, which goes on to proclaim: "After the ordeal he has endured, he will see the light and be content. .. my servant will justify many by taking their guilt on himself. Hence I shall give him a portion with the many, and he will share the booty with the mighty, for having exposed himself to death and for being counted as one of the rebellious, whereas he was bearing the sin of many and interceding for the rebellious" (53,11-12).

Although the word covenant is not mentioned in or just after this Song, there is talk of the servant's sufferings "reconciling us" effectively, for "we have been healed by his bruises" (53,5). The servant's mission of reconciliation was overwhelming, since "we had all gone astray like sheep, .. and Yahweh brought the acts of rebellion of all of us to bear on him" (v.6). More than any other chapter in the Old Testament, this one foreshadows the path to be trodden by the servant of Yahweh in order to introduce a new covenant for Israel and a light for all nations. Already it sheds light on earlier prophecies which depicted the covenant as preceding liberation and even preceding forgiveness. In the fourth Song the servant dies in order that reconciliation might be granted to the rest of his people. The forgiveness of sin, promised by Jeremiah as a characteristic of the new covenant, will be granted in response to the self-sacrifice of the servant. A new dimension has been added to the role of covenant-maker. Nor is it doing violence to the text to discern here that "rebels" may be moved to accept the new covenant after it has been established, rather than before its ratification as at Sinai.

As for any subsequent rebellions, there is no indication that they could terminate the new covenant once it has been established. On the contrary, Deutero-Isaiah has in mind an "everlasting covenant", as we shall now see. Using the imagery of married love, God declares: "For your Creator is your husband, Yahweh Sabaoth is his name, the Holy One of Israel is your redeemer. .. In a flood of anger, for a moment I hid my face from you. But in everlasting love I have taken pity on you.. For me it will be as in the days of Noah when I swore that Noah's waters should never flood the world again. .. For the mountains may go away and the hills may totter, but my faithful love will never leave you, my covenant of peace will never totter" (54,5-10). Not only does this promise a covenant as everlasting as Yahweh's love, but it also implies that the new covenant will be as sweeping as the universal and cosmic covenant granted after the Flood. Mention of the "Creator" here acting like a redeeming husband is a way of stressing the greatness of the reconciliation and the unshakeable permanence of the new relationship, a genuine covenant of peace. In this case the marriage will not break up due to unilateral desertion. Since Yahweh had never granted Israel a divorce, the past separation and suffering were due solely to Israel's fault (cf. 50,1-2). One of the greatest lessons to be learnt by the marginated exiles was that Yahweh's saving presence by no means depended on a particular city or temple, nor even on having a big welcome among the exiles. No! Yahweh remains always present and searching for them; to speak of a "return" is really to speak of a unilateral return, parallel to the unilateral desertion.

Fittingly, the last text to speak explicitly of covenant occurs in the final chapter, in which it is depicted as a precious gift to which Yahweh urgently invites the people. Several urgent, double-barrelled imperatives ring out: "Oh, come ..! come! .. buy and eat! .. buy .. without money! .. Listen carefully to me! .. Pay attention, come to me! listen! and you will live" (55,1-3; some exclamation marks added to N.J.B.'s text). Then the purpose of such a pressing invitation is announced: "I shall make an everlasting covenant with you in fulfilment of the favours promised to David. Look, I have made him a witness to peoples, a leader and lawgiver to peoples. Look, you will summon a nation unknown to you" (vv.3-5).

This single explicit mention of the "favours" (**hesed**) promised to David gives a surprising re-orientation to that promissory covenant. Here its fulfilment is to be achieved in the whole new people — "I shall make an everlasting covenant with you", in the plural. The rest of Deutero-Isaiah is silent about any reestablishing of the Davidic monarchy back in Jerusalem. The royal role of David as witness, leader and lawgiver "to peoples" will be continued, but through all the "kingdom" rather than just the king and his dynasty[20]. Von Rad considers that "in thus 'democratizing' the tradition, Deutero-Isaiah actually robbed it of its specific content. Indeed, the Messianic hope had no place in his prophetic ideas"[21]. Notwithstanding his opinion, we can maintain that the promise to David, far from being emptied of its main content, is here purified, so that Israel will not be afflicted again by any king "like other nations have". Because the Davidic dynasty had failed badly to uphold the wider covenant between Yahweh and all Israel, a new role must be assigned to David with regard to the new covenant. The suffering servant and new covenant-maker is not identified with a new David; nor is such an identification excluded[22].

The book of consolation closes by recalling the note on which it opened, consolation and confidence in the creative word of Yahweh, who insists that "it will not return to me unfulfilled or before having carried out my good pleasure and having achieved what it was sent to do" (55,11)

C. DURING THE PERSIAN EMPIRE

1. TRITO-ISAIAH (IN JERUSALEM)

The liberation of the Judean deportees was granted by Cyrus the Persian shortly after he occupied Babylon in 539 B.C. Because Babylon surrendered without any fight, it was able to continue intact, but completely under Persian control. Cyrus permitted those who so wished to return to rebuild Jerusalem and its Temple, in a greatly reduced Judah. Some forty thousand returned immediately with Zerubbabel, a Davidic leader, and the priest Jeshua, plus ten other organizers. After about twenty tough years battling away to restart their little territory, their city and their public worship, they eventually opened the new Temple in 515 B.C. (cf. Ezra cc.1-6).

Many modern scholars are inclined to assign Trito-Isaiah (= Is cc.56-66) mainly to the period leading up to the completion of the Temple, then perhaps for another few decades after that. However, the chapters concerned contain such diverse oracles and styles that they can hardly have come from only one author. In speaking of Trito-Isaiah, therefore, we have in mind the literary work and not one particular prophet[23]. The central block comprising cc.60-62 shows most affinity with Deutero-Isaiah, hence it could be from one of his closest disciples among the repatriated Jews around Jerusalem. It also tells of a prophet's mission to set the people free, and it gives a splendid vision of Jerusalem as the city of God. The four chapters either side of the central section contain many disparate oracles, but in general they are concerned about repentance, justice and holiness in the new Jerusalem, which again is portrayed in glowing terms, opening the way for apocalyptic writers.

The first explicit mention of covenant comes at the end of a section calling for full social justice and an end to rebellion against Yahweh. The kind of fast that God wants is very much oriented towards true fellowship and respect for the freedom of others: "Is not this the sort of fast that pleases me: to break unjust fetters, to undo the thongs of the yoke, to let the oppressed go free, and to break all yokes? Is it not sharing your food with the hungry, and sheltering the homeless poor?" (58,6-7).

Next, a kind of penitential liturgy, admitting the widespread rebellion against Yahweh, concludes: "Then for Zion will come a redeemer, for those who stop rebelling in Jacob, declares Yahweh" (59,20). Attached to this comes the additional promise, in prose: "For my part, this is <u>my covenant</u>, says Yahweh. <u>My spirit</u> with which I endowed you and <u>my words</u> that I have put in your mouth, will not leave your mouth, or the mouths of your children .. henceforth and <u>for ever</u>" (59,21). The wording recalls the Davidic covenant as presented in 2 Sam 23,1-5, where the dying David reviews the benefits he had received: "The <u>spirit of Yahweh</u> speaks through me, <u>his word</u> is in on my tongue; .. Yes, my House stands firm with God: he has made <u>an eternal covenant</u> with me". The juxtaposition of the two texts certainly helps us to appreciate the implications of the later one. It refers to an everlasting covenant along the lines of that with David, hence a covenant which will bring the gifts of God's spirit and effective word. This is offered to all the people and not just to the royal house, so that renewed Israel may be an inspired, prophetic nation.

The only other explicit mention of covenant occurs as a high point within the central block (cc.60-62). The lead up to it is a description of renewed Jerusalem, to which God promises: "I shall make Peace your administration and Saving Justice your government. Violence will no longer be heard of in your country. .. You will call your walls 'Salvation'" (60,17-18). Then comes the chapter describing the prophet's mission in words which were later to be used by Jesus to inaugurate his own mission in Nazareth. As in some of the Servant Songs, here too a servant prophet tells of his call and mission: "The spirit of the Lord Yahweh is on me for Yahweh has anointed me. He has sent me to bring the [good] news to the afflicted, to soothe the broken-hearted, to proclaim liberty to captives, release to those in prison, to proclaim a year of favour from Yahweh and a day of vengeance from our God, to comfort all who mourn" (61,1-3).

This mission is also along the lines just mentioned for David, with its emphasis on spirit, word (of good news), and also interior anointing for a special mission. Here the mission is of the prophet, not the (usual) king. There is also great insistence, as in c.58, on bringing comfort and full freedom to the afflicted, brokenhearted, captives, prisoners, and mourners. "To proclaim a year of favour from Yahweh" must be to declare a Jubilee Year as outlined in Lev 25, whereby there was a "release" of all the enslaved Hebrews and of ancestral properties. Here the panorama includes the release of Hebrews in any way enslaved, despoiled or imprisoned by foreigners. The released and restored Israelites will be called "priests of Yahweh, .. ministers of our God" (61,6) in line with their original call to be a "priestly kingdom", but again the horizon is much wider, envisaging the new Israel ministering in God's name to the other nations as well.

To crown the mission of the prophet comes Yahweh's promise: "I shall reward them faithfully and make an everlasting covenant with them. Their race will be famous throughout the nations and their offspring throughout the peoples. All who see them will admit that they are a race whom Yahweh has blessed" (61,8-9). The talk of "reward" has to be taken in the context of so much talk of "punishment", since Yahweh is by no means indifferent to uprightness; the just will be "rewarded" with life. The "everlasting covenant", however, will not be withheld until the people have merited it as a reward for their own virtue. On the contrary, the reference to the nations and peoples recognising Yahweh's blessing on the new Israel harks back to the entirely gratuitous promise made to Abraham (Gen 12,1-3). The ongoing fulfilment of that promise will be granted through an everlasting covenant equally gratuitous. In confirmation of this, the famous chapter concludes: "..so Lord Yahweh makes saving justice and praise spring up in sight of all nations" (61,11).

The prophet breaks into a beautiful song rejoicing in the new beginning of fruitful relations between Zion and its Builder, "for Yahweh will take delight in you, and your country will have its wedding. Like a young man marrying a virgin, your builder will wed you, and as the bridegroom rejoices in his bride, so will your God rejoice in you" (62,4-5). The newness of this covenant of love is portrayed by the imagery of the young couple and the joyful celebration of the wedding. This is something beyond the return of the adulterous wife as depicted since Hosea. "Even the allusions to the past serve to highlight the newness and freshness of this event. The power of love, its capacity to rejuvenate, its inexhaustible novelty, could not be stated with greater force"[24].

The following chapter, looking back perhaps at the reference to Abraham, appeals to God as Father, who must keep on owning even those whom Abraham would disown. It will also serve to conclude our reflection on covenant in all of Isaiah, for it relies on bonds of spiritual kinship that outlast those of race: "After all, you are our Father. If Abraham will not own us, if Israel will not acknowledge us, you, Yahweh, are our Father, 'Our Redeemer' is your name from of old" (63,16).

2. ZECHARIAH (IN JERUSALEM)

Zechariah was active as a prophet in Jerusalem for a short while around 520 B.C. and encouraged the returned Jews to finish building the new Temple. From this concern have emerged cc. 1-8, which we are now considering. It is common to speak of the remainder of the book, cc.9-14, as being from Deutero-Zechariah some time during the Greek period[25]. Zechariah's personal ministry was therefore addressed to somewhat the same audience as that of Trito-Isaiah. It likewise contains a promise of what seems to be the same covenant that we have just been considering in Trito-Isaiah, hence also in line with the new covenant as foretold by Jeremiah and Ezekiel.

It occurs in ch.8, as one of ten promises in favour of Jerusalem, and presupposes a homecoming of exiles from all directions. "Yahweh Sabaoth says this: Look, I shall rescue my people from the countries of the east and from the countries of the west. I shall bring them back to live in the heart of Jerusalem, and they will be my people and I shall be their God, faithful and just" (vv.7-8). The formula "my people/their God" is the one used by the earlier prophets to sum up the result of the new covenant. As here, they speak of it as something in the future ' "they will be my people.."

Echoes of those earlier prophets can also be heard in Zechariah's lead up to this promise. Before the exile, Yahweh had requested "faithful love (**hesed**) and compassion towards one another", with no oppression of the widows, orphans, poor or strangers (7,9-10). But the people "had made their hearts adamant rather than listen to the teaching" (7,12). So for lack of covenant kindness and for hard-heartedness, they were scattered abroad. Now they have returned to Jerusalem, but there is still something more in store for the future, to ensure that they will be truly and permanently God's people.

3. MALACHI (IN JERUSALEM)

Malachi seems to be a name imposed on an anonymous prophet who spoke about God sending "my messenger" (**malachi**). He was probably active in Jerusalem about 450 B.C., when the enthusiasm and fidelity of many had waned. Malachi's preaching against abuses, especially in connection with worship at the Temple, points to a period before the reform of Ezra and Nehemiah in the latter half of that century.

He has only one passage that appears to refer to a new covenant, and it, too, is connected with the Temple[26]. The announcement begins: "Look, I shall send my messenger to clear a way before me. And suddenly the Lord whom you seek will come to his Temple; yes, the angel of the covenant, for whom you long, is on his way" (3,1). Since Malachi has mentioned the existing covenant with Levi (2,4.8), and then presents the "angel of the covenant" as coming to the Temple to purify the Levites, he obviously expects the (new) covenant to bring about a great purification of Temple worship and sacrifices, as well as Levitical teaching. Yahweh will also call to judgment "those who oppress the wage-earner, the widow and the orphan, and who rob the foreigner of his rights and do not respect me" (3,5). In the light of the N.T. we can see in John the Baptist the messenger (cf. Mt 11,10), and in Jesus the "angel of the covenant", that is, the one who proclaimed and inaugurated the promised new covenant. By offering himself to the Father, he "purified" the Levites to the extent of becoming our "compassionate and trustworthy high priest" (Heb 2,17), replacing the old order of Levites.

Another text of Malachi which merits attention is one which reproaches the men of Judah for breaking their own marriage covenant with their wives by marrying women "of an alien god" (2,10-16). The violation of the individual human covenant is firmly set within the framework of the wider human-divine covenant: "Is there not one Father of us all? Did not one God create us? Why, then, do we break faith with one another, profaning the covenant of our ancestors?" (v.10). He goes on to explain why divorce and remarriage with gentile women goes against the God of creation and of the covenant: "Because Yahweh stands as witness between you and the wife of your youth, with whom you have broken faith, even though she was your partner and your wife by covenant. Did he not create a single being, having flesh and the breath of life? .. For I hate divorce, says Yahweh, God of Israel" (vv.14-16). Malachi begins a train of thought here which Jesus could take up in defence of marriage(cf. Mt 19,3-9), and and which Paul was to develop in presenting the divine covenant as a model to be consciously reflected by Christian couples (cf. Eph 5,21-33).

4. JOEL (IN JERUSALEM)

Joel gives very few indications of the historical period in which he was preaching, making it difficult to date his work with any certainty. We accept the arguments of those who propose a date around 400 B.C., without insisting on it too much[27]. What catches our attention is that Joel, after various reflections arising from a bad plague of locusts and leading on to the Day of Yahweh, opens out a vista of the new age. Its characteristic will be the abundance of the spirit communicated to all the people: "After this I shall pour out my spirit on all humanity. Your sons and daughters shall prophesy, your old people shall dream dreams, and your young people see visions. Even on the slaves, men and women, I shall pour out my spirit in those days" (3,1-2). This can be taken as a further glimpse of how God will achieve that change of stony hearts as promised in Jeremiah and Ezekiel, and how the charisms usually associated with great leaders like prophets, judges or kings, will be granted to all the new community, including the slaves.

We may be disappointed that room is left for slaves in the new Israel, but for Joel the emphasis is on their sharing in the marvellous outpouring of God's spirit, so that they too may "dream dreams" and "see visions" of full liberty as people of God equal to all the other people. Let us remember the great prominence given in those earlier prophets, especially Deutero-Isaiah, to the breaking of every yoke, the ending of all slavery and unjust captivity. Peter proclaimed the arrival of that new age of the Spirit at Pentecost (cf. Acts 2,14-21).

D. DURING THE GREEK PERIOD

1. BARUCH (AMONG EXILES OF THE DIASPORA)

Two centuries of Persian rule came to a rapid end once Alexander the Great set out to take over all their empire and well beyond it. By 331 B.C. he controlled practically all the territory from his native Macedonia across to the Indus River and down to Egypt. Once more, little Judah was simply overrun by the conquering army, which added it to the many states which Alexander dreamed of welding into one vast kingdom unified through Greek language and culture. It meant that Greek became the common official language. The Jews in Judah and those still scattered in the "diaspora" (=dispersion) were drawn into the Greek world of language and ideas. Some of the final books of the Old Testament were written in Greek instead of the traditional Hebrew.

One such book is that of Baruch, which ostensibly addresses the original exiles in Babylon, but that seems to be a literary device to encourage the dispersed Jews of much later times. They were still scattered far and wide in the last century or so before Christ, which some take to be the period for the final redaction of Baruch[28]. Although it may be a slightly later work than that of Daniel, we will consider it now, partly due to its many links with the exile and the longing for a return to Jerusalem, and partly because Daniel must take us into the apocalyptic world.

The most relevant section for our theme is a long prayer in the form of **toda** (Heb. = confession), in Bar 1,15 - 3,8. In the Jewish community prayer, the "confession" on the part of the sinful (and accused) people corresponded to the "lawsuit" instituted by God against them[29]. The humbled people pleaded guilty and, in the penitential setting, "to <u>confess</u> their own infidelity signifies immediately to <u>confess</u> the superiority of the ever faithful partner"[30]. Here the prayer begins by admitting that Israel has been disobedient "from the day when the Lord brought our ancestors out of Egypt until today" (1,19), with "each following the dictates of his evil heart" (1,22). But"<u>now</u>, Lord", they confess, "we have sinned .. Listen, Lord, to our prayers and entreaties .. and think of us" (2,12-16). They remind God of the warning through Moses about punishment for disobedience, and at the same time of the promise that after suffering exile they would repent. Then God's later promise through the prophets is recalled: "I shall give them a heart and an attentive ear, and they will sing my praises in the country of their exile .. and will turn from their evil deeds. Then I shall bring them back to the country which I promised on oath to their ancestors Abraham, Isaac and Jacob, and make them masters in it. ... And I shall make an everlasting covenant with them, so that I am their God and they are my people" (2,31-35).

The prayer is a forerunner of our Christian eucharistic prayer, as shall be seen in more detail when discussing the new covenant in the Gospel. What stands out here is the way God is reminded respectfully that the promises as well as the threats are to be fulfilled. Israel has become keenly aware that its complete restoration and the establishing of a new covenant must depend on God's mercy and fidelity, not on any merits of the Israelites. It is not by accident that the promise to Abraham is recalled, since that was unconditional and irrevocable. We also note that many of the characteristics of the new covenant coincide with those given by the other prophets evaluating the effect of Israel's rebellion against the demands of the Mosaic covenant.

2. DANIEL (BABYLONIAN BACKGROUND ACTUALIZED FOR JERUSALEM)

This book is named, as Hartman & Di Lella observe, "not after its author, but after its protagonist"[31]. Daniel is depicted in the book as among the exiles in Babylon for most of the 6th century B.C., from the time of the mighty Nebuchadnezzar until a mysterious "Darius the Mede" reigned in Babylon. More than half the book as we have it recounts stories about Daniel in that kind of Babylonian setting, showing him as a fully faithful Israelite blessed with wisdom and the interpretation of dreams. These are edifying stories to inculcate confident loyalty towards a supremely wise God, who controls all human affairs, especially empires.

The remainder of the book (cc.7-12) contains visions which are described and interpreted in apocalyptic form. Actually the whole work (leaving aside the additional stories about Daniel which have been tacked on in cc.13-14) has been welded together to serve the interest of the apocalyptic writer. He orchestrates all the material to hand so that a central message emerges with great force: all human kingdoms, typified by those that have overrun Israel, must inevitably give way to the everlasting kingdom of God. That will be a kingdom comprising "the holy ones of the Most High" (9,25.27).

As the book of Daniel is the most sustained apocalyptic work in the Old Testament, a few words must be said about the special features of an apocalyptic writing. Although Daniel and the N.T. Apocalypse(= Revelation) are the only two major apocalyptic works received into the Bible, the Jews wrote some forty apocalyptic works between 200 B.C. and 100 A D.[32]. From all such material - biblical and non-biblical — we can gather that the apocalyptic is a fruit of prophecy, for a time when new prophets are not to be heard. It is significant that at the time of the Maccabees the people were very conscious of the lack of a prophet to guide them in crucial decisions (cf. 1 Mac 4,46; 9,27; 14,40). This was precisely the period during which the book of Daniel took final form, probably between 167-164 B.C. The apocalyptist therefore takes up what earlier prophets have foretold and attempts to "reveal" how it is now being actualized by God, who lets the visionary grasp it secrets in order to reveal them to his contemporaries. This is done through writing, not by preaching as in the case of the prophets[33]. The Hebrew Bible did not include Daniel among the Prophets, but among the Writings.

The apocalyptic avails also of the whole wisdom tradition, in an attempt to organize, codify and actualize the promises of God[34]. Once the order predetermined by God has been grasped, then the steps along the way to fulfilment can be pointed out, thus leaving only a final step until the "time of the End" (cf. 11,40; 12,4.9). Daniel himself is presented as a wise young Jewish exile educated also in the wisdom of the Babylonians, whose wise men he surpassed. He, like Joseph of old, reached high offices because his wisdom was so outstanding. The story of his intervention in the trial of Susanna also attests his wisdom and keen sense of justice (cf.c.13).

Yet another area that greatly concerns the apocalyptist is the unfolding of history until it reaches its ultimate and definitive goal, which obviously must correspond to God's great plan for all human history. Certainly a striking feature in Daniel is the ease with which the author can conjure up one great empire after another, symbolised now as parts of a colossal statue (c.2), now as a fierce animal (c.7), now as a domestic animal or horns thereof (c.8). In each case the once mighty gentile empires, which for a while overwhelmed Israel, will pass away until the definitive kingdom of God emerges and remains.

This leads us into the heart of the matter. The Assyrians may have conquered and dethroned the Israelite kings of Samaria, then the Babylonians may have conquered and dethroned the Davidic kings of Jerusalem. But, reveals Daniel, God has by no means been conquered or dethroned as King, nor rendered powerless by those victories over his people. On the contrary! Those gentile kingdoms are the ones who are utterly powerless to withstand what God has decided to bring about. They will rise and fall in their allotted times, but when God's kingdom is fully established, nothing will ever be able to overthrow it. This theme is well stated early in the book: "In the days of those kings, the God of heaven will set up a kingdom which will never be destroyed, and this kingdom will not pass into the hands of another race: it will shatter and absorb all the previous kingdoms and itself last for ever" (2,44). Here we need to realise that for Daniel, the reign of God is envisaged particularly from God's point of view. The will of God will prevail, even over the proud, the mighty, the impious, those quite unwilling to yield top place to God.

On the other hand, Daniel does leave room for the voluntary acceptance of God's will, by the "holy ones of the Most High". The wise teachers have as their special mission to "instruct many in uprightness" (12,3). That is the aspect of the reign of God we often concentrate on these days, i.e. the voluntary and loving acceptance of God's will by the human will, or, in covenant terms, an irrevocable mutual commitment of both parties. Daniel shows how Ezekiel's promise of a retribution according to each one's personal conduct can become a reality, for there will be a resurrection unto "everlasting life" for those who have been faithful, or unto "everlasting disgrace" for the impious (12,2-3). In this sense also the kingdom of God can be everlasting for each of its citizens granted everlasting life through a bodily resurrection.

The concern for the End (Greek **eschaton**) is another aspect borrowed from the prophets, whose eschatology normally presumed the working out of God's salvation in human history and through human servants of God, who would be empowered to overcome all the human opposition eventually. Special attention was given to an anointed king, a messiah, from the line of David. In Daniel, the symbol of the kingdom of God is "as it were a son of man"(7,13), who comes on the clouds of heaven (and not born on earth from any royal family). Again, this stresses God's part in providing all that is necessary to establish the everlasting kingdom among people on earth. This is extending still further the line of thought noted early in Deutero-Isaiah (55,3), where the special favours promised to David were extended to the people as a whole. In Daniel, "the son of man" is a symbol, but as such it was open to be taken up and enriched, until it was eventually accepted by Jesus as a fitting way to describe himself without stressing kingly claims.

The apocalyptic needed to stress God's inexorable control over all empires, because it was a literature especially for times of religious persecution or other great trials of the faithful. Daniel alludes to the persecution going on at the time of writing, when the Seleucid king Antiochus IV Epiphanes was trying to impose Greek language and customs by force of arms upon the Jews. Some Jews were willing to enter into an alliance with the Seleucids (cf.9,27), which meant breaking their covenant with God (cf.11,30.32). Others like the Maccabees were willing to die rather than forsake the covenant (cf.1 Mac 1,57; 2,20.27). It is against that background of a deadly persecution that we will now look more closely at Daniel 9, which illustrates well how an earlier prophetic theme can be reworked in an apocalyptic key. It also presents, at least implicitly, a rethinking or updating of what Jeremiah promised about the restoration, including the new covenant.

Ch.9 is set in Babylon, but in the reign of a king Darius the Mede who does not square with history as we know it. The vagueness about historical facts is already a pointer to a literary form other than that of history. By the end of the chapter we will realise that the writer is really reviewing history from about the time when the Medes and Persians took over Babylon until the time of Antiochus Epiphanes' persecution throughout Judah. This is another characteristic of the apocalyptic, to seem to be foretelling how periods of history will work out, whereas the early periods have already come and gone. What really matters is to try and make known the final big step. So we find Daniel in 6th century Babylon pondering the prophecy of Jeremiah about the seventy years of desolation for Jerusalem. The time has elapsed and yet Jerusalem is still in the hands of the desecrating gentiles.

Daniel's prayer for further light on the deeper meaning of that prophecy leads him to make a "confession" such as we looked at in Baruch[35]. It is again the counterpart of God's "lawsuit" against Israel, for Daniel, accepting solidarity with his sinful people, confesses that God is just and completely faithful to their covenant: "you keep the covenant and show faithful love towards those who love you and who observe your commandments: we have sinned.." (v.4). The fault is all on Israel's part, but now (v.15) , he pleads, "Hear Lord, and act! .. - since your city and your people alike bear your name" (v.19). The prayer itself indicates that Jeremiah's promise has not yet been completely fulfilled, for there is little evidence of a properly restored Jerusalem or of a people distinguishable for their new heart or covenant loyalty. It also offsets the supposed determinism in the apocalyptic, for Daniel is obviously praying here in "an attempt to mobilize God's compassion so as to change the history" currently unfolding[36].

While Daniel was still confessing his own sins and those of his people, the angel Gabriel was sent to teach him to understand, for Daniel was "a man specially chosen" (vv.20-23). That adds solemnity to the revelation that follows, namely that it is no longer a matter of 70 years, but "seventy weeks are decreed" (v.24), i.e. 7 times 70 years. Only when that time has elapsed will there be "an end to transgression" and the introduction of "everlasting uprightness" - the biblical "justice" so frequently demanded through the prophets that its definitive establishment will truly be "setting the seal on vision and prophecy" (v.24).

The final week, i.e. 7 years, brings us down to the bitter years of persecution by Antiochus IV, from 171 to 164 B.C. The second half of that period was to be forever remembered because of the "appalling abomination" by which he desecrated the Temple (v.27). The real prediction of Daniel is that the impious king will soon meet the doom in store for him. Then once that tyrant had been killed and the Temple rededicated to God, later generations were tempted to extend the "weeks" of Daniel to provide further clues to the date of the messiah's arrival. However, only God knows when "the fulness of time" has come; to humans it is not foretold beforehand with mathematical accuracy.

NOTES

1. Cf. New Jerusalem Bible, 1175.
2. Cf. Alonso Schökel & J. Sicre, op.cit. II, 667-681 for dates and location of Ezekiel's ministry. Also E. Beaucamp, Prophetic Intervention in the History of Man (New York: Alba House, 1970) 141-149. For a summary of events influencing Ezekiel's preaching in Babylon, see L. Boadt, "Ezekiel" in NJBC, 305-309.
3. Cf.C.T. Begg, "b^{e}rit in Ezekiel", in Ninth World Congress of Jewish Studies, Division A (Jerusalem: World Union of Jewish Studies, 1986) 77-84. He finds that of the 18 occurrences of the term in Ezekiel, 7 "denote a

future arrangement which YHWH announces he will initiate with (or on behalf of) Israel" (77-78).
4. Cf. L. Boadt, art.cit. 316-317.
5. J. Sicre, Los Dioses Olvidados, 149-152.
6. Id. Con Los Pobres, 401-404, explaining the implications of Jerusalem being a city of blood (Ez 22).
7. Alonso Schökel & J. Sicre, op.cit. II, 817, where Ez 36,16-30 is described as "a great oracle of restoration", for "Dios decide la restauración, una nueva alianza que se realiza primero internamente y después se realiza en diversas bendiciones."
8. Cf.: C. Stuhlmueller, The Book of Isaiah Chapters 40-66 (Collegeville: O.T. Reading Guide, Liturgical Press, 1965); id. "Deutero-Isaiah and Trito-Isaiah" in NJBC, 329-344.
Also: Alonso Schökel & Sicre, I, 263 ff., where the opening paragraph mentions that many consider Deutero-Isaiah "the greatest prophet and best poet of Israel".
9. Cf. C. Stuhlmueller, Creative Redemption in Deutero-Isaiah, esp. c.5 on "Yahweh-go'el, Israel's Creative Redeemer", 99-131, e.g. 107: "We thus recognize more clearly the persistent context of redemption and love within which Dt-Is introduced the idea of Yahweh-creator. Because the **go'el** idea of kinsman, father and spouse is applied analogically to Yahweh, this new series of terms can be considered practically synonymous with [the Heb. root] **g'l** and an indirect witness to the 'kinship' between Yahweh and Israel." Finally: "In the Bk Con [= Book of Consolation], therefore, the idea of creation helped to bring out the colossal proportions of redemption, but the redemptive context kept that idea of creation within the bond of personal love"(236).
10. Cf. G. von Rad, The Message of the Prophets, 238: "In the last resort, the question was whether the contemporaries of this prophet could still understand themselves as the Israel which had once been brought to life by God. God's history with his people did not continue automatically, once it had begun."
11. Cf.: H. Renckens, Israel's Concept of the Beginning (New York: Herder, 1964) 20-22: "In short, it was equally characteristic of Israel to live on the past as it was to hope in the future. ... The more difficult it becomes to go on believing in the future, the more tenaciously faith hangs on to its footing in the past. We find all this summed up in the thought of the greatest of Israel's prophets, Isaias 40-55. .. [Yahweh] is not only 'the First' who created 'all things of old'; he is also 'the Last' who will create 'all things new'." Also G. von Rad, op.cit, 210: "Indeed, Deutero-Isaiah sees the whole course of world-history from the viewpoint of its correspondence with a previously spoken prophetic word." And J. Bishop, The Covenant: A Reading, 116, where he draws attention to the way interest in creation came after the great national disaster; the Priestly account of creation would have been emerging about the same time as Deutero-Isaiah.

12. Cf. C. Stuhlmueller, The Book of Isaiah cc.40-66, 20: "[Dt-Is's] style follows the form of liturgical hymns, and his poems can never be fully appreciated unless they are sung or heard. We think to ourselves: they are ideal for Sabbath ceremonies in the first Jewish meeting-halls or 'synagogues' of Babylon."
13. Cf. New Jerusalem Bible, 1169 on "Book of Consolation".
14. Cf. S. Porubcan, Il Patto Nuovo in Is.40-66, esp. pp.88-134 which deal with the new covenant as found in the first two Servant Songs.
15. Cf. New Jerusalem Bible, 1169 for extension of the Songs; also Alonso Schökel & J. Sicre, Profetas, I, 271.
16. C. Stuhlmueller, op.cit., 40.
17. S. Porubcan, op.cit. 130-131: " Abbiamo concluso che alle 'cose nuove', di cui al v.9 appartiene anche il 'patto del popolo'(v.6) .. ne è la base oggetiva. De qui un solo passo per considerare e chiamare, anche formalmente, questo patto 'patto nuovo'" (author's emphasis). Cf. P. Buis, "La Nouvelle Alliance" in Vetus Testamentum XVIII (1968) No 1, 1-15, where he looks systematically at the recurring "themes" in the O.T. texts about the new covenant. Of Deutero-Isaiah he notes the special contribution: "Il réintroduit le médiateur dont on avait noté l'absence dans la nouvelle alliance. Le message isaïen est donc indispensable à une théologie complète de la nouvelle alliance" (14-15).
18. Cf: C. Stuhlmueller, Creative Redemption, 13-15; 206-208. Also: B. Anderson, The Living World of the O.T., 456-470 for a good presentation of the extent and meaning of the Servant Songs.
19. Cf.: B. Anderson, op.cit. esp. 457-462 on both individual and corporate interpretation of the Servant of these Songs. Also: W. Harrington, Record of the Promise: The Old Testament (Dublin: Helicon, 1966) 224-226, e.g. 225-6: "It is hard to deny that the Servant figure has both corporate and personal characteristics; he is at one and the same time, the Messiah and the messianic people."
20. Cf: C. Stuhlmueller, The Book of Isaiah cc.40-66, 109-110: "The benefit or 'gift of love' which God promised to David five centuries ago is now being granted to all the people. Royal blood is not required, only obedient faith to God's word." Also: Alonso Schökel & J. Sicre, Profetas, I, 338, where they see in Is 55,3-5 a kind of divine reply to the questions raised in Psalm 89 because of the dethroning of David's line. That promissory covenant with David will be honoured by God, but in a new way that benefits all the people.
21. G. von Rad, op.cit. 208. He also remarks: "This bold reshaping of the old David tradition is an example, though admittedly an extreme one, of the freedom with which the prophets re-interpreted old traditions." Cf. E. Beaucamp, Les Prophètes d'Israel ou le drame d'une Alliance (Quebec: Université Laval, 1968^2) 273-4 on the extension of the future Kingdom to all civilisations; and 267 on the role of the Servant as Mediator of the new covenant, a role beyond that of David.

22. S. Porubcan, op.cit. 292: "Per il patto [nuovo, di Is. 40-66] e il regno davidico tale identificazione viene posta in termini espliciti in Is.55,3-5 e parall. ..; per la persona del Servo e del Re Davidico l'ultima equazione, esplicita, non viene posta, ma manca esa sola, tutti gli altri elementi e le premesse d'identificazione esistono." Cf.: W. Brueggemann, The Land, 148: "Second Isaiah makes a connection which will be important to the NT and for every homeless group. Kingship of Yahweh leads to homecoming. Rule by Yahweh means the end of homelessness because he is a God who wills land for his people." Also: H.H. Rowley, The Servant of the Lord and Other Essays on the O.T. (Oxford: B. Blackwell, 1965^2) Essay 2: "The Suffering Servant and the Davidic Messiah", 61-93,, e.g. :"There is no serious evidence, then, of the bringing together of the concepts of the Suffering Servant and the Davidic Messiah before the Christian era"(90). "They [scholarly endeavours] have made much clearer the relation between these conceptions, and also their relations to the conception of the Son of Man, and enabled us more clearly to perceive that in our Lord's bringing of them together He was doing no violence to them, but was uniting ideas that had a common root and had many points of connexion with one another" (93).
23. Cf: C. Stuhlmueller, art. cit. (in NJBC) 344-348. Also: Alonso Schökel & J. Sicre, op.cit. I, 341-347. For a wider range of possibilities with regard to origins of cc.56-66, see O. Eissfeldt, The Old Testament, 341-346.
24. Alonso Schökel & J. Sicre, op.cit. I, 373: "Expresamente se habla de jóvenes que se casan, no de adultos que se reconcilian; de modo que incluso las alusiones al pasado sirven para realizar la novedad y frescura del acontecimiento. No se puede decir con más fuerza la fuerza del amor, su capacidad de rejuvenecer, su novedad inagotable."
25. Cf: R.J. Coggins, Haggai, Zechariah, Malachi (Sheffield: JSOT Press, 1987) 60: "As will shortly be seen, the book of Zechariah, although this has attracted less attention [than that of Isaiah], has been divided by critical scholars in a comparable way, with the first part (1-8) containing a nucleus of material going back to Zechariah himself, though with extensive editorial elaborations, and the remainder of the book, which cannot be attributed to Zechariah or his immediate circle, consisting of two collections, chs. 9-11 and 12-14. It has thus become customary to think of 'Deutero-' and 'Trito-Zechariah'". Nevertheless, Coggins accepts that the book as we have it evidences a certain unity between the different parts (cf.61 and 68).
26. Cf. D. McCarthy, Institution and Narrative, 310: "Still in the post-exilic period, Malachi is even more clear. With all its concern about worship — no mean thing in Itself — a set of verses like Malachi 3,1-10 sounds like the earliest prophets in its insistence on justice and its emphasis on judgment." Also 407-408 on the strong denunciation by Malachi (2,13-16) of those who have broken faith with the wife of their youthful "covenant".

NOTES

27. Cf. Alonso Schökel & J. Sicre, op.cit. 926. Also: E.D.Mallon, "Joel [&] Obadiah", in NJBC, 400, who concludes from the fragmentary indications available for the dating of Joel: "A date between the last half of the 5th and the first half of the 4th cent. seems best to fit the context."
28. Cf. New Jerusalem Bible, 1173, where the date suggested for Baruch is mid-first century B.C. Alonso Schökel & J.Sicre, op.cit. II, 1312 consider the evidence too jejune to date it with any confidence; they mention C.A.Moore's recent conclusion dating it between 1st and 2nd cent. B.C.
29 Cf. C. Giraudo, La Struttura Letteraria, 118-122.
30. Ibid. 388, where he brings out well the twofold meaning of the Heb. **toda** : "Infatti in contesto sacrale 'confessare la propria infedeltà' significa immediatamente 'confessare la superiorità del partner sempre fedele'" (author's emphasis).
31. L. Hartman & A. Di Lella, "Daniel", in NJBC, 406.
32. Cf: R.H. Charles: The Apocrypha and Pseudepigrapha of the O.T. in English (Oxford: University Press, 1963-4). E. Hennecke, The N.T. Apocrypha: Vol.II: Apostolic and Early Church Writings (London: Lutterworth Press, 1965). D. Russell, The Method and Message of Jewish Apocalyptic (London: S.C.M., 1964). G. Vermes, The Dead Sea Scrolls in English (Harmondsworth: Pelican pb., rev.ed., 1968). M. McNamara, The N.T. and the Palestinian Targum to the Pentateuch (Rome: Pontifical Biblical Institute, 1966), esp. 189-237 for its influence on the apocalyptic.
33. Cf. B. Vawter, "Apocalyptic: Its Relation to Prophecy" in Catholic Biblical Quarterly XXII(1960) 33-46, e.g. 41:"The transition from prophecy to apocalyptic was an effortless one, for the prophets shared the eschatological tradition of which the apocalyptic is the elaboration." Again: 44: "With the disappearance of prophecy, apocalyptic was left its heir, a literary form in its own right. It retained the prophetic message without the prophetic vision." Cf. G. von Rad , op cit. 271-274 for reasons why apocalyptic seems to owe more to wisdom than to prophecy. The view of history found in the apocalyptic is sharply different from that of the prophets.
34. Cf. Alonso Schökel & J. Sicre, op.cit. I, 1223-1224 re influences at work in the emergence of apocalyptic at the time of composition of Daniel.
35. C. Giraudo, op.cit. 116-125.
36. Alonso Schökel & J. Sicre, op.cit. II, 1282: "Interceder no es simple desahogo ni estímulo hacia dentro; es un intento de movilizar la compasión de Dios para que cambie la historia, demasiado determinada por un sistema de pecados. Esto es más notable cuando el autor piensa que el destino está definido, aun temporalmente, por Dios: si hasta la fecha está señalada, ¿para qué rezar?"

CHAPTER 8: COVENANT IN CHRONICLER'S AND MACCABEAN HISTORY, IN WISDOM AND PSALMS, AND IN QUMRAN COMMUNITY

INTRODUCTION

We have now seen something of the development in understanding, living out and renewing the covenant well into the Greek period. What we still need to look at, in a more summary way, is the attitude to covenant manifested in the Chronicler's history and then in the Maccabean history. After that will come a brief reflection on the rich wisdom literature, which generally does not appeal to "salvation history" nor the divine covenants for its norms. Finally we must catch at least a few strains of the sacred songs of Israel now preserved for us as the Psalms, which express in praise, lament and confident supplication all the main biblical concerns, including the Mosaic and Davidic covenants. By way of transition from the Old to the New Testament we will glance at the Qumran community, which strove fervently to be a "community of the new covenant" by renewing the Mosaic covenant.

A. COVENANT IN THE CHRONICLER'S HISTORY

We accept with many commentators that the books of 1 & 2 Chronicles, Ezra and Nehemiah, in their final form, are the work of the same author. He is commonly termed the Chronicler, because 1 & 2 Chronicles constitute the largest part of the whole composition[1]. These first two books open with 9 cc. of genealogies, beginning from Adam, recording especially the house of David till the exile and even beyond it. After a brief account of Saul's death in battle, "in the infidelity of which he had been guilty towards Yahweh" (10,13), the remainder of both books concentrate on David and his successors on the throne in Jerusalem, "until Yahweh's wrath with his people became so fierce that there was no further remedy" (2 Ch 36,16). The last few lines mention the destruction of the city and its Temple by the Babylonians, then the proclamation of Cyrus permitting the exiles to return to Jerusalem and rebuild the Temple[2].

The books of Ezra and Nehemiah, so called after their two principal characters, take up the story from that crucial decree of Cyrus. They tell of the immediate return of tens of thousands of Jews from Babylon to reoccupy Judah and rebuild Jerusalem, especially its Temple. Ezra cc.1-6 tell how the return was organised and the Temple rebuilt by 515 B.C. The rest of Ezra and Nehemiah tells of the period from about 445 - 428 B.C. (or possibly 398 B.C., if Ez 7,7 refers to the "7th year of Artaxerxes" II). The genealogies of David and the high priest seem to reach at least 400 B.C. In short, the Chronicler reviews the history of the Davidic kings and their relation to the Temple, to worship, and to the whole worshipping community around Jerusalem, until its destruction. All that part we can compare with what the Deuteronomic historian has concerning the same period. For the post-exilic section, from about 538 to 400 B.C., the Chronicler is our only guide. A comparison of 1 & 2 Chronicles with the Deuteronomic history indicates that the former has selected and adapted material to suit his obvious theological point of view about the Temple in Jerusalem being central for the people of God. Knowing that the general history was already available, the Chronicler chose to present more of a sustained reflection on it, which some refer to as a kind of O.T. **midrash** (= searching, meditating upon, interpreting)[3]. In Ezra and Nehemiah the writer obviously draws on the written memoirs of both leaders, and the overall result is somewhat closer to other biblical history. Some would even posit an author or redactor for Ezra and Nehemiah distinct from that of 1 - 2 Chronicles[4]. The Chronicler's work is to be dated about 400 B.C. and before the inroads of Hellenism as from 330 B.C.[5]. The author is presumed to be a Levite, so great is his interest in the Levites (who are mentioned some 160 times throughout the work[6]). J. Meyers sees good reasons supporting the theory that the author was really Ezra the scribe in person, at least for the major part of the composition: "Ezra appears a more and more likely candidate for authorship"[7]. The same Ezra is credited with having based his renewal programme on the Pentateuch, and his spiritual leadership has won for him the title of "the father of Judaism"[8].

A big concern of the Chronicler is to show the continuity of the little Judean community with the Israel of old. In fact he goes back to show the link with Adam (1 Ch 1,1), and also recalls the covenant sworn to Abraham, Isaac and Jacob —"an eternal covenant for Israel" (1 Ch 16,17). Although he gives such prominence to the role of David's house in promoting proper Temple worship, he by no means neglects Moses and the sacred **Torah**. Indeed, he names Moses some 30 times and the Torah 40 times, referring to it several times as the "Torah of the Lord". He likewise refers to covenant more than 30 times and to **hesed** more than 20 times[9]. With regard to the promissory Davidic covenant, the Chronicler presents the continued security of the throne as conditional for Solomon, e.g.: "I shall make his sovereignty secure for ever if he sturdily carries out my commandments and ordinances as he does now" (1 Ch 28,7; cf. 2 Ch 7,17-22).

Writing a couple of centuries after the last good Davidic king (Josiah) had ruled in Jerusalem, the Chronicler clearly accepts that the line of David had forfeited their right to a secure throne. Nor does he show any great yearning to see their throne set up and occupied again in Jerusalem. The house of God is what really holds top priority, and David's house is given such prominence because of its great contribution in getting that Temple and its worship properly established. The Chronicler has such a deep respect for the Torah of God that he must assess even the Davidic kings as bound by its demands —and subject to its sanctions. In that sense the kings were never promised immunity from the consequences of violating the Mosaic covenant. The contemporary situation of the worshipping community centred around the Temple and acknowledging Yahweh as their only King once again clarified in what sense

COVENANT AND LIBERATION

Israel was meant to be "a kingdom of priests, a holy nation" (Ex 19,6). There was a broad messianic hope kept alive within that sort of kingdom, and the frequent references to David showed that the promise to him was not to be forgotten.

Several of the Davidic kings are singled out for special mention because they led their people to renew the Mosaic covenant. For instance, in the days of king Asa all the people assembled in Jerusalem, where they "made a covenant to seek Yahweh .. with all their heart and soul. .. They pledged their oath to Yahweh in ringing tones, with shouts of joy ..; Yahweh gave them peace all round" (2 Ch 15,12-15). King Hezekiah (in the time of Isaiah the prophet) declared: "I am now determined to make a covenant with Yahweh, God of Israel, so that his fierce anger may turn away from us" (2 Ch 29,10). The public renewal of the covenant by Josiah(in the days of Jeremiah the prophet and Hulda the prophetess) is retold almost in the same words as we have earlier noted in 2 K 23(2 Ch 34,14-33). Such passages express the ideal that the king should be an active viceroy of Yahweh the King, encouraging the loyalty of all his people to the covenant, which alone would maintain Israel as a genuine people of God.

Likewise, both Ezra and Nehemiah were outstanding for their zeal to have the Mosaic covenant renewed in a restored Jerusalem. The most striking account of this is found in Nehemiah cc.8-10. Ch.8 tells of a great gathering of "men, women and all those old enough to understand", who came to hear Ezra reading "the Book of the Law of Moses which Yahweh had prescribed for Israel". Ezra read and explained the Book "from dawn till noon" (vv.1-3). The governor Nehemiah is mentioned as being present(v.9). The reading continued each morning for the seven days of the feast (of Tabernacles or Shelters), culminating in a "solemn assembly" on the eighth day(v.18).

Ch. 9 describes at length the fast and confession of sin (**todah**), which recalls the giving of the Mosaic covenant and the many subsequent violations of it by the Israelites down to the time of this public national confession. As in other examples of this kind of confession, the people admit their corporate infidelity, but with a view to begging forgiveness and reconciliation with the offended partner: "<u>Now</u>, our God, the Great God, .. maintaining the covenant and your faithful love —count as no small thing this misery which has befallen us, our kings, our princes, our priests, our prophets, and all your people.. .. Despite the wide and fertile country which you had lavished on them, they did not serve you.. See, we are slaves today, slaves in the country which you gave to our ancestors for them to eat the good things it produces" (vv.32-36).

That confession highlights with great clarity how the serious violations of the covenant led Israel right back to slavery, but not in Egypt this time. The slavery had engulfed the Israelites right in the middle of the Land so generously entrusted to them by Yahweh. Their Land had not been properly cherished nor shared by them in freedom and fellowship. The latest attempt of Jewish "nobles and officials" to reduce to slavery "their brother Jews" had been strongly reprimanded and successfully stopped by an angry Nehemiah. The victims had protested to him that "though we belong to the same race as our brothers, and

IN POST-EXILIC HISTORY, IN PSALMS & WISDOM

our children are as good as theirs, we shall have to sell our sons and our daughters into slavery; some of our daughters have been sold into slavery already. We can do nothing about it, since our fields and our vineyards now belong to others" (Neh 5,5).

Hence arose their humble appeal to Yahweh to have compassion on them and liberate them anew from their continuing slavery as a tiny nation held subservient to the powerful Persian empire. Ch.10 tells of the signing and sealing of a solemn promise under oath "to follow the law of God given through Moses, servant of God, and to observe and practise all the commandments of Yahweh our Lord, with his rules and his statutes"(v.30). This solemn commitment was made by "all those who had reached the age of discretion" (v.29) and were willing to accept the standards set by Ezra and Nehemiah in their reforms. It was basically a renewal of the Mosaic covenant to meet the new conditions around Jerusalem and a reorganized Judah.

B. COVENANT IN THE MACCABEAN HISTORY

Unlike 1 & 2 Samuel, 1 & 2 Kings, 1 & 2 Chronicles, the two books we are about to consider arose independently of each other. 1 Maccabees was probably written originally in Hebrew, or possibly in Aramaic, although it has come down to us only in the Greek translation. On the other hand, 2 Maccabees was originally written in Greek and intended for the Jews living around Alexandria in the Nile Delta of Egypt. What is still more surprising for the modern reader is that 2 Maccabees deals in detail with the period already covered by 1 Maccabees 1-7, then it stops! Both books take their title from Judas Maccabee, the most outstanding of the three brothers who, one after the other, led the armed rising against the Seleucid kings of Antioch in Syria. The proper name, Judas Maccabee, appears in 1 M 5,34 and throughout 2 M. The Hebrew term "Maccabee" could mean "hammer", or it may mean "designated by Yahweh"[10]. Although only Judas was the real "Maccabee", the name was extended to his brothers as well.

The Chronicler's history which we have just considered brought us down to the end of the 5th century, or perhaps into the start of the 4th century B.C. After that vigorous beginning of "Judaism" the O.T. is practically silent on life around Jerusalem for the following two hundred years. Although 1 M casts an eye back over the reign of Alexander the Great (336-323) as the root cause of the spread of Hellenism (e.g. Greek culture, bearing on government, language, religion, attitudes and way of life, including gymnastics), the main focus of attention for both 1 and 2 M is the period beginning with the reign of Antiochus IV Epiphanes(175-164 B.C.). Both books cover the events till 160 B.C., but 2 M stops before the death of Judas Maccabee that year. 1 M continues on till the time of John Hyrcanus(134-104), who became high priest and ethnarch, maintaining the practical autonomy and religious freedom won through the long years of armed rebellion by the Maccabee brothers.

The rebellion was provoked by the Seleucid king, Antiochus IV, whose capital was Antioch by the river Orontes in Syria. He had himself proclaimed

171

"god made manifest, bearer of victory", encapsulated in his title "Epiphanes". He wanted to impose Greek language and religion on all his subjects, including the Jews around Palestine. On learning of the courageous opposition of many Jews, he stepped up the efforts to smash all resistance, even if it meant killing off all those unwilling to submit to his decrees. He disgusted the Jews by defiling their Temple with a statue and sacrifices to Zeus ("the abomination of desolation"). He also issued an edict that "anyone not obeying the king's command was to be put to death" (1 M 1,50).

The Jewish revolt against Antiochus IV was sparked off by Mattathias, a priest who lived in Modein. He slew a Jew who was offering sacrifice to Zeus, and he slew the king's agent who had come to enforce the edict. Defiantly Mattathias cried out throughout the town: "Let everyone who has any zeal for the Law and takes his stand on the covenant come out and follow me" (2,27). His zeal for the covenant was again displayed in his farewell exhortation to his sons: "This is the time, my children, for you to have a burning zeal for the Law and to give your lives for the covenant of our ancestors" (2,50). Three years after the Temple had been desecrated, Judas Maccabee was able to purify it and rededicate it, in December of 164 B.C.(cf. 1 M 4 and 2 M 10). From then on the Jews gradually won more concessions and eventually they achieved religious freedom and national autonomy.

It is clear, therefore, that the Maccabees' determined stance on the covenant provided a strong enough basis to withstand the most blatant systematic attempt to assimilate and absorb their fragile nation into a more powerful gentile empire. In this case we may justly claim that the covenant proved to be an adequate motivation and source of courage to secure liberation through armed revolt accompanied by wise negotiations.

The Jewish independence was maintained amidst many difficulties until the Romans decided it was time to incorporate Palestine into their expanding empire in 63 B.C. It was to remain under Roman control until long after the time of Christ.

C. COVENANT IN WISDOM LITERATURE

In speaking of wisdom literature of the O.T. we have in mind the following six books: Proverbs, Job, The Song of Songs, Ecclesiastes (or Qoheleth), Ecclesiasticus (or Ben Sira), and The Book of Wisdom. The list follows the chronological order of composition for the main part of each book, in so far as it can be deduced, in some cases from scanty indications. The central part of Proverbs (cc.10-29), for example, could well be mainly from the time of Solomon, the great patron of wisdom in Israel. That puts its composition back round 950 B.C. At the other extreme, the Book of Wisdom was written in Greek, presumably in Alexandria of Egypt, some time between 100 to 50 B.C.. The earlier chapters of Proverbs, plus Job and The Song of Songs emerged about 500-400 B.C., followed by Ecclesiastes perhaps 300 B.C., and ben Sira about 180 B.C.[11]. The dates are given in an effort to indicate that wisdom was a constant factor in the life and conduct of Israel, expressing attitudes and values not linked explicitly to sacred history or to the covenant in particular. The human person as human, firmly set within all creation as its masterpiece and principal voice, was considered worthy of the sage's attention[12]. It also reflects an international heritage that Israel was not ashamed to make its own and to enrich, gradually linking it to the unique wisdom found in and communicated only by Yahweh[13].

The wisdom literature seems to me to have blazed the trail for ongoing reflection (and dialogue or dialectic) between theory and practice. The sages of Israel did not, like the prophets, await a special "word of the Lord" before they spoke to the community. Instead, they reflected night and day on all the world around them; their gaze took in all creation, all the rhythm and changes of nature, all the experiences of daily life. They also gathered and reflected on the wisdom already accumulated by their predecessors from many of the nations surrounding Israel, e.g. the Egyptians, the Assyrians, the Aramaeans, the Canaanites, the Edomites. Wisdom was truly an international treasure, considered by such nations as indispensable for the proper government of a country and the right ordering of daily life in harmony with nature and the gods responsible for nature[14].

The sages of Israel, therefore, were the voices articulating daily experience —daily **praxis**, to use the Greek term now commonly adopted by liberation theologians. By reflecting on the accumulated attitudes, customs, wise sayings, legal precedents, etc. already operative within their community, they were enabled to confront new situations and so refine still further, if necessary, the wisdom of their ancestors. Having received new insights that way, they strove diligently to communicate their practical wisdom to kings and commoners, recording it in writing for a wider and also a later audience[15]. It is noteworthy that the tendency in wisdom literature of the O.T. was the opposite to that of our Christian theology, which is "faith seeking understanding" (from reason). For the sages, wisdom in Israel entailed, after reason had done its part, "understanding seeking (more light from) faith." This can be perceived in Proverbs, for instance, since the proverbs more directly dependent on Solomon are about natural observations and remarks on how community life should be lived by Yahweh's people. Then in cc.1-9, which would be mainly post-exilic, we find wisdom is personified and placed beside the Creator of the universe —"when he fixed the heavens firm, I was there" (8,27). The close relation with Yahweh is further emphasised: "Whoever finds me finds life, and obtains the favour of Yahweh" (8,35).

R. Murphy can speak about the "theologizing of wisdom", especially after the exile, when there was no longer a royal court in Jerusalem, but instead a religious school in which wisdom was further drawn in to the expression of Israel's unique heritage[16]. G. Gutiérrez does not hesitate to acknowledge the contribution which (Christian) wisdom has made and still can make towards liberation theology. "Theology as a critical reflection on Christian praxis in the light of the Word does not replace the other functions of theology, such as wisdom and rational knowledge; rather it presupposes and needs them"[17]. Not merely does theology of this kind not replace biblical wisdom, but it also follows in wisdom's footsteps when it directs the Christian's attention to daily socio-political and economic affairs in order to evaluate them. In evaluating them, the Christian must at the same time be ready to gain new insights into what God is doing or demanding in the midst of such daily events that affect so many of the community.

In this regard the example of both David and Solomon are very instructive. When Joab wanted to persuade David to allow his rebellious son Absalom to return from exile, he sought out a wise woman of Tekoa. The wise woman made a good case for Absalom under the guise of a "dramatic fiction" about two sons of her own[18]. As soon as David let her know that he sensed the mind of Joab in the little scheme, the woman had to exclaim to David that "my lord has the wisdom of the Angel of God" (2 Sam 14,20). David then granted the implicit petition of Joab by allowing Absalom to return. The wise woman effectively prodded the wise king to practise with regard to the rebellious son the same kind of wisdom he had shown in dealing with the fictitious case. In modern terms, she was able to persuade the king to adopt a praxis in keeping with his theory. All that was in a case of considerable political importance, since Absalom was still a strong contender for the throne of David, as Joab well knew.

Due to further rebellion, Absalom was killed by Joab, and eventually Solomon succeeded to the throne shortly before David died. At the beginning of his reign, Solomon pleased Yahweh by his prayer for wisdom at Gibeon: "So give your servant a heart to understand how to govern your people, how to discern between good and evil, for how could one otherwise govern such a great people as yours?"(1 K 3,9). Solomon was then granted exceptional wisdom to help him govern Yahweh's covenanted people. In this way his wisdom, acquired through contact with the surrounding nations and increased by reflection on daily experience within Israel, was open to enrichment through the guiding light of Yahweh's boundless wisdom. The covenant standards served as a permanent criterion whereby Israel could judge and, when necessary, adapt what was borrowed from other nations[19].

The book of Job provides a gripping example of traditional wisdom seeking more light from God in the face of a human situation that seemed to contradict the sages' teaching. Job was a just man who suffered profoundly despite his innocence, and his reputedly wise comforters could do no more than try to persuade him to admit that somehow he was guilty. There was no way Job could lie to himself or his comforters, being a noble-minded citizen aware of his abiding attitude towards the poor, the widowed, the orphans, the oppressed. He had constantly helped them, not harmed them in any way. Job appealed to God to come down to settle his case personally, so sure was he that a just God could not but give the verdict in his favour.

At last, "from the heart of the tempest, Yahweh gave Job his answer" (Job 38,1). The substance of the answer was that Yahweh's wisdom far surpasses that of Job, who must therefore accept the way God runs the universe and directs human affairs. Job admits humbly that he has spoken out of turn, as one less wise. Having now seen God with his own eyes, he readily confesses that "you have told me about great works that I cannot understand, about marvels that are beyond me, of which I know nothing. .. I retract what I have said" (42,3-6). Yahweh then rebuked the comforters "for not having spoken correctly about me as my servant Job has done" (42,7). This, together with the way Yahweh blessed Job again with health, family and double his previous wealth, indicates that Job had done well in appealing for divine intervention, even if his attitude called for some modification[20]. Or, in our earlier phrase, his too-limited understanding was right to seek more light from faith.

The long centuries of reflection on the relation between wisdom and the Law led ben Sira to link wisdom inseparably with the Mosaic Law. The emphasis given to that strong link between the gifts of wisdom and Law came at a time when little Judah was in danger of being completely overwhelmed by Greek culture[21]. We have touched on that in our treatment of the Maccabean history. What the Maccabees had to resist with the sword, ben Sira only a few decades earlier had tried to forestall through his words of wisdom. His advice was given with full clarity and conviction, e.g. "If you desire wisdom, keep the commandments, and the Lord will bestow it on you" (1,26).

Then ch. 24 opens with a long discourse of wisdom personified, who claims:"I came forth from the mouth of the Most High .. From eternity, in the beginning, he created me, and for eternity I shall remain" (vv.3.9). Next, ben Sira declares: "All this is no other than the Book of the Covenant of the Most high God, the Law that Moses enjoined on us.. This is what makes wisdom brim over like the Pishon" (v.23-25). Here we have a view of the Law which regards it as making God's will known to the people, who are thus enabled to live well-ordered lives in conformity with that will. For earlier sages, virtue was the fruit of wise conduct; for ben Sira, wise conduct is ensured by keeping the Law.

Ben Sira also shows keen interest in salvation history as summed up in its leading "illustrious men", from Enoch down to Simon the high priest(cc.44-50). With regard to theory and praxis, it is significant that this long section concludes by exhorting the reader to take to heart "instruction in wisdom and knowledge" as found in the whole book: "Blessed is he who devotes his time to these and grows wise by taking them to heart! If he practises them he will be strong enough for anything, since the light of the Lord is his path" (50,27-30). Blessing is not promised for mere possession of wisdom, even that taken to heart from an inspired book. Such precious wisdom must be lived out in daily life. A close parallel was to be given by Jesus at the Last Supper concerning his own teaching: "Now that you know this, blessed are you if you behave accordingly" (Jn 13,17).

The last sapiential writing, which is also the last book of the O.T., bears the distinguished title of Wisdom. Composed about 100-50 B.C., probably in Alexandria, the flourishing Greek city founded by Alexander the Great in Egypt, it reflects the merging of Jewish traditions and their response to Greek culture. The streams of Law, prophecy, divinely guided history and wisdom in Israel were already merging, as we noted for the work of ben Sira. That work also was directed to a Jewish people in danger of being engulfed and completely absorbed by the strong Hellenic culture, which had the force of arms to impose its values and even its gods. In the book of Wisdom we have, as is noted in the New Spanish Bible, the O.T.'s "most important treatise on 'political theology'. If we prefer, it is a treatise concerning justice in government, with theological argumentation and doctrinal orientation. .. The prophetic denunciation becomes here a sapiential critique"[22].

That was part of the inevitable evaluation of the daily life of Jews in the midst of a successful city famous for its Greek learning, libraries and search for new ideas. That city also had Hellenic government, which tolerated Judaism but obviously subjected the faithful Jews to a lot of adverse comments and even hostile treatment at times. The anonymous author of Wisdom took up the huge challenge of strengthening his fellow-Jews and at the same time presenting a reasonable case for acceptance of their wisdom by the Greeks. He was familiar enough with Greek to compose his work in that language, and knowledgeable enough of the current Greek philosophies and terminology to avail of them to express his traditional faith and shrewd critical assessments.

Like practically all the preceding wisdom literature, Wisdom is also written in poetic form for cc.1-9, then cc.10-19 are more like ornate prose interspersed with poetry. Those opening chapters tell of the importance of wisdom for the present and future life, with everlasting retribution(1-5). Next is a stirring invitation to seek wisdom, which is personified and said to be of divine origin, yet wanting to give herself to the sincere seeker (6-9). There follows a long midrashic description of divine wisdom's role in the history of Israel, above all at the time of the exodus from Egypt(10-19)[23].

That last section is interrupted with a condemnation of idolatry as practised in Egypt, with its worship of kings, heavenly bodies, animals and statues (13-15). A midrashic reflection was intended above all to describe and evaluate a current situation in the light of ancient traditions and terminology. Thus the contemporary government in Egypt was being cleverly assessed from a biblical viewpoint. It is shown by means of sharp contrasts that, under God's guidance, what harmed the Egyptians helped the Israelites till they emerged free at the other side of the Red Sea: "For the whole creation, submissive to your commands, had its very nature re-created, so that your children should be preserved from harm" (19,6).

One great contribution made by the book of Wisdom is its insistence on the immortality of humans and a just retribution from God in an ongoing life beyond the grave(cc.1-5). Here we find some basic answers to the anguished questioning of sages like Job and Ecclesiastes. Their sense of justice and a well-ordered world had run into big obstacles because the wise and the upright did not always reap much more benefit in this world than the foolish or the unjust. Such obstacles are overcome by the new vista of the upright destined to live on with God while the unjust receive fitting punishment. In fashioning men and women to his own image, the Creator made them "to be immortal; Death came into the world only through the Devil's envy" (2,23-4). Hence: "The souls of the upright are in the hands of God.. If, as it seemed to us, they suffered punishment, their hope was rich with immortality; slight was their correction, great will their blessing be. .. They will judge nations, rule over peoples, and the Lord will be their king for ever. .. those who are faithful will live with him in love; .. But the godless will be duly punished for their reasoning, for having neglected the upright and deserted the Lord" (3,1-10).

That rather lengthy text also throws fresh light on how the the kingdom of God and the new covenant can be truly everlasting for the individual, as well as for the whole community "from generation to generation". Now it becomes much clearer that the generations of the faithful who have died also live on, united in love to the Lord as their king for ever. Covenant love may be seen as described in the Song of Songs: "For love is strong as Death... Love no flood can quench, no torrents drown" (8,6-7). The reward promised by Wisdom is above all to be for ever with the Beloved. That aspect is at least suggested by the way personified wisdom is depicted as a bride: "Wisdom I loved and searched for from my youth; I resolved to have her as my bride, I fell in love with her beauty. She enhances her noble birth by sharing God's life, for the Master of All has always loved her" (Wis 8,2-3). But such an appreciation of wisdom and immortality does not lead to escapism into "the other world". On the contrary, wisdom is eagerly sought in order that rulers may be fitted "to govern the world in holiness and saving justice, and in honesty of soul to dispense fair judgement" (Wis 9,3).

In conclusion, the great heritage of wisdom in Israel offers us a wide basis for our own reflections on daily life. It also presents a valid method for appreciating what is best in each culture's traditional wisdom when related to the reign of God.

D. COVENANT IN THE PSALMS

The Psalms are often loosely linked for treatment with the wisdom literature, since they often express the cry of human hearts in the face of daily life. Several Psalms do treat explicitly of wisdom themes, in poetry and hymns, e.g. Pss. 1; 34; 49; 112[24]. However, the Psalms as a whole form a special kind of literature, which arose from the daily prayer of Israelites, as individuals and as a worshipping community. While wisdom has Solomon as its royal patron, the Psalms have David as theirs. David was remembered as a skilled harpist in the court of Saul (1 Sam 16,18-23), and later as "the singer of the songs of Israel" (2 Sam 23,1). Nearly half the Psalms came to be related "to David" in the introductory headings assigned to them in the Hebrew Bible. That simply indicates that they are in line with the great tradition of worship in David's city and according to his spirit.

The collection of those sacred songs and poems was made over some seven centuries, from David's time till about 300 B.C., although the great majority of them would have been composed by the end of the exile (about 538 B.C.)[25]. The Greek translation (LXX) termed the whole collection **Psalterion** (= a stringed instrument), since the hymns were to be sung to that kind of instrument. It needed only another step to refer to each of the hymns or poems as a Psalm. Music obviously added an important element to the whole atmosphere of joyful praise or heartfelt cries for help in distress. The title of B. Janecko's book, "The Psalms —Heartbeat of Life and Worship" is already a summary of what we find on reading and praying the Psalms. "First and foremost", as he remarks, "the psalter is a collection of songs of the people of God. .. They have the power and magic to evoke and to arouse the feelings of the reader or audience, since song and poetry have the innate ability to identify with the other and with the Totally Other"[26]. Along the same lines, R. Murphy argues that "the high dramatic and poetic level of the Psalms", with such rich "symbolism and imagery" is really a value in itself, and ought not be an obstacle to the modern reader. Symbolism has also "preserved the Psalms from details that would limit their outreach to all peoples". Furthermore, "The poetic is a 'prerequisite' in the sense that there is an innate poetic potential in all of us to react to reality by means of imagery"[27].

The Psalms reflect covenant concerns in myriad ways, of which we can take up only a few of the most outstanding examples. The collection itself has been carefully divided into five books, each one ending with a doxology and crowned by Ps 150, which is a doxology "to end all the other doxologies". — "The final psalm is a fitting conclusion to the entire psalter, a book of hymns of praise. .. The division of the psalter into five books seems to be analogous with the five books of Moses and was probably used in conjunction with them at the temple and synagogue services"[28]. Hence the final collection itself reflected an awareness that the worshipping Israel was responding to the Yahweh of the whole Torah, with the promise, the covenant and its demands of loyal love. "From the very first, Israel was a covenant community whose primary bond of unity was the worship of Yahweh. .. [Hence] the book of Psalms lies at the very heart of the Old Testament"[29] (author's emphasis).

Given that the Psalms arose from a covenant community praising and pleading with Yahweh as their Creator, Redeemer and ever-faithful partner, it is not surprising that they constantly recall God's loving-kindness - **hesed**. According to R. Sorg, "the whole psalter is bathed in its colour and light", for the word occurs 128 times in the Psalms, slightly more than in all the rest of the Hebrew Bible[30]. A beautiful Psalm to illustrate this and many of the preceding remarks is Ps 23: "Yahweh is my shepherd" —and also my generous host, and the goal of life's pilgrimage towards "my home .. for all time to come" (vv.1.5.6). Its appealing image of the shepherd leading a flock to green pastures and restful waters, is followed by another of the desert host welcoming, anointing, and sharing rich fare with the threatened wanderer. Then, as if escorting the guest safely beyond reach of the waiting enemies, "kindness and faithful love (**hesed**) pursue me every day of my life" (v.6).

The Israelite who responds well to God's **hesed** is said to be **hasid** (= godly, holy, saint), a term which also occurs much more frequently in the psalter than in all the remainder of the Hebrew Bible[31]. Ps.149 merits special attention in this regard, for it has a stirring call, "Sing a new song to Yahweh: his praise in the assembly of the faithful" (**hasidim**). That particular "congregation of the faithful" could be related to the loyal and militant group who quickly threw in their lot with the Maccabees. Shortly after the Maccabees had called for an armed uprising against the Seleucid persecutors, "they were joined by the Hasidaean party, stout fighting men of Israel, each one a volunteer on the side of the Law" (1 M 2,42)[32].

Those Hasidaeans have been proposed with good reason as the ones giving rise to the Essenes, since that title comes from an Aramaic word meaning much the same thing as pious, faithful, loyal[33]. We will return to the Essenes in connection with the Qumran community. They are mentioned here in anticipation in order to draw attention to the bonds between covenant loyalty and a special group of "loyal ones" who were to set themselves apart in the wilderness as the community of the new covenant.

Many Psalms praise Yahweh as king, so much so that S. Mowinckel posits that there must have been an annual feast proclaiming the "enthronement of Yahweh"[34]. A good example is found in Ps 47, in which Yahweh is enthusiastically hailed as "the great king over all the earth" (v.2). .. "God reigns over the nations, seated on his holy throne" (v.8 —where the Ark of the Covenant may well be alluded to, being regarded as the footstool of Yahweh's throne and also sufficiently portable to be carried in a liturgical procession back to the Temple). Pss.96 to 99 are in the same vein, praising Yahweh as king and judge "who will judge the nations with justice" (96,10).

There are also Psalms which recall the covenant granted to David, of which Ps 89 is the most striking example. It recalls God's promissory covenant several times, e.g. "I shall maintain my faithful love for him always, my covenant with him will stay firm. I have established his dynasty for ever" (vv.28-29). Then the psalmist protests, after the end of the monarchy in Jerusalem: "you have repudiated the covenant with your servant, dishonoured his crown in the dust. .. Lord, what of those pledges of your faithful love?"(vv 39 and 49). Despite the human dead-end as far as the house of David was concerned, messianic hope grew stronger in the centuries following the destruction of Jerusalem. Several messianic Psalms, such as Pss. 2, 21, 72, and 110, were retained, expressing a lively expectation of a king who would be anointed by Yahweh to carry out his projects and thereby establish a kingdom of real justice.

So many of the Psalms manifest covenant themes that A. Weiser has rejected S. Mowinckel's theory of an annual enthronement festival in favour of an annual covenant renewal festival. This shifts the focus of attention from what happened in other kingdoms to what happened in the public worship of Israel itself. Weiser therefore holds that "the <u>cult of this festival</u> [of the Israelite Covenant] must be assumed to be the <u>Sitz im Leben</u> for the vast majority of the individual psalms and their types"[35](author's emphasis). The annual feast most likely to have included a Covenant Festival would have been that of the autumn New Year, hence tied in also with the feast of Booths (or Tabernacles)[36]. The enthronement Psalms would have served well during such a festival, obviating the need for a separate enthronement feast to explain their origin. Both Yahweh as king and his Davidic viceregent were deeply involved in the outcome of each New Year for all Israel. The ordinary people likewise were personally involved, hence they were called on specifically to review their conduct and renew their loyalty to Yahweh as king and covenant partner for the coming year.

A fine example of calling the worshipping community to review its conduct and to renew its commitment to Yahweh is found in Ps 81. In the eyes of D.J. McCarthy, its vv.7-11 "could be a miniature covenant-renewal". Concerning the importance of worship, he remarks: "The expression of society's unity with its LORD was in worship, the service of the LORD alone. Hence arose the concern not just for loyalty in general, but for proper worship and the rules, including those of moral purity, to be kept by those who would join in the worship"[37](author's emphasis).

On looking closely at Ps 81, we see it begins with a call to "sing for joy to God our strength", to "strike up the music", to "blow the trumpet for the new month, for the full moon, for our feast day" (vv.1-3). Added significance can be seen in its opening verse in M. Dahood's translation: "Ring out your joy to the God of our Fortress", for he then notes in his commentary that "'Fortress' is a name for the ark of the covenant"[38].

The community recalls how it heard Yahweh's voice in the midst of its Egyptian slavery: "I freed his shoulder from the burden, his hands were able to lay aside the labourer's basket. You cried out in your distress, so I rescued you. Hidden in the storm, I answered you" (vv.5-7). It goes on to express Yahweh's warning, which is also a compelling invitation to pay careful heed this time, in the new meeting between "my people" (vv.8.11.13) and "Yahweh ..your God who brought you here from Egypt" (v.10). The basic demand of the whole covenant is recalled: "You shall have no strange gods" (v.9), and the relentless pursuit of Yahweh: "If only my people would listen to me, if only Israel would walk in my ways" (v.13). The blessing promised for sufficient change of stubborn hearts and a genuine practice of covenant loyalty is the subduing of all Israel's enemies, together with an abundance of finest wheat and choicest honey(vv.14-16). For A. Weiser, this Psalm is certainly one related to the feast of Tabernacles and covenant renewal. "Within the covenantal relationship the promise of divine salvation is tied up with loyalty and obedience in religion; for this reason, in contrast to the Ten Commandments, God's affirmation of his faithfulness to his people follows the manifestation of God's will in the present context"[39]. In many ways, therefore, this short Psalm does encourage covenant renewal in a festival setting. Hopefully it will serve as a key for our fuller appreciation of numerous other Psalms, such as A. Weiser's large commentary has ably indicated.

Psalms 50 and 51 seem to have been placed together because one complements the other[40]. Both also serve well to draw together fundamental aspects of the covenant relationship which we have already been alerted to by the prophets and historians. Ps 50 is another vivid poetic presentation of Yahweh conducting a court-case against Israel regarding its empty sacrifices, whose offerers are still intent on robbery, adultery, lies and slander of brothers. Such conduct openly contradicts the words of the covenant coming from their lips. Ps 51 then gives a profound cry for forgiveness of sin humbly acknowledged, with full confidence in God's "faithful love" and "great tenderness" (v.1). The sinner, so conscious of being "born guilty" and always inclined to sin, beseeches God to bring about the necessary change of heart and to grant a new spirit. That comes very close to requesting explicitly what Jer 31 and Ez 36 had promised concerning the new covenant.

Considering each of those two Psalms in a little more detail will illustrate how deftly Israel's prayer could depict the basic challenges arising from its covenant commitment. They also reveal an ever-watchful Yahweh immeasurably more concerned for the honouring of the covenant than were the Israelites. Ps 50 opens with an awesome description of "the God of gods, Yahweh", coming to "judge his people", calling on heaven and earth to be witnesses. The divine summons goes out: "Gather to me my faithful, who sealed my covenant by sacrifice". Then the case opens, with Yahweh acting both as judge and accuser, calling the court to order: "Listen, my people, I am speaking, Israel, I am giving evidence against you, I, God, your God" (vv.1-7). Yahweh wants to be heard so that Israel, the unfaithful partner, may come to realise and publicly admit that the charges being laid against her are true[41].

In this case the central charge is that the animal sacrifices being offered to God are quite unacceptable(vv.8-13). This is not a rejection of all animal sacrifices, but of those not accompanied by genuine thanksgiving and fulfilling of "the vows you make to the Most High" (v.14). Then the following verses make more explicit some of the objections, e.g. God's case against the wicked: "What right have you to recite my statutes, to take my covenant on your lips, when you detest my teaching and thrust my words behind you?(vv.16-17). Their conduct indicates their practical denial of the covenant demands which the cult calls forth from their mouths. They side with thieves and adulterers, their talk is of evil, full of lies and slander even of their own family(vv.18-20). God confronts them to their face: "You do this, and am I to say nothing?(v.21). The time of reckoning is at hand, hence a final urgent invitation to think well about the two options —to be torn apart for continuing in wickedness, or to receive salvation through honouring God sincerely with "a sacrifice of thanksgiving" (vv.22-23).

Ps 51 is the most striking of the penitential Psalms, still frequently prayed by Christians who can easily identify with its sentiments of deep sorrow for sin coupled with great trust in God's enduring love, perceived as capable of creating in the sinner a "clean heart" (v.10). The oppressive weight of sin and guilt stands out as the psalmist twelve times over admits his sin[42], so that God might show his "saving justice". What is uppermost is the saving aspect, and yet justice is effective in the sense that the unjust sinner admits that God is just in judging him a sinner. Mercy is sought from a just judge whose justice is above all to be true to the inner nature of the God of love and compassion. Once again, we are confronted with the unique biblical idea of a justice that seeks reconciliation rather than a death sentence through the divinely instigated lawsuit.

Almost in the same breath as mercy and forgiveness, also a radical change of heart is also sought in order to put an end to sin's domination there. "God, create in me a clean heart, renew within me a resolute spirit, do not thrust me away from your presence, do not take away from me your spirit of holiness" (vv.10-11). The religious experience of the psalmist, who can speak also from the long experience of the entire community, makes him long for a "new creation" within himself. This is right in line with the promises concerning the new covenant, based on centuries of experience concerning the sinfulness which rendered the Mosaic covenant ineffective. The renewed psalmist, again speaking also for the worshipping community, promises to proclaim God's saving justice. He also offers to God "a broken spirit", a "contrite heart", confident that such a sacrifice is acceptable(vv.14-17). The closing verses plead for the rebuilding of Jerusalem's walls, which gives a further indication that the final form of the Psalm is post-exilic, hence later than the promises of Jeremiah and Ezekiel.

The more we pray the Psalms, especially those recalling kingship and covenant themes, the more we become aware of how the risen Jesus could declare, "This is what I meant when I said, while I was still with you, that everything written about me in the Law of Moses, in the Prophets and in the Psalms, was destined to be fulfilled" (Lk 24,44). Jesus had no doubt frequently used the Psalms as his own prayer and in his discussions with the people, as well as with his chosen band of disciples. The N.T. certainly bears witness to a constant reflection on the Psalms, now read in the light of the crucified and risen Messiah. Sabourin is able to list nearly half the Psalms as being used in the New Testament, some of them several times over[43]. Following the example of Jesus and his disciples, we can make the Psalms our own prayer, as has been amply explained in works such as those of T. Worden and A. Gelin[44]. The daily liturgy of the word related to the eucharist provides a good atmosphere for listening to Yahweh's call to renewed commitment to the new covenant being celebrated anew in our midst "today".

One example of this from the liturgy of Friday within the Easter Octave will illustrate well how the Psalms are able to bear witness to Jesus as the Messiah and only Saviour. Ps 118 has been chosen as the Responsorial Psalm that day, because it contains the verse quoted by Peter in Acts 4,11, as recalled in the first reading of the day: "The stone which the builders rejected has become the cornerstone" (Ps 118,22). The whole Psalm is set within the refrain, "Give thanks to Yahweh for he is good, for his faithful love (**hesed**) endures for ever" (vv.1 and 29). It is also the Psalm which rounds off the **Hallel** (=Praise) Psalms (113-118), which were sung by the participants in great feasts such as Passover and Shelters(or Tabernacles)[45].

In Ps 118 we find "a king's hymn of thanksgiving for delivery from death and for a military victory"[46]. Praise of God for salvation from certain death is expressed, for instance, in the lines: "Yahweh's right hand is triumphant!. I shall not die, I shall live to recount the great deeds of Yahweh" (vv.16-17). But the liturgical adaptation calls for alternating voices to praise Yahweh in the name of the king, of Israel, of the "House of Aaron", and of "those who fear Yahweh" (whom A. Weiser identifies as proselytes[47]). The setting is a festival procession with "branches in hand, up to the horns of the altar" (v.27). The joyful spirit in recalling the past is also actualized for the contemporary participants: "This is the day which Yahweh has made, a day to rejoice and be glad. We beg you, Yahweh, save us, we beg you, Yahweh, give us victory! .. I thank you for hearing me, and making yourself my Saviour" (vv.24 - 28). The whole Psalm also illustrates clearly the ease with which cultic celebration could pass from the individual (king) to all the people (kingdom) and to an individual worshipper facing a similar situation.

The prayer given in the Roman missal for Friday within the Easter Octave also captures excellently the spirit of the Psalms that we have been considering : "Almighty, ever-living God, you offer the covenant of reconciliation to mankind in the mystery of Easter. Grant that what we celebrate in worship, we may carry out in our lives."

E. COVENANT COMMUNITY OF QUMRAN

Since the initial discovery in 1947 of ancient scrolls in a cave overlooking Wadi Qumran, close to where it runs into the Dead Sea, the world has come to know a great deal about those and a rich variety of biblical and other manuscripts from that same area. At first they were popularly known as the Dead Sea Scrolls, whereas today they are more often referred to in general as the Qumran writings. Despite troubled times in Palestine, a team of archaelogists, under the direction of Lancaster Harding and Père Roland de Vaux, moved in to search the original cave and surrounding ones. Remains of hundreds of manuscripts were found and this aroused a keen desire to find the source of such a wealth of literature. From 1951 till 1956 annual "digs"were made at Khirbet Qumran, some 5 kilometres from the original cave and close to the Dead Sea[48].

Gradually a whole complex of buildings and cisterns was uncovered, dating back to about 140 B.C. and showing evidence of being suddenly abandoned in 68 A.D. Viewed in the light of the manuscripts found near them, the ruins provided compelling evidence that they had once been a community centre for as many as two hundred members. A large writing room deepened the conviction that many of the manuscripts had originated right there, and had then formed part of the community's library. Fortunately they had been hidden for safekeeping in times of danger, hence their presence in about a dozen different caves. Some thirty caves in the neighbourhood also showed signs of having been occupied, presumably by solitary disciples related to the large "monastery" (as several have called it). Beyond the east wall of the complex was a cemetery with more than a thousand simple graves.

Among the better preserved documents were found copies of the Rule of the Community , also the Damascus (Covenant) Document, which gave a somewhat different rule of life, the community's Hymns, and the War Scroll (for a war of the "sons of light against the sons of darkness"). There were also many substantial sections of the Book of Jubilees, which helped to bridge the gap between the book of Daniel(of which several texts were also found) and the original compositions stemming from Qumran itself[49]. These were apart from the marvellous collection of manuscripts (or fragments thereof) containing all or part of every book of the Hebrew Bible except Esther. There were also parts of deuterocanonical books such as Tobit and Sira. For this it is rightly regarded as the greatest discovery ever of biblical manuscripts. This must be kept in mind when seeking the principal inspiration of those who had withdrawn to the wilderness to devote so much time and effort to copy biblical texts and compose their own religious literature.

A study of their literature, which comes from the period between the Maccabees and the destruction of Jerusalem, points very strongly to the Essenes as the group responsible for both the big centre and the manuscripts of Qumran. The most plausible explanation of their origin is found in the Hasidaeans, the faithful or pious ones who had quickly thrown in their lot with the Maccabees' armed rebellion(1 M 2,42). The very name Essenes seems to come from an Aramaic word, **hasen**, which also means the pious ones[50]. Their break with the Maccabees was probably begun when Alcimus, a high priest of Aaron's line, treated the Hasidaeans treacherously, having sixty of them executed despite his oath of peace with them(1 M 7,12-18). Then when Jonathan, brother and successor of Judas Maccabee as civil ruler, assumed the high-priesthood as well, even though he was not from the line of Aaron, the Hasidaeans presumably turned completely against him. A Qumran commentary of Habacuc speaks of a "wicked priest", who could have been Jonathan or else his brother Simon, who became high priest in 140 B.C.[51].

The indications are that about that time(140) one zealous group of the Hasidaeans gathered round an outstanding priestly leader, the "Teacher of Righteousness" and/or "Righteous Teacher". He and many other priests who decided to retire with him to the wilderness must have regarded themselves as descendants of Zadok, high priest in Solomon's time(1 K 2,35). The "sons of Zadok" are the most prominent authorities mentioned in both forms of the Rule. Their complete dedication to living out the covenant in Qumran was partly a rejection of Temple worship while that was controlled by high priests from the Maccabee family. Among the many fervent Jews who joined them were many Pharisees, whose roots were also to be found in the Hasidaean movement. However, the majority of Pharisees were able to accept regular Temple worship in Jerusalem. The ruins of Qumran suggest that at the height of this influx of candidates the complex was enlarged so as to accommodate nearly two hundred members. It has been suggested that a sizable group went off from Qumran to found a similar community near Damascus, which would explain the Damascus (Covenant) Document. Others think that Damascus was a symbolic name for Qumran itself. The somewhat different Rule contained in it would then be intended to cater also for Essenes still living in ordinary society[52].

The second stage of Qumran was from about 40-4 B.C., when it was inexplicably empty. That was during the reign of Herod the Great, but as he was reported by Josephus to have been friendly towards the Essenes, the big threat must have come from an enemy like the Parthians. During that period the Essenes continued to live according to their convictions in the towns.

The third and final stage of Qumran was from 4 B.C. till 68 A.D. As not all the buildings were restored for use, the community must have been reduced in size. Its writings, such as the Rule of War, manifest intense anti-Roman and zealot tendencies. For us it is of considerable importance that for nearly forty years the Qumran covenant community co-existed with the initial Christian covenant community so attractively described in Acts. It was the Romans who finally destroyed Qumran in 68 A.D., as part of the same war which resulted in the destruction of Jerusalem.

The Qumran community's life did have many features that manifested a truly remarkable zeal to take the covenant ideal seriously in every detail of life. For instance, the community held their goods in common. When a candidate, after two years of probation, was being accepted as a full member, he had to take an oath to enter the covenant and observe the Law of Moses, as directed by the Zadokites. At that stage he also renounced his private property. Strict discipline was maintained by an "Inspector" or "Overseer", in co-ordination with a Community Council of priests and laymen[53]. Breaches of the Rule were assigned various penalties, including expulsion or up to seven years custody. There was a year's penance for a deliberate lie about property. Celibacy was also required, partly to minimize legal impurity where the whole community wanted to act as "a priestly kingdom", always ready to offer sacrifice of praise to God. It was also in view of the imminent Holy War of "the sons of light" against "the sons of darkness", since tradition required such abstention in the face of battle for the Lord of Hosts[54].

It is only in the Damascus (Covenant) Document (designated in references as CD) that the sectarians speak of themselves as members of the new covenant, e.g. CD VI and VII. In the other documents there are frequent mentions simply of entering the covenant, e.g. in Rule of the Community (QS I and II)[55]. There was provision made for an annual renewal, which was probably to be at Pentecost[56]. From what is said as a whole in their Rule and in other writings, it is clear that for them the new covenant promised by Jeremiah could be entered into by a whole-hearted renewal of the Mosaic covenant and fidelity to all its demands(cf. QS VIII and XI). Their Hymns also show a keen awareness of the need for God's spirit to purify the heart and help humans keep the Law (cf.QH VII and XVII)[57].

In line with their being the renewed covenant community, they also regarded themselves as the true Israel (cf. QS VII and IX). Likewise they refer to themselves as the faithful remnant (cf. CD III; and Rule for the War - QM XIV). Being estranged from the Temple, they also found in their own community an adequate "House of Holiness for Aaron", i.e. a temple or even a "holy of holies" (cf. QS VII and IX)[58]. They were strongly exhorted to live as men of holiness walking in perfection (cf. QS IX; CD VIII). In that way the congregation would be truly the "holy nation" such as Israel was called to be. Since even one sinful member was considered a risk to the purity and holiness of the community, a serious violation of the Law could lead to expulsion. And so could murmuring against the authority of the community! (cf.QS VI -IX).

Their prevailing outlook was eschatological, hence their fervent and unremitting preparation for the final intervention and judgment of God. It was also heavily influenced by apocalyptic ideas as to the time and manner already predetermined by God. The apocalyptic strain that we saw emerging in the book of Daniel flowed on into non-biblical books such as Jubilees (with its pattern of God's plan from creation to the Sinai covenant neatly spread over 49 periods of 49 years each, like a jubilee of jubilees). The Qumran literature includes at least twenty works which have some apocalyptic features, hence they now provide us with a reliable bridge between Daniel and the N.T. Apocalypse. "These writings", says D. Russell, "assume many literary forms — commentaries, psalms, books of rules, liturgies, anthologies, and the rest; but in their teaching and beliefs they have much in common with those generally known as 'the apocalyptic books', especially in their expression of messianic hopes, their beliefs concerning good and evil spirits, and their conception of 'the last things'"[59].

The apocalyptic intervention of God was expected to be sudden, irresistible, cosmic and definitive for all people alive at the time. God's faithful community would be granted the victory, their sinful enemies would be destroyed. In that context there was not much emphasis on the role of a human messiah, nevertheless Qumran was awaiting two messiahs, as well as the prophet like Moses (cf. Dt 18,18). The Rule urges the members not to depart from any counsel of the Law until the coming of the Prophet and the Messiahs of Aaron and Israel (QS IX). In the light of their documents R.E. Brown can reasonably interpret this text as meaning, "The Messiah of Aaron would be the anointed High Priest, and the Messiah of Israel would be the anointed Davidic king. .. It is quite plausible that in a priestly group like the Qumran community a hope for a priestly Messiah may have accompanied the more general hope for a Davidic Messiah"[60]. In another "Rule of the Community" there is an interesting description of how the sacred meal of bread and wine is to be blessed first by the Priest when the Messiah of Israel arrives (QSa II). There is no indication that the Messiah would proclaim and inaugurate a new covenant different from the Mosaic covenant. The "sons of Zadok" had already been chosen by God to renew and confirm the covenant for ever.

While retaining a high esteem for the consistent dedication of the Qumran community to the Scriptures and to the strictest observance of the Mosaic covenant, we cannot pass over in silence some features which distinguish them from a Christian covenant community. Since fraternal love has been singled out by Jesus as the mark of his disciples, we can start by looking at the kind of love inculcated at Qumran. We must be impressed by the lofty ideal of fraternal love within the community, with its corollary of sharing all goods in common. However, their attitude to those outside the community was far too exclusive and hostile. Their Rule urged them to love "the sons of light" but to hate all "the sons of darkness" (cf. QS 1). At least in some texts it sounds as though even Jews outside the covenant, together with any sinners, were to be exterminated in the apocalyptic-style battle (cf.QS VIII-IX; also CD VII). We must realise, though, that conversion of sinners was not expected when all was so fixed beforehand in God's plan. Qumran members waited with faith and asceticism for the script to be played out on earth. They were ready to join battle for God when the appointed moment came.

Others who were to be excluded from the congregation of God were the crippled, the blind, the lame, and the infirm (QSa II). Their regulation would have been based on that of Leviticus concerning priests: "No descendant of the priest Aaron may come forward to offer the food burnt for Yahweh if he has any infirmity" (21,21). At Qumran they wanted every member to be like a priest entitled to approach God to offer sacrifice. This kind of exclusion is far from the openness of Jesus expressed, for example, in the parable of the banquet: "Go out quickly into the streets and alleys of the town and bring in here the poor, the crippled, the blind and the lame" (Lk 14,21).

As for inviting in the Gentiles, the Essenes as a sect were outstanding for their resistance to the inroads of Hellenization. Once the Romans replaced the Greeks as the Gentile oppressors of the small Jewish nation, the Essenes longed for the day when their Holy Land would be cleansed of such defilement(cf. QS VIII-IX; QM I-VII). That was their ardent commitment to removing what today we would call sinful and oppressive structures. They were even less inclined than other Jews to admit Gentiles unless they were willing to accept and follow the Law in all its implications, as explained by the "sons of Zadok". Which meant that their prevailing attitude was rather to increase the distance between their community and the Gentiles, whereas the Christian covenant was to break down the wall of division between Jew and Gentile (Eph 2,14).

In short, the Qumran covenanters were not driven outwards in a missionary project such as the Christians were to undertake well before the destruction of Qumran by Roman troops. The two views of what constituted the "new covenant" were radically different, mainly because Jesus' whole presentation of it was such an all-embracing perfection of what the prophets had promised that only the Messiah in person could inaugurate it. There are plenty of hints in the N.T. that once he had established the new covenant, some of the covenanters of Qumran were among those who accepted it and contributed to its form of community life[61]. Pauline and Johannine writings in particular also reflect some Qumran concerns and language, e.g. the struggle of light against darkness, baptism, evil spirits, inner temple, interior sacrifice. The Christian Apocalypse, drawing on the literary form dear to Qumran, also depicts the final battle to end the reign of "Babylon"(= Rome as an empire opposed to the reign of God and the Lamb).

NOTES

1. Cf.: J. Meyers, I & II Chronicles (2 Vol.) (Garden City, N.Y.: Anchor Bible, Doubleday, 1965); and id., Ezra Nehemiah (1 Vol.) (also Anchor Bible, 1965). Also: R. North, "The Chronicler: 1-2 Chronicles, Ezra, Nehemiah", in NJBC, 362-398. J. Mulcahy, "1 & 2 Chronicles" in New Catholic Commentary on Holy Scripture (London: Nelson, 1975^2) 352-379. P. Simson, "Ezra-Nehemiah",ibid. 402-438.
2. Cf.: P. Ackroyd, Exile and Restoration. A Study of Hebrew Thought of the Sixth Century B.C. (London: S.C.M., 1968); and id., Israel Under Babylon and Persia (Oxford: New Clarendon Bible, O.T. Vol.IV, Oxford University Press, 1970). Also: J. Bright, A History of Israel, c.9 on "Exile and Restoration", and c.10 on "The Jewish Community in the 5th Century".
3. H. Lusseau: "Esdras and Nehemias" and "The Books of Paralipomenon or the Chronicles", in Robert & Feuillet (Ed.) Introduction to the O.T. (New York: E.T., Desclée, 1968) 485-493 and 495-504 resp.
4. Cf. D. McCarthy, "Covenant and Law in Chronicles-Nehemiah", in Institution and Narrative, 92-111, where he finds sufficient differences in the way 1-2 Chronicles present covenant renewal when compared to Ezra-Nehemiah to make him wonder if distinct authors would not provide the most satisfactory explanation (cf.esp.108-111).
5. Cf.: Nueva Biblia Española (Madrid: Tr. L. Alonso Schökel & J. Mateos, Ediciones de Cristiandad, 1975) 542 (Introd. to Chronicles). Also: R. North, art. cit. 363-4, where he mentions the wide variety in dating composition and reediting from 515 to 200.
6. R. North, ibid.
7. J. Meyers, I Chronicles, LXXXVI-LXXXVII, and Ezra-Nehemiah, LXVIII.
8. B. Anderson, The Living World of the Old Testament, 493-501.
9. J. Meyers, I Chronicles: for information on Moses and Torah, LXXVIII-LXXX; on Covenant and **hesed**, LXVI.
10. N. McEleney, "1-2 Maccabees" in NJBC, 421. Cf.: M. Schoenberg, 1 & 2 Maccabees, (Collegeville, Minn.: O.T.R.G., Liturgical Press, 1966). T. Corbishley, "1 & 2 Maccabees" in NCCHS, 743-758. C.J. Roetzel, The World that Shaped the New Testament (Atlanta, Georgia: Knox Press, 1985) 8-9 on Alexander the Great, e.g. "He freely used indigenous leadership. .. Wittingly or not, he cleared away barriers to a lively reciprocal exchange of culture, ideas, religion, social forms, and political institution between Hellenism and the Eastern traditions." H. Koester, Introduction to the New Testament, Vol 1: History, Culture, and Religion of the Hellenistic Age (Philadelphia: E.T. by author, Fortress Press, 1982) esp. 205-228 on the Maccabees and successors.
11. For dating of sapiential books, cf. New Jerusalem Bible's "Introduction" to them in general (749-752), then each one in particular, beginning with Job

(753-756). Similarly in Nueva Biblia Española, which treats the Psalms and Canticle of Canticles under "Poesía" (1159-1272), and begins "Sapienciales" with Proverbs (1283).
12. Cf. B. Anderson, op.cit., re Wisdom, 528-562, e.g. 528: "Wisdom is the concern of Man as Man: Greek or Jew, Babylonian or Egyptian, male or female, king or slave. The quest for wisdom is the quest for the meaning of life. And this quest is the basic interest of every human being."
13. Cf. C. Westermann, Mille Ans et Un Jour (Paris: F.T. by A. Chazelle, Cerf, 1975) 343-345 on "le caractère supranational de la sagesse", as well as Israel's openness to universal wisdom.
14. Cf. J. Crenshaw, "Murphy's Axiom: Every Gnomic Saying Needs a Balancing Corrective" in The Listening Heart — Essays in Honour of R.E. Murphy,O.Carm. (Sheffield: JSOT Press, 1987) 1-17. Crenshaw does not think that the ancient sages accepted the world view of Yahwism (13, ftn.20). Also: C.V. Camp, "Woman Wisdom as Root Metaphor: A Theological Consideration", ibid. 45-76, where it is pointed out that after the exile the sociological and theological changes gave rise to significant female imagery, e.g. Prov. 9 and 31.
15. D. McCarthy, Institution and Narrative, 354-362, on the part of wisdom in government and every-day life in Israel. The central conviction was that "the world is an ordered place", and furthermore, "creation works according to the plan of a personal God" (357).
16. R.E. Murphy, Introduction to the Wisdom Literature of the Old Testament (Collegeville, Minn.: Liturgical Press, 1965), e.g. 44-55 on the "theologizing of wisdom" after the exile. Cf. id. "Introduction to Wisdom Literature" in New Jerome Bibl.Comm., 447-452, where theologizing is related to the invitation to seek wisdom in openness to all God's creation, readily acknowledged by Israelites as an important source of wisdom.
17. G. Gutiérrez, A Theology of Liberation, 13.
18. Cf. L. Alonso Schökel, Hermenéutica Biblica, 217-230, which concludes a reflection on David and the wise woman by saying that the Bible really demands of its readers that they "enter into dialogue with the text while sharing personally in the drama of human existence, ready to take decisions for the good and accept the consequences."
19. D. McCarthy, op.cit. 283: He asserts of Israel's wisdom writings: "If not explicitly from, they were certainly for, Yahweh's chosen community. ... Hence, if they lack an explicitly Yahwist source, they have an explicitly Yahwist end, and so a place in the tradition of Yahweh's people." Cf: G. Witaszek, I profeti Amos e Michea nella Lotta per la Guistizia Sociale nell'VIII Sec. A.C. (Roma: Pontificia Universitas Gregoriana, 1986), 61, where he finds that the basis of Amos's social criticism stemmed from the fact of the election of Israel and from wisdom, plus the universal power of Yahweh and the idea of the covenant.
20. Cf.: G. Gutiérrez, Hablar de Dios —desde el sufrimiento del inocente. Una reflexión sobre el libro de Job (Lima: CEP, 1986), in which the inadequacy of traditional wisdom in the face of unmerited suffering is well

related to modern sufferers. Insufficient, unsatisfactory answers to the problems of real life should be put frankly before God for further enlightenment. J. Vermeylen, Job, Ses Amis et Son Dieu —La légende de Job et ses relectures postexiliques (Leiden: E.J. Brill, 1986), on the other hand, concentrates more on the attitude displayed towards Job by each of the three "editions" of the work between 5th to 3rd cent. B.C. No "edition" approves of the way Job questions God, although the 2nd redactor shows sympathy for Job as one weighed down by suffering. Job readily admits he has spoken foolishly and accepts God's viewpoint once God has answered his appeal for a hearing. E. Dhorme, A Commentary on the Book of Job (Nashville: E.T. by H. Knight, T. Nelson, 1984[2]) is a large and still helpful commentary.

21. Cf. E. Beaucamp, Man's Destiny in the Books of Wisdom (New York: E.T. by J. Clarke, Alba House, 1970, 120-121) e.g. : "It is natural that all gather round the Torah at a time when Judaism, conscious of what threatens it, is on the alert. They will prove their fidelity to their national Wisdom by conforming their conduct to the Mosaic Law." B. Vawter, The Book of Sirach —With a Commentary (2 Parts) (New York: Pamphlet Bible Series, Paulist Press, 1962), 2, 5-6 where he speaks of Sirach's "identification of wisdom and Judaism", which is more nuanced than simply identifying wisdom and the Law as such.

22. Nueva Biblia Española, 1458.

23. Cf. P. Ellis, Men and Message of the Old Testament (Collegeville, Minn.: Liturgical Press, 1963), e.g. 451: "In the O.T. the best example of haggadic midrash is found in Wisdom 10-19." New Jerusalem Bible, 1044: "Secondly, and more significantly, he [author of Wisdom] manipulates the biblical narrative in the interests of his thesis. In ch. 16-19, a sustained contrast between the fortunes of Egyptian and Israelite, the author fills out the narrative with imaginative elements, draws together episodes which in effect were disconnected, makes the facts more than lifesize. All this is an excellent example of **midrash**, the exegetical method practised later by the rabbis." Similarly R. Murphy, The Seven Books of Wisdom (Milwaukee: Bruce, 1960), 130: "This is a devotional, edifying interpretation of historical events in order to point moral or spiritual lessons." E. Maly, The Book of Wisdom —With a Commentary (New York: Pamphlet Bible Series, Paulist Press, 1962), esp. the introduction, 1-13, in which he brings out well the effort made to confront the challenge of Greek philosophers by drawing on the wisdom granted in various ways to Israel.

24. Cf. J. Kselman & M. Barré, "Psalms" in NJBC, 523-552. R.Murphy, Seven Books of Wisdom, ch.3: "An Approach to the Psalms". Id. The Psalms, Job (Philadelphia, Penn.: R.R. McCurley [Ed.], Proclamation Commentaries, Fortress Press, 1977), 11-57 being on the Psalms; the remainder is devoted to Job.

25. M. Dahood, Psalms (3 Vol.) (New York: Anchor Bible, Doubleday, 1970) III,XXII , where he asserts that "the vast majority of the psalms may be

ascribed to the period 1000-539 B.C.". Cf. XXXVI, where he considers that the literary differences between the biblical psalms and those of Qumran "seem to preclude a late date of composition(i.e., after the sixth century B.C.) for the biblical Psalter."
26. B. Janecko, The Psalms... (St Meinrad, Indiana: Abbey Press, 1986.
27. R. Murphy, The Psalms, Job, 12-13 and 55: "We have argued that the psalms, with all the cultural limitations they have, are more transcultural than most other prayers."
28. B. Janecko, op.cit. 81.
29. B. Anderson, op.cit. 504-505.
30. R. Sorg, **Hesed** and **Hasid** in the Psalms. —A story of the marvellous relation between God and the blessed ones of His election and love (St Louis, Mo.: Pio Decimo Press, 1953) 11.
31. Ibid. 12. Cf. C.F. Whitely, "The Semantic Range of **Hesed**" in Biblica 62(1981), 519-526, where he claims that in several psalms there are passages which show that "**hesed** has an obvious and basic meaning of 'strength' quite irrespective of whether it is in a 'covenant' context or not." He finds that it can also mean protection, assurance, confidence.
32. L. Alonso Schökel, Treinta Salmos: Poesía y Oración (Madrid: Ediciones Cristiandad, 1986^2) 431-438 on Ps.149 and the Faithful Ones.
33. Cf. H. Koester, op.cit. 234-235. See also below under Qumran.
34. Cf.: S. Mowinckel, The Psalms in Israel's Worship (2 Vol.) (Oxford: E.T. by D.R. Ap-Thomas, Blackwell, 1962). P. Drijvers, The Psalms —Their Structure and Meaning (London: E.T., Burns & Oates, 1965), e.g. 164-182 on "The Processional and Enthronement Psalms". R. de Vaux, Ancient Israel — Its Life and Institutions (London: E.T. by J. McHugh, Darton, Longman & Todd, 1961) 502-506, where he rejects the theory that there was a New Year feast in Israel or any corresponding "Enthronement Feast of Yahweh".
35. A. Weiser, The Psalms (London: E.T. by H. Hartwell, S.C.M. 1962) 35; cf. 27; 56-57; 90; 93.
36. Ibid., 375.
37. D. McCarthy, Institution and Narrative, 105.
38. M. Dahood, op.cit., II, 262-263.
39. A. Weiser, op.cit., 554-555.
40. Cf. L. Alonso Schökel, op.cit. 190-230, where he treats Pss.50 and 51 in the same section, while maintaining that they were originally autonomous.
41. P. Bovati, Ristabilire La Giustizia, has several keen observations about the language used in Pss. 50 and 51, for he discerns the terminology of lawsuit, admission by covenant people that they have been unfaithful, repentance and reparation as a plea for reconciliation, e.g. 84-6; 121-123; 178-181; 276-280; 312-313. Cf. A. Weiser, op.cit. 391-410 on both these Psalms.
42. L. Alonso Schökel, op.cit. 214-215; and 227 for aspects of sacramental reconciliation in the new covenant, "which has the Gospel as its charter".

43. L. Sabourin, The Psalms: Their Origin and Meaning (Staten Is., N.Y.: Alba House,1969) I, 169-175. (A P-b. rev. ed. in 1 Vol., 1974.)
44. T. Worden, The Psalms Are Christian Prayer (London: G. Chapman, 1964). A. Gelin, The Psalms Are Our Prayers (Collegeville, Minn.: E.T. by M.Bell, Liturgical Press, 1964).
45. A. Weiser, op.cit. 722-730, on Ps.118.
46. M. Dahood, op.cit. III, 155.
47. A.Weiser, op.cit. 725 concerning proselytes being mentioned in Ps. 118.
48. Cf.: R. de Vaux, Archaeology and the Dead Sea Scrolls (London: Oxford University Press, for British Academy London, 1973). J. Milik, Ten Years of Discovery in the Wilderness of Judaea (London: S.C.M., 1959). M. Burrows, The Dead Sea Scrolls, (London: Secker & Warburg, 1956); and More Light on the Dead Sea Scrolls (Ditto, 1958).
49. Cf. A. Jaubert, La Notion d'Alliance dans le Judaisme aux abords de l'Ere Chretienne (Paris: Ed. de Seuil, 1963) 87-88, where she regards Jubilees as post-Maccabean but pre-Qumran. Likewise R.E. Brown, P.Perkins & A.Saldarini, "Apocrypha; Dead Sea Scrolls; Other Jewish Literature", in NJBC, 1055-1082, esp. 1059 where dates of composition for Jubilees between 176 and 140 B.C. are mentioned.
50. Cf. J. Milik, op.cit. 8O on derivation of Essenes from an Aramaic word. Likewise R. Brown, art.cit.1074, and H. Koester, op.cit. 235.
51. Cf. R. Brown, ibid., where Jonathan is regarded as more likely to have been the "Wicked Priest" referred to. But others like H. Koester, op.cit. 235-236 favour Simon. J.Sicre, Los Dioses Olvidados, 102 follows authors who would apply the title to Hyrcanus II or Alexander Jannaeus. That, however, seems much too late for a persecutor of the "Righteous Teacher", who is presumed to have been the founding father of Qumran.
52. Cf.: R. de Vaux, op.cit. 113: "The Damascus Document is certainly at home at Qumran. In the light of this one is tempted to agree with those authors who interpret the 'land of Damascus' as a symbolic name for the Qumran area."   H. Koester, op.cit. 237 considers that the Damascus Document "seems to have been written for members who lived in various places of the country, were married, and lived more like ordinary citizens."
53. Cf. R. Brown, art.cit. 1076 on parallels between a Qumran "Overseer" and an early Christian bishop.
54. H. Koester, op.cit. 237: "Old Testament concepts of the holy war obviously influenced this idea of the ritual purity of the community's members: the members are all soldiers in the holy war of God and must therefore observe all the relevant biblical commandments including abstinence from sexual intercourse."
55. D. Hillers, Covenant: The History of a Biblical Idea, 169-178 on Qumran, where references to covenant surpassed those in the N.T. Hillers justifiably concludes: "Yet for all their sincerity, Essene ideas about covenant are essentially conservative and recapitulate familiar patterns. Their new covenant is a renewal of the old" (178). K. Baltzer, The

Covenant Formulary — In O.T. Jewish and Early Christian Writings (Philadelphia: E.T. by David Green, Fortress Press, 1971) xiii on the liturgy at Qumran for entry into the covenant (as in QS I-II) —"it preserves the covenant formulary so completely that the individual elements of the O.T. texts can simply be inserted as they stand." Again, 167-9, where an English translation of that liturgy for entry into the covenant is given, he remarks: "As we have shown, it preserves almost in its entirety the formulary of a covenant renewal".   A. Vanhoye, La Nuova Alleanza nel N.T., A.27-28, likewise insists that even in the Damascus Document, where new covenant is mentioned three times, the call is to renew the Mosaic covenant and swear utmost fidelity to the Law. F. Peters, "Children of Abraham", 14, remarks of the Essenes: "They were a purified people of a New Covenant, who were elected for survival in wicked days".
56. Cf.: A. Jaubert, op.cit. 214-216.   R. Brown, art.cit. 1076.
57. Cf. A. Jaubert, op.cit. 239.
58. Ibid. 152-162.
59. D. Russell, The Method and Message of Jewish Apocalyptic, 39. Cf. G. Vermes, The Dead Sea Scrolls in English (Harmondsworth: Pelican P-b, 1968^2) (rev. ed. 1975 not to hand for present writer).   A. Dupont-Sommer, The Essene Writings from Qumran (New York: Meridian P-b., World Publishing Co., 1962).
60. Cf. R. Brown, art.cit. 1077.
61. Cf.: G. Graystone, The Dead Sea Scrolls and the Originality of Christ (London: Sheed & Ward, 1956) 59-96.   J. Danielou, The Dead Sea Scrolls and Primitive Christianity (New York: Mentor P-b., 1962).   M. Black, The Scrolls and Christian Origins —Studies in the Jewish Background of the N.T. (Chico, California: Scholars Press, 1983 —being reprint of New York: Scribner, 1961) e.g. 97: "We have thus a significant point of contact with the NT in its general presentation of the baptism of John as a baptism of repentance for the forgiveness of sins. .. What is new is that these rites [of Qumran] were practised in relation to a movement of repentance, of entry into a new Covenant (and a new Covenanted Israel, the sect itself) in preparation for an impending divine judgment."

CHAPTER 9: NEW COVENANT IN MARK AND MATTHEW

From the long and often troubled marriage between God and Israel was born Jesus of Nazareth, true Son of God and true son of Israel. Through him the Father chose to fulfil, in many surprising ways, everything that had been promised to Israel and the family of nations. The new covenant promised through the prophets was gradually delineated by Jesus throughout his ministry. In keeping with this he also gathered round himself a little group of disciples whom he carefully formed into the nucleus a new covenant community. He taught them about the reign of God being ushered in through the mission entrusted to his own person in order to lead the human family back to the Father[1]. To carry out the Father's will was to accept his reign over human hearts, homes, and all society.

The Twelve, representing the nascent community, were present at the Last Supper when Jesus formally inaugurated the new covenant, which he went on to seal in his own life-blood on Calvary. Through the outpouring of the Spirit the new covenant was to become fully effective till the Parousia. The Spirit of Jesus would empower the community of disciples to promote, celebrate and live out joyfully a new kind of partnership with the Divine Persons and with one another.

On looking at the Synoptic Gospels we find that there is only one explicit mention of covenant attributed by each of them to Jesus. The text in each case is that describing the words of Jesus over the cup of wine at the Last Supper. Even there, only in Luke's account do we find the combination "new covenant"; Matthew and Mark have simply "covenant". As for John's Gospel, it does not mention covenant explicitly in any text. First impressions, therefore, are that the new covenant was rather a marginal theme within the Good News[2]. Much more prominence was given to the kingdom of God[3], the compassion of the Father for the afflicted and for sinners, who were urged to seek the forgiveness of sin. What was emphasised for Jesus was his profound filial love for his Father, his spirit of loving service and self sacrifice on behalf of his brothers and sisters, especially the poor[4], all in accord with his role as Messiah, Son and King, Prophet, Saviour, Suffering Servant and Liberator. The role of the Spirit was also prominent, especially in Luke and John. The disciples, for their part, were called to faith and the following of Jesus in loyal love, as well as to an abiding love for one another, while excluding nobody from their love.

Our reflection on the gospels, therefore, will need to concentrate on such texts in order to show how they do recall important characteristics of a divine covenant such as we are now familiar with from the Old Testament. Each text will also be considered in relation to the special concern of the gospel in which it occurs. In that way we should be able to see how each evangelist was actually laying a good foundation for the solemn inauguration of the new covenant, having mentioned its substance without naming it. We must bear in mind that the Mosaic covenant remained in force until the "hour" of Jesus struck, which it did precisely during his final celebration of the Jewish Passover. Furthermore, throughout the lifetime of Jesus there was already that Jewish sect at Qumran which called itself the community of the new covenant. It was better for Jesus to clarify for his disciples what kind of a new covenant was to be granted, since it was to be radically different from Qumran's renewed Mosaic covenant.

A. THE NEW COVENANT IN MARK'S GOSPEL

We begin with Mark's gospel, because it is now generally accepted as the first gospel to have been written. Mark rightly gets the credit of giving the world the actual literary form of gospel. His pioneering work was then used extensively for the composition of Matthew and Luke, which will enable us to leave aside the common material once it has been discussed in our consideration of Mark. Being in vivid narrative style, with few long discourses, Mark's is a good gospel to start with. Like all four gospels, this one is the end result of the public preaching of Jesus himself, followed by that of the apostles and other disciples, and finally committed to writing in its present form under divine inspiration. The date of composition is difficult to determine, hence we can work with a flexible date between 65 and 75 A.D.

A 1. The gospel of Jesus Christ

The main lines to be followed through in Mark appear in the opening sentence: "The beginning of the gospel about Jesus Christ, Son of God" (1,1). The term "gospel" here means the good news about Jesus himself, proclaimed as the Messiah and as Son of God. Mark develops the meaning of gospel to embrace the good news about the kingdom of God(1,14.15), then to be virtually equivalent to Jesus, so that disciples may suffer or sacrifice themselves for the sake of him "and the gospel" (8,35; 10,29). Finally, the gospel to be preached to every creature after Easter must include the crucified and risen Jesus Christ - he reproached those who had been unwilling to believe that he had risen (16,14-16).

A 2. Jesus as a suffering Messiah

The title of Christ or Messiah is also at the centre of Mark's story. The first half of the gospel is the gradual teaching and convincing of the Twelve that Jesus is the Christ, a high point being reached when Peter declares "You are the Christ" (8,29). But that is still only half the truth. From that point onward Jesus opens their eyes and ears gradually to perceive something of his determination to accept the role of a suffering Messiah. Peter's first reaction on hearing the prediction of Christ's passion and death was to oppose the whole idea strongly (8, 31-33). However, Mark presents the "journey to Jerusalem" in a way that brings out Jesus' complete commitment to follow his Father's will. Then he gives such a detailed passion account that it could well have served at first for reading at eucharistic celebrations. Such celebrations were preparing for and anticipating the full messianic feast with their risen Lord, to share with him for ever "the new wine in the kingdom of God" (14,25).

A 3. Jesus Christ as Son of God

Parallel to Mark's gradual unfolding of Jesus as the suffering Messiah goes the gradual revelation of him as Son of God. At the inauguration of his public ministry, on the occasion of his baptism by John, "he saw the heavens torn apart and the Spirit, like a dove, descending on him. And a voice came from heaven, 'You are my Son, the Beloved; my favour rest on you'"(1,10-11). At the crucial juncture in his mission, when the Twelve still needed a much deeper understanding of the need to suffer, the transfiguration was granted to strengthen Jesus and the chosen three. They heard a voice speaking from the cloud which had overshadowed them: "This is my Son, the Beloved. Listen to him"(9,7). Then in the trial before the Sanhedrin, when Jesus was asked bluntly by the high priest, "Are you the Christ, the Son the Blessed One?", he replied, "I am."(14,61-62). Finally, the Gentile centurion who witnessed how Jesus died expressed what Mark wanted his readers to conclude with faith: "In truth this man was Son of God"(15,39).

A 4. Jesus as one teaching with authority

Mark also lets his readers see how Jesus' constant teaching as one having compelling authority was a window through which something of his hidden Sonship could be glimpsed. More than thirty times Mark uses words that refer explicitly to Jesus as "teacher", "teaching" others, with his own special kind of "teaching" or "doctrine"(**didache**) for varying audiences. His words had particularly evident authority when they cured the sick, cast out unclean spirits, stilled the storm, converted and forgave the sinner (confirmed in one case by healing the paralytic whose sins he had forgiven in a crowded room - 2,1-12).

A 5. The Twelve as disciples accompanying Jesus

For Mark, teacher is used of Jesus in preference to prophet, although in Nazareth Jesus comments on his rejection there: "A prophet is despised only in his own country"(6,4). Jesus is depicted as a unique, inspired and itinerant teacher who draws a band of willing disciples to form a permanent community around his own person. He formally names the Twelve who "were to be his companions and to be sent out to proclaim the message, with power to drive out devils"(3,14-15). Only once in Mark are the Twelve referred to as apostles(6,30); normally they are disciples being taught in depth by Jesus, being drawn more fully to share in all aspects of his unique mission[5]. They have accepted his call to leave all and follow him(1,18). They walk behind him, however apprehensively, on the road (or the way) that goes up to Jerusalem(10,32). For Mark, every true disciple is called to follow that same road[6]. As soon as the blind man of Jericho, for instance, had his sight restored by Jesus, "he followed him along the road"(10,52).

A 6. The way prepared by John the Baptist

The preparatory role of John the Baptist is one of the cardinal points in the whole gospel tradition. According to Mark, the Baptist was proclaiming "a baptism of repentance for the forgiveness of sins"(1,4). His baptism would have been in the line of the purification by water so strongly promoted at Qumran. There the repentance for sin was certainly expected to be an inner change and a humble begging of forgiveness from God. The external cleansing with water manifested outwardly what they desired within. The difference between John's baptism and that to come through Jesus is acknowledged by the Baptist himself: "I have baptised you with water, but he will baptise you with the Holy Spirit." Thus the theme of forgiveness of sin is related to baptism with the Holy Spirit, in a way that Jesus will introduce. We should recall here the aspects of forgiveness and the gift of God's spirit as characteristics of the new covenant promised by Jeremiah and Ezekiel.

A 7. The meaning of baptism in Jesus' mission

Jesus' own baptism in the Jordan by John was certainly marked by a striking manifestation of the Spirit coming to inspire him for the vital mission he was undertaking. It was the Spirit who, immediately after that baptism, "drove him into the desert" for forty days. Forty days recalls the forty days of Moses on Mt Sinai when the covenant was first sealed and when it had to be renewed shortly afterwards (Ex 24,18; 34,28). It also recalls the forty years of Israel in the desert before they could enter the promised land. Such allusions are suggested also by the text chosen to describe the mission of John the Baptist as one sent into the desert to prepare "a way for the Lord" (1,2-3 - which helps explain Mark's fondness for the way or road to describe the path of discipleship). The quotation is from Deutero-Isaiah, for whom the return of the exiles from Babylon was to be like a second exodus. Within Mark, therefore, we are entitled to see it as announcing the imminent beginning of yet another exodus, this time having "Jesus Christ, the Son of God" to lead it along the road so earnestly prepared by John the Baptist. We may even ponder the imagery of Jesus "coming up out of the water" of the Jordan(1,10), for it can remind us of Moses leading Israel safely through the Reed Sea, and also of Joshua leading Israel through the Jordan into the Promised Land (cf. Ex 14 and Jos 3-4).

As well as having deep significance for Christian baptism, Jesus' baptism is a symbolic acceptance of all the cost involved in his mission. Mark is able to bring that out through the answer given to the ambitious sons of Zebedee. They are asked by Jesus, "Can you drink the cup that I shall drink, or be baptised with the baptism with which I shall be baptised?"(10,38). The cup is the one he was to ask the Father in Gethsemane to take away if possible (14,36); the baptism is likewise his complete immersion in suffering and death. With that in mind Jesus quickly defuses the indignant jealousy aroused by the petition of James and John. He urges his disciples to a spirit of self-sacrificing service of their people, since "the Son of man himself came not to be served but to serve, and to give his life as a ransom for many" (10,45). We will return to the imagery of the cup in reflecting on the Last Supper, where it is directly linked with "the blood of the covenant" (14,24).

A 8. Jesus proclaiming the kingdom of God

Having finished his forty days in the desert, and aware of the Baptist's arrest, Jesus began to preach "the gospel from God", saying to the people of Galilee: "The time is fulfilled, and the kingdom of God is close at hand. Repent and believe the gospel" (1,14-15). This takes us back to what Jesus himself preached, the gospel of God, whereas Mark's opening line, introducing the gospel of Jesus Christ, reflects what the Christian communities emphasised. There was no contradiction, and for Mark the good news about God was centred on the good news about Jesus, the Son, the Beloved, the Teacher, the messianic King and Saviour. The content of Jesus' gospel revolves around the kingdom of God[7].

That was a concept rich in meaning for the Israelites, who could remember the stories of great kings like David and Josiah, or the wisdom and magnificence of a king like Solomon. However, prior to the monarchy in Israel, Yahweh was recognised as the great king over Israel. Again, after the loss of the monarchy with the destruction of Jerusalem, the messianic hopes still envisaged some kind of Messiah from the line of David. The emphasis, though, shifted to the apocalyptic level, in which God was expected to intervene in an irresistible manner. We have seen how Daniel was already speaking confidently about a kingdom which God would establish for ever, embracing "the saints of the Most High" (2,44; 7,18), putting an end to all human kingdoms opposed to the designs of God.

In declaring that "the time is fulfilled", Jesus proclaimed that the time had come for the inauguration of the reign of God so long awaited by those attuned to all the promise and preparation summed up in the Scriptures. Mark attempts no definition of the kingdom, but the remainder of his gospel is a vivid portrayal of what it meant in practice for Jesus and his disciples, as well as the widely differing reactions it stirred up throughout the country. It meant that the power of God at work through Jesus was actively breaking the stranglehold of sin and its consequences for human life and human institutions. The misery of sickness, grinding poverty, imprisonment, rejection and alienation was being confronted with great concern, compassion, solidarity with the sufferers, and a fearless challenging of those in any way responsible for the misery of their fellow-Jews or any neighbour.

A 9. Kingship and kinship for the covenant community

The reign of God, however, has to be accepted voluntarily by the people, hence it is only discernible little by little[8]. Having given free will to all people, God fully respects their freedom, even though that means they may refuse to acknowledge God or live according to revealed values. In Mark, to belong to the kingdom is to belong also to the family of God, as Jesus declared on the occasion of a visit from his mother and cousins. He had just been told that they were waiting outside to see him. "And looking at those sitting in a circle around him, he said, 'Here are my mother and my brothers. Anyone who does the will of God, that person is my brother and sister and mother'"(3,33-35). That is one of the most illuminating texts of all with regard to the relation of the kingdom to the new covenant.

We know from the O.T. that one of the principal goals of entering into a covenant was to draw both parties into a family relationship, so that they would ever afterwards treat one another with loving kindness and fidelity. As we have noted more than once in reflecting on Yahweh's covenant with Israel, the Israelites were bound to treat each other that way, too, over and above honouring Yahweh by loyal love. Therefore when Jesus declares that his disciples have entered into his special family through fidelity to God's will, he is really drawing attention to a marvellous characteristic of the new covenant as well as of the kingdom. While the kingdom presupposes God acknowledged as King, kinship stems from being accepted as brothers and sisters of Jesus, indeed even as his mother.

A 10. God as **Abba**, Father

This awareness in turns leads on to accepting his Father as their own Father, of whom Jesus taught them so much because of his own deep personal experience of God as **Abba**, Father[9]. The most striking use of that term of filial affection in Mark's account is found in the scene following on immediately after Jesus' announcement concerning "the blood of the covenant". During his feeling of "terror and anguish"(14,34) in Gethsemane, Jesus prayed, "**Abba**, Father! .. Take this cup away from me. But let it be as you, not I, would have it"(14,36). Jesus here gives the perfect example of what it means to do the will of God the Father, however hard it may be. He was willing to obey unto death, shouldering the responsibility of a kinsman (**go`el**). Thanks to that voluntary offering of himself as "a ransom" for all his human family, the new covenant was sealed in his blood.

It should not escape us that Jesus himself was the first of the human family to accept fully the terms of the new covenant between the Father and mankind. In this way Jesus crucified and risen is the new covenant, fulfilling what the Servant Songs had glimpsed: "I, Yahweh, have called you in saving justice,..I have made you a covenant of the people and light to the nations"(Is 42,6)[10]. Once that new covenant had been sealed in his own sacrificial blood on the hill of Calvary, it was an everlasting covenant, which no later human violation of commandments could render null and void for others. On the other hand, nobody who knowingly rejected the terms of the new covenant could lay claim to membership of the kingdom of God proclaimed by Jesus. The gospel to be proclaimed to the whole world carries a striking option: "Whoever believes and is baptised will be saved; whoever does not believe will be condemned"(16,16). In stressing God's respect for freedom, we should also point out the heavy responsibility of using freedom to opt correctly in life.

A 11. Jesus as bridegroom

Another image stressing close kinship is that of Jesus as the bridegroom. That is the image which we found used so tellingly by many prophets of Israel, beginning with Hosea. It became so well known that when we find an account of Jesus referring to himself four times as "the bridegroom", we can be morally certain that he is using covenant language. Our presumption is strengthened when we find that the context is a discussion as to why the disciples of Jesus were not fasting like the disciples of the Pharisees and of John the Baptist. That drew Jesus' explanation: "Surely the bridegroom's attendants cannot fast while the bridegroom is still with them? As long as they have the bridegroom with them, they cannot fast"(2,19). The bridegroom's "attendants"in this case were none other than the small group of disciples who were really being prepared as the new Israel to become the bride pledged to the bridegroom in a new alliance of love and fidelity[11]. Theirs were the "new skins" into which the new wine of the gospel had to be put(2,22).

A 12. The new covenant's all-embracing commandment

That Jesus had in mind a covenant of love is made evident by his declaration concerning the greatest commandment[12]. In answer to a scribe's question, "Which is the first of all the commandments?", Jesus replied partly with the biblical text (Dt 6,4-5) so well known to Jews as **shema** (= listen!): "This is the first: 'Listen, Israel, the Lord our God is the one, only Lord, and you must love the Lord your God with all your heart, with all your soul, with all your mind and with all your strength.'" Then Jesus added something not contained in the **shema**, but found in Lev 19,18: "The second is this: 'You must love your neighbour as yourself'. There is no commandment greater than these" (12,29-33). When the scribe publicly commended Jesus for such a good answer, Jesus commented to him, "You are not far from the kingdom of God"(12,34).

By joining on the second part concerning love of neigbour, which was not listed as such among the ten commandments, then saying of both parts as a whole, "There is no (single) commandment greater than these", Jesus formulates the central obligation of the new covenant[13]. The extent to which love of God must permeate all thought and action bearing on the neighbour has to be learnt from following the road of compassion and self-sacrificing service taken by Jesus personally. For this reason the scribe, who acknowledged the force of such a penetrating answer, was "not far from the kingdom of God" - nor far from accepting that all-embracing clause of the new covenant.

A 13. Love of riches as opposed to love of poor people

The case of the rich young man brings out clearly the cost of discipleship with regard to love of riches, love of the poor, and love of Jesus. We can discern here the new dimensions of the road to "eternal life" as sign-posted by the ten commandments and explained by Jesus. When the rich young man was told that the way to eternal life was indicated by the commandments (especially those concerning the neighbour), he was able to state, "Master, I have kept all these since my earliest days" (10,20). Because Jesus "was filled with love for him", he invited him further, saying, "You need to do one thing more. Go and sell what you own and give the money to the poor, and you will have treasure in heaven; then come, follow me" (10,21). In that moment of his call to full discipleship in Jesus' company, the young man decided against it. "He went away sad, for he was a man of great wealth" (10,22)[14].

The demand made to share all his wealth with the poor as the prelude to following Jesus full-time is another basic aspect of genuine kinship with the poor. In his compassion and practical concern for the poor, Jesus insisted that the accumulated wealth of the rich should be made available to those reduced to oppressive poverty. It is a practical step to undo the damage done to the poor by the ruthless efforts of the rich to acquire far more than their share of the human family's resources. This factor must underlie Jesus' comment which astonished his own disciples: "It is easier for a camel to pass through the eye of a needle than for someone rich to enter the kingdom of God" (10,25). It is not a discussion on how to be perfect, but on how to submit to God's reign, God's will, God's values and priorities. Mark goes on to illustrate the Christian response by recalling Peter's attitude to personal possessions and family ties: "'Look', he said to him, 'we have left everything and followed you'" (10,28). Jesus assures Peter that those who leave everything for the sake of him and the gospel will receive a hundredfold now, "and in the world to come, eternal life" (10,30).

A 14. Sharing bread and the eucharist

Jesus compassion for needy and his insistence on sharing food with the hungry shines through the two miracles of loaves and fishes described by Mark. On both occasions the disciples were asked to take out their little supply of food so that it could be shared with thousands of other hungry listeners. Both miracles are also retold in language redolent of a eucharistic celebration, such as taking the loaves and fishes in his hands, looking up to heaven, blessing and breaking the loaves, handing them to the disciples to share out among the people (6,41; 8,6). The first occasion is set within Jewish territory, the second in Gentile territory[15]. It has been suggested that baptism and eucharist played such a leading role in the early Christian community that Mark's whole gospel sets them like two magnets around which the other material is gathered. Baptism serves as the initial focus, then the eucharist provides the final focal point[16]. The suggestion has the merit of relating gospel material to the liturgical setting in which it was being continually celebrated as stemming directly from Christ's own life and teaching. We can rightly regard baptism as a solemn entry into the new covenant community, with the eucharist as a constant renewal and nourishing of that covenant commitment[17].

A 15. Jesus as messianic king

Throughout his ministry Jesus stressed the importance of God and was extremely reluctant, especially in Mark's account, to stress any claims of his own as Messiah or king. Nor would he permit others to acclaim him publicly along those lines. He preferred the unassuming title of "Son of man", which he used especially when speaking of his death and resurrection. However, when he reached the end of his "road" at Jerusalem, he arranged to enter that city of David amid the acclamation of an enthusiastic crowd gathering for the Passover. The people were shouting "Hosanna! Blessed is he who is coming in the name of the Lord! Blessed is the coming kingdom of David our father!" (11,9-10). That entry certainly had implications of Jesus being the "coming" messianic king from the house of David, hence the one who would procure the "coming" of the everlasting kingdom promised to David.

That the kingship of Jesus loomed large in the minds of the Sanhedrin can be deduced from the way Pilate, after hearing their charges against Jesus, asked him directly, "Are you the king of the Jews?" To which Jesus replied, "It is you who say it" Which was a guarded way of affirming a truth that he had not been preaching. Pilate also asked the crowd, "What am I to do with the man you call king of the Jews?" Later the soldiers mocked him as "king of the Jews", even putting on him a makeshift crown of thorns. The charge for which he was crucified read, "The King of the Jews". Those who had instigated proceedings against him mocked him on the cross, taunting him, "Let the Christ, the king of Israel, come down form the cross now, for us to see it and believe"(15,1-32)

A 16. Jesus' concern for the Temple

Like David and Solomon of old, Jesus showed great concern for the Temple once he had entered Jerusalem. He proceeded immediately to cleanse it of the money-changers and merchants who had made it into a den of thieves. He reminded the people there of the promise given through Trito-Isaiah (56,6-7) concerning even foreigners, who will become God's servants and "cling to my covenant": "My house will be called a house of prayer for all peoples" (Mk 11,17). That authoritative stand taken in the Temple was certainly a challenge to the "chief priests and scribes", who regarded that holy precinct as doubly their own domain. The Sanhedrin, which was a council of some seventy priests, scribes and Pharisees, ruled the Jewish nation under the tutelage of Rome. It exercised ordinary civil power as well as religious authority.

The challenge of Jesus was definitely seen as a danger to their political power over the nation, as well as a breaking of their religious power over the lives of the Jewish people as believers and Temple worshippers[18]. While it is becoming more common to describe Jesus as a political agitator[19], it would seem more accurate to say that he agitated politicians. He was the greatest prophetic critic ever of dehumanising conditions, of unjust people and their unjust use of power over others. By his clear proclamation of the kind of family spirit and truly just society to which God was calling all Israel, as by his forthright denunciations of leaders who were hindering the establishment of God's reign on earth, he also stirred up the victims of injustice and neglect. He brought them a new vision and motivation to join together to change what contradicted the plan of God made known through Jesus' entire mission.

His prophecy concerning the destruction of the Temple was in line with those earlier prophecies given by Micah and Jeremiah. Prophets like them were sent to warn the people of Jerusalem to change their unjust conduct, instead of presuming that empty sacrifices in the Temple would shield them from any disaster. For his part, Jesus foretold the destruction of the Temple only in the hearing of Peter, James, John and Andrew: "You see these great buildings? Not a single stone will be left on another; everything will be pulled down" (13,2). When they questioned him further about when all that would happen, Jesus delivered an eschatological discourse. The "last days" it treats of seem to be mainly the crucial period between his resurrection and the destruction of Jerusalem.

Some sections of it are clothed in apocalyptic imagery in the style of Daniel. Apocalyptic style does not mean that the content of the message can only be something quite other-worldly. On the contrary, as in Daniel, so also here in Mk 13 the impact of God's intervention will be very much upon empires and cities of this world. God's kingdom is a reality in this world, able to transform human institutions, even though the full flowering will only be seen beyond the last day of human history. It is worth noting the trials in store for the disciples, who are warned: "You will be beaten in synagogues; and you will be brought before governors and kings for my sake, as evidence to them, since the gospel must first be proclaimed to all nations"(13,9-10). Just as governors and kings are obviously political figures, opposed to the heralds of the gospel, likewise the synagogues wielded political power, capable of beating, imprisoning, even stoning opponents to death. Hence the disciples will need to follow the lead of their Teacher in confronting such political authorities. He promises them the special help of the Spirit when they have to bear witness to him and the gospel before such leaders (13,11)

A 17. Giving "the blood of the covenant"

Mark's Passion account opens with the remark that, when the Passover was two days off, "the chief priests and the scribes were looking for a way to arrest Jesus by some trick and have him put to death"(14,1). Judas then offered to betray him for money. In that hostile situation Jesus arranged to celebrate the Passover meal with the Twelve. When it was under way, Jesus revealed that one of his table-companions was going to betray him. "It is one of the Twelve", he said, "one who is dipping into the same dish with me"(14,20). That was a most painful betrayal of the close personal friendship and mutual commitment summed up for the Israelites in a shared meal, all the more binding because this was one of the most sacred meals of the Jewish year.

In the course of that paschal meal, Jesus took some bread, said a blessing, broke it and gave it to the disciples saying, "Take it, this is my body". Next he took a cup of wine, gave thanks, and handed it to them saying, "This is my blood, the blood of the covenant, poured out for many". He remarked: "In truth I tell you, I shall never drink wine any more until the day I drink the new wine in the kingdom of God"(14,22-25). In those few cryptic sentences Mark depicts the great moment when Jesus, during his farewell meal with the disciples, gave them his own body and blood, while indicating that this gift was part of his total self-giving for them and "for many" in sacrifice. The Greek word used for "having given thanks" over the cup is **eucharistesas**, from which comes the traditional word "eucharist". Blessing and thanksgiving were part of the celebration of the Passover, but on this occasion Jesus, acting as head of the family, gives an astonishingly new significance to the meal[20].

His words over the cup do not refer directly to the Passover lamb, but they take us back to the sealing of the covenant at Sinai, where Moses sprinkled sacrificial blood over the Israelites and explained it: "This is the blood of the covenant which Yahweh has made with you, entailing all these stipulations" (Ex 24,8). By speaking of "my blood .. poured out for many", Jesus clearly refers to his imminent sacrifice on the cross, when the last drop of his blood would be poured out, voluntarily, "for many". As he had foretold earlier to his disciples, his life would be given "as a ransom for many" (10,45). Remember that the phrase of a sacrifice "for many" is taken from the prophecy concerning the Suffering Servant (Is.53,10-12), where the many are unlimited. The point is that one Servant is willing to die for the forgiveness and healing of the rest of his sinful people.

It is not hard to perceive in the Last Supper a covenant meal, deepening the table-fellowship of the Twelve (except for Judas) with Jesus, and through him drawing them into communion with the Father as well. The demands of the new covenant had been made known gradually as the demands of following Jesus along the road to the cross and resurrection. Now the covenant and the cross are inseparably linked, for the blood of the covenant is the blood shed on the cross. In this light we can see that Mark's gradual revelation of Jesus as the suffering Messiah includes the aspect of establishing the new covenant and the eucharistic celebration of it till the fulness of God's reign has come.

A 18. The new covenant can extend God's reign to every land

As for the covenant announced by Jesus, it is certainly a new covenant, even though in Mark the word "new" is not used here[21]. The sentence which follows the giving of "my blood, the blood of the covenant" looks forward to the day when Jesus will "drink the new wine in the kingdom of God". That is another way of emphasising that his self-sacrifice and the covenant it establishes between God and mankind is a vital step towards the fulness of God's reign over all. The fellowship it makes possible between Jesus and the disciples will reach its joyful goal when they join him in the final messianic banquet[22].

The Passover itself was a memorial meal recalling the liberation from Egypt and the long journey towards the Promised Land. For the disciples Jesus gives the kingdom of God as the goal to which he is leading them. It can be entered wherever God is, therefore is not limited to one particular country or race. In fact there are several indications in Mark that "the many" are to comprise people from all the world (cf.13,10; 14,9; 16,16). It is not that a disciple has to leave this world to enter the kingdom of God, but that a disciple's own land can and should become a land where God is joyfully acknowledged as King and Father over the land and its people.

A 19. The new covenant is the way to full resurrection

The covenant is also strongly linked to the resurrection, since the ongoing celebration of the Eucharist is always with the awareness of the risen Christ present in the midst of each celebrating community. Mark leaves open the symbolism of the road ahead when he records the message of the young man at the empty tomb: "He is going ahead of you to Galilee; that is where you will see him, just as he told you"(16,7). The miracle of raising Jairus's daughter to life (Mk 5,21-43) was retold as a reminder of Jesus' power to raise the dead to new life. Later on, when correcting the view of some Sadducees in Jerusalem, Jesus strongly affirmed the power of God to raise the dead. His closing remark was, "He is God, not of the dead, but of the living. You [Sadducees] are very much mistaken" (12,27). Jesus' own death and resurrection, therefore, opened the way to eternal life for all his brothers and sisters. As true Son he invites them to enter voluntarily into the new covenant of mutual love with the Father and with one another, moved and guided by the Spirit. That is the road leading them towards the true homeland intended for them by the God of the living.

B. THE NEW COVENANT IN MATTHEW'S GOSPEL

This gospel in its final form is now generally considered as being about ten years later than that of Mark, hence from about 80 A.D. It is the most Jewish of the four gospels, displaying throughout a great concern for the fulfilment of biblical promises and of the Mosaic Law in all its implications for interior fidelity. While Mark has been traditionally regarded as reflecting the preaching of Peter in Rome, Matthew is thought to have been written "in Syria by an unknown Greek-speaking Jewish Christian, living in the 80s in a mixed community with converts of both Jewish and Gentile descent"[23]. A comparison of those two gospels show that Matthew has much in common with Mark, but is much longer because it adds several discourses of Jesus which are not found in Mark. It also adds two colourful chapters about the infancy of Jesus, which serve as a good prelude to his public ministry.

The good news preached by Jesus is again the kingdom of "heaven" (with capital H in New Jerusalem Bible, since Heaven is used in this phrase as a synonym for God). Jesus' preaching of the kingdom, however, is depicted as intimately related to the little community or "church" which he builds on Peter and other disciples[24]. This has to be viewed in the light of fifty years of development in the understanding of the apostolic Church after the original preaching, death and resurrection of "the Christ, the Son of the living God" (Mt 16,16)[25].

We shall pay special attention to the way Matthew presents Jesus bringing to perfection the roles of both Moses and David, till at the Last Supper he speaks in the same breath of "<u>the blood of the covenant</u>" and drinking "the new wine with you in <u>the kingdom of my Father</u>" (26,28-29). The first phrase underlined recalls Moses' role, the other that of David as viceroy of Yahweh and recipient of a promissory covenant concerning an everlasting throne(and hence a kingdom to go with it). What follows are important aspects of the new covenant discernible particularly in Matthew.

B 1. The Infancy Narrative: Jesus as son of David

Cc.1 - 2 open with a genealogy, a feature of considerable importance in Jewish circles, as we have already noticed right from Genesis through to the Chronicler's history. For Matthew it provides an opportunity to recall all the preparation for the birth of Jesus from the line of Abraham down through David and his successors till the exile, then through David's descendants after that until Joseph, the husband of Mary and legal father of Jesus. In that one genealogy, David is named five times, beginning with the solemn opening line of the whole gospel: "Roll of the genealogy of Jesus Christ, son of David, son of Abraham" (1,1). For those who know that the name of David in Hebrew has a numerical value of 14, the division of the genealogy into 3 groups of 14 names makes the emphasis on David even more thought-provoking[26].

Why David has a special importance for the author soon emerges in the first of many quotations from the O.T. to indicate how Christ's coming has fulfilled the promises. Reflecting on what the angel had told Joseph about Mary having conceived a son "by the Holy Spirit", Mt says that all this was to fulfil the prophecy: "Look! the virgin is with child and will give birth to a son whom they will call Immanuel"(1,23). That prophecy is drawn from the "Immanuel Cycle" in Isaiah (7-12), where the promise concerns a child to be born from the house of David as a sign of the survival of that royal house and of the introduction of a reign of justice. Mt emphasises the significance of Immanuel by explaining that it means "God-is-with-us". For Mt, the coming of Jesus begins a unique form of God-with-us as one conceived and born of woman into our human family. That in turn opens the way to a whole new dimension of the covenant relationship often summed up as "your God - my people"[27]. Mt is sufficiently struck by the implications of Immanuel to use it again to close his gospel, this time with the farewell words of the risen Jesus, "And look, I am with you always; yes, to the end of time"(28,20). The unique presence and relationship of God-with-us in Jesus Christ, "son of David", will never be withdrawn, nor can it be terminated by us.

The Davidic origin of Jesus is further emphasised by his birth in Bethlehem, which was well known as David's home-town. To that town the wise men were directed when they asked Herod in Jerusalem, "Where is the infant king of the Jews?"(2,2). In this, as in what now follows about Jesus as a new Moses, the infancy narrative serves as an accurate prelude to the main body of the gospel[28]. The gentiles are represented by the wise men coming to find the new-born king, whereas king Herod foreshadows the local rulers who want to eliminate Jesus as a threat to their own power over the people.

B 2. The Infancy Narrative: Jesus as a new Moses

The birth of Jesus — so named "because he is the one who is to save his people from their sins" — readily suggests a parallel with the birth of Moses, the first saviour of Israel from slavery. Mt tells how the infant Jesus escaped a killing of male babies as Moses had been spared in his infancy. To make the parallel unmistakable, Mt says that Jesus' return from Egypt with his parents would fulfil "what the Lord had spoken through the prophet: 'I called my son out of Egypt'"(2,15). In Hosea those words were said of Israel's exodus, so their use by Mt here implies that Jesus sums up in himself the Israel that the Lord is setting free.

Then an association with the time of the exile is ingeniously suggested by a passage from Jeremiah about Rachel mourning her children who had all been killed or taken away. In the original context Rachel is told to stop weeping, because Yahweh declares, "Your children will return to their homeland" (Jer 31,17); later in the same chapter the new covenant is promised. Let us not forget that Jesus as an Israelite had solidarity with the people who were still in need of liberation and the new covenant.

B 3. Sermon on the Mount: the spirit of the new covenant

Cc.5-7 contain the first and longest discourse of Jesus recorded in Mt. By means of it, Mt concludes his first section or "book" of the public ministry with an admirable charter of the kingdom of Heaven, which we can also recognize as a synthesis of the new spirit demanded by the new covenant. The setting itself, with Jesus seated "on the mountain" teaching his disciples and "crowds", recalls Moses on Mt Sinai receiving the Law, then passing it on to all the Israelites as basic for their covenant with Yahweh.

a) The Beatitudes:
The eight beatitudes with which the Sermon begins seem to be deliberately parallel to the ten commandments. The first four beatitudes, clustering around evangelical poverty, can be taken as proposing the right attitude before God; the next four, revolving around loving kindness, are concerned with attitudes toward the neighbour[29].

However, there is also a great contrast between the commandments and the beatitudes, since the latter are not in the form of laws but of revolutionary declarations. They resound from "the mountain" as the programme being launched through Jesus to overturn existing assessments of the way to lasting happiness. The beatitudes present positive ideals, whereas most of the commandments were couched in the form of "thou shalt not..". They leave no doubt that the inauguration of God's reign will bring happiness to the poor, the meek, the humble, as well as to those who long for justice or suffer persecution on its behalf. Those gospel values and spirit were in direct contrast to the commonly accepted Jewish view that God must have blessed the rich, the powerful, those secure in their possessions and never troubled by fights over justice.

In the light of covenant language, it is also noteworthy that here Jesus does not threaten any curse for failure to live up to the ideals being proposed. They carry only the assurance of happiness to those whom the world normally would consider most unfortunate. In Lk the antithesis is made explicit, by recording four "woes" awaiting the rich, the well fed, those laughing now and praised in public(6,24-26). Even a "woe" is more like an urgent warning to change while there is still time, rather than a covenant curse or a death penalty to be carried out by the community.

— The poor and the kingdom: The opening beatitude provides a key example of the new outlook: "How blessed are the poor in spirit: the kingdom of Heaven is theirs"(Mt 5,3). Mt is often said to have practically substituted a "spiritual" poverty (such as detachment from wealth) for real economic poverty. The way Luke gives the beatitude: "How blessed are you who are poor: the kingdom of God is yours" (Lk 6,20), probably reflects more closely the original saying[30]. However, Mt is really quite close to Lk in the meaning of poverty, since his whole gospel brings out that for him the poor are in the tradition of the O.T.'s "afflicted poor", those who put their trust entirely in Yahweh. They are the lowly, the meek and humble, the little ones open to God. Jesus own example is mentioned shortly after the Sermon is concluded. In alerting a would-be follow of the poverty involved, Jesus told him simply, "Foxes have holes and birds of the air have nests, but the Son of man has nowhere to lay his head" (8,20). Jesus also indicates to the Baptist's disciples some of the signs that the messianic era has begun - "the blind see again, the lame walk, .. and the good news is proclaimed to the poor" (11,5).

In wording it as "the poor in spirit", Mt does emphasise a spiritual, and therefore a voluntary, aspect of poverty, whereby economic poverty leaves the poor person really open to God. After all, the reign of God normally brings happiness only to those who accept it personally. God, not poverty, is the source of happiness. Riches, on the other hand, all too often stifle acceptance of God's will. As Jesus expounds within the Sermon, "You cannot be the slave both of God and of money" (6,24). Again, in the following discourse of parables, Jesus explains how "the worry of the world and the lure of riches choke the word and so it produces nothing" (13,22). In short, the poor whose spirit trusts in God and not in riches is the outstanding beneficiary of God's reign that has come to reverse the situation of the selfish rich and the trusting poor.

It also implies quite sweeping changes in the social and political systems of Israel first and eventually of all nations. S. van Tilborg has a fine study on the impact of the ideology of the ruling class on the Sermon on the Mount. He holds that through its text "a new way of living arises, a way of living which wants to change the whole society. Different forms of possession, the other forms of relationships and a new mentality .. will bring God's covenant with Israel to reality"[31]. Under that aspect, all the afflicted poor who have not yet heard of God's plan as proclaimed through Jesus are also meant to benefit greatly from the social revolution it is introducing.

— The subjugated and the land: One inescapable dimension of such social change is the occupation of the land and the full rights to the products produced on this or that block of land. The second beatitude says explicitly, "Blessed are the gentle: they shall have the earth as inheritance"(5,4). The word used here for "earth" also means "land", as it is translated in the N.A.B. We have already considered the implications of the Jubilee Year, with its ideal of returning ancestral land to its dispossessed owners, and setting free from slavery the many little farmers whom hard times had forced to sell everything, including themselves and their families. There is a growing convictions among commentators that Jesus fully intended to declare open an unending Jubilee(Year), one obviously much more profound and widespread than the original one[32].

W. Brueggemann, for example, insists that the theme of the kingdom of God "clearly includes among its nuances the idea of historical, political, physical realm, that is, land. .. However rich and complex the imagery may be in its various articulations, the coming of Jesus is understood with reference to new land arrangements"[33]. The "gentle" who are to inherit the earth are very closely allied to the "afflicted poor", but the Greek word used implies that they are submissive because they have been subjugated, broken in like the domestic animals. So they have been broken down and yoked up to work the land that used belong to them, but which they now have to work for Roman or Jewish landlords[34]. Jesus can declare them blessed because the arrival of God's reign will restore the land taken away from them by the powerful.

This is still a happiness lacking to hundreds of millions of the "gentle", including the yoked farmers of today and shanty town dwellers who were the little farmers of yesterday. The gospel continues to herald God's reign on earth as intent on a much more equitable sharing of the land, which is God's gift to all his family. For the Jews, the Land meant what had been given in fulfilment of the promise to the patriarchs, obtained in Joshua's day, lost through the exile, and partially regained by those who returned to it. Because so many Israelites remained in the Dispersion outside Palestine, while even those within Palestine were rarely the real masters of their Land, the Jews of Jesus' day had already begun to spiritualize "the land". It could be used by them as a synonym for the kingdom of God, as W. Davies has observed[35].

Because Mt was written for Jewish and Gentile Christians living outside the original Land, it is understandable that "the land" could also be regarded as closely allied to the kingdom. In that context, to belong to the kingdom and to be heirs of the land are parallel ideas. Many exegetes, in fact, see the second beatitude (about the meek inheriting the land) as a doublet for the first one (that the kingdom of heaven is for the poor). The fact that the second beatitude has been included should draw our attention to the prominence of the promised Land in the Torah and the rest of the O.T. As the new Moses and rightful heir of David, Jesus assures the dispossessed that such a fundamental promise will be honoured through the arrival of God's reign. Once again it is worth insisting that the happiness of the subjugated stems from the assurance that their yoke will be removed, that their land will be restored to them in accord with God's original gift to Israel (as to every nation given their land by the Creator).

— New horizons for covenant kindness: The four beatitudes concerning attitudes and conduct towards others all recall essential characteristics of covenant kindness. "Blessed are the merciful"(5,7) is the equivalent to saying, "blessed are those who practise **hesed**"[36]. Twice in Mt Jesus confirms the demands of **hesed** expressed by the prophet Hosea —"Mercy is what pleases me, not sacrifice" — when defending his table-fellowship with Matthew and other sinners, or when defending the picking of some grain by his disciples (Mt 9,13 & 12,7). As the Sermon itself unfolds, Jesus will indicate a new horizon for the exercise of such mercy by his disciples.

"The pure of heart" (5,8) are those who harbour no malice in their heart toward their neighbour. This emphasises still further that true mercy must spring from a noble and undivided heart. "The peacemakers" (5,9) are not content simply to enjoy the peace that exists within a good covenant community as one of its distinguishing features. They also want to do everything in their power to encourage peace with and among all their neighbours.Today we should be more earnest than any previous Christians about peacemaking, for now we know that the likely alternative to peace on earth is the destruction of at least the major part of our human family and our planet home.

"The persecuted in the cause of uprightness" (5,10) or God-inspired justice, which reflects God's saving justice, are those willing to proclaim and practise such justice themselves. They are always ready to defend the right of their neighbours to share fully in it with freedom and dignity. The mention of persecution against such committed upholders of justice presupposes that public leaders are going to demand other standards under pain of severe sanctions. The following verses expand on the kind of abuse and calumny to be expected during a persecution, but it also offers the consolation of a great reward in heaven after suffering like the earlier prophets did (5,11-12).

B 3. b) Bringing to perfection the Law and the Prophets:

With full authority as the new Moses, Jesus explains his unique mission, saying, "Do not think that I have come to abolish the Law or the Prophets. I have come not to abolish but to complete them" (5,17). The beatitudes are already striking examples of how the purpose of the Law is to be achieved through a radical change in attitudes. The rest of the Sermon continues to illustrate the kind of changes necessary. We limit our consideration in this section to the clear examples given in the second half of ch.5.

"You shall not kill" requires the constant avoidance of anger against another person and a willingness to seek reconciliation, which is to be sought before daring to offer a sacrifice on the altar (vv.21-26). Similarly, to avoid adultery it is necessary to avoid any "adultery in the heart" (vv.27-30). Divorce is forbidden on the grounds that remarriage of a divorced person would be a form of adultery. On a later occasion Jesus bases the permanence of marriage on its divine origin, as described in the first chapters of Genesis. He maintains that "what God has united, human beings must not divide" (19,6). The kind of divorce permitted by Moses is no longer permitted by Jesus, who wants marriage restored to its original sacredness and indissolubility. Which makes Christian marriage that much better able to reflect the new covenant of love being established through and with the messianic bridegroom. That this is within Mt's context can be seen from the other allusions to Jesus as the bridegroom (9,14-16; 22,1-14; 25,1-13). Marriage should be permanent, not provisional.

If enduring love of one partner for the other was so difficult that the disciples considered marriage inadvisable once divorce was ruled out (19,10), then Jesus' call to "love your enemies" must have sounded quite incredible. The motivation for it is directly linked to their status as God's children, who are granted sun and rain independently of what they do. It is what they are that makes them always precious in the eyes of their Father. It is not for any of God's children to hate other members of the same family. On the contrary, Jesus demands a kind of love which also reaches out with compassion and the offer of reconciliation to the enemy.

W. Klassen expresses well the positive steps demanded by such love: "To love the enemy means to live for the enemy, to share with the enemy that which you have, rather than seeking to destroy the enemy, to do that which will enhance the good of the enemy and enrich the life of the enemy. To love the enemy means to place yourself at his service"[37]. Such service must follow the path set by Jesus and always remain subject to the Spirit of love. At no stage did Jesus abandon his Father's will in order to serve an enemy. An important strategy for opening the way to dialogue and reconciliation with an enemy is to leave him or her with room to choose what the next step will be and to take it freely, out of conviction or at least in the interests of further communication[38].

B 3. c) The prayer of the covenant community:
The prayer which Jesus taught his disciples is another admirable summary of the basic attitudes and sentiments that are acceptable to "our Father in heaven". Once again the first half lifts the mind and heart to God as our Father, then the second half is concerned with the needs of the human family, with all petitions in the plural. It is a family prayer, addressed with great confidence to the heavenly Father and showing concern for the fundamental needs of all the family. In teaching us to address God as "our Father", Jesus was inviting us to share in his own direct, familiar, loving approach whereby he spoke to God as "**Abba**". That is a word retained from the Aramaic language spoken by Jesus and his people in those days. **Abba** was the form of address used by children to speak to their father and was considered a term of endearment and intimacy. Presumably for that reason Jewish prayers never addressed God as **Abba**[39].

Christians, taught by Jesus and moved by his Spirit, were enabled to cry out "**Abba**, Father!" (Rm 8,15). The opening words, "our Father", govern and enrich all that follows in the prayer. The predominant attitude to God, therefore, is that of loving children toward the Father rather than of loyal subjects toward the great King. Or we could say that this prayer pinpoints what makes the kingdom of God so distinct, namely that its King is also the compassionate Father of all the people being invited to become its citizens.

The first of the three petitions (in Mt 6,9-10) is really asking that the name "Father" be held in honour, by those who already recognise him and by an ever increasing number who will do so. The convinced family members must help others to recognise God as Father of all nations and peoples[40]. The second petition introduces the kingdom theme, for it prays "your kingdom come". The Father's reign over all our race is something we want to come about, but only the Father can draw people to enter freely into it. The Christians' part is to pray for it constantly and to carry out the mission entrusted to them by the risen Christ. The following petition is rightly regarded as requesting the same thing: "your will be done". To do the Father's will is to enter the kingdom (7,21); it is also to enter the family of God, because it makes disciples into brothers and sisters of Jesus, the beloved Son (12,50; cf.17,5).

Accepting that the first half of the prayer articulates a longing for the honour and voluntary acceptance of our Father by all, we can readily discern in the second half a confident request that the Father provide for the basic needs of all the family (6,11-13). The petition for "daily bread" can be taken to include the ordinary material food, plus aspects of "the bread of life" within the community keenly interested in the definitive messianic kingdom[41]. In today's world it is vital to realise that, in asking for "our" daily food from the Father, we are committing ourselves to share that food as soon as it is given.

Not by accident does the following petition link the forgiveness of our own debts with a willingness on our part to forgive the debts of those who owe us something. All too quickly we limit the meaning to our "sins", and our willingness to forgive those who have "sinned" against us. When it comes to hard cash, there's no thought of telling the debtor that he does not have to repay it.

For Jesus, however, the forgiveness or setting free was to be in the spirit of the Jubilee release, which definitely involved releasing slaves and cancelling their debts, as well as returning to them their homes and small fields. Because the Jubilee traditions were concerned with rectifying dehumanising aspects of the socio-political and economic order, Jesus was able to take them up to proclaim how the reign of God was, to quote S. Ringe, "breaking the stranglehold of the old order on those we have come to recognize as 'the poor'". .. ... "The petition concerning the 'forgiveness of debts' portrays in a condensed and economical way the radical change in relationships and behavior that is both required and made possible in the reign of God proclaimed by Jesus the Christ"[42] (emphasis added).

Jesus' parable to illustrate the kind of forgiveness expected among disciples tells of a king who forgave his servant an enormous cash debt, whereas that servant refused to forgive someone who owed him a small amount of money. The king then punished severely the unforgiving servant, from which the lesson is drawn: "And that is how my heavenly Father will deal with you unless you each forgive your brother from your heart" (18,35; cf. 6,14-15).

In covenantal terms, we may say that the first half of the "Our Father" expresses our loyal love toward the Father, whereas the second half expresses at the same time our trusting dependence on the Father and our loving concern for all the other members of the family, including ourselves but excluding nobody. This prayer has to be as wide as the love of enemies already mentioned: "You must therefore set no bounds to your love, just as your heavenly Father sets none to his" (5,48). This prayer sums up the distinctive spirit of the new covenant, as it comes from the mediator of that covenant and was intended for his new community.

B 4. Jesus himself as messianic king rejected by Israel

The third "book" (Mt 11 - 13), being in the centre of the five "books", carefully delineates a central issue for Mt and one which we must touch on, even if briefly. The kingdom of Heaven is shown to be closely related to the person of Jesus as the promised messianic king, who alone has been sent to usher it in. Cc. 11 - 12 recount the growing opposition to Jesus himself, which for Mt amounts to the rejection by Israel's leaders of the promised kingdom. D. Verseput, The Rejection of the Humble Messianic King — A Study of the Composition of Mt 11-12, finds that "Mt has placed the Davidic Messiahship at the heart of his presentation. .. Jesus is the royal Messiah, but he is antecedently the divine Son." His disciples, by accepting the Father's will, stand in contrast to Israel, who as a nation rejected Jesus and therefore the kingdom as well. "To her, the covenant people, had been given the promises of the kingdom. And yet at the moment of decision, she stumbled"[43].

The Baptist's envoys to Jesus raise the leading question that governs the rest of this narrative section (cc.ll & 12): "Are you the one who is to come, or look for another? (ll,3). Jesus was able to praise John, but he made it clear that the Baptist was not in the same era as "the least in the kingdom of Heaven" (11,11). On the other hand, Jesus could only reproach the crowds from favoured towns like Chorazin, Bethsaida and Capernaum, who were so unresponsive to his preaching and miracles. The "little ones" and the heavily burdened are those to whom the Son can reveal the Father and bring them relief (11,25-30). Jesus himself is described in the language of the Suffering Servant, quiet and extremely sensitive to the crushed and the faltering (12,18-21).

He can promise forgiveness of all kinds of sin, but not deliberately insulting speech against the Holy Spirit (12,31-32). That is a declaration of fact, in the sense that such blasphemers will not accept any light from the Spirit whom they are insulting. Not even the promise of the Spirit in relation to the new covenant can overcome the voluntary and insulting rejection of the Holy Spirit. Tyre, Sidon, Sodom, Nineveh, and the Queen of the South are all mentioned as having been more open than the Israel to which Jesus was preaching the kingdom of Heaven. They will be judged accordingly, because the freedom to reject God's full reign by no means brings an exemption from personal responsibility or God's judgment.

The corresponding discourse is one of parables (c.13), each one being a comparison of the kingdom with a familiar country scene. The parables teach the small, humble, hidden beginnings of the kingdom, together with its sure and enduring growth till "harvest time". There will be a crop, despite difficulties. In explaining the parable of the darnel, Jesus says that the field is the whole world, and the good seed is "the subjects of the kingdom". He also promises that "the upright will shine like the sun <u>in the kingdom of their Father</u>" (13,38.43). The last pregnant phrase confirms what was implied in the prayer to "our Father" for the coming of his kingdom. Our Father's kingdom or reign will endure, for those who have accepted it, beyond "the end of time" (13,40), and in that phase the full glory of our kingly Father and the royal family will be seen.

B 5. The Church as the new covenant community accepting God's reign

The fourth "book" (13,53 - 18,35) presents the Church as being "the first-fruits of the kingdom of Heaven"[44], through the narrative section with the disciples quite prominent, then through the discourse about the spirit of humble service expected within the community. In both sections the term "church" is used to denote the little community of disciples gathered around Jesus (16,18; 18,17).

B 5. a) The narrative section (13,53 - 17,27)

It gives, for example, both accounts of the miracle of the loaves and fishes, as in Mk. After Peter's confession of Jesus as "the Christ, the Son of the living God", comes a promise recorded only in Mt: "You are Peter and on this rock I will build my community" (16,18)[45].. The Greek word used for "community" is **ekklesia**, which is frequently used in the LXX (= Septuagint translation) for the "solemn assembly"/"congregation"/ "covenanted community of Israel". For instance, **ekklesia** is used in texts where Moses recalls "the day of the assembly at Horeb" to receive the commandments and all the covenant

(Dt 4,10 - 14; 9,10-11; 31,30), and where Solomon blesses "all the assembly of Israel" at the dedication of the Temple (3 Kings 8,14)[46].

In some texts of the LXX there is reference to the **ekklesia** "of the Lord", for instance when specifying who could enter that assembly (Dt 23,2-9), and when David gives a farewell exhortation: "So now in the sight of all Israel, the assembly of Yahweh .. I charge you to observe and adhere strictly to all the commandments of Yahweh your God, so that you may retain possession of this fine land and leave it to your sons after you as a heritage for ever" (1 Ch 28,8). For Mt, therefore, when Jesus as Messiah and Son of God announces that he will build "my church" on the rock of Peter's divinely given faith, the promised community must be regarded as succeeding to Israel as the "assembly of the Lord". As such, the church will also realise what Yahweh promised through Jeremiah concerning Israel of the new covenant: "Then I shall be their God and they will be my people" (31,34).

The special relationship of Peter to Jesus is illustrated by the delightful little story of how Peter was permitted to pay the Temple tax for Jesus and himself as "sons of the kingdom" [and so by rights exempt] (17,24-27).

In the transfiguration scene, set on "a high mountain", Mt suggests another comparison with Moses on Mt Sinai. Jesus' face "shone like the sun and his clothes became dazzling as light" (17,2). For Moses, a veil over his face was sufficient to conceal the radiance of his face (Ex 34,29-35); for Jesus, the brightness lit up not only his face but was so dazzling that it shone through his clothes. After seeing both Moses and Elijah speaking with Jesus, the chosen trio of disciples heard a voice declaring, "This is my Son the Beloved; he enjoys my favour. Listen to him" (17,5). Mt thus indicates that Jesus is the "prophet like Moses", to whom Israel is told to listen or be ready to render an account to God (Dt 18,17-19).

B 5. b) A new community spirit (18,1-35)

The discourse which is used to conclude the fourth "book" stresses the need for child-like humility in order "to enter the kingdom of heaven" (18,1-4). It also demands deep respect for all the "little ones" of God's family, because their "Father in heaven" never wants to lose even one of them (vv.5-14). Any family member who errs is to be admonished kindly by the others, and as a last resort his case can be put before the "church". If the offender disregards correction suggested by the community as a whole, then he will have to be treated "like a gentile or a tax collector". That kind of decision by the community on earth is backed up "in heaven", namely by Jesus Christ, whose "church" has his authority to speak on the standards demanded of its members. To treat an obdurate offender like a tax collector does not mean to hate him or shun him, but rather to approach him as one still to be evangelized, in the same way that Jesus evangelized Matthew himself (cf.9,9).

In teaching the efficacy of community prayer to the Father, Jesus declares that, "where two or three meet in my name, I am there among them" (18,20). The Greek word used for "meet" means literally "having been called together" [as a "synagogue" or congregation]. To meet as an assembly in the name of Jesus, in Mt, is to meet as the new "assembly of the Lord" that brings to perfection the earlier assembly of Israel as God's people.

God's forgiveness of sin, which is a characteristic of the new covenant, entails for all the community members likewise a willingness to forgive without limit. This is emphasised by a parable in which the kingdom of heaven is compared to a king who cancelled the debt of a servant, who then refused to do likewise to his own debtor. The lesson leaves no doubt that the king stands for "my heavenly Father" and the small debtor who must be forgiven from the heart is "your brother" (18,21-35). In concluding the "book" on the church with that parable, Mt discreetly confirms that requirements for the kingdom are to be observed by the disciples who form the church. Furthermore, all forgiveness is to be viewed within the family context.

B 6. The parousia and last judgment

The fifth "book" (cc.19-25) captures some of the tension and final crisis as Jesus moves courageously right into Jerusalem. Both narrative and discourse reflect the challenge to Jesus by the Jewish leaders. He also persistently challenges them to accept the reign of God before it is "taken away" from them and "given to a people who will produce its fruit" (21,43).

B 6. a) The narrative section (cc. 19 - 23)

In scathing language Jesus denounces, by means of seven "woes", the scribes and Pharisees. He warns them about over-concern for small details while they neglect "the weightier matters of the Law - justice, mercy, good faith" (23,23). Mercy, or "covenant kindness", as we have seen, was strongly inculcated for his own little community, together with faith and justice. In fact, the "keys of the kingdom" entrusted to Peter presupposed those qualities in leaders of the new "assembly of the Lord", otherwise they would not differ from the scribes and Pharisees, who "shut up the kingdom of Heaven in people's faces" (23,13).

The narrative section closes by a touching reproach to Jerusalem, the city that kills the prophets. The imagery of the hen gathering together her chickens under her wings is one of many instances in the Bible where God and God-incarnate manifests a maternal love. Despite the loving invitation, Jerusalem refused it, and thereby prevented its entry into the kingdom or new covenant community. Part of God's love is to leave freedom of choice and responsibility for conduct to all peoples and nations. Some day, Jesus implies, the people of Jerusalem will exclaim, "Blessed is he who is coming in the name of the Lord!" (23,37-39).

B 6. b) The concluding discourse (cc.24 - 25)

Jesus leads the disciples on from his prediction of the destruction of the Temple to an announcement of his own "coming" (**parousia**) the end of the world (24,1-51). As D. Stanley has noted, the 5 major "discourses" in Mt start with the charter of the kingdom and hence for the church or "assembly" convoked by the new Moses. Then in the final discourse the destruction of the Temple is to mark the passing of the old Israel with its old institutions[47]. Heading the list of old institutions would have to be the old covenant, which prophets had said would be replaced by a new one. On this point the N.J.B.

succinctly comments, "The destruction of Jerusalem marks the end of the old covenant - Christ has thus manifestly returned to inaugurate his kingly rule. Such a decisive intervention will not occur again until the end of time"[48].

Because the day of the parousia is not known, members of the community must live and work loyally with all their talents, like wise and trustworthy stewards. "When the Son of man comes in his glory, escorted by all the angels, then he will take his seat on his throne of glory. All nations will be assembled before him" (25,31-32). The second coming of Jesus Christ will be truly an epoch-making event, a definitive intervention of the king as judge over all nations. It will mark the end of human history as we know it, but not necessarily of the world. The last days have begun with the first coming of Christ; the last day will be that of his second coming. With full glory and manifest authority, Christ "the King" (25,34) will declare those who are blessed by the Father and admitted to take possession of the kingdom prepared for them "since the foundation of the world". He will also indicate those who must go away from him, with their curse upon them, to everlasting punishment.

That is the only time in the gospel when Christ is said to mention a curse upon any person[49]. Even in this case, it is to impose the sanction for a curse already incurred. Blessing and curse are common elements in covenant language of the O.T., whereas we noted that the Sermon on the Mount offers many blessings but threatens no curse. The criterion which Jesus will invoke to divide the blessed from the cursed is that of practical love towards all his brothers and sisters in need of food, drink, clothing, shelter, medicine, or a compassionate human presence. The extent of Christ the King's kinship with all humans stands out unmistakably in the way he identifies himself with each poor and needy person. Could we possibly devise a clearer expression of loving loyalty to the entire human family? The new covenant demands a corresponding universal love on our part (cf.22,37-40).

B 7. "The blood of the covenant" for the forgiveness of sins

Mt's account of the institution of the Eucharist is close to Mk's, but it adds an important phrase to the words over the cup. Jesus handed the cup to the disciples saying, "Drink from this, all of you, for this is my blood, the blood of the covenant, poured out for many <u>for the forgiveness of sins</u>" (26,28). The phrase underlined takes the mind beyond "the blood of the covenant" as at Sinai, where it sealed the Mosaic covenant. We are led to recall Yahweh's promise concerning the new covenant: "I shall forgive their guilt and never more call their sin to mind" (Jer 31,34). The theme of offering his life as a sacrifice of atonement for the sins of many is also in line with the fourth Song of the Servant of Yahweh (Is 53,10-12). Mt in this way is able to link up "the blood of the covenant" with the fundamental mission of Jesus already latent in his name. An angel of the Lord had told Joseph that, "you must name him Jesus, because he is the one who is <u>to save his people from their sins</u>" (1,21). For Mt, therefore, the blood of Jesus is poured out to save "his people" from the whole gamut of slavery imposed by sins, and the new covenant sealed in that blood is open to all "his people", all the human family.

The voluntary commitment of Jesus to the covenant sacrifice is made quite explicit by his prayer in Gethsemane. "My Father", he prayed, "if this cup cannot pass by, but I must drink it, your will be done!" (26,42). The essence of the new covenant is to love God the Father unreservedly and live according to his will - or to die rather than disobey it. The human will of Jesus was therefore perfectly attuned to his Father's will at the moment of entering into the new covenant offered to all our race. Because Jesus accepted the conditions of that covenant on our behalf, he could announce that it was being sealed in his blood. He gave consent for all the human family, expressing it intensely three times over: in the cenacle, in Gethsemane, and on Calvary[50].

B 8. The commission to offer the new covenant to all nations

The final verses of Mt (28,16-20) serve as a fitting climax to Jesus' mission as Son of God, as Son of man, as son of David, as Saviour from sin and Liberator from its enslaving consequences, and as a new Moses mediating the new covenant. Those verses also contain an ongoing commission to the apostolic church to carry the good news to all nations until "the end of time"[51]. The setting for the commission to the "eleven disciples" is, as we have come to expect in Mt, "the mountain" (28,16), somewhere in Galilee. The meeting had been arranged through the faithful women whom Jesus had met as they left his empty tomb. He directed them, "Go and tell my brothers that they must leave for Galilee; there they will see me" (28,10). To hear the risen Lord speak of his disciples as "my brothers" already sums up one important aspect of the new covenant.

After they had met and worshipped the risen Jesus, he summed up the fruits of his mission up to that point, saying, "All authority in heaven and on earth has been given to me" There is no difficulty for Mt to have Jesus claiming such authority, since the resurrection has confirmed that it now pertains to him as the Son of God and beloved co-regent with the Father "in heaven". Jesus the Christ is also doubly entitled to the promised throne of David "on earth".

Now that the new covenant has been inaugurated, the mission of the disciples is no longer to be restricted to Israel, as it was beforehand. D. Senior wisely treats of the missionary discourse to the twelve disciples in Mt 10 in relation to the final commission we are now considering[52]. While the Mosaic covenant was still in force and the first invitations were being sent out for acceptance of the new covenant, Jesus instructed his disciples, "Do not make your way to gentile territory, and do not enter any Samaritan town; go instead to the lost sheep of the House of Israel" (10,5). Jesus made every effort to uphold the deepest meaning of the existing covenant between God and Israel.

All dividing walls between Israel and the other nations were torn down like the curtain of the Temple was torn asunder. Now the risen Jesus can commission his disciples, "Go, therefore, make disciples of all nations; baptise them in the name of the Father.. .., and teach them to observe all the commands that I gave you" (28,19-20). In short, the mandate is to evangelize, to baptise the believers, and catechise them more fully on all the "commands" given by Jesus. This presupposes that his "church" is of its very nature a missionary church, a community open equally to people of "all nations", eager to invite them to share more completely in the good news that the reign of God has entered into the final age of human history[53]. The joyful confidence to carry out the commission comes from the risen "Immanuel" (28,20).

NOTES

1. Cf. J. Navone, The Jesus Story: Our Life as Story in Christ (Collegeville: Liturgical Press, 1979) 22 , where he explains how the Christ story reveals the desire the Father to be Father of all through their acceptance of union with the Son.
2. Cf. J. Bishop, The Covenant: A Reading, 155-156, e.g. 156: "Covenant has not even seemed a satisfactory way of connecting 'Judaism' with 'Christianity', much less of explaining Christianity to itself."
3. Cf.: D. Senior & C. Stuhlmueller, The Biblical Foundations for Mission, 141-160 and 211-232, where D. Senior treats perceptively "Jesus and the Church's Mission", then "The Mission Theology of Mark" resp., giving good insights into why "the kingdom of God" was so central to Jesus' preaching. Also: J. Fuellenbach, Kingdom of God —Central Message of Jesus (Nemi, Italia: Mimeographed class notes, 1986).
4. Cf.: C. Duquoc, Messianisme de Jésus et Discrétion de Dieu — Essai sur la limite de la christologie (Genève: Labor et Fides, 1984), 145-151, esp. on the way theologies of liberation have focused attention on the poor and called the Church to make much more its own the cause of the poor. Also: E. Dussel, Historia General de la Iglesia en América Latina, Tomo I/1: Introducción General a la Historia de la Iglesia en América Latina (Salamanca: Sigueme, 1983) 11, where his preliminary remarks indicate that this history of the Church must include a theological dimension: "Se entiende teológicamente la historia de la Iglesia en América Latina como la historia de la institución sacramental de comunión, de misión, de conversión, como palabra profética que juzga y salva, como <u>Iglesia de los pobres</u>" (Emphasis added to mark the phrase taken from "**Laborem Exercens**", N.8.) Also: M. Farina, Chiesa Di Poveri E Chiesa Dei Poveri — La fondazione biblica di un tema conciliare (Roma: Libreria Ateneo Salesiano, 1986), developing the theme that, just as Christ redeemed our race through poverty and sufferings, so likewise the Church is called (and sent) to take the same path. The authoress also provides a wide bibliography on the theme, 15 - 44.
5. S. Freyne, The Twelve: Disciples and Apostles (London: Sheed and Ward, 1968) esp. 106-150 on Mark and the Twelve.
6. Cf. E. Best, Disciples and Discipleship - Studies in the Gospel According to Mark (Edinburgh: T.& T. Clark, 1986), e.g. 5: "Mark's Gospel is the Gospel of the Way. It is a way in which Jesus the Lord goes, and it is a way to which he calls his followers."

NOTES

7. Cf.: R. Schnackenburg, God's Rule and Kingdom (New York: Herder and Herder; London: Burns & Oates, 1968^2), esp. part II (77-258) on "The Reign of God in the Preaching of Jesus". Also: T. Sheehan, The First Coming — How the Kingdom of God Became Christianity (New York: Random House, 1986), in which he himself asserts that his interpretation of the kingdom "is certainly not traditional or orthodox" (223); his reinterpretation proposes "recovering the kingdom without Christ or Jesus" 224). His approach at least invites the reader to try and imagine the kingdom before Jesus was being preached as Christ the King, etc.
8. Cf. the parables of growth in Mk 4, - the sower and the seed, the mustard seed, and the seed that keeps growing by itself. They imply a mysterious, slow, but steady growth to maturity.
9. B. Byrne, 'Sons of God' - 'Seed of Abraham' (Rome: Biblical Institute Press, 1979), esp. p.224: "Finally, the birth of the 'messianic community' enjoying a filial relationship to God, corresponds to the central proclamation in the synoptic gospels — the twin realities of the fatherhood of God and the arrival /imminence of the kingdom."
10. Cf. J. Fuellenbach, op.cit. 61: "Jesus is the covenant in person, that means he is God's self-communication to us, but he is also the one who gives on our behalf the response that we could never give."
11. Cf. R. Schnackenburg, The Gospel According to St. Mark (London: E.T. by W. Kruppa, Sheed & Ward, 1971, in series of J.L. McKenzie (Ed.) New Testament for Spiritual Reading) 1, 45-47 on the bridegroom, e.g. 46: "For the young church Jesus himself was the bridegroom and she also recalled his death" (author's emphasis).
12. Cf. C. Spicq, Agape in the New Testament (London and St.Louis: E.T. by Sisters M.A. McNamara & M.H. Richter, B. Herder, 1963) Vol.1, 62-66.
13. Cf. V.P. Furnish, The Love Command in the New Testament (London: S.C.M., 1973), esp. 22-90, e.g. 25 -30 re Mk 12,28 - 34. Furnish comments (27): "The 'second commandment' is not 'of second importance'. It is, simply, the second of two mentioned as together comprising the 'chief' commandment about which the scribe had initially inquired."
14. Cf.: C. Spicq, op.cit. 1,59-62. Also: John Paul II's Apostolic Letter to the Youth of the World, 1985, NN.7-9 on the call of the rich young man; and "**Sollicitudo Rei Socialis**", 1987, NN.37-40 on the desire for exclusive profit and power, whereas solidarity with every fellow human is called for.
15. Cf. Q. Quesnell, This Good News (London: G. Chapman, 1964), 171-173.
16. Cf. Bo Reicke, The Roots of the Synoptic Gospels (Philadelphia: Fortress, 1986), esp. 65-67 on "Life Setting in Baptism and in the Eucharist", e.g. 66: "First of all, it was no coincidence that context-

parallel pericopes of three synoptic texts reached a maximum in the magnetic fields of the Lord's baptism and last supper."

17. Cf.: J. Bishop, op.cit. 297-300 on the Eucharist and covenant. Also: J. Delorme, P. Benoit, J. Dupont, M. Boismard, & D. Mollat (Ed.s), The Eucharist in the New Testament — A Symposium (London: E.T. by E.M. Stewart, G. Chapman, 1965) esp. 21-101 on the bearing of the Jewish Pasch and the Christian liturgy on the the texts of institution.

18. Cf. E.P. Sanders, Jesus and Judaism (London: S.C.M., 1985) 61-119 on aspects of Jesus and the Temple. Sanders finds an accumulation of evidence that Jesus' public acts and words concerning the Temple had a major bearing on his execution. E.g. 293: "Jesus offended many of his contemporaries at two points: his attack on the temple and his message concerning sinners. On both points he could be said to be challenging the adequacy of the Mosaic dispensation."

19. Cf.: J.L. Segundo, Jesus of Nazareth Yesterday and Today (2 Vol.), Vol.II, 1: The Historical Jesus of the Synoptics (Maryknoll, N.Y.: E.T. by J. Drury, Orbis, 1985) esp. 71-85 on "Jesus and the Political Dimension", e.g. 77: "If Jesus did not agitate the political scene in Israel, then we must label the Gospels false in their most obvious prepaschal data." Again, 80: "The only sound explanation is that prophetism comes into conflict with established authority and power. It threatens the latter and the latter responds with violence, provoking the death of the prophet" (author's emphasis). Also: E.P. Sanders, op.cit. 231: "It is now virtually universally recognized that there is not a shred of evidence which would allow us to think that Jesus had military/political ambitions, and .. the same applies to his disciples. .. they knew that an army was not being created. .. They expected something, but not a conquest."

20. Cf. R. Schnackenburg, The Gospel According to St. Mark, vol.2, 116-122 on "The Institution of the Eucharist", e.g. 121: "A further saying is added to the words that institute the covenant, and this announces the ultimate fulillment of this covenant in the future kingdom of God (v.25). ... His death serves to bring about the kingdom of God which he had proclaimed" (emphasis added).

21. Cf. I.H. Marshall, Last Supper and Lord's Supper (Exeter: Paternoster Press, 1980) , esp.77 on the way the Passover was "one of the ways in which the covenant between God and Israel was maintained in being." Then 92: Even if Jesus did not use the word "new" at the Last Supper, "the fact remains that in talking of a covenant sealed with his own blood Jesus was undoubtedly talking of another covenant, different from the one made in the wilderness, and hence a new covenant" (author's emphasis).

22. Cf. D. Senior & Stuhlmueller, op.cit. 226, where D. Senior observes concerning discipleship in Mk: "The life-giving service of Jesus sets the pattern for the church's own existence, including the style and intent of its mission. Thus the degree to which the disciples are able to comprehend the cross is the degree to which they comprehend the

meaning of the kingdom of God." Also: A. Ambrozic, The Hidden Kingdom (Washington D.C.: C.B.A.A., 1972) 181. Also: L. Morris, The Cross in the New Testament (Exeter: Paternoster Press, 1967^2), which presents the evangelical tradition concerning "Atonement by the Cross", e.g. 365: "The cross stands as the divine answer to the fundamental problem, the problem of man's sin. Each N.T. writer writes as one who has come to know salvation by way of the cross." The author uses the term "substitution" (cf. 380; 404-405) where Catholics would speak rather of Christ's solidarity with those for whom he gave his life on the cross.
23. R.E. Brown, The Birth of the Messiah, 45.
24. Cf: D. Stanley, The Apostolic Church in the New Testament (Maryland: Newman, 1965) esp. on "Kingdom to Church", 5-37, e.g. 36: "Mt has attempted in one volume what Lk has accomplished in two books: to show the coming of the kingdom of heaven as realized in the organization of the apostolic Church." Also: D. Senior, Matthew: A Gospel for the Church (Chicago: Herald Biblical Booklet, 1973).
25. Cf. J.L. McKenzie, "The Gospel According to Matthew", in J.B.C. II, esp. 64-5 on "The Theological Character of the Gospel", which has been influenced by "the controversies of Christians and Jews in the apostolic Church". Cf. B.T. Viviano, "The Gospel According to Matthew", NJBC 630-632.
26. Cf. R.E. Brown, op.cit. 74-81.
27. Cf.: J.L.McKenzie, art.cit. 67. Cf.B. Viviano, art. cit. 632: "<u>The whole Gospel, finally, is framed by a covenant formulary</u> in which God is united with his people through Jesus Christ (1:23 and 28:18-20)" (emphasis added). Also: O.P. Robertson, The Christ of the Covenants, 46-52 on common aspects of all four historical covenants (Abrahamic, Mosaic, Davidic, and of Christ), e.g. 51: "He[Christ] is the head of God's kingdom and the embodiment of God's covenant. ... He becomes the unifying focus of all Scripture. Both <u>'kingdom' and 'covenant' unite under Immanuel</u>" (emphasis added).
28. Cf.: R.E. Brown, op.cit. 232: "If the infancy story is an attractive drama that catches the imagination, it also is a substantial proclamation of the coming of the kingdom and its possible rejection." Also: A. Paul, L'Évangile de l'Enfance Selon St Matthieu (Paris: Cerf, 1968), e.g. 174, where the first two chapters of Mt are said to agree wonderfully with his two-fold concern throughout his gospel, namely to safeguard the Davidic royalty of Jesus and the Mosaic aspect of his mission.
29. Cf.: S.A. Panimolle, Il Discorso Della Montagna (Mt 5-7) — Esegesi e vita (Milano: Edizioni Paoline, 1986), esp. 17-28 on the structure of Mt 5,3-12 which gives the beatitudes. Also: W. Harrelson, The Ten Commandments and Human Rights (Philadelphia: Fortress Press, 1980) 161, where he notes the great influence of the Deuteronomic tradition on Jesus and the Gospels, in which "there are 77 quotations from the Book

of Deuteronomy alone". "It is Deuteronomy and not Exodus that is the best counterpart and foil for the Sermon on the Mount."
30. Cf.: S.A. Panimolle, op.cit. 46-49. Also: A. Gelin, Les Pauvres que Dieu Aime (Paris: Cerf, 1967), esp. Ch.7 on effective/economic/social poverty and spiritual poverty. Real poverty is fertile ground in which openness to God and "spiritual" poverty can flourish.
31. Cf. S. van Tilborg, The Sermon on the Mount as An Ideological Intervention — A Reconstruction of Meaning (Assen: Van Gorcum, and New Hampshire: Wolfeboro, 1986), a penetrating study which helps considerably to recognise what ideology was being replaced by the "Jesus-movement". He says that the ruling ideology will be that of the ruling class, "where the class distinctions are based on oppression and domination". With regard to the Sermon on the Mount, he asserts that via its text "a new way of living arises, a way of living which <u>wants to change the whole society</u>. Different forms of possession, other forms of relationships and a new mentality .. <u>will bring God's covenant with Israel to reality</u>: that is the message of the Sermon on the Mount (emphasis added). Again: "The S.M.(sic) has <u>a political and social direction</u> which no one will want to deny" (emphasis added).
32. S. Ringe, Jesus, Liberation and the Biblical Jubilee, esp. 33-64 on "Jesus as Herald of Liberation" and "Jubilee Images Elaborated". E.g. 32: "In other words, <u>God's reign</u> and <u>humankind's liberation</u> go hand in hand" (emphasis added).
33. W. Brueggemann, The Land, 171.
34. Cf. S. Tilborg, op.cit. 23-27, e.g. 27: "'The meek' are people who have been made subject. .. Submissiveness is for the common people, but this humiliation will come to an end." Cf. 85 on the sabbath year as "the most important economic institution", because it was meant to "maintain the the fiction that all were equal: <u>the land belonged to all Israelites equally</u>" (emphasis added).
35. Cf. W.D. Davies, The Gospel and the Land. — Early Christian and Jewish Territorial Doctrine (Berkeley: University of California Press, 1974) 128: "It was the Pharisaic understanding of Judaism that made this [historic] continuity possible — an understanding that placed Torah above political power and control of the land." Cf. 362; and 367: "By implication .. the NT finds holy space wherever Christ is or has been." Also: C.J. Roetzel, The World That Shaped The N.T., 1-23 on "Political Setting", in which he says that the kingdom of God for first-century Jews was "no mere spiritual concept", hence to proclaim its arrival would be "electrifying". 22: "The kingdom envisioned by Jesus gave priority to the powerless and those without status. .. Jesus' inclusion of those on the fringe of power, without status or recognition, carried distinct political overtones." Also: J.G. Gager, Kingdom and Community (Englewood Cliffs, N.J.: Prentice-Hall, 1975), a work on the importance of social factors for the shape of the kingdom of God on earth.

36. S. Tilborg, op.cit. 31, on Mt 5,7: "First of all, it has to be noticed that 'the mercy' primarily refers to the biblical covenant practices in which the partners bind themselves mutually in fidelity to help one another steadfastly and forever, to stand by one another, to assist the weaker partner in the covenant."
37. W. Klassen, Love of Enemies. — The Way to Peace (Philadelphia: Fortress Press, 1984) 86. Also: V. Furnish, op.cit. 45-69, e.g. 66: "It is Jesus' commandment to love the enemy which most of all sets his ethic of love apart from other 'love ethics' of antiquity, and which best shows what kind of love is commanded by him" (author's emphasis). Also: N. O'Brien, Seeds of Injustice (Dublin: The O'Brien Press, 1985) in which the author recounts that, while in Bacolod prison as one of the "Negros Nine" awaiting trial, he realised that "so too are the guards our brothers, even if they don't know it. That's the Good News, and we must bring it to them." He also reflected: "Non-violence is a sensible and truly human solution; Christ adds the dimension of the brotherhood and sisterhood of the human. The eventual purpose of struggle is not only justice; it is reconciliation, which is a much more difficult achievement."
38. W. Klassen, op.cit. 89: (Jesus did not use parables to confront and trap his opponents.) "The reason for this would seem to be that in the way that Jesus told his stories, his opponents were always allowed room to maneuver. .. He was instead a peace-maker who forged weapons of peace in such a way that he could express his love to those who were God's and his enemies."
39. Cf.: J. Jeremias, Abba y El Mensaje Central del Nuevo Testamento (Salamanca: S.T. by Fernando-Carlos Vevia et al., Sigueme, 1983^2) 215-235 on the Our Father in current exegesis. Also 37-42 on influence of that prayer on the rapidity with which the first Christians adopted "our Father"/"the Father" as the name of God. Also: J. Fuellenbach, op.cit. 46-59. Also: W. Barclay, The Gospel of Matthew (2 Vol.) (Edinburgh: St. Andrew Press, 1958^2) 1, 197-234, e.g. 200: "The great value of this word Father is that it settles all the relationships of this life."
40. Cf. J.A.T. Robertson, Twelve More New Testament Studies (London: S C M , 1984) 44-64 on the Lord's Prayer. He notes that Jn 17 could be used as a meditation on the "Our Father".
41. Cf. J. Jeremias, op.cit. 228-231.
42. S. Ringe, op.cit. 66 and 80. Cf. S. van Tilborg, op.cit. 122: On Mt 6,12: "As in the main sentence, the basic metaphor in this comparative sentence is taken from the financial reality of remitting debts. That connects it with the other texts in the S.M., which deal with loans and repayments. .. Whoever is not prepared to remit his neighbour's debt cannot expect that God will remit his." Also: Pontifical Commission "Justitia et Pax", At the Service of the Human Community: An Ethical Approach to the International Debt Question (Vatican City: Vatican Press, 1986). E.g. 30-31 stress the need to give priority to "the human

factor", because "at stake are human lives, the development of peoples, and solidarity among nations".
43. D. Verseput, The Rejection of the Humble Messianic King (Frankfurt am Main/ New York: Peter Lang, 1986) 35 and 302.
44. New Jerusalem Bible heading, 1632.
45. Cf. R.E.Brown, K.P. Donfried, J. Reumann (Ed.s), Peter in the New Testament (Minneapolis: Augsburg Publishing House; N Y: Paulist Press, 1973) 83-107 on the promise to Peter and on paying the Temple tax.
46. In the Septuagint translation, 1 & 2 Samuel of the Hebrew text is called 1 & 2 Kings, so the following books become 3 & 4 Kings (instead of what we now call 1 & 2 Kings).
47. Cf. D. Stanley, op. cit. 36-7: "Gk Mt .. has carefully marked the beginning and the end of the continuous movement which is the founding of the Church, by means of the first and last of five great discourses. The **terminus a quo** is the Sermon on the Mount, by which Jesus inaugurates His preaching of the kingdom; the **terminus ad quem** is the destruction of the Temple, the divine manifestation of the coming of the glorified Son of Man in His kingdom-become-Church."
48. New Jerusalem Bible, 1649, ftn. 24a.
49. Cf. C. Westermann, Genesis 1-11, 193: "There is only one other passage in the Bible which is parallel to Gen 2-3 and where God passes judgment directly on human sin by trial and sentence. It is the world judgment scene in Matt 25."
50. Cf. John Paul II, Letter of Holy Thursday, 1987 (Vatican City: Vatican Press, 1987) brings out clearly the unity of the announcement, acceptance and sealing of the new covenant in the cenacle, in the garden of olives, and on the cross, e.g. par.4 (p.6): "The prayer in Gethsemane is to be understood not only in reference to everything that follows during the events of Good Friday, namely Christ's Passion and Death on the Cross; it is also to be understood, and no less intimately, in reference to the Last Supper. .. The words which institute the sacrament of the new and eternal Covenant, the Eucharist, constitute in a certain way the sacramental seal of that eternal will of the Father and the Son, the will which has now reached that 'hour' of its definitive accomplishment" (author's emphasis). Cf. 6-8.
51. Cf. J. L. McKenzie, art.cit., II, 113-114, e.g. 114: On 28,20: "The object of the teaching is 'all that I have commanded you'. This phrase echoes Mt's habitual presentation of Jesus as the new Moses of a new Israel" (emphasis added). Cf. T. Viviano, art. cit., NJBC 674 on same verse: "The covenant formulary forms an **inclusio** with 1:23; cf. 18:20. Jesus is Emmanuel, the divine presence (**shekinah**) with his people..." (emphasis added). Also: D. Patrick, Old Testament Law (Atlanta: John Knox Press, 1985), in which the newness of Christ's covenant and abiding presence as "Immanuel" is apparently not seen as very convincing. E.g. 246: "It sounds very much as though the N.T. falls back into the track of the old covenant, wherein 'I will be their God and they

NOTES

shall be my people' is a statement of principle and commitment, not of accomplished fact."
52. Cf. D. Senior & C. Stuhlmueller, op. cit., 250-254, which also includes a bibliography. E.g. 252: "Taken together the discourse of chapter 10 and the final commission of chapter 28 do indeed synthesize the mission theology of Matthew."
53. Cf. Pastoral Statement of U.S. Catholic Conference (N.C.C.B.) on World Mission, To the Ends of the Earth (N.Y.: The Society for the Propagation of the Faith, 1987) #3: "Jesus' great commission to the first disciples is now addressed to us. Like them, we must go and make disciples of all the nations ..." Also #75: "Jesus is 'the missionary of the Father': each Christian is his witness. Let his voice proclaim the Gospel through us as we bring the good news of salvation to the ends of the earth."

CHAPTER 10: NEW COVENANT IN LUKE AND ACTS OF THE APOSTLES

A: NEW COVENANT IN LUKE'S GOSPEL

Luke's gospel is the only one to come to us from a non-Jewish writer. The author is thought to have been the companion mentioned by Paul as "my dear friend Luke, the doctor" (Col 4,14), as a "fellow-worker" (Phm 24), and also mentioned as being with Paul during his final imprisonment in Rome (2 Tim 4,11). It is generally presumed that Luke was also one of Paul's travelling companions on at least three distinct journeys, since they are written up in Acts with "we" as the subject (e.g. 16,11ff.). The common opinion is that Acts and Lk come from the same author, hence as Acts comes from Luke, so does the gospel of Lk[1].

Both works are dedicated to Theophilus, and have a great deal in common. Luke's gospel presents the infancy and then the ministry of Jesus through to his ascension; Acts takes up the story from there to present the life of the risen Christ continuing to manifest itself in the church, while the Spirit of Jesus transforms the first Christians into joyful witnesses reaching out to the ends of the earth (cf. Acts 1,8). The gospel of Lk has much of what is in Mk, as well a good deal in common with Mt only, and some material akin to that found in Jn. Lk also has an infancy narrative (cc.1-2) and a lengthy "journey to Jerusalem" (9,51 - 18,14) with a great deal of material proper to Lk. Both Lk and Acts probably reached their final form somewhere between 75 - 90 A.D.[2].

Tradition and the two books themselves indicate that the author was a non-Jew, well skilled in writing Greek, anxious to present the good news of salvation in Christ to a predominantly Gentile community. He shows the continuity running through from Adam, Abraham, Moses, David, holy women like Leah, Miriam, Hannah, and Judith, until the promises are fulfilled in Jesus Christ. The risen Christ in turn is proclaimed with "tongues of fire" imparted by the Holy Spirit to the emerging Christian community, which is viewed as a renewed Israel. Now it is sent out to let all the families of earth experience the blessing promised through Abraham and his descendants.

Every page of Lk leading up to the Last Supper manifests the preparation for the new covenant, which subsumes and surpasses all that was best in the preparatory covenants. With the sealing of the new covenant and the entry of Jesus Christ into his kingdom at the Father's right hand, Acts can go on to show the fervent community living out that covenant. It could truly be said that Acts is to Lk what the Deuteronomist's history is to Deuteronomy. There is a big difference, however, between the two histories depicted. Whereas the Deuteronomist's evaluation closes with the Mosaic covenant so broken as to bring on the exile, Luke's account in Acts depicts such an abundance of the Holy Spirit that the new covenant is being observed joyfully by Gentiles and Jews alike. A generous spirit of fellowship and sharing pervades the widely scattered Christian communities.

A 1. The Infancy Narrative in Lk
Like Mt, Lk has an Infancy Narrative as a prelude to the public ministry of Jesus. It serves very well as a bridge between the old Israel and the humble arrival of its Messiah. There are solid reasons for R.E. Brown's opinion that, in the case of Lk, the Infancy Narrative was attached to the remainder of Lk-Acts after that major composition had been finished[3]. While this allows Lk to bring out implications realised after the resurrection and Pentecost, the narrative recaptures the atmosphere of the faithful Israelites who encountered Jesus in his infancy. Their welcome to him and their canticles of praise help to identify them with the "poor of Yahweh", the **'anawim**, those afflicted poor who put all their trust in God and the promises of salvation/liberation. The lowly "handmaid" of the Lord, Mary, who figures so prominently in Lk 1-2, "responds obediently to God's word from the first as a representative of the Anawim of Israel"[4]. What bears most directly on our theme is the way Lk explicitly links up the arrival of the Saviour with the promissory covenants granted to Abraham and David.

A 1. a) The consent of Mary to the mighty word of God:
Lk 1,5-25 describes how the angel Gabriel, in the Temple of Jerusalem, foretold to Zechariah the birth of a son to be called John. Then comes Gabriel's announcement, in Nazareth of Galilee, to the virgin Mary that she was to bear a son, to be called Jesus. He could also be called "Son of the Most High", he would be given "the throne of his ancestor David", and "his reign" would have no end. After being assured that the child would be conceived by the power of the Holy Spirit, Mary gave her consent freely, saying, "You see before you the Lord's servant, let it happen to me as you have said" (1,26-38).

Mary was at that time "betrothed to a man named Joseph, of the House of David" (1,27). It was through Joseph, as the legal father, that Mary's child would be born into the House of David, but it was only God who could and would grant him David's throne for ever. In Jesus would be found the solution to that constant friction, if not contradiction, between Yahweh as King and his human viceroy, called to rule over Israel but under Yahweh's covenant. Mary's own attitude of obedient compliance with the will of God constitutes the initial acceptance of God's plan for redemption, liberation and salvation through her unique child. She will remain faithful to God and her Son till "the forgiveness of sins" (1,77) and the outpouring of the Spirit (Acts c.2) have been accomplished, ushering in the final age of the new covenant.

A 1. b) The promissory covenant with Abraham recalled:
In the **Magnificat** (1,46-55), Lk depicts Mary as expressing the confident and joyful spirit of the early Jewish Christian "poor of Yahweh" as they praised God for coming to their help[5]. Mary rejoices in God's "faithful love" as displayed by the way "he has routed the arrogant", "pulled down princes from their thrones" and "sent the rich away empty". In so doing, he "raised high the lowly" and "filled the hungry with good things". This is attributed to God being "mindful of his faithful love — according to the

promise he made to our ancestors — of his mercy <u>to Abraham and to his descendants</u> for ever".

The phrases underlined serve to extol the wonderful kindness of God in making the promise to Abraham and his descendants (including therefore Mary's generation and "all generations"), then the fidelity of God in keeping that promise. This canticle contains a striking expression of God's "preferential option for the poor", the lowly, the starving. The remainder of Lk and Acts will bear out that this is a theme dear to Luke, who brings out the connection between Jesus' deep concern for the poor and his severe warnings to the rich. Mammon so easily becomes an idol that replaces the one true God and leads to human sacrifice.

The **Benedictus** (1,68-79) is a canticle "prophesied" by Zechariah, on the occasion of the birth and circumcision of John the Baptist, glimpsed here as a "prophet of the Most High". Like the **Magnificat**, this canticle praises God for what has been done through the coming of Jesus and his precursor, e.g. "the God of Israel has visited his people, he has set them free, and he has established for us a saving power in the House of his servant David". Note that the House of David is again recalled, and that in turn is also said to have been in fulfilment of "his holy covenant", namely "the oath he swore to our father Abraham" (1,72- 73).

Both these canticles follow the traditional line of Jerusalem which, as we touched on when dealing with the Davidic covenant there, stressed that it was dynastic, unconditional, and everlasting. It was looked on as being of the same character as the earlier Abrahamic promise/covenant/oath. In short, both were unconditional promissory covenants, dependent on the "loving kindness and fidelity" of Yahweh for their permanence and the granting of what had been promised. Luke has little about the Mosaic covenant in the Infancy Narrative, apart from the evident commitment of his characters to live according to the Law and worship God in the Temple. They certainly base their confidence on God's faithful love and not on their own merits in living according to the Law. In this, Lk is close to Paul's view.

With regard to the kind of salvation and liberation for which God is blessed in this canticle, it certainly includes the fulfilment of Yahweh's covenant commitment "that he would save us from our enemies and from the hands of those who hate us" (1,71), and "that he would grant us, free from fear, to be delivered from the hands of our enemies, to serve him in holiness and uprightness" (1,74). It is precisely in fulfilment of this that, with the coming of Jesus, "the rising Sun has come from on high to visit us, to give light to those who live in darkness and the shadow dark as death" (1,78-9).

In short, the Saviour has come like the "rising Sun" in order to set us free from all the enemies who hate us and therefore subject our whole lives to fear, darkness, injustice and death. Part of the liberation comes from "knowledge of salvation through the forgiveness of sins", which brings with it new light to lead us "into the way of peace". It is important to note that the goal of liberation is said to be the service of God in holiness and justice (1,74). For Luke, the coming of the Saviour and the new covenant has made effective for his people both liberation from enemies and the free service of God in a new light, resulting in a new peace. The new covenant is set firmly within the long history of Israel, with Jesus as the descendant **par excellence** to bring to fruition those promissory covenants granted to his ancestors Abraham and David, and to extend the benefits to all nations.

The birth of Jesus took place in "David's town called Bethlehem", as befitted the heir to David's throne. However, his birthplace was a stable, and he soon experienced the lot of the poor when he was laid in a manger as his cradle. The first people to hear the good news of his birth as their "Saviour" were likewise lowly shepherds, to whom the angels sang the original **Gloria in excelsis Deo**, with its assurance of peace on earth "for those he favours". We are told that, after hearing the enthusiastic reports of the shepherds, "Mary treasured all these things and pondered them in her heart" (2,1-20). This is a fine illustration of the way God's handmaid was open to learn through listening to others, knowing that God can speak through them. Once she had recognised God speaking to her through them, she treasured those words in her heart, where God's word must take root and be permitted to produce its full impact over the years.

As faithful Israelites, Mary and Joseph had the baby circumcised and gave him the name Jesus, in keeping with what Gabriel had told Mary to do. Then for the purification of Mary and the redemption of her first-born son, they went to the Temple. Once more Lk depicts the welcome given to the Saviour through the lips of a lowly just man, Simeon. His canticle, **Nunc Dimittis**, expresses well the joy at knowing — and seeing with his own eyes — the salvation so keenly awaited by Israel. Lk again emphasises the universal dimension of the "salvation", perceived by Simeon as bringing "a light of revelation for the gentiles and glory for your people Israel" (2,29-32). This wording is close to what was said to the Suffering Servant: "I have made you a covenant to the people and light to the nations" (Is 42,6)[6].

Then the holy prophetess Anna also came on the scene in the Temple and was moved to speak of the child to all "who looked forward to the deliverance of Jerusalem" (2,36-38). The word here for "deliverance" means basically "redemption", the setting free of a slave by paying the price demanded for his release. The significance of "the redemption of Jerusalem" will be seen from what follows.

A 1. c) The importance of Jerusalem in Lk-Acts:

As noted above, this gospel opens with Zechariah serving in the Temple, and it closes after the ascension with the disciples being "continually in the Temple praising God" (24,53). Acts opens with the disciples remaining in Jerusalem until Pentecost, but gradually they went out, as Jesus had told them, to bear witness to him to the ends of the earth. Acts closes with Paul "proclaiming the kingdom of God" in Rome, the capital of the most powerful empire known in those times. For Luke, Jerusalem stood as the centre and symbol of Israel's life as a theocracy, that is, a nation whose religious and civil life was governed in God's name.

Lk presents Jesus as coming in God's name, with full authority to claim David's throne and hence also to claim David's city of Jerusalem. Only Lk tells of the visit of the boy Jesus to Jerusalem to celebrate the Passover and tarry in his "Father's house" (2,41-50). The third temptation at the start of the public ministry is set "on a parapet of the Temple" (4,9). During the transfiguration, Moses and Elijah were speaking to him about his approaching death in Jerusalem (9,30-31). From then on, "he resolutely turned his face towards Jerusalem" (9,51), explaining to his disciples that "it would not be right for a prophet to die outside Jerusalem" (13,33). Lk attaches to that saying the reproach to Jerusalem for killing the prophets and refusing his own efforts to gather its people into unity round himself (13,34-35).

After reaching Jerusalem, "he shed tears over it" and lamented that it had not recognised "the way to peace" (19,41-42) — which for Lk would imply the voluntary acceptance of the new covenant he was about to announce and seal in that recalcitrant city. His claim to its loyalty was made explicit during his triumphal entry there, when the disciples cried out, "Blessed is he who is coming <u>as King in the name of the Lord</u>!" (19,38). Shortly after that Lk tells how Jesus drove out the traders from the Temple, with such obvious authority that "the chief priests and the scribes" challenged him about it, as well as about continuing to teach the crowds there without any permission (19,45 - 20,8). It was also in Jerusalem that he appeared to the disciples after the resurrection, telling them to await the Holy Spirit there before going out as witnesses from Jerusalem "to all nations" (24,47-49; Acts 1,8). In Luke's eyes, therefore, Jerusalem did become the centre of salvation through Jesus' death and resurrection there, as well as by the subsequent outpouring of the Holy Spirit upon the new community gathered there in prayer.

A 2. The inaugural address in Nazareth

The text which Jesus chose to read and comment upon in the synagogue of his home town, Nazareth, is rightly regarded as "programmatic"[7] for his entire mission, giving priority to the poor, the captives, the oppressed, and the infirm in his proclamation of the good news(4,18-21). It is the favourite N.T. text for liberation theology, because it indicates so convincingly that Christ's mission is fundamentally to "the afflicted poor", in order to set free "captives" and "the oppressed"/the crushed[8]. Its explicit proclamation of a "year of favour from the Lord" is increasingly accepted as an ongoing Jubilee Year, with all the socio-economic implications for both oppressors and oppressed[9]. An aspect rarely given attention, however, is the covenant spirit underlying the original Jubilee ideal and carried over into "the year of favour from the Lord" publicly inaugurated by Jesus. This can be confirmed by a closer look at the texts involved.

Before going into details, it is essential to note that the "inaugural address" is set within 4,16-30 as part of a crucial visit to Nazareth. Actually two, or possibly three, different visits seem to have been woven into this narrative, making its message extremely concentrated[10]. It serves as an example of how Jesus, known in his home town as "son of Joseph", emerges "in the synagogue" there as the special spokesman of God. After a favourable reception at first, anger mounts as his mission and mercy are considered to be going outside his own "country" and even to the Gentiles. He is therefore rejected, even threatened with death. I think Lk articulates more fully what is at stake by giving us the parable of the elder brother, who "was angry" and refused to welcome home his prodigal brother, despite the welcome offered by their father (15, 25-32).

The major part of the text quoted by Jesus is taken from the central section of Trito-Isaiah, which we saw to be the closest in spirit and content to the Servant Songs. The opening declaration is the mission of a prophet: "The Spirit of the Lord is on me, for he has anointed me to bring good news to the afflicted [poor]." Acts has Peter saying of Jesus at the start of his ministry that, "God had anointed him with the Holy Spirit and with power" (10,38). Great prominence is given by Luke to the Holy Spirit, who is mentioned 17 times in Lk and 57 times in Acts. In noting this, J. Fitzmyer points out: "More than either of the other Synoptic evangelists Luke has made the Spirit an important feature of his Gospel and its sequel"[11]. We must recall that the transforming role of the Spirit was also promised as a feature of the new covenant.

Jesus is therefore "the Christ" — a title used more than twenty times in Lk[12] — because anointed as prophet as well as king and priest. In fact Jesus says openly in Nazareth that "no prophet is ever accepted in his own country" (4,24). A prophet was not as likely to stir up nationalistic ambitions as was a claimant to David's throne, so Jesus could claim the attention due to a prophet in Israel. He was also well aware that there were leaders in Jerusalem who knew how to silence prophets.

The next two phrases (of 4,18), "He has sent me to proclaim liberty to captives, sight to the blind", are likewise from Is.61 (in its LXX translation). The captives were primarily those taken in war, and many of the blind could also have been war victims in one way or another. There were still plenty held captive because Palestine was under Roman domination, which gave rise to constant uprisings and repressions.

Then comes a phrase, "to let the oppressed go free", which has been borrowed from Is.58,6. There it is part of a cluster of phrases all calling for release as the kind of fast that would please Yahweh, namely, "to break unjust fetters, to undo the thongs of the yoke, to let the oppressed go free, and to break all yokes". For good measure it goes on to demand sharing of food, shelter and clothing with the needy, instead of turning away from "your own kin" (Is 58,7). That is very much in the spirit of the Jubilee Year with its release of "the oppressed", who had became slaves on losing their homes and lands[13]. The word used here (and retained in Lk 4,18) for "the oppressed" means literally the broken, the shattered, not by foreign enemies, but by those trying to please Yahweh with a fast. Such a fast cannot be "acceptable" (**dektos**) to God while the crushing process continues. This is also very close to the "commentary" following the second Servant Song, in which Yahweh speaks of helping the Servant at an "acceptable" (**dektos**) time, which is also "a day of salvation", a day on which "I have formed and appointed you to be a covenant for a people, to restore the land, to return ravaged properties, to say to prisoners, 'Come out'" (Is 49,8-9).

Lk concludes the quotation by returning to the text taken from Is 61,1-2, which serves as a solemn promulgation of the prophet's mission: "to proclaim a year of favour from the Lord". We find that here, too, the year is declared to be **dektos**, acceptable to the Lord, but this must be on condition that it is used to set all people free from their unjust chains and shattering burdens or "yokes". In that vein Jesus, having rolled up the scroll of Isaiah, announced to the privileged congregation in Nazareth, "This text is being fulfilled today even while you are listening" (4,21). By emphasising "today", Jesus lets his fellow-townspeople know that he is the Servant-prophet sent to "fulfil", to bring to its fulness the mission described in the book of Isaiah. He is the one chosen personally by God to act as the special envoy and herald of the "year of release" (which is the basic meaning of Jubilee Year[14]). He is authorised to declare, in God's name, an acceptable year, a year in which God's compassionate favour must be made obvious through the release of all those suffering from oppression or imprisonment.

God as supreme King does not have to wait for the fiftieth year, nor does he have to declare the Jubilee Year closed after twelve months. By saying "today", Jesus declares the "acceptable year" open, and further reflection will convince his hearers that it remains open always. No generation is to be deprived of their year of "release". J. Fitzmyer draws attention to the way Lk shifts the emphasis from the **eschaton**, the End, to "today"[15]. This is because Lk-Acts open up an indefinite age of the church, through which the kingdom of God is being proclaimed and bearing fruit, while the second coming of Christ is not sensed as so urgent or imminent as in Mk or Paul's writings. That is an added reason for granting "release" immediately, instead of saying that God will grant it in the world to come. Jesus is undeniably talking about daily life in this world, of the rich and powerful, of mortgaged farms, evicted families, harsh prisons, destitute widows and orphans[16]. Even the obviously spiritual release from sin which he grants is granted on condition that the person forgiven is willing in turn to forgive others their "debts" (Lk 6,37; 11,3)[17].

After further discussion with those in the synagogue, it became obvious that Jesus as a prophet was not acceptable (**dektos**) to them (4,24). Such wording in Lk hints that if the prophet is not acceptable, then God's special year will not be acceptable, either. Later on, Jesus will make explicit the implications of such a rejection, when his own disciples were being sent out in his name: "Anyone who rejects you rejects me, and those who reject me rejects the one who sent me" (10,16).

Which confirms that "a year of favour from the Lord" is a gracious offer to rich and poor alike, but it demands a generous response in return. Jesus' historic mission is already the greatest manifestation of God's "favour" and willingness to welcome home all Israel, and through them, all other nations as well. His mission, proclaiming God's word, pardoning sinners, healing the afflicted, and liberating the oppressed, will achieve what he was sent to do. As such, the programme he has launched in Nazareth is irrevocable and unstoppable, as is typified by what happened when that town tried to stop him — "he passed straight through the crowd and walked away" (4,30). For this or that person, even for this or that town, faith, love and permanent commitment are indispensable to "enter the kingdom of God". For all, as for Jesus himself, it means accepting the terms of the new covenant.

A 3. Beatitudes and parables

To savour something of what is specifically Lucan in the presentation of Jesus' teaching on the kingdom and covenant values, we will now select a few of the most striking passages from the Sermon on the Plain, and from some of the parables found only in Lk.

A 3. a) The Sermon on the Plain:

In Lk, the first major discourse to a crowd in the open-air takes place on a plain in Galilee. Included in the audience are the Twelve "apostles" (6,14), also "a large gathering of his disciples", together with a large crowd of people "from all parts of Judaea and Jerusalem", as well as from the Gentile regions of "Tyre and Sidon". Many sick people and those "tormented by unclean spirits" have come to be healed, because they have heard that power comes out of him to heal all the sick and the tormented (6,17-19). As in Mt, Lk opens the discourse with beatitudes, but with only four of the eight that we found in Mt. Jesus tells his disciples that the blessed are the poor, the hungry, the weeping and those hated and treated as criminals "on account of the Son of man" (6,20-23).

Lk gives no grounds for not taking the situation of each group quite literally, e.g. "you who are poor" has no rider such as Mt's "poor in spirit", nor are the hungry said to be hungering "for justice". The denunciation of disciples as criminals arises from religious motives, but leads to civil sanctions, not to mention the hatred and margination suffered by the victims. On the other hand, Lk has Jesus addressing his disciples, and that opening information colours the beatitudes. In other words, it is Jesus' own disciples who are called blessed because they are poor and can be assured that "the kingdom of God is yours" — Lk uses the present tense here. The beatitudes are offered to all willing to follow the ideals being proposed here, and must reflect the kind of communities expected (and already experienced) by Luke.

Each beatitude has a corresponding woe for those in the opposite group, namely those who are rich, well fed, laughing and well spoken of by everybody (6,24-26). Although some regard these woes as curses, they are rather a stern warning and a call to radical rethinking on the part of those enjoying their opulent comfort and popular acclamation. The reign of God calls for a reversal of the popular human values and ambitions, especially if the road to achieve human goals is strewn with broken brothers and sisters. Wealth, luxury, pleasure and power over others, maintained at the expense of other people, must be overthrown by the implementing of God's will, of God's plan, for the entire human family. Those who love themselves and their own gratification more than their brothers and sisters will bring upon themselves the woes mentioned. In this sense Lk here does come close to Mt 25, where a curse on the uncharitable is mentioned. The love required to comply with the new covenant cannot be elicited by the threat of a curse carrying the sanction of eternal punishment.

An adequate motivation is suggested in the rest of the discourse. After calling for love of enemies deep enough to make us treat them as we would like to be treated ourselves (6,27-35), Jesus announces the sublime ideal, "Be compassionate as your Father is compassionate" (6,31-36). Through "compassion" we suffer interiorly with others who are suffering. Compassion is an abiding attitude that manifests itself in acts of mercy, of loving solidarity with those suffering. God called out to Moses on Mount Sinai, "Yahweh, God of tenderness and compassion" (Ex 34,6). Moses was then graciously instructed to renew the covenant which Israel had so quickly broken. We may confidently interpret the call to "be compassionate" as a call to exercise in our faltering way something of the immeasurable compassion of the Father, the one whose family we are privileged to join and love. Because the compassion called for is in this family atmosphere, it is also a distinguishing feature of the new covenant.

A 3. b) Three Lucan parables:

— The Good Samaritan (10,29-37): This parable is given to answer the question as to "who is my neighbour?" The reply is drawn from the lips of the questioner himself at the end, when he answers that the genuine neighbour to the robbers' victim was "The one who showed pity towards him". The text here means literally "doing mercy". Furthermore, in the parable it was a Samaritan who showed pity to the wounded stranger, whereas a priest and a Levite had already passed by without helping him. The parable brings out clearly that the basis of compassion and mercy is not a written law but our common humanity. Nobody is to be regarded as outside the demands of "love of neighbour".

— Parable of the prodigal son (15,11-32): This parable comes in reply to complaints of "the Pharisees and scribes" that Jesus "welcomes sinners and eats with them" (15,1-3). To share a meal was regarded as a sign that those at table had accepted one another as members of the same family, either by blood or by adoption. It was virtually sealing a pact of friendship[18]. So Jesus wished to clarify the motives underlying his table-fellowship with people branded as "sinners".

The parable shows the persevering love of a father towards his wandering and profligate son. With warmth and joy the father welcomed back his son when he returned looking for work as a hired labourer. The joy had to be celebrated with a big feast, because the lost son had been found again, alive and well. The thrust of the parable is that erring sons and daughters of God always retain that standing despite what they may have done. Jesus, therefore, is making manifest the compassion, concern, and mercy of his Father towards them. His offer of friendship with them is an open invitation to come back home and enter with him into the full joy of their Father's house. As noted in relation to Jesus' rejection at Nazareth, those criticising his friendship with "sinners" (and other outsiders) are like the elder brother, who refused to go in to celebrate the return of his wasteful but repentant brother.

— Parable of the rich man and Lazarus (16,19-31): This time the parable comes to illustrate Jesus' attitude with regard to riches. He had even been jeered by the Pharisees "who loved money" and could not take seriously his astonishing dichotomy between God and "Mammon": "You cannot be the slave both of God and of money" (16,13-14). In the parable that follows, the rich man is an example of "one of the most perfect adorers of Mammon with his attitude of egoism"[19]. Nothing explicit is said on how the rich man acquired so much wealth as to be able to live in completely selfish luxury. There is no indication that he was in any way concerned for the poor sick man who was dying at his gate, where "even dogs" showed some interest in healing his sores.

The second scene shows a complete reversal of the lot of the rich man and Lazarus after they died. Lazarus was warmly welcomed by Abraham, whereas the rich man was "in his torment in Hades", crying out to Abraham to send Lazarus with a drop of water to relieve his burning thirst. Abraham told the rich man firmly that the gulf between them was wide and final, with no crossing from either side. The option for Mammon — and all the sumptuous living that the idol allows its worshippers — is a rejection of the true God, and after death there is no opportunity to escape the consequences of that bad option.

In the final scene, the rich man pleads on behalf of his five brothers who are obviously heading for the same punishment unless they change their way of life immediately. He asks Abraham to send Lazarus back to warn them! But Abraham says that, "They have Moses and the prophets, let them listen to them". That reply indicates that the rich man and his brothers were acting contrary to the basic demands of Moses and the prophets — which included covenant kindness to all Israelites and special compassion towards the poor, the oppressed, the homeless and strangers. To say that this parable prescinds "from moral and religious reasons"[20] is to overlook that it does tell us how such idolatry could be avoided by taking seriously the Law and the Prophets.

A 4. The transfiguration — "Speaking about his exodus"

Lk 9,28-36, in recounting the transfiguration, gives one striking addition to the accounts in Mk and Mt. It tells us that Moses and Elijah were "speaking of his passing which he was to accomplish in Jerusalem" (9,31). The Greek word used for "passing" is **exodos**, which means a going out, a departure, a death. It is used here in a passage in which the first character speaking about it is Moses, who led the exodus out of Egypt, and the other is Elijah the prophet, who went back to Sinai to have his hope in the covenant renewed. By adding that the exodus of Jesus was to be accomplished by him in Jerusalem, the text certainly encourages us to ponder why his death there will be another exodus[21].

Those familiar with the original exodus as a paradigm or model will ask themselves what were the harsh conditions from which Jesus needed to lead out his people. And what was the goal, the promised land, to which he was to lead them after liberating them? In this connection is is helpful to recall the way John the Baptist heralded the "entry" (**eis-odos**) of Jesus: "God raised up for Israel one of David's descendants, Jesus, as Saviour, whose coming was heralded by John" (Acts 13,24)[22]. Then Lk also emphasis the "road" or "way" (**'odos**) which Jesus courageously followed right to Jerusalem. Through his passion, death, and resurrection in Jerusalem, followed by the ascension, he accomplished his "exodus". The glory of Jesus which the chosen three observed at the transfiguration was a glimpse of the glory that he would enter through the resurrection. Then he would ask the two disciples, "Was it not necessary that the Christ should suffer before entering into his glory?" (24,26)[23]. From all of which we may conclude that the "exodus" was especially the liberation from the power of sin, suffering and death; the new goal was life with the Father, a life to be communicated to the rest of the human family through the powerful love of the Spirit.

There is also emphasis on the role of Jesus succeeding Moses as God's normative spokesman and leader of a renewed Israel, indeed of a more universal people. Moses and Elijah withdraw, leaving the stage clear for Jesus to be confirmed in his role as leader of the new exodus. Then a voice from the cloud declares, "This is my Son, the Chosen One. Listen to him." The Son is the one designated to tell the disciples and the world the terms of the new covenant and to seal it in the very hour of accomplishing the new "exodus". In Hebrews, as we shall see in our Chapter 12, the entry of Jesus into the heavenly sanctuary, as mediator of the new covenant, is said to have opened likewise for his followers an entrance (**eis-odos**) into heaven (Heb 10,19).

A 5. "This cup is the new covenant in my blood.."

It is tempting to take up many confirmatory texts that can be found between the prediction of the Jesus' "exodus" and the hour of its accomplishment to be considered now. Hopefully this direct transition from the transfiguration to the solemn announcement and sacramental sealing of the new covenant will increase our awareness of the direct connection between the new exodus and its new covenant. In Lk, the Last Supper is depicted explicitly as the Passover, first in its preparation (22,1-13), then when Jesus took his place at table with the apostles and said to them, "I have ardently longed to eat this Passover with you before I suffer" (22,15). In this way Lk gives added emphasis to the first exodus, which was recalled and actualized each Passover. We shall devote most attention to the Last Supper, then comment very briefly on a few salient points concerning the agony, death and resurrection.

A 5. a) Eating the Jewish Passover and drinking the festal wine:

Lk 22,14-18 provides us with another of his literary diptychs. The first leaf gives a picture of the usual Jewish Passover meal being celebrated by Jesus and the apostles; the corresponding leaf describes the institution of the new rite to supersede the paschal sacrifice, the Passover meal, and the blood of the old covenant. In referring to the paschal meal and again after telling the apostles to share a cup of wine, Jesus announces that he will not eat the Passover meal nor drink wine until the kingdom of God comes. The initial resumption of "eating and drinking" a paschal meal with the disciples could well be found within the eucharistic celebration, at the Last Supper by anticipation and afterwards in honouring the mandate to continue celebrating it as a reminder of "Christ our Pasch"[24].

A 5.b) "My body given for you. .. the new covenant in my blood":
Lk 22,19-20 is the other half of the diptych. In this scene, Jesus gives new significance to his farewell meal by taking some bread, giving thanks, breaking it and saying, "This is my body given for you; do this in remembrance of me." Lk differs from Mt and Mk by two additions here: "given for you", stressing the sacrifice as well as the gift of the eucharistic food; and "do this in remembrance of me", which underlines that a new form of remembrance is being instituted, as a perpetual reminder of the new exodus and its new leader[25]. Since Paul's wording for the institution has words to the effect of "do this as my memorial" said over the cup as well (cf. 1 Cor 11,23-25), we will return to the phrase after we see what Lk has concerning the cup.

Perhaps Lk implies what Paul has made explicit, for Lk says, "He did the same with the cup after supper, and said, 'This cup is the new covenant in my blood poured out for you'." In any case, the final part of Lk's wording is a key to his understanding of the covenant mentioned here. By including the word "new", Lk links up this covenant with the new covenant promised explicitly in Jer 31,31-34. In saying, "this cup is the new covenant in my blood", Jesus would be referring also to the way the old covenant was sealed in sacrificial blood. Lk's arrangement of the words then suggests that the cup given to be shared by the disciples contains within it the essence of the new covenant, namely the life-blood of the living Jesus, which (at the time of the Last Supper) is being poured out voluntarily in self-sacrifice.

The blood poured out in response to the Father's will thereby seals the new covenant. To say that "the cup is the new covenant in my blood " is coming close to the idea of the Servant in person being made "a covenant of the people" (Is 42,6). Blood was regarded by the Israelites as "the seat of life", and as such it was reserved to the Author of life. Even a sacrificial meal, such as that of paschal lamb, could be prepared only after the animal's blood had been removed. For Jesus to leave as his memorial a celebration permitting the sharing of his own blood, in sacramental form, was something astonishingly new. No more compelling symbol could be devised, in that setting, for the unlimited life now made accessible by the sealing of the new covenant and actively communicated through its celebration[26].

A 5. c) "Do this as my reminder":
Here we must look briefly at the phrase which Lk gives with the words over the bread (22,19), and which Paul also gives in connection with the bread, then repeats it with regard to the cup. In what follows I am indebted to the thorough work of F. Chenderlin, 'Do This as My Memorial' — The Semantic and Conceptual Background and Value of **Anamnesis** in I Cor 11:24-25[27]. He presents a convincing case in favour of taking the "memorial" as a cultic reminder which is intended to remind God and to remind the worshippers of Christ's self- oblation. The Greek word, **anamnesis**, which is used in exactly

the same phrase by Lk and Paul, means a calling to mind, or a reminder. In the literature used by Greek-speaking Jews in those days, it was frequently used in texts about calling to mind the covenant. "In this covenant context, the word group [of **anamnesis**] recalls the widespread and persistent mode of petition coupled with thanksgiving in which God is asked by people in unison or individually to 'remember your covenant promises', a practice that simultaneously underlines the fact the petitioners are themselves remembering them"[28].

We must also refer the reader again to the magisterial work of C. Giraudo on the literary structure of the earliest known eucharistic prayers. Part III of that work shows clearly how those prayers stand in continuity with the extremely rich O.T. "confession" supplications and the Jewish "blessings"[29]. The "reminder" bequeathed to the Church by Jesus is great enough to remind both "partners" of the whole sacred history of Israel and the new covenant community arising from it. Lk carefully prepares the ground for that dimension by the canticles that praise God for the way he has "remembered" his covenants with Abraham and David (1,54-5; 1,72-3). Because the human partner is still weak and subject to the daily attrition of life in a world where God's reign is often rejected, the faithful need to "remind" God and themselves of the great gift already given in and through Christ, the beloved Son who has made possible the full family reunion[30].

A 5. d) "And now I confer a kingdom on you":

After two short discussions, one on the betrayer, Judas, and the other on the spirit of humble service that must characterise Christian leaders, Jesus encourages the faithful apostles by telling them, "And now I confer a kingdom on you, just as my Father conferred one on me: you will eat and drink at my table in my kingdom" (22,29-30). The Greek verb used here for "to confer" can also mean "to dispose", and from it has come the word **diatheke** (= disposition, arrangement, last will, covenant). Because that verb is used twice in the context of the new covenant just announced, we are entitled to ask if Lk is suggesting that there is close connection between the "conferring of the kingdom" and the acceptance of the new covenant[31].

There is much evidence in Lk that the reign of God requires a voluntary acceptance of God's will, and that Jesus himself did accept the Father's will totally, even unto death on a cross. For Lk, therefore, the new covenant is established when the Father's will is made known and publicly accepted by Jesus on behalf of all his brothers and sisters. Lk surpasses Mt and Mk in impressing on us the depth of Christ's agony in the garden as he accepted the Father's will, with such intensity that "his sweat fell to the ground like great drops of blood" (22,44). Having accepted his part of the covenant demands, Jesus is able to speak of conferring an important share in the kingdom, which is now also his kingdom. As crucified and risen Lord, he is to be forever co-regent with the Father. In his person, thanks to the full conformity between the divine and the human will, the new covenant is established and guaranteed. The disciples, drawn by the example of Jesus, also accept the basic demand of the new covenant when they accept the Father's will as made known to them through their Master.

A 5. e) The words spoken from the cross:

Lk has three sentences spoken by Jesus from the cross. They therefore help to articulate the mind of Jesus in the supreme hour of sealing the new covenant in his own blood. The first word begs forgiveness of those responsible for the unjust execution. Jesus prays, "Father, forgive them; they do not know what they are doing" (23,34). This is a striking example of love of enemies and of willingness to forgive others. It confirms his own teaching, while at the same time it highlights his mission of winning forgiveness of sin through his suffering and death[32].

The second word is addressed to the penitent criminal crucified beside him. It develops further the kind of salvation which "the Christ" makes possible for others. While one criminal is hostile, because somebody reputed to be the Christ should be able to save himself and his fellow-victims from their crosses, the other defends the innocence of Jesus. He then asks him respectfully, "Jesus, remember me when you come into your kingdom". The favour is granted in words that open up new vistas for the good thief and all repentant sinners: "In truth I tell you, today you will be with me in paradise" (23,43).

At the start of the public ministry, the human origin of Jesus is traced back to "Adam, son of God" (3,38); at its close, the Son of man, whom Paul calls the second Adam, can declare that he has won access to paradise for the human family. Instead of the cross proving that the Christ could not save anybody, not even himself, it opens the way for Christ and others into the everlasting kingdom of God[33]. This is not a return to the garden of Eden, but a going forward to the perfection of what was started at creation.

The third word on the cross recorded in Lk expresses the complete filial commitment of Jesus at the moment of death, when he says, "Father, into your hands I commit my spirit" (23,46). D. Coffey explains well the relation of the Holy Spirit to the spirit of Jesus throughout his mortal life. Then at his death "his whole being was now concentrated in a single act of love of God, which was the return of the Holy Spirit by the incarnate Son to the Father. But, as love of God is love of neighbour, the death of Jesus released the Holy Spirit as his love of neighbour, thus bringing the Church into existence. The content of the first Christians' experience of the Spirit was Christ himself"[34]. Luke, as we noted earlier, gives remarkable attention to the Spirit, especially in Acts. In Lk, John the Baptist foretells that there will be a baptism "with the Holy Spirit and fire" (3,16). After the resurrection, Jesus tells his disciples to wait in Jerusalem until they have been "clothed with power from on high" (24,49).

If some of the spirit of Moses could be given to seventy elders (Nb 11,16-25), and if a double share of the spirit of Elijah could be given to his successor, Elisha (2 K 2,10), then the spirit of Jesus could be committed to the Father for imparting to whomsoever he chose. Acts tells us of some of the outpouring of the Holy Spirit, who is also called "the Spirit of Jesus" (Acts 16,7). It is no exaggeration to say that Lk's presentation of the last words of

Jesus on the cross sets in bold relief the forgiveness of enemies, the welcome to repentant sinners, and the voluntary release of his Spirit-filled spirit to be bestowed on stony hearts to transform them into hearts "burning within" the disciples (Lk 24,32). In short, the blood of the new covenant has not been shed in vain, nor will the new "exodus" fail to save and liberate all who freely choose to participate in it[35].

B: THE NEW COVENANT IN ACTS

Acts provides us with the most sustained account of the emergence and spread of the primitive Church during the three decades following the death and resurrection of Jesus. This second part of Luke's unified work enables him to describe the life and convictions of the new community gathered together in the name of the risen Lord and vivified by the Holy Spirit. Acts is both a witness to the inauguration of the age of the Church and "the gospel of the Holy Spirit"[36]. Both those aspects are important for our own reflection, because the Church described in Acts manifests the characteristics of a distinctly new covenant community.

Although Acts does not mention the new covenant by name, there are plenty of indications that the members of the new community are truly "the heirs of the prophets [and] the heirs of the covenant God made with your ancestors" (through Abraham) (Acts 3,25). Christ's disciples appear as fully committed to God and to one another in loyal love. There is also a remarkable change of attitude with regard to the admission of Gentiles into their community, and then comes a vigorous missionary effort reaching out "to the ends of the earth". We will now look briefly at four stages in the growth of the new covenant community, which is often called "the Church" in Acts, and whose members become known as "Christians".

B 1. Entry into the new covenant community

In fulfilment of the promises made by Jesus before and after the resurrection, the Holy Spirit was poured out at Pentecost upon the little group of disciples, including Mary, the mother of Jesus, and other women. Filled with new enthusiasm, courage and eloquence, Peter promptly began to explain the good news about Jesus the Nazarene and the Spirit to many of the pilgrims who had come to Jerusalem from more than a dozen countries. It was the manifestation that the crucified Jesus had risen and been made "Lord and Christ" (2,1-36). When many were moved to ask Peter, "What are we to do, brothers?", Peter told them, "You must repent, .. and be baptised in the name of Jesus Christ for the forgiveness of your sins, and you will receive the gift of the Holy Spirit" (2,37-38). This was the rite of reception into the new community. It entailed repentance, which was basically a change of heart with regard to any conduct unacceptable to God. The baptism in Christ's name brought the forgiveness of sins, and the gift of the Holy Spirit was given generously to the new disciples.

After Peter had healed the lame beggar at the entrance to the Temple, he took the opportunity to explain how the miracle was due to the power of Jesus.

In him, God had kept the promise of sending another prophet like Moses, to whom all God's people must now listen. Peter went on to tell them that they were the heirs of the prophets and of the covenant made with Abraham, when God told him, "All the nations of the earth will be blessed in your descendants" (3,25). Peter let them know that Jesus was the "descendant" whom God had raised up to bless them, but on condition that they turned from their "wicked ways" (3,26).

Peter and John were quickly arrested and brought before the Sanhedrin, where Peter again insisted that the miracle had been worked in the name of Jesus crucified and risen. "Only in him is salvation; .. for [his name] is the only one by which we can be saved" (4,12). Through such scenes, Acts presents Christ as the descendant of Abraham who brings with him the promised blessing to "all the nations of the earth". He is also the "prophet like Moses", as well as the new occupant of the throne of David, not in Jerusalem, but at the right hand of the Father. He offers the world its only possible source of "salvation" and integral liberation. With Christ's coming, the history of salvation must include all nations, and likewise it must include all dimensions of personal and social life. It is highly significant that Peter had to defy the ruling Sanhedrin, who tried to silence the apostles as it had wished to silence Jesus before them. Despite all difficulties, "the word of the Lord continued to spread: the number of disciples in Jerusalem was greatly increased" (6,7).

B 2. Community fellowship and sharing

The early chapters of Acts contain three summary descriptions of life in the new covenant community in Jerusalem (2,42-47; 4,32-35; 5,12-16). Taken together they give an appealing picture of common concern for the things of God and for the daily needs of all in the community[37]. One sentence is almost a synthesis of the summaries, for it tells us: "These [newly baptised] remained faithful to the teaching of the apostles, to the brotherhood, to the breaking of the bread and to prayers" (2,42). Fidelity is a keynote of their commitment. "The teaching of the apostles" brings them God's teaching made known through the Lord Jesus and now handed on by his apostles. "The brotherhood" or "fellowship" is an excellent word for summing up the prevailing family atmosphere. G. Panikulam's study, **Koinonia** in the New Testament — A Dynamic Expression of Christian Life, concludes that fellowship which has Christ as its focal point "expresses the real sense of Christian life. And as such could it not be interpreted as the quintessence of the new covenant community of the New Testament?" (emphasis added)[38].

To be faithful "to the breaking of the bread" implies in Lk-Acts the special meal associated with the eucharist. The two disciples at Emmaus recognised Jesus "at the breaking of the bread" (24,35). At Troas Paul devoted a whole Sunday night to a meeting "for the breaking of bread", at which he preached till midnight, and restored to life the young man who had dozed off during the sermon and fallen to his death. After that, Paul "broke bread and ate", and carried on talking till daybreak (Acts 20,7-12). This "reminder" of Christ's self-offering that sealed the new covenant must be considered as a constant help to make each meal an occasion of genuine covenant fellowship.

To share bread broken at the one table also has many implications for sharing all the necessities of daily life with the com-panions (= fellow bread-eaters).

That the Christians took fellowship seriously can be gauged from the way they "owned everything in common; they sold their goods and possessions and distributed the proceeds among themselves according to what each one needed" (2,44-45). It is repeated in the next summary that "everything they owned was held in common", with such a spirit of sharing that "none of their members was ever in want" (4,32-34). They were putting into practice what Jesus had requested about selling possessions, giving the proceeds to the poor, and following him. In that way the ideal of God's people, as expressed in connection with the "remission" or "release" for each sabbatical year, could be realised: "There must, then, be no poor among you. For Yahweh will grant you his blessing.." And again: "Always be open handed with your brother, and with anyone in your country who is in need and poor" (Dt 15,4.11). As T. Mworia comments on this point, "The early Christians, conscious of being the Messianic community of the final times, began quite early to apply this promise to themselves, since by their way of living they eliminated poverty among themselves"[39]. Their spirit of sharing resources and extending table-fellowship to all disciples was also a flowering of what their Master had done[40]. For Luke, the Jerusalem community's life-style was obviously an ideal to inspire later communities as well[41].

Another aspect of the community is its close association with the Temple, as a place for united prayer and for giving a challenging witness to all the Jewish nation(2,46; 4,12). Moreover, the Lord worked miracles through the apostles to confirm their witness to Jesus' resurrection and confirmation as Saviour. For instance, "The apostles worked many signs and miracles among the people" (5,12). Their reputation became so great that crowds from all sides brought to them the sick and the tormented, "and all of them were cured" (5,16). The healing, as well as the teaching mission of Jesus was being continued through his apostolic community. It is important to note that the lead-up to the final summary of what went on in that community speaks for the first time in Acts of the "church". Having narrated the way Ananias and Sapphira had been struck dead for deceiving the apostles on the amount received from selling their property, Acts remarks that "a great fear came upon the whole church" (5,11). Each local church, therefore, is called to reproduce something of the generous fellowship and sharing proper to a new covenant community.

B 3. Admission of Gentiles to the new covenant community

The stoning of Stephen the deacon in Jerusalem marks the beginning of a more general persecution against Christians, and because of that, a dispersion of Christians to centres well away from Jerusalem. For the first time we catch a glimpse of Saul, a zealous young Jew who participated in the execution of Stephen. His subsequent conversion while persecuting Christians provides Acts with its outstanding "apostle of the Gentiles". However, the opening of the Christian community in Jerusalem to non-Jews is shown to have been gradual. Acts is at pains to tell of the way Peter himself was led by the Spirit to go to the

Gentile Cornelius, remain in his house, and baptize all his household. Peter later defended his decision by asking his critics back in Jerusalem, "And who was I to stand in God's way?" He carried the day, helping the others to realise that, "God has clearly granted to the gentiles too the repentance that leads to life" (11,17-18).

Several years later (about 49 A.D.), an important meeting of apostles and elders had to clarify the position of Gentile Christians with regard to observance of the Mosaic Law, and probably their right to mix freely at all levels with Jewish Christians (who may still have shunned such fellowship on the grounds of the legal impurity it would cause them). Peter supported the freedom of Gentile converts from the Law, while James pleaded for sensitivity to Jewish consciences as formed by centuries of traditional teaching (cf. Acts 15). The final decision incorporated Peter's viewpoint and respected the plea of James. Paul and Barnabas went back to Antioch very encouraged by the confirmation of what had been their own basic teaching for Gentile converts.

B 4. Mission to the Gentiles and "to the ends of the earth"

Before that crucial meeting of Jerusalem, Paul and Barnabas had already completed a missionary journey from Antioch of Syria to the area around Antioch of Pisidia. Reassured in their apostolate, Paul and Silas set off for another missionary journey that took them as far as Macedonia and Achaia, which meant that they had begun to proclaim the good news in Europe. Paul's speech in the Areopagus of Athens is well fitted to the cultural capital.

Paul stresses the universal lordship of the true God, "who gives everything". "From one single principle he not only created the whole human race so that they could occupy the entire earth, but he decreed the times and limits of their habitation" (17,25-26). Paul goes on to mention the general judgment which will be conducted by one risen from the dead. The speech is important for its insistence on the unity of the human race, that all are "the children of God", and that the land of each people has been assigned to it by the Creator. Like the Land entrusted to the Israelites, the land entrusted to each nation is to be used for the good of all its citizens in accord with the Creator's plan. Whether it is acknowledged or not, all live and move and have their being in God. Paul invites them to take the step from honouring "An Unknown God" to acknowledging the one true God.

From Athens Paul went on to Corinth, where he remained for some eighteen months, establishing an important church there. We will glimpse in our next chapter something of its many charisms and growing pains. After returning briefly to Antioch of Syria, Paul set off for Ephesus, where he stayed for more than two years, consolidating the churches there and in the vicinity. In Ephesus he met a dozen disciples of John the Baptist and was able to baptise them all. "At the moment Paul laid his hands on them, the Holy Spirit came down upon them, and they began to speak with tongues and to prophesy" (19,1-7). In that way Luke illustrates how fully the promise of John the Baptist was fulfilled in favour of his own faithful disciples.

Another notable feature of Paul's evangelization of Ephesus was the way he decided to change from teaching in the synagogue to teaching in "the lecture room of Tyrannus" (19,9). There he continued for two years, "with the result that all the inhabitants of Asia, both Jews and Greeks, were able to hear the word of the Lord" (19,10). F. Pereira brings out well the import of this step: "In the narrative of Acts, this step had never been taken before. Its implications, we feel, are far-reaching and truly universal. .. .. All, Jews as well as Gentiles, are thus treated on an equal footing <u>as hearers together</u> of one and the same message"[42] (author's emphasis).

In his farewell discourse to the elders and "overseers" of the Church of Ephesus, who had come to see him off from the port of Miletus, Paul recalled their responsibility towards "the Church of God which he bought with the blood of his own Son" (20,28). By that phrase, in its context of an apostle exhorting the leaders of the young church, Paul conjures up a parallel between the blood of the new covenant and that which sealed the Sinai covenant, which confirmed Israel as Yahweh's "personal possession" (cf.Ex 19,5; 24,8). The phrase of Paul, therefore, serves well in Acts to suggest that the "Church of God" is the community called into being by the sealing of the new covenant in the blood of Jesus Christ[43].

The final journey described in Acts is that of Paul going to Rome to stand trial there, as he had "appealed to Caesar" rather than be tried in Jerusalem (25,12). As a Roman citizen Paul several times received favourable treatment from the authorities, so much so that P.W. Walaskay finds Acts to be be an "**apologia pro imperio**"[44]. The sea voyage, in which Luke seems to have been involved as one of Paul's companions, led to shipwreck on Malta, but eventually they reached Rome safely. Paul spent the next two years in his own hired lodgings in Rome, guarded by a soldier but free to receive visitors. Some of the Jews who came along to listen to his explanation of the gospel were impressed, but "the rest were sceptical". Their general reaction led Paul to pass a final remark to them: "You must realise, then, that <u>this salvation of God</u> has been sent <u>to the gentiles</u>". Acts closes with Paul spending his two years there "<u>proclaiming the kingdom of God</u> and teaching the truth about the Lord Jesus Christ with complete fearlessness and without any hindrance from anyone" (28,23-31).

The phrases underlined merit our attention. "Salvation of God" refers to what has been achieved and offered by God through "the Lord Jesus Christ"; it can be accepted by those deprived of political and socio-economic freedom. Paul himself was at that stage nearing the end of five years in chains! His own arrival in Rome, the heart of the Roman empire, was a means of bringing the good news of salvation "to the Gentiles". By "proclaiming the kingdom of God" he was inviting Jew and Gentile alike to accept the will of God and to enter through baptism into the "Church of God", an organised community of the new covenant.

As such, the Church must be pledged to bring all the new covenant values to bear on civil societies like the powerful Roman empire. The new covenant is powerful enough to bring liberation from any pharaoh in any country or over any race. The confrontation with Roman emperors and the subsequent fear for the unlimited power of Caesar led to the execution of both Jesus and his apostle Paul. Jesus was condemned to the death of a slave or rebel on a cross; Paul as a citizen of the empire was condemned to die by the sword. Luke's great literary work, nevertheless, closes on a note of complete confidence that God's reign and gift of salvation are effective for all peoples. From that stems our own confidence today that the new covenant and integral liberation are becoming a reality for the entire human family.

NOTES

1. J.A. Fitzmyer, The Gospel According to Luke (Garden City, N.Y.: Anchor Bible, I-IX and X-XXIV, 1981 and 1985) 8, where he says that Lk/Acts "emerged toward the close of the second last decade of the first Christian century." Cf. Nueva Biblia Española, 1589, where the most probable date is set between 75-90 A.D.
2. Cf.: R.E. Brown, The Birth of the Messiah, 236, where a date in the 80s, "give or take ten years", is proposed for the composition of Lk/Acts. He also notes the questioning of the force of the "we" passages in Acts to establish authorship. The New American Bible, 1107, accepts a date of composition around 75 A.D.
3. Cf. R.E. Brown, op.cit. 239-241.
4. Cf. ibid. 499; also 346-366; 378; 391.
5. Cf.: A. Gelin, Les Pauvres que Dieu Aime, 91. N. Lemmo, Maria, 'Figlia di Sion' a Partir da Lc 1,26-38 — Bilancio esegetico dal 1939 al 1982 (Roma: Marianum, l985) esp. 32...
6. Cf. R.E. Brown, op.cit. 459 on the **Nunc Dimittis**: "This opening to the Gentiles.. brings to the Lucan infancy narrative a theme that we saw in Matthew's account of the magi. .. [It is] the theme of Gentiles who are attracted by the light of God's Son."
7 Cf. W. Pilgrim, Good News to the Poor — Wealth and Poverty in Luke-Acts (Minneapolis, Minnesota: Augsburg, 1981) 64-84, e.g. 64: "No text is more important for understanding Luke's two volumes than this one. Recent scholarship is in general agreement that here we find the programmatic text for the Lukan writings." Again, 67: "The idea of being anointed to carry out a divinely commissioned task is central to the O.T., and in Isaiah is linked with the proclamation of good news to a captive people." (And it is addressed specifically to the poor in our text.)
8. Cf. D. Senior, "The Mission Perspectives of Luke-Acts" in The Biblical Foundations for Mission, 255-279, esp. 255: "Luke's theology has become a central focus of contemporary biblical scholarship. Some of this interest is generated by the third world churches. Luke's stress on the prophetic character of Jesus' ministry as well as his confrontation with issues of justice fit the powerful concerns of liberation theology."
9. Cf. S.H. Ringe, Jesus, Liberation and the Biblical Jubilee, esp. 33-80 on Jesus and "Jubilee Images", e.g.48: "In both cases [Lk 4 and 7], Luke depicts Jesus as making that power [mentioned in Is 61] known especially

to people outside the community with which the covenant promises were generally associated. .. At issue is the acceptability (ch.4) and the recognition(ch.7) of Jesus as the one in whom people meet the inaugural celebration of God's reign."

10. Cf. R.J. Karris, "The Gospel According to Luke", in NJBC 690, where he comments on the phrase used in Nazareth, "Scripture <u>has been fulfilled</u>": "The adult Jesus' first words in Luke deal with the theme of <u>God's fidelity to promise</u>" (emphasis added).

11. J. Fitzmyer, op.cit., 227. Cf.: J. Navone, Themes of St Luke (Rome: Gregorian University, 1970) 151-169, on the Holy Spirit, e.g. 156: "In the Lucan account, the Spirit and power do not come upon Jesus as a charismatic force; rather, because Jesus is conceived by the power of the spirit of God, he is penetrated by them to the depth of his being." Also D. Coffey, "A Proper Mission of the Holy Spirit", in Theol. Studies 47 (1986), 227-250, e.g. 232: "The Holy Spirit, as the Father's love for the Son, moves out from the Father to the Son, but as the Son's love for the Father returns to the Father, its ultimate source. He is the 'bond' uniting the Son to the Father in love."

12. Cf. J. Fitzmyer, op.cit. 197, where he notes that in Lk the word "Christ" is used 24 times in a titular sense.

13. Cf. W. Pilgrim, op.cit. 70: He draws attention to the fact that in Is 58,6 "four successive verbs express the one idea of supreme importance, <u>the liberation of the oppressed</u>" (emphasis added).

14. Also R. North, Sociology of the Biblical Jubilee, 2, where he accepts that the basic meaning behind the Hebrew word for "jubilee" is "release".

15. Cf.: J. Fitzmyer, op.cit. 235 on use of "today" in Lk. Also I.H. Marshall, Commentary on Luke (Grand Rapids: Eerdmans, 1978) 184: "The 'today' of Jesus is still addressed to readers of the Gospel and assures them that the era of salvation is present."

16. Cf. M. Hengel, Property and Riches in the Early Church — Aspects of a Social History of early Christianity (London: E.T. by J. Bowden, S.C.M. 1973) 23: "This negative picture [of social conditions] is supplemented by rabbinical accounts of the avarice and despotism of the leading high-priestly families, among whom pride of place was taken by the house of Annas. This family used their privileged position to exploit those who came to Jerusalem on pilgrimage at festival times and they oppressed the more humble ministers of the temple; they often worked hand in hand with the Roman prefects." Also: R.J. Karris, art. cit., 685 on the power of Annas and family under Rome.

17. Cf. John Paul II's addresses during his visit to Lima, May 14-16, 1988, in which he recalled that the liberation offered by Christ is not limited to this world. On the other hand, the gesture of the Pope kissing the soil of each new land that he visits is a clear indication of the importance of "earthly" things, as gifts of God to be rightly used by all those "on earth".

18. Cf.: D. Senior, op.cit. 265: "The parable of the banquet in Lk.,14:15-24 seems to use the table-fellowship theme as an object lesson on salvation

NOTES

history." J. Navone, Themes of St Luke, 11-37 on the importance of the banquet theme in Lk. E.P. Sanders, Jesus and Judaism, 44 on the opposition aroused by Jesus's table-fellowship with sinners.
19. J. Sicre, Los Dioses Olvidados, 168. Cf. D.L. Meadland, Poverty and Expectation in the Gospels (London, S.P.C.K., 1980) 60, where he wisely relates the teaching of Jesus about wealth to his deep concern for "the sufferer, the outsider and the poor". Also 61-83.
20. Cf., J.L. Segundo, The Historical Jesus of the Synoptics, 114.
21. Cf. J. Fitzmyer, op.cit. 800; 1359; 1367 on "exodus" in the transfiguration. J. Navone and T. Cooper, The Story of the Passion (Rome: Gregorian University, 1986) 226: "Salvation for Lk is a following of Jesus along his way so that by sharing in his **exodos** one may come to share in his assumption to glory."
22. Cf. I.H. Marshall, op.cit. 384-385.
23. Cf. J.S. Croatto, Historia de la Salvación, 351.
24. Cf.: I.H. Marshall, op.cit. 797: "It is, therefore, possible that Luke saw in the saying [of Lk 22,16] a hint of the fellowship between Jesus and his disciples in the 'new Passover' of the Lord's Supper." F. Chenderlin, 'Do This as My Memorial', 5; 233 against J.Jeremias's interpretation of this section in Lk.
25. Cf. R.J. Karris, art. cit., 716: "The dying Jesus has bequeathed to his community of reconstituted Israel the eucharist to replace the Passover meal."
26. Cf.: X. Léon-Dufour, 'Le Partage du Pain Eucharistique' Selon le N.T. (Paris: Seuil, 1982), 161-183, e.g. 161: "La parole sur la coupe est d'une densité exceptionnelle, recapitulant en quelques mots le sens et la portée de l'existence de Jésus de Nazareth. .. D'abord, non plus l'annonce simple du 'règne' de Dieu, mais l'alliance, ce mot qui évoque le long itinéraire d'Israël au cours de l'histoire ..: au terme de son existence, Jésus proclame que l'alliance avec Dieu est définitivement renouée.." (author's emphasis). M. Braconnot and many others (Ed.), L'Évangile selon saint Luc — Avènement (Paris: Desclée de Brouwer, 1984), 296: "Ainsi se trouve davantage précisé le sens de la mort de Jésus: le sang versé, c'est la vie donnée, et donnée de telle sorte qu'une relation durable est établie entre Dieu et l'homme dans le Christ" (emphasis added). J.S. Croatto, Historia de la Salvación, 365.
27. F. Chenderlin, 'Do This as My Memorial' — The Semantic and Conceptual Background and Value of **Anamnesis** in 1 Cor 11:24-25.
28. Ibid. 216-217; also 146; and 227: "Into this kind of picture, when the past events involve covenant promise and command, reminding-man and reminding-God fit as the spontaneous, yet traditional expression of both the humanization and the divine vitalization of the pattern" (emphasis added).
29. Cf. C. Giraudo, La Struttura Letteraria della Preghiera Eucaristica, 271-355; 357; 364. J. Fitmyer, op.cit. 1401.

30. Cf. C. Giraudo, op.cit. 369: "Tanto la **toda** [=O.T. "confession"] quanto la preghiera eucaristica dicono la marcia nel deserto, ossia il tempo della Chiesa che attende fiduciosa, pur tra infedeltà e mormorazioni, il pieno compimento di una relazione già sancita." Also 370.
31. Cf.: I.H. Marshall, op.cit. 816. J. Fitzmyer, op.cit. 1418-1419.
32. Cf. J. Navone and T. Cooper, The Story of the Passion, 255: ['Father forgive'..] are "two words which sum up his message and meaning and mission."
33. Cf.: W. Klassen, Love of Enemies — The Way to Peace, 91. M. Hengel, The Cross of the Son of God (London, S.C.M. 1986) 154: "Death on the cross was the penalty for slaves, as everyone knew; as such it symbolized extreme humiliation, shame, and torture". Also 180-181 on the impact of Jesus not only taking on "the form of a slave" but also accepting the death of a slave, in solidarity with others subjected to similar suffering, torture and death.
34. D.M. Coffey, Art. cit., 238.
35. Cf. J. Fitzmyer, op.cit. 1502: (On crucifixion:) "The climax of his suffering has been reached; his **exodos** (9:32) from this life has moved to its definitive stage. 'The power of darkness' has closed in against him."
36. Cf.: N.J.B.'s introduction to the Synoptic Gospels, 1608 re prominence of H.Spirit in Lk. J. Delorme, "Diversité et Unité des Ministères d'Après le N.T.", in Le Ministère et les Ministères Selon le N.T. (Paris: Seuil, 1974) 328: "L'action divine dans le présent est celle du Christ ressuscité dans l'Esprit."
37. Cf. R. Dillon, Acts of the Apostles, in NJBC 724; 734-739. T. Mworia, The Community of Goods in Acts: A Lucan Model of Christian Charity (Rome, Pontifical Urban University, 1986) 89-122 on the three "major summaries" of the early Christian community life in Jerusalem.
38. G. Panikulam, Koinonia in the N.T. — A Dynamic Expression of Christian Life (Rome: Biblical Institute Press, 1979) 142. Cf. M. Hengel, Property and Riches in the Early Church, 131-134.
39. T. Mworia, op.cit., 163. Cf. E. Schüssler Fiorenza, Bread Not Stone — The Challenge of Feminist Biblical Interpretation (Boston: Beacon Press, 1984) 146-147 indicates the importance of seeing in the believing community a "discipleship of equals". She considers that such a vision has been obscured by "androcentric scholarship".
40. Cf. D. Senior, op.cit. 273, where he notes the "strong follow-through from table-fellowship in Lk to the sharing of goods and meeting the needs of all the community in Acts".
41. Cf. W. Pilgrim, op. cit. 148: "What Luke intends is not just a historical glimpse of the earliest community, but a working vision of what every Christian community ought to be like."
42. Cf. F. Pereira, Ephesus: Climax of Universalism in Luke-Acts — A Redaction-Critical Study of Paul's Ephesian Ministry (Acts 18:23 - 20:1) (Anand, India: Gujarat Sahitya Prakash, 1983) 148. Cf. 136; 138; 176.

43. Ibid. 210: "The blood of Jesus which is mentioned [in Acts 20,28] is to be understood, as Lyonnet observes, as the blood by which the <u>new</u> covenant, just as the <u>old</u> one at <u>Sinai</u>, has been 'ratified' " (author's emphasis).
44. P.W. Walaskay: 'And so we came to Rome' — The Political Perspective of St Luke (Cambridge: Cambridge University, 1983) ix: "Are there passages in Luke-Acts that not only indicate a pro-Roman bias, but suggest an **apologia pro imperio**? I answer this last question in the affirmative, a conclusion supported by an investigation of the text of Luke-Acts." Cf. 67: "Luke was a theologian .. who could not divorce theology from history. If God was truly at work in the world, then he did his work not only through the church but through the secular realm as well. God has called both church and state into his service."

CHAPTER 11: NEW COVENANT IN JOHN'S GOSPEL AND EPISTLES

A. NEW COVENANT IN JOHN'S GOSPEL

John's gospel is so different from the Synoptic gospels that it merits separate treatment. This is all the more necessary with regard to our theme, because the word covenant is never mentioned in Jn, nor in any of the three Johannine epistles. (Because the Apocalypse or Revelation is very likely from another author within the general Johannine circle, it will be treated in the next chapter.) It would be easy to leave out Jn and 1-3 Jn from any further consideration, but that would be to miss some of the richest material in all the Bible concerning the fulfilment of the goals proposed by biblical covenants. The predominant aim has always been to establish an abiding relationship of mutual love between God and the human family, overflowing into mutual love between all the members of the family. John's gospel and first epistle are outstanding in their presentation of the new relationship with the Father made possible through his "only begotten Son". Thanks to the abiding presence of Father, Son and Holy Spirit within those who become "the children of God" (Jn 1,12; 14,15-24), the human heart is enabled to receive and respond consistently to the love of God revealed in the Son who "became flesh" and "pitched his tent among us" (Jn 1,14)[1].

John's presentation of the gospel differs greatly from that of the Synoptists (Mt, Mk and Lk). This is due above all to the way in which Jn writes consistently from the viewpoint of a disciple immersed in the love and life of the risen Jesus, fully recognised as Son of God and Messiah. The Jesus whom we meet in Jn moves calmly, majestically, in full control of every situation, speaking openly as the Son, as the Messiah, as the Good Shepherd, even as the divine "I AM". Jn has therefore carefully selected some miracles (only seven or eight) as "signs" of what Jesus was making manifest to the world. Generally, the context and the ensuing discourse (or public discussion) allow Jn to bring out the deep significance of the sign. The purpose of Jn is to lead the readers to realise and ponder more thoughtfully the meaning of every "sign" given by Jesus to reveal the Father and his own standing as the Son sent by the Father. Some commentators see this feature as so important that they speak of the first half of this gospel (cc. 1-12) as "the book of signs"[2]. Then the other half of the gospel (cc.13-20), in the view of R.E. Brown, is "the book of glory", followed by the addition of an epilogue (c.21)[3].

Jn in its final form is generally regarded as the last of the gospels to be written, and it can be dated around 90-95 A.D. Because the gospel was being preached, applied and refined during some sixty years, it is not surprising that commentators can find indications of considerable editing, re-editing and the incorporation of extra material. The guiding spirit behind the whole work was undoubtedly the "beloved disciple", but it is extremely difficult to establish with certainty his part in the actual composition of Jn. It is feasible to hold that the evangelist was an author in his own right who availed of other sources as well as the precious witness of the "beloved disciple". It is also being increasingly asked these days if the "beloved disciple" should be identified with John the apostle, the son of Zebedee. It is possible that the "beloved disciple" came from Jerusalem and was distinct from John the apostle[4]. In any case, there is still a strong insistence on the first-hand witness of a disciple close to Jesus, especially for the climactic "hour" in Jerusalem. He could possibly have been one of the disciples considered to replace Judas, when Peter called for nominations from among "the men who have been with us the whole time that the Lord Jesus was living with us" (Acts 1,21).

For our purposes it is sufficient to take Jn as it has been finally handed over to the Church and received into the N.T. It has a unity that does credit to the main evangelist and the final redactor, in fact it is now difficult to take up any major theme of Jn without finding that much light is thrown on it by practically every chapter. In what follows, the seven topics have been selected because they each illustrate what is announced so solemnly in the prologue: "For the Law was given through Moses, love and loyalty became a reality in Jesus the Messiah" (Jn 1,17)[5]. In other words, Jn is certainly interested in the way loyal love — the key factor in a biblical covenant — has become a reality in Jesus Christ. All of Jn draws attention to the various ways in which Jesus brings "the fulness" of what God was preparing through creation, through Abraham, Moses, and David. The fulness of the covenant relationship is really to be seen in the gathering together of all "the scattered children of God" (11,51-52), to form one great family reunited through the Son with their Father.

A 1. The Prologue (1,1-18).

"In the beginning was the Word, .. and the Word was God" (v.1). Mention of the beginning takes us back to the opening words of the Bible concerning God's creation of the universe. Now we learn that it was through the Word that "all things came into being" (v.3). Life and light came to the human race through the Word. Finally, "the Word became flesh and lived among us", so that in him his disciples have seen "the glory that he has from the Father as the only Son of the Father, full of grace and truth" (v.14).

To call the Son of God "the Word" is to associate him not only with creation by the mighty word of God, as in Genesis c.1, but also with the word of God made known constantly through the prophets and preserved for the people of God in their sacred Scriptures. It is also to link the Son with biblical wisdom, which was with God and yet could "pitch her tent" in Sion (Sirach 24,8-10). As the Word, the Son made flesh is able to reveal the Father more perfectly to all the human family. I. de la Potterie justifiably claims that the Johannine synthesis of Christology "is built around the theme of the Incarnation and of the revelation made to us in Christ: in Jesus, the Word made flesh, we are shown the glory of the only-begotten Son and of his relationship with the Father"[6]. Since God has graciously decided to speak to the world through this Word-made-visible, Jn is consistent in looking for a deeper meaning, a sign value, in every public gesture of Jesus. Jn does not need to invent miracles or personal encounters with Jesus, but he does need to dwell on their value as a revelation of both Jesus and the Father who sent him — and to whose "bosom" he returned when "lifted up" on the cross (cf. 1,18; 12,32).

The Father-Son relationship announced in the prologue is certainly central to the whole gospel. In Jn, "Father" is used of God a hundred and fifteen times[7], while "the Son" by itself is used of Jesus eighteen times[8]. R. Schnackenburg notes concerning the frequency with which Jesus (in Jn) addresses or speaks of "my Father" or "the Father" : "There can be no doubt that we have here an essential theme of Johannine theology and Christology. The 'Father-Son relationship' is the key to the understanding of Jesus as portrayed by the evangelist"[9].

The prologue itself makes clear that the coming of the Word into the world also makes it possible for those who accept him "to become the children of God" (v.12). Thanks to the Son becoming one of our human family, we in turn can receive "from his fullness". M. Vellanickal comments well on this text: "Hence 'to receive from His fullness' means to accept the Revelation in Christ and consequently to share in His sonship"[10]. Jer 31,9 has Yahweh's declaration, "For I am a father to Israel, and Ephraim is my first-born son" in the general context of the promised restoration and new covenant[11].

That the prologue itself is thinking of the fulfilment of such a promise can be discerned in the ensuing description of the fulness that we have received — "one gift replacing another, for <u>the Law was given through Moses, grace and truth have come through Jesus Christ</u>" (vv.16-17). "Grace and truth", or "love and loyalty" as translated earlier, or "this enduring love" (N.A.B.). Jn uses these two words to recall the pair of Hebrew words (**hesed** and **'emeth**) frequently used as the quintessence of covenant commitment. However, for Jn the "fullness" received in Jesus Christ is what makes such loyal love a reality in human hearts[12]. It had never been lacking in God; neither will it be lacking any longer among God's children. The glory of the Word incarnate has already been seen as that of the "only Son of the Father, <u>full of grace and truth</u>" (v.14).

R.E. Brown accepts that this section of the prologue recalls "the enduring covenant love of God" as manifested at Sinai, and that "now the supreme exhibition of God's love is the incarnate Word, Jesus Christ, the new Tabernacle of divine glory." Brown concludes: "If our interpretation of 'love in place of love' is correct, the hymn comes to an end with <u>the triumphant proclamation of a new covenant replacing the Sinai covenant</u>"[13] (emphasis added). This is in line with the opinion of E.M. Boismard concerning the prologue: "The Evangelist's design is therefore clear: he wants to show that <u>Christ is the new Moses of the New Covenant</u> and that just as Moses had been the mediator of the ancient Covenant, so Christ, though in a much more perfect way, had been constituted by God the mediator of the New Covenant"[14].

The universal scope of the Word should not escape us, either, for P. Lamarche is well justified in taking the Word to be practically equivalent to the Plan or Mystery of God in Col (c.1) and Eph (c.2). Just as those epistles speak of God's plan to bring all races together again through union in Christ, "so too in the Prologue of John, God through his **Logos** [= Word or Plan] conceived, prepared and effected the salvation both of the Gentile world .. and of Israel. .. Right from the beginning, despite certain rebuffs.., he planned to unite them in the single community of the children of God. .. This then is the controlling idea of the Prologue"[15].

A 2. The Spirit of the new covenant (cc.1 - 20)

We do not have to wait long for Jn to tell us that an essential part of the "fulness" of Jesus is his possession of and by the Holy Spirit. Like the Synoptics, Jn has the public ministry of Jesus opening with an epiphany to confirm the divine mission entrusted to him as "the Chosen One of God" (Jn 1,34). But in Jn the witness of the Baptist twice proclaims that the Spirit had come down on Jesus and "rested" on him or remained (1,32-33). The more we read of Jn, the more we are struck by the prominence of the Spirit, for instance in talking to Nicodemus about baptism (c.3), to the Samaritan woman about the gift of "living water" (c.4), and again to the crowds in Jerusalem (c.7). The fact that it is the "glorified" Jesus (7,39) who gives the Spirit is a feature proper to Jn.

In his farewell discourse at the Last Supper, Jesus repeatedly promises to send the Paraclete, the Spirit of truth, to be with the disciples, to help them from within to "remember" all that he has told them[16]. Here again Jesus promises quite clearly that both the Father and he himself will send the Paraclete (14,16.26; 16,7). Then in Jn even the cross takes on also the aspect of a royal throne, from which the messianic king "handed over the spirit/Spirit" (19,30), to give a literal translation[17]. That initial giving was made quite explicit on the day of his resurrection, when with the breath of his risen body he breathed on the disciples and said, "Receive the Holy Spirit.." (20,23).

For Jn that giving of the Spirit by the risen Jesus corresponds to the Pentecost described in Acts. It likewise empowers the disciples to carry out the mission now entrusted to them, just as Jesus himself had been empowered to carry out his mission from the Father thanks to the Spirit "resting" on him (20,21). In Jn the blending of the twofold mission of Son and Holy Spirit is such that neither mission is conceivable without the other. Moreover, Jn envisages the indwelling of the Father, Son and Holy Spirit always perfectly united within the disciples. Indicative of this is the way in which the explicit promise of the indwelling of Father and Son within loving disciples is set between the first two promises about the coming of the Paraclete (cf.14,16-26)[18]. The remark of D. Senior is apposite in this regard: "The Paraclete .. does not simply replace the presence of the risen Christ in the community, but intensifies it"[19] (author's emphasis). In many ways, therefore, Jn proclaims that the "fullness" of Jesus Christ includes an abundance of the Holy Spirit which even surpasses anything promised in the O.T. for the new covenant[20].

A 3. Messianic nuptials between Jesus and his disciples (c.2)

This is a theme which we have already met in Mark's gospel, so here we need only note what is special in Jn's treatment of it. The wedding feast of Cana provides the scene for the first "sign" performed by Jesus, and centuries of reflection on it have helped to discern many things of which it is a sign. Jn notes carefully that the wedding was "on the third day", which puts it at the end of the first week of Jesus's ministry, hence the first week of the new creation, the new "beginning" parallel to Gen c.1[21]. Representing the beginnings of the messianic community are Mary, "the mother of Jesus" and "his disciples" (vv.1-2). On being told by his mother that their hosts for the wedding feast had run out of wine, Jesus simply replied, "Woman, what do you want from me? My hour has not yet come" (v.4).

The words just underlined can now be seen as pointing forward to the "hour" of Calvary, when Mary would again be addressed as "woman". At the foot of the cross she would be given a unique role within the new community on whom her dying Son was to confer the Spirit (cf. 19,25-30). There she and "the disciple whom Jesus loved" would symbolise the nascent Church, the humble bride destined to be united to Jesus for ever in the new alliance of love[22]. R. Brown notes that Mary "symbolizes the Church", while the beloved disciple "symbolizes the Christian"[23]. J. Navone and T. Cooper also comment perceptively on that situation: "John and Mary represent the community of faith that prays the 'Our Father' with the recognition that they have been given to one another by the Father and the Son through the gift of their Spirit"[24].

John the Baptist's fine testimony to Jesus, in the chapter following on that of the Cana wedding feast, illuminates what Jn has in mind. When the Baptist was told that everybody was going to Jesus, he declared magnanimously: "It is the bridegroom who has the bride; and yet the bridegroom's friend .. is filled with joy at the bridegroom's voice" (3,29). There can be no doubt, therefore, that Jn wishes to present Jesus as the bridegroom "who has the bride" — in the form of the growing number of disciples gathering around him instead of around the Baptist as formerly.

A 4. The solemn declarations of "I AM" (cc.4 -18)

According to R. Schnackenburg, there are twenty six instances in Jn when Jesus declares, "I AM" , and in contexts which indicate that it "has become a highly compressed formula"[25]. Seven times Jesus affirms that, "I

AM .. something" (metaphorical, e.g. the bread of life; the light of the world; the good shepherd; the true vine). There are also some eight texts in which Jesus affirms absolutely that, "I AM". These are on such solemn or crucial occasions that we have to consider them as a deliberate re-echoing of the famous occasion when God revealed himself to Moses as "I AM" (Ex 3,13-15), so that the exodus and the Sinai covenant are inseparably linked to the divine name of Yahweh, "He who IS". It is one of the disconcerting aspects of Jn that, when we look for comparisons between Jesus and Moses, Jesus tends to emerge as "I AM", placing him on quite a distinct level of being to that of Moses.

The best chapter to illustrate some of the links (for Jn) between "I AM" and Moses' mission is ch.6. It has the advantage of letting us discern how Jn could take up an incident treated by the Synoptists and spotlight a profound truth which they had already suggested. It was after the feeding of the five thousand that Jesus came walking on the stormy sea towards the struggling disciples in their boat. To calm their fear he assured them, "I AM" (literal translation). "Don't be afraid" (v.20; cf. Mk 6,50 for similar wording).

There are hints of the Reed Sea crossing in Jn's description of the crossing from "the shore of the sea" to "the other side of the sea", with the darkness, the threatening sea, the fear of the disciples, then the divine presence to reassure and accompany them until their boat "reached the shore at the place they were making for" (vv.16-21)[26]. The 'crossing' took place when "the Jewish Passover was near" (v.4), and immediately after the big crowd had been fed with bread and fish in the wilderness (vv.5-13). The crowd had been so impressed that there was talk about Jesus being the long awaited prophet, presumably "the prophet like Moses" (Dt 18,18). (We recall that Moses' role as preparatory for that of Jesus has already been mentioned explicitly in Jn 1,17; 3,14; and 5,46 — "it was about me that Moses was writing"). There was even a plan to make Jesus king, from which he "fled" (6,14-15).

Having led his disciples safely "across the sea", away from the temptations of mistaken expectations about him as Messiah, Jesus is in a position to pronounce a programmatic discourse in the synagogue of Capernaum. In that discourse he makes it clear that he is much more than a "prophet like Moses". Jesus points out to them that the manna given in Moses' time was not really true "bread from heaven", the kind of bread which "gives life to the world". Then comes the astonishing claim of Jesus: "I AM the bread of life" (v.35). The whole discourse (vv.35-58) unfolds this central point in something like concentric circles, with each circle giving greater light on what is being offered as "living bread". Jesus' claim is based on the way he is given "from heaven" as the revelation of the Father and also as the eucharistic food and drink[27].

The essence of Jesus' commitment to the new covenant is expressed in his words, "I have come from heaven, not to do my own will, but to do the will of him who sent me" (v.38). He explains that his Father's will is to ensure that believers in Jesus have eternal life and that they be raised up on the last day (vv.39- 40). Only the Father can draw a person to Jesus, and it is precisely in doing so that the messianic promise is fulfilled: "They will all be taught by God" (v.45; that promise is directly related to the new covenant in Is 54,10-13 and Jer 31,31-34).

Then the extent of Jesus' sacrifice to carry out the Father's will is indicated when he makes more explicit the eucharistic promise: "Anyone who eats this bread will live for ever; and the bread that I shall give is my flesh, for the life of the world. .. Anyone who does eat my flesh and drink my blood has eternal life" (vv.51 and 54). Those who refuse this gift cannot have life in them, so Jesus here recalls the offer of "life or death" which was made through Moses with regard to fidelity to the Sinai covenant (Dt 30,15-20). However, going far beyond what Moses knew about, Jesus is now offering his disciples a new way of sharing personally in the common or "family" life of himself and the Father: "Whoever eats my flesh and drinks my blood lives in me and I live in that person. .. [as] I draw life from the Father, so whoever eats me will also draw life from me". The discourse concludes by emphasising the vast difference between the bread now offered by Jesus and the manna given through Moses, for "it is not like the bread our ancestors ate: they are dead, but anyone who eats this bread will live for ever" (v.58).

That Jn considers Israel to be faced again with a momentous choice is confirmed immediately. Like the Israelites of old who "murmured" against Moses, so too do many of Jesus' followers complain that his offer and demands are quite intolerable. The result is that "many of his disciples" go away, unwilling to return (vv. 59-66). Instead of sending the Twelve hurrying after the departing crowd, Jesus confronts them also with the same crucial option, asking, "What about you, do you want to go away too?" Simon Peter answered nobly for them that they would stay, because they did believe that Jesus could give them eternal life, as "the Holy One of God". R. Schnackenburg's comment brings out well the significance of Peter's confession: "'Holy' expresses the closest possible intimacy with God, a participation in God's deepest and most essential being. Peter's confession is therefore the appropriate responsory ['thou art'] to the revelatory formula ['I AM'] which John transfers from God to Christ, who reveals himself and the Father"[28]. Unfortunately, Peter is not speaking for Judas, as Jesus has to make known, but without naming the one who will betray him (vv.67-71).

In short, the bread of life is inseparably bound up with the free decision of Jesus to carry out his Father's will, plus the free decision of his disciples to accept the revelation and self-sacrifice of Jesus with loyal faith. This is the new covenant commitment in a nutshell. Commentators often note that Jn does not really need to mention the institution of the Eucharist at the Last Supper, as ch. 6 says enough. We are justified in thinking much the same concerning the new covenant. In fact we shall see that Jn's account of the Last Supper stresses the "new commandment", the principal clause of the new covenant. It also expands considerably the way the disciples "will all be taught by God" thanks to the abiding Spirit to be bestowed on them by the Father and the risen Christ.

A 5. "If the Son sets you free, you will indeed be free" (c.8)

Before dealing with the key passage about the way the Son will set free his disciples (8,31-36), it is necessary to situate it within its wider context of the important feast of Booths or Shelters, during which Jesus confronts "the Jews" in the Temple of Jerusalem (7,1 - 10,21). During that feast the people erected temporary Shelters to remind them of the nomadic life with Moses in the wilderness. It was a feast celebrating the gifts of light and water, in a joyful atmosphere of messianic expectation[29].

The public exchanges between Jesus and the Jews during the feast certainly remind one of the O.T. "lawsuits". There is such evident hostility and threatening attitude on the part of "the Jews" (= the Jews who reject Christ and his followers) that it has to be seen as a reflection also of the situation between Christians and Jews when Jn was being written. Jesus again mentions the preparatory mission of Moses by "accusing" the Jews, "Did not Moses give you the Law? And yet not one of you keeps the Law!" (7,19).

As if in response to the expectation of abundant water, Jesus invites those who are thirsty to come to him and drink, for he offers "streams of living water" — a reference, as Jn tell us, to the Holy Spirit, to be given to believers after Jesus has been "glorified" (7,38-39). As for the gift of light, he declares to the people that, "I am the light of the world; anyone who follows me will not be walking in the dark but will have the light of life" (8,12). We shall now follow that theme through the remainder of ch.8. The Pharisees challenge such an astounding claim, to which Jesus retorts that there are two reliable witness to back it up — himself and his Father! In the same vein Jesus warns them that, "If you do not believe that I am He [literally: I AM], you will die in your sins" (v.24). He insists that, once they have "lifted up the Son of man" (on the cross, and through the cross to his glory with the Father), then they will know that "I AM" (v.28).

Against that background Jesus, as light of the world, urges "the Jews who believe in him" to welcome his word and and so become truly disciples. In so doing, he assures them, "you will come to know the truth, and the truth will set you free" (v.32). The Jews reply indignantly that they are children of Abraham and "have never been the slaves of anyone". How can there be any talk of setting them free now? (vv.33-34). Jesus' answer takes up his earlier warning about them dying in their sins. He now explains the connection between their sins and slavery, saying, "Everyone who commits sin is a slave" (v.34). The liberation in question is basically liberation from sin, and in particular the kind of sin due to rejection of the supreme revelation of Yahweh now offered through Jesus himself. Neither the Law given through Moses nor physical descent from Abraham is sufficient to "set them free" from the slavery of sin.

As slaves who in fact serve sin instead of God, they have no real claim to be part of God's household or family, whereas the Son certainly does belong to it by right, and "for ever". "So", he assures them, "if the Son sets you free, you will indeed be free" (vv.35-36). As I. de la Potterie points out, there is a close parallel between becoming "truly disciples" at the start (v.31) and being "really free" at the close of the section (v.36). Furthermore, the theme of liberty is tied in with that of filiation through the revelation and liberating activity of the Son[30]. Following this lead, M. Vellanickal comments: "In the context, as the parallelism shows, it is a freedom that is identified with discipleship. Hence 'to be free' is not simply to be free from sins, but 'to be a disciple'"[31](emphasis added).

When this kind of free person is permanently guided and inspired by the truth accepted interiorly, "the truth thus becomes the law written within the heart which Jeremiah announced as a distinctive trait of the new covenant"[32] (author I. de la Potterie's emphasis). It is therefore as the truth and the life that Jesus is the way to the Father's house (Jn 14,6); he goes ahead to prepare a place, a "mansion", for his brothers and sisters. This is also the fulfilment of an Exodus theme, especially the aspect of God at the head of the Israelites to lead them to a suitable place[33].

The Jews persist in claiming that they have Abraham as their father, and hence that "the only father we have is God". The prolonged debate leads up to the striking declaration of Jesus that, "Before Abraham ever was, I AM" (v.58 — emphasis added to last word). The following chapter continues the theme of light, aptly symbolised by the healing of a blind man, who in turn proves to be a marvellous witness to the significance of that "sign" (c.9). The whole Shelters section is rounded off by the double affirmation of Jesus that, "I am the gate of the sheepfold" and "I am the good shepherd" (10,7.11). Once more he emphasises that he is going to lay down his life voluntarily for his flock — and for those yet to be led into his one flock — in obedience to the "command" received from the Father who loves him (10,17-20).

A 6. The new commandment of love (cc. 13 - 17)

The Last Supper is firmly situated by Jn in an atmosphere of love by the opening comment: "Before the festival of the Passover, Jesus, knowing that his hour had come to pass from this world to the Father, having loved those who were his in the world, loved them to the end" (13,1). "To the end" can also mean "to the very limit", so it could well be that Jn wants us to realise that both meanings are correct. Jesus begins proceedings for the supper by washing the feet of his disciples, then explaining to them that they, too, "must wash each other's feet" (13,2-17). He has to remark pointedly, though, that one of those present is still not "clean", because "he knew who was going to betray him".

A sharp contrast is made between the total love of Jesus for "his own" and his betrayal by Judas, a chosen disciple who has shared his table and his mission. Now Judas is told to leave quickly, so out he goes, away from "the light of the world" and into "the night" (13,28-30).

Once Judas Iscariot has gone off to betray his "Lord and Master", Jesus can expand his farewell instructions to the loyal disciples. Through these disciples Jesus is also speaking, as the Son of man now glorified by the Father, to later disciples. It is a feature of the Farewell Discourse that it is really addressed to true disciples, whereas the first half of Jn had a wider audience in view[34]. That feature must colour our interpretation of the "new commandment" which Jesus announces in connection with his imminent death. He says to his disciples: "I give you a new commandment: love one another; you must love one another just as I have loved you. It is by your love for one another that everyone will recognise you as my disciples" (13,34-35).

The newness of this commandment can be understand in several complementary ways, each of which helps us to appreciate why it is the key commandment for distinguishing the new covenant from the old one. R.E. Brown rightly comments: "The newness of the commandment of love is really related to the theme of covenant at the Last Supper — the 'new commandment' .. is the basic stipulation of the 'new covenant' of Luke xxii 20"[35]. W. Furnish also notes: "It would be fully consonant with his stress on Jesus' mission as one of transforming love, if indeed the Fourth Evangelist is interpreting the 'new covenant' as the 'new commandment' to love one another"[36]. The interior nature of mutual love as described in Jn (and amplified in 1 Jn) is practically identical with the kind of commitment-oriented "knowledge" of God to be given with the new covenant (Jer 31, 31—34). M. Vellanickal notes, "As love is a participation in the life of God, a life of love makes one <u>know God more and more</u>, because 'God is love'"[37].

What is new, therefore, in this commandment to love one another is closely connected with the newness brought by Jesus himself, first as revealer of the greatness of the Father's love. Both by word and conduct Jesus has borne witness to that love, which he knows and experiences personally by being "in the bosom of the Father" (1,18). This leads on to the newness of the standard set by Jesus' own love towards his disciples. In calling on them to love "just as I have loved you", he is asking for a love to the very limit, a self-sacrificing love generous enough to lay down their lives for their friends (cf. 15,12-13).

Closely linked to the above is the newness of the indwelling Paraclete to "remind" them of Jesus' teaching and practical example in many situations. And where the Spirit is dwelling, there too are to be found the Father and Son (14,15-23). The whole Farewell Discourse concludes with Jesus' prayer that the love of the Father towards him might also be in the disciples, and that Jesus himself might be in them(17,26). Hence the new commandment is also a new commitment of Jesus to help his disciples from within to carry out the commandment that will let the whole world recognise them as his disciples.

That the new commandment is presented within a context of inaugurating the new covenant is confirmed by the many passages of the Discourse which speak of the new and everlasting relationships being established between the disciples and God[38]. The predominant relationship is certainly one of loyal love, not only between the disciples themselves, but also with Jesus their "friend" (cf.15,14-15). That in turn is closely linked to both Jesus and the disciples being loved by the Father and loving him in return. Their love of Jesus must be made manifest by keeping his commandments, just as he has kept his Father's commandments (14,31; 15,10).

A strong emphasis is also placed on the unity made possible through fully committed love. So close is the union of the parties involved in the new covenant that they may remain permanently with one another, thanks to the abiding presence of the Paraclete and of the glorified Jesus. In the parable of the true vine, Jesus exhorts the disciples to remain in him as he remains in them to maintain in them the sap of life and love (15,1-17). The close dependence of the disciples' unity upon the unity of Father and Son is brought out in the culminating prayer of Jesus(esp.17,22-23). Furthermore, the goal of the new covenant is to ensure that its faithful members may remain united for ever in the Father's house. Jesus' imminent departure will make it possible for him to secure this for his disciples (14,2-3). He also intercedes for them: "Father, I want those you have given me to be with me where I am" (17,24). Such a reunion does not have to wait till each disciple gets to heaven. There are many indications that through union with the risen Lord, who has replaced the old Temple (2,21-22), the disciples are already "in the Father's house"[39].

There is also the abiding peace promised and experienced thanks to the new relationship of faithful love. Their departing Friend assures them, "Peace I bequeath to you, my own peace I give you, a peace which the world cannot give, this is my gift to you" (14,27; cf.16,33). After "passing to the Father", the risen Jesus can greet them with the salutation, "peace be with you"

(20,19.21.26). Suffice it to recall here that peace sums up the fruits of a well kept covenant.

Finally, the divine covenants each had a "sign" to remind people of the continuing commitment of both parties. For the covenant with Noah's family, the sign was the rainbow; for that with Abraham's family, it was circumcision; for the Mosaic covenant it was the sabbath rest. For the new covenant, the sign is to be loyal family love within the entire community. The Discourse's concentration on mutual love among the disciples, however, is far from making theirs a closed community. On the contrary, their manifest mutual love should act as a constant invitation drawing "everyone" (13,35) to interest themselves in the Christian community[40].

A 7. The risen Lord confirms the new covenant (cc. 20-21)

In this section we will consider only the appearance to Mary Magdalene in Jerusalem and the other to Simon Peter at the Sea of Galilee. The first indicates how Mary's loyal love was reciprocated by the risen Jesus, whereas the second portrays the reconfirmation of Peter in his love for the Master whom he had denied under pressure.

A 7. a) The appearance to Mary Magdalene (20,1-18)

It was "still dark" in more ways than one when Mary came back to the tomb where she had seen her beloved Lord laid to rest. Yet another blow struck her grieving heart when she saw that the tomb had been opened, presumably to "take away the Lord", as she rapidly reported to Peter and the beloved disciple (vv.1-2). After those two disciples had investigated the situation and confirmed that the tomb was empty, Mary remained "standing outside near the tomb, weeping". Two angels inside the tomb asked her why she was weeping. Then she saw Jesus himself standing nearby, without recognising him. He also asked why she was weeping. Soon he spoke her own name,"Mary!", and with joyful recognition she exclaimed, "Rabbuni!"(vv.11-16).

As Mary, in her joy at finding Jesus alive again, was clinging to him, he commissioned her to go as his apostle to the other disciples, saying, "Go and find my brothers, and tell them: I am ascending to my Father and your Father, to my God and your God" (v. 17). A. Feuillet describes the ascending mentioned here as "the definitive conclusion of the new covenant in virtue of which Christ will be the brother of men, his Father will be their Father, and his God their God"[41](emphasis added). Mary Magdalene thus becomes the herald of the immediate fruits of the passion and glorification of Jesus, namely that he has now become the elder brother who can lead all his brothers and sisters to the one great God and Father of them all. Through him God is proclaiming in effect, "I am your Father, and your are my family" — the perfect form of covenant.

A 7. b)   The renewal of the covenant for Simon Peter (c.21)

Ch. 21 comes as an epilogue to the gospel, which already has a conclusion at the end of c.20. It seems to be from a writer other than the main evangelist, but obviously from the same circle of disciples as the evangelist[42]. Because it has been added on to a completed gospel, the epilogue may actually be describing the first meeting of Peter with the risen Jesus, and that would explain the need to let Peter renew his allegiance and be reassured of his standing as a disciple[43].

The setting is "by the Sea of Tiberias", after a breakfast graciously prepared and handed by Jesus to the seven fishermen, as soon as they have managed to drag ashore their great netful of big fish. Something in the way Jesus gives them the bread and fish helps those astonished disciples to recognise him. It is also an excellent occasion on which to let Peter know that sharing such a meal implies that he is again an acceptable disciple and companion of Jesus (vv.1-14). Nevertheless, Peter's triple denial, after protesting that he would be willing to die for Jesus, calls for an equally strong affirmation of his loyal love from now on. It is noteworthy that Peter's profession of sturdy faith in Jesus had been elicited after the first miracle of the loaves and fishes, and somewhere along the bank of this same lake (6,67-69).

"When they had eaten, Jesus said to Simon Peter, "Simon son of John, do you love me more than these others do?" Peter, avoiding any "odious comparisons", promptly replies, "Yes, Lord, you know I love you." Jesus obviously accepts this as true, for he commissions Peter, "Feed my lambs" (v.15). Instead of concluding the exchange at that high point, Jesus asks Peter twice more, "Simon.., do you love me?" Peter is understandably "hurt" by the persistence of the soul-searching. He equivalently swears the truth of his declaration: "Lord, you know everything; you know I love you" (vv.16-17). This time Jesus not only reiterates Peter's special role in feeding the flock, he also predicts that Peter will be led by others to his death. That is a gentle way of accepting that now Peter's protestation about being willing to lay down his life for his Lord (13,37) can be taken seriously. His commitment to the covenant of love is now "to the end"; henceforth he will be able to follow the way shown so impressively by his crucified and risen Master.

Peter's faith and love — we might word it as his loyal love — are closely related in the epilogue to the nourishing of the whole Church, described by Jesus as "my lambs" and "my sheep". In Jn, as we have seen, the "bread of life" indispensable for eternal life is Jesus himself, especially as the revelation of God and as the Eucharist. R.E. Brown gives good reasons for considering the epilogue as a mature attempt on the part of the redactor to show that Peter's special pastoral role and martyr's witness is compatible with the beloved disciple's role in his particular community. In that community the emphasis was evidently on the constant witness of love given by "the disciple whom Jesus loved", together with great reliance on the inner teaching by the Paraclete[44]. The fourth gospel thus closes with the assurance that ample provision has been made by Jesus for the members of his flock to live out fully his new commandment and, by so doing, to draw others into their fellowship.

B. NEW COVENANT IN THE EPISTLES OF JOHN

Like the last chapter of John's gospel, so too the three epistles of John present many indications that the author was distinct from the main evangelist of Jn. On the other hand, it is feasible to regard all three epistles as the work of a single author[45]. Although different writers were probably involved, there is no doubt about a common tradition and outlook underlying Jn and the three Johannine epistles. R. E. Brown has worked through the plausible theory that 1 Jn was written after Jn cc.1-20, and in order to tackle the serious problem caused by a break-away group from the Johannine circle, that is, from the beloved disciple's community[46].

1. Love of God demands and inspires love of one another

The main themes in 1 and 2 Jn develop what we have already seen in Jn, but their stress on love of one another as the inescapable demand of divine love warrants further attention. The epistles describe an interior communion with God and a corresponding love for one another which reach the ideal relationship expected between partners pledged to the new covenant. E. Malatesta has fully justified the promising title of his book on such aspects of 1 Jn — "Interiority and Covenant"[47]. He finds that, "The structure of the author's theology thus seems to be based upon the actual fulfillment of the promises of the New Covenant as announced by Jeremiah and Ezekiel. The realities promised are received in terms of the new relationships thus created between the members of the Christian community with each other, with God, and with the universe"[48]. Following the same line, G. Panikulam finds: "The three main divisions [of 1 Jn] successively and ever more profoundly treat the general theme of the criteria of fellowship. They are arranged almost in parallel and <u>develop the new covenant themes</u> of forgiveness of sins, knowledge of God and the observance of the commandments understood in terms of faith and love"[49](emphasis added). All that we can take up here is 1 Jn's insistence on genuine love as the criterion of a real Christian.

The theme of loving one another occurs in strategic places throughout 1 Jn. For example, in c.2 the "new commandment" is mentioned (v.8), then comes the sharp contrast: "Anyone who loves his brother remains in light .. But whoever hates his brother is in darkness" (vv.10-11). The following chapter is still more forceful on the contrast: "We have passed over from death to life because we love our brothers. Whoever does not love, remains in death. Anyone who hates his brother is a murderer" (3,14-15). Love must be practical like that of Christ, who "laid down his life for us". Important for today's world is the question springing from Christ's example: "If anyone is well off in worldly possessions and sees his brother in need but closes his heart to him, how can the love of God be remaining in him?" (3,17).

The section with the most sustained reflection on love runs from 4,7 to 5,13. It opens with the moving exhortation: "My dear friends, let us love each other, since love is from God .. Whoever fails to love does not know God, because <u>God is love</u>" (4,7-8). Knowledge of God in the O.T. sense includes an inner conviction and personal commitment. In that sense, a person who lacks love simply cannot know God. Then we are told that God has taken the initiative to give us that kind of experiential knowledge by sending "his only Son into the world" (4,9), revealing how much he loved us. When we love one another, "<u>God</u> <u>remains</u> in us, and <u>his love comes to its perfection in us</u>" (4,12). Having empowered us to love properly, God sustains our love by remaining within us.

2. The Spirit brings Christians an indwelling and knowledge of God

The proof of his abiding presence within us is "that he has given us a share in his Spirit" (4,13). Here again there is a prominent feature of the promised new covenant, namely the imparting of God's own Spirit to transform hardened hearts into truly human hearts, hearts open to God and compassionate towards others. Reference has been made earlier (2,20.27) to an anointing of the community members, which would include the action of both the word of Jesus and the counsel of the Spirit[50]. In this epistle, as E Malatesta comments, "The Holy Spirit mediates our communion with Jesus, with the Father and with each other"[51]. The Spirit really inspires us to relate properly to all involved in the new covenant, and to be open towards those who have not yet entered into it. The universal aspect of love within the community is seen in its public testimony that "the Father has sent the Son as <u>Saviour of the world</u>" (4,14).

The abiding presence of God in the believer is intimately connected with mutual love, because "<u>God is love</u>, and whoever abides in love <u>remains in God</u> and <u>God in him</u>" (4,16). This kind of relationship of "mutual remaining" is justifiably hailed as "perhaps the most perfect expression the N.T. gives us of our life in this world according to the New Covenant"[52]. God's presence <u>within</u> the people is transforming, enlightening, and inspiring. It "casts out fear" (4,18), and rules out hatred of a brother or sister — "whoever loves the father loves the son" (5,1). As in Jn, so also here we are told that love of God is shown by "keeping his commandments" (5,2-3; also 2 Jn 6). As F.F. Bruce comments on this verse, "the test of love and the test of obedience are seen to be not two tests, but one"[53]. In the same vein R.E. Brown comments that God "gives the commandment to love because He is love. The Word that became flesh and the word that says we should love one another are intertwined in Johannine thought"[54].

After recalling the primacy of love, the section then concentrates on the origin and importance of faith. Here again we note that both Jesus and the Spirit are involved in giving the testimony on which true faith must be grounded. In saying that "Jesus Christ [came] with water and blood, and it is the Spirit that bears witness, for the Spirit is Truth" (5,6), the author recalls the scene on Golgotha so solemnly attested by Jn 19,34-37, together with the solemn promises of Jesus to send his disciples "another Paraclete .. the Spirit of truth" (Jn 14,16-17).

The blood and water coming from the pierced side of Jesus, who had voluntarily offered himself as a paschal sacrifice on the cross, have enormous significance because Jesus was "the Son of God" (1 Jn 5,5) right through to death (and glorification). The water and blood are also symbols of the Spirit and life that welled forth from Jesus as he sealed the new covenant by his sacrifice. Because 1 Jn stresses communion and not covenant, many commentators see allusions to baptism and eucharist, the visible community celebrations through which the life of the glorified Jesus Christ is imparted to his disciples[55]. The role of the Spirit is to help the disciples from within to grasp and appreciate always more fully the revelation given in Jesus. This is summed up in the closing lines of the epistle: "We are well aware also that the Son of God has come and has given us <u>understanding</u> so that we may know the One who is true" (5,20).

The word "understanding" has been underlined in the preceding text because it recalls quite literally "the heart" of Jeremiah's promise concerning the new covenant: "<u>Within them</u> I shall plant my Law, writing it <u>on their hearts</u>" (31,33). The Greek (LXX) text for that sentence in Jeremiah uses the same word, "understanding", that is used by 1 Jn, and only used in this one text. Both E. Malatesta and R E. Brown draw attention to the covenantal aspects of its use here. The latter comments: "5:20 echoes in several ways covenantal vocabulary and imagery. God is referred to as 'the One who is true', even as **'emet**, 'truth, fidelity', is the primary attribute of the covenanting God of the OT. .. As we have seen before, knowing God is a motif fulfilling the promise of Jeremiah about a renewed covenant where 'they shall all know me from the least to the greatest'"[56].

Another more general observation of Malatesta merits attention. He asserts: "<u>With the Incarnation</u> of the Son of God <u>the New Covenant was inaugurated</u> in the Person of Jesus. .. <u>Through the Paschal Mystery</u> the most perfect expression of the communion between the Father and the Son, <u>the New Covenant, was extended</u> to all those who would accept Jesus in faith and love"[57] (emphasis added). My own view throughout this present work is that the new covenant was not sufficiently inaugurated to replace the Mosaic covenant until it had been adequately proclaimed, accepted, and sealed with "the blood of the new covenant". With that in mind I have stressed the essential part played by the complete and frequently articulated acceptance of the Father's will by the human will of Jesus.

The events of the Last Supper, Agony, and Calvary all united to express that acceptance "to the limit", on his own behalf and on behalf of the entire human family. It was only then that, as Son of man, Jesus fulfilled all the "commandment" of the Father necessary to inaugurate, and not merely to extend, the new covenant. Needless to say, I fully accept that the Incarnation was the giant step towards "the hour" of Jesus, but until that "hour" had come and been voluntarily accepted, the new covenant had not been formally established either. As we shall see in the following chapter, even after the new covenant had been publicly inaugurated and then confirmed by the abundant outpouring of the Spirit at Pentecost, the disciples needed a long time to realise that it was adequate to replace the Mosaic covenant and not simply to renew it or complement it.

NOTES

1. Cf. C.H. Dodd, The Interpretation of the Fourth Gospel (Cambridge: Cambridge University Press, 1968) 199: "If now we are thinking of union with God, is not love, as a matter of fact, the only kind of union between persons of which we can have any possible experience?(author's emphasis)."
2. Cf.: Ibid. 297-389 on "The Book of Signs". R.E. Brown, The Gospel According to John, I-XII (New York: Anchor Bible, Doubleday, 1966). Apart from the Prologue, the text is treated as within "The Book of Signs".
3. Cf. R.E.Brown, The Gospel According to John, XIII-XXI (continuation of the above Anchor Bible Commentary, 1970). In this volume, all the text apart from the Epilogue (c.21) is treated as part of "The Book of Glory".
4. Cf.: Id., I-XIII, XCVIII -CII where "the authority behind the Fourth Gospel tradition" was considered by an ancient tradition to have been John, the son of Zebedee. In any case, a "disciple-writer" was used, and then a final redactor was a different close disciple. However, R.E. Brown, The Epistles of John (Anchor Bible 30, 1982) 510 is less inclined now to identify the Beloved Disciple as John, son of Zebedee.
5. Nueva Biblia Española, 1649.
6. I. de la Potterie, Studi Di Cristologia Giovannea (Genova: Marietti, 1986^2,261. Id., La Vérité Dans Saint Jean (Rome: Biblical Institute, 1977

- 2 Tomes), I, 2-3, where he claims that for John's theology, revelation is central, and that God has revealed himself in Jesus Christ. The Incarnation therefore commands all the thought of John. Cf. R. Schnackenburg, The Gospel according to John (3 Vols.) (New York: Vol. 1: E.T. by K. Smyth, Herder and Herder, 1968) 160: "In John, however, the stongest motive is the Christology, which shows the glory of the Logos still dwelling in the earthly Jesus, and the power of the exalted and glorified Lord already present in his word and work of salvation. In John, Christ is really the 'eschatological present'."
7. Cf.: M. Vellanickal, The Divine Sonship of Christians in the Johannine Writings, 127, where he says that "Father" for God occurs 115 times in Jn and 16 times in John's Epistles.
8. Cf. R. Schnackenburg, op.cit. Vol.2 (New York: E.T. by C. Hastings and others, The Crossroad, 1982) 172.
9. Ibid.
10. M. Vellanickal, op.cit. 161. Cf. p.1: "Taking as the determinative concept Jesus' favorite name for God, Father, John interprets the ideal relationship of men to God as that of spiritual children, having the life — eternal — from the Father."
11. Cf.: Ibid., 14-15. W. Marchel, '**Abba**, Père!'— La Prière du Christ et des Chrétiens (Rome: Biblical Institute, 1971^2)165.
12. Cf. D. M. Stanley, 'I Encountered God' — The Spiritual Exercises with the Gospel of St John (St. Louis: Institute of Jesuit Sources, 1986) 47-48: "'He pitched his tent among us' recalls the desert experience of Israel, when her God dwelt under canvas as a divine camper in her midst, and so serves to introduce the covenant theme, which is shortly to be discreetly suggested by the author" (emphasis added). Stanley proceeds to comment on the phrase, "full of graciousness and truth" (which he gives as "the poet's rendering" of **hesed** and **'emeth**).
13. R.E. Brown, The Gospel according to John, 35. Cf. 16: (On his translation, "love in place of love"): "This idea of replacement .. connotes the **hesed** of a New Covenant in place of the **hesed** of Sinai." Cf. I. de la Potterie, La Vérité.., 160 (on Jn 1,17): "Si Moïse avait été le médiateur choisi par Dieu pour la première révélation, celle du Sinaï, Jésus Christ, par le don de la vérité, est devenu le médiateur de la révélation définitive, celle de la nouvelle Alliance."
14. Cf. Cf. M.E. Boismard, St. John's Prologue (London: Blackfriars, 1957), 139-140. Cf. 142.
15. P. Lamarche: "The Prologue of John" in J. Ashton (Ed.), The Interpretation of John (London, SPCK, 1986), 36-52; quotation is from 39. Cf. N.A. Dahl: "The Johannine Church and History", in same

publication, 122-140), esp. 123: "From the beginning it is made clear that the mission of Jesus is a mission to the world."
16. Cf. D. Stanley, op.cit., 21.
17. Cf. I. de la Potterie, La Passion de Jésus selon l'évangile de Jean — Texte et Esprit (Paris: Cerf, 1986) 167-181, e.g. 1180: "Le dernier souffle de Jésus symbolise le don de l'Esprit."
18. Id., Studi di Cristologia.., 287. Also 288, where he notes that (in Jn) both Jesus and the Spirit are in the disciples after the glorification of Jesus. Moreover, "L'insegnamento dello Spirito coinciderà quindi con l'insegnamento interiore di Gesù." Cf. id., La Vérité.., I,279—471 on close bond between the Spirit and the Truth in Jn.
19. D. Senior, The Biblical Foundations for Mission, 287.
20. W. Marchel, 'Abba, Père!'.., 217: "Ramener les hommes a la maison du Père et leur conférer l'adoption filiale, c'était le but de la mission de Jésus. Or, l'activité intérieure de Christ ressuscité dans le chrétien est inséparable de celle de l'esprit Saint: elle ne s'exerce que par lui. C'est l'Esprit qui réalise et achève l'oeuvre du Christ."
21. Cf. footnotes to Jn 1,29-2,1 in the N.J.B. (re "first week").
22. Cf. I. de la Potterie, La Passion.., 11; and 148-149.
23. R.E.Brown, op.cit. 931; cf. 913; 926. Cf. C.H.Dodd, op. cit., 142: "(Yet) in the development of the argument we discover that Christ's work of giving life and light is accomplished in reality and actuality, by the historical act of His death and resurrection. In that sense, every **semeion** [=sign] in the narrative points forward to the great climax."
24. J. Navone and T. Cooper, The Story of the Passion, 414; cf. 296.
25. R. Schnackenburg, op.cit. 2,79 (which is the opening page of a good Excursus, 79-89, on the "I AM" texts in Jn).
26. Cf.: P.F. Ellis, The Genius of John: — A Composition-Critical Commentary on the Fourth Gospel (Collegeville: Liturgical Press, 1984), 107-111, on Jn 6,16-21, esp. 110: "The walking on the waters serves in John, therefore, as a transition (it happens at night) between the multiplication of the loaves on the one day and the explanation of the loaves as the Eucharist on the next day. .. It allows him to place greater emphasis on the sea scene as a new exodus event" (emphasis added). Also: J. Huckle and P. Visokay, The Gospel according to St John, Vol. 1 (New York: Herder & Herder, 1981), 84 where they also draw attention to the reminiscences of the exodus sea crossing and the subsequent manna in the wilderness — events recalled by the Passover that Jn 6 refers to explicitly. On 92 they also note the connection between Jesus' promise to give his blood as drink and the Sinai blood-sprinkling.
27. Cf. R.E. Brown, op.cit., 272.

28. R. Schnackenburg, op.cit. 2,77.
29. Cf.: I. de la Potterie, La Vérité., II, 816-825.   R.E. Brown, op.cit., 319-327 (on Tabernacles as a feast of "light and water").   P. Perkins, "The Gospel according to John", in N.J.B.C. 963-9.   R. Russell, "St John" in N.C.C.H.S., 1023-1026, where he points out the main factors which create the impression that "the Gospel is a kind of vast lawsuit between the Jews (or 'the world') and Jesus".
30. Cf. I. de la Potterie, op.cit., II, 827.
31. M. Vellanickal, op. cit., 290.   Cf. V-M. Capdevila i Montaner, Liberación y Divinización del Hombre — Teología de la Gracia, Tomo I: La Teología de la Gracia en el Evangelio y en las Cartas de San Juan (Salamanca: Secretariado Trinitario, 1984), 81-86.   R. Schnackenburg, op.cit. 3,394: "Johannine theology does mankind (which has to withstand the threatening future) an invaluable service. For it turns our gaze on man's inner powers, providing him with something to cling on to — a foothold in the darkness and turmoil of the world. .. In Jesus Christ the believer who understands the message of John's gospel gains a firm hold on the present and the future, and is directed to <u>brotherly love as the decisive norm</u> of his action" (emphasis added).
32. I. de la Potterie, La Vérité ..II, 849; cf. 850-866.
33. Ibid., I,241-278.
34. J. Blank, The Gospel according to St John, Vol.2 (New York: E.T. by M. O'Connell, The Crossroad, 1981) 39: "The first farewell discourse begins after the departure of Judas the traitor. Now that a division has been effected in the inner circle of disciples, Jesus is in the presence only of those who are his truly faithful followers, his own in the full sense of the words. This fact determines the group to whom the discourse is addressed."
35. R.E. Brown, op.cit. 614.
36. V. Furnish, The Love Command in the N.T., 138.   Cf.:   D. Senior, op.cit. 282.   S. Lyonnet, In Dialogo Col Mondo (Roma: AVE, 1987) 94: After recalling how the O.T. already reveals the law of love, in teaching that men and women are created in the image of God, a God of love, Lyonnet notes what is new: "Il precetto di Cristo, qual è stato da lui <u>promulgato durante l'istituzione eucaristica</u>, offre, rispetto a quello in cui 'si compendiavano la legge e i profeti', una significativa differenza. .. Proprio quando si offre per noi alla morte e alla morte in croce, Cristo dichiara ai discepoli: 'Amatevi gli uni agli altri come io vi ho amato' " (emphasis added)."
37. M. Vellanickal, op.cit., 316. Also 300: "Hence the brotherly love is the very expression of the communicated divine life which unites the children

of God into one family of God, which, though actually realized in the Christian Community, is virtually and dynamically oriented to the whole of mankind through Christ."

38. Cf. V. Furnish, op.cit., 200, who points out that the noun **agape** [=love] is used 116 times in the N.T., and the verb **agapan** [to love] occurs 141 times, whereas it it is not found in Greek sources prior to the LXX.
39. Cf.: P. Perkins, art.cit., N.J.B.C. 978-9. V-M Capdevilla i Montaner, op.cit. 122: "Veremos que [en Jn] la unión con Jesús lleva consigo la unión con el Padre. Y se realiza per el don del Espíritu Santo."
40. Cf. R. Schnackenburg, op.cit., 3,53-55, e.g. 55: "Love as a sign by which Jesus's disciples can be known points to the future of the community. ... There are many patristic texts which bear witness to [the] high esteem in which brotherly love was held in the early Church as well as the way in which it was realized."
41. A. Feuillet, "Le Recherche du Christ Dans la Nouvelle Alliance D'Après la Christophanie de Jn 20,11-18", in Mélanges offerts au Père Henri de Lubac: L'Homme Devant Dieu. I: Exégèse et Patristique (Aubier: Montaigne, 1963) 93-112. Part quoted is from 101. Cf. J. Alonso Schökel, '¿Dónde está tu hermano?', 323, commenting on Jn 20,17: "La hermandad es pues contenido fundamental del mensaje pascual. ... La hermandad que establece Cristo, por su fuerza, exigencia, y extensión, es más profunda y más alta y más consistente que la hermandad simplemente humana." R. Schnackenburg, op.cit., 3,319: "Now is the hour of Jesus' ascent to the Father, and that means for his 'brethren' that he is preparing a place of them also with the Father, that he mediates that fellowship with God for them, which he had foretold them to be the fruit of his departure."
42. Cf.: R.E. Brown, op.cit., 1080-1081. R. Schnackenburg, op.cit., 3,349-351, e.g.350: "Looked at on the whole, the origin of 21:1-23 as being from the evangelist cannot be defended. At the most, the editors who are here at work, could have received some traditions from him (and then, presumably orally)."
43. Cf. R.E. Brown, op.cit. 1085-1087.
44. Cf. Ibid., 1112-1122. Id., The Epistles of John (New York: Anchor Bible, Doubleday, 1982) 70-71: "How a need for structure and a reluctant Community tradition were ultimately reconciled may be illustrated symbolically by John 21, which assigns to Peter, one of the Twelve, an authoritative pastoral care of Jesus' sheep, but still gives preference to the Beloved Disciple who received no such role." Also 110-112 and 510. R.E. Brown, K.P. Donfried and J. Reumann (Eds.), Peter in the New Testament, 146: (On Jn 21): "No confession of love needs to be drawn

from the Beloved Disciple who has never denied Jesus, but neither does he receive a specific commission as a shepherd. In a certain sense he needs no special commission to be what he is, for he is the Beloved of Jesus. Yet both these men are witnesses. Simon's martyrdom is a witness consonant with his shepherd's duty of laying down his life." R. Schnackenburg, op.cit., 3, 369: "Without belittling Peter's authority, the Johannine circles want to enhance the reputation of their founder and master, precisely through Peter who receives Jesus' answer."

45. Cf. R.E. Brown, The Epistles of John, 19; 30; 35.
46. Ibid., 1-3. Id.. The Community of the Beloved Disciple (London: C. Chapman, 1979) 31-34; and 93-144 on "When the Epistles were written — Johannine internal struggles."
47. E. Malatesta, Interiority and Covenant — A Study of 'einai 'en and menein 'en in the First Letter of St John. He divides the Epistle into three Parts, each Part having a heading which begins: "Interiority and the New Covenant Communion with God.. "who is Light" (I), "who is Just" (II), "who is Love" (III) (emphasis added). In other words, he considers the entire epistle as revolving around the interiority and communion with God which are characteristic of the new covenant.
48. Ibid., 78. Also 79: "The author's theology of the interiority of the New Covenant is thus itself an experience of this interiority, a mirror in which the author sees himself, a mirror which he places before his readers, inviting them to see themselves with him as sharers in the communion with God proper to the New Covenant" (emphasis added).
49. G. Panikulam, Koinonia in the N.T., 130.
50. Cf. I. de la Potterie, "Unzione..", in La Vita Secondo lo Spirito (Roma: I.T. by T.Federici, A.V.E., 1971^2) 199: "Il termine chrisma [=anointing] non s'applica esclusivamente ad uno dei due insegnamenti, ma si applica coestensivamente alla Parola de Gesù ed all'illuminazione dello Spirito Santo."
51. Cf. E. Malatesta, op.cit., 304.
52. Ibid. 308. Also 24 and 29.
53. F.F. Bruce, The Epistles of John (Grand Rapids: Eerdmans, 1970) 117.
54. R.E. Brown, op.cit. 554.
55. Ibid., 594-599.
56. Ibid., 639-640. Cf. E. Malatesta, op.cit., 319-321.
57. E. Malatesta, op.cit., 323. Also 324: "John teaches us that Christian interiority and Christian community are complementary and inseparable dimensions of life according to the New Covenant."

CHAPTER 12: NEW COVENANT IN THE EPISTLES AND APOCALYPSE

In this final chapter on the new covenant as described in the New Testament, we will be looking at some of the earliest and latest texts of the N.T., namely from 1 Thessalonians through to the Apocalypse (or Revelation). The former was written about 50 A.D., the latter about 95 A.D. In between those extremes came the other Pauline epistles, plus Hebrews and the seven "catholic" (or general) epistles. The most explicit and penetrating treatment of all the N.T. on the new covenant is found in the epistle to the Hebrews. In other epistles there are also plenty of indications that the early Christian churches were being urged to live according to the new covenant. As for the Apocalypse, it is almost overwhelming in its picturesque presentation of Jesus Christ as the Alpha and Omega of all creation, leading the people of Israel and the Church to their definitive liberation and perfection in the new city of God. There God "will make his home among them; they will be his people, and he will be their God" (Apoc 21,3).

With regard to the authorship of the Pauline epistles, P.F. Ellis has summed up the opinions of modern scholars: "Of the fourteen letters attributed to Paul, only seven are unanimously accepted today as authentic: 1 Thessalonians, Galatians, Philippians, 1 and 2 Corinthians, Romans and Philemon. Three letters are debatably authentic: 2 Thessalonians, Colossians, and Ephesians. Three are very doubtful: 1 and 2 Timothy, Titus. One is certainly not authentic: Hebrews"[1]. Here we follow the traditional opinion that those three "debatably authentic" letters are from Paul, whereas the Pastoral epistles (1 and 2 Tim., Titus) show more signs of being from an author distinct from Paul. The letter to the Hebrews is reasonably classed as certainly not from the hand of Paul. All of which serves to underline the freedom of God to inspire the writers whom he considered best suited to convey his message in writing. To accept the evidence that writers other than Paul were responsible for the Pastorals and Hebrews permits the reader to perceive a different orientation and emphasis in them, when they are compared with the more obviously authentic letters of Paul.

We will consider first some of the more striking passages of the Pauline epistles, mainly in the order of their composition, then Hebrews and the catholic epistles, leaving the Apocalypse till the end.

A. IN 1 THESSALONIANS

Paul helped to found the church in the port city of Thessalonica in Macedonia (northern Greece) during his second missionary journey. Fairly soon after leaving that little community Paul received good news of their progress in the faith. It was about 51 A.D. when he wrote them his first known letter, which is also the earliest of the N.T. writings. With the happiness and kindly concern of a father he wrote to encourage the Thessalonians "to live a life worthy of God" (2,12). What is highly significant for our theme is the way

Paul bases his appeal for a worthy Christian life on the fact that the Thessalonians have been called to become the "church of God". As such they are enabled by God's Spirit to show forth the holiness and love which should characterise the new covenant people.

The letter is addressed "to the Church in Thessalonica which is in God the Father and the Lord Jesus Christ" (1,1). That description enriches the O.T. phrase, "the assembly of God", by adding the title of "Father" to God and by speaking of the Church as being at the same time "in the Lord Jesus Christ". Paul also takes it as understood that God the Father is calling them "into his kingdom and glory" (2,12). He also goes on to recall that they have modelled themselves "on the churches of God in Christ Jesus which are in Judaea" (2,14). In other words, the little Christian Community just formed in Europe is a church that looks on the earliest churches founded around Judaea as models that it is now capable of following. Commenting on the use of "church" and other related terms in these opening chapters of 1 Thess, T. J. Deidun remarks: "Thus within a few months of the evangelisation of Thessalonica, Paul can address the community there in terms which presuppose that its members think of themselves as belonging to God's chosen People"[2]. The whole of Deidun's study highlights "the centrality of the New Covenant in Paul's theology"[3].

In ch.3 Paul mentions Timothy's report of their faith and love (v.6), then he prays that "the Lord may increase and enrich your love for each other and for all" (v.12). Clearly, Paul is as aware as John of the importance of mutual love within the community, and that Christian love must at the same time be universal in its outreach to "all" Such love is inseparably linked to holiness, hence Paul's prayer continues: "And may [the Lord] so confirm your hearts in holiness that you may be blameless in the sight of our God and Father when our Lord Jesus comes" (v.13).

It is in ch.4 that we find the most striking references to the interior action of God as promised for the people of the new covenant, and as being fulfilled in the faithful church at Thessalonica. In his exhortation to them, Paul is urging them to "make more progress still" (v.1). God's will is that they be holy (vv.3 and 7), a demand which they cannot reject without rejecting God, "who gives you his Holy Spirit" (v.8). God's will requires a corresponding acceptance of it by the Christian's will. In the knowledge and carrying out of God the Father's will we have the basic acceptance of the new covenant, as well as the practical manifestation of both the holiness and love mentioned earlier. Paul himself adds here: "As for brotherly love, there is no need to write to you about that, since you have yourselves learnt from God to love one another, and in fact this is how you treat all the brothers" (vv.9-10).

The way Paul speaks in this chapter of God giving his Spirit to help the Thessalonians live up to God's calling of them to holiness, is quite close to the promise: "I shall put my spirit in you, and make you keep my laws" (Ez 36,27; cf. 37,6). The way the Thessalonians have been taught by God is also a reference to the promises concerning the new covenant (cf. Is 54,13 and Jer 31,34). T.J. Deidun is justified in saying that, "by utilising the parallel texts of Jeremiah and Ezechiel in 1 Thess. 4,8b-9, Paul wishes to recall to the

Thessalonians their unique Covenant relationship with God"[4]. To be taught by God is much more than abstract or theoretical knowledge; it is the kind of biblical knowledge which results in action consistent with personal conviction and commitment to what is properly known. God's giving of his Holy Spirit and God teaching the Christian are therefore two aspects of the same inner power at work in the heart and mind of the Christian, who must voluntarily make his own the holiness and love stirring his heart to a wholehearted surrender to God and a generous commitment to the whole community. As Deidun rightly insists, "it is only in the light of the People theme — that is, for Paul, in the light of the New Covenant — that we can understand why Paul's exhortations to christian love most frequently envisage love within the community. .. Christian **agape** [=love] is the fulfilment of the New Covenant, whereby God puts his own will in the hearts of the members of his Church to make of it the beginning of a transformed humanity"[5].

B. IN 1 - 2 CORINTHIANS

The church in Corinth, a bustling port city of Achaia (southern Greece), was also founded by Paul and his fellow-workers during the second missionary journey, only a few months after Paul had left Thessalonica. His two surviving letters to the Corinthians were written during the third missionary journey (c.54-58 A.D.), during which he was able to revisit those Christians as well as write to them. In both these major epistles Paul deals directly with the many divisions and questions that had arisen during his absence, hence both letters are primarily his response to particular questions and local anxieties, including the serious questioning of Paul's own standing as a genuine apostle of Christ.

The new covenant is mentioned explicitly only once in each of these epistles, but it can be discerned as the basis of many other passages as well. The introduction to the first epistle speaks of "the church of God in Corinth" being called by God to fellowship "with his Son Jesus Christ our Lord" (1 Cor 1,2.9), then the second epistle closes with the wish that "the fellowship of the Holy Spirit be with you all" (2 Cor 13,13). It is no exaggeration to say that Paul bases his teaching concerning the Corinthians' call to holiness and unity on their "fellowship" in both Jesus Christ and the Holy Spirit, just as he bases his own apostolate on being a "minister of the new covenant, a covenant .. of the Spirit" (2 Cor 3,6). The communitarian (and equally covenantal) dimension of "fellowship" is well brought out by G. Panikulam: "Paul never uses **koinonia** for the individual sharing of someone in Christ. It is always used for someone's sharing in Christ with others. .. and fellowship with one another in Christ for him is the ideal Christian community"[6].

B 1. 1 Corinthians

In the opening lines, Paul addresses the letter to "the church of God in Corinth, .. called to be God's holy people" (1,2). As in 1 Thessalonians, so also here, the church of God corresponds to the O.T. "assembly of Yahweh", as we see confirmed here by Paul's remark that this church in turn is now called to be

"God's holy people". Paul's very frequent use of "church" in this particular epistle serves to emphasise his concern that the Corinthian Christians realise the implications of being the people of the new covenant. The remainder of the epistle tells them some of those implications.

The first problem to be tackled is that of the divisions and factions at Corinth, a contradiction of their commitment to Christ and to one another in real fellowship (cc.1-4). Paul explains that his manner of preaching the gospel to them in the first place had relied on the power and wisdom that comes from God. In fact, he insists, Jesus Christ for us was made wisdom from God (1,30). As J.A. Davis rightly notes, "it is quite possible to interpret the manifestation of wisdom at Corinth and Paul's critical response to its phenomena against the background of later sapiential Judaism"[7]. In later Judaism, wisdom is presented not only as coming from God to his people, but also as being enshrined in the Law and being imparted to those open to the spirit of Yahweh. What is new here in Paul is that divine wisdom is now being made available more abundantly through Christ Jesus and through the gift of the Holy Spirit to those who accept Christ with faith and love[8].

Convinced that true wisdom is a gift freely imparted through Christ and the Spirit, Paul had not posed as an ordinary Greek "lover of wisdom" — the familiar academic philosopher — but as an obedient servant offering "the mysterious wisdom of God" (2,7). The Corinthians who have formed factions around Paul or Apollos show thereby that they still do not appreciate God's form of wisdom. God is the "farmer", the "architect", the "builder", who alone can bring the plant to full growth, or the building to be a living temple wherein the Spirit may dwell (c.3). That dignity makes its demand on the individual Christian, too, so that sexual immorality is a desecration of the Holy Spirit's dwelling place (6, 12-20). Hence the abundance of the Spirit brings with it a more serious demand on the Christian to live according to the Spirit. The demands of Christian fellowship are also operative when any dispute is to be settled "between brothers". They must not drag one another before non-Christian tribunals (6,1-11).

Cc. 8-10 answer difficulties arising out of the way meat offered to idols could become available for Christians to eat. Paul explains how Christians may eat such meat as long as it does not associate them with the idol to whom it was originally offered. An idol is really a non-existent god and so cannot change the meat in itself. However, scandal must be avoided, including scandal to Christians who cannot tolerate any use of such meat. The answer leads Paul to recall lessons from Israel's experience in the desert, which lets us see that he regards the Corinthian community as continuing in the same line as those people of God. He brings out well that the eucharist entails a close fellowship with the Lord Jesus, by "drinking the cup of the Lord" and sharing "at the Lord's table" (10,14-22). He also insists again on the unity and fellowship which the sharing brings to those who partake of the one loaf and so are drawn together into the one body of Christ (10,16).

Speaking of the eucharist enables Paul to pass easily to other questions that have reached him concerning the Christian meetings held to celebrate the

Lord's Supper as part of an "**agape**" (= Christian love celebration). Those meetings were also an occasion for the Christians to exercise publicly their many charisms, such as prophecy, teaching, tongues and interpretation of tongues, (cc.11-14). The section that concerns us most is found in 11,17-34. There Paul recalls what he had "received from the Lord" and faithfully "handed on" to the Corinthian community, namely the way the Lord had instituted the eucharist. We have already reflected on the words of institution in the gospels. Suffice it now to recall how Paul's account is close to that of Lk: "This cup is the new covenant in my blood. Whenever you drink it, do this as a memorial of me" (11,25) — or a more literal translation: "as my memorial". We need to recall those words of institution here in order to appreciate how the new covenant colours all the epistle, especially in its treatment of charisms and "love" within the Christian assemblies. To approach the Lord's table without proper fraternal love will bring condemnation (11,28-33), just as to exercise any other charism while lacking love will empty the charism of its value before God (13,1-3).

Paul stresses the close link between the eucharist and unity within the whole body of Christ, for "we were baptised into one body in a single Spirit, Jews as well as Greeks, slaves as well as free men" (12,13). His whole treatment of the public exercise of different charisms is governed by those considerations of unity among members of the one body, all animated by the one Spirit. Each one has been granted a particular gift to be exercised for the good of the whole community. After his "hymn to true love" (c.13), Paul urges all his readers: "Make love your aim" (14,1). Love is to guide them all in sorting out the priority to be assigned to the exercise of seemingly clashing charisms during assemblies (14,2-40). It is remarkable how smoothly Paul uses apostolic authority to ensure that individual gifts of the Spirit are not simply used in an individualistic or self-seeking way. The modern efforts to harmonise the hierarchical with the charismatic can find sound guidelines in these rich chapters. Paul's concern is plainly stated at the conclusion of the section: "Make sure that everything is done in a proper and orderly fashion" (14,40).

Questions about the resurrection of the dead call forth from Paul a magnificent chapter on the good news of Christ's resurrection as the source and guarantee of the Christian's own bodily resurrection on the last day(c.15). This, too, is part of the tradition which Paul received and has handed on the the Corinthians (vv.1-3). There is no room for doubt about physical resurrection now that Jesus Christ has risen from the dead "as the first fruits of all who have fallen asleep"(v.20). The salvation accomplished by Christ is an integral liberation from everything that held humans as captives, including death and physical disintegration[9]. "The last of the enemies to be done away with is death" (v.26), but the risen Christ has certainly broken the power of death over his brothers and sisters.

Through Christ the God of life confers a life that is abundant and unending, so that what is mortal in us may be clothed with immortality (cf. v.53). This kind of liberation far surpasses any political liberation, but it also provides great motivation for treasuring life and working for its maximum development. Paul easily connects the final goal of the risen Christ with that of "handing over the kingdom to God the Father" (v.24). The resurrection of Christians is therefore presented here as a "kingdom value" which must always be kept in mind when explaining what complete liberation entails. The universality of the resurrection is not made explicit in this chapter, but the basis is firmly set by proclaiming Christ as the new and perfect Adam, the newly appointed head of all our human family(vv.45-49). It is also made abundantly clear that he who has conquered sin has also conquered death (e.g. vv.54-56). This is motivation enough for Christians to continue with unbounded energy "for doing the Lord's work"(v.58), inviting others to share in the good news.

B 2. 2 Corinthians

This epistle was written only a couple of years after 1 Corinthians, but it was much more controversial in tone, mainly because "pseudo-apostles" were posing a serious threat to the unity of the church at Corinth. Paul's own standing as an apostle was seriously challenged by his rivals there, which provoked some stinging evaluations of them in Paul's letter. They also provoked Paul into reminding the whole community there of the many signs that he was a genuine apostle, so much so that he speaks about boasting "of the Lord" (10,17). Because the false apostles were Judaizing Christians, Paul is forced to remind the community he founded there of the characteristics which distinguish the new Israel from that of the Old Testament.

It is especially in cc.1-6 that we see the main characteristics being recalled to explain Paul's own apostolate and priorities. The opening lines of the epistle refer to the "church of God" and to "all God's holy people in Achaia" (1,1). Then Paul's delay in coming again to visit Corinth is not due to fickleness, for he is keenly aware of being an apostle of Christ Jesus, and in Christ is "found the Yes to all God's promises". There is no double-talk where Christ and his genuine apostles are concerned, but complete constancy and trustworthiness. Paul and his collaborators have been "anointed and marked with God's seal", giving them "the pledge of the Spirit". This is an indispensable foundation for their ministry as "envoys of God" (2,17), so dependent on the guidance, power and constancy of the Spirit.

Paul realises that his self-defence might begin to sound like self-commendation, and that possible taunt moves him to unleash his most sustained — and most brilliant — explanation of what it really means to be accredited by God as "ministers of the new covenant, a covenant which is not of written letters, but of the Spirit" (3,6). In the first place, Paul and his collaborators like Timothy do not need any letters of recommendation either to or from the Corinthian community: "You yourselves are our letter, written in our hearts, that everyone can read and understand" (3,2).

Although this unique letter may have been composed verbally in the hearts of the apostles of Corinth, its content was also inscribed deep in the hearts of the Corinthians themselves. The same Spirit that compels the apostles to proclaim the new covenant insistently has also moved the Corinthians to accept it in their own hearts. That letter was written "not with ink, but with the Spirit of the living God; not on stone tablets but on the tablets of human hearts" (3,3). The covenant clauses at Sinai were written with a strong chisel on tablets of stone; the new covenant is written by the Spirit as "the finger of God" on human hearts, which thereby cease to be hearts of stone. Paul here combines several of the features of the new covenant as foretold by Jeremiah, e.g. "Within them I shall plant my Law, writing it on their hearts" (31,33), and by Ezekiel, e.g. "I shall give you a new heart, and put a new spirit within you; I shall remove the heart of stone from your bodies" (36,26).

The vast difference between the Sinai covenant and the new covenant leads Paul to speak about Moses' role as a "ministry of death", in the sense that Paul will explain more fully in Romans and Galatians. Briefly, he is alluding to the situation in which the Law of God was made clear to Israel, and yet Israel was liable to the death penalty for violating God's Law now clearly known. In that context God had promised a new covenant as referred to in the previous paragraph, a covenant that would give also the change of heart and abiding inner strength to live in keeping with God's demands. I. Da Conceicäo Souza points out how circumcision was something external to man under the Sinai covenant, but now is a change of heart effected by God. Similarly, "in the old dispensation love of Yahweh was given as a commandment, in the new era it is presented as Yahweh's gift, as his activity. ... The Spirit will be the characteristic of the new covenant"[10]. He also claims with justification that "this new covenant is really a New Creation"[11]. The claim of a new creation is taken directly from Paul's own wording in the part of 2 Corinthians under discussion here: "So for anyone who is in Christ, there is a new creation: the old order is gone and a new being is there to see. It is all God's work" (5,17-18). He also speaks of "a new creation" in contrast to circumcision in Galatians: "It is not being circumcised or uncircumcised that matters; but what matters is a new creation" (6,15).

Since ministry of the new covenant is a collaboration in the new creation and is truly a "ministry of the Spirit" (2 Cor 3,8), it must be caught up into a glory much greater than that which shone on the face of Moses in his ministry of the old covenant. The old covenant was preparatory and transitory, even though it endured more than a thousand years. Now the new covenant is final and everlasting (3,8-11). The full contrast is between the glory shining on the face of Moses and "the glory on the face of Christ", who is "the image of God" (4,4-6). For the Jews who do not accept Christ, it is as if a veil still hides his glory from them as they read the Old Testament (3,14). For Christians, on the other hand, not only is there no veil hiding Christ's glory from them, but his glory can be openly reflected by their own faces: "And all of us, with unveiled faces like mirrors reflecting the glory of the Lord, are being transformed in to the image that we reflect in brighter and brighter glory; this is the working of the Lord who is the Spirit" (3,18).

Saul's own dramatic meeting with the glorious Christ Jesus on the road to Damascus was so overwhelming that Saul was left blinded until his baptism. Ananias on that occasion linked Saul's baptism with the recovery of his sight and the reception of the Spirit. "Brother Saul", said Ananias, " I have been sent by the Lord Jesus .. so that you may recover your sight and be filled with the Holy Spirit". With that, "it was as though scales fell away from his eyes and immediately he was able to see again" (Acts 9,17-18).

That beginning of his new mission as a Christian and of his special "ministry" of the new covenant is recalled gratefully by Paul, who tells the Corinthians: "Such by God's mercy is our ministry. ... It is God who said, 'Let light shine out of darkness', that has shone into our hearts to enlighten them with the knowledge of God's glory, the glory on the face of Christ" (2 Cor 4,1.6). In the same vein Paul continues: "It is all God's work; he has reconciled us to himself through Christ and he gave us the ministry of reconciliation. .. So we are ambassadors for Christ; it is as though God were urging you through us, and in the name of Christ we appeal to you to be reconciled to God" (5,19 - 20). As ambassadors of Christ they are making known God's appeal to all people to return to the God who has never ceased to love them all. The ministry of the new covenant is basically one of reconciliation with God and with all those redeemed by Christ.

In cc.6-7 Paul speaks easily to the faithful of Corinth as to people called to form the holy people of God, to be as a living temple of God, and also to be as God's "sons and daughters" (6,14-18). As such the Christians are urged to cooperate with God so that their sanctification may be brought to completion(7,1). Just as easily Paul can go on to invite them to "a share in the fellowship of service to God's holy people" (8,4), namely the afflicted poor Christians in Jerusalem. Cc. 8 and 9 are fully taken up with motivating the Corinthians to contribute generously and quite voluntarily to the collection being organised in Achaia as well as in Macedonia. It is clearly presented as a fellowship within the people of God now found in several countries. In this particular instance, it is the turn of Christians in a Gentile setting to manifest their fellowship and solidarity with those in the Jewish capital of Jerusalem.

In view of the growing tendency to disparage giving of material aid to the poor, for fear that it will be dubbed "paternalism", we need to be as clear-minded as Paul in seeing that material aid, given in the right spirit, can still be an acid test of covenant fellowship and generous sharing (cf.8,8). As a cheerful sharing among members of the one family, it should reflect the generosity of the Lord Jesus: "although he was rich, he became poor for your sake, so that you should become rich through his poverty"(8,9). When such a "help to God's holy people"(9,1) is known to be the expression of "the generosity of your fellowship with them", the recipients can accept it with gratitude to God for bringing about such an unselfish sharing and mutual affection between the different communities (9,10-15). "God loves a cheerful giver" (9,7), today as much as then.

In short, giving material help to the poor in their emergency situations need not be paternalistic; it can and should be the expression of a genuinely cherished equality and fellowship that makes us one in the Lord Jesus and in God's household. Helping those of different faiths to our own must follow the same lines, while striving even harder to avoid any airs of superiority or presumption that the giver has any new rights over the receiver. We must want to share because we know we are only stewards entrusted with God's gifts, so that any surplus is meant to provide something for our most needy brothers and sisters as well. There may also come a moment when we will be looking to others to help us in our need (cf. 8,13-14).

The conclusion of the epistle is rich in expressions summing up the ideals of the people of the new covenant: "have a common mind and live in peace"; "the God of love and peace will be with you"; "all God's holy people send your their greetings"; the final wish is that "the love of God and the fellowship of the Holy Spirit be with you all"(13,11-13). Both letters to the Corinthians are therefore truly witnesses to a profound sense of covenant.

C. IN ROMANS AND GALATIANS

The Epistles to the Romans and to the Galatians were written not long after 2 Corinthians, for Romans at least can be dated to the time when Paul was wintering in Corinth before terminating his third missionary journey, hence probably 57-58 A.D. As Romans gives the impression of being a more comprehensive and calmer treatment of the major issues dealt with rather brusquely in Galatians, it is reasonable to presume that Galatians was written shortly before Romans. Galatians was a pastoral response to the big questions raised by Judaizers who were telling the new Christians that circumcision and the Mosaic Law were still necessary for salvation. Romans, on the other hand, was more like a theological reflection on the relation of the Law to the new covenant. The striking synthesis which emerged was intended as an introduction of Paul to that important church, which he intended to visit for the first time by passing through Rome on his way to Spain[12].

Paul shows how the promise to Abraham is fulfilled in Christ, and how the Mosaic Law served to make clearer the kind of life required in the midst of God's people. However, the inner strength necessary to live up to those standards consistently calls for the "saving justice of God" made known through Christ and poured forth into human hearts by the Holy Spirit. For Paul, God has acted with great consistency, for the plan of salvation has always been based on God's own merciful initiative as shown in calling Abraham, then on fidelity to the promises made to Abraham and his descendants. The human response has to be one of confident faith in God promising and imparting a share in the divine life and justice, to be fully communicated only through the coming of Christ and the gift of the Holy Spirit.

For Paul, the love and faithfulness of God loom much larger than the faith of this or that individual. The Judaizers' big mistake is to underestimate the full import of Christ's voluntary sacrifice to bring about what the Law by itself was unable to do. For the Son of God "loved me and delivered himself up for me... if saving justice comes through the Law, Christ died needlessly" (Gal 2,20-21; cf. Rm 5,8). Moreover, the question being treated is about the continuity between the children of Abraham, the people of the Sinai covenant, and the people of the new covenant, "the Israel of God" (Gal 6,16). We will concentrate on a few of the major sections of Romans which throw most light on Paul's understanding of the new covenant, and which also indicate a corresponding familiarity with those ideas among his Galatian and Roman readers.

Romans 1,1-17 is an excellent introduction to the "gospel" of Jesus Christ, which Paul has been called to preach, and through which the Roman community has already been called by God "to be his holy people" (v.7). This gospel "is God's power for the salvation of everyone who has faith — Jews first, but Greeks as well — for in it is revealed the saving justice of God" (vv. 16-17). A similar wholehearted commitment to the gospel can be seen in the first two chapters of Galatians, where Paul insists that he had received it "through a revelation of Jesus Christ" (1,12). The Galatians had been given a share in the justice of God through accepting the gospel with faith and so being open also to receive the Holy Spirit (2,15 - 3,5).

Rm 1,18 - 3,31 is a strong assertion that all people, be they Jew or Greek, are sinners before God, in need of the saving justice which God has now made available through the mission of Christ Jesus. Forgiveness of sin and reconciliation with God, indeed salvation itself, depend on accepting the gospel through faith. This is to say that all must accept the need to enter into the new people of God who accept the new covenant sealed in the blood of Christ. For, "God appointed him as a sacrifice for reconciliation, through faith, by the shedding of his blood, and so he showed his justness" (3,25)[13]. The loving obedience of Jesus unto death outweighs all sins of disobedience and suffices to seal the new covenant. All his brothers and sisters can accept that covenant by faith in Jesus Christ, a faith "working through love" (Gal 5,6). T. Deidun is quite right in deducing that, for Paul, the new covenant "is synonymous with the Gospel", and that "Christians are the beneficiaries of the New Covenant"[14].

Rm c.4 then takes up the example of Abraham in order to show that his basic response to God's promise was one of faith, which came before he was circumcised and centuries before the Law was given through Moses (cf. Gal c.3). It is important for our theme to note how Paul is contrasting a justice based on faith in God promising, with a kind of justice that the Jews strove to achieve by observing the Law. In other words, the basis of justice and friendship with God is the unconditional promise to Abraham, and not the conditional covenant of Sinai. Moreover, Paul insists that those who have faith in Christ are so united to him that they form with him the "offspring of Abraham" — "the heirs named in the promise" (Gal 3,29).

An integral part of that promise concerns the gift of the Spirit (Gal 3,14), and the fulfilment of this aspect is eloquently described by saying, "The love of God has been poured into our hearts by the Holy Spirit which has been given to us" (Rm 5,5). The marvel of this is again the initiative of God, who loved us so much that "Christ died for us while we were still sinners" (5,8). There is no doubt that the new covenant of reconciliation was established through Christ's voluntary sacrifice, before the rest of the human race had agreed to follow his example and proclamation of twofold love(5,9-11). Furthermore, only by voluntary association with Christ crucified and risen can any sinner be set free from sin and death (5,12-21), from sinful self-centredness (c.6), and from the Law, in so far as its violated demands bring death to the offender (c.7). Those three chapters (5-7) are a compendium of the liberation which Jesus Christ has accomplished for all the family of Adam. It is a liberation far wider and deeper than the liberation of one small nation from slavery to an Egyptian pharaoh.

On the other hand, it does demand a corresponding acceptance of the new covenant made possible for peoples of all nations on earth. But this time the clauses of the covenant are written deep in the human heart, and the inscribing Spirit remains within each believer to sustain the inner force necessary to live according to the new covenant. "If the Spirit of him who raised Jesus from the dead has made his home in you, then he who raised Christ Jesus from the dead will give life to your own mortal bodies through his Spirit living in you" (8,11). It is highly significant that this central chapter of Romans is devoted to the role of the Holy Spirit, "the spirit of adoption enabling us to cry out, '**Abba**, Father'" (8,15)[15]. Thanks to the outpouring of the Spirit upon those who believe in Christ, they can now live according to "the law of the Spirit which gives life in Christ Jesus" (8,2). The indwelling Spirit gives the inner strength necessary to live consistently according to the will of the Father, and thereby reach bodily resurrection as well. In this way "the Law has found its fulfilment in Christ" (Rm 10,4; cf.3,31: "We are placing the Law on its true footing").

The liberation of mankind by Christ is so complete, and the power of his transforming Spirit is so all-embracing, that the bodily resurrection to which believers are now heading gives a sure hope that "the whole creation itself might be freed from its slavery to corruption and brought into the same glorious freedom as the children of God" (8,21). F. Menezes in his study of Rm 8, 18-30, "Life in the Spirit: A Life of Hope", draws attention to the way in which Paul's theology of hope is presented in the context of suffering: "This global situation of suffering is presented in the triple groaning of creation, Christians and the Spirit"[16].

Creation "groans" because of human sin, which has broken the proper relationship between the stewards and the beautiful creation they are meant to guard, cherish and develop in harmony with God's design and human destiny[17]. The sinful corruption of humankind has led to the pollution and "enslavement" of our natural home, our **"oikos"**, hence of our whole "eco-system", the ecological balance within all parts, especially living parts, of our planet and our universe[18]. Thus the new covenant established by Christ and sustained by his Spirit affects all creation, in fact it is the basis of a new creation. We may make our own Menezes' finding: "The resurrection of Christ inaugurates the new creation, and the entire universe shares the destiny of the human nature assumed by the Son of God"[19].

Rm 9-11 take up the objection that God cannot reject Israel without violating his promise to Abraham and his commitment to Israel at the time of the Exodus. Paul does not hesitate to admit that, "They are Israelites; it was they who were adopted as children, the glory was theirs and the covenants; to them were given the Law and the worship of God and the promises" (9,4). Paul does not for a moment accept that God has rejected Israel: "Is it possible that God abandoned his people? Out of the question!" (11,1). The only rejection has been that of God's plan by Israelites; it is not enough to be a physical descendant of Abraham or of Jacob to be assured of receiving in full the blessing promised to those patriarchs and their descendants. God has always manifested the freedom to choose those to whom special mercy will be granted. Now, with the coming of Christ, God has called the gentiles, as well as a faithful remnant of the Israelites, to become the new people of God, a much more international people than Israel alone (c.9).

Paul's deep and loyal love for his own Jewish people enables him to sum up their situation by means of a striking allegory, that of an olive tree and its different branches (11,16-24). Far from suggesting that God has decided to root up the chosen tree, Paul develops the imagery of some natural branches being broken off, and other "wild olive branches" being grafted on, against nature. The normal procedure is to take a wild stock and graft on branches from a good fruit-bearing tree. The gentile Christians are reminded of the Jewish root that sustains them as newly grafted branches (11,18)[20]. To such gentiles can be applied the prophecy of Hosea: "I shall tell those who were not my people, 'You are my people'" (Rm 9,25). As for the Jews who have failed to believe the gospel and therefore become like branches broken off from the good olive tree, they will one day be fully restored. "It is within the power of God to graft them back in again" (11,23). God will fulfil the prophecy about the Redeemer coming to purify Jacob and establish "my covenant with them" (11,27).That Christ is an essential part of the good olive tree is not stated explicitly, but it is presupposed once Paul has recalled of Israel: "To them belong the fathers and out of them, as far as physical descent is concerned, came Christ who is above all, God, blessed for ever" (9,5). The allegory serves well to illustrate the continuity and the unexpected in God's merciful initiatives with regard to both Israel and the gentile world[21]. Well might Paul close the whole doctrinal section of the epistle with a hymn of praise to the unbounded wisdom and knowledge of God, from whom everything comes and to whom everything is drawn (11,33-36).

Rm 12-16 is the final section containing many practical exhortations that flow easily from the earlier teaching concerning the new people of God. Christians are to be outstanding in their spirit of self-sacrifice guided by an inner discernment of God's will (12, 1-2). Likewise their love of others is to be sincere, humble and generous, ready to "share with any of God's holy people who are in need" (12,13). So essential is love that, "The only thing you should owe to anyone is love for one another, for to love the other person is to fulfil the law. .. and so love is the fulfilment of the Law" (13,8-10). The words underlined express the synthesis worked out by Paul concerning members of the new "holy people of God" and the Law. To be inwardly attentive to the will of God and to manifest a generous, unrestricted love of fellow Christians is to accept the saving justice of God. That is "the Law in its fulness" (as S.

Lyonnet has suggested[22]). It is also living according the "law of the Spirit" proper to the new covenant.

D. IN EPHESIANS AND PHILEMON

Of the four epistles written during some imprisonment of Paul, namely Philippians, Colossians, Ephesians and Philemon, the last two mentioned bear most directly on our theme. Ephesians presents a masterly and jubilant synthesis of the "mystery" that all races can now be united in Christ, whereas Philemon teaches clearly that masters and slaves can become brothers in Christ. It is still feasible to accept that both these epistles were written by Paul while he was awaiting trial in Rome about 63 A.D., but admittedly the Pauline authorship of Ephesians is now being widely questioned by scholars[23].

D 1. New covenant in Ephesians

Ephesians treats explicitly the central covenant theme of belonging to the people of God, formerly the privilege of Israelites but now open to the Gentiles as well. The anguished searching of Rm 9 - 11 to find consistency in God's treatment of Israel has prepared the way for a more joyful, prayerful and complete proclamation of the "mystery" made known through Jesus Christ. The general vision shares with Romans and Galatians that non-Jews who believe in Christ form part of "God's holy people" (Eph 1,1.15.18), chosen gratuitously to be "adopted sons, through Jesus Christ", "in whom, through his blood, we gain our freedom, the forgiveness of our sins" (Eph 1,4-7).

While Romans was wrestling with the big difficulty of the many Israelites who have not accepted Christ with faith, Ephesians concentrates on the unity that has been achieved between the many believing Gentiles and the believing Jews. Romans was concerned with the original branches broken off and the wild branches grafted in; Ephesians is concerned more directly with Jesus Christ as head and unifier of all the branches/races chosen to become as one in him. For he "has made the two into one entity and broken down the barrier which used to keep them apart" (2,14).

The whole section of Eph 2,11-22, in which is found the text just quoted, is profoundly influenced by the ideals of covenant. M. Barth justifiably alludes to this section as "the key and high point of the whole epistle"[24]. Paul reminds those who were "gentiles by physical descent, termed the uncircumcised..", how they were formerly "excluded from the membership of Israel, aliens with no part in the covenants of the Promise" (vv.11-12). An enormous change has occurred, because "now in Christ Jesus, you that used to be so far off have been brought close, by the blood of Christ. For he is the peace between us.." (vv.13-14). "The covenants of the promise" are not identified precisely, but they would include the promissory covenants with Abraham and David, for through them all peoples now have the Messiah (cf. vv.12 and 13), and very probably also the blessings promised to those who keep the commandments of the Sinai covenant.

With Christ's sacrificial death and the shedding of his blood, the dividing wall between Jews and Gentiles has been broken down. That wall was due particularly to "the Law of commandments with its decrees" (v.15). The blood of sacrificial bulls at Sinai had sealed the covenant which made Israel a people set apart from Gentiles and a people committed to live according to the Law. Now the sacrificial blood of Jesus Christ has sealed a new covenant which is open to all races without distinction, be they Jew or Gentile. The old Law as such has therefore been superseded by the new law of Christ. Christ has died so that both Jew and Gentile might be reconciled in him, to live in peace. "Through him, then, we both in the one Spirit have free access to the Father" (v.18).

That verse, in the opinion of D. Stanley, "may be considered one of the most complete and summary statements of Pauline soteriology and of the function of Christ's resurrection in effecting man's salvation. Salvation is described as an access"[25]. It is an access to the Father's own home, for thanks to the new covenant sealed in Christ's blood, the gentiles "are no longer aliens or foreign visitors; you are fellow-citizens with the holy people of God and part of God's household" (v. 19). To belong to "the holy people of God" and to "God's household" is to belong to the people of the covenant. That is possible now for Gentiles who become members of "the Church" with Christ as its head (cf. 1,22; 2,10.21; 5,23-32). The mystery proclaimed by Paul is that "the gentiles now have the same inheritance and form the same Body and enjoy the same promise in Christ Jesus through the gospel" (3,6). In short, the gospel for Paul is precisely this access to the Father and universal covenant fellowship between all peoples thanks to Christ's sacrificial blood and consequent status as head and creator of the one "New Man" (2,15).

That Paul is steeped in the imagery of covenant is further confirmed by his original approach to Christian marriage in Ephesians 5. The Old Testament frequently availed of human marriage to describe aspects of the covenant between God and Israel. Here Paul avails of the union of love between Christ and the Church as a model for Christian marriage. It is noteworthy that the chapter opens with a general appeal to Christians to live as God's children and to "follow Christ by loving as he loved you" (vv.1-2). Because they are "the holy people of God" they must avoid "sexual vice" (v.3).

Vv.21-33 give the very original approach to the implications of the divine covenant with regard to Christian marriage. Once again, the general tone is set by the opening verse: "Be subject to one another out of reverence for Christ" (v.21). This exhortation sets the governing spirit of all that follows. It calls for a spirit of humility in the presence of others, and encourages a spirit of esteem for fellow-members of Christ. This kind of "subjection" is voluntary, concerned for others and sacrificial, inspired and sustained by a common union in Christ. M. Barth rightly explains: "The single imperative of vs 21 ['subordinate yourselves to one another'] anticipates all that Paul is about to say not only to wives, children and slaves, but also to husbands, fathers and masters, about the specific respect they owe because of Christ to those with whom they live"[26].

In this light must be seen the ensuing exhortation: "Wives should be subject to their husbands as to the Lord, since, as Christ is head of the Church and saves the whole body, so is a husband the head of his wife" (vv.22-23). To concentrate solely on the subjection of wives to their husbands and then reject Paul's attitude to Christian marriage as distorted by male chauvinism is to miss the heart of his exhortation. Far from encouraging male chauvinism, Paul lays sure foundations for remedying it and replacing it in keeping with the guideline given for all the exhortations in cc. 4 - 6: "With all humility and gentleness, and with patience, support each other in love. .. There is one Body, one Spirit .. There is one Lord, one faith, one baptism" (4,2-5). The Christian husband and wife are already one and equal in Christ through faith and baptism; together they form part of the body, part of the Church, subject to Christ voluntarily and united to him by the bonds of mutual love.

Through Christian marriage the couple are called into a new covenant of love which, as Paul realises, can have the splendour of the new covenant itself in miniature[27]. The emphasis is not on subjection of one partner to the other, but on their mutual commitment in love. That shines through the repeated urging: "Husbands should love their wives, just as Christ loved the Church and sacrificed himself for her" (v.25; cf. vv.28 and 33). Furthermore, the husband must love his wife as he loves his own body, for the two have become "one flesh". Just as Christ loves and nourishes his body, the Church, so also must the husband love and cherish his wife (cf.vv.28-33).

In short, Paul's treatment of Christian marriage certainly takes up the accepted culture and social attitudes of his own day with regard to the relationship between husband and wife. He proceeds from the presumption that the husband is the head of the family and, by relating this to the kind of headship which Christ practised and proclaimed, he presents a vastly different ideal to that current among non-Christians. So much so that M. Barth concludes from his thorough study of the section : "Instead, the reality of the New Covenant dominates the picture — totally, radically, radiantly. If ever there was a joyful affirmation of marriage, without any shadow and misgiving, then it is found in Eph 5. .. A greater, wiser, and more positive description of marriage has not yet been found in Christian literature"[28]. It is to be hoped that such a view of marriage will break down the wall of division between husband and wife, just as the new covenant breaks down all division between Jew and gentile.

D 2. New covenant in Philemon

This short letter was sent by Paul from prison, about the same time as the sending of Colossians. The probable date would have been about 63 A.D., towards the end of the Paul"s first house arrest in Rome. The letter is friendly, fraternal, and tactful, pleading for a kind reception to Onesimus, Philemon's runaway slave whom Paul had baptised in prison. As Paul sends him back to his Christian master, he courteously invites the master to welcome the slave back into the household as a brother in Christ. Such treatment is not ordered by Paul, who wants it to be quite spontaneous and done out of personal conviction (14). Although Paul does not ask Philemon to set Onesimus free from slavery, he does express the hope that Philemon will do "even more than I ask" (21).

To understand Paul's seeming reticence in denouncing slavery or demanding the manumission of all slaves by Christian masters, we need to be aware of how widespread slavery was in the Roman Empire of his day. According to G.S. Bartchy, up to two-thirds of Corinth's population, for instance, could have been slaves at the time Paul was preaching there (as a free Roman citizen)[29]. Likewise in Rome itself and on its farmlands, there would have been more slaves than free citizens. From the New Testament, especially from the Pauline letters (including the Pastorals) and 1 Peter, we get the impression that the Christian "household" included free family members and their slaves, hence the need to give instructions on how to regulate relations between Christian masters and slaves (cf. Col 3,9 - 4,1; Eph 6,5-9; 1 Tim 6,1-2; Tit 2,9-10; 1 Pet 2,15-25).

The passage in Col is particularly illuminating, for it declares that among those whose very self has been "renewed in the image of the Creator, .. there is no room for distinction between Greek and Jew, .. or between barbarian and Scythian, slave and free. There is only one Christ" (3,10-11; cf. Gal 3,28). As God's chosen, holy and beloved people, they are to be outstanding in compassion and love, "the perfect bond", so that "the peace of Christ" may reign in the hearts of those "called together in one body" (3,12 -15). Slaves are urged to be obedient to those who "according to human reckoning, are your masters" (whereas before God they have only one Master, whom they are to serve by their work for human masters). Christian masters, for their part, are also under the same Master as their Christian slaves, hence all slaves (Christian or otherwise) must be given "what is upright and fair" (4,1). The standing of the runaway slave, Onesimus, is striking in this whole context: "I am sending Onesimus, that dear and trustworthy brother who is a fellow-citizen of yours" (Col 4,9).

I Tim 6,1-2 takes it for granted that Christian slaves know quite well that their Christian masters are also their brothers in the Lord: "Those whose masters are believers are not to respect them less because they are brothers". Such an exhortation is fully in line with what Paul said of Onesimus directly to Philemon, namely that he was receiving back "something much better than a slave, a dear brother" (16). It is also significant that Paul can write to Philemon about "the church that meets in your house" (2), since this is evidence enough that a Christian household could be envisaged as a small domestic church, a portion of "the holy people" (Col 3,12). Slaves therefore have equal standing as their masters within the community of the new covenant. There can be no doubt that for Paul the freedom given to slaves by Christ enables them to serve God quite freely and out of conviction, with a faith "working through love" (Gal 5,6). He tells the slaves: "It is Christ the Lord that you are serving" (Col 3,24).

Christian slaves, therefore, by no means have to await a manumission from human emperors or slavemasters before they can serve the one true God. As with the Israelites of old, so too with the Christian slaves, their liberation is at the same time a call to wholehearted service of God. Unlike the rescued Israelites, Christian slaves have to await full civil liberation from their status as slaves at the beck and call of harsh masters. The little pharaohs are right in the midst of the people of the new covenant. Paul does urge Philemon to do more than take back the runaway slave, hinting that he might be set free (21).

The relative unimportance of being bond or free when called to union with Christ and fellowship with other believers can be gauged from the advice given to slaves in 1 Cor 7,20-24. Paul's guiding principle, which he says is "the rule that I give to all the churches" (v.17), is that each is to stay in the state in which they were called by God, e.g. circumcised or uncircumcised, slave or free, single or married. Nevertheless, Paul faces up to the question as to when it could be a good thing, even the better thing, for a Christian slave to change his or her state in civil society. In any case, "what is important is the keeping of God's commandments" (1 Cor 7,19), for that is the way to manifest covenant loyalty to God and neighbour.

However, says Paul, if Christian slaves have a chance of freedom, let them use it. Unfortunately for interpreters, the text remains ambiguous, for we are not told precisely what is to be used — the state of slavery in which they were at the time of their call? or their vocation, their call to be Christians? or the new status as manumitted people? The careful study by S. Bartchy has led him to conclude that in 1 Cor.7,21 the pithy phrase, "use it", refers to using or accepting God's call completely. The text may reasonably be interpreted: "But if, indeed, your owner should manumit you, by all means (now as a freedman) live according to God's call"[30].

In the light of this attitude we can deduce that Paul, even while inviting Philemon to treat Onesimus like a dear brother in all things, did not consider it necessary to insist that the slave be manumitted immediately. The basic liberation for both Philemon and Onesimus was being set free by Christ so effectively that they could now serve God freely, out of personal conviction and not because of any external force or fear.

1 Peter 2,18-25 adds the dimension of voluntary participation in the mission of Jesus as the suffering Servant, who was innocent and yet accepted death on the cross to set free his brethren from sin. "Christ suffered for you and left you an example for you to follow in his steps" (v.21). The good slave, like Christ the shepherd, can thus accept harsh treatment out of love for God and for all those still in need of reconciliation with God. That is clearly set within the framework of Christians forming the new people of God: "But you are a chosen race, a kingdom of priests, a holy nation, a people to be a personal possession to sing the praises of God.. Once you were a non-people and <u>now you are the People of God</u>" (1 Pet 2,9-10).

An echo of this wonderful change is heard at the conclusion of the exhortation to slaves: "You had gone astray like sheep, but now you have returned to the shepherd and guardian of your souls" (1Pet 2,25). This is nothing less than a call to heroic solidarity with the suffering Christ and with all those still urgently in need of liberation from sin, especially their harsh slavemasters[31]. In this way Christian slaves are already free to follow the example of Christ and, in union with him, to overcome evil with good, injustice with fraternal love. We will come back to 1 Peter and the covenant after reflecting on the extremely rich treatment of the new covenant in Hebrews.

E. NEW COVENANT IN HEBREWS

While this writing was attributed to Paul in some parts of the early Church, in other parts that claim was disputed. Now there is general agreement among biblical scholars that Hebrews is from an author distinct from Paul[32]. The anonymous author displays a profound knowledge of the Old Testament and a keen insight into the way Jesus Christ has brought to perfection such basic institutions as priesthood, sacrifice and covenant. The writer also manifests great mastery of the Greek language and forms of argument, as well as familiarity with the style of Philo, a Jewish philosopher who wrote for the Greek-speaking world around Alexandria.

A penetrating exposition of doctrine is constantly accompanied by fervent exhortations to live according to such convictions. The writer justifiably refers to the work as "words of encouragement" (13,22), making quite clear its main purpose. Unlike Pauline epistles, it is not addressed to a particular community nor does it mention the writer's name anywhere. In fact, the whole work is more like a sermon than an epistle[33]. Some suggest that it was intended for reading during the celebration of the Lord's Supper, which would give added force to its central theme of Jesus as the new high priest and perfect offering, as well as the mediator of a new covenant sealed in his blood[34].

Hebrews provides the most sustained and explicit treatment of covenant in the N.T., in fact the word **diatheke** occurs 17 times in Hebrews and only 16 times in the rest of the N.T.[35]. However, its treatment of covenant is so closely associated with that of Christ as high priest that we need to consider it now within that same framework. The literary structure of the entire work is so carefully and strikingly arranged with innumerable interlocking parts that it must be respected in order to grasp the message being communicated. In this area the meticulous work of A. Vanhoye over the last 30 years is a sure guide, especially "La Structure Littéraire de l'Epître aux Hébreux"[36].

E 1. Jesus as Son of God and brother of us all (Heb 1 - 2)
The solemn opening affirms that finally God "has spoken to us in the person of his Son, whom he appointed heir of all things", and who "has taken his seat at the right hand of the divine Majesty on high" (1,2-3). The Son is superior to the angels, as he has been given a throne at the right hand of God. The teaching of the Lord must therefore be heard attentively.

At the same time, Jesus is truly "a child of Adam" (2,6), one who submitted to death to "benefit all humanity" (2,9). As befits our leader, he has first been made perfect through suffering, so that he could lead us to perfection, setting free "all those who had been held in slavery all their lives by the fear of death". He has thus been made "completely like his brothers so that he could become a compassionate and trustworthy high priest for their relationship to God" (2,10-17).

As Son, Jesus is close to God the Father, and as our brother he is close to us, having solidarity with us and deep compassion for those suffering. He is "trustworthy" in what he reveals of God; he is "compassionate" in his dealings with all his human family. He is ideally situated to act as high priest, enabling God to enter into dialogue with mankind, and enabling mankind to draw near to God with full confidence.

E 2. Jesus, as Son over God's household, is its high priest (3,1 - 5,10)

In this role, Jesus is superior to Moses, who was a servant whereas Jesus is "trustworthy as a son is, over his household. And we are his household" (3,5-6). We must listen to Christ more effectively than the Israelites listened to Moses in the desert, for they did not enter into the "rest" promised them by God. Nor did Joshua give his people complete rest, since in David's time God could still promise to give rest to those who listen properly to his voice. Jesus can lead his people more effectively than did Joshua into this promised rest. But the word of God which he brings is "something alive and active", demanding a personal response. We need help to live according to its demands, so "let us have no fear in approaching the throne of grace to receive mercy" (4,16). Jesus has been called by God from among his fellow-humans to be our high priest, and through suffering unto death "he learnt obedience". His voluntary self-sacrifice was accepted by God, so that he was made perfect, with power to perfect the rest of his human family, becoming "for all who obey him a source of eternal salvation". It was God who acclaimed him high priest "according to the order of Melchizedek" (5,1-10).

E 3. Jesus as high priest is perfect, unique and eternal, superseding the priesthood of the Mosaic covenant (5,11 - 8,13)

Here we enter into the central part of the work, which A. Vanhoye has identified as 5,11 - 10,39[37]. Because it is so rich in its treatment of covenant, we are subdividing it into two sections, E 3 and E 4.

A strong exhortation alerts the audience to the importance of the high point, the "solid food" (5,14) now to be offered. Let there be no falling away! Instead, let them press on as "heirs of the promises" (6,12). Furthermore, God's promise to Abraham has been confirmed by an oath, so that it is doubly sure. Very adroitly the author situates the salvation brought by Jesus within the context of God fulfilling the promise to Abraham. That promise is not annulled by the annulment of the Mosaic covenant. Our hope is even stronger because now Jesus has already gone ahead as our "forerunner" into the heavenly sanctuary, being confirmed as "high priest for ever" (6,13-20).

Ch. 7 is a profound treatment of the priestly role of Jesus in which a new reality is described in the light and language of O.T. figures and promises. The mysterious non-Israelite priest-king, Melchizedek, provides the key for explaining how Jesus could be a genuine high priest, not merely independent of the tribe of Levi, but also superseding all levitical priesthood. Furthermore, "any change in the priesthood must mean a change in the Law as well" (v.12).

Quite explicitly the author argues that, "the earlier commandment is thus abolished, because of its weakness and ineffectiveness, since the Law could not make anything perfect; but now this commandment is replaced by something better" (vv.18-19).

In other words, the Levitical priesthood was basic to the whole Mosaic Law and the covenant binding Israel to live according to that Law. God's sworn promise to establish a different kind of priesthood — "You are a priest for ever of the order of Melchizedek" (Ps 110,4) — was already pointing the way to a new and more perfect covenant. In this connection comes the first explicit mention of covenant in Hebrews: "The very fact that it occurred with the swearing of an oath makes the covenant of which Jesus is the guarantee all the greater" (v.22). Such a reference to the (new) covenant as being directly related to Jesus' role as a new kind of priest alerts us to the author's conviction that priesthood includes the capacity to mediate effectively between God and the human race. Christ's mediation is perfect and enduring "for ever", since he has been raised up after offering himself in sacrifice and now lives on "as the Son who is made perfect for ever", to intercede before God for all people (vv.20-25).

Ch.8 announces: "The principal point of all that we have said is that we have a high priest of exactly this kind". Christ is now appointed by God as the minister of the heavenly sanctuary, of which the earthly Tent or Holy of Holies was only a faint reflection. Jesus has gained immediate access to God, being seated "at the right of the throne of divine Majesty" (vv.1-5). Again, the connection between his priestly ministry and the new covenant is stressed: "He has been given a ministry as far superior as is the covenant of which he is the mediator, which is founded on better promises" (v.6). To insist more emphatically on the excellence and superiority of the new covenant, the author does not hesitate to argue that it has replaced the former (Mosaic) one. Giving the longest quotation of all those found in the N.T., he recalls the full text of the promise of a new covenant made through Jeremiah. He concludes relentlessly: "By speaking of a new covenant, he implies that the first one is old. And anything old and ageing is ready to disappear" (v.13).

E 4. Jesus, "mediator of a new covenant", has offered himself as the perfect sacrifice (9,1 - 10,39).

The levitical high priest was the only one allowed to enter the Holy of Holies of the earthly Tent, and that but once a year, with sacrificial blood of animals. Such blood, however, could not bring any worshipper to perfection, for it could not cleanse the conscience of sin (9,1-10). Christ, however, has now entered the heavenly dwelling place of God, taking his own sacrificial blood. The blood of Christ, who offered himself to God "through the eternal Spirit" (instead of through the old fire of holocaust[38]), is truly effective to "purify our conscience from dead actions so that we can worship the living God. This makes him the mediator of a new covenant ..." (9,11-15).

As we saw when dealing with Exodus, an important objective of the liberation from slavery to an Egyptian pharaoh was to free the Israelite to worship Yahweh. The sealing of the Sinai covenant in sacrificial blood was a mutual commitment of Yahweh and Israel. The subsequent history of Israel manifested that the service, the worship of God remained fitful and inadequate, too frequently made unacceptable because of sin. Only the new mediator's self-sacrificing death was adequate "to redeem the sins committed under [that] earlier covenant" so that now "those called to an eternal inheritance may receive the promise" (9,15). Here again it is made quite clear that God's promise endures and is actually the explanation of why a new covenant should be granted to a sinful people. The new covenant is as gratuitous and everlasting as the original promises recorded in Genesis and amplified in succeeding books. Because Christ's blood has secured the cleansing of the inner conscience of sinful humans, it opens the way for them to offer a truly acceptable worship of God.

The part played by the new covenant in ensuring access to "an eternal inheritance" leads the author to bring out the aspect of "testament", which was the more common secular meaning of the term **diatheke**. In the sense of a last will and testament, such a "disposition" takes effect only after "the death of the testator", and "that is why even the earlier **diatheke** was inaugurated with blood" (9,16-18). As for the "testament" of Christ, it came into effect when he sacrificed himself "once and for all" (9,26), and was thereby able to enter "heaven itself", to remain for ever "in the presence of God on our behalf" (9,24). Entry into that presence of God, to join Christ there, is actually to receive the "inheritance" that he has bequeathed to all his human family. His "last will" is definitive and even more irrevocable than ordinary human testaments. Individuals may deny or despise or ignore such a momentous testament, but they can never annul or modify it — nor can they prevent others loyal to Christ from receiving their proper inheritance[39].

Ch. 10 concentrates attention on the sacrifice offered by Christ as our high priest and mediator of a new covenant. By comparing and contrasting the sacrifices of the Law with that of Christ, the author puts his finger on the outstanding feature of the unique sacrifice which far surpasses and replaces all the others for ever[40]. Instead of continuing to offer the kinds of sacrifice laid down by the Law, Christ made his own the words of Ps 40: "You gave me a body. ... then I said, 'Here I am, I am coming,' .. to do your will, God" (vv.5-7). The mission of Jesus amounts to abolishing the old inadequate sacrifices by presenting to God a sacrifice that is fully acceptable in every way. In offering himself, Christ "has offered one single sacrifice for sins, and then taken his seat for ever, at the right hand of God" (vv. 10-12). So perfect is his sacrifice that "by virtue of that one offering, he has achieved the eternal perfection of all who are sanctified" (v.14).

Although Jeremiah did not specify in his famous prophecy how sins would be taken away, now the connection between Christ's voluntary offering of himself and the forgiveness of sins is made: "The Holy Spirit attests this to us, for after saying: 'No, this is the covenant I will make with them, when those days have come.' the Lord says: 'In their minds I will plant my Laws, writing them on their hearts, and I shall never more call their sins to mind' " (vv.15-17).

This connection is alluded to again in the transitional summing up of the central doctrine: "We have then, brothers, complete confidence through the blood of Jesus in entering the sanctuary, by a new way which he opened for us, a living opening through the curtain, that is to say, his flesh" (vv.19-20). We should therefore be "sincere in heart .. our hearts sprinkled and free from any trace of bad conscience. .. Let us be concerned for each other, to stir a response in love (literally 'a paroxysm of love') and good works" (vv.22-24). Furthermore, if violations of the Law of Moses could bring death, then "any one who tramples on the Son of God, and who treats 'the blood of the covenant' which sanctified him as if it were not holy, and who insults the Spirit of grace, will be condemned to a far severer punishment" (vv 28- 29). Here the promises in Ezekiel concerning a new heart and a new spirit can also be perceived as fulfilled through the "sprinkling of hearts" with the blood of the new covenant, plus the gift of "the Spirit of grace" to transform the stoniest of hearts. With such a marvellous gift comes also an awesome responsibility to honour this new — and final — covenant.

The author's use (10,19) of 'eisodos (= a way into, entry, entrance, a right of entrance) to sum up the result of Christ's covenant should be taken as closely related to the original 'exodos achieved through Moses and oriented towards entrance into the promised land. Moses died without actually entering that promised land, and even Joshua's occupation of it still left much to be desired concerning full entry into "God's rest". The 'exodos which Jesus has now achieved personally and to which he calls all people is primarily a liberation from all forms of sin and its enslaving consequences in daily life.

The 'eisodos, at the other end of the road, is the positive goal of redemption and liberation. It is the unrestricted entry into the presence of God, to be there with the risen Christ, whose very body has become the "living way", the 'odos (10,20; cf. Jn 14,6), by which all of us in turn may enter into the abiding household of God[41]. Liberation theology has much to say about modern forms of exodus, but not so much on the ultimate goal, which is the 'eisodos, towards which the crucified and risen Lord is the only road or 'odos. Others may achieve a striking liberation from human tyranny, but as Christians we should urge those so liberated to march onwards to the final goal, the full entry into God's company and into fellowship with all God's people.

E 5. A pilgrim people called to follow faithfully the example of Jesus, mindful of "the blood of the covenant" (Cc. 11 - 13).

Ch. 11 is a great review of the faith displayed by the outstanding servants of God as they responded to their vocation. The theme of pilgrimage is prominent, for such servants were aware of being "only strangers and nomads on earth"; "they were longing for a better homeland, their heavenly homeland" (vv.13 and 16). Ch. 12 calls for persevering and courageous imitation of Jesus, "who endured the cross, disregarding the shame of it" (v.2). If God is disciplining Christians, it is a Father correcting his children. Instead of coming into an atmosphere of fear and trembling, such as surrounded the sealing of the covenant at Sinai, Christians have come to Mount Zion, "and the city of the living God, the heavenly Jerusalem". There is assembled "the whole Church of first-born sons, enrolled as citizens of heaven". The readers are told (and therefore it is true of those still on earth): "You have come to God himself, .. and to Jesus, the mediator of a new covenant, and to a purifying blood which pleads more insistently than Abel's. Make sure you never refuse to listen when he speaks. .. We have been given possession of an unshakeable kingdom" (vv.18-28).

The phrases underlined are highly significant in the way that they relate the Church to both the new covenant and to the kingdom now possessed by those who have accepted that covenant. The text also refers again to Jesus as "the mediator of a new covenant", then goes on to urge complete obedience to him when he speaks. In that way Christians can make their own the obedience of Jesus to the Father's will, which is clearly proclaimed through him as Son. Christ's blood "pleads" as a reminder both to God and to humankind of the covenant of love which it sealed. The blood of Jesus, like the blood of innocent Abel, cries out, not for vengeance on the killers, but for an end to unjust killing, to be replaced by a profound respect for human life as something precious and sacred.

Ch. 13 concludes the work with further exhortations, e.g. "Continue to love each other like brothers, and remember always to welcome strangers .. Keep in mind those who are in prison .. Marriage must be honoured by all" (vv. 1-4). Those are all basic demands of the new covenant on Christians, especially that of mutual love. Solidarity with Christ calls his followers to "go to him outside the camp and bear his humiliation. .. Through him, let us offer God an unending sacrifice of praise" (vv.13 -15). The sacrifice is by no means restricted to words, but includes "doing good works and sharing your resources" (v.16).

The final prayer brings out excellently the central concern of the writer: "I pray that the God of peace, who brought back from the dead our Lord Jesus, the great Shepherd of the sheep, by the blood that sealed an eternal covenant, may prepare you to do his will in every kind of good action; effecting in us all whatever is acceptable to himself through Jesus Christ" (vv.20-21). The prayer relies on the power of God, manifested by the resurrection of "the great Shepherd", to prepare and effectively move human hearts to comply with "his will". For the Christian, as for Jesus, to do the will of God in a spirit of self-offering is what pleases God because it accepts his reign. It amounts to living according to the basic demand of the new covenant. God wants primarily not our external offerings but ourselves. With Jesus as our great high priest, we are invited and enabled to offer our whole being and daily life as an acceptable sacrifice to God[42].

In this way Hebrews closes on the same note with which it opened, namely that God has spoken — and continues to speak — through his Son. As Son, he makes known God's word and will, revealing the demands of the new covenant. As our elder Brother, and on our behalf, as our fully accredited representative, he has accepted and carried out completely the will of God the Father. It was because he persisted in proclaiming the will of God that he was called on to lay down his own life rather than become a disobedient Son or a retired prophet. It was his voluntary self-sacrifice which marked the acceptance and sealing of the new covenant, which must remain as an everlasting covenant because it expresses his last will and testament at the hour of sacrifice. Now risen and glorified forever in the real dwelling place of God, he has become thereby the living way to the Father. To follow him as the way is to accept the will of God, to live up to all the demands of the new covenant, and hence to sacrifice oneself for God and for the whole family of God.

While it is true that the central theme of Hebrews is Christ as high priest, the author convincingly argues that the change of priesthood has brought with it such a radical change from the Law of Moses that Jesus is in fact the mediator of a new covenant.

F. NEW COVENANT IN 1 PETER

This epistle opens with a greeting from "Peter, apostle of Jesus Christ, to all those living as aliens in the Dispersion" (of Asia Minor). The author later on speaks as "a witness to the sufferings of Christ" (5,1). There are sufficiently solid grounds for accepting that this writing does come from Simon Peter, while admitting that his secretary, Silvanus (5,12), probably had considerable influence on its language and style. Its many exhortations to accept suffering inflicted on the innocent "for doing right" (3,17) point to a time fairly close to the outbreak of persecution, as in Rome under Nero in 64 A.D. The letter sends greetings from "Babylon" (5,13), which is an apocalyptic title for Rome, the current empire threatening the people of God.

The epistle gives the impression of being addressed especially to the newly baptized in the communities, especially up to 4,11 which closes the section with a doxology and "Amen". Being for beginners in the Christian life, it exhorts them: "Like new-born babies all your longing should be for milk — the unadulterated spiritual milk" (2,2). This is a prior stage to that envisaged in Hebrews, which has in mind those already maturing in the faith and participating in the eucharistic celebration — "solid food is for adults with minds trained by practice" (Heb 5,14).

Another striking difference between I Peter and Hebrews is the way the former concentrates on the results of the new covenant on the Christians, including their new standing as "a holy priesthood" and "a kingdom of priests" (1 P 2,5.9). This supplements the concentration of Hebrews on Christ as the one and eternal high priest, the mediator of the new covenant. Although 1 Peter does not mention the word "covenant" explicitly, it certainly keeps using explicit covenant language to describe the reality of those who believe the gospel.

Right from the opening greeting the recipients are said to be "obedient to Jesus Christ and sprinkled with his blood" (1,2). Thanks to him and the gospel, they are now receiving the fulfilment of what was foretold by the prophets (1,12). Like Israel of old, they are called to holiness, "after the model of the Holy One who calls us : 'Be holy, for I am holy' " (1,16). For Christians this entails being "obedient children", who address God as "Father" and who regard the present life as a time of exile, until they reach their abiding home (1,16-17). The price of their ransom from former bondage was nothing less than the "precious blood as of a blameless and spotless lamb, Christ" (1,19). Here, both the sprinkling of the blood of the paschal lamb on the door-posts (Ex 12,7) and the sprinkling of the people to seal the covenant (Ex 24,8) seem to be relevant. They are immediately told that, since their purification enables them to "experience the genuine love of brothers , they should "love each other intensely from the heart" (1,22). Apparently related to baptism is the reference to their "new birth .. from .. the living and enduring Word of God" (1,23). Furthermore, "this Word is the Good News that has been brought to you" (1,25). As "new-born babies" they should long for the unadulterated "milk", the gospel, through which they have tasted how good the Lord is (2,2-3).

Having accepted the gospel of the Lord and membership of his people through baptism, these neophytes are to unite themselves ever more closely with him. He is "the living stone", upon which they too can be as "living stones making a spiritual house as a holy priesthood to offer the spiritual sacrifices made acceptable to God through Jesus Christ" (2,4-5). U. Vanni draws attention to the double use of "spiritual" in the phrase underlined, for the Greek adjective **pneumatikos** in this whole context is best translated as "pervaded by the Spirit"[43]. Unlike Hebrews, 1 Peter does not make an explicit comparison with the former sanctuary, but it certainly indicates the present reality of the Christian community being both a priestly group and a living sanctuary wherein acceptable sacrifices are offered to God "through Jesus Christ".

This leads to a ringing affirmation of the fulfilment of what was only mentioned at Mount Sinai in the future tense and as conditional: "So now, if you are really prepared to obey me and keep my covenant .. for me you shall be a kingdom of priests" (Ex 19,5-6). In contrast, Peter assures the Christians that, "you are a chosen race, a kingdom of priests, a holy nation" (2,9)[44]. This puts beyond doubt that Peter is alluding to the Sinai covenant and affirming that through Christ the proposed ideal has been accomplished. Each "new-born" member of Christ's people belongs to the "kingdom of priests" having him as its living link. Moreover, the link with both God and with one another is so strong that A. Vanhoye remarks: "Since it is at the same time Temple of God and community of believers, the 'spiritual house' appears as the perfect realization of the New Covenant, under its two inseparable aspects: communion with God and communion among human beings"[45] (emphasis added).

It is worth noting the kind of "Spirit-pervaded" sacrifices that this new priestly group is called on and enabled to offer in union with Christ, "who suffered for you and left you an example for you to follow in his steps" (2,21). An important part of their priestly role concerns daily life in the midst of the unbelieving "gentiles". To them they must give constant witness by their acceptance of public authority and by their good deeds, as they "sing the praises of God" (2,9). The phrase is taken from a description of a new exodus after the Babylonian exile: "The people I have shaped for myself will broadcast my praises" (Is 43,21). Yet another allusion to the renewal of a covenant of love between Yahweh and his people is drawn from Hosea and declared to be fulfilled in the Christian community: "Once you were a 'non-people' and now are the People of God" (2,10).

Slaves, for their part, are called on to obey their masters and even to accept unjust punishment in the spirit of Christ. In this way Christian slaves can share in the vicarious sufferings of Christ, who "had done nothing wrong" (2,22). Such a humble acceptance of unjust suffering may seem at first to be better left aside these days in the interests of getting everybody to denounce unjust punishments and oppose them at every turn. Nonetheless, there is still an enormous amount of suffering inflicted on innocent people today, hence the need to help them realise the value of suffering borne in union with the crucified Lord [46]. He died because he would not desist from denouncing injustice, and yet he accepted his extremely unjust execution as a sacrifice worth making for the sake of his friends, those for whom he wanted more justice and a more abundant life. The Father was pleased to accept that sacrifice and grant the final victory over sin and death to his beloved Son (cf. 1,21).

Through him a share in that victory is assured to others who share in his unjust sufferings, moved by his Spirit (cf. 3,13 -4,19). This seems to be the framework within which Peter was writing, precisely as "a witness to the sufferings of Christ" (5,1). Incidentally, we note a radical change from the Peter who wanted the Christ to put aside his talk about having to suffer (Mk 8,32). If evil is to be overcome by good, rather than by force of arms, there is still need for Christians willing to stand up unarmed in defence of all their brothers and sisters, whatever the cost. Unjust punishment or suffering is accepted, not to please or enrich the unjust people causing it, but rather to help other victims of sin and injustice. In Peter's eyes, the cost can be regarded and offered as a pleasing sacrifice to God, on behalf of our troubled human race[47].

G. NEW COVENANT IN THE APOCALYPSE

The Apocalypse, or Revelation (the English meaning of the term) comes as a fitting conclusion to the whole Bible, reminding us of the imagery of the creation and deluge stories [48]. The same Creator is at the beginning and the end of our universe, as well as of our human history in particular. "I am the Alpha and the Omega', says the Lord God" (1,8). The risen Christ, too, speaks to the seven churches as "the First and the Last" (1,17; 2,8). Indeed, Jesus Christ, "the First-born from the dead" (1,5), is so completely the Lord of history that he is its centre as well as its beginning and end. He is seen constantly in the visions of the Apocalypse as the Lamb that was slain and is alive, sharing the Father's throne, actively and successfully directing all human history towards the "end" desired by Almighty God.

The apocalyptic literary form chosen to convey the message allows the author, John, to present an enormous wealth of images and symbols drawn from the Old Testament. Ugo Vanni mentions that the Apocalypse contains some 500 allusions to the O.T.[49]. Not only is this work an heir of the prophets, like the abundant Jewish apocalyptic works written during the three hundred years preceding it[50], but it is a prophetic work in its own right. John is the spokesman of Jesus Christ, who speaks through him to the churches (cf. Rev 1,2; cc.2-3;10,11; 22,10.19). At the end of each of the seven letters to the churches, the recipients are urged to "listen to what the Spirit is saying to the churches" (2,7.11.17 etc.), implying that they have access to an inspired prophetic message.

Like its forerunner, Daniel, Revelation emerges from a severely persecuted community, whose hope and courage need to be sustained by the consoling vision of a God and a Redeemer in full control of all human battles. What is assured is not freedom from opposition and suffering, but the final victory which will usher in the definitive reign of God and his Christ over all nations. "Babylon" is again the great city opposed to God and persecuting the servants of God, but John has in mind the city of Rome (seated on seven hills — 17,9) and its mighty empire. The date of the final redaction of Revelation would be about 95 A.D., at a time when Domitian was persecuting the Church.

The resistance to emperor worship is parallel to what was happening in the days of the Maccabees when they had to resist Antiochus IV Epiphanes. It is also parallel to the resistance of the Hebrews to the Egyptian pharaoh who regarded himself as divine, the son of the sun-god Re. These parallels are hinted at in the innumerable allusions to themes of Exodus and to battles against "the kings of the earth". Our interest lies especially in the more obvious references to Exodus and the Sinai covenant, through which the reality of the new covenant is constantly described, without ever being named explicitly as such.

Revelation also avails of the prophet Hosea's imagery of betrothal and marriage to describe the reality of the covenant of love between Jesus Christ and his faithful servants, redeemed by him to become a kingdom and a celebrating Church. The forward thrust of the whole book of Revelation comes from the "one who loves us" (1,5) guiding his people to become a truly beautiful bride properly prepared for "the marriage of the Lamb" (19,7). The Spirit fills the bride's heart with deep yearning: "The Spirit and the Bride say, 'Come!' .. Amen; come, Lord Jesus" (22,17. 20). To the bride and the bride-city, the new Jerusalem, is opposed the harlot and the harlot-city, Babylon. The utter defeat and destruction of Babylon is presented as the final victory to free the bride from all persecution and permit the definitive marriage to take place (17-19).

G 1. The blood of the Lamb inaugurating a new covenant

In the opening "liturgical dialogue" (1,4-8)[51], the assembled Christians give glory "to him who loves us and freed us from our sins by his own blood, who has made us a royal nation of priests in the service of his God and Father" (1,5-6 — N.A.B.). The blood of Christ serves like that of the paschal lamb in Egypt to save the chosen people from death and to bring about their escape from slavery. It also serves like the sacrificial blood at Sinai to seal the covenant whereby the people can become "a kingdom, priests to God " (to give a literal translation of Rev.).

The remainder of Revelation makes it clear that the "kingdom" is called and enabled by Christ to participate with him in the mission of bringing all the world to accept the reign of the Father. Even more than 1 Peter, this work presents Christians as "reigning" with Christ precisely as priests giving personal and community witness, which helps orient the world towards God the Father[52]. The family nature of the kingdom as ruled by the Father is further emphasised by presenting Jesus as "the Son of God" (2,18), and Christians as those on whose foreheads is written the Lamb's name and that of his Father (14,1). As if to emphasise the family relationship thus established between the Christians themselves, John refers to himself as "your brother and partner in hardships, in the kingdom" (1,9).

The next explicit mention of people of God bought with the blood of "a Lamb that seemed to have been sacrificed" (5,6) occurs in a new hymn being sung to him before the throne of God: "You are worthy to take the scroll and break its seals, because you were sacrificed, and <u>with your blood you bought people for God of every race</u>, language, people and nation and made them a line of kings and priests for God to rule the world" (5,9-10). The hymn emphasises the universality of the people redeemed by the blood of the Lamb and thereby admitted into membership of the new covenant. In union with the Lamb, as "kings and priests" they are empowered "to rule the world".

Their titles are no mere honorary ones repeated because they were used of those called into the Sinai covenant. On the contrary, it is strongly asserted through symbolism that the Lamb is the only one capable of taking the scroll of human history as planned by God and bringing it to pass. His people receive through him an active role as subordinate "kings and priests" concerned with bringing all their human family to know and accept the reign of God in their lives. As priests, their special mission is to bring God to all the world, especially by their witness, and strive to lead the world to God by their example. The sacrifice they offer in union with the Lamb must be their whole self, even if called on to make the supreme sacrifice.

Before the Lamb opens the seventh seal of the scroll, John is granted a vision of 144,000 Israelites and of a vast white-robed multitude "of people from every nation, race, tribe and language" (7,9). The latter people are said to be those who have come through "the great trial " and "have washed their robes white again in the blood of the Lamb" (7,14). Significantly, they are able to stand before God and serve him continually. God "will spread his tent over them", obviously to protect them, while the Lamb "will be their shepherd" (7,15-17). The effectiveness of the Lamb's leadership is brought out clearly in a later vision concerning the final battle between Babylon and the Lamb. Because the Lamb is "Lord of lords and King of kings", "<u>he and his followers</u>" will defeat all kings allied to Babylon (17,14).

The aspect of a struggle unto death emerges in the third and final explicit reference to the new people of God as "priests", for it is the martyrs whose souls are seen sharing in "the first resurrection" — "the second death has no power over them, but they will be priests of God and of Christ and reign with him for a thousand years" (20, 5-6). The "thousand years" is presented as the period before the final resurrection and judgment of everybody (cf.20,11-15). Each is to be held responsible for his or her "deeds". Christians in particular are expected to "obey God's commandments and have in themselves the witness of Jesus" (12,17; cf. 14,12)[53]. Or another way of relating their good works to the new covenant is to regard them as a personal contribution towards the wedding dress being prepared for the bride of the Lamb, "because her linen is made of the good deeds of the saints" (19,8). The emphasis given by John to Hosea's imagery of husband and wife merits closer attention as a fitting conclusion to the biblical presentation of the covenant between God and Israel, between Christ and the Church.

G 2. The Church as the bride of the Lamb

The book of Revelation is set between the first liturgical refrain giving glory "to him who loves us" (1,5) and the final one expressing the yearning of the Church as bride: "Amen; come, Lord Jesus" (22,20). Although the book keeps returning to the same themes presented under different symbols, there is also a definite progress towards the final, complete, and everlasting establishment of God's reign over all our universe through Jesus Christ. The people of all tribes and tongues are shown to be led effectively toward the final "marriage of the Lamb" : " Alleluia! The reign of the Lord our God Almighty has begun; let us be glad and joyful ... for this is the time for the marriage of the Lamb. His bride is ready, and she has been able to dress herself in dazzling white linen" (19,7-8).

Jesus Christ, as "the one who loves us", is seen in John's opening vision "on the Lord's day" as "one like a Son of man" standing in the middle of seven golden lamp-stands. The lamp-stands are the symbols of the seven churches, and hence are also equivalent to the whole Church. In that way Jesus is shown as one anxious to be personally present within the Church, following closely and critically the response of each community to his love. His first reproach to one of the seven churches, Ephesus, is "that you have less love now than formerly" (2,4). In the letter to Philadelphia, the reward promised is to become as a pillar in God's sanctuary, bearing God's name and the name of the new Jerusalem,the city coming down from God in heaven (3,10-13).

The city of God on earth is a place of persecution, symbolised by the three and a half years of persecution (11,2; 12,6), as in Daniel. In connection with the persecution, the Church is presented as "a woman robed with the sun", a woman "crying aloud in the pangs of childbirth". The son she brings forth safely is the Christ, who is taken up to God, whereas the mother and "the rest of her children" are furiously assailed by the huge red dragon (12,1-17). The woman is a symbol broad enough to include the people of Israel from whom the Messias was born, and the Church which likewise was born from Israel. There are good grounds for seeing Mary as the individual "virgin daughter of Sion" who sums up in herself the more collective role of Israel and the Church[54].

In complete contrast to the woman clothed with the sun stands the prostitute-city of Babylon, "mother of all the prostitutes .. on the earth" (17, 5). The total destruction of Babylon signifies that the reign of God has triumphed, and that the time for the "marriage of the Lamb" has arrived (19,7). The new Jerusalem is also depicted as a city "coming down out of heaven from God, prepared as a bride dressed for her husband" (21,2). One of the seven beatitudes given in Revelation[55] says: "Blessed are those who are invited to the wedding feast of the Lamb" (19,9).

In his work on Israelite marriage, A. Tosato explains well the two stages, betrothal and wedding[56]. During the betrothal the bride and bridegroom live apart, even though pledged to marriage. Then comes the actual wedding, with the departure of the bride from her own home to go to live with the bridegroom in his home. This is the occasion for the wedding feast, whereby the marriage is celebrated as something now fully concluded and binding in law. Revelation accepts that general progression in the relationship between the Lamb and his bride. In the final vision of the new Jerusalem John is invited by one of the angels, "Come here and I will show you the bride that the Lamb has married" (Greek has literally: "the bride the wife of the Lamb") (21,9). It is through the wedding that the ancient promise reaches its perfect fulfilment: "They will be his people, and he will be their God, God-with-them" (21,4). Furthermore, of anyone who is victorious God declares, "I will be his God, and he will be my son" (21,7). Down the middle of the new Jerusalem flows "the river of life", having on either side of it "the trees of life" (22,1-2). What the first couple had failed to grasp, the Lamb and his wife will enjoy forever. This is the global dimension of the personal reward promised earlier: "those who prove victorious I will feed from the tree of life set in God's paradise" (2,7).

A question not settled by Revelation is the location of the new Jerusalem, which is seen by John as "coming down out of heaven from God" (21,2). Moreover, this is immediately after the mention of John's vision of "a new heaven and a new earth" (21,1). Here the pair, "heaven and earth", are equivalent to all our universe, so the vision is equivalent to seeing a new — or thoroughly transformed — universe. The new Jerusalem, the final kingdom of God in its everlasting perfection and inviolable union of love, could be located on this duly "regenerated" earth. The longed for coming of the Bridegroom may but mark the stage when the Bride is fully prepared to recognise him present in the midst of all the redeemed on earth, united through the communion of saints with all who have died in God's friendship.

One of the most striking aspects of Christ's role in Revelation as the Lord of all history and controller of all empires is that he invites and enables all his disciples to rule with him actively in order to establish God's reign over all. This gives "eschatological urgency"[57] to their loyal service.

NOTES

1. Peter F. Ellis, Seven Pauline Letters (Collegeville, Minnesota: 1982), 11. Cf. Nueva Biblia Española, 1750: "De las catorce cartas de Pablo, siete se consideran auténticas: Rom, 1 y 2 Cor, Gal, Flp, 1 Tes, Flm; la autenticidad de las otras se discute."
2. T.J. Deidun, New Covenant Morality in Paul, 12.
3. Ibid. Preface, xi.
4. Ibid. 21.
5. Ibid. 147-149; cf. 217; 63; 86-87; 101-103.
6. G. Panikulam, **Koinonia** in the N. T., 5.
7. J.A. Davis, Wisdom and Spirit — An Investigation of 1 Cor. 1.18 - 3.20 Against the Background of Jewish Sapiential Traditions in the Greco-Roman Period (Lanham & New York: University Press of America, 1984), 81; also 44: "At Qumran, as in Sirach, there is a connection between the acquisition of wisdom, and the aid, or activity of God's Spirit."
8. Ibid. 146-147 : "But our study does indicate that in terms of maintaining one's place within the covenant of grace established as a result of the Christ-event, Paul was firmly opposed to the attempt to maintain covenantal righteousness through adherence to the law of Judaism."
9. David Stanley, Christ's Resurrection in Pauline Soteriology (Rome: Biblical Institute Press, 1961), e.g. 286: "The inhabitation of the Holy Spirit, which is also the presence of the risen Son of God, makes man God's adoptive son. One day, through this indwelling Spirit, the Father 'who raised Jesus from death' will give man the fulness of salvation, by imparting Life to mortal man in the glorious resurrection of the just."
10. Ivo Da Conceicäo Souza, The New Covenant in the 2nd Letter to the Corinthians. A Theologico-Exegetical Investigation on 2 Cor 3:1-4.6 and 5:14-21 (Rome, Gregorian University Press, 1978), 68.
11. Ibid. 106.
12. Cf. New Jerusalem Bible, 1856-1858 for dating of Romans.
13. The phrase in Rom 3,25 — "a sacrifice for reconciliation" translates the Greek **'ilasterion**, which was the word used also for the "mercy seat" or "propitiatory" above the ark of the covenant (Ex 25,17-18). The high priest sprinkled it with sacrificial blood annually on the Day of Expiation (Lev 16,14). Cf. Heb 9,5-14 for the way Jesus as the new high priest brings to perfection the expiation of sin through his own sacrificial blood.
14. T. Deidun, op. cit. 50.
15. Cf. B. Byrne, 'Sons of God' — 'Seed of Abraham', 226 on Paul's concern throughout Romans and Galatians to show that through Christ Jew and Gentile alike are called to be children of God and heirs to the blessings promised to the descendants of Abraham.
16. Franklin Menezes, Life in the Spirit: A Life of Hope (Rome: Pontificia Universitas Urbiana, 1986), 5.
17. Ibid. 9: "As a result of the sin of man, the physical consequences of death and corruption that affect him consequently affect the material creation as it is gradually involved in a process of deterioration, corruption and

death." Cf. 77 on the intimate connection likewise between the redemption of our body and the redemption of all creation.
18. Cf. S. McDonagh, To Care for the Earth, e.g. 128: "The creative challenge for soteriology in our time is to reflect on how to link the continuing redemption of human beings, both individually and socially, with the redemption of the earth."
19. F. Menezes, op.cit. 80.
20. Cf. Terrance Callan, Forgetting the Root — The Emergence of Christianity from Judaism (New York: Paulist Press, 1986), a work taking its title from the text in Rom 11. Callan argues that "the adoption of a liberal policy toward Gentile converts by the greater part of the early church was the decisive factor which separated it from Judaism" (p.2).
21. Cf. Karl Kertelge, The Epistle to the Romans, in series "N.T. for Spiritual Reading", E.T. by Francis McDonagh (New York: Herder and Herder, 1972), 126-127: (On how Paul in Rom 11 sees the situation:) "In the light of the gospel the People of Israel appear as 'enemies' of God, because they have rejected his revelation in Christ. But in the light of their own history they appear as beloved by God, and they retain their position in spite of their present rejection of him."
22. Cf. S. Lyonnet, La Carità pienezza della legge (Roma: Ave Minima, 1971^2). This is consistent with his translation of Rom 13,10 in the original Bible de Jerusalen.
23. Cf. Markus Barth, Ephesians (New York: Doubleday Anchor Bible, 1974) e.g. 3-4: "The following thesis will be proposed for consideration: The apostle Paul himself wrote the epistle to the Ephesians from a prison in Rome toward the end of his life. .. Ephesians represents a development of Paul's thought and a summary of his message which are prepared by his undisputed letters and contribute to their proper understanding." Cf. New Jerusalem B., 1860: "In the knowledge, then, that the genuine Pauline authorship of these two letters is the strongest but not the only possible hypothesis, we can attempt to reconstruct the genesis of Paul's thought in Col and Ep." For another viewpoint, see the Nueva Biblia Española, 1816, where the date posited for the writing of Ephesians is "between the years 80 and 100".
24. M. Barth, op.cit. 275. Cf. P.J. Kobelski, "The Letter to the Ephesians", in NJBC 888: "In Pauline writings .. the reconciliation accomplished through the death of Christ brought peace and union with God. .. In Eph, this understanding of reconciliation is expanded to include peace and unity between Gentiles and Jews."
25. Cf. D. Stanley, op.cit. 226; cf. 286 where he points to this same verse (Eph. 2,18) as the one which "adequately sums up [Paul's] soteriological thought and represents its most mature expression".
26. M. Barth, op.cit. 609.
27. Cf. C. Baker, "The New Covenant in Miniature", in Manna (Sydney), No.5 (1962) 85-97.
28. M. Barth, op.cit. 715.

29. Cf. S.Scott Bartchy, First-Century Slavery and the Interpretation of 1 Cor. 7:21 (Atlanta, Georgia: Scholars Press, 1985), 58-59.
30. Ibid. 159.
31. Cf. Ugo Vanni, "La promozione del regno come responsabilità sacerdotale dei Cristiani secondo l'Apocalisse e la Prima Lettera de Pietro", in Gregorianum 68,1-2 (1987) 9-56; texts of 1 Peter are treated 34ff.
32. Cf. Ceslaus Spicq, L'Epître aux Hébreux, 2 Vol. (Paris: Gabalda, 1952 and 1953), I, 253-261; cf. 196, where Apollos is proposed as the most likely human author of Hebrews. Cf. A. Wikenhauser, N.T. Introduction, 465-470 for a brief account of arguments against Pauline authorship.
33. Cf. Albert Vanhoye, Struttura e Teologia nell' Epistola agli Ebrei (Class Notes for Students) (Rome: Biblical Institute Press, 1987), 19: "E proprio lo studio della struttura sarà uno degli argomenti più validi per dimostrare che la lettera agli Ebrei non e una lettera ma un discorso, una predica, perchè possiede una struttura letteraria de discorso, perfettamente conformata, alla quale non manca niente." Cf. Nueva Biblia Española, 1858, where it is suggested that Heb. was a sermon spoken in a eucharistic gathering.
34. Cf. James Swetnam, "Form and Content in Heb. 1-6", in Biblica 53(1972) 368-385, e.g. 381-2: "Putting all these indications together, the suggestion seems warranted that in 3,14 the **'upostasis** alludes to Christ present in the eucharist. In the eucharist the presence of Christ is the divine reality which lies hidden beneath a transitory and shadowy appearance. In the eucharist there is a reality which was begun by the words of Christ and is continued on by those who heard him either immediately or mediately." Cf. reference in preceding footnote to N.B.E., 1858. Cf. A. Vanhoye, La Nuova Alleanza Nel N.T., Class Notes for Students (Rome: Biblical Institute, 1984) 137, commenting on 10,19-22, says that there is good reason for thinking that the whole homily of Hebrews was given during a eucharistic celebration. Cf. Pierre Grelot, Le Ministère de la Nouvelle Alliance (Paris: Cerf, 1967), esp. 131-135 on how quickly the Lord's Supper came to be seen in N.T. as the summit of community life, so that the "centre of gravity" shifted to that celebration.
35. Cf. A. Vanhoye, ibid. 62.
36. A. Vanhoye, La Structure Littéraire de l'Epître aux Hébreux (Lyons: Desclée de Brouwer, 1976^2). Cf. id., Our Priest is Christ; and O.T. Priests and the New Priest, according to the N.T. (Petersham, Mass.: E.T. by B. Orchard, St Bede's Publications, 1986).
37. Cf. Id., La Structure..., 55-56; ;59. Also: Our Priest.., 12-13.
38. Cf. id., La Nuova Alleanza .., 116; 120-123. Cf. Luigi di Pinto, Volontà di Dio e legge antica nell'epistola agli Ebrei - Contributo ai Fondamenti Biblici della Teologia Morale (Napoli: [Excerpts from a doctoral dissertation in Fac. of Theol., Gregorian University, Rome], 1976), 64: "Ci sembra che l'Autore veda trasposta, per analogia simbolica, la funzione del fuoco, che coopera all'esecuzione dei sacrifici, allo **pneuma** [= Spirit], che interviene nell'offerta del Cristo" (author's emphasis).

NOTES

39. Cf. L. Pinto, op.cit. 14: "Il Risorto è l'uomo nuovo della nuova alleanza. In lui il patto è inviolabile" (emphasis added).
40. Ibid. 9, where he insists that the will of God emerges in Hebrews as central and as the foundation for moral and religious life under the new covenant. Also 46, commenting on Heb 10,10 as getting to the heart of the christology of Hebrews, "nella nuova relazione che si crea fra Gesù e i fratelli, e nel senso che assume per loro la volontà di Dio come base dell'esistenza" (emphasis added). Also 49.
41. Cf. C. Spicq, op.cit. 109-138 for common points in John and Hebrews (and Apocalypse).
42. Cf. A. Vanhoye, O.T. Priests..., 233: "Christ, by his total and perfect personal offering, became in his own person 'the new and living way'. His priesthood is situated at the highest level of reality; it is in the hearts of human beings that he establishes the New Covenant with the heart of God. 'A high priest, worthy of faith and merciful', Christ fills to perfection all the functions of the priesthood .."
43. Ugo Vanni, art. cit., 37-39, e.g. ftn. 47 : "tutta la vita cristiana è, come tale, animata dallo Spirito e diventa una offerta sacrificale."
44. A. Vanhoye, O.T. Priests..., 254. Cf. Philip Rosato, "Priesthood of the Baptized and Priesthood of the Ordained", in Gregorianum 68.1-2 (1987), 215-266. And in the same special issue of Gregorianum, 267-305, Félix-Alejandro Pastor, "Ministerios laicales y Comunidades de Base — La renovación de la Iglesia en América Latina."
45. A. Vanhoye, O.T. Priests.., 259.
46. U. Vanni, art. cit. 50; also the Conclusion, 55. Cf. Angel Anton, "Principios fundamentales para una teología del Laicado en la Eclesiología del Vaticano II", in same issue of Gregorianum, 103-155; likewise Jean Beyer, "Le laïcat et les laïcs dans l'Église", 157-185.
47. D. Senior, ch.13 on "Witness and Mission", in The Biblical Foundation for Mission, 300: "Two situations are singled out [in I Pet. 2] for detailed comment: household slaves and wives of nonbelieving husbands. These community members were likely to pay a special price for their mission of witness and they are held up to the whole community as an example of redemptive suffering" (emphasis added).
48. Cf. C. Westermann, Genesis 1-11, 50-51; and 606: "The creator holds his creation in his hands; he can destroy it again. ... Talk about the end of the world is taken up again in the Apocalyptic. .. At the end as at the beginning, the world and humankind are in God's hands. .. It is only in this broader context the work of Jesus Christ can be seen in its full significance as God's action in the 'middle of time'."
49. U. Vanni, Note Introduttorie all'Apocalisse (Rome: Class Notes for students, Biblical Institute, 1985) 32.
50. Cf. D.S. Russell, The Method and Message of Jewish Apocalyptic. 200 B.C. - AD 100 . E. Hennecke, N.T. Apocrypha: Vol.II: Apostolic and Early Church Writings . G. Vermes, The Dead Sea Scrolls in English.

R.E. Brown, P. Perkins, & A.J. Saldarini, "Apocrypha ...", in NJBC 1055 - 1082.

51. Cf. U. Vanni, La Struttura Letteraria dell'Apocalisse (Brescia: Morcelliana, 1980^2) 311, where the opening "liturgical dialogue" of 1,4-8 is taken to be balanced by the final one in 22,6-21. Cf. id., Il Simbolismo nell'Apocalisse (Rome: Gregorian University Press, 1985) 483 and 504-506 on the importance of the liturgy. Vanni says in the Summary, 505: "The Book of the Apocalypse is explicitly written for liturgical reading." Id., Apocalisse: Esegesi dei Brani Scelti, Parte XVI, Fasc. I (Rome: Gregorian University, 1986-7) 4-13, where the dialogue is made obvious.

52. Cf. id., art. cit. Gregorianum (1987), 56 (Summary) "The relationship between kingship and priesthood is primarily studied in the Apocalypse where the three occurrences of the term 'priests' [are] always accompanied with a reference to kingship.. The conclusion, where the Apocalypse is concerned, is that, having become 'kingdom' through a specific action of Christ, the Christians cooperate with him towards the progressive building up on earth of the kingdom, and thus mediate between the 'mystery' intended by God's design and its concrete actuation in history" (emphasis added).

53. Cf. Thomas Collins, Apocalypse 22:6-21 As the Focal Point of Moral Teaching and Exhortation in the Apocalypse (Rome: Gregorian University Press, 1986), esp. 42-44, where author affirms that the word "work" (Greek 'ergon) occurs 19 times in Apocalypse and that, "In the Apocalypse the term 'work' refers to human behaviour insofar as it has an enduring effect. A person's actions leave a mark. They are substantial, almost tangible, like the works of a person's hands. .. Once a person acts, his works remain, and he can be held accountable for them." Also 61: "The ethics of the Apocalypse is a function of the Christology. Christ exercises a divine role as judge and source of moral guidance." See 78 for other aspects of "good works" as desired, requested and encouraged by John.

54. Cf. Bernard Le Frois, The Woman Clothed with the Sun — Individual or Collective? (Rome: Biblical Institute Press, 1954), in which it is well argued that the "woman clothed with the sun" designates Mary as an individual, the mother of the Messias. She is at the same time the noblest member and outstanding representative of the two collectives, Mother Sion and Mother Church. Cf. Nunzio Lemmo, Maria, 'Figlia de Sion' A Partir da Lc 1,26-38 (Rome: "Marianum", 1985), esp. in the introductory remarks of Ignace de la Potterie, v-vi: "Si cerca piuttosto di comprendere meglio il mistero di Maria sullo sfondo della teologia biblica del Popolo di Dio, sotto il simbolo della Figlia di Sion, cioè di quella figura femminile che, nella tradizione profetica, rappresentava la Sion messianica, nella sua triple funzione di sposa, di madre, e di vergine. .. Maria viene descritta qui come la città santa di Dio, perchè in Lei, come in Israele prima e nella Chiesa dopo, era presente Dio stesso (emphasis added)." Then Lemmo's own observation, 27: "Niente di inaudito, dunque, nel vedere attribuita a

Israele una maternità nei riguardi del Cristo. Tale idea era nell'aria. Questa sfocerà nell'Apoc 12, dove la Donna sembra essere <u>ora la Chiesa, ora Maria</u>" (emphasis added).

55. Cf. T. Collins, op.cit. 208: (John) "lays a trail of beatitudes throughout the book" (1,3; 14,13; 16,15; 19,9; 20,6; 22,7.14). Also 205: "The whole series of beatitudes stretches from the first to the last verse of the Apocalypse, and reaches its culmination in the concluding dialogue."

56. Angelo Tosato, Il Matrimonio Israelitico — Una Teoria Generale (Rome: Biblical Institute Press, 1982), esp. 109 - 110: "Possiamo designare questo secondo momento, per meglio distinguerlo dal primo che abbiamo designato come 'sposalizio', col nome di 'nozze'. .. Nulla di nuovo viene ora stipulato con le nozze. Si dà soltanto adempimento agli impegni presi con lo sposalizio. .. Si può dire che ora con esso il matrimonio viene completamente concluso e pienamente posto in essere il coniugio." Cf. Donal McIlraith, The Reciprocal Love Between Christ and the Church in the Apocalypse (Rome: Columban Fathers, 1989). This dissertation in biblical theology at the Gregorian University arrived when the present work was ready for the press. It is an excellent presentation of the covenant love which culminates in "the marriage of the Lamb". It follows through the Apocalypse the two stages of a Jewish marriage as mentioned by Tosato. Concerning the final stage McIlraith says (188): "This individual, the Risen Jesus Christ, holds the destiny of all humanity. This one individual is the partner of the wife. Conversely, the whole of humanity is presented as finding eschatological fulfilment in the relationship with this one individual, the Risen Jesus Christ." ... ... "The term Wife is purely eschatological." Also 202: "This one love is both the gift of the Lamb and the task of the Wife. Only the Spirit makes this possible."

57. Cf. T. Collins, op.cit. 22-23. Many times in Revelation the words "quickly" or "soon" occur. For instance, five times Christ is said to be coming "soon". "This is the context in which the Christian lives and acts, a context of urgency." Also 24: "The Lord is coming soon. Time is short. There is hardly a more effective way of motivating a person to examine his life than to remind him of that." On the question of what happens to the earth <u>after</u> the Parousia, cf. Carlos H. Abesamis, Where are we going: heaven or new world? (Manila: Foundation Books, 1984), esp. 38-55 on the "new world".

CHAPTER 13 : COVENANT DIMENSION IN LIBERATION THEOLOGY

INTRODUCTION:

The introduction to this book drew attention to some of the harshest realities of the world in which we are living today. These were seen to be closely connected with the scandal of a rich and powerful minority cornering for themselves a vast proportion of the world's resources, at the cost of indescribable suffering among the majority. Hundreds of millions today are left hungry, sick, homeless, landless, illiterate, politically marginated, and threatened with premature death. On the other hand, there is now a heightened awareness of the unity of the human family and more international cooperation in searching for solutions to its gravest problems. The Church for its part entered explicitly into these areas of common concern when, at the conclusion of Vatican II, it addressed a stirring message to the whole of humanity on the Church in the Modern World. Since then Christians around the world have sought to follow up that call to relate faith more effectively to the transformation of this world and its structures in keeping with the plan of God.

Keeping in mind that kind of emphasis and pastoral priority, especially in the Third World, we have looked again very closely at what the Scriptures have to say about covenants. From the opening pages of Genesis to the closing pages of Revelation we have followed the gradual unfolding of God's plan to draw all the human race into a family-like community, bonded to God and to one another through loyal love. Yahweh has constantly taken the initiative as Creator, as Lord of history, as King and Father (with mother-like qualities as well), demanding that a chosen people be freed from all forms of slavery and injustice so that they could develop freely in communities inspired by love. For this reason covenant has emerged as a goal of liberation, as well as a motivation for preserving and extending freedom. It also gave hope to Israel on many occasions when political freedom had been trampled underfoot by invading empires. M. Walzer shrewdly observes: "The Hegelian and the Leninist views of the Exodus have no place for the covenant, but it is central to the Jewish tradition" (emphasis added).[1]

We are left with no doubt about covenant being central not only to the Old Testament but also to the New. We have noted the continuity from one covenant to the next, as Yahweh extended the covenant from one family(in the days of Abraham) to one nation (in the time of Moses) and to all nations when Christ's hour arrived. Patriarchs like Abraham, liberators like Moses, military leaders like Joshua and the Maccabees, kings like David and Josiah, prophets like Amos, Hosea, Isaiah and Jeremiah, scribes like Esdras, and wisdom teachers like Sirach all found in covenant a criterion for daily living, as well as a strong incentive for renewal of commitment to God and their own people.

There were also surprising differences and new elements that entered into such covenants as the history of salvation gathered momentum, above all in the new covenant which superseded the old. In the person of Jesus Christ we have found the embodiment of all that covenant implies as a historical reality, as a religious symbol, and as a powerful inspiration for continuing commitment to liberating praxis in the world of today. Redemption and salvation are seen to include the integral liberation of the whole person and of every person, within a social context. Covenant without community and a family spirit of sharing would contradict the central biblical message that we have been perceiving anew as we reread all the Scriptures.

We have discerned that a biblical covenant carries with it a serious obligation, voluntarily accepted, to promote social justice and a generous family loyalty willing to make big sacrifices for the other community members, especially those enslaved or oppressed. Jesus is the supreme example of an elder brother willing to act as redeemer for all his brothers and sisters oppressed by sin and its multiple consequences. In calling us into the new covenant and sending us out to all nations as his witnesses, he is really calling on us to share in his own mission. As covenant partners inspired by his example and fired by his Spirit, we want to take an active part in his continuing mission of transforming this world, so as to make more manifest the reign of God over all of modern life and our history in the making. It is my contention that what distinguishes the kingdom of God from any merely human kingdom is well expressed in terms of the covenant relationships of loving fidelity and mutual concern between all the partners. The new covenant is as enduring as the kingdom of God, especially as it is an alliance of love, and "love never comes to an end" (1 Cor 13,8).

The preceding chapters have therefore been an attempt of an exegete to present a synthesis of the biblical covenants in a way that should throw considerable light on many of the biggest issues being raised these days in liberation theology. I have tried to avoid the reproach of Hugo Assmann: "The usual views of exegetes who 'work on the sacred text' are of little use to us, because we want to 'work on the reality of today'".[2] J.L. Segundo claims that liberation theology calls for a "hermeneutic circle", since "each new reality obliges us to interpret the word of God afresh, to change reality accordingly, and then to go back and reinterpret the word of God again, and so on".[3]

Well aware of the gaps in communication between theologians of the First and Third Worlds[4], the present writer wishes to facilitate the building of bridges between them. Likewise in what follows there is an ecumenical spirit, a call to ecumenism in socio-economic and political action. It also takes into account the growing possibility of frank dialogue between some Christians and Marxists in the same areas of public life. To achieve this, our final chapter will outline as briefly as possible the distinguishing characteristics of liberation theology for those not yet familiar with it. Fortunately the many fine works now available on it in English can serve to confirm and expand enormously what is said here[5]. The main thrust of this chapter will be to pick out those aspects of covenant which throw most light on the biblical themes, events and symbols very widely used in liberation theology. Hopefully liberation theologians and the evangelizing poor themselves will be persuaded to give more prominence in future to the covenant dimension in their reflections on liberating praxis.

A. WHAT IS LIBERATION THEOLOGY?

Liberation theology arose in Latin America as a pastoral response to the challenge thrown down by Vatican II when it called on the Church to be at the service of all humanity in this modern world. The Church was urged to direct the light and energy of the Gospel towards many huge problems facing the human race. In Latin America the most ubiquitous problem was that of a dehumanizing poverty and the enslaving dependence on international financiers and their local agents. It was the feeling of being oppressed and even enslaved that led to the longing for liberation and subsequent pastoral efforts to accompany the people's struggles for liberation from all that was oppressing them. This in turn led to a new searching of the Scriptures to discern what God has said and is saying to the oppressed poor. The Episcopal Conference of Latin America, meeting in Medellin in 1968, reflected this concern by using liberation language.

Three years later Gustavo Gutiérrez published his influential "Teología de la Liberación"[6]. In that work he speaks of liberation theology as "a critical reflection on Christian praxis in the light of the Word"[7]. On the basis of that description, as it is fleshed out in the whole work and widely expanded in other works, we can take as distinctive of liberation theology the following aspects:

1. A critical reflection

As in any genuine theology, faith in God is presupposed, then theology seeks to grasp better the implications of faith and to explain it convincingly to others. It is called <u>critical</u> because it constantly measures Christian praxis by means of the tools of analysis now offered by the social sciences. If the praxis is judged to be deficient in any way, the reflection will include practical considerations on how to improve the praxis. The Greek word **praxis** has been retained in English, as in Spanish, because it is a technical term with no satisfactory single word to translate it in modern languages. It is still being used here in something the same sense that Aristotle gave it, namely that kind of knowledge which is directed towards public and political action. Theory for him, on the other hand, was the knowledge concerned with the contemplation of (unchanging) truths, the realm of philosophers[8].

It was Karl Marx who gave great prominence and primacy to praxis as the kind of practical knowledge capable of <u>changing</u> the world instead of merely interpreting it[9]. In liberation theology, therefore, the praxis to be reflected on is the actual pastoral commitment of the local Church to change whatever is found to be contrary to Gospel values. Is the current praxis adequate to meet the challenge and set free the oppressed? What are the root causes of the oppressing situation, and what more should be done to eradicate them? Praxis is more than Christian practice, for it includes a continuing critical reflection on what is being done. It also connotes a readiness to modify any pastoral practice found to be still inadequate or even harmful to people, especially the poorest[10].

2. On liberating praxis

From this it can be seen that liberation theology turns its attention first to liberating praxis in a given ecclesial community rather than to this or that revealed truth[11]. It is worth noting that the Instruction on Christian Liberty and Liberation also insists that the Church's social teaching is essentially oriented towards action, and it speaks of "Christian praxis" as the fulfilment of the commandment of love[12]. To work towards a "civilization of love" is said to demand precisely a new reflection on the relation of that commandment to the present social order[13]. What is not mentioned explicitly is the need for never-ending reflection on that relationship, accompanied by a constant reconsideration of the inspired word on which it has been based, with a willingness to modify — or amplify — the accepted "directions for action"[14].

3. Accompanying a personal commitment to and with the poor

Latin American theologians also maintain that a personal commitment to participate with the people themselves in the whole liberating praxis is indispensable in order to produce a genuine liberation theology[15]. It is not enough to be working for the poor and trying to persuade the authorities to treat them better. What is of prime importance is an awareness of the dignity and capacity of the oppressed poor to be the principal agents in their marathon struggle to win full freedom. They, too, must be enabled to reflect critically on their dehumanizing situations, to evaluate what has caused it and why it is being maintained.

Pablo Freire's work in this area has given great prominence to "conscientization", whereby the down-trodden become more conscious of their rights and of the grave injustices being committed against them[16]. Through this process the oppressed can and, in growing numbers, already have become Christian communities committed to confront the modern Pharaohs. Courageously they demand release from their bondage, in order to serve the Lord of life in full liberty.

4. A praxis to challenge and change political decisions

Once a local church, or the whole Latin American church, becomes more fully aware of the need for liberation from many oppressive situations and structures, it inevitably finds that it must confront political powers in order to bring about the necessary socio-economic and political changes. One of the distinguishing features of liberation theology is its insistence that our faith urges us to tackle and change whatever is wrong in politics. To leave politics outside Christian commitment is in fact a surrender to the reign of insatiable greed and ruthless structures of domination. The political theology developed in Europe helped provide some of the general framework and terminology for liberation theology, but the latter soon emerged as a distinct form of theology. However, A. Fierro is justified in treating as inter-related the theologies of revolution, liberation, exodus, hope, and violence. "There are three common features", he finds, "in these latest theologies. They agree in projecting a theology that is practical, public and critical"[17].

The importance of politics in the mission of committed Christians has been emphasised recently by John Paul II in **"Rei Socialis"** (1987) and **"Christifideles Laici"** (1988). The first is significant for our purposes, as it draws attention to the positive values of liberation theology [18]. It also stresses that all the goods of this world are destined for common use, and their just distribution must be achieved through solidarity, equality, liberty, participation, political involvement, and a preferential love of the poor[19].

The second document is an apostolic exhortation which followed up the Synod of Bishops on the vocation and mission of the laity in the church and in the world. It insists even more strongly that Christian love and justice cannot leave aside an active participation in political affairs[20]. In recalling the common destination of all goods, it places private property firmly within that context[21]. A practical pastoral step is to ensure a more adequate preparation of the faithful for political affairs. For this important apostolate, the social doctrine of the Church provides principles of reflection, criteria of judgments and directions for action[22].

5. A praxis which wants all history to reflect God's reign

Throughout the entire Scriptures God acts in the midst of families and nations to help them escape in this world from the consequences of sin made painfully obvious in slavery, oppression, injustice, imprisonment, hunger and broken health. The laws given to God's people called for the setting up of better structures and fairer practices to defend the rights of the humblest people. The Old Testament makes it abundantly clear that Yahweh is Lord of history, who intervened in critical moments to help the Israelites attain and maintain freedom in socio-economic and political matters. In that way they could serve God freely, without idolatry — and without having their lives sacrificed to other people's idols.

During the twelve centuries from Moses to Christ, Israel was a theocracy, a nation in which religious and civil rule were merged. Identification of the people of Yahweh with the State of Israel (or Judah) was unquestioned. Their salvation was not outside their history as a nation seeking survival in the midst of many other growing nations. On the contrary, as Ignacio Ellacuria repeatedly asserts, it was "salvation in history"[23].

Likewise the kingdom of God proclaimed and inaugurated by Jesus is very much concerned with a change of heart that demands a radical change in the whole of society. It has set in motion a profound transformation of public life, including politics[24]. Because Jesus came to inaugurate a kingdom open to peoples of all States and countries, he did not leave any one State responsible for the maintenance and extension of God's kingdom. Citizens of every State are invited to modify their whole of way life in line with the Gospel values. Far from being an opium that dulls people into accepting unjust situations, biblical religion as it is now being lived in Latin America has ended any monopoly that Marxism may have had in arousing the oppressed to challenge and eradicate unjust systems[25]. Ernesto Cardenal can even see emerging in Latin America "a Christianity that is not anti-revolutionary, and a different Marxism — one that is not anti-Christian"[26].

It is in this world that Christians are called on to share actively in Christ's mission of directing all human life and history in harmony with the will of God. Our human race has only one destiny, and in guiding human history God encourages all people to become partners in making it truly a salvation history[27]. Obviously, not all that occurs within history can be identified as salvation history, in so far as there are people who reject and actively oppose the will of God in the shaping of history[28]. Considerable importance is given to piecing together the whole known history of Latin America, from the point of view of the conquered, the despoiled, the forced labourers, the marginated left to be perpetually hungry and dependent on untouchable authorities at home and abroad[29].

6. Continually evaluated in the light of the Word

Although liberation theology gives attention first to liberating praxis, it springs from a committed faith which seeks light constantly from the word of God, especially the Word incarnate. The Gospel is accepted as the power of God to save, and hence to set free effectively, those who believe (cf. Rom 1,16). What the Scriptures tell of the liberation and prolonged formation of God's people provides the light necessary to guide the present efforts (praxis) to promote the integral liberation of each person. Biblical salvation is by no means limited to getting people into heaven once their exile in this valley of tears has ended. It is especially by rereading pertinent passages of the Bible in reflection groups that oppressed people themselves become more deeply convinced that full human freedom in this world is an integral part of redemption and eternal salvation.

One of the most inspiring and encouraging developments in Latin America, particularly for a lover of the Scriptures, is the hunger of the humblest people here for the word of God. As the Boff brothers point out, the real roots of liberation theology are the innumerable poor people who, at their own level of generous faith, are reading the Scriptures in order to relate their daily struggles more directly to the reign of God[30]. Any parish in the poorer areas needs a big supply of Bibles to meet the constant demand of people in such groups, be they basic Christian communities, catechists, charismatic renewal groups, neocatechumens, marriage encounter couples, or members of mothers clubs. Professional exegetes like Carlos Mesters in Brazil have made great efforts to provide popular guidelines to help such groups link up their own lives and local history with the God speaking to them through the Bible[31].

In short, liberation theology is firmly set within a faith rich in compassionate love of the neighbour, especially the most afflicted, and a continual reflection, in the light of God's word, on the liberating praxis of one's (local) church inspired by such faith. What this present work has sought above all to do in the previous chapters has been to explain biblical covenants in a way that makes their rich contribution to human freedom and solidarity more obvious for our people of today. Hopefully that will serve to strengthen faith and make it more committed, because covenant demands wholehearted commitment to both God and all the family of God. It should also serve to encourage the local church, as a covenant community, to commit itself fully to the redeeming, liberating, and unifying mission of Jesus Christ, until no brother or sister of his remains enslaved or dying because of social injustice.

Finally, in the remainder of this chapter we can concentrate on that feature of liberation theology which is most explicitly biblical, namely, critical reflection in the light of the Word. Covenant morality, as we have discerned it from the the story of our first parents until its perfection in Christ Jesus, is undeniably one of the most basic criteria when it comes to making a critical reflection on what is being done or omitted. We shall now recall, by way of summary and conclusion, those aspects of biblical covenants which throw most light on the liberating praxis of the Church, especially as it is being experienced in Latin America. This, of course, is done with a keen awareness that the universal Church is being moved by the same Spirit in many other areas, too. In no country today can a Christian afford to ignore the invitation to "listen to what the Spirit is saying to the churches" (Rev 2,7). There is an appreciable stirring everywhere of hearts and minds concerning the plight of a billion people who are suffering unjustly.

B. COVENANT AND ALL CREATION

The initial rudimentary covenant discernible in the opening chapters of Genesis serves to highlight the special dignity bestowed on human beings and their unique role within all of creation. They are created capable of entering into dialogue with one another and with their Creator[32]. Free dialogue makes possible a mutual commitment of friendship and concern, with due regard to the vast difference between the Creator and the created. Failure to respect the instructions of the Creator led to the rupture of that initial friendly relationship, and affected adversely the marriage union between husband and wife. It also upset their harmony with the rest of the world, which they were meant to cherish and develop according to its God-given possibilities.

The alarming spread of sin and corruption soon threatened the continuation of humankind and of any living creature. The purifying flood that spared Noah and family moved God to grant the Bible's first explicit covenant or disposition, whereby the new human race was promised a future unthreatened by any similar natural disaster. The rainbow becomes a constant reminder to God and the human family of that gratuitous disposition. The importance of "remembering" a covenant is already touched on here; both parties are to remember the arrangement and relate to one another accordingly. Today the ecologists can rightly appeal to that universal covenant as a powerful symbol of the Creator's concern to preserve in a habitable condition the only planet home in which humans may continue to live. What God will not destroy, let no human folly destroy. Covenant morality today demands that the present human family take good care not to doom the next generation to death for lack of a home that can sustain human life.

C. COVENANT CONFIRMING THE PROMISE

In the story of Abraham and Sarah we have seen how God intervened suddenly and decisively to initiate a new stage in the history of salvation. God promised quite gratuitously to bless Abraham and his descendants so effectively that they would be the channel of blessing for the other "families of the earth". To reassure Abraham concerning the promise, God granted a covenant in such a way that it simply confirmed the promise already given. Nevertheless, it deserved to be called a covenant, in that it made more manifest, as it ritually sealed, a firm mutual commitment to friendship between God and Abraham (together with his wife and their promised heir).

The rest of Genesis, and indeed the remainder of the Bible, tells how the promise was gradually fulfilled. Through Isaac and Jacob came the large family of descendants as bearers of the promise, for to each of them the promise was renewed. The land of Canaan, where they lived as nomads, was promised to their descendants. That promise of land and universal blessing is a great source of encouragement for the millions of country people who are left landless today. Such people are left rootless and desperate, as their way of life and the future of their families is tied up with a plot of land, no matter how humble, to work as their own.

D. COVENANT CROWNING THE EXODUS

Thanks to Joseph's spirit of family loyalty and his willingness to forgive the harm done to him by his brothers, he was able to get the family settled in Egypt in the time of a great famine. In the following centuries that clan grew to be such a numerous people that the Pharaoh took repressive measures against it to ensure the national security of Egypt. He enslaved the Hebrews and instigated genocide against them by ordering the death of any male baby born to them. Through the courage of some midwives one baby boy, Moses, was saved from death, and through him Yahweh was later to set free the entire people.

The liberation of the Israelites from their slavery in Egypt is one of the highpoints of the Old Testament. It is the paradigm or model for modern liberation from socio-economic and political bondage. God, remembering the promises to Abraham, Isaac and Jacob, took the initiative in calling the exiled Moses to go back to set his people free, then Moses, with the help of his brother Aaron, went to confront the tyrant face to face. They also had a difficult task to convince their fellow-Israelites that they could walk out of their slavery and march safely to the promised land. The big crisis came at the Reed Sea, until eventually Yahweh enabled the Israelites to cross it in safety, whereas the charioteers of Pharaoh were all drowned.

That decisive victory over Pharaoh and his army "won glory" for Yahweh, who taught the Egyptians to "know that I am Yahweh" (Ex 14,4.18).

The "glory" was the public manifestation of God's saving presence in the midst of slaves whose liberation was achieved in direct defiance of the powerful slavemaster. Pharaoh was led, despite his hard-heartedness, to "know" Yahweh by experiencing the devastating effects of that saving power on those who persist in opposing it.

Another basic aspect of the liberation from Pharaoh's slavery was the opportunity it gave the Israelites to serve Yahweh, the one true God, instead of false gods like the Pharaoh. They had really been subject to a form of idolatry, since the Pharaoh was regarded as the son of the sun god. Slaves were to serve the State which the Pharaoh kept in harmony with all the gods and the whole of nature. It galled Pharaoh tremendously to be forced to set free the Israelites so that they could worship their own God, Yahweh, out in the desert, clear of Egypt. The highly organised State capitalism of Egypt was a forerunner of many modern forms of capitalism, State or private, that depend on unpaid or underpaid workers for national development. The workers, especially in the economically dependent Third World, are treated as though their lives can be sacrificed to increasing production and profits. Their children — girls as well as boys — die by the thousands as a direct result of the inhuman poverty which is the other side of the coin.

At Mount Sinai the Israelites freely agreed to the terms of the covenant which Yahweh offered them through Moses the mediator. In reflecting on modern efforts to set free oppressed peoples, we should never forget that the goal of the original exodus was the freedom to enter into a covenant with their liberating God[33]. One of the basic contentions of this present work is that liberation theologians have not yet given sufficient attention to this aspect of the exodus. For instance, J. Croatto concentrates on Exodus 1-15 in an article on liberation, prescinding from the covenant described in later chapters of Exodus[34].

One also finds something of this in the work of an exegete such as J. Topel aimed at determining "the scriptural bases of a liberation theology"[35]. He deals at first with the exodus and the journey to the promised land without mentioning the Sinai covenant, claiming that, "It is generally agreed that the Hebrews really became one nation when God delivered them from bondage as a slave class in Egypt"[36]. However, in a later chapter on laws, he explains that Yahweh did give laws to promote justice while Israel was in the desert, and gradually that was expressed as a covenant between the nation and Yahweh[37].

Some writers are even wondering what would be the point of liberation theology if there were no longer people to be liberated. A. Fierro, for instance, asks pointedly, "But what will happen when oppression disappears and there are no more people to liberate? ... Right now theologians need captive peoples in order to be able to talk about the gospel as liberation." He goes on to conclude that "liberation theology as such is destined to disappear"[38].

This means in practice that we must try to evaluate and orient any modern attempt at socio-political liberation in the light of the Sinai covenant. Liberation from political bondage must be seen as only the beginning of the road to full freedom, which needs the covenant dimension to consolidate it within the freed nation, as well as to extend it generously to others. Sinai's ten commandments (in the Catholic listing) comprise three demanding a proper relationship with Yahweh, and seven directed towards the rights and well-being of the neighbour. Other O.T. laws give more detailed protection to the widow, the orphan, the stranger and the slave.

These laws or "instructions" were seen as the demands of living in covenant with the just and compassionate Yahweh, who kept reminding them to treat others with something of the liberating compassion which they themselves had experienced. The promise to Abraham was unconditional and everlasting, whereas the Sinai covenant was conditional and could terminate if the conditions were not observed by Israel. A helpful observation is made by L.J. Topel, who finds that the promise can be attributed to the maternal love of God, while the conditional covenant reflects the paternal love, which demands a response from the child[39].

In view of a family relationship being so vital to every biblical covenant, here we may add a recent remark of John Paul II on anthropomorphic language in this area. He says that the eternal "generating" of God "has neither 'masculine' nor 'feminine' qualities. ... Thus every element of human generation which is proper to man, and every element which is proper to woman, namely human 'fatherhood' and 'motherhood', bears within itself a likeness to, or analogy with the divine 'generating' and with the 'fatherhood' which in God is 'totally different'"[40].

As we turn to the more perfect ideals proposed within the new covenant, we are guided by the insistence on mutual love, willing service of others, and solidarity with all our brothers and sisters. Christian solidarity should make us particularly concerned for those with whom we have covenant fellowship and for the very poor, with whom our Lord himself has proclaimed such complete solidarity[41].

E. COVENANT AND LAND

Joshua, as a valiant companion of Moses and his designated successor, led the Israelites into the promised land. After gaining control of large areas of Canaan, Joshua distributed the land to each of the tribes except Levi. What held the Israelites together in those days was not merely a certain amount of common family blood but also their experience, as a nation, of Yahweh liberating them from slavery and calling them to be a special people bonded together by the Sinai covenant[42]. To consolidate that commitment and to extend it to other inhabitants who had rallied to the ranks of the incoming Israelites, Joshua renewed the covenant at Shechem. He reminded the people there that the land was God's gift to Israel, and yet it carried a heavy responsibility, for abuse of such a precious gift could bring disaster on the people and make them disappear from the land (cf. Jos 23 - 24).

We have also given considerable attention to the Jubilee Year, with its ideal of giving back ancestral land to any family who had lost it through hard times and the vicious circle of increasing debts in order to survive. If survival were achieved, it would often have been through forfeiting family property and accepting a form of slavery. The legislation of the Jubilee Year was intended to safeguard the family inheritance, which was also a precious heritage from Yahweh. It is feasible to regard the period shortly after Joshua as a crucial period in which that practical side of the covenant was formulated. The aim was obviously to confront the spirit of greed and merciless grabbing of all properties by the richer and more powerful few.

Subsequent history down to the present day has confirmed the need to safeguard the rights of the rural families to their humble home and plot of land. "**Laborem Exercens**", for instance, draws attention to the millions of farm workers forced to work for landlords, exploited by them, and without any hope of having even a little piece of land as their own some day[43]. "**Sollicitudo Rei Socialis**" also condemns as one of the greatest injustices of the modern world the fact that those who possess much are relatively few, whereas those who possess almost nothing are many[44].

The small farmer who owns the land generally works it with a keen love of nature and a deep sense of improving a heritage which will be handed on to the next generation, to support them and their children. This is far more in harmony with ecology than those big business enterprises whose aim is quick profit, irrespective of the ruined land that may be left behind, not to mention irreparably ravaged jungles and polluted rivers[45]. That is far from treating the land as a precious gift of God destined for the common good and for generations yet to come. Moreover, big agribusinesses are usually not interested in growing the kind of food necessary to feed the starving millions of today. They grow the sort of cash crop that those with most money will want to buy. A worse crime against the starving millions is not bothering to cultivate the land at all. For instance in Brazil, where there are many millions of rural workers without land, only a small fraction of the arable land is being cultivated[46].

Third World countries are also forced to export food to service their foreign debts, instead of being free to grow the food urgently needed to feed their own badly undernourished people. It is ominous that a rich and well nourished nation like the United States is now investing so much in "low intensity conflict", to meet or bring about insurgency in other countries, on the grounds of defending (North) American interests there. However, in a country like El Salvador the costly and destructive impact of low intensity warfare has not brought about peace, because, according to D. Siegel and J. Hackel, "the United States and Salvadoran governments have not addressed the root causes of the rebellion: poverty and landlessness"[47] (emphasis added).

To deprive the majority of humble country people of their own block of land is to deprive them also of the source of their life and dignity. A basic paper for the Week of the Indian, in Brazil in 1984, asserted: "The land is the

Bible of the Indian, because it is the soil of his history, of his culture, of his cohesion, of his survival. The land is not private property. It is not for buying and selling. It is for living on"[48].

The O.T. ideal of a Jubilee "release" of land to its dedicated but dispossessed rural workers still has much to teach us about the ownership and cultivation of land today. It reminds us forcefully that the Lord of all the earth entrusts land as a gift to those who will use it carefully to provide for their own families and for other families. The Jubilee Year therefore continues to be an important manifestation of the spirit of the covenant with regard to restoring the freedom, the dignity, the equality and social participation of rural families.

F. KINGS UNDER COVENANT

The hundred and fifty years following Joshua's death turned out to be very turbulent years for the young Israelite nation trying to consolidate its hold on the promised land. That period was remembered as a cycle of sin, disaster, and a repentant crying out to Yahweh, who then raised up Judges to bring about the needed liberation. The prolonged experience led many in Israel to look for a king who would be able to lead all the tribes in their struggle for survival against the surrounding enemies. The king would also be able to maintain peace and defend justice once the kingdom had been secured. However, the prophet and last Judge, Samuel, made it quite clear that Yahweh would not grant Israel a king the same as any other king of the neighbouring nations. The king of Israel would have to be a king subordinate in everything to Yahweh, hence faithful to all the demands of the Mosaic covenant.

Saul as the first king over all the tribes proved to be disobedient and so lost the throne for his descendants. David was called and anointed by Samuel to replace the line of Saul. To David was given a great promise that his throne would endure forever. When David violated the covenant by adultery and murder, the prophet Nathan courageously rebuked him, and David repented of his twofold sin. Not even the king, to whom so much had been promised unconditionally, was exempted from the conditions of the covenant in his daily conduct. Nor was the prophet exempted from denouncing that king once he had seriously violated the rights of his subject, Uriah the Hittite.

From beginning to end of the monarchy, kings were confronted by prophets speaking in the name of Yahweh. We have seen the examples of Shemaiah telling Rehoboam to refrain from civil war, of Ahijah denouncing Jeroboam for idolatry, of Elijah denouncing Ahab for murdering Naboth in order to get his vineyard, and of Jeremiah denouncing Jehoiakim for not paying the workers extending his palace. In that way the kings were constantly reminded of their obligation to uphold the values of the covenant not only among their subjects but also in their personal lives. Some of the best kings, such as Hezekiah and Josiah, even led their kingdom into a public renewal of the Mosaic covenant. The bad kings were more frequently denounced for violations of social justice than for offences in their public worship of God.

The prophets just mentioned and many others like them did not hesitate to interest themselves in the political arena, in which the king held undisputed civil power. The prophets did not try to take over political power in the country, but they certainly were critical of its employment by the king and his officials. Elijah was called the scourge or troubler (equivalent to agitator) of Israel(1 K 18,17) by king Ahab. Amos was told to stop prophesying at the royal sanctuary in Bethel, because he was warning that king Jeroboam would die by the sword (Am 7,10-13).

This brings into proper perspective the role of political leaders today, for their power remains always subordinate to the will of God, and therefore it must also respect the rights of the people. For their part, modern Christian prophets cannot remain silent when they become aware of serious abuses committed by a government or politicians against the people whom they should be serving instead of oppressing. Like the biblical prophets, modern prophets are not political agitators, but rather faithful witnesses whose words agitate kings and other politicians. As Elijah remarked, the real disturbance in the kingdom stems from the king unfaithful to Yahweh. The genuine prophet speaks out in the hope of restoring justice and peace within the realm.

G. COVENANT AND THE PROPHETS

In addition to their critical evaluation of kings, the prophets of Israel constantly conveyed God's word of warning or consolation directly to the people. Fearlessly they spoke out against abuses that were threatening the continuation of Israel as the covenanted people of Yahweh. The earliest of the prophets whose preaching has been preserved for us in book form, namely Amos, Hosea, Micah and Isaiah, all spoke out vehemently against social injustices that were reducing the innumerable victims to misery and new forms of slavery[49]. Those prophets warned both the kingdoms of Israel and of Judah that such infidelity was leading them to disaster, not excluding the destruction of their capital cities and the exile of their people. Because their infidelity was a kind of adultery, a desertion of their Partner, Hosea began to call them to a renewal of their original covenant of love. That image of the divine Husband seeking to bring back an unfaithful wife was to receive much attention in the rest of Scripture right through to the book of Revelation.

Despite all the efforts of the prophets, who were mentors to many of the kings from start to finish of the monarchy, neither kingdom, Israel or Judah, remained faithful to the covenant. As we have seen, several prophets like Jeremiah, Ezekiel and Deutero-Isaiah looked beyond the destruction and exile. They foretold yet another intervention of Yahweh to set free the exiled people, granting them forgiveness and a new covenant. The new covenant would be more effective than the old, thanks to God putting a new spirit, a new heart, within the covenanted people. The motive for offering a new covenant was obviously not to be sought in the Mosaic covenant as such, but rather in God's fidelity to the promises made to Abraham and to David. Nonetheless the disposition made with both Abraham and David was also called a covenant, because it had the effect of drawing those leaders, with their people, into the special friendship and family of God. The new covenant was also to be in line with the promissory and unconditional character of those covenants.

Another feature of the prophetic ministry was a definite forerunner of liberation theology. The prophets were constantly engaged in a critical reflection on the community's (liberating) praxis, in the light of the word of the Lord remembered within Israel. Our contention is that much of the critical reflection of the prophets was in the light of the word of God as crystallized and articulated by the various covenants[50]. The prophets measured Israel's conduct (rather than "praxis" in the highly technical sense it carries today) by the criterion of the Mosaic covenant. The changes of heart and public morality which the prophets called for were in keeping with the traditional values of Israel as Yahweh's chosen people. The elements of special love, of compassionate mercy, of fidelity to the earlier promises, plus some new promises — all of this was also interwoven in the prophetic preaching.

While the practical conduct of Israel was not viewed as "liberating", there can be no denying that the prophets were keenly aware that Yahweh's liberation of the nation was jeopardized by so many violations of the commandments which specified the way to live out the covenant. In other words, the prophets wanted to defend and extend the true liberty of their people, by announcing God's point of view and by denouncing those who oppressed anybody within the community. Through their charism as prophets they grasped clearly the word of judgment which Yahweh moved them to give on a particular situation within Israel's long and troubled history.

It is instructive in this regard that the six books we now call the Deuteronomist's History (Joshua, Judges, 1 & 2 Samuel, 1 & 2 Kings) were termed "the Former Prophets" in the Hebrew Bible. They merited that title because the finished works convey a critical evaluation of each stage of Israel's history from the time of the occupation of the promised land until the time of its loss to the Assyrians and Babylonians. The kings especially were judged in the light of their fidelity to the Mosaic covenant. Only a few were found to have been very good by that criterion, some were fairly good, whereas the majority were bad (including every king of the northern kingdom, "Israel"). In short, inspired writers, basing themselves on the prophets, gave Israel in written form a critical reflection on the nation's performance as a covenanted community.

The final redactor(-s) found that far too often the Israelites, from the king down, had not practised coherently their faith nor honoured their national commitment to Yahweh. Because they chose instead to live just like the other nations surrounding them, Yahweh let them experience the full oppression of those nations. At the same time, however, he raised up prophets like Amos and Hosea for the northern kingdom, then later on Jeremiah, Ezekiel and Deutero-Isaiah for Judah. Those prophets reviewed the past, judged the sinful situation of their own day, and encouraged the battered people by giving them a glimpse of the power of Yahweh's word to bring about a new Israel in the future. Prophets were not critical only because they wanted to vindicate the wonderful justice of God; they also wanted to make known the saving and liberating aspect of that justice. Their criticism was therefore a continual appeal to their people to bring their conduct into line with their covenant commitment. Their threats were nearly always conditional, threats which could be averted by a change of heart.

H. COVENANT AND CULTURE

We cannot pass on to the sealing of the new covenant without recalling, at least briefly, the importance of traditional wisdom and liturgical celebration for the incorporation of covenant values into the culture of Israel. This factor seems to me all the more necessary in view of the disdain of philosophers expressed by Marx. For him, they were a failure when it came to changing the world, since their concern was only to understand the world. As for religious celebration, it meant little for Marx, who thought it deadened worshippers to the injustice of the real world by focusing attention on a world to come. In the O.T., on the other hand, we have seen how strong was the pursuit, the "love of wisdom", which is the root meaning of philosophy. Even more general was the involvement of the ordinary people in religious celebrations and sacred songs such as the Psalter has preserved for universal appreciation.

Wisdom in Israel generally seemed to develop the themes common to international wisdom and fairly independent of the usual biblical current of salvation history, Mosaic law and prophetic proclamation. However, wisdom was very concerned about the right way to relate to nature, to the Creator, to government, to people in authority, to parents and to friends. Much of the advice given by the sages was intended to guide daily conduct, and there was obviously a presumption that personal conduct should be brought into conformity with what was recommended as wise. The advice was based on the experience of many generations and the critical reflection of the sages, who were also concerned with expressing the lesson as pithily as possible.

Such traditional wisdom preserves and articulates much of the value and meaning of life, hence the world-view and accepted ethics of a particular people or nation. An enormous amount of what is known and cherished by a tribe or nation is worth preserving. There is no need to change it radically. On the contrary, to despise that rich wisdom and overturn its bases is to bring a new form of alienation, degradation, anomie, and — all too often — virtual annihilation of the people "changed" by outsiders. The grim story of hundreds of once flourishing tribes around Latin America bears out the need to respect their indigenous wisdom and way of life.

In ancient Israel, its deep religious convictions had a continuing impact on the national wisdom. God was acknowledged as the only source of genuine wisdom, and little by little wisdom was personified as a companion of God who could be sent to dwell in the midst of Israel, inviting all to imbibe wisdom freely. At times the sages themselves called into question some tenets of traditional wisdom, such as the prosperity of those faithful to God (cf. Job), or the advantages of working hard to improve one's standing economically or intellectually (cf. Ecclesiastes). Some wisdom writers did reflect on Israel's history as a source of inspiration for their contemporaries (cf. Sirach), or as a lesson on God's intervention being a saving experience for the Israelites but a punishing judgment on the Egyptians (cf. Wisdom). In those writings the covenant experience was not given any prominence, but the conduct called for was kept in line with the ten commandments. For Sirach, however, wisdom was practically identified with the Torah, of which the Mosaic covenant formed an essential part.

While the wisdom literature kept alive the fame of Solomon, the Psalms preserved the memory and the messianic hopes of David. As a king, David had made of Jerusalem a capital in which the Ark of the Covenant was lodged and the worship of Yahweh was enthusiastically celebrated. David personally led the way in praising and petitioning Yahweh through sacred songs. Through the words or titles of the Psalms used in its religious celebrations, Israel was reminded of David and the promise made to him. The nation was also reminded of the whole gamut of its special relation with Yahweh, especially that arising from promise and covenant. Many Psalms expressed sorrow for the people's infidelity to God, coupled with confidence in the unfailing love of God for them. There is strong evidence that many Psalms emerged from the annual cycle of feasts which featured a cultic celebration, including at times a public renewal, of the covenant.

The cyclic nature of Israel's celebrations was by no means a contradiction of its sense of an unfolding and "linear" history[51]. In this respect, the people of Israel were also like a tree, as the opening Psalm says of a just person (Ps 1,3). Every year a living tree adds another ring to its trunk, but at the same time its roots sink deeper into the soil, its branches reach further upwards and outwards. Ezekiel attached immense importance to the fact that trees watered by the stream flowing from the new sanctuary in Jerusalem would have abundant good fruit and medicinal leaves (Ez 47,12). Oft repeated celebrations to deepen communion with Yahweh as the fount of life and liberty for Israel certainly did not rule out severe pruning or new growth reaching out to the future.

Israel, like Latin America today, had its "popular religion", the religion with which the ordinary people could readily identify. In fact, a religion which is not "popular" in the sense of letting the ordinary people express their common faith meaningfully in public could well be an unpopular religion, a religion which would seem to the people to be too remote from their daily experience[52]. Although the Psalms come from a different cultural background to that of most Christian people of today, they should still guide us in expressing community prayer.

I. THE NEW COVENANT AND THE KINGDOM OF GOD

Jesus Christ, the Son of God made man, the Word of God made flesh like the rest of the human family, has been sent as the "Yes!" to all God' promises. In Jesus of Nazareth God has granted the descendant of Abraham in whom all nations are to be blessed, the prophet like Moses who surpasses Moses in bringing the world "grace and truth", the son of David whose just rule will never end, and the Suffering Servant who has become a covenant bringing together in himself the scattered peoples of the world. The scarcity of explicit references to a new covenant in the N.T. has given many the impression that covenant had become almost a marginal concern in the mission of Jesus.

This work has devoted considerable attention to the many N.T. writings in which implicit references to the new covenant, and occasional explicit ones, are found. Our rereading of the texts has made it clear that Jesus himself and then his disciples were deeply interested in the new covenant. They frequently mentioned this or that distinguishing feature of it. Jesus explicitly declared the sealing of it in his own blood at the solemn paschal supper, leaving the eucharist as his unique memorial. It is a reminder to both God and the community of the sacrifice which achieved their reconciliation and inaugurated the time of the new covenant, the last times, leading up to the parousia.

Given that liberation theology looks so much to the kingdom of God as its guiding light, here we will recall briefly how inseparable the kingdom of God is from the new covenant. No one can fully accept the reign of God without accepting the new covenant, with its basic commitment to the Father and to all members of his family now headed by the beloved Son. We have seen in the Gospels that the reign of God means essentially that the will of God is accepted voluntarily through faith and love, in a personal and communitarian commitment. What is often not realised these days is that such a commitment implies the acceptance of the essential demand of the new covenant, which is the twofold love of God and neighbour. The commitment is mutual, because "God loved us first", and once we respond with love, we have accepted our responsibility under the new covenant. Jesus has made it plain that compliance with the Father's will is the way to admission into his family (Mk 3,33-35). The spirit of the new covenant is well captured by that image and symbol of the family.

The family prayer is undoubtedly the "Our Father", in which we pray that the Father's kingdom may come and that his will may be done. Lk's version, however, sees no need to include the latter petition, as though it were included in praying for the coming of the kingdom. The second half of the prayer calls for a spirit of sharing the bread available and of forgiving one another's "debts". Never before has this prayer carried such a strong plea for a compassionate, Christ-like attitude towards those whose debts have become as huge millstones, grinding millions of our human family into inhuman misery and an early grave. First World creditors must ask themselves seriously if they are not denying food, drink, clothing, medicine, housing and liberty to Christ when they demand repayment of debts by his (and their own) impoverished brothers and sisters (cf. Mt 25).

Closely associated with this is the content of Jesus's inaugural discourse in the synagogue of his home town, Nazareth. There he declared open a never-to-be-closed Jubilee Year, the Lord's year of release from slavery, from prison, from sickness, and from otherwise unpayable debts (cf. Lk 4,16-22). As we noted in dealing with the O.T. ideal of the Jubilee Year, the purpose of "release" was to restore the impoverished and enslaved poor people to their ancestral properties, allowing them to be be once again free, dignified and independent citizens, able to participate in the public affairs of their city or country town. Jesus therefore proclaimed in Nazareth that his mission was to bring to perfection, through the new covenant, that ideal already presented to restore freedom and dignity under the old covenant.

The Sermon on the Mount proclaims the charter and the inner spirit of the new covenant. The beatitudes expand the ideals of life in harmony with God and with one another. Those ideals are often just the opposite to what the world without Christ regards as indispensable for happiness and security. The poor, the gentle, the merciful, the peacemakers, those who mourn and those who long for justice, and the persecuted — all are "blessed", because the kingdom of God and its happiness is now made available to them. The reign of God, inaugurated with the preaching and example of Jesus, is a reign of justice and compassion. It will overturn unjust thrones and sinful systems that have brought such suffering and margination to the poor and the little ones.

One of the first fruits of the promulgation of the kingdom by Jesus and its acceptance by some disciples was the Church, as we have seen especially in reflecting on Mt. The disciples called and instructed by Jesus were gradually formed into the community of the new covenant, with strong emphasis on a loving service of the others. All were to be accepted and treated as brothers and sisters, while the leaders were to be outstanding for serving and never for lording it over their community. In Lk and Acts the emerging Church is remarkable for its spirit of fellowship (**koinonia**), resulting in an effective sharing of material resources to prevent serious want among any of the Christian household. There was also regular sharing of the teaching of the apostles and of the eucharist.

Perhaps the most astonishing characteristic of the new covenant community was its zeal to reach out to all the surrounding nations and invite them to come into the community through faith and baptism. No race or class was excluded, and a special solidarity was shown towards the poorest and the most afflicted. Thanks to the new creation in Christ, the wall of division between any group and another has been broken down, so that all may live as one family if they freely choose to do so.

It was from the Pauline epistles that we have received some of the best insights into the usual life, convictions and difficulties of the recently formed communities, the local churches. Paul has let us discern in the recipients of his letters a great openness to the guidance of the Holy Spirit. Terming himself "a minister of the new covenant" (2 Cor 3,6), Paul emphasised what had been promised by Jeremiah and Ezekiel as a distinguishing feature of the new covenant, namely that the Spirit will give the inner strength necessary to live consistently according to that covenant (e.g. 1 Th 4,1-12; 2 Th 2,13; Ph 2,13).

The Spirit stirs up a generous commitment to the "law of Christ", who has summed up the ten commandments in his new commandment of love. For Paul, Christians are those into whose hearts the love of God has been poured by the Holy Spirit, the living gift of God. Those moved by the Spirit of the Son can make their own his confident appeal to "**Abba**", Father . Through Christ and his Spirit has come the integral liberation from sin, selfishness, merely external law, and from death itself (Rm 5 - 8; Gal 4). Each local church is therefore regarded by Paul as a portion of the holy people of Yahweh, for whom the new covenant is now a reality. The family atmosphere which pervades each community stems from the close relationship established with the eternal community of Father, Son and Holy Spirit[53].

J. THE NEW COVENANT COMMUNITY AND POLITICS

What has been said above concentrated on the Church as a visible fruit of the kingdom of God, which was introduced effectively into human society by the whole mission of Christ and the Spirit. The emphasis was on the inner nature of the Church freely accepted as part of the new covenant. This by no means implies that Jesus and the community he founded were not also deeply concerned about the whole civil society in which they lived — and by which many of them were executed as enemies of the political rulers, or as a menace to the existing power structures.

Liberation theology rightly insists that Jesus himself confronted the civil authorities of his day, as well as the religious leaders. This was almost inevitable, given that in Jerusalem the Jewish Sanhedrin wielded both religious and political power. It was also subject in many civil matters to the approval of the Roman procurator, who was quick to suppress any threat of revolt against the empire. Against that background Jesus proclaimed God's intervention to establish a kingdom which would challenge and insist on changing whatever was unjust or dehumanising in the kingdoms of this world. It was not long before those leaders whose power was threatened begun to seek some way to silence that sort of preacher for good.

Jesus appeared all the more dangerous as a prophet of the kingdom because he was being widely discussed as the long awaited Messiah, the anointed son of David who would establish Israel as the golden centre of God's kingdom on earth. The other nations would stream into Jerusalem with tribute. Correcting those (partly) mistaken expectations, Jesus told Pilate that his kingdom was not *of* this world. He was setting it apart from the ordinary human kingdoms of this world, with merely human kings and the commonly accepted standards of this world without Christ. He did not wish to deny that his unique kingdom was *in* this world and was open to people living in this world.

Furthermore, the will of God was being made known to rulers and ruled alike, for nobody was to be left in ignorance of God's plan for this world and for all its inhabitants. Kings and other leaders, like everybody else, retained their freedom to opt for or against God's will, but each person now had the responsibility to evaluate his or her life in the light of the Gospel. Even socio-economic and political affairs had to be assessed in that light, and changed if found wanting. Pilate was acting with political acumen when he chose as the charge to nail over the head of Jesus crucified: "Jesus of Nazareth, King of the Jews". The kind of kingdom which Jesus was talking about was obviously extremely disturbing to the Jewish leaders. It could easily have caused difficulties for the procurator himself with the Roman emperor, if the strange king had not been executed as requested.

The disciples of Jesus likewise ran into stiff opposition after Pentecost, when they had to defy the orders of the Sanhedrin in order to continue proclaiming the Gospel. Later on, Peter had to be rescued by an angel from the power of Herod Agrippa I, who was all set to execute him, as he had already executed James. Those first preachers of the Gospel were well aware that its values contradicted many commonly accepted values in the society around them. That did not deter them from devoting all their talents and energy to proclaiming the arrival of God's reign over human affairs, with its upsetting public demands for a change of heart and conduct. It also implied a change of the sinful structures that helped to perpetuate and extend injustice.

The kingdom of God was known to be like a leaven that would gradually have its impact on the whole mass of human society. The reticence of the first Christians to denounce by name particular rulers or systems should not blind us to the great courage with which they did announce the positive values of the kingdom. They stressed the all-embracing spirit of the new covenant, demanding a Christ-like concern for the whole of God's human family and an end to the selfish use of goods or power. By the time Revelation was being written, the persecuted Church was strongly denouncing the Roman empire for its various forms of idolatry and its unjust treatment of anyone opposing the system. Committed Christians of today are likewise bound to work in solidarity with one another for the full liberation of all their people, including their political and economic liberation whenever necessary[54]. The reign of God definitely demands a full acceptance of the Gospel values in those areas of public life, but it also has eternal dimensions that go far beyond politics or economics.

One of the most striking indications of the uniqueness of the kingdom being inaugurated by Jesus has been seen in the kind of exodus of which he was, and still is, the leader. Suffice it to recall here how Moses and Elijah, at the time of the transfiguration of Jesus, spoke about the "exodus" which Jesus was to accomplish in Jerusalem (Lk 9,31). Events have shown that exodus to have been passing from this world to the Father, through death and resurrection.

That entry, the **eisodos**, into the true fatherland, the definitive promised land, has been brilliantly presented in Hebrews as fulfilling the entry into the Holy of Holies. Jesus, as Mediator of the new covenant, and bearing the blood that won reconciliation, has opened up a living way ('**odos**) to the Father (Heb 10,19 -20) . What is central here is that we can all avail of this access to the Father, as we can also share in the risen and unending life of Jesus Christ. All that is far beyond the possibilities of a merely socio-political liberation limited to ordinary life in this world. The access to God, however, can begin for us in this world and can inspire us to work tirelessly to orient all life on earth towards God and the common good of our race. The general resurrection may well permit permanent access to the Father while we remain, risen and transformed, on this planet duly prepared as "a new earth"[55].

K. THE NEW COVENANT AND ITS EUCHARISTIC RENEWAL

All four N.T. accounts of the institution of the eucharist mention the blood of the covenant being shed by Jesus. We also saw that the fullest treatment of the new covenant is to be found in Hebrews, a writing that resembles a stirring homily on the occasion of a eucharistic celebration. In extolling Jesus as our compassionate and trustworthy high priest, Hebrews stresses his solidarity with the human family from which he has been called as mediator. It avails of liturgical language to describe how the blood of the new covenant has been offered to God in the heavenly sanctuary. It also mentions explicitly the serious responsibility accepted by those who have been sprinkled with the blood of the new covenant (Heb 12,24-25; 13, 12-16). We may reasonably link this with the Lord's command concerning the eucharist: "Do this as my memorial" (1 Cor 11,24-25), accepting the translation of F. Chenderlin[56].

Here we want to point out the great pastoral possibilities when each eucharist celebrated by a community "reminds" them of their covenant commitment in Christ to the Father and to each other. Every celebration can and should become an occasion to renew their commitment as a community. At the same time, they should realise that the eucharistic celebration also serves as a "reminder" to the Father of the heroic love with which Jesus accomplished the definitive exodus for himself and all his family. With good reason this "memorial" can be regarded as keeping fresh a "subversive memory" in the people of God, for it renews the commitment to break free with Christ from all the bondage caused by "the sin of the world"[57].

As well as individual sin, there are many man-made structures today that stem from sin and hence demand of the committed community a sustained effort to replace them with structures that promote justice and defend the rights of all the people[58]. This should be seen as an active participation in the mission of Christ as **go'el** (redeemer of captive family members). At times it may involve carrying the cross to the ultimate consequences on behalf of others. Of this especially the eucharist is the "reminder", Christ's memorial.

L. NEW COVENANT SPIRITUALITY AND LIBERATION

By way of conclusion, this section will draw together a few of the most outstanding features of the new covenant which offer rich possibilities for our spirituality, as individuals and as a local church committed to the integral liberation of every person[59]. Any genuine Christian spirituality must flow from a conscious union with Christ and the Holy Spirit abiding within the person. A spiritual life is not really the life lived by a spirit, but the life lived by a whole person immersed in the Spirit of God. As we have seen, the efficacious presence of the Spirit is one of the greatest gifts of the new covenant. It is the powerful love of the Spirit which changes stony hearts into truly human hearts, making them wide open to love of God and neighbour, as well as to a liberated love of self as one of God's living masterpieces.

What follows is only a minimal outline of some of the most pertinent aspects and general orientations of the kind of spirituality that we have now seen to be encouraged by the whole biblical presentation of covenant, especially of the new covenant. It is not meant to be in competition with other accepted spiritualities. On the contrary, it should enrich them, since it stems from a thoroughly biblical perspective. To simplify a vast field, we shall concentrate on Jesus' public life as our model of a covenant spirituality translated into daily dealings with the Father and with fellow members of the human family. Once again it is necessary to insist that the fundamental purpose of biblical covenants was to establish a family relationship between the parties voluntarily entering into such an arrangement. Both parties undertook to trust and treat one another from then on as belonging to the same extended family. For that reason covenant spirituality extends to every dimension of the family's honour and well-being.

The communion of the divine Persons is the source of all community life, of self-communication to others, and of mutual love. Through the Trinity's gratuitous initiative, our race has been called to share in the divine life, knowledge and love. We have been given the capacity to enter into a loving relationship not only with other humans but also with the divine Persons themselves. The covenants were offered by God to encourage the human family to live in stable friendship with the divine Persons and with each other, as in one large but united family.

Jesus' proclamation and personal prayer centred on the Father, fondly addressed as "**Abba**", a term which Jesus also taught his disciples to use in praying to the Father. God as Father stands out as the dominant intuition of Jesus and hence inspired his loving obedience to the Father's will in every crucial moment. In preaching the Kingdom of God, Jesus could emphasise now the decisive intervention of the King, now the compassionate invitation of the Father. The members of the kingdom are really those who generously accept and carry out the will of the Father, following in this the unwavering example of Jesus himself. Zeal to extend God's reign to all nations means a strong desire to have the Father draw those nations into the family that recognises him as Father (or Parent, having qualities reflected in human mothers and fathers). The new covenant is a way in which each person can respond with faith and love to that invitation.

Jesus was also "filled with the Holy Spirit" and "led by the Spirit" (Lk 4,1) from start to finish of the public life. Jesus' evangelizing mission to the afflicted, the imprisoned, the oppressed and the poor was inseparably linked with the anointing he received from the Spirit of the Lord (Lk 4,18). He also rejoiced in the Spirit as he blessed the Father for revealing so much to the little ones (Lk 10,21). At the Last Supper he promised several times to send the Holy Spirit from the Father to enlighten and strengthen the disciples, so that they could carry out the mission handed on to them (cf. Jn 14-17). On Easter Sunday, when Jesus sent them as the Father had sent him, "he breathed on them and said: 'Receive the Holy Spirit'" (Jn 20,22). The Acts and many epistles record how great was the role of the Spirit of Jesus in the primitive Church. The fervent communities listened to the Spirit speaking within them, as well as to what the Spirit was saying to all the churches and through other signs of the times.

It is evident that Jesus was nourished by the Scriptures, which he used in his prayers, which he recalled and explained in his preaching, and which he intended to bring to fulfilment and perfection through his whole mission. The fulfilment of the promise was related to a particular moment in the history of Israel, e.g. "This text is being fulfilled today even while you are listening" (Lk 4,21). He opened up the Scriptures still more convincingly to his disciples after the resurrection. That has set the pattern for disciples of every age, as they search the O.T. for more light on the meaning of Jesus and his liberating mission. It has also alerted the Church to recognise and cherish the inspired writings of the N.T., which emerged from its own members.

Jesus as the Son of Man (his favourite self-identification) continually manifested an admirable solidarity with all his brothers and sisters (cf. Mk 3,31-35; Mt 25,31-46). His own example of living in poverty, having "nowhere to lay his head", gave added force to his preferential treatment of the poor, and to his firm request to the rich that they give away their wealth to help the poor. He denounced Mammon for the idol that it was then and has increasingly shown itself to be in our own day. He acted as the elder Brother, compassionate towards sufferers, a friend of sinners, tireless in proclaiming the Good News of the Kingdom to all and sundry. No authority could deter him from demanding full recognition of the dignity, the heritage, and above all the right to a fullness of life for all his people[59]. In this line we have seen how Jesus did confront political leaders and perilously agitated them over what they regarded as touchy political issues.

Going counter to the practice of his day, Jesus entered into dialogue with a Samaritan woman; he allowed a sinful woman to show her gratitude for reconciliation by washing his feet with her tears; he forgave the adulterous woman whom others might have stoned to death; he was so moved by compassion for the widow of Naim that he restored to life her only son; after the resurrection he appeared first to Mary Magdalene and sent her as a convinced apostle to the still doubting Eleven. As John Paul II notes: "In all of Jesus' teaching, as well as in his behaviour, one can find nothing which reflects the discrimination against women prevalent in his day. On the contrary, his words and works always express the respect and honour due to women"[60]. He was truly the servant of all, men, women and children alike, even to the extreme of being willing to lay down his life as a sacrifice of expiation for all the family.

In anticipation of that supreme sacrifice Jesus announced, during the Passover meal, that he was sealing a new covenant in his own blood. His sense of mission, of solidarity, of divine and social justice, of self-sacrificing service, of being the elder Brother willing to redeem the rest of the family from slavery — all that found its culmination in the promulgation of the new covenant. The actual sealing took place on Calvary, after he had confirmed in Gethsemane the complete acceptance of the Father's will. On our behalf Jesus expressed the acceptance of the essential stipulation which unifies kingdom and covenant, namely the agreement to conform our life and our society to the will of our Father. As a stirring "memorial" of his redeeming sacrifice which established the new covenant, he has bequeathed to the Christian family the eucharist. Its proper celebration "reminds" both God and the community of the twofold love expressed by Jesus "to the very limit" as he sealed this covenant.

The spirituality of Jesus moved him to welcome those from nations other than Israel, although only after the resurrection did he send out his disciples to carry the Gospel to the ends of the earth. There was also an eschatological dimension to his spirituality, as can be deduced from its impact on his preaching. He proclaimed God's reign as being already inaugurated through his own mission, to be crowned by the coming of the Holy Spirit after the resurrection and ascension. On the other hand, the reign of God will not be complete and definitive over the human family and its world until the last day, the day of general resurrection and judgment. Jesus lived on earth aware that he and all his people were still like pilgrims heading towards fuller access to the Father, in order to enter into uninterrupted possession of risen life.

He was concerned that all of human life, including political and national affairs, should be oriented according to God's plan. Daily life and the history of this world were therefore being led towards their proper goal. The full transformation of this world could be achieved only through a final intervention of God on the last day. But the "new creation" had begun in Christ himself and he prepared his disciples to be willing agents in promoting the transformation of their own society and of the entire world.

We can find no better image for this than that of the bridegroom and the bride working together to prepare their future home, in this case, their eternal home. The eschatological vision of Revelation is dominated by "the Lover" (Rev 1,5), whose death as the Lamb (Rev 5,6 ff.) has won him full control over all nations as "Lord of Lords and King of kings" (Rev 17,14). When the reign of God has been definitively established and all opposition broken for ever, then the "wedding of the Lamb" will be joyfully celebrated. The bride will also have been properly prepared, clothed in dazzling white, symbolising "the good deeds of the saints" (Rev 19,7-8). Surely Christian praxis is glimpsed here in its true role.

That wedding represents the final and unbreakable covenant of love between Christ and his Church, between the Father and a fully reconciled family. Moreover, God announces what could be the surprise dowry for the bride of the Lamb: "Look, I am making the whole of creation new" (Rev 21,5). Perhaps in that way our own planet earth at last, and for ever, may serve as our home for living out the divine covenant in all its glorious fulness.

NOTES

1. Exodus and Revolution, 70. Cf. review of this book by D. Wall, in Review of Religious Research, Vol. 28, No. 3 (March, 1987), 279-280, where the reviewer queries the term "revolution" for what was more an escape from the slave-masters. However, for the Hebrew slaves it was a radical turn about in their whole relationship to the oppressors, who were defeated.
2. H. Assmann, Practical Theology of Liberation (London: E.T. by P. Burns, Search Press, 1975) 105.
3. J.L. Segundo, The Liberation of Theology (Dublin: E.T. by J. Drury; Gill and Macmillan, 1977) 8.
4. Cf. S. Galilea, "Liberation Theology and New Tasks Facing Christians", in R. Gibellini (Ed.), Frontiers of Theology in Latin America (New York: E.T. by J. Drury; Orbis, 1979) 170: "My feeling, then, is that much of the present opposition to liberation theology is due to faulty logical jumps and a lack of basic information."
5. Cf.: R. Haight, An Alternative Vision — An Interpretation of Liberation Theology. L.J. Topel, The Way to Peace — Liberation Through the Bible (New York: Orbis, 1979), esp.146-156 where the author's conclusions are briefly correlated with the Latin American way of presenting liberation theology. A. McGovern, Marxism: An American Christian Perspective (New York: Orbis, 1980), esp. 172-209 on "Liberation Theology in Latin America". D.A. Lane, Foundations for a Social Theology — Praxis, Process and Salvation (Dublin: Gill and Macmilllan, 1984). R.C. Montalba, Evangelization and the Liberation of the Poor: Theology and Praxis (Roma: [Dissertation] Pontifical University of St. Thomas, 1987).
6. Teología de la Liberación — Perspectivas (Lima: CEP, 1971; 5th ed. 1987); first British ed.— E.T. by Caridad Inda and J. Eagleson — (London: SCM, 1974).
7. Op.cit. (E.T.) 13; cf. id.: — "Introduction: Liberation, Theology and Proclamation", in H. Assmann, op.cit., 5-24, e.g. 17: "To reflect on the faith as liberating practice is to reflect on a truth which is made, and not just affirmed; it is to start from a promise which is fulfilled throughout history and at the same time opens history beyond itself." — The Power of the Poor in History (London: E.T. by R. Barr, SCM. 1983). — La Verdad los Hará Libres — Confrontaciones (Lima: CEP, 1986).
8. Cf. D. Lane, op.cit. 34; and 56: "The second view of praxis, which could be called the Critical-Marxist view, affirms the primacy of praxis over theory. In this view praxis is the source, ground and goal of theory, theory is subordinated to critical praxis."
9. Cf.: A. McGovern, op.cit., 179-181. A. Fierro, The Militant Gospel (New York: E.T. by J. Drury; Orbis, 1977), esp. 76-126; 182-256 on "Looking at the Present: Political Praxis and Theological Representations". R. Haight, op.cit. 41: "Praxis is behaviour that is participation in this movement of history; it is a practice or behaviour or struggle to increase freedom in society."

NOTES

10. Cf. H. Mottu, "Jeremiah vs. Hananiah: Ideology and Truth in O.T. Prophecy", in N.K. Gottwald (Ed.) The Bible and Liberation — Political and Social Hermeneutics (New York: Orbis, 1983) 235-251, e.g. 249: "..the strength of Marxism has always consisted of its insistence that one succeeds in putting human thought at a distance from its conditioning — a conditioning that it never ceases to reflect — only to the degree that human thought proves itself capable of transforming the world, of transforming the very conditioning that it reflects. That is the deepest meaning of the philosophy of praxis, innovating praxis" (author's emphasis). Also: R. J. Siebert, "Jacob and Jesus: Recent Marxist Readings of the Bible", ibid. 497-517, esp. 513.
11. Cf. G. Gutiérrez, "Liberation Praxis and Christian Faith", in R. Gibellini (Ed.), op.cit. 1-33, e.g. 22: "(Liberation theology) is a process of reflection which starts out from historical praxis. It attempts to ponder the faith from the standpoint of this historical praxis and the way that faith is actually lived in a commitment to liberation." R. McAfee Brown, "Liberation Theology: Paralyzing Threat or Creative Challenge?", in G.H. Anderson and T.F. Stransky (Ed.s), Mission Trends No 4 (Liberation Theologies), (New York: Paulist Press, 1979) 3-24, e.g. 6: "The key word here .. is praxis. Thinking must be engaged thinking; it must come out of doing and not just cogitating" (author's emphasis). — A. Fierro, op.cit. 23: "This open acceptance of Marx's thesis cited above is the first trait shared by present-day theologies: They are oriented basically towards a praxis that will alter the world."
12. 2nd. Instruction from S. Cong. for the Doctrine of the Faith, **Libertatis Conscientia** (1986), #71, saying that Christian praxis is the fulfilment of the great commandment of love.
13. Ibid. #81, asserting that to realise the civilization of love requires a new reflection on the relationship between the commandment of love and the social order.
14. Ibid. #72, recalling that the Church offers "principles of reflection, criteria of judgement, and directives of action".
15. Cf. J.L. Segundo, op.cit. 84: "Curious and shocking as it may seem, then, various Latin American theologians have come to the conclusion that it is impossible to know what a specifically Christian contribution to liberation might be, prior to a personal commitment to liberation."
16. Pedagogy of the Oppressed (Harmondsworth: E.T. by M. Bergman Ramos; Penguin, 1972).
17. A. Fierro, op.cit. 19; cf. 34. Cf. I. Ellacuria, Freedom Made Flesh — The Mission of Christ and His Church (New York: E.T. by J. Drury; Orbis, 1976) , e.g. 10: "Secularization is a historical process, and the historical form it takes today can be given a name at least. It is 'politicization'." Also 109: "At the present stage of history this [Christian] liberation must be liberation from injustice and for love. .. Strictly speaking, there is only one historical process: It is one of liberation from injustice leading towards liberty in love."

18. **Solicitudo Rei Socialis**, ##41-48, which relate the Church's social teaching to political and economic issues of the day. It is also noted that in some areas of the Church, especially in Latin America, "liberation" has become its fundamental category and its first principle of action (#46).
19. Ibid. #39.
20. **Christifideles Laici**, ##42-43, which spell out many aspects of the right and duty of Christians to participate actively in political affairs.
21. Ibid. #43.
22. Ibid. #60.
23. I. Ellacuria, op.cit. e.g. 17-18: "Post-Marxist theology has the task of seeking out a new alternative in the task of making sure that salvation will be salvation in history." See also 88; 108; 140 (on risen Christ as Lord of history). Cf.: G. Gutierrez, The Power of the Poor in History, esp. 3-22; 75-107. — Id., Líneas Pastorales de la Iglesia en América Latina (Lima: CEP, 1986^8) 11-12; 29-31. Leonardo y Clodovis Boff, Como Hacer Teología de la Liberación (Madrid: Sp.T. by E. Requena Calvo, Paulinas, 1986^2) 18; 39-40; 50-51; 69-73; 112; 116.
24. Cf. H. Echegaray, The Practice of Jesus (New York: E.T. by M.J. O'Connell, Orbis, 1984), 23-38. The notes after each chapter give a good bibliography.
25. Cf.: D. Lane, op.cit. 110-140, e.g. 139-140: "It does seem strange at times that a Church which can be so sure-footed about the place of certain moral issues in the political arena can, at the same time, be so shy about political involvement when it comes to social praxis in the name of justice on behalf of the poor and the oppressed." L. and C. Boff, op.cit. 110, where they justly claim that Marxism now has no monopoly on historic transformation, since Christians are moved by their own faith to take up that cause.
26. In Preface to H. Assmann, op.cit., 2. Cf. P.J. Klaiber, Religión y Revolución en el Perú, 1824 - 1988 (Lima: Centro de Investigación Universidad del Pacífico, 1988^2) 109-134, on José Carlos Mariátegui, founder of the Peruvian Communist Party, but a source of inspiration for both Marxists and Christians in the field of social reform. Mariátegui himself regarded the religious instinct of the Indians as a "vital impulse" that should be channelled into secular and political affairs. Also 231-236 on theology of liberation in Peru. Cf. J.L. Idígoras, "'El factor religioso' en los 7 Ensayos de J.C. Mariátegui", in Revista Teológica Limense, Vol.XXI, No.3 (1987) 303-324, where he notes that, for Mariátegui, it was the mystical dynamism of the religious myth that mattered, not its content, hence it could give way to a revolutionary myth directed to political change. Cf. also J. Equiza: "Teología de la liberación y religiosidad popular" in Lumen (Victoria, España) Vol.XXXVI, No.1 (1987) 53-91, where he suggests that the liberating values of popular religion be recognised in the Church's liberating praxis.

27. Cf.: H. Echegaray, op.cit. 39-73. L. Boff, Trinità e Società (Assisi: Collana: Teologia e Liberazione, 1987) 157-194, where he reflects on the trinitarian communion as the foundation of a social and integral liberation.
28. Cf. R. Haight, op.cit. 38; 41-2; 62; 99: "God has not only relativized history, but also made it the field for the co-creativity of human freedom."; 107.
29. Cf.: E. Dussel (Gen. Ed.) Historia General de la Iglesia en América Latina — a big project proposed by CEHILA, a commission related to CELAM; the history is planned to appear in 11 Vols.). E. Dussel, in Vol. I,1, p.11 notes that the interpretation of Church history in the light of faith is a theological task. Id., Historia de la Iglesia en América Latina — Coloniaje y Liberación {1492-1983} (Madrid: Mundo Negro, 1983^5), esp. 15, underlining the great need of today's Latin Americans to be aware of their own culture and history.   Also: G. Gutiérrez, Dios o el Oro en las Indias (Lima: CEP, 1989), a work containing 4 cc. of a proposed larger work of 16 cc. on Bartolomé de las Casas, who did publicly evaluate the events of the Conquest as a true pastor defending the rights of the uprooted and decimated Indians. This kind of history is essential in view of the call of John Paul II to a "new evangelization" to mark 500 years of evangelization in Latin America (1492-1992 A.D.) e.g. in his Message to the Bishops of Peru, 1988, in: Constructor de la Civilización del Amor [Lima: Conferencia Episcopal Peruana, 1988] 130-131.
30. L. and C. Boff, op.cit. 55 (where they mention three levels of liberation theologians — professional, pastoral, and popular, of which the last two necessarily involve working together with many faithful on the same issues.
31. Cf. C. Mesters, Flor Sin Defensa — Una Explicación de la Biblia a Partir del Pueblo; id., Lecturas Bíblicas: Guías de trabajo para un curso bíblico (Estella [Navarra]: Sp.T. by N. Darrical, Verbo Divino, 1986).
32. Cf. John Paul II, **Mulieris Dignitatem** (On the Dignity of Women), ##6-7 on Gen 1-2, e.g. #7, p.24: "It is a question here of a mutual relationship: man to woman and woman to man. Being a person in the image and likeness of God thus also involves existing in a relationship, in relation to the other 'I'." And #7, p.27-28: "To say that man is created in the image and likeness of God means that man is called to exist 'for' others, to become a gift. ... Already in the Book of Genesis we can discern, in preliminary outline, the spousal character of the relationship between persons" (emphasis added). Also #11, p.43 on Gen 3,15 as alluding to the "woman" in whom "the new and definitive Covenant of God with humanity has its beginning, the Covenant in the redeeming blood of Christ."
33. Cf. M. Walzer, op.cit. 80-81 on the importance of the interplay (at Sinai, then in later revolutionary politics) of "divine willfulness and popular choice, providence and covenant" (emphasis added). Cf. again G. Gutiérrez, A Theology of Liberation, 157: "The Covenant and the liberation from Egypt were different aspects of the same movement, a movement which led to encounter with God."

34. J.S. Croatto, "Liberar a los Pobres: Aproximación Hermenéutica", in L. Brummel et al.(Eds.) Los Pobres — Encuentro y Compromiso (Buenos Aires: ISEDET, Aurora, 1978), 15-28. In fuller works, however, Croatto includes the covenant dimension of biblical liberation.
35. L.J. Topel, op.cit. 14.
36. Ibid., 2.
37. Ibid., 20-22.
38. A. Fierro, op.cit. 210-211. Cf. John Newton, "Analysis of programmatic Texts of Exodus Movements", in Concilium 189, Feb. 1987, 56-62, esp. 62 where he warns that "the Exodus pattern, construed in literalist O.T. terms, has exacted a heavy toll in human suffering". For me, that is bound to happen when a misguided "chosen people" treats others as enemies to be conquered and kept down as inferiors.
39. L.J. Topel, op.cit. 42: "Again, the unconditioned nature of God's invitation reminds us of the unconditioned nature of motherly love."
40. Cf. **Mulieris Dignitatem**, #8, pp.31. Also: **Dives in Misericordia**, #4, ftn.52.
41. Cf. Basil Hume, Towards a Civilisation of Love, (London: Hodder & Stoughton, 1988) 124: "It is helpful to regard the Extraordinary Synod and the Synod on the Laity as two parts of a single whole. Theologically they embrace the same ecclesiology and the same understanding of the Church as **koinonia** or **communio**." On p.16 some approximate English translations of **koinonia** are suggested, such as "fellowship", "shared life", "partnership", "joint partaking". Solidarity is yet another facet.
42. Cf. N.K. Gottwald, "The Theological Task after 'The Tribes of Yahweh'", in id. (Ed.), The Bible and Liberation, 194, where he speaks of the covenant as a bonding of scattered groups of equals "committed to cooperation without authoritarian leadership". Thus united, the Israelites proved that social struggle could change harmful social conditions.
43. **Laborem Exercens** (On Human Work) #21.
44. #27.
45. Cf. **Christifideles Laici**, #43.
46. Cf. A. Gispert-Sauch de Borrell, Brasil ¿Para Quién es la Tierra? — Solidaridad de la Iglesia con los 'sin tierra', (Lima: CEP, 1984), 165-168, where the various kinds of rural workers with too little or no land are seen to total about 15 million. Cf. Ivo Poletto, "La Pastoral de la Tierra en el Brasil" in Informes de Pro Mundi Vita América Latina, 46 (1987) 1-25.
47. "El Salvador: Counterinsurgency Revisited", in M.T.Klare & P. Kornbluh (Eds.), Low Intensity Warfare — Counterinsurgency, Proinsurgency, and Antiterrorism in the Eighties (New York: Pantheon, 1988), 133.
48. Cf. A. Gispert-Sauch de Borrell, op.cit., 160.
49. Cf. L.J. Topel, op.cit., 68.
50. Cf. Instruction "**Libertatis Conscientia**" (1986), #46, which states that the prophets did not stop reminding Israel of the demands of the covenant. They denounced the unjust situation of the poor as "contrary to the covenant".

51. Cf. S. Frick & N.Gottwald, "The Social World of Ancient Israel", in The Bible and Liberation, 149-165, esp. 152 on Max Weber, "who was remarkably successful in anticipating the significance of the cult, the covenant and the role of the Levites in early Israel".
52. Cf. B. Lovett, Life Before Death : Inculturating Hope (Quezon City: Claretian Publications, 1986).
53. Cf. : B. Hume, op.cit. 124: "The primary **koinonia**, from which the Church draws its life, is the Trinity itself." L. Boff: Trinità e Società, esp. 13-25 on the divine Persons' participation, equality and communion as the basis for a just human society. Also 157-194. **Mulieris Dignitatem**, #7.
54. Cf.: I. Ellacuria, op.cit. 85: "Liberation can be viewed as a process of liberty, justice and love. These three categories are explicitly biblical and explicitly secular." Also 108: "Christian liberation is simultaneously salvation in history and salvation above and beyond history." H. Assmann, op.cit., 32; 37: "Pastoral thinking is beginning to take note ... that in the present situation in Latin America pastoral action must have a political bent, or risk leaving the Gospel outside the course of history." R. Durand Florez, Observaciones a 'Teología de la Liberación' [y] 'La Fuerza Histórica de los Pobres' (Callao: Obispado del Callao, 1985); id. La Utopia de la Liberación — Teología de los Pobres? (Callao: Obispado del Callao, 1988), two works in which the author persistently expresses concern at the Marxist flavour of liberation theology as expounded by Gutiérrez and others in the same current. Personally, however, I find that those theologians are simply availing of useful insights of Marx that can help in public dialogue concerning God's plan for the world of today. Any serious dialogue involves listening carefully to what the other party is saying, and at times admitting that it has a good point.
55. Cf. C.H. Abesamis, Where Are We Going: Heaven Or New World?, e.g. 26-27: "The expression new heaven and new earth then means 'new world'. And this new world according to the simple (or is it grandiose?) faith of biblical religion is the ultimate destiny which God has promised!" Also 47: "Where are we going? To the new world of fullness of life. This is the clear and distinct message of the Bible."
56. F. Chenderlin, Do This as my Memorial..
57. Cf.: D. Lane, op.cit. ch.6: "The Eucharist and the Praxis of Social Justice", 141-169. C. Giraudo, La Struttura Letteraria della Preghiera Eucaristica, in Part 3 and Conclusion (273-370), which shows convincingly the continuity between the Jewish **toda** (=confession) and the eucharistic celebration as a "memorial". Through their celebration the people of the covenant receive pardon, reconciliation and new hope as "partners" of the ever faithful God (e.g. 369). **Mulieris Dignitatem**, #26, p.94: "As the Redeemer of the world, Christ is the Bridegroom of the Church. The Eucharist is the Sacrament of our Redemption. It is <u>the Sacrament of the Bridegroom and of the Bride</u>" (emphasis added). #27, p.96: "In the context of the 'great mystery' of Christ and of the Church, <u>all are called to</u>

respond — as a bride — with the gift of their lives to the inexpressible gift of the love of Christ" (emphasis added).
58. Cf.: S. Galilea, art. cit. (in Frontiers of Theology), 174-175 on "institutionalized violence" : "It is the most deep-rooted sociological source for the resultant repressive violence on the one hand and the subversive violence on the other. Both types of violence are symptoms of the established disorder. .. Liberation from violence is one of the most important tasks confronting Christianity today." Cf. R. Haight, op.cit. 149 on structural, social sin; and 152-153 on the power of Spirit-inspired love to establish good structures, replacing the sinful ones. **Reconciliatio et Paenitentia** (On Reconciliation and Penance, 1984), #16 on social sin as the fruit or accumulation of personal sin.
59. Cf.: G.Gutiérrez, We Drink from our own Wells: The Spiritual Journey of a People (New York: E.T. by M.J. O'Connell, Orbis, 1984). J. Espeja, Espiritualidad y Liberación (Lima: CEP; /Salamanca: San Esteban; 1986). M.O'Sullivan, "Liberation Spirituality", Furrow Vol.39,No.10 (Oct.1988), 649-652, e.g. 649: "The task of liberating world order from forces of death and destruction has given rise to a new theology, the theology of liberation. It also gives rise to a new anthropology and a new spirituality. All three are interrelated." R. Haight, op.cit. 233-256 on "Liberationist Spirituality".
60. **Mulieris Dignitatem**, #13, p.51.

BIBLIOGRAPHY (OF WORKS UTILIZED)

Abbott, W., The Documents of Vatican II (London: G. Chapman, 1966).

Abesamis, C., Where are we going: heaven or new world? (Manila: Foundation Books, 1984).

Ackroyd, P., Exile and Restoration. A Study of Hebrew Thought of the Sixth Century B.C. (London: SCM, 1968).

————, Israel Under Babylon and Persia (Oxford: New Clarendon Bible, O.T. Vol.IV, Oxford University Press, 1970).

Alonso Schökel, L., "Sapiential and Covenant themes in Genesis 2-3", in Theology Digest 13 (1965) 3-10.

————, ¿Dónde està tu hermano? — Textos de fraternidad en el libro de Génesis (Valencia: Institución San Jerónimo, 1985).

————, Hermenéutica de la Palabra, 1: Hermenéutica Bíblica (Madrid: Cristiandad, 1986 [2]).

————, Treinta Salmos: Poesía y Oración (Madrid: Cristiandad, 1986 [2])

———— & Sicre, J. (con Breton, S. & Surro, E.): Profetas - Introducciones y Comentario, 2 Vol. (Madrid: Cristiandad, 1987 [2]).

Ambrozic, A., The Hidden Kingdom (Washington DC: Catholic Biblical Association of America, 1972).

Anderson, Bernhard, The Living World of the Old Testament (Harlow, Essex: Harlow, 1978 [3]).

————, The Eighth Century Prophets — Amos: Hosea: Isaiah: Micah; Proclamation Commentaries [Editor: F.R. McCurley] (Philadelphia: Fortress Press, 1978).

Anderson, G.H. & Stransky, T.F. (Ed.s), Mission Trends No. 4: Liberation Theologies (New York: Paulist Press; and Grand Rapids: Eerdmans, 1979.

Anton, Angel, "Principios fundamentales para una teología del Laicado en la Eclesiología del Vaticano II", in Gregorianum 68.1-2 (1987) 103-144.

Arens, E., "La Biblia Es Para Todos", in El Quehacer Teológico desde el Perú (Ed.s Arens,E. & Thai Hop,P., Lima: ISET, 1986) 73-95.

Ashton, John (Ed.), The Interpretation of John (London: SPCK, 1986).

Assmann, H., Practical Theology of Liberation (London: ET by P. Burns, Search Press. 1975).

Baker, C.J., "The New Covenant in Miniature", in Manna, (Sydney) No.5 (1962) 85-97.

Baltzer, K., The Covenant Formulary — In O.T., Jewish and Early Christian Writings (Philadelphia: ET by David Green, Fortress Press, 1971).

Barclay, W., The Gospel of Matthew (2 Vol.) Edinburgh: St Andrew Press, 1958 ^{2}).
Bartchy, S. Scott, First-Century Slavery and the Interpretation of 1 Cor. 7:21 (Atlanta, Georgia: Scholars Press, 1985).
Barth, M., Ephesians (New York: Doubleday Anchor Bible, 1974).
Barthes, R. & others (Ed.s), Exégesis y Hermenéutica (Madrid: Sp.T. by T. Ballester, Cristiandad, 1976).
Beaucamp, E., Les Prophètes d'Israël ou le drame d'une Alliance (Quebec: Université Laval, 1968 ^{2}).
—————, Prophetic Intervention in the History of Man (New York: Alba House, 1970).
—————, Man's Destiny in the Books of Wisdom (New York: ET by J. Clarke, Alba House, 1970).
Beauchamp, Paul, L'Un et l'Autre Testament — essai de lecture (Paris: Editions du Seuil, 1976).
Begg, Christopher, "Berit in Ezekiel", in Ninth World Congress of Jewish Studies, Division A (Jerusalem: World Union of Jewish Studies, 1986).
Best, Ernest, Disciples and Discipleship — Studies in the Gospel According to Mark (Edinburgh: T. & T. Clark, 1986).
Beyer, Jean, "Le laïcat et les laïcs dans l'Église", in Gregorianum 68 (1987)157-185.
Beyerlin, W., Origins and History of the Oldest Sinaitic Traditions (Oxford: ET by S. Rudman, Blackwell, 1965).
Bishop, Jonathan, The Covenant: A Reading (Springfield, Illinois: Templegate Publishers, 1982).
Black, Matthew, The Scrolls and Christian Origins — Studies in the Jewish Background of the NT. (Chico, California: Scholars Press, 1983 — a reprint of New York: Scribner, 1961).
Blank, J., The Gospel according to St John (2 Vol.) (New York: ET by M. O'Connell, The Crossroad, 1981).
Blenkinsopp, J., "Deuteronomy" in The New Jerome Biblical Commentary (NJBC) 94-109.
Boadt, L., "Ezekiel", in NJBC 305-328.
Boff, Leonardo, Trinità e Società (Assisi: Collana: Teologia e Liberazione, 1987); [ET, from Portuguese, by P. Burns, Trinity and Society (Maryknoll, N.Y.: Orbis, 1988)]

————, Leonardo & Clodovis, Como Hacer Teología de la Liberación (Madrid: Sp.T. by Requena Calvo, Paulinas, 1986²); ET from Portugese: Introducing Liberation Theology (N.Y.: ET by P. Burns, Orbis, 1987).

Boismard, M.E., St John's Prologue (London: Blackfriars, 1957).

Bouillard, H., "Exégesis, Hermenéutica y Teología. Problemas de Método", in Exégesis y Hermenéutica (Ed.s R. Barthes & others) 213-224.

Bovati, P., Ristabilire la Giustizia (Rome: Biblical Institute, 1986).

Braconot, M., L'Évangile selon saint Luc — Avènement (Paris: Desclée de Brower, 1984).

Bright, J., Jeremiah (New York: Anchor Bible, Doubleday, 1965).

————, A History of Israel (Philadelphia: Westminster, 1972²).

————, Covenant and Promise — The Future in the Preaching of Pre-exilic Prophets (London: SCM, 1977).

Brown, R.E., The Gospel According to John, I-XII & XIII-XXII (New York: Anchor Bible, Doubleday, 1966 & 1970).

————, & P. Perkins & A. Saldarini, "Apocrypha; Dead Sea Scrolls; Other Jewish Literature", in NJBC 1055-1082.

Brown, R.E., The Community of the Beloved Disciple (London: G. Chapman, 1979).

————, The Birth of the Messiah — A Commentary on the Infancy Narratives in Matthew and Luke (New York: Image Books, Doubleday, 1979.

————, The Epistles of John (New York: Anchor Bible, Doubleday, 1982).

————, Recent Discoveries and the Biblical World (Wilmington: Delaware, Glazier, 1983).

————, & Fitzmyer, J.A., & Murphy, R.E., The New Jerome Biblical Commentary (hereafter NJBC) (London: G. Chapman, 1989; Englewood Cliffs,N.J.: 1990).

————, & Donfried, K.P., & Reumann, J. (Ed.s), Peter in the New Testament (Minneapolis: Augsburg Publishing House; New York: Paulist Press, 1973).

Bruce, F.F., The Epistle of John (Grand Rapids: Eerdmans, 1970).

Brueggemann, W., Ed.'s Foreword to S. Ringe: Jesus, Liberation and the Biblical Jubilee.

————,The Land — Place as Gift, Promise and Challenge in Biblical Faith (Philadelphia: Fortress Press, 1977).

Brummel, L., and others (Ed.s), Los Pobres — Encuentro y Compromiso (Buenos Aires: ISEDET, Aurora, 1978).
Buis, Pierre, "La Nouvelle Alliance" in Vetus Testamentum XVIII (1968) No.1, 1-15.
―――――, La Notion de L'Alliance dans l'Ancien Testament (Paris: Cerf, Lection Divina, 1976).
Burns, R., "The Book of Exodus", in Concilium 189 (Feb. 1987) 11-21.
Burrows, M., The Dead Sea Scrolls (London: Secker & Warburg, 1956).
―――――, More Light on the Dead Sea Scrolls (London: Secker & Warburg, 1958).
Byrne, Brendan, 'Son of God' — 'Seed of Abraham' (Rome: Biblical Institute, 1979).
Callan, Terrance, Forgetting the Root — The Emergence of Christianity from Judaism (New York: Paulist Press, 1986).
Camp, Claudia, "Woman Wisdom as Root Metaphor — A Theological Consideration ", in The Listening Heart (1987) 45-76.
Campbell, Anthony, Of Prophets and Kings — A Late 9th-Century Document (1 Sam 1 - 2 K 10) (Washington DC: CBAA Monograph Series 17,1986).
Capdevilla i Montaner, V-M., Liberación y Divinización del Hombre — Teología de la Gracia, Tomo I: La Teología de la Gracia en el Evangelio y en las Cartas de San Juan (Salamanca: Secretariado Trinitario, 1984).
Cardenal, Ernesto, Preface to H. Assmann's Practical Theology of Liberation.
Charles, R.H., The Apocrypha and Pseudepigapha of the OT in English (Oxford: University Press, 1963-4).
Chenderlin, F., 'Do This as My Memorial' — The Semantic and Conceptual Background and Value of **anamnesis** in 1 Cor. 11:24-25 (Rome: Biblical Institute, 1982).
Clements, R.E., Prophecy and Covenant (London: SCM, 1965).
―――――, "Covenant and Canon in the Old Testament", in R. McKinney (Ed.), Creation Christ and Culture — Studies in honour of F.F. Torrance (Edinburgh: T. & T. Clark, 1976) 1-12.
Coffey, David, "A Proper Mission of the Holy Spirit", in Theol. Studies 47 (1986) 227-250.
Coggins, R.J., Haggai, Zechariah, Malachi (Sheffield: JSOT Press, 1987).
Collins, Thomas, Apocalypse 22: 6-21 As Focal Point of Moral Teaching and Exhortation in the Apocalypse (Rome: Gregorian University Press, 1986).
Da Conceicão Souza, I, The New Covenant in the 2nd Letter to the Corinthians. A Theologico-Exegetical Investigation on 2 Cor 3:1—4:6 and 5:14-21 (Rome: Gregorian University Press, 1978).
Cook, James I. (Ed.) Grace Upon Grace (Essays in Honor of L.J. Kuyper) (Grand Rapids: W. Eerdmans, 1975).

Corbishley, T., "1 and 2 Maccabees", in New Catholic Commentary on Holy Scripture (hereafter NCCHS) 743-758.
Couturier, G.P.,"Jeremiah" in NJBC 265-297.
Crenshaw, J., "Murphy's Axiom: Every Gnomic Saying Needs a Balancing Corrective", in the Listening Heart — Essays in Honour of R.E. Murphy, O.Carm. (Sheffield: JSOT Press, 1987) 1-17.
Croatto, J.S., Alianza y Experiencia Salvífica en la Biblia (Buenos Aires: Ediciones Paulinas, 1964).

———, "Liberar a los Pobres: Approximación Hermenéutica", in L. Brummel & others (Ed.s) Los Pobres — Encuentro y Compromiso (Buenos Aires: ISEDET, Aurora, 1978) 15-28.

———, "The Socio-historical and Hermeneutical Relevance of the Exodus", in Concilium 189, pp.125-133.

Cunliffe-Jones, H., Deuteronomy — The Preaching of the Covenant (London: Torch Bible p-b, SCM, 1964).
Curran, C.E. & McCormick, R.A. (Ed.s) Moral Theology No. 4: The Use of Scripture in Moral Theology (New York: Paulist Press, 1984).
Curtis, J. (Ed.), Fifty Years of Mesopotamian Discovery (London: British School of Archaeology in Iraq, 1982).
Dahl, N.A., "The Johannine Church and History", in J. Ashton (Ed.), The Interpretation of John, 122-140.
Dahood, M., Psalms (3 Vol.) (New York: Anchor Bible, Doubleday, 1970).
Daly, Robert, & others (Ed.s) Christian Biblical Ethics (New York: Paulist Press, 1984).
Danielou, J., The Dead Sea Scrolls and Primitive Christianity (New York: Mentor P-b, 1962).
Davies, W.D., The Gospel and the Land — Early Christian and Jewish Territorial Doctrine (Berkeley: University of California Press, 1974).
Davis, James A., Wisdom and Spirit — An Investigation of 1 Cor. 1.18 — 3.20 Against the Background of Jewish Sapiential Traditions in the Greco-Roman Period (Lanham & New York: University Press of America, 1984).
Deidun, T.J., New Covenant Morality in Paul (Rome: Biblical Institute, 1981).
De la Potterie, Ignace, La Verité dans Saint Jean (Rome: Biblical Institute, 1977 — 2 Tomes).

———, Introduction to book of Nunzio Lemmo, Maria 'Figlia de Sion' A Partir da Lc 1.26-38 (Rome: Marianum, 1985).

———La Passion de Jésus selon l'évangile de Jean — Texte et Esprit (Paris: Cerf, 1986).

———, Studi Di Cristologia Giovannea (Genova: Marietti, 1986^2).

———, & Lyonnet,S., La Vita secondo lo Spirito (Rome: IT by T. Federici, A.V.E., 1971^2).

Delorme, J., "Diversité et Unité des Ministères d'Après le NT", in Le Ministère et les Ministères Selon le NT (Paris: Seuil, 1974) 283-346.

———, & Dupont,J., Boismard, M., & Mollat, D. (Ed.s), The Eucharist in the New Testament — A Symposium (London: ET by E.M. Stewart, G. Chapman, 1965).

Dhorme, E., A Commentary on the Book of Job (Nashville: ET by H. Knight, T. Nelson, 1984^2)

Dillon,R., "Acts of the Apostles", in NJBC 722-767.

Dodd, C.H., The Interpretation of the Fourth Gospel (Cambridge: Cambridge University Press, 1968).

Dorr, Donal, Option for the Poor — A Hundred Years of Vatican Social Teaching (Dublin: Gill & Macmillan, 1983).

Drijvers, P., The Psalms — Their Structure and Meaning (London: ET by author, Burns & Oates, 1965).

Dumbrell, W.J., Covenant and Creation — An OT Covenantal Theology (Exeter, Devon: Paternoster Press, 1984).

Dupont-Sommer, A., The Essene Writings from Qumran (New York: Meridian P-b, World Publishing Co., 1962).

Duquoc, C., Messianisme de Jésus et Discretion de Dieu — Essai sur la limite de la christologie (Genève: Labor et Fides, 1984).

Durand Florez, R., Observaciones a 'Teología de la Liberación' (y) 'La Fuerza Hisórica de los Pobres' (Callao: Obispado de Callao, 1985).

———, La Utopia de la Liberación — ¿Teología de los Pobres? (Callao: Obispado de Callao, 1988).

Dussel, E., Ethics and the Theology of Liberation (New York: ET by B.F. McWilliams, Orbis, 1978).

———, Historia de la Iglesia en América Latina — Coloniaje y Liberación [1492-1983] (Madrid: Mundo Negro, 1983^5).

———, Historia General de la Iglesia en América Latina, Tomo I/1: Introducción General a la Historia de la Iglesia en América Latina (Salamanca: Sígueme, 1983).

———, "Exodus as Paradigm in Liberation Theology", in Concilium 189 (1987) 83-92.

Echagaray, H., The Practice of Jesus (New York: ET by M.J. O'Connell, Orbis, 1984).

Eichrodt, W., Theology of the Old Testament, 2 Vol. (Philadelphia: ET by J. Baker, Westminster Press, 1961 & 1967).

Eissfeldt, Otto, The Old Testament — An Introduction (New York: ET by P. Ackroyd, Harper & Row, 1965).

Ellacuría, I., Freedom Made Flesh — The Mission of Christ and His Church (New York: ET by J. Drury, Orbis, 1976).

Ellis, Peter F., Men and Message of the Old Testament (Collegeville, Minnesota: Liturgical Press, 1963).

———, The Yahwist — The Bible's First Theologian (Notre Dame, Indiana: Fides Publishers, 1968).

———, Seven Pauline Letters (Collegeville: Liturgical Press, 1982).
———, The Genius of John: — A Composition-Critical Commentary on the Fourth Gospel (Collegeville: Liturgical Press, 1984).
Episcopal Conferences:
1) CELAM (Conferencia Episcopal Latino-Americana):
———, The Medellin Conclusions — The Church in the Present-day Transformation of Latin America in the Light of the Council(Washington, D.C.: ET by Division for Latin America — USSC,1968).
———, Puebla — III Conferencia General del Episcopado Latinoamericano (Lima: Editorial Labrus, 1982^4).
Cf. Dar Desde Nuestra Pobreza — Vocación Misionera de América Latina (Bogotá: Departamento de Vocaciones de CELAM, 1986).
2) U.S. National Conference of Catholic Bishops:
———, The Challenge of Peace: God's Promise and Our Response. A Pastoral Letter on War and Peace (Washington, D.C.: U.S. Catholic Conference 1983).
———, Economic Justice for All: Catholic Social Teaching and the U.S. Economy (Washington, D.C.: National Catholic News Service, 1986).
———, To the Ends of the Earth (Washington, D.C.: U.S. Catholic Conference, 1986).
Epsztein, Leon, La Justice Social dans le Proche-Orient et le Peuple de la Bible (Paris: Cerf, 1983). Translation: Social Justice in the Ancient Near East and the People of the Bible (London: ET by John Bowden, SCM, 1986).
Equiza, Jésus, "Teología de la liberación y religiosidad popular", in Lumen (Victoria, España) Vol. XXXVI, No.1 (1987).
Erman, A., & Ranke, H., La Civilisation Égyptienne (Paris: FT by C. Mathien, Payot, 1985 — Photocopy of 1963 ed.).
Espeja, J., Espiritualidad y Liberación (Lima: CEP; Salamanca: San Esteban, 1986).
Farina, F., Chiesa di Poveri e Chiesa dei Poveri — La fondazione biblica di un tema conciliare (Roma: Libreria Ateneo Salesiano, 1986).
Fensham, F.C., "The Covenant as Giving Expression to the Relationship Between Old and New Testament", in Tyndale Bulletin 22 (1971) 82-94.
Feuillet, A., "Le Recherche du Christ Dans la Nouvelle Alliance D'Après la Christophanie de Jn 20,11-18", in Mélanges offerts au Père Henri de Lubac: L'Homme Devant Dieu. 1: Exégèse et Patristique (Aubier: Montaigne, 1963) 93-112.
Fierro, A., The Militant Gospel (New York: ET by J. Drury, Orbis, 1977).
Fitzmyer, Joseph A., The Gospel According to Luke (New York: Anchor Bible, Doubleday, I-IX & X-XXIV, 1981 & 1985).
Flanagan, N., Amos, Hosea, Micah (Collegeville: OT Reading Guide, Liturgical Press, 1966).
Fohrer, G., Introduction to the Old Testament (London: ET by D. Green, SPCK, 1970).

Freire, P., Pedagogy of the Oppressed (Harmondsworth: ET by M. Bergman Ramos, Penguin, 1972).
Freyne, S., The Twelve: Disciples and Apostles (London: Sheed & Ward, 1968).
Fuellenbach, John, Kingdom of God — Central Mesage of Jesus (Class Notes, Nemi; and Rome: Gregorian University, 1986).
Fuller, R.C., Johnston L., and Kearns, C., (Ed.s) A New Catholic Commentary on Holy Scripture [NCCHS] (London: Nelson, 1969).
Furnish, Victor P., The Love Commandment in the New Testament (London, SCM, 1973).
Gager, J.G., Kingdom and Community (Englewood Cliffs, NJ: Prentice-Hall, 1975).
Galilea, Segundo, "Liberation Theology and New Tasks Facing Christians", in R. Gibellini (Ed.), Frontiers of Theology in Latin America, 163-183.
Galloway, A.D., "Creation and Covenant ", in R. McKinney (Ed.), Creation Christ and Culture — Studies in Honour of F.F. Torrance (Edinburgh: T. & T. Clark, 1976) 108-118.
Galot, Jean, Gesù Liberatore (Rome: IT by C. Ciani & A. Cappelli, Florentina, 1978).
Gelin, A., The Psalms are Our Prayers (Collegeville, Minn.: ET by M. Bell, Liturgical Press, 1964).
———, Les Pauvres que Dieu Aime (Paris:Cerf, 1967). Translation: The Poor of Yahweh [from 1963 ed.] (Collegeville: Liturgical Press, 1964).
Gerbrandt, Gerald E., Kingship According to the Deuteronistic (sic) History (Atlanta, Georgia: Scholars Press, 1986) .
Gesmer, B., "The **RIB** or Controversy-Pattern in Hebrew Mentality", in M. Noth and W.W. Thomas (Gen Ed.s), Wisdom in Israel and in the Ancient Near East — issued as supplement III to Vetus Testamentum (Leiden: E.J. Brill, 1960) 120-137.
Gibellini, R. (Ed.), Frontiers of Theology in Latin America (New York: ET by J. Drury, Orbis, 1979).
Giraudo, C., La Struttura Letteraria Della Preghiera Eucaristica (Rome: Biblical Institute, 1981).
Gispert-Sauch de Borrell, A., Brasil ¿Para Quién es la Tierra? — Solidaridad de la Iglesia con los 'sin tierra' (Lima: CEP, 1984).
Gordon, R.P., 1 & 2 Samuel — A Commentary (Exeter: Paternoster Press, 1986).
Gottwald, Norman K. (Ed.) The Bible and Liberation (Maryknoll: Orbis, 1983^2).
Graystone, G., The Dead Scrolls and the Originality of Christ (London: Sheed & Ward, 1956).
Grelot, Pierre, Le Ministère de la Nouvelle Alliance (Paris: Cerf, 1967).
Gurney, O.R., The Hittites (Hammonsville: Penguin, 1952).

Gutiérrez, Gustavo, Teología de la Liberación (Lima: CEP, 1971; 1984^4).
Translation: A Theology of Liberation (London: ET by Sister Caridad Ida & John Eagleson, SCM, 1974).
―――――"Introduction: Liberation, Theology and Proclamation", in H. Assmann, op.cit. 5-24 (ET 1975).
―――――, "Liberation Praxis and Christian Faith", in R. Gibellini (Ed.), op. cit., 1-33.
―――――, The Power of the Poor — Selected Writings (London: ET by R.R. Barr, SCM, 1984).
―――――, We Drink from our own Wells: The Spiritual Journey of a People (New York: ET by M.J. O'Connell, Orbis, 1984).
―――――, Líneas Pastorales de la Iglesia en América Latina (Lima: CEP, 1986^8).
―――――, Hablar de Dios — desde el sufrimiento del inocente. Una reflexión sobre el libro de Job (Lima: CEP, 1986); ET from Spanish: On Job — God Talk and the Suffering of the Innocent (New York: Orbis, 1987).
―――――, La Verdad los Hará Libres —Confrontaciones (Lima: CEP, 1986).
―――――, Dios o el Oro en las Indias (Lima: CEP, 1989).
Haight, Roger, An Alternative Vision. An Interpretation of Liberation Theology (New York: Paulist Press, 1985).
Häring, Bernard, The Law of Christ ; 3 Vol. (Cork: ET by E. Kaiser, Mercier Press, 1963 - 1967).
―――――, The Liberty of the Children of God (London: ET by P. O'Shaughnessy, G. Chapman, 1967).
―――――, Free and Faithful in Christ — Moral Theology for Clergy and Laity (3 Vol.) (New York: Seabury Press, 1978; 1979; 1981).
Harrelson, W., The Ten Commandments and Human Rights (Philadelphia: Fortress Press, 1980).
Harrington, W., Record of the Promise: The Old Testament (Dublin: Helicon, 1966).
Hartman, L. & A. Di Lella, "Daniel", in NJBC 406-420.
Hengel, Martin, Property and Riches in the Early Church — Aspects of a Social History of Early Christianity.
―――――, The Cross of the Son of God (London: SCM, 1986).
Hennecke, E., The N.T. Apocrypha: Vol. II: Apostolic and Early Church Writings (London: Lutterworth Press, 1965).
Hillers, D.R., Covenant: The History of a Biblical Idea (Baltimore: John Hopkins Press, 1969).
Hodgson, Peter C., New Birth of Freedom — A Theology of Bondage and Liberation (Philadelphia: Fortress Press, 1976).
Huckle, J. & Visokay, P., The Gospel according to St John, Vol. 1 (New York: Herder & Herder, NT for Spiritual Reading series, 1981).
Hume, Basil, Towards a Civilisation of Love (London: Hodder & Stoughton, 1988).

Idígoras, J.L., "'El factor religioso' en los 7 Ensayos de J.C. Mariátegui", in Revista Teológica Limense, Vol XXI, No.3 (1987) 303-324.
Iersel, Bas van, & Weiler, Anton (Ed.s), Concilium 189 (Feb. 1987) devoted to the theme: Exodus — A Lasting Paradigm.
Janecko, B., The Psalms — Heartbeat of Life and Worship (St Meinrad, Indiana: Abbey Press, 1986).
Jaubert, Annie, La Notion d'Alliance dans le Judaisme aux abords de l'Ere Chrétienne (Paris: Ed. de Seuil, 1963).
Jensen, J.J. & Irwin, W.H., "Isaiah 1 - 39", in NJBC 229-248.
Jeremias, Joachim, Abba, y El Mensaje Central del Nuevo Testamento (Salamanca: ST by A. Ortiz & others, Sígueme, 1983^2). Earlier ET, The Prayers of Jesus; and, The Central Message of the NT (London: SCM, 1967 & 1965 resp.).
Jocz, Jakob, The Covenant — A Theology of Human Destiny (Grand Rapids: Eerdmans, 1968).
John Paul II, **Dives in Misericordia** (Rich in Mercy), 1980.
————, **Laborem Exercens** (On Human Work), 1981.
————, **Reconciliatio et Paenitentia** (Reconciliation and Penance), 1984.
————, To the Youth of the World (1985).
————, A weekly Instruction (1986).
————, Letter for Holy Thursday (1987).
————, Message for Word Day of Youth (1987).
————, **Sollicitudo Rei Socialis** (The Social Concern of the Church),1987.
————, Discourses in Peru, collected in: Constructor de la Civilización del Amor (Lima: Conferencia Episcopal del Perú, 1988).
————, **Mulieris Dignitatem** (The Dignity of Women), 1988.
————, **Christifideles Laici** (On the Vocation and Mission of the Lay Faithful), 1988.
————, "Peace with God the Creator, Peace with all Creation" (Message for World Peace Day, 1990).
Kalluveetil, Paul, Declaration and Covenant — A Comprehensive Review of Covenant Formulae from the OT and the Ancient Near East (Rome: Biblical Institute, 1982).
Karris, R.J., "The Gospel according to Luke", in NJBC 675-721.
Kertelge, Karl, The Epistle to the Romans, in the series NT for Spiritual Reading (New York: ET by Francis McDonagh, Herder and Herder, 1972).
Kirkpatrick, E.M., (Ed.) Chambers Twentieth Century Dictionary (Edinburgh: W. & R. Chambers, 1983).
Klaiber, P.J., Religión y Revolución en el Perú, 1824-1988 (Lima: Centro de Investigación, Universidad del Pacífico, 1988^2).
Klassen, William, Love of Enemies — The Way to Peace (Philadelphia: Fortress Press, 1984).
Kobelski, P.J., "The Letter to the Ephesians", in NJBC 883-890.

Koester, H., Introduction to the New Testament, Vol.1: History, Culture, and Religion of the Hellenistic Age (Philadelphia: ET by author, Fortress Press, 1982).
Kramer, S.N., The Sumerians: Their History, Culture and Character (Chicago: University of Chicago, 1963).
Krinetzki, L., L'Alliance de Dieu avec Les Hommes (Paris: Editions du Cerf, 1970).
Kselman, J.S. & Barré, M.L., "Psalms", in NJBC 523-552.
Lamarche, P., "The Prologue of John", in J. Ashton (Ed.), The Interpretation of John, 36-52.
Lane, Dermott, Foundations for a Social Theology — Praxis, Process and Salvation (Dublin: Gill & Macmillan, 1984).
Lapide, P., "Exodus in Jewish Tradition", in Concilium 189 (1987) 47-55.
Le Frois, Bernard, The Woman Clothed with the Sun — Individual or Collective? (Rome: Biblical Institute, 1954).
Lemmo, N., Maria, 'Figlia di Sion' a Partir da Lc 1,26-38 — Bilancio esegetico dal 1939 al 1982 (Rome: Marianum, 1985).
Léon-Dufour, X., 'Le Partage du Pain Eucharistique' Selon le NT (Paris: Seuil, 1982).
Lockhead, D., "Liberation of the Bible", in N. Gottwald (Ed.), The Bible and Liberation (New York: Orbis, 1983^2).
Lohfink, N., "The Kingdom of God and the Economy in the Bible", in Communio 13 (1986) 216-231.
Lovett, Brendan, Life Before Death: Inculturating Hope (Quezon City: Claretian Publications, 1986).
Lusseau, H., "Esdras and Nehemias" and "The Books of Paralipomenon or the Chronicles". in Robert & Feuillet (Ed.s), Introduction to the OT (New York: ET, Desclée, 1968) 485-493 and 495-504 resp.
Lyonnet, S., La Carità Pienzza della Legge (Rome: AVE minima, 1971^2).
———, Il Nuovo Testamento alla luce dell Antico (Brescio: Paideia, 1971).
———, In Dialogo col Mondo (Roma: AVE, 1987).
Lyonnet, S. & De la Potterie, I., La Vita Secondo lo Spirito (Roma: IT by T. Federici, AVE, 1971^2).
Malatesta, E. Interiority and Covenant — A Study of 'einai 'en and menein 'en in the First Letter of St John (Rome: Biblical Institute, 1978).
Mallon, E.D, "Joel Obadiah", in NJBC 399-405.
Mallowan, M.E.L., Nimrud, 2 Vol. (London: Collins, 1966).
Maly, E., The Book of Wisdom — With a Commentary (New York: Pamphlet Bible Series, Paulist Press, 1962).
Marchel, W., 'Abba, Père' — La Prière du Christ et des Chrétiens (Rome: Biblical Institute, 1971^2).
Marshall, I. Howard, Commentary on Luke (Grand Rapids: Eerdmans, 1978).
———, Last Supper and Lord's Supper (Exeter: Paternoster Press, 1980).

McAfee Brown, R., "Liberation Theology: Paralyzing Threat or Creative Challenge?", in G.H. Anderson & T.F. Stransky (Ed.s) Mission Trends No.4: Liberation Theologies, 3-24.

McCarthy, Denis J., Treaty and Covenant: A Study in Form in the Ancient Oriental Documents and in the OT (Rome: Biblical Institute, 1963).

———, Kings and Prophets (Milwaukee: Bruce, 1968).

——— & R.E. Murphy, "Hosea", in NJBC 217-228.

———, Old Testament Covenant (Oxford: B. Blackwell, 1973).

———, Institution and Narrative (Rome: Biblical Institute, [posthumously]1985).

———, & Mendenhall,G., & Smend, R., Per una Teologia del Patto nell'Antico Testamento (Torino: IT by M. Bracchi & others, Marietti, 1972).

McComiskey, T.E., The Covenants of Promise — A Theology of OT Covenants (Nottingham: Inter-Varsity Press, 1985).

McDonagh, Sean, To Care for the Earth (London: G. Chapman, 1986).

———, The Greening of the Church (London: G. Chapman; Maryknoll,N.Y.: Orbis, 1990).

McEleney, N., "1-2 Maccabees", in NJBC I, 421-446.

McGovern, A., Marxism: An American Christian Perspective (New York: Orbis, 1980).

McIlraith, Donal, The Reciprocal Love Between Christ and the Church in the Apocalypse (Rome: Dissertation in Biblical Theology, Gregorian University; Columban Fathers, 1989).

McKenzie, J.L., Myths and Realities: Studies in Biblical Theology (London: G. Chapman, 1963).

———, "Aspects of Old Testament Thought", in NJBC 1284-1315.

McKinney, R. (Ed.), Creation Christ and Culture — Studies in Honour of F.F. Torrance (Edinburgh: T. & T. Clark, 1976).

McNamara, M., The NT and the Palestinian Targum to the Pentateuch (Rome: Biblical Institute, 1966).

Meadland, D.L., Poverty and Expectation in the Gospels (London: SPCK, 1960).

Mendenhall, G.E., Law and Covenant in Israel and in the Ancient Near East (Pittsburgh, Pa.: The Biblical Colloquium, 1955).

Menezes, Franklin, Life in the Spirit: A Life of Hope (Rome: Pontificia Universitas Urbiana, 1986).

Mesters, Carlos, Abraham y Sara (Madrid: ST by W. Alvarez, Ediciones Paulinas, 1981).

———, Flor Sin Defensa — Una Explicación de la Biblia a Partir del Pueblo (Bogotá: ST by CLAR, CLAR, 1984); E.T. as Defenseless Flower (Maryknoll, N.Y.: Orbis).

———, Lecturas Bíblicas — guías de trabajo para un curso bíblico (Estella, Navarra: ST by N. Darrical, Verbo Divino, 1986).

Meyers, J., I and II Chronicles; 2 Vol. (New York: Anchor Bible, Doubleday, 1965).

———, Ezra Nehemiah; 1 Vol. (New York: Anchor Bible, 1965).
Milik, J., Ten Years of Discovery in the Wilderness of Judaea (London: SCM, 1959).
Miranda, José, Marx and the Bible — A Critique of the Philosophy of Oppression (New York: ET by J. Eagleson, Orbis, 1974).
Moltmann, J., The Future of Creation (London: ET by M. Kohl, SCM, 1979).
Montalba, Robinson C., Evangelization and the Liberation of the Poor: Theology and Praxis (Rome: Dissertation, Pontifical University of St Thomas, 1987).
Moran, W.L., "Ancient Near Eastern Background of Love of God in Dt.", in Catholic Biblical Quarterly (hereafter CBQ) 25 (1963) 77-87.
Moreno, F., Salvar la Vida de los Pobres — aportes a la teología moral (Lima: CEP, 1986).
———, Teología Moral desde los pobres — La moral en la reflexión teológica desde América Latina (Madrid: PS Editorial, 1986).
Moriarty, F. "Isaiah 1-39", in Jerome Biblical Commentary, I, 265-282.
Morris, Leon, The Cross in the New Testament (Exeter: Paternoster Press, 1967^2).
Most, W., "A Biblical Theology of Redemption in a Covenant Framework", in CBQ 29 (1967) 1-19.
Mottu, H., "Jeremiah vs Hananiah: Ideology and Truth in OT Prophecy", in N.K. Gottwald (Ed.) The Bible and Liberation — Political and Social Hermeneutics.
Mowinckel, S., The Psalms in Israel's Worship, 2 Vol. (Oxford: ET by D.R. Ap-Thomas, B. Blackwell, 1962).
Mulcahy, J., "1 and 2 Chronicles", in NCCHS 352-379.
Murphy, Roland E., The Seven Books of Wisdom (Milwaukee: Bruce, 1960).
———, Introduction to the Wisdom Literature of the OT (Collegeville, Minn.: Liturgical Press, 1965).
———, "Psalms", in JBC I, 569-602.
———, The Psalms, Job (Philadelphia, Penn.: R.R. McCurley (Ed.), Proclamation Commentaries, Fortress Press, 1977).
Mworia, T., The Community of Goods in Acts: A Lucan Model of Christian Charity (Rome: Pontifical Urban University, 1986).
Myrdal, K. G., The Challenge of World Poverty. A World Anti-Poverty Programme in Outline (Hammonsville: Penguin, 1970).
Navone, John, Themes of St Luke (Rome: Gregorian University Press, 1970).
———, The Jesus Story: Our Life as Story in Christ (Collegeville: Liturgical Press, 1979).
———, "The Dynamic of the Question in the Search for God", in Review for Religious 45 (1986) 876-891.
———, & Cooper, T., The Story of the Passion (Rome: Gregorian University Press, 1986).
Newman, Murray, The People of the Covenant (New York: Abingdon Press, 1962).
Nielsen, E., The Ten Commandments in New Perspective (London: SCM, 1968).

Noone, Martin J., The Islands Saw It (Dublin: Helicon Press, n.d.).
North, Robert, Sociology of the Biblical Jubilee (Rome: Biblical Institute, 1954).
―――――, "The Trauma of King Saul", in The Bible Today, 1967, 2048-2059.
―――――, "The Chronicler: 1-2 Chronicles, Ezra, Nehemiah", in NJBC 362-398.
Noth, Martin, The History of Israel (London: ET by P. Ackroyd, A. & C. Black, 1960^2).
O'Brien, Niall, The Seeds of Injustice (Dublin: The O'Brien Press, 1985).
―――――, Revolution from the Heart (Dublin: Veritas Publications, 1988).
O'Sullivan, M. "Liberation Spirituality", in Furrow 39, No.10 (October 1988) 649-652.
Panikulam, George, **Koinonia** in the NT — A Dynamic Expression of Christian Life (Rome: Biblical Institute, 1979).
Panimolle, S.A., Il Discorso Della Montagna (Mt 5-7) — Esegesi e Vita (Milano: Edizioni Paoline, 1986).
Pastor, Felix-Alejandro, "Ministerios laicales y Comunidades de Base — La renovación de la Iglesia en América Latina", in Gregorianum 68 (1987) 267-305.
Patrick, Dale, Old Testament Law (Atlanta: John Knox Press, 1985).
Paul, A., LÉvangile de l'Enfance Selon St Matthieu (Paris: Cerf, 1968).
Pederson, J., Israel, Its Life and Culture, I-II (Oxford: Oxford University Press, 1926).
Pereira, Francis, Ephesus: Climax of Universalism in Luke-Acts — A Redaction-Critical Study of Paul's Ephesian Ministry (Acts18:23-20:1) (Anand, India: Gujarat Sahitya Prakash, 1983).
Perkins, Pheme, "The Gospel according to John", in NJBC, 942-985.
Peters, F.E., Children of Abraham — Judaism/ Christianity/ Islam (New Jersey: Princeton University Press, 1982; p-b. 1984).
Pilgrim, Walter, Good News to the Poor — Wealth and Poverty in Luke-Acts (Minneapolis, Minn.: Augsburg, 1981).
Pinto, Luigi di, Volontà di Dio e legge antica nell'epistola agli Ebrei — Contributo ai Fondamenti Biblici della Teologia Morale [Excerpts from a dissertation in Faculty of Theology, Gregorian University, Rome] (Napoli: 1976).
Plastaras, J., The God of Exodus — The Theology of the Exodus Narratives (Milwaukee: Bruce, 1966).
Poletto, Ivo, "La Pastoral de la Tierra en el Brasil", in Informes de Pro Mundi Vita América Latina 46 (1987) 1-25.
Porubcan, S., Il Patto Nuovo in Is. 40-66 (Rome: Biblical Institute, 1958).
Pritchard, J.B., Ancient Near Eastern Texts Relating to the Old Testament (Princeton, N.J.: Princeton University Press, 1950).
Prussner, F., "The Covenant of David and the Problem of Unity in OT Theology", in J.C. Rylaarsdam (Ed.), Transitions in Biblical Scholarship, 17-41.

Quell, G., "**Diatheke**", in G. Kittel (Ed.), Theological Dictionary of the NT (Grand Rapids: ET by G.W. Bromiley, Eerdmans, 1964) II, 114.
Quesnell, Q., This Good News (London: G. Chapman, 1964).
Reade, Julian, "Nimrud", in J. Curtis (Ed.), Fifty Years of Mesopotamian Discovery, 99-112.
Reicke, Bo, The Roots of the Synoptic Gospels (Philadelphia: Fortress Press, 1986).
Renckens, H., Israel's Concept of the Beginning (New York: Herder, 1964).
─────, The Religion of Israel (New York: Sheed and Ward, 1966).
Ricoeur, P., "Hacia una teología de la Palabra", and " Bosquejo de Conclusión", in R. Barthes (Ed.) Exégesis y Hermenéutica, 33-50 and 237-253.
Ringe, Sharon, Jesus, Liberation and the Biblical Jubilee (Philadelphia: Fortress Press, 1985).
Robertson, O.P., The Christ of the Covenants (Grand Rapids: Baker Book House, 1980).
Robinson, John A.T., Twelve More NT Studies (London: SCM, 1984).
Roetzel, C.J., The World That Shaped the New Testament (Atlanta, Georgia: Knox Press, 1985).
Roman Documents:
    1) Vatican II: On the Church; and On the Church in the Modern World. ET in W. Abbott, The Documents of Vatican II (London: G. Chapman, 1966).
    2) The Extraordinary Synod — 1985 (Boston: ET in St Paul Editions).
    3) S. Cong. for Doctrine and Faith: Instruction on Some Aspects of the "Theology of Liberation" (1984); and Instruction on Christian Liberty and Liberation (1986).
    4) Pont. Comm. for "Justice and Peace": At the Service of the Human Community: An Ethical Approach to the International Debt Question (1986).
Rosato, Philip J., "Priesthood of the Baptized and Priesthood of the Ordained", in Gregorianum 68 (1987) 215-266.
Rowley, H.H., The Servant of the Lord and Other Essays on the OT (Oxford: B. Blackwell, 1965^2).
Russell, D., The Method and Message of Jewish Apocalyptic (London: SCM, 1964.
Russell, R., "St John", in NCCHS, 1022-1074.
Rust, E., Covenant and Hope: A Study in the Theology of the Prophets (Waco, Texas: Word Books, 1972).
Rylaarsdam, J.C. (Ed.), Transitions in Biblical Scholarship (Chicago: University of Chicago Press, 1968).
─────, "Jewish-Christian Relationships: The Two Covenants and the Dilemmas of Christology", in J.I. Cook (Ed.) Grace Upon Grace (Essays in Honor of L.J. Kuyper) 70-84.
Sabourin, Leopold, The Psalms: Their Origin and Meaning (Staten Is., N.Y.: Alba House, 1969).

―――, The Bible and Christ — the Unity of the Two Testaments (New York: Alba House, 1980).
Sanders, E.P., Jesus and Judaism (London: SCM, 1985).
Schnackenburg, R., The Moral Teaching of the NT (London: ET by J. Holland-Smith & W.J. O'Hara, Burns & Oates, 1965).
―――, God's Rule and Kingdom (London: ET by J. Murray, Burns & Oates, 1968^2).
―――, The Gospel According to St John, 3 Vol. (London: ET by K. Smyth, C. Hastings & others, Burns & Oates, 1968-1982).
―――, The Gospel According to St Mark (London: ET by W. Kruppa, Sheed & Ward, 1971).
Schoenberg, M., 1 & 2 Maccabees (Collegeville: Old Testament Reading Guide, Liturgical Press, 1966).
Schumacher, E.F., Small is Beautiful (New York: Harper and Row, 1973).
Schussler Fiorenza, Elizabeth, Bread Not Stone — The Challenge of Feminist Biblical Interpretation (Boston: Beacon Press, 1984).
Segre, C., Avviamento all'Analisi del Testo Letterario (Torino: Einaudi, 1985).
Segundo, J.L., The Liberation of Theology (Dublin: ET by J. Drury, Gill & Macmillan, 1977).
―――, The Historical Jesus of the Synoptics (New York: ET by J. Drury, Orbis, 1985).
Senior, D., Matthew, A Gospel for the Church (Chicago: Herald Biblical Booklet, 1973).
―――, & Stuhlmueller, C. (see below).
Sheehan, T., The First Coming — How the Kingdom of God Became Christianity (New York: Random House, 1986).
Sicre, José, Los Dioses Olvidados — Poder y Riqueza en los Profetas Preexílicos (Madrid: Ediciones de Cristiandad, 1979).
―――, Con los Pobres de la Tierra (Madrid: Ediciones de Cristiandad, 1984).
Siebert, R.J., "Jacob and Jesus: Recent Marxist Readings of the Bible", in N.K. Gottwald (Ed.) The Bible and Liberation, 497-517.
Siegel, D., & Hackel, J., "El Salvador: Counterinsurgency Revisited", in M.T. Klare & P. Kornbluh (Ed.s), Low Intensity Warfare — Counterinsurgency, Proinsurgency, and Antiterrorism in the Eighties (New York: Pantheon, 1988).
Simson, P., "Ezra-Nehemiah" in NCCHS 380-396.
Ska, Jean-Louis, " 'Je vais lui faire un allié qui soit son homologue' (Gn 2,18) — A propos de terme **ezer** - 'aide' ", in Biblica 65 (1984) 233-238.
―――, Le Passage de la Mer (Rome: Biblical Institute, 1986).
―――, Class Notes on Gen 1-11 (Rome: Biblical Institute, 1986-7).
Sklaba, R., "The Redeemer of Israel", in CBQ 34 (1972) 1-18.
Soggin, J.Alberto, Le Livre de Juges (Génève: FT by C. Lanoir,1987).
Sorg, Dom Rembert, **Hesed** and **Hasid** in the Psalms — A Story of the marvellous relation between God and the blessed ones of His election and love (St Louis, Mo.: Pio Decimo Press, 1953).

BIBLIOGRAPHY

Spicq, C., L'Épître aux Hébreux, 2 Vol. (Paris: Gabalda, 1952 & 1953).

———, Agape in the New Testament, 3 Vol. (London & St Louis: ET by Sisters M.A. McNamara & M.H. Richter, B. Herder, 1963, 1965 & 1966).

———, Théologie Morale du NT, Tome I & II (Paris: Gabalda, 1970^4).

Spohn, William C., What Are They Saying About Scripture and Ethics? (New York: Paulist Press, 1984).

Stanley, David, Christ's Resurrection in Pauline Soteriology (Rome: Biblical Institute, 1961).

———, The Apostolic Church in the New Testament (Maryland: Newman, 1965).

———, 'I Encountered God' — The Spiritual Exercises with the Gospel of St John (St Louis: Institute of Jesuit Sources, 1986).

Stuhlmueller, C., The Book of Isaiah Chapters 40-66 (Collegeville: OT Reading Guide, Liturgical Press, 1965).

———, "Deutero-Isaiah and Trito-Isaiah", in NJBC 329-348.

———, Creative Redemption in Deutero-Isaiah (Rome: Biblical Institute, 1970).

———, & Senior, D., The Biblical Foundations For Mission (London: SCM, 1983).

Swetnam, James, "Form and Content in Heb.1-6", in Biblica 53 (1972) 368-385.

Talmon, S., King, Cult and Calendar in Ancient Israel (Jerusalem: Magnes Press, 1986).

Thornhill, John, "Is Religion the Enemy of Faith?", in Theol. Studies 45 (1984) 254-274).

Tilborg, S. van, The Sermon on the Mount as an Ideological Intervention — A Reconstruction of Meaning (Assen: Van Gorcum; and New Hampshire: Wolfeboro, 1986).

Topel, L.J., The Way to Peace — Liberation Through the Bible (New York: Orbis, 1979).

Tosato, Angelo, Il Matrimonio Israelitico — Una Teoria Generale (Rome: Biblical Institute, 1982).

Tracey, D., "Exodus: Theological Reflection", in Concilium 189 (1987) 118-124.

Trible, Phyllis, God and the Rhetoric of Sexuality (Philadelphia: Fortress Press, 1978).

Vanhoye, Albert, La Structure Littéraire de l'Épître aux Hébreux (Lyons: Desclée de Brouwer, 1976^2).

———,Our Priest is Christ (Rome: ET by M.I. Richards, Biblical Institute, 1977).

———, La Nuova Alleanza Nel Nuovo Testamento (Rome: Biblical Institute, Class Notes, 1984).

———, Old Testament Priests and the New Priest, according to the NT (Petersham, Mass.: ET by B. Orchard, St Bede's Publications, 1986).

———, Struttura e Teologia nell'Epistola agli Ebrei (Rome: Class Notes for Students, Biblical Institute, 1987).
Vanni, Ugo, La Struttura Letteraria dell'Apocalisse (Brescia: Morcelliana, 1980^2).
———, Note Introduttorie all'Apocalisse (Rome: Class Notes for Students, Biblical Institute, 1985).
———, Il Simbolismo nell'Apocalisse (Rome: Gregorian University, 1985).
———, Apocalisse: Esegesi dei Brani Scelti, Parte XVI, Fasc. I (Rome: Gregorian University, 1986-7).
———, "La promozione del regno come responsabilità sacerdotale dei Cristiani secondo l'Apocalisse e la Prima Lettera de Pietro", in Gregorianum 68 (1987) 9-56.
de Vaux, Roland, Ancient Israel — Its Life and Institutions (London: ET by J. McHugh; Darton, Longman & Todd, 1961).
———, Archaeology and the Dead Sea Scrolls (London: Oxford University Press, for British Academy London, 1973).
———, Histoire ancienne d'Israël, 2 Vol. (Paris: Gabalda, 1971 & 1973).
Vawter, Bruce, "Apocalyptic: Its Relation to Prophecy", in CBQ XXII (1960) 33-46.
———, The Conscience of Israel — Pre-exilic Prophets and Prophecy (New York: Sheed & Ward, 1961).
———, The Book of Sirach — With a Commentary (2 Parts) (New York: Pamphlet Bible Series, Paulist Press, 1962).
———, On Genesis: A New Reading (London: G. Chapman, 1977).
Vellanickal, Matthew, The Divine Sonship of Christians in the Johannine Writings (Rome: Biblical Institute, 1970).
Vergote, J., Joseph en Égypte (Louvain: University of Louvain Press, 1959).
Vermes, G., The Dead Sea Scrolls in English (Harmondsworth: Pelican, rev.ed. 1968). [Now 1987^3]
Vermeylen, J., Job, Ses Amis et Son Dieu — La Légende de Job et ses relectures postexiliques (Leiden: E.J. Brill, 1986).
Verseput, D., The Rejection of the Humble Messianic King — A Study of the Composition of Matthew 11-12 (Frankfurt am Main/ New York: Peter Lang, 1986).
Viviano, B.T., "The Gospel according to Matthew", in NJBC 630-674.
Vogels, Walter, La Promesse Royale de Yahweh Preparatoire à l'Alliance — Étude d'une forme littéraire de l'A.T. (Ottawa: L'Université d'Ottawa, 1970).
———, God's Universal Covenant — A Biblical Study (Ottawa: University of Ottawa Press, 1979).
Von Rad, G., The Message of the Prophets (London: ET by D. Stalker, SCM, 1968).
Walaskay, Paul W., 'And so we came to Rome' — The Political Perspective of St Luke (Cambridge: Cambridge University Press, 1983).

Wall, David, Review of M. Walzer's book (see below), in Review of Religious Research, 28, No.3 (March, 1987) 279-280.
Walzer, Michael, Exodus and Revolution (New York: Basic Books, 1985).
Wansbrough, H. (Ed.), New Jerusalem Bible (London: Darton, Longman & Todd, 1985).
Ward, Barbara, & Dubos, Rene, Only One Earth: The Care and Maintenance of a Small Planet (Harmondsworth: Penguin, 1972).
Weinfeld, M., "Traces of Assyrian Treaty Formulae in Deuteronomy", in Biblica 46 (1965) 417-427.
Weiser, A., The Psalms (London: ET by H. Hartwell, SCM, 1962).
Westermann, C., Mille Ans et Un Jour (Paris: FT by A. Chazelle, Cerf, 1975).
———, Genesis 1-11 (London: ET by J. Scullion, SPCK, 1984).
———, Genesis 12-36 — A Commentary (London: ET by J. Scullion, SPCK, 1985).
Whitely, C.F., "The Semantic Range of Hesed", in Biblica 62 (1981) 519-526.
Wikenhauser, A., New Testament Introduction (Dublin: Herder, 1967).
Wilson, J.A. The Culture of Ancient Egypt (Chicago: Chicago University Press, p-b. 1963).
Winter, Francis X., "After Tension, Detente: A Continuing Chronicle of European Episcopal Views on Nuclear Deterrence", in Theol. Studies 45 (1984) 343-351.
Witaszek, G., I profeti Amos e Michea nella Lotta per la Giustizia Sociale nell'VIII Sec. A.C. (Rome: Gregorian University, 1986).
Worden, T., The Psalms are Christian Prayer (London: G. Chapman, 1964).
World Council of Churches, Final Document: Justice Peace Integrity of Creation (Geneva: WCC Central Committee, 1990), a document from the Convocation in Seoul, Korea.
Wyschogrod, Michael, "La Torah en tant que Loi dans le Judaisme", in SIDIC XIX, no.3 (1986), Ed. Francaise (Rome) 10-16.

George MacDonald Mulrain

Theology in Folk Culture
The Theological Significance of Haitian Folk Religion

Frankfurt/M., Bern, Nancy, New York, 1984. 423 pp.
Studies in the Intercultural History of Christianity. Vol. 33
ISBN 3-8204-7467-6   pb. DM 78.--/sFr. 65.--

The theology which has for long monopolized the world scene is a reflection of God-talk by people of the rich western nations. By contrast, the religious experiences of people within the poorer countries have often been regarded as having little or nothing worthwhile to contribute to the mainstream of the developed world as well as those from the so-called "third" world to appreciate the wealth of theological insights which emanate from folk cultures across the world. A truly multicultural approach to theology will emerge only when we admit that each culture has something unique to offer in our understanding of God.

Contents: There is more to Haitian vaudoo than "black magic" – Spirits constitute a reality within folk culture – True theology remembers its commitment to the poor.

Verlag Peter Lang Frankfurt a.M. · Bern · New York · Paris
Auslieferung: Verlag Peter Lang AG, Jupiterstr. 15, CH-3000 Bern 15
Telefon (004131) 321122, Telex pela ch 912 651, Telefax (004131) 321131
- Preisänderungen vorbehalten -